The Doctors Book
of
Pain Remedies

The Doctors Book
of
Pain Remedies

Over 1,000 At-Home Ways
To Cure Or Relieve
Whatever Hurts You

the Editors of

PREVENTION
Health Books™

RODALE

Printed in Italy by Rotolito Lombarda S.p.A.

ISBN 1-57954-156-9 hardcover

2 4 6 8 10 9 7 5 3   hardcover

RODALE

WE INSPIRE AND ENABLE PEOPLE TO IMPROVE
THEIR LIVES AND THE WORLD AROUND THEM

The Doctor's Book of Pain Remedies

Editor: Mark Bricklin
Writers: Rick Chillot
Researchers: Staci Ann Sonder
   Nancy Duin
   Barbro Truyen
   Marie-Jeanne Voysey
Interior Designer: Mary Ellen Curry
Cover Designer: Christopher Rhoads
Indexer: Barbara Long
Studio Manager: Leslie Keefe
Manufacturing Coordinator: Christa Gronbech

Rodale Healthy Living Books

Vice President and Publisher: Brian Carnahan
Vice President and Editorial Director: Debora T. Yost
Editorial Director: Michael Ward
Vice President and Marketing Director: Karen Arbegast
Product Marketing Manager: Denyse Corelli
Book Manufacturing Director: Helen Clogston
Manufacturing Managers: Eileen F. Bauder, Mark Krahforst
Research Manager: Ann Gossy Yermish
Copy Manager: Lisa D. Andruscavage
Production Manager: Robert V. Anderson Jr.
Office Manager: Jacqueline Dornblaser
Office Staff: Julie Kehs, Suzanne Lynch, Mary Lou Stephen

Contents

About Prevention Health Books

The editors of prevention Health Books are dedicated to providing you with authoritative, trustworthy, and innovated advice for a healthy, active lifestyle. In all of our books, our goal is to keep you thoroughly informed about the latest breakthroughs in natural healing, medical research, alternative health, herbs, nutrition, fitness and weight loss. We cut through the confusion of today's conflicting health reports to deliver clear concise, and definitive health information that you can trust. And we explain in practical terms what each new breakthrough means to you, so you can take immediate, practical steps to improve your health and well-being.

Every recommendation in Prevention Health Books is based upon interviews with highly qualified health authorities, including medical doctors and practitioners of alternative medicine. In addition, we consult with the Prevention Health Books Board of Advisors to ensure that all of the health information is safe, practical, and up-to-date. Prevention Health Books are thoroughly factchecked for accuracy, and we make every effort to verify recommendations, dosages, and cautions. The advise in this book will help keep you well-informed about your personal choices in health care—to help you lead a happier, healthier, and longer life.

Notice

This book is intended as a reference volume only, not as a medical manual. The information given here is designed to help you make informed decisions about your health. It is not intended as a substitute for any treatment that may have been prescribed by your doctor. If you suspect that you have a medical problem, or if you are pregnant or nursing, we urge you to seek competent medical care. The supplements in this book should not be given to children. Pregnant women should consult their doctors and use caution when taking supplements, as some may affect their health, cause miscarriage, or affect the health of the unborn child. If you are taking prescription medications or being treated for a chronic health condition, it is advisable to consult your doctor before taking supplements.

Introduction

The Doctors Book of Pain Remedies is the most complete guide for relieving pain of nearly every type ever made available to the public. Wherever you hurt, however you hurt, the experts in this book give you the smartest ways to find blessed relief.

Make no mistake. Pain is not just for the old. Even the youngest and most active can be tormented by pain. Sports injuries, headaches, backaches, urinary infection and many more forms of pain are no respecter of youth and vigor!

Despite all our medical advances and easier lifestyles, there is certainly no shortage of pain today. The mere fact that we tend to weigh more these days is a major contributor to pain. Ever suffer knee pain? Consider this: if you've gained just 10 pounds, you're putting an extra 60 pounds of pressure on your knees with every step you take, as an orthopaedic surgeon explains in the chapter on Knee Pain. If you shed 10 pounds, he says, the relief you experience could feel miraculous!

And while long, back-breaking shifts of industrial labor are mostly forgotten, the advent of the electronic workplace has brought its own, new forms of pain. One is called "repetitive strain injury," affecting the wrist and hands. Incredibly, the incidence of this pain has increased some 600 percent just in the last decade! This epidemic coincides perfectly with the near-universal use of computers at work and home, where we spend hour-upon-hour frozen in one (often awkward) position. In this book you will discover not only how to "chase" this pain, but how to prevent it from ever attacking you.

This is not a book that denies the wisdom and relief that can come from medical care. Far from it! Most important, we must all see a physician to determine the underlying nature of our problem. It's all too easy to make a mistake and treat symptoms when we need to understand the real reason we are suffering pain.

But once that is done, the help you can give yourself is enormous. As described in this book, a study in Ireland showed that giving people advice on home care resulted in less pain, and a much shorter recovery period, than giving medical devices or even professional physiotherapy. There is no substitute for informed self-care—and that is what this book is all about!

Some people have endured pain for years because they fear surgery or strong pain-killers. But this book is entirely about what you can do at home—certainly no mind-numbing or potentially addictive drugs are involved!

No drugs...no surgery...no pain! That is our philosophy.

And there are so many ways presented here to achieve that, we can say," From head to toe, your pain must go!"

Mark Bricklin
International Editor

Anal Pain
(fissures, haemorrhoids and abscesses)

The pain: A person with anal fissures will experience two kinds of pain: a knifing pain at the time of a bowel movement and then a dull pain caused by spasms of the underlying muscle that can last for hours. Haemorrhoids may cause anal pain or itching. An abscess is a tender, red lump near the anus that's incessantly painful and may be accompanied by a fever. After two or three days it becomes too painful to sit or walk.

The cause:
Anal fissures: Small tears in the skin around the anus, anal fissures are usually caused by trying to pass hard, large stools. There are doctors who think that the cause is obvious. "Most patients who develop anal fissures also have chronic constipation," says William B. Ruderman, MD, a practicing physician in gastroenterology.

Haemorrhoids: Despite their prevalence, no one knows what causes haemorrhoids to appear in the first place. Scientists do suspect, however, that "straining at stool"—pushing too hard when you're trying to have a bowel movement—may combine with certain genetic tendencies to cause the problem. Just inside the anus are collections of blood vessels that act like inflatable cushions, forming a tight seal that helps prevent stool, flatus and mucus from leaking from your rectum. But if one of these vessels gets inflamed or droops out of its normal position on the rectal wall—often from intense straining during a bowel movement—it becomes a haemorrhoid. Besides itching or hurting, haemorrhoids can also bleed.

Anal abscess: Abscesses start when one of the small lubricating glands around the anus gets infected. The infection creates a cavity that fills with pus. The infection spreads through the sphincter muscle and usually surfaces one to three inches from the anus. In some cases, the abscess moves in reverse and never surfaces.

See a doctor if:
...you notice blood in the stool or experience any bleeding while trying to pass your stool. See your doctor as soon as possible. While some bleeding occurs because of haemorrhoids or trying to pass hard stools, rectal bleeding may be a warning sign of colon cancer or another serious problems. But you'll need a doctor's examination to find the cause.

...your anus feels swollen.
...the pain persists for more than two to three days.
...you have a fever.
...you have changes in bowel habits, such as chronic diarrhoea or constipation.
...you've tried self-help measures and still have anal fissures.

Medication:

In 10 percent of fissure patients, scarring or sphincter spasms will prevent a fissure from healing. A 15-minute outpatient operation called sphinctero-tomy can correct a fissure that continues to bleed or cause pain. More than 90 percent of such patients have no further fissure problems.

If haemorrhoids remain painful, injection and banding are two treatments that may eliminate troublesome symptoms. In the doctor's office, the haemorrhoid is tied off with a rubber band and then injected with phenol and almond oil, a treatment that prevents the band from slipping off, or with local anaesthesia.

A second procedure that doctors sometimes use is infrared coagulation. It's probably just as effective as injection and banding, but the procedure itself -in which several infrared beams are aimed inside the anus to burn an internal haemorrhoid-may generate a considerable amount of pain in a certain number of patients.

Outright surgery is a third option. It was once used to treat about 50 percent of all haemorrhoids, but today it's usually reserved for those who have haemorrhoids that are far advanced, with severe protrusion, bleeding, irritation, and spoilage. Less than 10 percent of patients suffering from haemorrhoids that are seen in a doctor's office require surgery, since banding handles most haemorrhoids effectively.

Fixing an abscess is usually simple, but you need a doctor to do it because of its out-of-sight location. "You just lance it," says Olaf Johansen. MD, a colorectal surgeon. "It can usually be done in the office by injecting some local anaesthetic, and then you open up the abscess. You drain it out and that will take care of about 60 percent of abscesses." Forty percent of abscesses will leave a small tunnel, called a fistula, leading from the rectum to the skin. Fistulas can run with pus, blood and even feces. When necessary, they are repaired with surgery to remove the infected gland.

Nutritional remedies:

Fibre up. "Constipation is the most common cause of anal fissures," agrees Randolph M. Steinhagen, MD, associate professor of surgery at Mount Sinai Medical Centre. He recommends a high-fibre diet, which, besides bran, includes lots of fruits, vegetables, beans, and grains. Cultured buttermilk, yoghurt, and sweet acidophilus milk added to your diet will encourage stool-softening "friendly" bacteria in the colon.

A Danish study lends support to the high-fibre recommendation. In the study, Danish doctors divided 75 patients who had a history of the condition into three groups. To people in the first group the doctors gave high-fibre supplements; the second group received medium-fibre supplements; while the third, the control group, received a placebo—a dose that looked like a fibre supplement, but wasn't. Only 16 percent of the high-fibre group got anal fissures again. In the medium-fibre and placebo groups, however, about 60 percent of the patients got fissures.

Watch what you eat. Chew your food carefully and be aware that what goes in, must come out, even if you can't digest it. "It doesn't happen very often, but if a person swallows a small bone, it can cause cuts, tears and bleeding when it goes through the anus," says Philip Jaffe, MD, a gastroenterologist.

Gulp down water. "When you are eating more fibre, it is also very important to drink lots of liquids," says Dr. Steinhagen. "Without sufficient water, the fibre can become very thick and make constipation worse." He recommends eight eight-ounce glasses a day.

Prevent a fissure encore. Fissures heal, but they also tend to come back again. To prevent a fissure from returning, be sure to maintain your high-fibre diet, says Dr. Steinhagen.

Helpful vitamins and supplements:

Try a fibre supplement. If you have been eating a lot of fibre and drinking plenty of water but you are still constipated, maybe you need some extra help in the fibre department. "When a patient tells me, 'I eat a lot of fibre, but I'm still constipated,' I suggest a fibre supplement," says Dr. Steinhagen. Among his recommendations are Metamucil or Konsyl (Fybrogel)—both of which are psyllium-based high-fibre supplements—or Citrucel (Celevac), which uses methylcellulose as its source of fibre. "They are not laxatives or stimulants, which can damage your digestive tract. They just add more fibre into your system."

Take fibre with water. If you do need a fibre supplement, make sure that it doesn't get clogged up inside your digestive tract. Dr. Steinhagen tells his patients to take the fibre supplement by mixing a heaping spoonful in a glass of water or juice. He also tells them to drink a full glass of water right afterward. "This ensures that there is enough water so that the fibre doesn't thicken," he says.

Get the pluses without the wind. To avoid one possible side effect of fibre supplements, extra wind, Dr. Steinhagen says to start with small amounts of the supplement and gradually work up to the recommended amount. Some of his patients have told him that they prefer Citrucel (Celevac) because it produces less wind than the rival psyllium-based supplements.

Get fibre in pills. If you don't like the taste of powdered fibre supplements, you may be tempted to take fibre pills instead, but Dr. Steinhagen doesn't think the pills work as well. For those who can't stand the taste of the supplements, he recommends the product Perdiem Fibre (Fibrebran). "You don't have to mix this product with water," he says. "You just put a spoonful of the granules in your mouth and swallow them with a full glass of water, and that tends to go down easier. It docsn't have the sawdust consistency of the fibre supplements."

Try over-the-counter vitamin creams. To soothe the pain and help heal fissures, try over-the-counter ointments that contain vitamins A and D, suggests Marvin M. Schuster, MD, chief of the Department of Digestive Diseases at Francis Scott Key Medical Centre.

Over-the-counter relief:

Soften your stool. For some people, a stool softener is easier to take than fibre supplements. If his patients prefer to prevent constipation with a stool softener, even though the fibre supplement is likely to be more effective, Dr. Steinhagen suggests Colace (Dioctyl). This over-the-counter product keeps more water in the stool, making it softer.

Spray away the pain. To make personal hygiene a little easier on your tender bottom, there's ClenZone. This small cleansing device hooks up to your bathroom faucet; just spray your-self clean with a narrow stream of water aimed at the anal area. There's no need for toilet paper, except to pat yourself dry.

"This is a neat little appliance that offers a real nice way to get clean after a bowel movement," says colon-rectal surgeon John A. Flatley, MD It can be used for both fissures and haemorrhoids. (Hepp Industries, 687 Kildare Crescent, Seaford, NY 11783.)

Everyday prevention:

Soak your bottom in a tub or sitz bath (a sitz bath is sitting in three or four inches of warm bath water with your knees raised) of plain, warm water. Experts recommend several times a day, 20 minutes at a time. Be sure the water is not painfully hot. But remember that the warmer the water is, the greater and longer the pain relief will be. That's what doctors discovered at Cairo University in Egypt, where they tested 18 patients with fissures and 10 patients with haemorrhoids. The patients soaked in water at 104, 113' and 122 degrees F. Although the higher temperatures provided the greatest pain relief for those patients, test your water for your own personal comfort level.

Lube to soothe. You can protect your anal canal by lubricating it before each bowel movement. A gob of petroleum jelly inserted about an inch into the rectum may help the stool pass without causing any further damage, advises Edmund Leff, MD, a proctologist.

Wipe with facial tissue. The best toilet paper isn't toilet paper at all. Facial tissues coated with moisturizing lotion offer the least amount of friction to your fissure-plagued anal area, says Dr. Leff.

Let it slide. Say your diet slips while you're on the road. You're in a hotel facing a scary, rocklike bowel movement. You know straining to pass it will risk injury, but what else can you do? "You ought to give yourself a small enema," says David E. Beck, MD, Chairman of the Department of Colon and Rectal Surgery at Ochsner Clinic. "There are some on the market that have water and mineral oil in them, available over the counter. That will provide some fluid, and the oil tends to soften the stool."

If that doesn't work, try using a finger to break up the stool before it passes—yes, you can do it (doctors recommend you first put on a latex glove and trim your fingernail), or ask a doctor or nurse to help.

Leave the magazines in the living room. Sitting on the toilet reading your favourite book or newspaper may be a nice diversion, but it also puts unwanted strain on your anal muscles and leaves you vulnerable to discomfort caused by swelling. "If the bathroom is the only place in the house where you can find privacy, and you do like to read in there, then be sure to put down the toilet seat cover and use it as a chair," says Bruce Orkin, MD, a colon and rectal surgery specialist.

Trim your fingernails. Well-manicured fingernails may make a fashion statement, but long nails can be dangerous. "Once I was called to the emergency room because a woman was bleeding quite briskly," says Juan Nogueras, MD, a colon and rectal surgeon at the Cleveland Clinic. "It turned out she had accidentally stabbed a haemorrhoid with a long fingernail while wiping her bottom."

Easing the pain with exercise:

Exercise wisely. Exercise is an important way to help keep your bowel movements regular. When you experience anal pain, however, you should avoid exercises such as weight lifting that put a strain on anal muscles. Swimming is good because it's a non-weight-bearing exercise. Tennis and racquetball are okay, too, says Dr. Harig, a digestive and liver disease specialist. But you want to avoid doing squats or anything that increases pressure in the anal area.

Kegel it. Usually used to control certain types of incontinence, Kegel exercises also can help strengthen anal muscles and prevent painful haemorrhoids. Kegels work on the slinglike group of muscles that stretch from the pubic bone in the front to the anus and tailbone in the rear. Squeezing those muscles not only can cut off urinary flow but also can keep the rectal muscles in tone. Although it may vary according to your condition, a typical Kegel regimen might include 20 contractions of these muscles for ten seconds each, four times a day. Ask your doctor if Kegels may be right for you.

Herbal help:

Opt for Aloe Vera. Try snipping a leaf from an aloe vera plant, squeezing out the aloe and applying it liberally with a cotton swab or finger twice a day. You can also buy aloe gel at the pharmacy or health-food store. Medical researchers have found that aloe gel speeds the healing of surgical wounds, burns, pressure sores and frostbite. In addition to containing salicylates, the same anti-inflammatory painkiller found in aspirin, aloe vera also may inhibit the histamine reactions that cause itching and irritation.

Avoid antibiotics for an abscess. Merely taking antibiotics for an abscess is a mistake, says Richard M. Burg, MD, a colon and rectal surgeon. "As soon as a person has been diagnosed with an abscess, provisions should be made to drain it he says, "because it will only progress and damage more tissue and cause pain. An antibiotic can help with the surrounding inflammation of an abscess, but it won't ever cure it."

Remedies:

Nix citrus fruits and spicy foods. Doctors aren't sure why, but citrus fruits, such as oranges, grapefruits and tangerines, and spicy foods, like curry and hot peppers, can cause some people to develop irritating secretions at the anus. Other possible culprits are acidic foods like tomatoes and alcohol. To discover which foods are bothering you pay careful attention to what you eat-perhaps by keeping a food diary—and to what the effect is a day or two later.

Cut back on coffee. Coffee beans contain oils that you can't digest. The oils irritate the skin surrounding the anus when they are excreted from the body.

Turn off the wind. Anything that causes a person to pass a lot of wind rectally will also bring out moisture and contribute to itching. So cut back on the broccoli, cabbage, carbonated beverages, or anything else that toots your tuba.

Go easy on the drink. Your behind doesn't take kindly to more than six glasses of caffeine, alcohol or carbonated fluid a day, according to the American Society of Colon and Rectal Surgeons. Caffeine and alcohol actually remove fluid from the body and carbonated sodas give you wind you don't need.

Tame it with gauze. Place a thin strip of gauze or cotton up against the anal opening to absorb excessive sweat and mucus and to prevent rashes and itching, says Dr. Orkin.

Dress for the occasion. Loose cotton underwear is a better choice than clinging nylon or polyester because it absorbs moisture better and allows more air to pass through, keeping your bottom dry.

Sock it to pinworms. Pinworms generally infect young children, but other family members can attract the unwanted attention of these pests, which come out at night and cause infernal anal itching. Your doctor can prescribe an oral antiparasitic medication to relieve the problem, but you also should thoroughly wash all bedding in hot water to prevent a recurrence.

Check your medications. Some drugs can cause anal itching. Antibiotics, for example, often destroy harmless bacteria in the anus that fight off itchy yeast infections. Ask your doctor if your medications may be causing your problem.

Blow your itch away. Using a hair dryer set on low for 20 to 30 seconds after bathing or swimming is a good way to gently but thoroughly dry your bottom and prevent itching.

Bare your bottom to the sun. "The sun's ultraviolet light can help prevent and relieve itching and other irritations in the anal area and dry the skin. Nude sunbathing is a great way to get some of that sunlight into areas of your backside that are usually left in the dark," says Eric G. Anderson, MD, a family practice physician. As with more modest forms of sun worshipping, you should always apply a sunscreen to exposed skin and build up your time in the sun gradually.

Don't worry. Believe it or not, if you feel anxious or are under a lot of stress, you may develop an itchy anus. Relieving your stress through yoga, progressive relaxation or exercise might end your scratching.

Wash, don't wipe. Good hygiene is crucial to preventing anal itching. If possible, after each bowel movement wash your anus with a soft cloth dipped in warm water and mild soap. Rinse and pat dry; don't rub.

Wash up before bed. Anal itching is often worse at night. You can prevent that problem, however, by washing your anus with soap and water at the end of the day, even if you haven't moved your bowels since the morning.

Keep it clean. "First thing I tell people is try to keep the area clean, but don't over scrub," says Dr. Johansen. After a bowel movement clean yourself gently with wet toilet paper. If it's practical, get in the shower and wash with plain water no detergent soap. Then pat yourself dry.

Clean with lotion regularly. Dry toilet paper can be abrasive enough to damage the skin. "I usually recommend that patients clean with a lotion such as Balneol or Prax (Balneum or Lignocaine)," says Dr. Burg. Do this on a routine basis—not just when you need it—because itching notoriously tends to recur.

Cream it with steroids. If your symptoms are severe, one of the over-the-counter steroid creams, like hydrocortisone, might provide relief, says Dr. Johansen. "The steroid can break that scratch-itch cycle," he says.

Powder your bottom. After a shower apply cornstarch or other powder to keep your anus dry. To further absorb moisture, place a small wad of cotton near your anus. Leave it there, and change it several times a day.

Anal itching

Doctors call it pruritis ani. It is a fiendishly irritating itch, usually worse at night, in one of the body's most tender and hard-to-scratch spots. An itchy bottom usually is a signal that fecal material or body secretions are irritating nerve endings in the anus. However, the causes are numerous, and finding a specific reason for it can be elusive, doctors say. To make sure that the itching is a minor-league problem, first have a medical examination to be certain that there aren't any significant health problems. Definitely see a doctor if you feel a lump in the rectal area, you have diabetes, you are taking steroids, your children complain of anal itching.

Angina

The pain: Pressure-like pain or squeezing sensation in your chest. Often, the pressure comes on when you exert yourself and goes away once you stop. It's prone to happen when you're under stress, after big meals or in cold weather. If you're in your sixties or seventies, you might just feel pressure, shortness of breath, or a squeezing sensation in the chest as if someone was tightening a belt around your ribs, or even pain in some area that seems completely unrelated to your heart, for instance, in your jaw or even your left or right elbow.

The cause: Angina is usually a sign that your heart isn't getting enough oxygen-rich blood, because the arteries which supply it have been narrowed by cholesterol-laden plaque. Result: your heart muscle doesn't get enough fuel to meet its needs, so it sends out a painful distress signal. Angina is especially likely to come on when the heart needs to step up its pumping and so needs an extra dose of oxygen; for example during times of exercise or stress. Angina that is limited to times of exertion is called stable angina; when it happens during rest or for no apparent reason, it's called unstable angina.

See a doctor if...
...you're having an angina attack for the first time. It may turn out to be something minor, but a heart disorder is not something that you want to self-diagnose, says Peter M. Abel, MD, director of cardiovascular disease and prevention at a cardiovascular institute. Making a mistake can be disastrous, so see your doctor right away.

...you have chest pain, as opposed to chest pressure, that lasts for 15 minutes or is accompanied by shortness of breath and a sick-to-your-stomach feeling. Go to the emergency room immediately—you may be having a heart attack instead of an angina attack. The longer your heart goes without oxygen, the more likely you'll end up with heart damage, Dr. Abel warns.

...there's a change in the pattern. Stable and predictable angina attacks in someone who has been diagnosed with angina aren't a reason to see a doctor, says Robert March, MD, a cardiovascular surgery specialist. But if the pain comes on more frequently with less activity, see your doctor. If angina comes on in the middle of the night or when you haven't been doing anything active, you should call your doctor or go to the emergency room.

Medication:

Once your doctor knows you have angina, you're likely to get a prescription for nitroglycerin, which dilate blood vessels to reduce the workload for your heart.. This can drop your blood pressure very rapidly, putting you at risk of fainting. So the medication should only be taken while you're sitting down, says Dr. March. If you feel dizzy or faint, no harm done as long as you're not standing or walking around. Nitroglycerin is available in two forms: one that reduces the number of attacks, such as the patch (Nitro-Dur), and one that relieves an attack in progress, like the under-the-tongue tablet (Nitrostat). Your doctor may advise you to keep the tablet form of nitroglycerin with you at all times.

Nutritional remedies:

Eat less fat, more fibre, more veggies: "We found a reduction in the frequency of angina or chest pain within weeks of making severe changes in diet and lifestyle," says Dean Ornish, MD, director of the Preventive Medicine Research Institute in California, and author of *Dr. Dean Ornish's Program for Reversing Heart Disease.* Dr. Ornish recommends holding dietary fat to 10 percent of your calories and eliminating animal products. The move will do more than soothe your chest pain. Over time, it will open up your clogged arteries, preventing heart attack. Studies by Dr. Ornish have shown that a super-low-fat diet (less than 10 percent), when combined with exercise, giving up cigarettes, and reducing stress, not only lowers cholesterol but also may actually reverse existing blockages in the arteries.

Eat essential fatty acids: Doctors recommend two kinds of fatty acids—omega-3's and omega-6's—for people who have angina. These are found in fish oil, flaxseed oil, cold-pressed safflower or sunflower oil, and borage oil. Experts also advise people with angina to cut back on saturated fats (those that are solid at room temperature), hydrogenated fats (margarine and shortening), and polyunsaturated fats (corn oil). Your muscles, including the heart, choose fatty acids as their primary source of fuel, so if you provide your heart with omega-3's and omega-6's, you're giving it a healthier form of energy. Since fish oil may have some side effects, however, be sure to check with your doctor before taking high doses, particularly if you have a bleeding disorder, uncontrolled high blood pressure, or diabetes.

Quaff a cantaloupe: Those prone to angina attacks may benefit from regular doses of cantaloupe juice, suggests Michael Murray, ND, a naturopathic physician and author of *The Complete Book of Juicing.* Cantaloupe contains the compound adenosirle, which is used in heart patients to thin the blood and prevent angina attacks, according to Dr. Murray. Along with proper medical treatment, he recommends drinking two eight-ounce glasses of cantaloupe juice a day.

Helpful vitamins and supplements:

Ease the squeeze with magnesium: At the top of Dr. Weiss's prescription list for angina is magnesium, a mineral that helps to relax the muscles that wrap around blood vessels. "Magnesium dilates the coronary arteries, improving oxygen delivery to the heart," Dr. Weiss, a naturopathic doctor, explains. It also plays an important role in energy production in all cells, so having enough on hand is especially important to heart muscle cells, which are high energy producers, he says. If you have angina, you probably have heart disease, so it's best to consult a doctor who's knowledgeable in nutrition before taking supplemental magnesium. Dr. Weiss recommends two forms—magnesium orotate and magnesium glycinate—but check with your doctor before you settle on a dosage of either.

Queue up to coenzyme q10: Sharing top billing with magnesium for angina is coenzyme Q10, a vitamin-like substance that plays an essential role in producing energy. CoQ10 as it's commonly called, actually increases oxygen delivery to heart muscle cells. By boosting energy and improving oxygen delivery, it allows your heart to pump more efficiently and with less effort, Dr. Weiss says. Since the enzyme is fat-soluble, gel capsules are more potent and more readily absorbed than the tablet form of this supplement. If you opt for tablets, chew them with a fat-containing food such as peanut butter to maximise absorption.

Get E, C and Selenium: Certain vital nutrients help prevent cholesterol build-up in arteries and protect the cells lining blood vessels from damage that makes blockage more likely. These protective nutrients include vitamins C and E and the trace mineral selenium. "I routinely suggest these nutrients to someone with angina," Dr. Weiss says. In one study, supplements of vitamin E, along with vitamin C, vitamin A, and beta-carotene, reduced the incidence of angina and arrhythmia and improved heart function in people with suspected heart attacks.

Vitamin E affects both cholesterol and platelets in a way that reduces the risk of heart disease, Dr. Weiss explains. He recommends 400 to 800 international units (IU) a day (talk to your doctor before taking more than 400 IU).

Vitamin C helps keep blood vessels open because it prevents the breakdown of nitric oxide, which helps relax and dilate the blood vessel walls, says Dr. Weiss.

Selenium, when teamed with vitamin E, can also offer some protection from angina. One study found that people with heart disease who took 200 IU of vitamin E and 1,000 micrograms (a very large dose) of selenium had a significant reduction in angina pain compared with people taking placebos. (Doses of selenium over 200 micrograms must be taken under a doctor's supervision.) Doctors who recommend selenium supplements to their heart patients generally stick with no more than 50 to 200 micrograms a day.

Try a bromelain/curcumin combo: Bromelain (a protein-dissolving enzyme found in pineapple) helps reduce the formation of fibrous tissue and clots in damaged arteries, and curcumin (the yellow pigment in turmeric) acts somewhat like aspirin, Dr. Weiss says. It helps to reduce the tendency for blood to clot and also reduces inflammation. For the best therapeutic effect, take divided doses of this duo, says Dr. Weiss. A standard dose of bromelain is 125 to 450 milligrams three times a day on an empty stomach, he says. Do not take bromelain with food, or it will simply act as a digestive enzyme. Usual doses of curcumin are 400 to 600 milligrams a day, Dr. Weiss says. Ask your doctor what dosage is best for you.

Bring in the B's. Make sure that you're getting about 400 micrograms of folic acid, along with 1,000 micrograms of vitamin B12 and 50 to 100 milligrams of vitamin B6, says Dr. Weiss. These B vitamins help your body to process homocysteine, a by-product of protein metabolism that can damage arteries by creating rough spots on artery walls that can pick up fatty deposits.

Easing the pain with exercise:

Walk away from pain: Walk as much as you can, every day. "Walking is the best exercise," Dr. Francis says. The activity helps improve blood flow to the heart, which may help offset angina. Exercise also relieves the stress that helps trigger angina attacks. Unlike other activities, walking won't put much strain on your heart.

Can amino acids ease angina

The molecules that make up proteins, amino acids are sometimes used to treat angina and other types of heart and circulatory disorders—they include carnitine, taurine, and arginine, Dr. Weiss says. In several studies of people with heart disease, carnitine helped improve their ability to exercise. "Many people with heart disease need extra carnitine to utilise the essential fatty acids their hearts need," Dr. Weiss says. This amino acid helps transport fatty acids into the mitochondria, the tiny areas within cells where energy is produced. Carnitine may be deficient in people with reduced blood flow to the heart, and supplemental carnitine may help the heart muscle better utilise its limited supply of oxygen, studies suggest. The daily therapeutic dose for carnitine is 1,500 to 3,000 milligrams for an average person. Take three divided doses a day, advises Dr. Weiss.

Taurine is also important for the normal function of the heart and vascular system, says Dr. Weiss. It's the most abundant amino acid found in the heart. In Japan, taurine is widely used to treat various causes of heart disease.

Arginine is involved in the production of nitric oxide, a compound formed by the cells that line the arteries. With increased nitric oxide, the arteries can relax and dilate, which helps augment blood flow to crucial heart muscle.

Your best bet for using these amino acids is to ask your doctor to recommend a formula that contains a balanced mixture. Recommended doses will differ depending on your current and past history of heart disease.

Pose for yoga: For heart-healthy benefits, Dr. Rothfeld, author of *Natural Medicine for Arthritis*, recommends a yoga posture called the expansion pose. While standing, hold your arms out at your sides and slowly move them backward until you can interlace your fingers. Hold your trunk straight and without straining, slowly raise your arms behind you. Gently arch your back as you begin to lift your locked hands toward the ceiling. Hold for five seconds. Then slowly bend your body farther forward, lowering your head and raising your arms to shoulder level for ten seconds. Then return to an upright position, drop your arms to your sides and relax. Practising yoga postures daily or several times a week keeps you flexible, helps you to relax, and yoga improves circulation, says Dr. Rothfeld.

Play that funky music. Dancing is a sneaky way to get in some heart-strengthening exercise. Also, the music alone can relax you, soothing away heart-damaging stress. "You can't be angry and dance at the same time," says Stephen T. Sinatra, MD, heart specialist, and author of *Optimum Health and Heartbreak and Heart Disease*.

Seek out fresh air. Inhaling carbon monoxide can trigger an angina attack. In fact, just being exposed to everyday levels of carbon monoxide can cause angina prematurely in some people, says Sidney Gottlieb, MD, a cardiologist at Johns Hopkins Medical Institutions. So if your exercise routine includes running or walking, do it away from car exhaust. If you live in an urban environment, try to exercise indoors.

Everyday prevention:

Start out slowly: Take your time when you get up in the morning, Dr. Francis, a coronary intensive care specialist, suggests. Don't hop right out of bed. Stretch, get acclimated to being awake, and give yourself enough time to eat a nice breakfast and read the paper. Why the early morning slow down? Because the early hours of the day are the most dangerous for your heart. As people get older, their bodies can't handle the-jump-out-of-bed-grab-a-quick-bite-rush-to-work routine, Dr. Francis says. If you force it in the morning hours, you might put a lot of unnecessary pressure on the heart—additional pressure that could jump-start an angina attack. "Get up a little more slowly and don't rush around," Dr. Francis says.

Lift less: Leave heavy lifting to others. If you have to move something heavy, find someone else to do the job, Dr. March says. Heavy lifting is a common trigger for angina pain in many people, he adds. Even something as simple as lifting a suitcase and carrying it up a flight of stairs can cause angina pain.

Hike up your headboard: If you experience angina attacks at night, raising the head of your bed three or four inches can reduce the number of attacks, says cardiologist Gregory Sachs, MD. Sleeping in this position makes more blood pool in your legs, so less of it returns to the heart's narrowed arteries.

Stop when it strikes: If angina comes on during an activity, stop whatever you are doing. Sit down and prop up your feet, says Michael A. Brodsky, MD, a cardiologist. Don't try to work or push through the pain.

Take a few minutes to relax. "If you stop the activity, the pain should go away," Dr. March adds.

Sit up and say ahhh: If you are lying down or sleeping when you have angina pain, sit up on the edge the bed with your feet on the floor, or stand up. "Standing up takes the pressure off your heart," Dr. Francis says. Your body demands less from your heart, giving it time to recover from the angina episode.

Put out the butts: If you are a smoker, you're making things extra-tough for your heart, Dr. March says. Cigarette smoke steals oxygen from your blood and nicotine constricts your blood vessels. Your arteries shrink, less blood makes it to your heart, and the blood that does make it has less oxygen than it should. That's a recipe for angina.

Take an aspirin a day: With your doctor's permission take one adult aspirin (about 325 milligrams) tablet a day, Dr. March says. Aspirin is thought to decrease heart damage during an angina episode. While the drug may not prevent an attack of angina all the time, studies show that men with angina who take aspirin are less likely to have a heart attack or die of heart problems than men who don't take aspirin.

Be a heatseeker: When the weather is ice cold, make it a point to keep warm and stay inside as much as possible. Below-freezing days provoke angina in some people, Dr. Francis says. "On extremely cold days, it's dangerous for people with angina to go out."

Mind over malady:

Calm down: Mental stress can cause chest pain for the same reasons as physical stress: It increases the oxygen demands of the heart. So if you feel chest pain when you argue with your wife, worry about your taxes, or

---

Exercising with angina:

If you like other forms of exercise besides walking, such as swimming or bicycling, go ahead as long as it doesn't bring on angina, Dr. Francis says. "I encourage physical activity as long as you feel good doing it." Strive for at least 20 minutes 3 times a week. "When patients start an exercise program, they may experience angina with increased exercise levels,' says Dr. Beller. The answer: Exercise until you begin to feel the onset of discomfort, then stop until the pain subsides (which may require taking a pill). Often you can then continue, and the pain will not return. Ultimately, an exercise regimen will promote exercise tolerance, with angina occurring only with greater exercise stress than when you first started.

And don't have a heavy meal before taking your walk. If you're hungry, munch on a light snack such as an apple. Dr. Francis suggests. If you eat a big meal and then exercise, you are more likely to experience angina pain. (Be sure to consult with your physician before you start an exercise program.)

Herbs for Angina

Note: Always consult your physician before taking herbs for a serious condition like angina.

Ginkgo: "I absolutely recommend ginkgo for angina," says Dr. Weiss, noting that this herbal supplement can help stimulate blood flow around the damaged area of the heart. He recommends 60 milligrams of ginkgo biloba extract (standardised to 24 percent ginkgoflavoglycosides) up to three times a day.

Angelica *(Angelica archangelica)* and other herbs of the carrot family: Calcium channel blockers are a standard class of anti-angina drugs, and angelica contains 15 compounds that act much like these channel blockers. Similar compounds appear in other plants in the carrot family: carrots, celery, fennel, parsley and parsnip Try combining them all in a drink that consists of juiced angelica, carrots, celery, fennel, parsley and parsnips, with some water and spices added.

Bilberry *(Vaccinium myrtillus)* and other fruits: Bilberry contains compounds known as anthocyanins that have a cholesterol-lowering effect and help prevent formation of the blood clots that trigger heart attacks. This herb also opens blood vessels and lowers blood pressure. Other good anthocyanin sources include blackberries, black chokeberries, boysenberries, black currants, blueberries, cherries, cranberries, red grapes and red raspberries. "All of these fruits might help prevent and treat angina," says James A. Duke, PhD, author of *The Green Pharmacy.*

Garlic *(Allium sativum)* and onion *(A. cepa):* Both of these spicy herbs help treat heart disease by lowering cholesterol and blood pressure and by preventing formation of the blood clots that trigger heart attack. According to one study, eating one clove of garlic daily cuts cholesterol by 9 percent. Every 1 percent decrease in cholesterol translates to a 2 percent decrease in heart attack risk, so a clove a day reduces risk of heart attack by 18 percent. Onions have similar benefits, although not as pronounced.

Purslane *(Portulaca oleracea):* Purslane is extremely well endowed with artery-protecting antioxidants. In addition, it's our best leafy source of omega-3fatty acids, to help prevent heart disease.

Evening primrose *(Oenothera biennis):* Primrose is an excellent Source of gamma-linolenic acid (GLA), a compound that lowers both cholesterol and blood pressure.

Flax *(Linum usitatissinuan):* Flaxseed contains an abundant amount of alpha-linolenic acid, a compound that many claim has heart-protective ability.

chastise your kid for his bad report card, call a mental time-out and lie on the couch. Progressive relaxation, meditation and other relaxation techniques, used in conjunction with medication and with the knowledge and approval of your doctor, may help prevent angina, says Robert S. Eliot, MD, director of the Institute of Stress Medicine in Wyoming.

Breathe deep: It's not a coincidence that many angina episodes get started when someone's in a tense situation. Stress often precedes a bout with angina, Dr. Francis says. When in the midst of an angina attack, calm down by taking slow, deep breaths. That may help control your stress and stop the pain. (Deep breathing is when your abdomen expands outward as you inhale rather than your chest or shoulders rising.)

Manage a massage: Having your partner's hands against your skin can heal your heart, says Dr. Sinatra. His or her touch will help you let go of artery-clogging negative emotions such as anger, sadness, stress, and fear. It also will reduce your heart rate, creating less oxygen demands on your pinched arteries.

Take the good with the bad: Just like the rest of the world, people with heart problems have good days and bad days. Accept this and you may be able to stop some angina attacks. On the days when you don't feel right, take it easy. "If you just feel lousy, there's no need to go out and push it," Dr. Francis says. Leave chores and challenging activities for the good days.

Ankle Pain

The pain: Ankle pain or soreness following an injury. May be accompanied by swelling, tenderness and bruising.

The cause: A sudden twist or overextension of the ankle joint. A strained ankle involves damage to tendons, while a sprained ankle indicates damage to ligaments. If the injury produces immediate swelling, a big knot, and tenderness at the affected area, it's probably a sprain. Sprained ankles are caused by slipping or mis-stepping more often than they are by an athletic injury.

See a doctor if:

...your ankle is so swollen that you can't put on your shoe or put weight on your leg. You may have torn ligaments or even a fracture.
...you have a lot of tenderness right over the bone and it is extremely painful to stand. You may have a fracture.
...you have a significant amount of swelling in the back of the ankle. It may be a problem with the Achilles tendon and not a typical sprain..
...you feel pain directly on the ankle bone, not merely an ache or tenderness on a muscle or tendon.

Quick relief:

Serve up some RICE: For the first few days after an ankle sprain, doctors recommend the RICE (rest, ice, compression, and elevation) treatment plan. It works like this:

Rest. Completely rest the affected joint area for at least the first 24 hours.
Ice. Apply an ice pack wrapped in a towel to the injured area for 20 to 30 minute sessions, three to four times daily, for as long as you have swelling. (When all swelling is gone, you can switch to a heating pad for 20 to 30 minute sessions, three to four times daily, until the pain is gone.)
Compression. Wrap the joint area with a compression bandage, being careful not to cut off the circulation.
Elevation. Rest the joint in a raised position until the pain and swelling begin to lessen.

Experts agree that this procedure is important to follow as quickly as possible after the injury. How long do you use RICE? Most authorities say 48 hours. One way to tell is to put the back of your hand on one ankle, and then on the injured ankle. If the injured ankle feels warmer, you still have bleeding and swelling going on. Continue until the injured ankle is not longer warm. If it's swollen but not warm, it's okay to resume normal activities—but do so gradually, testing the ankle after a day or more has passed.

Take some tablets of relief. If your ankle really hurts, consider easing the pain with an over-the-counter nonsteroidal anti-inflammatory drug (NSAID) such as ibuprofen. " Follow the directions on the product label. But don't ignore lingering pain or try to cover it up with over-the-counter painkillers," says Phillip A. Bauman, MD, an orthopaedic surgeon. "You need to be aware of pain to keep from re-injuring vulnerable muscles or tendons," he says.

Give a sprain a pop. The commonest cause of ankle pain is a sprain, and the most basic treatment is to elevate the injury and apply cold and compression. Stephen G Motto, a musculo-skeletal physician with a speciality in sports medicine at London Bridge Hospital, offers a simple way of doing the last two: fill a plastic cup with water, freeze this, then cut off the rim of the cup – the cup is now like an ice lolly/popsicle. Invert the cup and apply the ice behind a towel firmly to the injury for 10–15 minutes, no more.

Wrap it up. Protect the injury from further damage for the next 2–3 days by wrapping it in a crêpe bandage or similar product, says Dr. Motto. Not only does this ensure that the ankle won't be wrenched painfully, it is also good for your mental state. "The presence of the bandage is a form of 'rubbing it better', and will make you feel more secure," he says.

Heat things up. Doctors advise that once swelling has subsided and your ankles are the same temperature, you may gradually mix heat and cold. Here's how: Apply heat for 5 minutes, then switch to cold for 5 minutes, then go back to heat for 5, then go to cold for 5, and again, for a 30-minute total. Try to do this at least two times a day. Epsom salt soaks are another warm option you may try once swelling has gone down.

Easing the pain with exercise:

Exercise is important because it reduces the amount of scar tissue that develops after a sprain. Too much scar tissue and you'll lose mobility in the ankle joint. Doctors recommend mild stretching to help resolve swelling and soreness, and strengthening exercises returning power to the ankle's ligaments, muscles, and tendons. Here are some to try (wait for a few days for the pain and swelling in your ankle subsides before you start):

Stretching exercises:

Wave bye-bye with your toes. Sitting on a chair, extend your legs in front of you, about three inches off the floor. Focus on your toes and try to turn them back toward you as far as you can. Hold for a few seconds. Then tip your toes forward so that they point straight out in front of you. Again, hold for a few seconds. Try 5 repetitions at first and work up to 15 twice a day, suggests Kim Fagan, MD, sports medicine physician. "This back-and-forth motion will get the muscles in the lower leg working and help dissipate any swelling," she says. "You should feel a little discomfort, but don't push to the point of pain."

Try the ankle alphabet. Slip off your shoes and sit on a chair or the floor. Using your big right toe as a pointer, rotate your ankle to air-write the letter "A." Be sure you pivot around your ankle. Don't just move your whole leg. Continue through the alphabet. For variety, write your name in the air.

Play foot tennis. Here's a sprain-recovery stretch recommended by Michael Ciccotti, MD, an orthopaedic surgeon. "Try this as soon as comfort allows," he says. "Some swelling is okay."

Sit on a chair with both feet flat on the floor. Tuck a tennis ball between the arches of your feet. Gripping the ball, raise and extend your legs so that your heels are three to four inches off the floor. Holding the ball between your feet, slowly rotate both ankles clockwise. Try 10 clockwise circles and then 10 circles counterclockwise. Remember to make the circles by rotating your ankles, not just by moving your legs and feet. Start and end your day with this stretch.

Table your pain. From a standing position, lean forward against a table with your hands palms down on the table edge. Stand far enough away so that you feel a moderate stretch in your calf muscles. Your arms should be straight .

Lock the leg with the sprained ankle at the knee. Slide the other leg forward and bend it so that your knee is directly over your toes.

Keep your heels on the floor.

Press your upper body forward (don't bend at the waist) until you feel a moderate stretch in the calf muscles of your back leg. Hold that stretch for 15 to 20 seconds.

Keeping both heels on the floor, bend your back leg until you feel a moderate stretch in your Achilles tendon. Hold that stretch for 15 to 20 seconds

To give your good ankle a healthy stretch, change your position and repeat the steps on the other side.

Strengthening exercises

After you complete these exercises to give your sprained ankle a workout, Dr. Fagan recommends that you repeat them with your good ankle to keep it in top shape. (And after your ankle has healed, these same exercises can keep both ankles in good shape, lowering the risk of future injuries).

Move it out and up. Sit barefoot on a chair with your aching foot directly facing the leg of a sturdy table. Loop one end of a resistance band (available at sporting goods stores; if that's not handy, a bike inner tube will do) around your foot at the base of your toes (your toes will have to be slightly flexed). Loop the other end around the table leg about two inches above the floor. Keeping your heel on the floor, raise your toes up and slowly turn your foot outward, pulling the band taut. Repeat this five times

Move it in and up. For the second band stretch, start with your feet in the same position as before. With your heel on the floor, slowly turn your ankle inward while flexing your toes as high as you can. Feel the resistance from the band. Try five stretches.

Pull straight. For this final strength-building exercise, start with your heel on the floor and your toes facing the table leg. This time, flex your toes straight back as far as you can. Feel the tug-of-war from the band. Try five repetitions.

Towel off. Sit on the floor with your legs straight out in front of you. Wrap a towel around the ball of the foot on the same side as your injured ankle and grip the ends of the towel in your hands. Pull the towel toward you, flexing your foot with it. Hold for 10 seconds and relax. Then point your toes forward into the towel, using your arms for resistance. Hold for 5 seconds. Repeat 10 times.

Walk in water: Seek a flat-bottomed pool with cool water. Begin by walking on the bottom of the pool. Then bounce up and down lightly. Gradually work up to jogging in the pool, then see if you can build up to running in the water. The water makes you more buoyant, so there's less weight on the ankle. Be sure to wait at least 72 hours after your initial injury to hit the pool.

Try a wobbly workout. The most common causes of ankle pain are ill-fitting shoes and high heels. But the answer to the problem is to exercise your ankles to increase their flexibility and strength, says Jenny Sutcliffe, former Senior Lecturer in Paediatric Neurology, Great Ormond Street Hospital, London, and chartered physiotherapist. Buy a wobble board from your local health store and stand on it twice a day, for five minutes to start with and working up to 20 minutes a session—it's fun and it helps strengthen the muscles surrounding the ankle. And when you are sitting down, try crossing one leg over the other and circling the top foot six times in each direction; then repeat with the other leg on top. Doing this increases the range of movement at the ankle joint, Dr. Sutcliffe says. Walk around barefooted as much as possible, too—this strengthens the ankle, and improves overall co-ordination and balance.

Everyday prevention:
Stand like a flamingo. Lots of sprains happen because you lose your balance, stumble, and land on one of your feet at an odd angle. To improve your balance, try standing on one leg. Keeping one leg slightly bent, simply lift your other leg off the floor. If you're nervous about being unsteady, put a chair in front of you as a security measure. After one minute of standing on your right leg, switch legs. If you're feeling brave, try the one-legged stance with your eyes closed. It will help you achieve better balance.

Choose sensible shoes. Poorly fitted or shoddily constructed footwear can make underlying foot problems worse, perhaps setting you up for an ankle injury. Here are some guidelines offered by the American Podiatric Medical Association for choosing proper shoes:

Have your feet measured, while standing, each time you try on shoes.

Shop for shoes in the afternoon. Your feet swell during the day.

Try on both shoes. If one foot is larger, choose the shoes that fit the bigger foot.

Allow a thumb's width between the end of your big toe and the tip of the shoe.

Be sure that the ball of your foot fits well into the widest part of the shoe. The heel should fit snugly.

Look for a shoe with a firm sole and a soft upper.

Shoe soles should be flexible and move when your foot moves. Look for thicker soles to soften the pressure placed on your foot if you walk on hard surfaces.

Avoid extreme, often uncomfortable styles.

Choose shoes made of leather or any fabric that allows your feet to breathe and that lets the shoe conform to the shape of your foot.

Select shoes that will match your activity, not your outfit. Try not to wear high-heeled shoes on a daily basis.

When buying athletic shoes, be sure to wear appropriate socks to guarantee a good fit. And consider your sport and its unique foot requirements before making a selection.

Herbal help:

Soothe gingerly. After two to three days, apply warm compresses, says Arthur H. Brownstein, MD, a physician, and clinical instructor of medicine. Here's his unusual remedy.

Boil fresh grated ginger, then let it cool a little.

Make a compress by soaking a washcloth in the warm brew.

Place the compress over the injured ankle.

According to Dr. Brownstein, ginger draws out toxins and hastens healing.

Arthritis

The pain: Achy, chronic joint pain and swelling that leads to limited movement and stiffness.

The cause: The word arthritis literally means "joint inflammation," but refers to a group of 100 rheumatic diseases that cause pain, stiffness, and swelling in those critical areas where bone meets bone throughout your body. Arthritis is basically a packaging problem. Your joints—remarkable and elaborate hinges—are cushioned by cartilage. They're held together with various other tissues, including muscles and tendons. Lubrication is in the form of some oily goo called synovial fluid, which is released by the synovial lining of the joints.

If you have osteoarthritis (the kind that most frequently coincides with ageing), the cartilage around the joints starts to thin down or disappear. Overuse may be the root of the problem—years of wear and tear of the joints. Obesity may contribute to the development of osteoarthritis in weight-bearing joints.

The runner-up, rheumatoid arthritis, is far less common, more mysterious, and equally pain producing. Rheumatoid arthritis is an inflammatory disease. With some people, the onset begins between the ages of 30 and 40, but more often it starts when people are between the ages of 40 and 60. For reasons that aren't fully understood, your own body's immune system attacks your own joints, which start to suffer dire consequences.

See a doctor if...
...you have pain, stiffness, swelling in and around joints, and limited movement that lasts more than two weeks. Don't delay because you think that all you have are minor aches and pains, says Howard R. Smith, MD, chief of rheumatology at Meridia Huron Hospital. Often, the sooner you see your doctor, the more options you have and the better the outcome, he says. As an arthritic condition worsens, the joint may become more painful and deformed; and, in some cases, you may need a joint replacement to regain movement and function. While some forms of arthritis can be cured, there are no cures for osteoarthritis and rheumatoid arthritis. But they can often be effectively controlled, says Dr. Smith, and there are things you can do to help manage them.

...any of the joints in your body appear red or swollen or if tenderness in them persists for several weeks, suggests Robert Swezey, MD, arthritis and back pain specialist. Also, be sure to schedule an appointment if your hands are bright red, swollen, and you can't grab things properly. "Whatever you do, don't put off seeing a doctor, if you're in pain," says Dr. Swezey. "An early, accurate diagnosis will help you immensely."

It takes a doctor to determine whether you have osteo- or rheumatoid arthritis—and your doctor will outline some courses of action. And before you begin any kind of regular exercise program, it's important to have your doctor's approval.

Medication:

Anti-inflammatory drugs can certainly help you deal with arthritis pain. But anti-inflammatory medicines like aspirin and ibuprofen may aggravate certain pre-existing gastrointestinal conditions, notes David Richards, MD, an orthopaedic surgeon. Be sure you talk to your doctor about taking these medications if you have ulcers or intestinal bleeding, any inflamed bowel disorder or an aspirin allergy. Also, exposure to toxic drugs such as hydroxychloroquine (Plaquenil), which is prescribed for rheumatoid arthritis, can cause anaemia.

Rheumatologists know that stress causes arthritis to flare up. Would drugs that block the effects of stress also impede the inflammation of arthritis? Apparently so. Drugs called beta-2-blockers, which inhibit the effects of a stress-related hormone, norepinephine (noradrenaline), also apparently calm the fires of arthritis. "Other drugs currently used for the treatment of arthritis help reduce the pain and swelling, but beta-2-blockers have been shown to arrest further damage to the joint," says rheumatologist Jon Levine.

According to recent research, a rapid treatment with the prescription drug sulphasalazine at the onset of rheumatoid arthritis could put the brakes on joint damage. A study in the Netherlands found that the progression of joint damage was significantly reduced when sulpha-salazine was given in the early stages of rheumatoid arthritis.

Quick Relief:

Try aspirin. The least expensive and most widely used antiarthritis drug is still aspirin, and most rheumatologists still recommend this ancient medicine as the first line of defence against pain and inflammation. According to arthritis expert James F. Fries, MD, the pain-relieving, or analgesic, effect of aspirin reaches its peak after two five-grain tablets and lasts about 4 hours. Dr. Fries says that "the anti-inflammatory activity," in which rheumatoid arthritis sufferers may be more interested, "requires high and sustained blood levels of the aspirin. A patient may need to take 12 to 24 five grain tablets each day, and the process must be continued for weeks to obtain the full effect." This intense a regimen is standard for people with rheumatoid arthritis and requires medical supervision.

Try a cold pack. If you have swelling, especially after any physical activity, put some ice with a thin towel wrapped around it on the area around the affected joint, says Keith Jones, head trainer for the Houston Rockets. "Ice the area for 15 to 20 minutes after exercise to reduce the discomfort and also minimise the amount of swelling," Jones says.

Or as an alternative to ice packs, recommends physical therapist Pesanelli applying a package of frozen peas to the affected area because they can contort to the shape of the hurting joint. After you've used the peas once, you can just toss them back in the freezer compartment, get them iced, and use the same bag again. But since bacteria can quickly multiply in food that has been thawed and refrozen, make sure to clearly label them so that you don't accidentally try to serve them for dinner.

Give yourself a hot wax. A hot-wax treatment can provide soothing relief if your hands are aching from arthritis, says Dr. Jane Katz, a professor of health and physical education. The treatment is available at many hospitals, he points out, but it's less expensive to treat yourself at home. A professional therapist should instruct you on its appropriate use before you use this at home.

For a hot-wax or paraffin treatment kit, call an orthopaedic supply store to check availability. "Heat the wax in the heating unit, apply it to your hands, and wrap them in plastic liner gloves for 10 minutes and you should feel some relief." Professional units are also available for home use. The beauty of the at-home hot-wax treatment is that the wax can be reused for several weeks.

Immobilise the achy area. Buy a splint and use it to immobilise the joints affected by arthritis. The splint will keep the area from being bumped or moved, says David Richards, MD, orthopaedic surgeon. But Dr. Richards cautions that a splint, sling, or other protective device shouldn't be used for more than a couple of days. If you start to rely on the splint, your muscles could weaken quickly. If the symptoms persist after a couple of days, see your doctor.

Pepper yourself. You may not like hot peppers on your sandwich, but you might like hot pepper cream for arthritis relief. Capsaicin cream, made from the active ingredient in hot peppers, has been shown in studies to ease arthritis pain when used regularly, according to Jeffrey R. Lisse, MD, rheumatologist. You can buy this cream over the counter. Follow instructions on the label, wash your hands thoroughly after application, and keep this stuff away from your eyes and other mucous membranes. It can really burn.

Blast your clothes. "Most arthritic pain responds to heat," says Charles Jones, D.P.M., a podiatrist. "Heat reduces the stiffness, too." During the winter, as Dr. Jones advises his patients, you can warm up your clothes in the dryer for a few minutes before dressing. The warmth will help loosen stiff morning joints.

Get a gadget. "The best quick fixes for arthritis are the ones you can do around the house or on the job to make life easier," says Valery Lanyi, MD, a rehabilitation specialist. "There are dozens of techniques and easy-to-use, inexpensive devices to help you conserve energy and save wear and tear on the joints. Thousands of gadgets and widgets can make your life easier," Dr. Lanyi says. "Some you can make yourself." For example:

Opening and closing things: Looping a cloth through the refrigerator door handle saves wear and tear on the fingers. Smaller loops through zippers make dressing easier. And, Dr. Lanyi says, there are even gadgets that will open doors with the flip of a switch.

Holding things: Wrapping foam rubber around the handles of eating utensils, razors, and hairbrushes makes them easier to grip and less stressful for sensitive, arthritic fingers. An extended mirror saves bending over while shaving, as can long-handled shoehorns and sock-pullers while dressing.

Go over the counter. Take two tablets of acetaminophen (paracetamol) every four hours to relieve pain. Avoid, however, the NSAIDs like ibuprofen and naproxen (Aleve or Naprosyn), except for occasional relief.

Play towel toss. Moist heat helps improve blood flow and relax tight muscles around joints, says Dr. Hamner a physiatrist. The next time your knee throbs or your elbow swells, try wetting a hand towel and then putting it in your dryer at a high temperature for about 10 minutes. Take it out while it is still wet and hot. Place it on your knee or elbow and then lay a dry towel on top to keep the heat from escaping.

Hit the showers. This "no-sweat-but-get-wet" technique can decrease muscular stiffness associated with arthritis in your neck and back, says Jane Sullivan-Durand, MD, a behavioural medicine physician. "Stand under a hot shower for 10 minutes with the water beading on the affected

---

Golfing with arthritis

If you're a golfer with arthritis, the Arthritis Foundation offers these exercise tips to stay on the links.

Before you tee off, walk for a few minutes to loosen your joints.

Devote 5 or 10 minutes to gentle stretches like trunk twists and hamstring stretches.

Be sure to spend some time on the practice range. Loosen your muscles with a few dozen swings.

If your playing partners aren't sticklers for the rules:

Use tees for every shot that you take, even on the fairway. This will help you avoid striking the ground and jarring your joints.

If you start feeling tired, skip the tee area and begin your pursuit of the hole from the 150-yard marker on the fairway.

area. Get the temperature as hot as you can stand," she says.

Go hot or cold. When arthritis flares up, you can use either cold or heat to help relieve the pain, says Howard R. Smith, MD, a rheumatologist. It depends on the problem. If your joints and muscles are stiff when you wake up or after a long period of inactivity, take a long, hot shower; dip your hands in a paraffin bath (talk to your doctor about getting one of these if you have rheumatoid arthritis in your hands); or apply a heating pad to the stiff area. If your joints are inflamed and swollen, apply ice or an ice pack wrapped in a thin towel. As a general rule, apply the heat or cold for 20 minutes, and repeat as needed, up to several times a day.

Request some rubbing. Ask your spouse or a friend for a 10-minute massage. Massage can reduce pain, says Dr. Hamner. It can push blood and other bodily fluids through the bloodstream to reduce swelling and eliminate waste products from tissues.

Nutritional Remedies:

Seek suspects with an elimination diet. For about one-third of all people with arthritis, sensitivity to one or more foods may be to blame for the pain, says John Irwin, MD,—author of *Arthritis Begone!* "It appears that, for some people, certain foods can spark an immune response that leads to the inflammatory condition of arthritis," he says. Eliminating those foods, which aren't the same for all food-sensitive people, can mean an improvement in both pain and swelling.

To discover if your arthritis is related to a food sensitivity, Dr. Irwin recommends that you follow the Class One diet for one week. This basic, limited diet is designed to rule out your most common trouble foods. If you are one of the people affected by food, this step alone will most likely give you some blessed-and quick-pain relief, according to Dr. Irwin.

In the Class One diet, the safe foods to eat are limited to the following: Fruits: Grapes, peaches, pears, plums, and prunes. Vegetables: Lettuce, avocado, celery, olives, parsley flakes, cauliflower, peas, spinach, and winter squash. Starch: Rice. Oils: Olive oil. Fish: Cod, flounder, salmon, tuna, and trout. Water and salt as needed.

If you experience significant relief on the Class One diet, you can start identifying which trigger foods you need to avoid. Reintroduce potential trouble foods into your diet one at a time. Those foods can include anything that is not in the basic diet, such as bananas, lamb, shellfish, dairy products, and caffeine. After you have reintroduced the food, eat a good amount of it during the next day or two. If you have no reaction, then you can add that food to the "friendly" list. But if arthritic symptoms flare up, mark down that food as a troublemaker.

Drop the trouble food from your diet forever, then wait until you are feeling painless again before you resume your food sleuthing. In time, you will have a range of safe foods to choose from and a list of pain-producing foods to avoid. This dieting should be safe for everyone, but people with diabetes or who are on other special diets should check with their doctors before trying it.

Enjoy some pineapple. Some intriguing research suggests that bromelain, a chemical in pineapple, helps prevent inflammation. For some time now, athletic trainers have been recommending pineapple to athletes to prevent and treat sports injuries. Bormelain can help the body get rid of immune antigen complex, compounds that are implicated in some arthritic conditions. It also helps digest fibrin, another compound suspected of being involved in some types of arthritis. if you need an excuse to indulge yourself with fresh, ripe pineapple, this is it.

Eat well. Many folks with arthritis just don't eat very well. Their diets are top-heavy with fat, prepared foods and sodium, says Dr. Morgan, a research scientist. "A good diet improves overall health, boosts your immune system, and provides minerals and vitamins that the body needs," she says. Because many arthritis drugs affect the way you absorb vitamins and minerals, you might get vitamin deficiencies if you don't eat a balanced diet, she explains. Eat lots of fruits, vegetables, and whole-grain cereals, suggests Dr. Morgan.

Chug black cherry. Black cherry juice is good for arthritis, says Eve Campanelli, Ph.D., a holistic family practitioner. She estimates that around 85% of her patients with arthritis get a least partial relief from drinking two glasses of this juice twice a day (each glass contains four ounces of juice diluted with four ounces of water). "Fresh is always best, but even black cherry juice from concentrate seems to benefit arthritis," she says. She adds that you can discontinue this treatment once the pain clears up.

Go fish. Eat more salmon or other cold-water fish such as herring and sardines and you just might take some of the sting out of rheumatoid arthritis, says Dr. Katz. That's because these fish are high in omega-3 fatty acids, a type of fat that actually eases the aches and swelling of an arthritic joint.

Gulp glutathione. Studies show that people who are low in the antioxidant compound glutathione are more likely to have arthritis than those who have higher doses. Vegetables rich in glutathione include asparagus, broccoli, cabbage, cauliflower, potatoes, tomatoes and purslane. Fruits with healthy amounts include avocados, grapefruit, oranges, peaches and watermelon.

Helpful vitamins and supplements:

Put on the brakes with vitamin C. Vitamin C may not be able to prevent osteoarthritis, but research shows that it may help prevent the rapid progression of the disease. In a Boston University study of 640 people with and without knee osteoarthritis, those eating the most vitamin C had three times less disease progression than the people eating the least amounts of that vitamin, the least being about 120 milligrams (the equivalent of two oranges) per day. These results suggest that the people eating more vitamin C lost less cartilage and were likely to develop less pain during the eight years of the study than did those who didn't get as much of the nutrient.

Study leader Tim McAlindon, MD, assistant professor of medicine at the Boston University School of Medicine, theorises that an antioxidant vitamin like vitamin C provides important protection when the inflammation from arthritis is in full swing. Vitamin C and other antioxidants earn their name by helping to prevent the ageing process, which is accelerated by cell-attacking free radicals that come from oxygen molecules. Inflammation is believed to release cell-attacking free radicals that do more damage to the joint, unless antioxidant vitamins are there to stop the radicals from doing harm. So while antioxidant vitamins may not stop you from getting arthritis, they may prevent the disease from becoming severe.

Try the fab four. Besides vitamin C, be sure to take the following four nutritional supplements. The two vitamins help prevent tissue damage, while the two minerals rebuild cartilage.

Vitamin A: 5,000 IU (international units) per day Vitamin E: 400 IU per day

Zinc picolinate: 30 milligrams per day

Copper: 2 milligrams per day.

Ask for alternative oils. If you're not a fish eater, Dr. Katz recommends a visit to the nearest health food store. Look for either evening primrose oil, flaxseed oil, or fish oil. All contain the same omega-3 fatty acids found in cold-water fish. If you take one teaspoon of either each day, it might lightly ease some of the inflammatory aspects of arthritis, Dr. Katz says. If you decide to take capsules, follow the manufacturer's instructions on the label.

Give glucosamine a go. Supplement with 500 milligrams of glucosamine sulfate three times daily-and give it time to act. Glucosamine is a naturally occurring chemical found in joints that stimulates connective-tissue repair and new cartilage growth. It also reduces pain and inflammation. It may take about six weeks before you start getting pain relief from it. If you get a stomach irritation, reduce the dose.

Everyday Prevention:

Dehumidify. If the humidity is kept constant in your house it can help calm arthritis pain caused by weather changes, says Joseph Hollander, MD, professor emeritus of medicine at the University of Pennsylvania Hospital. When rain is on the way, the sudden increase in humidity and decrease in air pressure can affect blood flow to affected joints, which become increasingly stiff until the storm actually starts. If you close the windows and turn on a dehumidifier—or an air conditioner in summer— you may be able to eliminate this short-term but significant pain.

Lighten the burden. Arthritis gets worse more rapidly in overweight individuals, according to Dr. Dale L. Anderson author of *Muscle Pain Relief in 90 Seconds.* "If you lose 5 or 10 pounds, it considerably lightens the load

A stinging solution

Would anyone in his right mind ever ask for a bee sting? How about 20 of them? If you sought out the care of an apitherapist, that is precisely what you would be doing. Apitherapy-the medicinal use of bee venom and other bee products-has been practised since the time of the ancient Greeks, and today is practised by more than 10,000 Americans.

Bee venom contains a variety of anti-inflammatory substances that can relieve the pain and stiffness of arthritis, according to Glenn S. Rothfeld, MD, author of Natural Medicine for Arthritis. To benefit from this unusual medicine, though, you need to be brave.

First, you will need to see a qualified apitherapist, a person who has been trained to use bees and their products for treating disease. The apitherapist uses tweezers to hold the bee and control stinging. Then he applies it to the area it is supposed to sting, either directly on the sore joint or in a trigger point-an area of your body identified by the apitherapist as being related to your aching joint.

The number of stings and the duration of the treatment depends on you and your arthritis. If your condition is ongoing and troublesome, you might require several stings at a time, two or three times a week, for up to three months.

Never try this if you know that you are allergic to bee stings. You should always have a bee-sting kit in readiness, in case you have an allergic reaction. Also be aware that the Arthritis Foundation does not endorse apitherapy for the treatment of arthritis.

on all your weight-bearing joints—hips, knees, ankles, and feet," Dr. Anderson says.

Shoe away the pain. To ease the impact on your hip, leg, ankle, and foot joints, invest in a pair of walking shoes, advises Dr. Anderson. Because these shoes have softer heels, walking will be easier on your arthritis. Leather-soled shoes and high heels are out if you do a lot of walking, he says.

Don't hurt—try HRT. If you are a postmenopausal woman, you probably already know that taking oestrogen during hormone-replacement therapy (HRT) helps protect you from osteoporosis, the bone-thinning disease that can shatter hips and spines. Researchers at the University of California, San Francisco, have discovered that oestrogen may help protect bones from another disabling bone disease—osteoarthritis. The scientists (led by Michael C. Nevitt, Ph.D.,) examined the hip x-rays of 4,366 women, age 65 and older. They found that the women taking oestrogen had a 38 percent lower risk of developing any osteoarthritis in their hips than women who weren't taking the hormone. Even better, oestrogen-takers had a 46 percent lower risk of moderate to severe hip arthritis.

Ease the pain with exercise:

Stretch things. Any kind of stretching is good as long as you do not bounce, which can lead to a muscle pull, says Emil Pascarelli, MD, professor of clinical medicine. Try to hold a slow, steady stretch for 15 to 20 seconds, then relax and repeat. It is best to limber up by stretching before any exercise, especially running and walking. But it is also a good idea to stretch each day. Ask your doctor to teach you stretches that focus on potential arthritis trouble spots, such as the knees or the lower back.

Move those joints. To keep the pain of arthritis from getting an even tighter grip on you, get yourself on an exercise program, says Dale L. Anderson, MD. "Folks suffering from osteoarthritis must stay active, otherwise the already affected joints will get weaker and the person's overall aerobic capacity will drop," says Dr. Anderson. If you're over 60, start with low-impact aerobic activities such as 20-minute walks or exercises in a swimming pool at least three or four times per week, says William Pesanelli, physical therapist.

Any aerobic exercise program should be matched to your physical capacity, says Pesanelli. "If a person has been inactive for a period of time, then we're not suggesting they go out and try and run a marathon. Instead, start with something like a five-minute walk a couple times per week and then slowly start to increase your distance as you feel more comfortable."

Vary your terrain. Walking is always recommended but it's important not to get in a rut. "If you walk the same exact path every day, then you're landing on the same part of your foot each and every day and you're putting stress on your knees and hips the exactly same way every day," says Dr. Dale Anderson. For the sake of interest as well as exercise, seek out new terrain like hills, fields, and pathways as well as flat road or sidewalk.

Walk softly. Dr. Anderson believes that there are two types of walkers in this world: soft walkers and hard walkers. Soft walkers glide across a room and don't put their heels, ankles, feet, or knees through much stress. Hard walkers are in the habit of hitting the ground with their heels or soles of their feet.

If you suffer from arthritis and are a hard walker, try out a softer, more gliding style. Try to place your feet when you walk, rather than plunk them or imagine that you're gliding on a layer of air or having puppetlike strings attached to your head and shoulders that straighten you up. "You'll feel like you're walking on air, and it will save serious wear and tear on your weight-bearing joints," promises Dr. Anderson.

The Morning-and-Evening Exercise Plan

"A daily routine that combines flexibility exercises with strength exercise reduces pain and stiffness," says Dan Hamner, MD, a physiatrist and sports medicine specialist. The following 10-minute exercise plan may help people with osteoarthritis. Try these exercises twice a day—right after you wake up and right before you go to bed. Start out by repeating each exercise 3 times and gradually work up to 10 repetitions.

The first half of Dr. Hamner's plan focuses on improving flexibility and range of motion.

For ankles: Before you begin, warm up by sitting on a chair and crossing one leg over the other. Slowly rotate the ankle of your top leg so that your foot moves in a circle. Then switch sides and repeat with your other ankle. Now you're ready to begin.

Stand facing a wall with your feet flat on the floor and shoulder-width apart.

Place both palms against the wall at shoulder height and lean forward from the waist.

Keeping your left foot in place and your heel on the floor, take one step forward with your right foot.

Keeping your left knee and hip straight, bend your right knee and lean forward a bit at the right hip.

Gently stretch forward and hold this position for two to five seconds. You'll feel a little stretch in your left ankle, but stop if you feel any pain.

Repeat this movement, reversing the position of your legs.

For knees: Warm up by standing with your feet and legs together and your hands on your knees (if you need more balance, you can keep your feet about six inches apart). Slowly move both knees in a circular motion, first clockwise and then counterclockwise.

Next, lie on your back and bend your right leg at the knee; keep your left leg straight.

Use both hands to pull your left knee to your chest. Hold for two to five seconds.

Push your left leg into the air, as close to vertical as you can manage.

Hold this position for a moment and then lower your leg slowly to the floor.

Repeat these steps with the right knee. Try doing five sets for each knee.

For hips: You can use the same basic warm-up for your hips that you used for your knees. Stand with your legs together, put your hands on your hips, and slowly move your hips in a circle as if you were playing with an imaginary hula hoop, first clockwise and then counterclockwise. Don't try the following exercise, though, if you have had a total hip replacement or if you have lower back problems or osteoporosis.

Lie on your back with your legs straight. Place your feet six inches apart with your toes pointed up.

Slowly slide your right leg out to the side as far as you can comfortably while keeping your toes pointed up. Hold for two to five seconds and then slowly slide your leg back to its original position.

Repeat with your left leg.

For shoulders: Standing straight, raise your left arm over your head, keeping your elbow straight and your arm close to your ear. Hold the stretch for two to five seconds. Then sweep your arm—like the hand of a clock—forward in a clockwise motion and bring it slowly back to your side. Repeat with your right arm.

The second half of Dr. Hamner's daily workout centres on maintaining and increasing muscle strength.

For ankles: Sit in a comfortable chair with both feet flat on the floor. Try to lift the toes of your left foot as high as possible while keeping your heel on the floor. Hold this position for 5 seconds. Then lift the toes on your right foot and hold for 5 seconds. Next, lift the front of your left foot and tap with your toes for 10 seconds, then tap the toes of your right foot for 10 seconds. Then tap both feet for 10 seconds. Try to work up to 60 seconds for each foot.

For knees: Sit in a comfortable chair with both feet on the floor and spread slightly apart. Move your left foot up and out until your leg is parallel to the floor. Tighten your leg muscles and hold for 10 seconds. Slowly lower your leg, then repeat the same steps with your right leg.

For hips: Stand straight and place your right hand on the back of a chair in front of you. Using your hip muscles, extend your left leg behind you while keeping your right knee fairly straight. Hold for two seconds, then slowly lower your leg. Raise it again for two seconds. Think up, one-two, down, one-two. Repeat with your right leg.

Work out in water. Exercising in water can be a great anti-arthritis option. The water not only keeps your aching bones from being jarred, it also offers resistance and thus helps you build strength. "Water is the mainstream alternative for low-impact, soft exercise," says Jane Katz, Ed.D., world Masters champion swimmer, and author of *The New W.E.T. Workout.* She suggests these pool exercises.

• **Follow your toes.** Sit on the edge of a pool and dangle your legs up to midcalf in the water, says Dr. Katz. Begin by making foot circles, rotating from the ankle clockwise and then counterclockwise. Next, move your feet forward and back, then left and right, keeping your legs slightly bent and your ankles loose. Repeat each five times.

• **Try a wet walk.** Stand in chest-deep water and simply walk forward normally, making sure to swing your arms as you would on dry land. Once you feel stable doing this, try walking backward and then sideways, says Dr. Katz. Begin with 1 minute, resting as needed, and progress to 10 minutes.

• **Step up the pace of your walk.** Pretend you're in a race and run in place, lifting your knees and moving your arms with each stride. As you get comfortable with this water jog, try to run faster and faster, says Dr. Katz. Begin with one minute, resting as needed, and progress to five minutes.

• **Try a wrist roll.** Standing in chest-deep water, extend your arms to the sides, keeping them underwater, and slowly close and open your fists six times. Then, to work your wrists, point your fingers up and then down, then keep your wrists straight as you move your hands from side to side. Finish by making clockwise and counterclockwise hand circles from the wrists, with both open hands and closed fists. Progress to three sets, resting briefly between sets.

Do lunges to build up the muscles that protect your hips and legs. Standing upright, step with your right foot farther forward than a normal step, while you bend your right knee. Do not let your right knee extend beyond your toes. Then push back against that leg, returning to the starting point. Repeat with your left leg. Do 10 repetitions with each leg. To increase resistance, hold hand-weights while you are doing the lunges if you can do so without pain.

Lift some light weights. An interesting, new way to treat arthritis takes the focus off the joints and strengthens the surrounding muscles instead, says Glenn S. Rothfeld, MD, author of *Natural Medicine for Arthritis.* "Gentle weight training makes a lot of sense for arthritis," he says. Stronger muscles at either end of an arthritic joint mean that the cartilage in between won't have to work as hard-and that translates into less pain.

To strengthen the muscles that protect your elbows, do concentration curls, suggests Dr. Rothfeld. Sitting in a chair, lean forward and hold a one-pound dumbbell in your right hand. Brace your right elbow against the inside of your right thigh, with your left hand on your left knee for support.

Head-to-toe check

There are specific arthritis treatments for specific body parts, according to Paul Caldron, D.O., a clinical rheumatologist and researcher at the Arthritis Centre in Phoenix.

Give your neck a break. Don't extend your neck by looking up for long periods. if you're painting, hanging curtains or doing other work that requires you to look up for long a time, get a ladder and bring yourself to the same level as the work.

Support your shoulders. Don't sleep with your arms over your head, because that strains your shoulders. Dr. Caldron advises women to lighten their handbags so that they carry only what they need. And big-busted women are advised to get bras with more support to ease shoulder strain.

Glove your hands. Wear gloves with a thick palm padding-like work gloves-whenever you're holding something tightly. With thick gloves you don't have to exert as much force on the hand joints to hold a heavy skillet, a broom or a wrench. Also, you can build up handles of tools and garden supplies with foam rubber padding or terry cloth, so you're exerting less force on the joints.

Never squat or kneel. That's about the worst thing you can do to arthritic knee and hip joints.

Ease your knees with a hydrocollator—a pad filled with silicon gel that you heat up in the microwave.

Wear running or walking shoes whenever possible. To ease the pressure on aching feet, you want footwear that provides comfort and support. When shopping for dressier footwear, look for shoes that have a wide toe box and good, built-in arch support. The best shoes have heels approximately 1 to 1½ inches high, and they come up high on the instep. For men, a lace-up oxford, as opposed to a slip-on, is the preferable dress shoe.

Soak your feet alternately in basins of cool and warm water; try five minutes in each basin and keep switching until the warm water cools.

Then bend the elbow to lift the weight, curling it up and in toward your body. Do 10 repetitions, then repeat with your left arm. You can increase to a three-pound weight if you don't feel any pain. You may continue to increase weight every two sessions until you are at a challenging, but not straining, weight. Try to engage in weight training every two to three days.

Herbal Help:

Sip some white willow bark. "Aspirin was discovered more than 100 years ago by a German chemist who studied white willow bark's pain-relieving properties," says Douglas Schar, a practising medical herbalist in London, editor of the British Journal of Phytotherapy, and author of

Backyard Medicine Chest. But white willow bark has an edge over aspirin—it doesn't cause stomach irritation, as aspirin can, adds Schar. It may not be the best-tasting beverage around, but a strong cup of white willow bark tea will do wonders to relieve the inflammation in a sore joint, he notes. To make the tea, steep 1 teaspoon of white willow bark in a cup of boiling water, covered, for 15 minutes. Strain out the bark and drink a cup three times a day.

Mix up an herbal rub-down. "A medicated rub made with pure essential oils can ease inflammation and joint pain," says Schar. "Here's my favourite: Get a small jar of petroleum jelly and discard 1 tablespoon's worth. To the jar, add 20 drops of essential oil of lemon and 20 drops of essential oil of sandalwood. Mix the oils well into the petroleum jelly and apply a dab to the sore joint four times a day."

Infuse yourself with some burdock and dandelion. "Herbalists know that if you stimulate liver function and improve the flow of bile, it helps to improve arthritis," says Schar. "Old medical books say that arthritis is caused by improper elimination of waste. While we don't know whether that's true scientifically, we do know that people feel that their arthritis improves when they use herbs like dandelion and burdock, which stimulate liver and kidney function."

To make tea, boil 1 teaspoon each of dried dandelion root and dried burdock root in 3 cups of water for 5 minutes, then sip it throughout the day. Drink it daily until you notice some improvement. Be prepared, though—the tea tastes bitter. You can add a little honey to make it more palatable, Schar says.

Try agrimony. "Known as a traditional medicine for what people used to call rheumatism, agrimony is a great herb for reducing pain and inflammation," says Margi Flint, a professional member of the AHG. Herbal textbooks recommend taking one to three drops of tincture one to three times a day as needed for pain.

Bathe in black cohosh. Add a few tablespoons of black cohosh infused oil to a tub of hot water, suggests Flint. The combination of the heat and the herbal oil will help relieve pain, she says. Traditionally, Native Americans used black cohosh for rheumatism; American colonists used it for similarly painful conditions such as lumbago, a type of back pain.

Concoct your own bath salts. "To ¼ cup of sea salt, add 1 tablespoon of either St. John's wort infused oil or black cohosh infused oil," says Flint. Used externally, St. John's wort helps reduce inflammation. Fill a tub with hot water and add the bath salts. "The salt absorbs the oil, and when the water dissolves the salt, the oil floats on top of the water," says Flint. "The combination helps remineralize your body and coats it with the therapeutic oil." Be careful getting out of the tub, though—the oil may make it slippery.

Take time for tea. Certain herbs can be very beneficial to joint health, says Glenn S. Rothfeld, MD, author of *Natural Medicine for Arthritis*. He recommends a mixture of nine herbs: white willow and nettle for their anti-inflammatory effect, calendula and white peony for their ability to detoxify joints, horsetail to strengthen connective tissue, and rosemary, yarrow, juniper berries, and cornflower for their overall anti-rheumatic effect.

Combine equal amounts of each dry herb in a large jar or other airtight container. Use one heaping teaspoon per cup of boiling water. Let the tea steep for 15 minutes to reach a healing strength. Strain, then drink two to three cups a day, says Dr. Rothfeld.

Or try ginger tea. Slice a piece of fresh ginger and put a few shavings of slivers of it in a tea ball. Put the tea ball in a cup, pour freshly boiled water over it and allow the ginger to steep for 10 minutes. Make sure tea has cooled off before sipping it.

Try ayurveda. "Arthritis takes many different forms," says David Frawley, O.MD, director of the American Institute of Vedic Studies in Santa Fe, New Mexico. "In Ayurveda, we're concerned with underlying energetic imbalances. Is the condition affected by heat or cold, dampness or dryness? An obese person with swollen joints, for instance, will be treated quite differently than a thin person with dry skin and brittle bones." Although long-term treatments differ, Dr. Frawley says the following remedies can soothe the pain of periodic attacks for most people. To loosen stiff joints and relieve pain, he suggests rubbing warmed sesame oil (available in most health food stores) onto affected areas once or twice a day, then taking a hot shower about 20 to 60 minutes afterward to heat the oil and drive it into the pores.

Also, add hot or spicy herbs such as cayenne, cinnamon and dried ginger to foods, he says.

For rheumatoid arthritis, Vasant Lad, B.A.M.S., M.A.Sc., director of the Ayurvedic Institute in Albuquerque, New Mexico, recommends taking 1/4 teaspoon of yogaraj guggulu three times daily, with a little warm water. This ancient herbal preparation is available by mail order. You can also add one tablespoon of castor oil to a cup of ginger tea and drink it before going to bed, he says.

Cure with curcumin. For rheumatoid arthritis, take 400 milligrams of curcumin three times a day until the flare-up subsides. Curcumin—the yellow pigment that gives turmeric its colour—may be nature's most potent anti-inflammatory agent, according to Joseph E. Pizzorno Jr., N.D., a naturopathic doctor and author of *Total Wellness*. Studies of people with rheumatoid arthritis have shown that it improves mobility, morning stiffness and joint swelling. Curcumin capsules are available at health food stores.

Order oregano. In a test of nearly 100 plants, oregano was the one that had the greatest total antioxidant activity. Like other antioxidants contained in fruits and vegetables, the compounds in oregano may help prevent the cell damage caused by free radicals—highly unstable oxygen molecules. Free radicals are probably involved in inflammation, degenerative arthritis and the ageing process in general. Considering how high it ranks for this kind of protection, oregano is definitely worth adding to your pizza or any other food, if you have arthritis.

Get help from homeopathy. For a homeopathic remedy, try Rhus tox. 6C or Bryonia 6C. For either remedy, take two pellets every 15 minutes for four doses, then two pellets every hour for four doses on the first day. After that, take two pellets every six hours for two to three weeks.

Mind over malady:

Try to relax. When you are feeling stressed, your muscles tense up, which can cause more pain. You can get caught in a destructive cycle where stress, pain, depression, and limited movement all work together to make you feel miserable. Learning how to relax is an important way to handle stress, advises Dr. Howard Smith. It's more than just sitting down and being quiet. It is an active process that takes practice. There's more than one way to relax, Dr. Smith says. Try deep breathing, progressive relaxation, or guided imagery and find out what works for you. Whichever one you try, pick a quiet place where you'll have at least 15 minutes to yourself. Get comfortable. Loosen tight clothing and sit or lie down, without crossing your legs, ankles, or arms. Try to do this daily, or at least four times a week.

Breathe deeply. To begin, sit comfortably with your feet on the floor, your arms at your sides, and your eyes closed, says Dr. Smith. Breathing in, say to yourself, "I am...." As you breathe out, say, "...relaxed." Continue breathing in and out silently saying positive things to yourself like "My hands...are warm" or "I feel calm...and relaxed." Co-ordinate your breathing with your words.

Be progressive. Progressive relaxation, in which you tense your muscles and then let them relax, is another helpful technique, says Dr. Smith. Close your eyes. Take a deep breath and hold it a few seconds. Breathe out, letting all your stress escape with the breath. Imagine that your muscles feel heavy and let them sink into the chair or floor. Starting with your feet and legs, tense your muscles for a few seconds and then let them relax. Work your way up your body, first tensing and then relaxing various groups of muscles. When you are done, remain sitting or lying quietly with your eyes closed for a few minutes and enjoy the feeling.

Use your imagination. Guided imagery and visualisation refocus your attention off stress and pain and on to more pleasant things, such as a day at the beach. Start by closing your eyes and taking a deep breath. Hold it a few seconds and exhale, letting go of your stress. Continue taking deep breaths and releasing your stress as you exhale, says Dr. Smith. Now think about a pleasant scene from your past or make one up. Imagine it in detail: the warm water lapping at your pain-free knees, the warm sun easing the aches in your hands and shoulders. Savor the image and enjoy feeling relaxed for a few minutes before you open your eyes.

You can also visualise painful body parts symbolically. Imagine your inflamed knees as bright red. Then try to change the picture. Make the red colour disappear as you imagine all stress and pain fading away.

Play mind games. Try to find at least 15 minutes of day of quiet time. Close your eyes and take deep, deliberate breaths. Inhale and exhale slowly and fully. Fifteen minutes of happy, healthy thoughts can ease muscle tension, say doctors.

Meditation, tai chi, visualization, and yoga are effective ways to counter pain and induce relaxation, say doctors.

Laugh the pain away. There's no need to be the Robin Williams or Jerry Seinfeld of your home or office. But frivolity can actively help, says Norman Harden, MD, a neurologist. "Laughter can trigger our wonderful endorphins, natural painkillers that also combat depression and anxiety," he says.

Athlete's Foot

The pain: Intense itching or burning between your toes or on the bottom or sides of your feet. The skin may turn white and soggy and may peel, or be raw, red, and inflamed. Sometimes you will even see cracking and oozing.

The cause: Microscopic, moisture-loving fungi that take up residence in the warm, dark, humid residence created by a foot in a shoe.

See your doctor (dermatologist) if:

Over the counter or other remedies don't work within five to seven days. Athlete's foot has the potential to bring on something more serious, like a bacterial infection.

The skin on your feet is so cracked that it's painful, or the cracks are beginning to look like cuts.

The fungus seems to have moved to the skin underneath your toes. At that point, it's tough to get rid of it without prescription medicine.

The infection is identical on both feet. It's probably eczema or an allergic reaction to your shoes.

It's only on the top of your toes. It may be contact dermatitis caused by shoe material.

It occurs on a child below the age of puberty. Athlete's foot rarely strikes before adolescence.

The foot is red, swollen, blistered and sore. Severe dermatitis is the likely culprit.

Nutritional Remedies:

Cut out the candy. Sugar feeds any sort of yeasty fungus, and that's what athlete's foot is. So if you cut out the sugar, you'll cut out one bit of sustenance to the gunk growing between your toes. "The remedies you put on the outside of your body will only help long-term if you're also feeding the inside of your body properly," says Nancy Dunne-Boggs, a doctor of naturopathy. "You need to cut at least simple sugars out of your diet." That means no candy, sugar, soda, maple syrup, ice cream, or other sweets, says Dr. Dunne-Boggs. "Do this until you can't see the fungus anymore and then for three weeks after that," she says. If you begin to eat sugar again and the fungus comes back, cut out the sweets again, then experiment with how much sugar you can eat without sending your feet back into fungus land.

Try antifungal teas. Scientists have demonstrated significant fungicidal activity for lemongrass oil against several common infection-causing fungi. Enjoy drinking lemongrass tea one to four times a day. And for additional fungal benefit, use the spent tea bags as compresses directly on the affected area. Other teas to try for an antifungal boost include cinnamon, fennel, peppermint, orange, sage and spearmint.

Over-the-counter aid:

Powder those puppies. "Using an antifungal foot powder every day is the best thing that you can do to prevent athlete's foot from recurring," says Thomas Helm, MD, dermatologist "One brand that I recommend is ZeaSORB, if it's not on your chemist shelf, ask your pharmacist to order it. It absorbs the moisture and has an antifungal ingredient that kills the organisms. After your morning shower, dry your feet carefully, sprinkle a little on your feet, put your socks on, and you're ready to go." Others are Desenex, Tinactin, and Micatin (Mycota and Mycil). Avoid cornstarch, it may set you up for a yeast infection. Powder the insides of your shoes too.

Slather on a lotion. "People who are prone to athlete's foot might also want to use a good medicated foot lotion or cream containing micronazole or clotrimazole. Check the product labels. These antifungals work very well to stop the itching and burning sensations that accompany athlete's foot," says Dr. Helm. To help prevent flare-ups of fungal activity, he recommends that you ask your doctor about a lotion called Lac-Hydrin (Compeed), which is available in prescription form. The lotion contains alpha hydroxy acids (AHAs), which remove the dead skin that is a perfect medium for the growth of the fungus. Hydrocortisone cream is an aggressive approach that should relieve extreme itching in a day or too. But using for more than a week may cause a "rebound" itch and rash.

Helpful hygiene:

Wash your dogs. Wash your feet at least once a day," says Jerome Z. Litt, MD, dermatologist and author of *Your Skin: From Acne to Zits*. Every time you wash well, you are flushing away some of those itch-producing fungi. "When you bathe, get in the toe webs and make sure that they are clean," he advises.

Use a tough soap. Sometimes the bacteria on your feet, coupled with the fungus, will start athlete's foot more readily. Try an antibacterial soap, instead of a perfumed kind, says Dr. Litt.

Dry your dogs thoroughly. This may be the most important anti–athlete's foot strategy, according to Dr. Litt. Dry the whole foot. Toe webs, too.

Blow the fungus away. Use your hair dryer on your feet dries them more effectively than you can with a towel. And blowing air from your hair dryer into your shoes is a good way to dry them out after you wear them.

Give 'em a soak. Soaking your feet in a solution of salt and warm water creates an unattractive environment for the fungus, and softens the

affected skin. (Use a mixture of two teaspoons of salt per pint of warm water.)
Remove dead skin. When your condition starts to improve, remove any dead skin. According to Frederick Hass, MD, author of *The Foot Book*, dead skin houses fungus that can reinfect you. To remove it, use a bristled scrub brush on the entire foot and a baby bottle "nipple brush" on toe webs. And brush in the shower, so the dead skin goes down the drain without touching other parts of your body.

Everyday prevention:
Divide to conquer. "To prevent and cure athlete's foot, keep your toe webs separated, particularly the last toe web (where athlete's foot is prominent)," says Dr. Litt. To do that, he suggests putting lamb's wool or any cotton material—"not cotton batting, but an old piece of linen shirting or sheeting cut into one-inch squares"—between the toes. "You can also use small corks and cut them in half," he says. "If you keep your toe webs open, you can't be tripped up by athlete's foot." If the day's almost over and you can kick back for a while, prop up your bare feet with some lamb's wool between your toes.

Get cooking with baking soda. Baking soda is a cheaper alternative to expensive foot powders, yet it does essentially the same thing. Either sprinkle it on dry or make a paste by moistening one tablespoon of baking soda with lukewarm water, suggests Suzanne M. Levine, D.P.M., clinical instructor of Podiatric Medicine. Rub the mixture on your feet and between your toes. After about 15 minutes, rinse it off and dry thoroughly.

Put on some antiperspirant. Rubbing or spraying antiperspirant on your feet can keep them from sweating. You can use the same brand you use on your underarms. As long as it contains aluminium chlorohydrate, the active drying ingredient, it will work.

Dress feet first. If your feet are infected, pulling on your underwear over your bare feet could transfer the fungus to your groin. Shield your feet with socks first.

Herbal Help:
Fend off fungus with tea tree oil. Mix an antifungal soak by diluting 5 to 7 drops of tea tree essential oil in 4 ounces of warm water in a tub large enough to accommodate your feet. Double the recipe if you need more water to cover the affected area. Soak once a day for 20 minutes. "In five days, the fungus should be gone," says Dr. Murray-Doran a naturopathic doctor. After each soak, dry the affected area well with a clean towel. "And then put that towel in the laundry immediately," Dr. Murray-Doran says. "Don't reuse it, because it could spread the fungus." Anyone with sensitive skin should dilute the oil, using about 7 drops of the essential oil to 3 drops of vegetable oil, to avoid skin irritation. Undiluted tea tree oil is toxic when applied to the skin, and it should be kept out of reach of children.

Stir in some garlic. For more fungus-fighting power, add 4 to 6 drops of garlic essential oil to the above formula, Dr. Murray-Doran suggests. Garlic is a traditional antifungal remedy, and its fungus-fighting abilities have been backed by laboratory studies.

Or you can concoct a simple garlic foot bath, suggests Paul Bergner, editor of *Medical Herbalism.* Puree 6 garlic cloves in a blender or food processor. Fill a small tub with enough comfortably hot water to cover your feet, then add the garlic and soak for 15 minutes. You may want to stay clear of loved ones, though. A garlic bath not only can make your feet odoriferous, but the offending compounds can travel through the bloodstream to your lungs, giving your breath that pungent smell. And don't apply garlic directly to the skin, as it can cause irritation.

Promote healing with calendula. After using an antifungal soak for three days, add calendula to your routine, Dr. Murray-Doran suggests. Research suggests that calendula petals, used traditionally to heal wounds, help promote the growth of new skin cells. After soaking and drying your feet, apply a light calendula cream or salve or rinse your tootsies with warm calendula tea. Make a calendula foot wash by adding 1 to 2 teaspoons of dried calendula flowers to a cup of boiling water, then steep for 10 to 15 minutes. Strain, if necessary, and cool. Use the calendula cream or rinse three times a day. "It's perfect for the stage when the fungus has died off, but you still have cracked skin because healing is slow," Dr. Murray-Doran says.

Stay dry all day with lavender. You can fend off fungus all day by sprinkling on some lavender, which Dr. Murray-Doran says can help discourage fungus growth. Grind 1/4 cup of lavender flowers in a coffee mill or food processor, then mix with 1/2 cup powdered bentonite clay. Sprinkle it onto your clean, dry feet or right into your clean cotton socks. "The clay helps keep your feet dry, and in my experience, the lavender works as a mild antifungal agent," she says. "And it smells nice."

Get ginger going. You can prepare a strong decoction by adding an ounce of chopped ginger root to a cup of boiling water. Simmer for 20 minutes and apply it directly to the problem areas twice a day with a cotton ball or clean cloth.

Lick the problem with licorice which contains 25 reportedly fungicidal compounds. You can brew a strong decoction using about five to seven teaspoons of dried herb per cup of water. Bring it to a boil, simmer for 20 minutes, then let it cool. Apply directly to the affected areas using a cotton ball or clean cloth.

Cool the burn with camomile. Camomile oil is also fungicidal. In Europe it's incorporated into many over-the-counter antiseptics. You can use camomile oil in the same way as teatree oil, or mix the two. If you have hay fever, however, you should use camomile products cautiously. Camomile is a member of the ragweed family, and in some people, it might trigger allergic reactions. The first time you try it, watch your reaction. If it seems to help, go ahead and use it. But if it seems to cause or aggravate itching or irritation, discontinue use.

Footwear and Fungus

What you put on your feet can have a big impact on athlete's food flare-ups. Follow this advice to give fungus the boot from your feet:

Choose the right shoes. Wearing light, ventilated footwear in the summer—when hot, moist weather increases the risk for athlete's foot—can help prevent the problem, says Dr. Helm. He recommends canvas boat shoes or sandals.

Give your shoes a break. Letting a pair of shoes sit out for a day or two gives them time to dry out. Ideally, you should wear the same pair only once every five days. If it's a sunny day, put your shoes outside to air dry. If not, stuff them with newspaper and let them dry inside.

Stay shod in showers. Wearing sandals or thongs in the locker room can help shield you from an infection, says Dr. Helm.

Kick out plastic shoes. "They are very bad for you because they don't breathe and the moisture just sits in them," Dr. Helm says. Kids, in particular, need to be careful about their choice of shoes: "I'm seeing a lot more athlete's foot in kids now that everybody is wearing high-top sneakers that don't allow the air to circulate."

Bare your feet. Sometimes the best strategy is no shoes at all. "Walking barefoot can be very helpful in preventing athlete's foot," says Dr. Helm. Unlike the locker room, where your bare feet are at risk, a clean environment like your home is a perfect place to air your toes. "Heat, sweat, and moisture aggravate the problem, and a cool, dry environment is helpful," he points out. "Obviously, you don't want to walk around outside in your bare feet because of rusty nails and other risks. But around the house—absolutely."

Cradle them in cotton. "Cotton socks are the best because they absorb all the moisture and perspiration and wick it away from your feet," says Dr. Litt. "Polyester, silk, or nylon socks retain the sweat." Change your socks two or three times a day to prevent moisture from building up.

Disinfect your footwear. Neal Kramer, D.P.M., a podiatrist, says that Lysol and other household disinfectants can kill off any living fungus spores. After you take off your shoes, rub the insides with a cloth or paper towel that has a dab of disinfectant. (Then use that hair dryer to dry out the insides of the shoes!) Also, when laundering socks and hose, add a capful of disinfectant to the final rinse.

Go for the goldenseal. This herb contains berberine, a powerful antifungal and antibacterial compound, which makes it an excellent antibiotic. Barberry, goldthread, Oregon grape and yellowroot all contain it and all have been used traditionally to treat yeast and other fungal infections. You might buy a goldenseal tincture and follow the package directions. Usually. the guidelines suggest adding it to juice three times a day. If you want to use it externally, you can make a strong decoction with the dried herb. Add five to seven teaspoons to a cup of water, bring it to a boll and let it simmer for 20 minutes. After the liquid cools to a tolerable temperature, use a cotton ball or clean cloth to apply it to the affected area. You'll probably want to repeat the application up to three times a day.

Take aim with arrowroot and other herb powders. Since moisture and darkness help the growth of foot fungus, you're more likely to prevent it if you put some drying powder inside your socks and even your shoes. You can get a number of powders made from the dried leaves, stems or roots of herbs, including arrowroot, comfrey and goldenseal.

Try turmeric. Pakistani studies show that oil of turmeric inhibits many common problem fungi, even at very low concentrations. Go with commercial oil of turmeric, diluting it with water (one part oil to two parts water) and apply it directly to the affect area using a cotton ball or clean cloth.

Say Aloe: For an Ayuverdic remedy, follow up tea tree oil treatment with a mixture of 1 teaspoon aloe vera gel and 1/2 teaspoon turmeric. Apply topically to the affected area every day in the morning and before bedtime. Since turmeric stains, wear old sock, and keep them on in bed to avoid staining the sheets. Discoloration of the skin should wear off in two weeks.

Back Pain

The pain: Chronic or sudden aches or spasms that occur most often in the lower part of the back. Pain may vary from minor to intense, and at worst, can bend you over with lightening-like stabs of agony.

The cause: Its source is the spine, which is a stack of bones called vertebrae and, between them, cushions of cartilage called disks. Disk problems cause 99 percent of all back pain, says Kenneth Light, MD, medical director of the San Francisco Spine Centre. When the disks are damaged, they develop rips, and little sections of the disk pop out and press on nerves. Or a disk can collapse, causing the vertebrae to shift.

The exact cause of back pain can be tough to track down. Pinpointing the cause and even the precise location of back pain often turns doctors into body detectives. "When one muscle in the back becomes inflamed or spasms, it affects a whole bunch of muscles that may have nothing to do with it, structurally," says Patrick Massey, MD, Ph.D., an internist at Alexian Brothers Medical Centre. "Sometimes, moving your skull will affect your tailbone." Consequently, the causes of back pain are numerous: pinched nerves, weak abdominal muscles, loss of flexibility, tight leg muscles, a big gut, trauma, sitting too long, poor overall fitness, and herniated disks.

See a doctor if:
...your pain is severe, lasts more than three days, or radiates to your hips or legs.
...you have sudden pain and you've never had backache before.
Your doctor can rule out serious injury and prescribe a course of action that can have you up and about quickly.
...the pain follows a traumatic accident.
...the pain is accompanied by bladder or bowel problems, severe illness or fever.

Medication:
If it's not poor muscle tone or improper movement that's got your lower back in knots, you may want to peek in your medicine cabinet. A few drugs can cause backaches, says W. Steven Pray, Ph.D., R.Ph., professor of non-

prescription drug products. They include:

- Temazepam (Restoril or Euhypnos), a central nervous system depressant that is prescribed to relieve tension
- Sumatriptan (Imitrex or Imigran), which is used to treat severe migraine headaches

Also, Vitamin D, especially when taken in high amounts, can cause muscle and joint pains, including backache.

To ease your pain, your doctor may recommend that you take acetaminophin (paracetamol), nonsteroidal anti-inflammatory drugs, such as ibuprofen, or aspirin. These types of medicine may interact with other drugs, so make sure you talk to your doctor about possible conflicts.

Quick relief:

Pack some ice. To relieve backache, reach for an ice pack, says Sheila Reid, therapy co-ordinator at the Spine Institute of New England. Apply it for 5 to 10 minutes at a time. Alternately, fill a paper cup with water, freeze it, peel back the paper, and rub the ice on sore spots, Dr. Wheeler, a neurologist, says. Don't hold the ice on the area for more than 20 minutes, and keep a thin towel between you and the ice to prevent damage to your skin.

Pack some heat. After the first couple of days, you may get more comfort from the warmth of a heating pad, bath, or shower. Try moist heat, Dr. Wheeler says. Rinse a small towel under hot water and wring it to near dry. Apply heat for up to 15 minutes at a time. If you use a heating pad on a medium setting, be careful not to fall asleep or leave it on too long, he says. You could burn your skin. Try hydrocollars, which are sold at chemists and look like little sandbags. Toss one into a pot of hot water and when the bag is heated, apply it to your sore spot for 15 minutes.

Go hot and cold. Its technical name is hydrotherapy, but all it means is using water to soothe your sore back. Alternate hot and cold packs for about 15 minutes on your back when it hurts, says Robert Edwards, a massage therapist. Get extra relief by soaking in a warm bath, then applying a cold compress. "A warm bath is relaxing and soothing," he adds, while the cold compress helps minimise pain.

Ease the pain with exercise:

Get out of bed. "Most people shouldn't be in bed for back pain," says Reid, therapy co-ordinator at the Spine Institute of New England. Movement helps the body heal faster, even after age 60.

That may contradict what you've heard in the past, but doctors no longer recommend more than a few days of bed rest for backache and only then if the pain is severe. Too much rest actually can make backache worse or lead to chronic pain that comes and goes for months or years. That's because muscles become lax and bones lose strength when they're not used. Resist the urge to rest in bed, especially for more than two to three days, says Steven Mandel, MD, a clinical professor of neurology. Studies show that light activity actually hastens healing. If you feel you need bed rest, take it but try walking around every few hours, even if you have a little pain, he says. A stroll around the house or yard will help strengthen muscles and keep them limber.

Until you're feeling better, though, avoid activities that may strain the lower back, such as vacuuming or gardening.

Reach for the home stretch. As soon as you're able, add some gentle stretches to your daily routine. This will speed healing and increase flexibility, says Dr. Mandel.

Try this exercise. Lie on the floor on your back and hug your knees to your chest. Hold for 15 seconds. Relax. Repeat two times.

Go to the point of stretch, not to the point of pain, Reid says.

If you can't get down on the floor, you still can stretch, Reid says. Sit in a sturdy chair with your feet flat on the floor. Lean forward from the waist, bringing your chest slowly toward your thighs. Breathe in on the way down, and let the air out with a sigh as you lower yourself near your legs. Hold the stretch for 15 seconds. You can do this stretch as often as you like, Reid says.

Or try this standing stretch, Reid suggests. Stand with your feet shoulder-width apart with your hands on the small of your back. Lean

---

How to act in the sack (when your back's out of whack)

Your hormones scream yes; your back says no way. You can win this battle by practising safe sex for backs, say physical therapists. The most important things are to keep the spine aligned properly and to use positions that don't require the partner with back pain to be active or bear weight. Try these back-safe positions.

Spoon your mate. In this position, both partners lie on their sides with their knees bent and the man behind the woman. Nobody bears any body weight, says Wendy Woods, P.T., a physical therapist.

Try a pillow prop. Here, the partner with the bad back lies on his back, using pillows to support the neck and lower back if necessary. This provides a more stable position for the back during sex, says Woods. If the man has a bad back, his partner should straddle him with her knees bent while supporting her upper body weight with her arms. If it's the woman who has a bad back, her partner should support himself with his arms and knees so that little weight falls on her.

Head for the hot tub. Let buoyancy and the warm, massaging bubbles of a hot tub keep both of you in the mood, says Woods. She recommends that the man sit in the tub with the woman sitting on his thighs and facing him. This position will work if either the man or the woman has a bad back, she notes. "The key here is to not make twisting motions," Woods adds.

backward as you breathe out, then ease off and repeat several times. This promotes a backward motion of the spine, Reid says.

Soothe with yoga. Yoga stretches, called asanas, may help relieve some back pain, says Alice Christensen, founder and executive director of the American Yoga Association in Sarasota, Florida. But be sure to get your doctor's approval before trying this or other yoga poses. With this pose, Christensen suggests, pretend that you're an ocean liner slicing through the deep blue. Lie on your stomach with your arms outstretched in front of you and your forehead on the floor Exhale completely, then inhale as you raise your legs, arms, and head all at once, looking up. Lift yourself up only as far as you can comfortably. Exhale and lower your body. Rest completely, then repeat two more times.

The classic knee-to-chest pose helps relieve common lower-back discomfort: Lie on your back with your arms at your sides. Place a folded towel under your head to keep your neck and head in line with the spine. Bring your right knee up to your chest. Place your clasped hands underneath your right knee. Relax the right foot. Straighten the left leg on the floor as you flex the left foot. Keep your head centred and relax your shoulders. Hold this pose for 20 to 60 seconds, and then do the same exercise with the left leg. Try to do at least two sets every day, suggests yoga instructor, Mara Carrico.

Add some aerobic options. As your pain diminishes, within the first few days or weeks, add some light aerobic activity, such as walking, swimming, or bicycling, Dr. Mandel suggests. Exercise is no guarantee you'll never have back pain, Reid says, but it can lessen the chances of a relapse by strengthening muscles and supplying them with oxygen.

Go slow. "When someone starts exercising, there's a tendency to say, 'I'll go until I can't go anymore,'" Reid says. "That's a recipe for failure." You may feel too sore to try again. Instead, start with short periods of exercise several times a day. Go for five minutes out and five minutes back. Build up to six minutes and then seven. "Before long, you're up to your first half-hour but you're doing it safely," Reid says.

Try a pseudo-sit up. Patrick Fallon, P.T., a physical therapist with the Texas Back Institute, suggests this modified sit-up. Lie on your back with your knees bent in a comfortable position and your hands on your thighs. Lift your head and shoulders off the floor slowly as you slide your fingertips to reach your knees. Hold for a count of three and gradually ease back down. Start slowly, but aim for three sets of 10 repetitions. Don't attempt this exercise, however, if you are currently experiencing back pain.

Stretch like an elephant. Pretend that you're Dumbo with this back stretch offered by Meir Schneider, Ph.D., a licensed massage therapist, founder of the Centre and School for Self-Healing in San Francisco, and creator of the Meir Schneider Self-Healing Method. Stand up and bend your torso forward as far as is comfortable. Let your arms hang separate and loosely at your sides. Next, swing your arms gently from side to side like the trunk of a contented elephant. This relieves pressure in the sacrum—the lower part of the spine—and loosens your hip and lower back muscles. After a minute of swaying, uncurl your spine and slowly straighten to a standing position. Bring your head up last. Repeat these steps at least six times a day, says Dr. Schneider.

Try tai chi. This "moving meditation" offers graceful movements that are relaxing and energising, says Lana Spraker, a master instructor who has taught tai chi for more than 25 years. "Tai chi is successful for older people because it is done slowly and gently, exercising all the muscles of the body in a balanced way," says Spraker, who is also a certified Alexander Technique instructor.

Slip into the pool. Water provides buoyancy and allows your tender muscles the chance to move freely without a lot of resistance, says Jane Sullivan-Durand, MD, a behavioural medicine physician. Here's a tip: Take gentle laps for at least 10 to 12 minutes in a pool with a water temperature of at least 83°F. Warm water helps relax back muscles.

Loosen the legs. You might think that the problem is in your back, where the pain is, but it could be in your legs. After sitting or bending all day, your leg muscles may be extremely tight or unbalanced (meaning that some muscles may be loose and relaxed but others are contracted or in spasm). Tight leg muscles pull oddly on the torso and put pressure on the back and abdominal muscles, says Jerome F. McAndrews, D.C., spokesman for the American Chiropractic Association. To rebalance your calf muscles, stand flat-footed on a stair step in flat, comfortable shoes with the balls of your feet on the very edge and your heels in the air, advises Dr. McAndrews. Holding on to a railing for support, slowly lower your heels until you feel a tightness up the back of the legs. Hold for a few seconds, repeat 5 to 10 times, and do as needed during the day, says Dr. McAndrews.

Extend those hamstrings. The same is true of those muscles running down the back of your thighs. Sitting for long periods—the bane of office workers—shortens the hamstring muscles in the back of your legs, which then yank on the pelvis and make other muscles compensate. Work your hamstrings by standing up and placing one heel on a steady chair or end table. (Hold on to a nearby table or chair for balance). Keep this leg straight and lean forward until you feel a pulling sensation in the back of your thigh. Hold for about 30 seconds, and then switch to the other leg, suggests Dr. McAndrews. Do this a few times a day, especially after you've been sitting for a long time. Don't try to "lock" the extended leg when first attempting this stretch. As the muscles stretch out, "locking" the leg will come naturally, advises Dr. McAndrews.

Keep your abdominal muscles strong. "The stronger your abdominal muscles, the less likely you are to injure your spine," says Dr. Light. When your abs are strong, they push up the abdominal contents, forming a cylinder of fluid that lifts and takes weight off the spine. To strengthen your abdominal muscles, Dr. Light suggests abdominal crunches, a special kind of no-stress sit-up. To do a crunch, lie on your back on a carpeted floor or an exercise mat with knees bent, feet flat on the floor, fingertips lightly touching the sides of the head, and elbows out to the sides. Tilt your pelvis so that your lower back stays flat on the floor, and then curl your body up so that your head and shoulders come off the floor. Keep the crunch slow—take three seconds to lift your head and shoulders, pause for a second with the abs fully contracted, and then take three seconds to lower your body. Dr. Light suggests that you do these crunches for a 10-minute session every day.

Stretch your spine. Carry on with your normal everyday activities, but avoid lifting and strenuous sports until the pain has subsided and your strength has returned, says Dr. Jenny Sutcliffe, former Senior Lecturer in Paediatric Neurology, Great Ormond Street Hospital, London. In the evening, she suggests you stretch out your spine by lying face up over a lumbar roll (also called a 'back archer')—most health stores stock them—but check the instructions carefully, because it should be placed under the sacrum (the lower back, at the top of your bottom). "If you can't get one, put a large, soft-backed book under your sacrum—a telephone directory is ideal," says Dr. Sutcliffe. Start with a lumbar roll about two inches high and gradually increase the height as your flexibility improves. You'll feel a powerful stretch, but try to relax so that the vertebrae can separate a little

---

The back pain sufferer's guide to gardening

There are plenty of twists in gardening—keep these thoughts in mind when you're doing earth work.

Pace yourself. If you're a weekend gardener who tries to get everything done on Saturday, you might want to be a little kinder to your back. "People tend to go from doing nothing during the week to gardening for four hours or more on the weekend," says Woods. You should take a break every half-hour, according to Woods.

Get the real hoe down. The smaller the chopping motions, the less strain on your back muscles. With hoes, brooms, or mops, keep your upper arms close to your sides. Use your leg muscles for power, not your back.

Weed with your knees. Get up close to those wicked weeds by getting down on your hands and knees. Crawling around on your hands and knees is a fine position for the back. It's much better than bending over and rounding your back to pull weeds. That position puts a lot of stress on your lower back."

Stop rake ache. Woods offers this leaf-raking tip for autumn weekends: When you're raking, be sure to stand really upright. Use your knees and hips so that the power of your legs can help your arms pull the leaves. And take stretch breaks every 15 minutes.

and the spine opens out. The first time you use the roll you may only manage a few seconds, but persevere and extend the time gradually until it feels relatively comfortable. Always do five curl-ups after this exercise to stretch out the opposing muscles and prevent any muscular spasm.

Try some "back-ups." If you have lower back pain, do the following exercise. Lying on your stomach, use your arms to push your upper body off whatever you are lying on. Do 10 of these in bed before getting up, and another 10 before bed at night. "It shouldn't hurt, but if it does, discontinue immediately and get medical advice," says Dr Stephen G Motto, a musculo-skeletal physician with a speciality in sports medicine at London Bridge Hospital.

Hang around. Try hanging off a door frame for do-it-yourself traction, but only if you're strong enough. "This is particularly good for chronic back pain, but only do it if it helps," says Dr. Motto.

Everyday prevention:

Give yourself a lift. Bending and lifting incorrectly are major causes of back pain, says John E. Thomassy, D.C., a chiropractor in private practice. "Even if you're not lifting anything, 70 percent of your body weight is above the waist," he says. That means a 150-pound person lifts about 100 pounds every time he bends.

Don't lift with your back, Dr. Thomassy says. Next time you reach for a suitcase in your car trunk, bend your hips and knees, keeping your back straight.

Hold on tight. When you're carrying luggage, keep it close to you. The further away you hold an object, the more it weighs, Dr. Wheeler says. And avoid lifting loads of more than 5 to 10 pounds, he advises.

Push rather than pull your loads. That way your legs bear most of the weight.

Stay straight. If you're moving a box, don't pick it up and twist your body. "Never bend and twist," Dr. Thomassy says. Instead, grasp the box diagonally from the bottom, keeping it close to your body. Lift with your legs and buttock muscles while keeping your back straight. Then face squarely to where you set it down.

Please don't be seated. Sitting can actually aggravate back problems, Dr. Thomassy says. Sleeping or sitting for long periods on soft, cushy sofas or recliners can cause your back to slouch or your neck and head to be held forced forward, he says.

Pick the right chair. "Sitting for prolonged periods can aggravate your back," says Dr. Light. "You should find a chair with a firm cushion on the seat and with armrests. Both of these will help support the spine."

Rise from the monitor. If you sit at a computer or desk for hours at a time, get up and do something else about every 30 minutes, Reid says. You'll provide your back with needed nutrients by keeping the circulation going. "It's really important to move around."

Get even. Position your computer monitor at eye level, even if you have to put it on top of a telephone book. Keep your elbows bent at 90-degree angles and your arms parallel with the floor. Your feet should be flat on the floor or on a low stool, Reid says.

Get out of a slump. When you're sitting at your desk, try not to slouch, Reid cautions. Tuck a pillow or rolled towel behind your lower back for extra support. Or invest in a high-end office chair with a seat height and seat pan (the forward-back tilt of your seat) that can be adjusted to meet your needs, Reid says.

Stand safely. When you're standing for long periods of time, that, too, can aggravate back pain. Vary your position, Reid says. While standing, keep one foot on a low stool. Or keep a taller stool nearby, so you sometimes can sit while you work, Dr. Wheeler suggests. Another option, of course, is to run errands during off-peak hours so you won't have to spend as much time standing in line.

Sleep right. To prevent or minimise back pain at night, keep your spine in a neutral position, Dr. Thomassy says. Don't prop your head and neck with a big pillow. Instead, choose one that keeps your head and neck in line with your upper back. "Sleep only on your side or your back, but never on your stomach," he says. Sleeping on your stomach twists your neck and back. Also, avoid extremes in surfaces, such as saggy mattresses or bare floors. A good mattress and pillow will maintain your neck and back in the correct posture even while you sleep. Pillows between your knees or along your back or sides may provide further comfort to your back and shoulders. Or, Dr. Wheeler says, if you're on your back, prop a pillow under your knees.

Pick the right pillow. Hardness is the enemy. A pillow only need be firm enough to keep its shape and support the lower neck when you sleep on your side.

Ease into the driver's seat. To get safely into your car, lower yourself backward onto the seat, keeping your feet on the ground. Bring one leg and then the other into the car, "even if you have to use your hands to pick up those legs." Dr. Thomassy says. To get out of the car, do the opposite. If you need to, carefully support yourself on the back of the seat as you rise.

Ride in style. If you're driving or riding in the car on a long trip, use a small pillow and vary its position on your back for comfort. Take a break about every two hours and walk a bit. Your back will thank you for it, says Dr. Thomassy. Don't lean forward with your upper body when you are driving, cautions Hope Gillerman, a board-certified teacher of the Alexander Technique. The Alexander Technique is a method for improving movement and posture. "You want your neck, shoulders, and back to be as free of tension as possible," she says. Slide your hips all the way into the back of the car seat and lean into the seat back. And position your seat so that you can hold the steering wheel comfortably. If you are too close, you will have to hunch your shoulders to hold the wheel. If you are too far away, you will have to round your upper back to reach it.

Advice for a hacker's back

Golf, because it involves so much twisting, can sometimes cause back pain. Try these strategies for dealing with 18 painful holes.

Slow down. In general, Wendy a physical therapist, recommends that golfers with bum backs slow down their strokes to reduce stress on the lower back. Remember the wisdom of Bobby Jones, the biggest name in golf during the 1920s: A golf club cannot be swung too slowly.

Shorten your swing. Everyone wants to blast the dimples off the ball. But a long backswing is not just bad golf strategy, it's also bad back medicine. Woods says that shortening your backswing by not pulling back so far with the club reduces twisting and the strain on your back.

Meet the tee. When it's time to tee up the ball or pull it out of the cup, posture is key, says Woods. "Don't bend from the back," she says. "Try to bend at the knees, keep your back in a neutral position, and slowly lower yourself down to put the ball on the tee or take it out of the hole."

Get symmetrical. If you carry your bag, be sure to use a strap that goes over both shoulders. That way, you distribute the weight evenly and can prevent some back problems caused by habitual overuse of one side of the back.

Do a sidewalk window-check. "When you are walking by a shop window, look at your reflection and check out how you are moving," says Gillerman. "If you are leaning forward, stop walking. Then bring your weight back on to your heels of your feet and feel the ground solidly underneath your whole foot.

Then watch your stride. After you have checked out your reflection, continue to pay attention to your posture as you start walking again. If you are slumping and tucking your hips forward, let your hips shift slightly backward and unlock your knees. While you are moving, think about lengthening your spine, like an arrow pointing up away from the ground, says Gillerman.

Wear well-cushioned shoes. "Any shoe with a cushioned sole and good arch support can help prevent back pain," says Dr. Light. But high heels are the worst shoe for your back. "They exaggerate the lumbar curve—the curve in the lower part of your back—and that can cause back pain," he says.

Belt up for safety. If your job requires frequent lifting, Dr. Light suggests that you wear an abdominal belt: "It pulls in the abdomen, helps support the spine, and it reminds you to lift correctly." Weight lifters wear these belts to protect their backs during exercise. The belts are available at sporting goods stores and most drugstores.

Use a stool when you stand. "If you are standing a lot, it is best to bend one knee and put it on a stool—that helps relax your back," says Dr. Light.

Bone up on supplements. "If you are a woman over the age of 40, you should consider taking calcium supplements," says Dr. Light. Calcium helps protect your spine and the rest of your skeleton from osteoporosis, the disease of eroding and weakening bones. In older women especially, there is the risk that vertebrae may fracture if they are weakened by osteoporosis. But calcium can help prevent the disease.

And if you have a family history of the osteoporosis, Dr. Light suggests talking to your physician about hormone-replacement therapy, which can also help protect the spine.

Don't smoke. "Smoking decreases circulation to the disks and causes them to degenerate sooner," says Dr. Light.

Hands-on help:

Find a hero. Attention all partners of back pain sufferers—here's your chance to be a real hero to your mate. When your partner begs for a gentle massage, rub to the rescue, says Dr. Sullivan-Durand. Using both your thumbs or the heels of your hands, rub up the centre of the spine, starting at the bottom of the back and stopping just below the shoulder blades. Then start over again at the bottom. Massage stimulates the circulation of blood and lymphatic fluid (which tends to accumulate around an injury site). If you do this kind of massage, it reduces swelling and promotes healing, says Dr. Sullivan-Durand.

Turn to a professional. Let someone else's hands do the walking—all over your aching back. Regular professional massages, as part of an overall treatment program, can significantly improve your back ailments, says Robert A. Edwards of the Somerset School of Massage Therapy. Check with your insurance company; they may even cover therapeutic massage. As you get your massage, don't just lie there and grunt, by the way. Be sure to tell your massage therapist what helps and what hurts, he adds.

Work on your feet. According to reflexology, the art of improving your health by manipulating pressure points in your feet, the midway point down the inner sides of your foot represent the spine and back area. By pressing on that special point, you can relieve some of your back pain. How do you find this precise spot? Instead of memorising the special reflexology chart, just give yourself a foot rub down those inner sides when you have back pain, Edwards says. "If you find a point that is extremely tender, then you know you have it," he says. Once you find that point, gradually increase the amount of pressure.

Roll around. If your game isn't up to par lately, you can still put all your tennis and golf balls to good use. Grab a tennis ball (for beginners) or a golf ball (for advanced folks) to give yourself a quick and easy back massage. Either sitting in a chair or lying down, take a tennis ball and place it behind your lower back or wherever you feel pain. Then roll around and move your back so that the ball rubs into your back muscles. "It will cause some relief," says Edwards. If at any time you feel pain, either let up on the ball or stop, he adds. Edwards suggests rolling around for two to three minutes twice a day.

Stretch back your back. This acupressure move stimulates several key trigger points in your upper back and loosens the knots that tend to cause pain, says the Acupressure Institute's Dr. Michael Reed Gach, author of *The Bum Back Book*. Interlace your hands with your palms facing each other behind your back near your buttocks. As you inhale deeply, stretch your arms away from your back, pressing your shoulder blades together. Hold for a few seconds. Repeat this exercise three more times, and do them twice a day, says Dr. Gach.

Make some heat. Using either your palms or the back of your hands, rub your lower back until you generate heat. "The friction will warm the area and increase circulation," Dr. Gach says. By rubbing the entire lower-back area, you inevitably stimulate many of the acupressure points located there, Dr. Gach adds. This will activate those points and will ease some of your pain.

Reach for your knees. An acupressure point located in the centre of the crease in the back of the knee can relieve back pain. Using your fingers, find the centre of the crease. Apply firm pressure with your fingers at different angles, until you feel a rather sharp sensation. "This usually takes some gentle poking around," Dr. Gach says. When you feel the sensation, you have the point. Hold that point for about two minutes, slowly inhaling and exhaling. After doing one side, switch to the other, Dr. Gach says. For best results, do both knees three times a day.

Press pain away. Another acupressure point for back pain is located on

Taking a Crack at Chiropractic

The way chiropractors see it, nobody knows more about your back than they do. The basis of their entire practice lies in the spine. According to chiropractic medicine, joints and vertebrae get knocked out of line, or lock in one position, and cause different conditions, including back pain.

Using his hands, the chiropractor pushes or adjusts the problem back into place or into a normal movement. "It is a gentle process. The motion is very easy and not deep," says Jerome F. McAndrews, D.C., a spokesperson for the American Chiropractic Association. Depending on the injury, it may take one session or it may take several, he says.

For back pain, several studies have been backing up chiropractic claims. An analysis of 17 different medical studies found that patients preferred chiropractors when it came to treating lower-back pain. Another study had 741 patients who were assigned to standard outpatient or chiropractic care for three years. Chiropractic care produced superior results, and the people who receive chiropractic treatment also reported an improvement in daily living. More medical doctors are referring patients to chiropractors than even before, Dr. McAndrews says.

the outside of your ankles between the ankle bone and your heel, Dr. Gach says. Place your thumb on the outside of your right ankle, and place your index finger on the inside of your ankle, as if you were pinching your ankles. Slide your thumb and press it into the soft tissue in the back of your heel bone. Hold the pressure for at least two minutes. Shake out the ankle before doing the same thing to your left side. Keep your breathing deep and slow during the exercise. Repeat this exercise three times a day for best results, suggests Dr. Gach.

Stick your finger in your ear. There is an acupressure point inside the top of your ear—called the neurogate point—that can control back pain, says certified acupuncturist Dr. David Nickel. The neurogate point is located in the middle of the upper part of the ear, just above the main ear opening. Press the point firmly for five seconds, then let go for five seconds, Dr. Nickel recommends. Stick with the five-second intervals for one full minute. Exhale through your mouth as you apply the pressure, and inhale through your nose as you ease off the pressure point. If you can't find the exact point, press all over your ear until you hit a tender spot, Dr. Nickel suggests. Repeat the exercises two or three times a day or as needed for relief of pain, he says.

Back Pain and Acupuncture

In the clenches of a back pain attack, sticking a bunch of needles all over your body may not sound like a viable solution. But it just might be what you're looking for. Back pain sends many people to the acupuncturist. "Back pain is the most common thing I treat with acupuncture. I get very good results. I like to treat patients before they go to surgery to see if we can relieve their pain without an operation. I have treated many patients for back pain after their back surgery. It would have been beneficial to spare them the surgery since they still had pain afterward," says Dr. Victor S. Sierpina of the University of Texas Medical Branch.

Although widely accepted as a medical practice in China, acupuncture has made its name world-wide as a treatment for back pain and other chronic conditions. In one study, 50 people with chronic lower-back pain were separated into two groups. One group received acupuncture treatment right away, while the other group had to wait a while. Eighty-three percent of the group treated immediately with acupuncture reported that their pain was cut in half. In the other group, only about 33 percent reported feeling better, and 25 percent reported that their pain got worse. Once the second group received acupuncture treatment, 75 percent of them reported that their pain was alleviated.

One theory behind acupuncture's success with back pain is that the pressure induced by the acupuncture needles triggers the release of endorphins, natural painkillers produced by your own body, says Dr. Sierpina says.

Engage in hand-to-hand combat. Two points on the top of your hand can ease the pain for lower-back strains, Dr. Nickel says. One point is about an inch or so down from your knuckles between your ring and pinkie finger, the other is at the same spot between your index and middle finger. Just like you would for your ear acupressure points, press down on the point with your thumb or finger for five seconds, then release for five seconds. Inhale through your nose as you let up, exhale through your mouth as you apply the pressure.

You can use this point to prevent back pain as well, Dr. Nickel adds. Press the points on the left hand, just like you would if you had an injury—five seconds on, five seconds off. While you do this, slowly move the upper part of the body into the range of discomfort as you press and then exhale. Then gently move your body back to a comfortable position. Visualise the ligaments and muscles growing stronger as you breathe. You should feel a "good" hurt, that is, a hot stinging sensation, when you do preventive acupressure for back pain. Then switch and apply the pressure points on the right hand.

Mind over malady:

Change the pain. You can try to relax into the pain so your perception of it changes. Just imagine that you smell cabbage cooking, Emmett Miller, MD, a mind-body specialist and author. At first the scent is overpowering, but before long, you don't notice it anymore. The sensation of pain, too, may be great. But if you can relax and "just hang out with it for a time," he says, your perception of the pain might lessen. "The pain is still there but it doesn't feel so bad."

Relax your mind and your back. Back pain can be an endless cycle. You have a spasm, or you feel a sharp stab of pain. Your mind goes through a quick checklist: "Is it serious? Will I have to take off work? Do I have to see a doctor? How am I going to get everything done? I don't need this." This stressed-out feeling sends your body into tense mode, and ends up tensing up muscles everywhere, including your back, explains Dennis C. Turk, Ph.D. The result? Your back muscles tighten even more, you end up with even greater pain, and the cycle repeats itself. When you feel back pain, you need to calm down your mind and your back, Dr. Turk says.

During your next back pain attack, try the following exercise: Sit in a chair and focus on your breathing. Slowly inhale, hold the breath for a second, then exhale as if you are blowing on a candle flame but you don't want to blow it out. As you do this, picture yourself sinking into the chair. Think about feeling warmth and heaviness near your back. "The warmth helps relieve pain and tension," Dr. Turk says. Do this for two to five minutes a few times a day, he suggests. "Whenever you feel tense or stressed or your pain increases, take a short break, even one to two minutes, at work, at home, wherever. This is a portable approach that can be done anywhere as needed," he explains. This should help relieve some of the pain as well as relax your entire body and mind, Dr. Turk adds.

Harp on your back. Listening to the quiet music of the harp has helped people deal with pain for ages, says Don Campbell of the Mozart Effect Resource Centre. In the Bible, David played the harp to rid Saul of an evil spirit. Monks played the instrument to assist the dying. You may just need it to quell some back pain. The harp has been used in music therapy to alleviate many types of pain, but especially back pain, Campbell says. Buy a tape or CD of harp music and have it ready to go the next time your back starts harping on you. Although music is therapeutic and aids in relieving or "masking" pain, Campbell stresses that it is a great complementary therapy, when used as an adjunct to your normal medication.

Herbal Help:

Pump in the blood flow. Getting fresh blood to an injury brings in nutrients needed for healing and also carries away waste products manufactured by injured cells, says Alison Lee, MD, a pain-management specialist and acupuncturist with Barefoot Doctors, an acupuncture and natural-medicine resource centre in Michigan. The herb ginkgo biloba has been shown to dilate blood vessels and may theoretically increase blood flow to your aching back, says Dr. Lee. You can buy the herb in capsule form in health food stores and over the counter at many chemists. Dr. Lee recommends a product with standardised extract. Follow the package directions for dosage information.

Try a combo. In some cases, a combination approach may be useful. Where ginkgo biloba increases blood flow, curcumin can add an anti-inflammatory effect, suggests Dr. Lee. Curcumin, a highly concentrated form of turmeric sold in health food stores, is a potent anti-inflammatory medicine that is very effective for a soft-tissue injury, like a sore back, says Dr. Lee. Look for a product (capsule form) with standardised extract of 95 percent, and follow the recommended dosage on bottle.

Pepper the pain. Red pepper contains a marvellous pain-relieving chemical-capsaicin-that is so potent that a tiny amount provides the active ingredient in some powerful pharmaceuticaltopical analgesics. You can buy a commercial cream containing capsaicin and use that or simply use red pepper. A hot pepper costs a few cents, while capsaicin drugs cost a few dollars. You can mash a red pepper and rub it directly on the painful area. You can also take any white skin cream that you have on hand—cold cream will do and mix in enough red pepper to turn it pink. Whether you use a cream or a hot pepper, be sure to wash your hands thoroughly afterward: You don't want to get it in your eyes. Also, since some people are quite sensitive to this compound, you should test it on a small area of skin to make sure that it's okay for you to use before using it on a larger area. If it seems to irritate your skin, discontinue use.

Try willow and other forms of natural aspirin. Aspirin originally came from compounds known as sallicylates that occur naturally in willow bark, meadowsweet and wintergreen. Any of these herbs can be made into pain-relieving teas.

Make pain vanish with mint. You will find the compounds menthol and camphor in many over-the-counter backache medications. They are chemicals that can help ease the muscle tightness that contributes to many bad backs. Menthol is a natural constituent of plants in the mint family, particularly peppermint and spearmint, although the aromatic oils of all the other mints contain it as well. Camphor occurs in spike lavender, hyssop and coriander. Dilute essential oils in a carrier base oil such as jojoba, baby, or castor oil (10 to 12 drops of essential oil per ounce of carrier oil). Then have someone massage them into your back to help alleviate pain. You can also put a few drops of peppermint on a compress and place it against the sore area of your back. Peppermint gets the circulation moving and the blood flowing to the injured area.

Strike oil. Treatment with essential oils can often help relieve the painful muscle spasms that contribute to back pain. Several of these-sage, rosemary, thyme, horsebalm and mountain dittany-are rich in thymol and carvacrol, compounds that help muscles relax. To use any of these oils, add a few drops to a couple of tablespoons of any vegetable oil and massage the oil mixture directly into the affected area. You might also add a few drops of the oil to a hot bath and soak for a while,. inhaling the vapours. (Remember, though, never to ingest an essential oil, as small quantities of some oils can be fatal.)

Bedsores

The pain: Pressure ulcers that start as a red spot on the skin; left untreated, the affected skin can blister, deteriorate and die. Eventually the sore can break through the skin and extend through the fat, into muscle and expose bone.

The cause: They occur when you sit or lie in a single position for so long that the sheer weight of the body pinches off blood flow to certain areas. Usually, the danger spots are bony areas of the body, especially the hips, buttocks, and heels. Anyone confined to a bed or wheelchair, especially those who have suffered paralysis or a stroke, is in danger of developing a pressure ulcer, says Mitchell Kaminski Jr., M.D., clinical professor of surgery at the Finch University of Health Sciences. And a bedsore can start a lot sooner than you might think. "Most experts say it takes about two hours to create a stage I bedsore, but you can start to see the changes that lead to an ulcer after about 20 minutes." Once a bedsore opens, the body's natural protective barrier has been compromised, leaving one vulnerable to bacteria, infection, and pain.

See a doctor if...
You notice a reddened area that doesn't go away. Get a doctor's help as quickly as possible," says Diane Krasner, R.N., who specializes in chronic wound care. Don't assume that if a bedsore doesn't hurt, it's not serious, adds Krasner. Constant pressure tends to numb the skin, and other conditions such as paralysis or diabetes may reduce the ability to feel pain.

Medication:
Your doctor may want to prescribe antibiotics to assist healing. The doctor may also want to remove, or debride, dead tissue that surrounds a bedsore. If the bedsores hurt continuously, you may want to ask about taking over-the-counter medication at regular intervals, not just when the pain flares. acetaminophen (paracetamol), aspirin, or another pain reliever may be appropriate. But be sure to consult your doctor before taking these medications regularly.

Nutritional remedies:

Eat right. "In a scientific study of nursing home patients, we have never found a pressure ulcer in anyone who was well-nourished," Dr. Kaminski said. "Along with pressure, malnutrition is the single biggest co-factor in the creation of bedsores."

When people think of malnutrition, they frequently think of people who are thin or even emaciated. "That's not the person who is at the greatest risk," he says. "The people who are most in danger of developing pressure ulcers are obese people, those who are eating lots of processed foods and processed carbohydrates that lack protein." Keep that from happening by getting your loved one the minimum daily requirement for protein, which is two to three servings of meat, poultry, fish, or eggs a day. In addition, doctors recommend that people eat 6 to 11 servings of unprocessed whole grains, 2 to 4 servings of fresh fruits, and 3 to 5 servings of vegetables a day.

Choose your oils wisely. If you're preparing food for anyone who is bedridden, be careful about the kinds of oils that may be in their foods, according to Dr. Kaminski. "Omega-3 oils, which are found in fish, canola oil and flaxseed oil, lower blood cholesterol and support good circulation," he says. Avoid using corn or safflower oil in your cooking because such oils can enhance inflammation, which decrease blood circulation and can increase bedsore risk, he adds.

Helpful vitamins and supplements:

Supplement against sores. Dr. Kaminski encourages people at risk for bedsores to take a multivitamin that contains vitamins C, E, and beta-carotene. These vitamins are antioxidants that can speed healing. Some research suggests zinc is also helpful.

Everyday prevention:

Get even relief. Try to keep the person on a mattress or cushion that distributes their weight more evenly, such as an air mattress, says Dr. Kaminski. "There are many kinds available, but a regular air mattress that you use at a lake or the beach can be used to help support a person who is bedridden." Be sure it's thickly covered with an airy cotton blanket and sheets to prevent sweating. Sponge mattresses and water beds are also good choices. Other experts recommend using cotton padding or wool to soften the mattress. The extra padding should be evenly distributed, however, to prevent bunching and increasing the likelihood of pinching blood vessels.

Add an extra layer. Cover the bed mattress with an air mattress or foam padding that is dense and at least four inches thick. "There are a lot of mattress overlay devices that put cushioning between the bony surface and the bed surface," says Carol Jones, R.N., a board-certified entero-stomal therapy nurse. "And these devices can help prevent pressure ulcers." For people in wheelchairs, she suggests an air or gel cushion. The egg crate paddings that were once used to prevent bedsores are not effective, she says. "These are not dense enough, so the bone would still lie on the surface of the mattress, and there would be tissue destruction."

Keep things moving. "You've got to rotate the person's body throughout the day," says Dr. Kaminski. "The person should be shifted at least once an hour, just to relieve the pressure on any area of the body." Not only is this an essential way to keep bedsores from worsening once they start, it's also one of the best ways of preventing them. Be sure to reposition the person so that pressure is relieved from any reddened area on the body.

Help out the hips. One problem with repositioning—for example, turning a person from his back onto his side—is that a person lying on his side can get a pressure ulcer from his hipbones. To prevent this, turn the person on his back part way toward his side, say, 30 degrees (a full turn onto the side would be 90 degrees). Then support his back with pillows so that he stays in the new position. This way, the pillow takes some of the weight.

Separate the knees and ankles. Pressure sores can also form when an ankle is pressing on an ankle, or a knee on a knee. Use pillows to keep them separated, says Jones.

Lower the head of the bed. People who are propped up in bed tend to slide down, says Jones. And if the person is older, the skin on the back and the buttocks can stretch and tear, creating an ulcer. This phenomenon is called shearing, and it can be prevented by keeping the head of the bed at the lowest angle possible and limiting the time it is elevated.

Do a "pushup." People who are confined to wheelchairs but still have the use of their upper bodies should do a slight pushup every four to five minutes on the arms of the wheelchair to relieve the pressure, says Jones.

Clean with care. A person in bed should be cleaned regularly, says Jones, since excess moisture—from elimination or perspiration—can weaken the skin. But clean gently, using a mild soap. And afterward, apply a moisturiser so that the skin doesn't become too dry. "Keep the skin lubricated, but not saturated," she says.

Caring for the wounds:

Maximise blood flow to existing ulcers. Make sure there is no pressure on any area where an ulcer already exists, warns Mary Ruth Buchness, MD, chief of dermatology at St. Vincent's Hospital and Medical Centre in New York City. If an ulcer appears on the heel, suspend the heel by raising the lower leg with pillows or soft blankets, she recommends. Once pressure is relieved, blood will flow to the existing wound and aid healing.

Keep the wounds clean. Pressure ulcers have to be kept clean in order to avoid infection and to heal properly. "Rinse the wound and surrounding skin with soap and water," says Dr. Kaminski. Do not use cleansing solutions containing disinfectants, such as povidone-iodine. Disinfectants generally slow the healing process.

Make the wound moist. To help speed healing, cover any existing sores with gauze bandages coated in petroleum jelly or similar moist, thick ointment. This encourages tissues to grow rapidly, Dr. Buchness says. There are special dressings such as Duoderm and Vigilon, which are available through your pharmacist, that dissolve into the wound and create a good environment for healing.

Keep the healthy skin dry. "Keep the wound moist and the surrounding skin dry," suggests Dr. Kaminski. Healthy skin that is allowed to remain moist is more susceptible to developing a sore and an open wound. For patients who are incontinent, undergarments must be changed when needed in order to keep skin dry.

Bee Stings

The pain: A local reaction to the attack of stinging insects, including honeybees, wasps, hornets or yellowjackets; intense pain accompanied by redness, swelling and itching at the site of the sting.

The cause: Stinging insects cause pain because of the venom they inject into your skin when they sting. Only honeybees have a barbed stinger and are unable to extract it after stinging, which means the stinger and stinger sac are left behind. This kills the insect, but the sac keeps pumping venom, making the sting worse. The other insects can remove their stingers, meaning they can sting repeatedly.

See a doctor if...
...you experience any symptoms of allergic reaction, such as: trouble breathing, tightness in the throat or chest, dizziness or nausea, hives, a drippy nose, a swollen mouth or tongue, and difficulty breathing. Seek medical attention immediately. Remember to observe for symptoms of allergic reaction for up to 60 minutes after a sting. Sometimes someone will look fine for the first 15 minutes or so and then develop a life-threatening reaction. If you know you're allergic to bees, get a prescription for an epinephrine kit from your doctor and always have it handy.
...the swelling spreads to a large area—for example, you entire arm or a large section of your trunk. Seek medical attention immediately.
...pain and swelling continue for more than 72 hours without relief.

Quick relief:
Scrape out the stinger. If the insect bite left a stinger behind, scrape it out. The sooner the better, says Mark Rosoff, an emergency medical technician and director of the Front Range Institute for Safety in Colorado. "Use the edge of a credit card, a knife, or your fingernail to scrape out or flick away the stinger," he explains. (Don't use your fingers or tweezers to pinch the fuzzy part sticking out—that's the venom sac.) If you squeeze it, you'll inject more venom into yourself.
Ice the bite. Put an ice pack wrapped in a thin towel on for 15 to 20 minutes to soothe the pain and keep down the swelling.
Slap on some soda. A paste of baking soda and water takes away the sting

of most bites, especially bee stings. "The baking soda neutralises the acidity of the bee sting," says Rosoff.

Neutralise a wasp attack. Unlike bee stings, however, Wasp bites are alkaline, so you'll need something acidic to neutralise them. Rosoff suggests applying some lemon juice or vinegar to soothe those stings.

Try some tenderness. You may soothe the itching by rubbing the area with meat tenderisers made with the enzyme papain.

Use paste against the pain. Rubbing toothpaste on a sting makes it feel better because the menthol in the paste has a cooling effect.

Calamine will feel fine. Applied as needed, calamine will help soothe the area.

Cream it. To soothe the savage sting, apply some over-the-counter lotion, such as After Bite or Wasp-Eze. For the itching that comes later, apply an over-the-counter cortisone cream.

Wipe it out with ammonia. Sometimes dabbing some household ammonia on the sting does the trick.

Ongoing aid:

Elevate the area. If a sting becomes so swollen that it actually aches, elevate the stung arm, leg or other body part so that gravity helps fluid leave the area, reducing swelling and the soreness that comes with it.

Go over the counter. To further relieve pain and itching, take an over-the-counter analgesic such as aspirin or acetaminophen (paracetamol), says Rosoff . Take as directed on the label. If you have itching near the sting, oral antihistamines like Cholor-Trimetin, Piriton or Benadryl may be taken every 4 to 6 hours to ease the itch.

Resist the urge to itch. Most bites and stings heal themselves after a few days. If you scratch open a bite, it has a good chance of getting infected, especially in warm, moist climates. Leave it be.

Put together a poultice. Poultices ease stings, help heal wounds, and reduce swelling, says Susan S. Weed, an herbalist and herbal educator, and author of the *Wise Woman* series of herbal health books. The simplest poultice for treating insect bites is a dab of mud. Or if you want to be more hygienic about it, you can buy powdered clay at a health food store and mix it with a little water.

Apply gentle heat. If you're still swollen after the first day on ice, try placing a warn compress or heating pad on the sting as often as possible.

Vitamins and supplements:

Increase the zinc. Certain nutrients appear to offer protection against some insects, possible by altering body odour. Try 60 mg of zinc a day (about four times the recommended dietary allowance). Dietary sources include oysters, red meats and fortified cereals. Thiamine (B1) may also help. Be sure to check with your doctor before taking either supplement, because high doses can cause problems.

Everyday prevention:

Shield your skin. If a bug can't light, a bug can't bite. Wear a long-sleeve shirt and long pants. Insects like bright colours and floral patterns, so choose white, green, tan, and khaki hues.

Tell bugs to bug off. Always apply bug repellent when you're out. On clothing, use a repellent containing permethrin (such as Permanone), the synthetic version of a natural insecticide found in chrysanthemums. Permethrin repels bugs even after several washings. On your skin, you can try a natural product that contains citronella, such as Natrapel or Wasp-Eze, which provides short-term protection from bugs. These products are available at most health food stores.

Get shots for protection. "If you have ever had a systemic reaction to an insect sting, you should see an allergist right away," says Robert Plancey, MD, assistant clinical professor of medicine at the University of Southern California. It is vital that an allergist test you to find out which insect venom you are allergic to. You can be placed on a regimen of allergy shots to lessen the intensity of or prevent allergic reactions in the future.

Carry a kit. People who are allergic to insect venom should also carry a special medical kit to prevent anaphylactic shock. It includes a chewable antihistamine and injectable adrenaline, both of which will help stop the symptoms. Your allergist can prescribe a kit to carry with you at all times, especially outdoors, and demonstrate its correct use. If you need to use the kit, you should go to the nearest emergency room via paramedic ambulance in case the reaction recurs.

Shun good scents. Bees are attracted to floral smells. So don't use perfume, aftershave, or even scented deodorant when you are headed for woods or fields or raking leaves and cleaning the gutters.

Choose plain soap. Use unscented soap and wash your clothes in unscented detergent. You don't want to smell like a daffodil.

Be sombre. Avoid brightly coloured clothing—no reds, yellows, blues, violets, oranges, or pinks. And no floral patterns either. Bees may mistake you for a garden.

Sip inside. A stinging insect is attracted to any beverage. If you leave a can of soda untended, a bee can fly into it. Getting stung in the mouth or throat can cause swelling that could obstruct the airway, even to a nonallergic person, says Dr. Plancey.

Look before you eat. Yellow jackets and hornets have splendiferous palates. Thus, keep a watchful eye on picnic foods during summer outings.

Drive with your windows closed. If your car is air-conditioned, leave the windows up all summer long, even when the car is parked. You never know when a stinging insect will make a beeline for the warm interior.

Always wear shoes. If you are allergic to bee stings, you can't risk a fancy-free barefoot amble through the meadow.

Try to stay calm. If a stinging insect approaches, walk calmly away. If you start flailing your arms and running away, the insect is more likely to sting.

Herbal Help:

Soothe the pain with Calendula. In her classic *Modern Herbal*, written in 1931, Maude Grieve writes picturesquely that calendula flower "rubbed on the affected part, is an admirable remedy for the pain and swelling caused by the sting of a wasp or bee."

Ease it with garlic and onion. Both contain enzymes that break down chemical substances known as Prostaglandins that the body releases in response to pain. Interestingly enough, garlic and onions work both internally and externally. You can make a poultice of these herbs and apply them directly to insect bites and stings. You can also get a measure of relief by eating them.

Stop pain with plantain. "Plantain is one of the first herbs my botanical friends mention for bug bites and stings," says James Duke, Ph.D., author of *The Green Pharmacy*. (You need to rub on the fresh herb for this remedy to work.)

Oil up and say ahhh. Try applying pure lavender, tea tree, helichrysum or blue camomile essential oil to the affected area. The oil can be reapplied every ten minutes until you feel better.

Going, going, pulegone. Both mountain mint and pennyroyal contain pulegone, a powerful insect repellent. If you have access to fresh mountain mint, just pick some leaves and rub them on your skin and clothing. (But don't use pennyroyal or mountain mint if you're pregnant, as the ingredients in these herbs have been known to increase the risk of miscarriage. Kids under age eight should also avoid pennyroyal.) Other repelling herbs include basil (Indians rub the leaves on their skin as an insect repellent, and Africans do the same) and citronella (available in candles and insect repellents, or dilutecitronella oil by adding several drops to a vegetable oil base, then apply to skin).

Debug with oil: Try half a cup of olive oil, five or six drops each of essential oils of citronella, eucalyptus, rosemary and lavender, and two drops of pennyroyal. Dab the mixture on as needed. Avoid contact with your eyes and wash your hands after applying.

Black Eye

The pain: A bruise over the eye, following a blow or other forceful impact.

The cause: Trauma, usually caused by something (like a ball) or someone (with a good right hand) breaks the skin or small veins under the skin near your eye. Blood leaks into the skin around the eye, causing swelling and discoloration. (Black eyes can also be caused by sinus infections or allergic reactions.) Black eyes usually fade away in two to three weeks.

See a doctor if...
...You have blurred or double vision or your eyesight is impaired in any way.
...You have pain in your eye as well as around it.
...You become light sensitive.
...You have "floaters" or other specks in your field of vision.
...You haven't walked into any doors or fists lately, and you have allergy symptoms like itchy eyes and sneezing, or your skull is pounding and your sinuses hurt along with the black eye. If so, your allergies or a sinus headache are more than likely the source for your shiner. Your doctor can these conditions with the proper medications, which should also clear up the black eye.

Quick relief:
Ice your eye. Besides reducing swelling, the cold will narrow blood vessels, limiting the amount of blood that will get pooled under the skin and cause a shiner, says Kevin Ferentz, MD, associate professor of family medicine at the University of Maryland School of Medicine. Wrap the ice in a towel and apply for 15 minutes every 2 to 3 hours. Don't leave the ice on for longer than 20 minutes, or your body will start thinking your eye area is too cold and send blood over there to warm things up, which actually increases swelling.
Chill with frozen veggies. Remember when tough guys used to slap a slab of raw steak over a black eye? Well, it isn't the steak that brings relief, it's the coldness of the piece of meat that helps decrease blood flow and relieve swelling. But you can save yourself some money (as well as a nice

piece of meat) by using anything icy ."I recommend you use a bag of frozen vegetables wrapped in a washcloth," advises Rodney Basler, MD, a dermatologist. It contours to your face better than a steak, and when you're done using it, you can just throw the bag back into the freezer and save it for the next day's treatment." Keep the cold compress on your blackened eye for about 20 minutes or until the skin begins to feel numb; then remove it for about 10 minutes. You may continue this procedure on and off for three days, or until swelling subsides.

Ongoing aid:

Warm it up. After three or four days of ice, put heat on your eye, says Dr. Ferentz. The pooled blood from the original shot you took needs to be reabsorbed back into the body so that your black eye will go away, and Dr. Ferentz says that heat will help. Soak a washcloth in comfortably warm water, wring it out, and then apply it for 15 minutes 2 or 3 times a day.

Pass on aspirin. The basic thing you need to do to heal a black eye is to stop the bleeding above or below the skin's surface and get that blood out of the area. Clots are what the body uses to stop bleeding, and the platelets in your blood stick together to form them, says Flip Homansky, MD, a ringside physician in Las Vegas who has worked more than 250 championship boxing matches. But if you take aspirin for the pain, your broken blood vessels will take longer to clot and heal. Instead of aspirin, take 500 to 650 milligrams of acetaminophen (paracetamol) every four to six hours for as long as you have pain. This kills the pain without interfering with the blood clotting, says Richard Roberts, MD, associate chair and professor of family medicine at the University of Wisconsin Medical School. People with liver disease must be careful about taking acetaminophen (paracetamol), so check with your doctor if you have liver problems, he cautions.

Nutritional remedies:

Have a Hawaiian punch. "Eating pineapple or papaya-or better yet, a fruit cocktail made of both-can help remedy a black eye," says Las Vegas orthopedic surgeon, Michael Rask, MD. According to Dr. Rask, "An enzyme found in those fruits changes the molecular structure of the blood, so it's more easily absorbed by the body." If you have a black eye, eat three papayas a day for faster healing. Or you can take up to 600 milligrams of papaya in capsule form (sold in health food stores) four times a day. Loading up on pineapple will also do the trick, according to Dr. Rask, and both fruits give you a healthy dose of vitamin C.

Helpful vitamins and supplements:

Try vitamin C. It's well documented that vitamin C promotes healing-and for anyone who bruises easily, getting plenty of vitamin C in your diet is a must. If you're sporting a black eye, take a daily vitamin C supplement and increase your intake of vitamin C-rich foods such as broccoli, mangoes, peppers and sweet potatoes, as well as pineapple and papaya, to speed the healing process.

Herbal help:
Get comfort from comfrey. For black eyes, Kristin Stiles, a doctor of naturopathy, recommends an herb poultice made from comfrey leaves, which she says soothes the eye, lessens pain, stops bleeding, and promotes wound healing. You can buy dried comfrey leaves at most health food stores. Boil four ounces of water, add a tablespoon of leaves, and stir. Shut off the heat, and put the mix in the refrigerator for 10 to 15 minutes so that it cools and steeps. Then soak a piece of cheesecloth or washcloth in the mix, wring it out, and apply to your eye for 20 minutes four times a day.

Other alternatives:
Pop some pellets. Arnica is a homeopathic remedy that would make you sick if you took it in massive doses. But in a diluted, pellet form, it actually stimulates your body to heal itself. It's "an all-purpose trauma remedy known to reduce haemorrhaging or bleeding from any particular area," says Dr. Stiles. You can get arnica at most health food stores. Dr. Stiles recommends taking one to three pellets of 30C potency arnica three or four times a day for two or three days. Dr. Stiles says that contact with your skin can reduce the homeopathic arnica's effectiveness, so for best results, shake out the pellets onto the lid of the bottle and tip them into your mouth without touching them.

Everyday prevention:
Protect your peepers. Since sports-related trauma can cause the black eye, Dr. Ferentz says that it's very important to protect those delicate orbs when playing sports like racquetball or basketball. He suggests using a pair of sports goggles. If you use glasses, these goggles are even available with prescription lenses. Look for goggles with polycarbonate lenses; they're far more impact-resistant than their plastic counterparts.

Stop and think. If you have a black eye from a fight, and it was in a bar or alley instead of a ring, Dr. Roberts says that you may want to sort through what got you in that situation. Sometimes it can be a problem dealing with anger, alcohol, or a domestic violence issue. He suggests facing the problem realistically to prevent future black eyes and seeking help if you need it because the next go-around in a bar might lead to something a lot more damaging than a black eye.

Blisters

The pain: Tender fluid-filled "bubbles" that usually occur at the site of a chronic irritation of the skin.

The cause: "Blisters are caused by heat, friction, and moisture," says Douglas Hale, D.P.M., a podiatrist at the Foot and Ankle Centre of Washington. To prevent those tender domes of pain on your feet, you have to minimize those three blister inducers.

See a doctor if:

...you develop a severe blister or blisters that are very painful and don't seem to be healing well.

...a blister suddenly shows signs of infection—pain, swelling, redness, weeping or a yellow crust—and you have a fever.

...you develop a wide-scale eruption of blisters.

...blisters continue to form over time without an obvious cause, such as friction or poison ivy.

...you develop a single or repeated episodes of a cluster of tiny blisters, often with tingling, which may represent herpes simplex.

...you develop blisters while pregnant.

Quick relief:

Pop it. If you pop the blister promptly, within the first couple of hours, the skin layer will adhere back quickly. To do it: Clean the area with alcohol, heat a clean needle or pin in a flame, and then pop the blister. "Afterward, be sure to leave the skin on" so it can heal over. As an added precaution, you may want to cover the remaining skin with a bandage or sterile piece of gauze or tape.

Wash with liquid soap. Gently clean the blister with soap and water to eliminate bacteria that could cause infection. Liquid soap is preferable to bar soap, which may contain bacteria from previous uses.

Fight the germs. If a blister is open, you must apply antimicrobial ointment, such as Bacitracin or Polysporin (Cicatrin or Polyfax), to kill bacteria and prevent infection.

Cover it. After you apply ointment, cover the blister with a bandage to cushion it from pressure and keep it clean. Gauze and surgical tape or a plain old adhesive bandage work fine. The bandage also keeps ointment from

ruining your clothes and helps absorb any fluid that leaks out of the blister.
Use a doughnut pad. If you want to protect a small blister from friction and pressure, cover it with a doughnut-shaped pad, called a soft corn cushion, which has a hole in the middle.
Silken your skin. "Wearing a silk undersock can help prevent foot blisters and relieve the pain once you get them, since silk is less damaging to the skin than other fabrics," says Nicholas J. Lowe, MD, clinical professor of dermatology at the University of California.
Give it air and water. You want to keep the blistered area protected with a bandage when you wear shoes all day. But when you can, take off your shoes, socks, and bandages and give the blister some breathing room. The best thing you can do for a blister is give it some air because the air will help it heal faster. A good 20-minute soak in lukewarm water will also speed up the healing process.

Everyday prevention:
Invest in sock options. To help prevent blisters during exercise, choose a sock with a synthetic material that wicks moisture away from the foot, such as Capilene, says Dr. Huppin a podiatrist. "The ideal sock is a Capilene/wool mixture. While the Capilene helps to keep the foot dry, the wool protects the foot from the shoe." You might also consider wearing two pairs of socks. The inner one should be a thin synthetic sock that wicks moisture away from the foot. The outer sock should be thick to absorb friction. "This is an old trick used by runners and hikers to prevent blisters," says Martin Lynn, D.P.M., a podiatrist at the Seattle Foot and Ankle Centre.
Nip it in the bud. If you feel or see a hot spot-the red, sore, inflamed area that announces a blister is on the way-stop the blister from developing by applying moleskin. This is a feltlike, synthetic padding with an adhesive backing, available at most chemists and sporting good stores. First clean the hot spot with rubbing alcohol to remove the oils on the skin so that the moleskin sticks better. Then cut a circle of moleskin slightly bigger than the hot spot and paste it on, following directions on the package.
Protect with petroleum jelly. If you know that you're prone to blisters In a certain site, prevent future friction by applying a coating of plain petroleum jelly, such as Vaseline. Runners and other athletes who are prone to blisters on their feet can try a variety of products, such as Skin Lube or Runner's Lube (PhysoSPORT), says Richard T. Braver, a sports podiatrist and director of the Active Foot and Ankle Care Centre. "They are ointments that reduce the friction and help prevent blisters." They work better than petroleum jelly, which has a tendency to melt inside the heat of a shoe.
Use powder power. Rubbing baby powder on your feet before any blister promoting activity is another good preventer. "Make powdering part of your daily routine," says Richard Cowin, D.P.M., director of Cowin Foot Clinic of Florida. Reason: Like petroleum jelly, it helps reduce friction and eases glide.

Turn up your toes at medicated pads. People with corns and hammer toes sometimes use so-called medicated pads for relief. But if you do, you put yourself at risk for a blister. These pads contain an acid that burns the skin and causes blisters, says Dr. Hale.

Carry tape. Prevention is much easier and faster than healing, says Frederic Haberman, MD, a sports dermatologist. That's why he takes a roll of adhesive tape to any marathon where he's serving as a doctor. Runners who feel a blister threatening to form should simply cut a small piece of tape and gently place it directly over the sore spot. The same trick, he says, will work on any part of the body where your skin starts to feel irritated from friction.

Soap your socks. If blisters are a frequent problem, here's what to do: Turn your socks inside out. Then take a bar of soap and rub it over them. Put the socks back on with the soaped side next to your skin.

Cushion your feet with drop-in shoe insoles. The extra padding can further reduce friction and perspiration.

Quit the cotton. Sorry, but much-ballyhooed cotton sweat socks don't offer the best protection against blisters. In fact, sports podiatrists say that manmade acrylic socks are best for preventing blisters. "Cotton fiber becomes abrasive with repeated use, and it also compresses and loses its shape and when wet," says Douglas Richie, Jr., D.P.M., a podiatrist. According to Dr. Richie, "The shape of the sock is critical when it's inside a shoe." So a sock that loses its shape is just what your blister-vulnerable foot doesn't need.

Shoe shopping for blister sufferers:

Shop for shoes in the afternoon. That is when your feet are most swollen, says Dr. Hale. If you pick your shoe early in the day, you may end up with a pair that is too small for your afternoon feet.

Have your feet measured. Even if you think you know your shoe size, get your feet measured every time you buy shoes, Dr. Hale says. Sometimes, feet spread out over time.

Remember your width. People tend to take the width of shoes for granted. You may need a different width than the standard, explains Dr. Hale. Not all brands come in all widths. If a shoe feels too narrow, ask the salesclerk for the next widest size.

Test it with your thumb. "Make sure that there is a thumb-width between the end of your shoe and your big toe when you are standing up," says Dr. Hale. Don't fall for the "it'll stretch" spiel. "Don't let the shoe salesclerk tell you that the shoes will stretch out," says Dr. Lawrence Z. Huppin. "If they feel tight in the store, they will feel tight in a couple of weeks."

Avoid looseness. A tight shoe isn't the only friction-cause. A loose shoe can cause blisters because of the friction the shoe creates as the foot moves around in it, says Arnold Ravick, D.P.M., a podiatrist.

Keep Your Hands Blister-Free

Jenny Stone knows hand blisters. She is a certified athletic trainer and the manager of clinical programs in the division of sports medicine for the U. S. Olympic Committee in Colorado Springs. Training gymnasts, discuss throwers, and volleyball players, she sees hands that get a lot of punishment. Here are her tips to keep your hands blister-free:

Ease into new activities. Start slowly. Don't go out and play 36 holes the first time you play golf in the spring. Play 9 holes instead," she says. "You don't want to jump into any activity that your body is unaccustomed to."

Use equipment that is right for you. Equipment that is inappropriately sized-for example, the grip of a tennis racket that is either too small or too large will have a tendency to cause blisters on the hands. "Ask your local pros to check if you have the proper size," Stone advises.

Protect the tender spots. "If you know that you get blisters on your hands when you do certain things, like play tennis or shovel, put some athletic tape or moleskin over that area before the activity," she says.

Wear gloves. "They will absorb the friction that normally would transfer to your hands," she explains.

Keep your hands dry. "If your hands are damp, they are more likely to get blisters. Powder your hands before exercise," says Stone. "And if you have a problem with excessive sweating, use an antiperspirant on your hands."

Shop with a sock. When you shop for shoes, slip on the type of sock that you actually plan to wear with your new shoes, says Dr. Hale.

Take a test-drive inside. Even if you follow all these tips, there is always a chance that your new shoes may not fit perfectly. That's why you should wear them around the house for an hour or two before you ever wear them outside. "If you do that, you will know very quickly if there is a hot spot in the shoes," says Dr. Lynn. "And if there are hot spots, you can still return them."

Break 'em in. "Probably the biggest cause of foot blisters in women comes from trying to break in a new pair of shoes," says dermatologist Joseph Bark, MD. "My advice to women who get a new pair of shoes: Wear them for only 30 minutes at a time. It's all fight to wear the shoes several times a day, but only for 30 minutes-at least for the first few days." (So carry an extra pair of broken-in shoes in your handbag and trade off a few times during the day.)

Herbal Help:

Aid it with aloe. This plant, usually used for burns, can also treat blisters, says Eric A. Weiss MD, assistant professor of emergency medicine at Stanford University Medical Centre and author of *Wilderness 911.* Aloe vera will help heal and protect a blister because it contains both anti-inflammatory and antibiotic properties, he says. But be certain that you use pure aloe vera gel, because some prepared products contain additives such as alcohol, which may sting, says Dr. Weiss. Smear some on before you bandage the area. For added benefit, put a thin coat of aloe on the blister and a thin coat of honey (it is a natural antibiotic) on a piece of gauze and tape it down with first-aid tape, says Dr. Weiss.

Be blister-free with comfrey. The herb comfrey contains allantoin, a compound that helps heal wounds, says Kathleen Maier, a physician's assistant and herbalist. You can buy an already-made comfrey cream at an herbal or health food store, or you can make a poultice by using the following recipe: Take a small handful of comfrey leaves and cut them up. Cover them with boiling water and let steep for 10 minutes. Let cool. Remove the leaves from the water and gently squeeze out excess water. Place a piece of gauze over the blister, put the moistened herb on top of the gauze and cover with another piece of gauze. Keep the gauze in place with an elastic bandage for a minimum of 20 minutes. Do this two times daily, Maier says.

Let E help. A mixture of the herb calendula and vitamin E will speed up the healing of your blisters, says Andrea D. Sullivan, Ph.D., a doctor of naturopathy and author of *A Path to Healing*. Both calendula and vitamin E can reduce inflammation of the blister. They also contain compounds that promote wound healing, Dr. Sullivan adds. How much of the mixture you need depends on the size of the blister. Mix equal parts of calendula and vitamin E oil (which can you can get by poking a vitamin E capsule with a pin if you don't have the actual oil on hand) and spread it on the blister. Reapply as needed for about a week.

Make a blister-busting cocktail. Obviously, vodka can relieve the pain of a blister-if you drink enough that you can't feel your feet anymore. But there's another way that vodka can help soothe a blister, according to James A. Duke, Ph.D., the world's foremost authority on healing herbs and author of *The Green Pharmacy*. Mix a handful of each of the following herbs: fresh thyme, rosemary, a mint that contains menthol such as peppermint or spearmint, and either cherry birch or wintergreen. Crush the herbs and put them in a glass jar and cover with vodka. After a few days, strain out the herbs and keep the liquid in your medicine chest or first-aid kit. Apply the liquid on your next blister. The mixture will help fight infection.

Boils

The pain: Red, painful, pus-filled bumps on the skin.

The cause: Bacterial infections of hair follicles. Boils originate deep in the layers of your skin but make their presence known as they rise to the surface. Any number of irritants can cause strains of the bacteria Staphylococcus aureus to get inside a hair follicle or pore and cause an infection. The body responds by deploying white blood cells to kill the infection. In some people—especially those with diabetes, compromised immune systems, and certain skin problems—the body's attack on the bacterial invaders causes pus, which gathers into an absccss right below the skin. The bacteria in a boil is highly contagious. It can plant a boil on somebody else. Prevention involves avoiding the boil-making four: heat, pressure, moisture, and bacteria.

See a doctor if...
...the boil is larger than a half inch in diameter, or is on the face, armpits, groin or breasts. (A woman with a boil on her breast should not breast feed until she's seen a doctor, since she may pass bacteria on to her child.)
...you develop a fever, chills, or an increasing red area surrounding the boil. You should see a doctor immediately because the infection may have spread, says Karl Kramer, MD, clinical professor of dermatology at the University of Miami School of Medicine.
...the boil is extremely painful. "Relief can be in achieved in seconds when treated," says Vail Reese, MD, a dermatologist with the Dermatology Medical Group.
...you have diabetes. You may need prescription antibiotics.
...you develop multiple boils.

Medication:
Injecting a boil with a steroid solution helps it to heal fast. The treatment can be performed in a doctor's office. Prescription antibiotics tackle a boil in three to four days. In fact, oral antibiotics are your best course of action for a boil that has lingered or for battling a persistent crop of boils.

Quick relief:

Apply warm compresses. Soak a washcloth or a compress in warm water and place it on the boil for 15 minutes three times a day, Dr. Reese says. The warm compress brings the boil to a head, causing it to drain naturally.
Take a bath. If you have the time to spare, take a warm bath for 20 minutes a few times a day, says Michael Carlston, MD, assistant clinical professor in the department of family and community medicine at the University of California. The warm water will bring the boil to a head and soothe your pain.
Get hot and cold. Alternating hot and cold compresses speeds the healing of a boil by increasing the flow of blood to the affected area, says Agatha Thrash, MD, a medical pathologist and co-founder and co-director of Uchee Pines Institute, a natural healing centre. Her instructions: Soak a washcloth in comfortably hot water and hold it against the boil, refreshing the heat as necessary to keep the cloth hot. After three to five minutes, apply a cold compress for 30 to 60 seconds. Dr. Thrash says to repeat this treatment three times daily until the boil comes to a head or goes away.

Ongoing care:

Keep it clean. The infection that causes a boil can easily spread to other areas of your body. Clean the boil area regularly with antibacterial soap, Dr. Reese says.
Leave it alone. Pinching, squeezing, or popping a boil yourself will only lead to a bigger chance of infection, says Don W. Printz, MD, a dermatologist. The squeezing motion will actually push the pus down deeper into the skin, possibly spreading the infection. Popping a boil can also lead to scarring, Dr. Reese adds.
Zap it with benzoyl peroxide. The over the counter acne preparation benzoyl peroxide may help dry it out. It can be used twice a day.

Nutritional Remedies:

Eat well. "Eat foods that are rich in vitamin A and zinc, because these nutrients aid in skin healing and repair and can help relieve boils," says Allan Magaziner, D.O., a nutritional medicine specialist. "Good sources of vitamin A include any fruit or vegetable that has a yellow or orange colour—squash, yams, sweet potatoes and carrots. Zinc is found in oysters, sunflower seeds and pumpkin seeds. Vitamin A is also found in dark green leafy vegetables such as spinach and kale."
Juice it. Like many other skin ailments, boils result from a build-up of toxins in the system, according to Eve Campanelli, Ph.D., a holistic family practitioner. To stimulate the liver and speed up the elimination of wastes, Dr. Campanelli recommends drinking a blend of 8 ounces of carrot juice, 1 ounce of beet juice, 4 ounces of celery juice and 1/2 to 1 ounce of parsley juice. "A large glass each morning and a smaller glass in the afternoon is an effective and a very nutritious way to get the liver moving," says Dr. Campanelli.

Helpful vitamins and supplements:

Try A to zinc. To relieve a boil, take 10,000 international units of vitamin A and 15 to 20 milligrams of zinc, advises Dr. Magaziner. If you're prone to boils, keep taking these nutrients, but cut the dosage in half after the boil disappears, he says. And if boils aren't a chronic problem for you, he advises that you stop taking the supplements after the boil has cleared up.

Everyday prevention:

Chill out. Excessive heat in a hair follicle can make infection more likely. Tight pants and sweatbands, for instance, create hot zones where boils can get started. So wear looser clothing for a cooler skin temperature, says Joseph P. Bark, MD, a dermatologist and author of *Your Skin: An Owner's Guide.*

Depressurize. Heat can also be created by pressure. "I see lots of boils on the lower backs and buttocks of salespeople," says Dr. Bark. "They sit on car seats for hundreds of miles a week, and their skin is chronically compressed." He suggests that people who spend a lot of time driving get a seat pad made of woven wire and wooden beads. "It distributes the weight more effectively and lets air passage occur."

Pick a little cotton. Since moisture leads to boils and cotton underwear helps wick away humidity, changing your polyester privies for all-natural undies may reduce your boil-risk, explains Dr. Bark.

Try shower power. Frequent showers with antibacterial soap may help by fighting the boil bacteria, according to Dr. Bark.

Lose a little weight. Boils tend to occur in intertriginous areas of the body—that is, places where skin is touching skin, like between the thighs, in the cleft of the buttocks, and underneath women's breasts, says Dr. Bark. People who are overweight not only have more folds of skin, but these areas are particularly pressurised and moist. "Losing weight is the most fundamental preventive measure in people who are overweight and get boils," says Guy F. Webster, MD, Ph.D., professor of dermatology at the Jefferson Medical College of Thomas Jefferson University in Philadelphia.

Try some talc. If you are overweight, be sure to dust some talcum powder in areas where the skin chafes, suggests Dr. Webster. It reduces moisture and prevents breaks in the skin where the staph bacteria might enter.

Don't Share That Sweater. Boils are not only painful but also contagious. "The most common way that boils are transmitted— particularly in teenagers—is by sharing clothing," says Guy F. Webster. So if someone in the family has a boil, don't steal his sweatshirt at the game. Also, you should launder his towels and washcloths separately.

Keep the hair. As the popularity of men having hair-free chests increases, so do boils. Dermatologists in the San Francisco area are seeing more patients who develop boils because they shave or wax their chest and abdominal muscles, says Dr. Reese.

Herbal help:

Make room for rumex. The herb Rumex crispus can help calm an erupting boil, says Steven Bailey, a naturopathic doctor. You can find the herb in capsule form at chemists or health food stores. Take two 100-milligram capsules three times a day for three to four weeks during and for three to four days past the boil's inflammatory stage, Dr. Bailey suggests. The inflammatory stage is over when the pain, redness, and swelling are gone. If your inflammation does not show improvement within two weeks, it's time to see your doctor, says Dr. Bailey. Rumex crispus may have a mild laxative effect.

Try tea tree. Tea tree essential oil is a natural antiseptic that speeds the healing of virtually any kind of skin irritation, says herbalist Jeanne Rose, author of *Aromatherapy: Applications and Inhalations*. She suggests applying a single drop of tea tree oil directly to the boil after bathing.

Other alternatives:

Seek homeopathic help. "If you have a boil that comes on quite suddenly, is very bright red and inflamed and is hot and very painful to the touch, then Belladonna is a good remedy choice for you," says Mitchell Fleisher, MD, a family practice physician and homeopath. "If it's a boil that comes on more slowly, looks more darkish blue than red and is extremely painful to touch and you feel quite chilled, then try Hepar sulphuris. Take a 6C or t 2C dose of the indicated remedy every three to four hours as needed until you feel relief." If the swelling and inflammation go down within 12 to 24 hours, then you're on the right track; otherwise, seek professional medical care, says John G. Collins, N.D., a naturopathic physician. Silica, another homeopathic remedy, helps bring stubborn boils to the surface. Use silica when the boil is red and swollen but pus isn't present. Take one dose of a 12C potency silica product once or twice a day until the boil comes to a head.

Try some kitchen cures. Applying pieces of warm, milk-soaked bread directly to the boil is an old folk remedy, and some people find it works quite well, according to Varro E. Tyler, Ph.D., professor and author of *The Honest Herbal.* Other home remedies: compresses of heated slices of tomato, raw onion, mashed garlic or the outer leaves of cabbage, or a warm tea bag of black tea.

Get aid from Ayurveda. Here's how to bring a boil to a head, according to Vasant Lad, B.A.M.S., director of the Ayurvedic Institute in New Mexico: Apply a paste made from 1/2 teaspoon each of ginger powder and turmeric and enough warm water to mix. Rub the paste directly on the affected area, cover with gauze and leave in place for a half-hour. Repeat as necessary until the boil breaks and begins to heal. Turmeric can stain skin and clothes, cautions Dr. Lad, so be sure to wear old garments when using this remedy. Any skin discolouration should wash off in two weeks, he adds.

Breast Pain

The pain: Swollen, tender, lumpy breasts that make movement painful. The condition usually occurs just prior to menstruation.

The cause: In 30 to 40 percent of women, fluid and extra breast cells that should be reabsorbed at the end of the menstrual period is retained in the breasts, creating cysts. You'll feel this as lumpiness. Cysts aren't the only problem. If the fluid isn't reabsorbed, or the breasts over-prepare for pregnancy, the swelling that results can be downright severe. (Swelling causes the nerve fibres to stretch, which can create significant pain.) Eight percent of women suffer from monthly breast changes so disabling it disrupts their lives.

See a doctor if:
...you try dietary or lifestyle changes for three months and your breasts still hurt.
...your breasts become tender and swollen over the course of a day or two.
...your breasts become painful after taking oral contraceptives or hormone replacement therapy.
...you have persistent tenderness accompanied by redness and you feel a mass.
...you have these three symptoms occurring at the same time: the breast is hot, hard and hurting.
...you have a bloody discharge from your nipple.
...you notice anything unusual during your monthly breast self-examination.

Quick relief:
Slip into a support bra. It will take you half a minute to change bras at the first sign of breast pain. The extra support can prevent the breasts from moving around, helping to reduce stretching of nerve fibres that can produce pain messages.
Warm gently. Holding a warm compress such as a heated towel or heating pad against the breast for 10 to 15 minutes can give some relief from breast tenderness, says Ellen Yankauskas, MD, director of the Women's Centre for Family Health in California.

Compress with castor oil. Hot compresses soaked in castor oil can be helpful. Soak a piece of wool flannel with castor oil. Wrap one side in plastic wrap, then in a towel, and hold the pack against your breast so that the oil soaked flannel touches your skin. Finally, cover the pack with a heating pad or hot water bottle. Warning: castor oil is toxic if ingested and this could harm a nursing infant. So don't rely on this remedy if you're nursing.

Have some hydrotherapy. Frequent water treatments can soothe tender, lumpy breasts, says Agatha Thrash, MD, a medical pathologist. She suggests applying a hot, moist compress to each breast for three to five minutes every time you shower. Follow each hot application with a cool sponging, she says.

Soak in a bathtub filled with comfortably hot water for at least 20 minutes. "Settle back into the tub so that your chest is submerged," suggests Rosalind Benedet, R.N., a breast health nurse specialist. The water soothes your breasts and relaxes your entire body.

As an alternative to heat, apply a cold pack to sore breasts for up to 20 minutes whenever you need relief. Use either crushed ice or a bag of frozen peas, since either will conform to the shape of your breasts, says Benedet. And remember to wrap the ice or bag of peas in a towel so that the extreme cold doesn't injure your skin.

Go the over-the-counter. If you prefer to go with an over-the-counter pain reliever, look for one containing the active ingredient pamabron, advises. Pamabron acts as a mild diuretic.

Nutritional Remedies:

Cut back on meat. "The more animal proteins you eat, the slower your body will excrete oestrogen," says Susan Doughty, R.N., a nurse practitioner. This excess oestrogen often winds up in breast tissue, which is particularly sensitive to hormones.

Dehydrogenate your menu. Besides reducing meat and poultry, eliminate or drastically cut back on your intake of margarine and other hydrogenated fats, advises Christiane Northrup, MD, an obstetrics and gynecology professor. Hydrogenated fats interfere with your body's ability to convert essential fatty acids from the diet into gamma linoleic acid (GLA). Since your body needs GLA to help prevent breast pain, you may be asking for discomfort if you overdo hydrogenated fats and suppress the production of GLA.

Drink up. Drink at least eight eight-ounce glasses of water a day. Paradoxically, the more water you drink, the less likely your breasts are to swell before your period. Water flushes salt out of your body, so you retain less fluid, says Benedet.

Cut back on salt. Salt makes your entire body retain fluid-including your breasts, which can swell up like water balloons. "Lots of women crave salty foods such as potato chips and pickles right before their periods," notes Benedet.

Serve up some soy. In societies where soybeans are a routine part of the diet, women have fewer breast problems, says Dr. Yankauskas. Soybeans, and foods made from soy, contain isoflavones-naturally occurring substances that are converted to hormonelike substances and may block certain unwanted effects of oestrogen in the body, thus mitigating breast discomfort. So the next time you order Chinese food, order an entrée with tofu instead of meat. Pour soy milk on your cereal. Or pick up some soy burgers for your next cookout. You can find soy milk, soy burgers and other soy products in health food stores.

Switch to sorbet. It has less fat than ice cream. And choose skim milk over whole, skinless poultry over beef, and low-fat salad dressing over the heavy stuff. In a Canadian study of 21 women who had persistent and severe cyclical breast discomfort, 6 of the 10 who cut their fat calories to 15 percent of total calories (they made up for the lost calories by increasing carbohydrates) found "significant relief" from pain, swelling, and lumpiness within six months. The remaining women in the study did not cut back on fat, and only 2 of them showed any improvement after six months. The body makes different forms of oestrogen, and one of them, estradiol, may be a suspected troublemaker. A high-fat diet may cause the ovaries to produce more estradiol than is good for the body, leading to an overproduction of breast cells and thus, lumpiness, he says.

Can the caffeine. The results of a Duke University study of 138 women with persistent monthly pain who made significant cuts in caffeine showed a decrease or total loss of pain within a year.

Fibre up. Reducing fat isn't the only way to lower oestrogen levels in your body. Eating more fruits and vegetables not only reduces fat but also provides more fibre in your diet. "Fibre can help reduce swelling and tenderness of the breasts by absorbing excess oestrogen and carrying it out of the body," says David P. Rose, MD, an endocrinologist. The daily value for fibre is 25 grams. That should be enough to reduce the oestrogen and help ease the pain of fibrocystic breast. One of the easiest ways to get more fibre is to eat bran containing cereals at breakfast. Eating vegetables, fruits, legumes and grains will also add fibre to your diet.

Helpful vitamins and supplements:

Get your vitamins. A good multivitamin/mineral supplement and a diet with plenty of foods rich in calcium, magnesium, vitamin C and B-complex vitamins are effective weapons against breast tenderness. Most of these vitamins indirectly affect the production of a hormone that can cause breast pain, says Dr. Northrup.

Ease with E. Another helpful nutrient is vitamin E. There isn't solid scientific evidence to prove that it works, but some women and their doctors say that getting more vitamin E can help reduce the pain of fibrocystic breasts. Since vitamin E helps stabilize fluctuations in a woman's hormones, it makes sense that it might help. "Many women find relief when they take a vitamin E supplement of 200 to 400 international units a day, particularly when they're experiencing pain," according to Dr. Yankauskas. If you plan to take more than 600 IU of vitamin E a day, you should talk to your doctor first.

Everyday prevention:

Exercise daily. Women who exercise get at least 30 minutes of aerobic exercise every day (the kind that elevates your heart and breathing rate) are less likely to have premenstrual symptoms, says Benedet. If exercise seems to aggravate premenstrual breast pain, switch to a low-impact activity (swimming, walking or biking).

Nurse your baby. Mothers who decide to nurse notice a softening of the breasts. Nursing cleans out the ducts system, so that whatever partial blockages are in the breast are washed out.

Massage away the pain. Daily massages can help ease breast pain. Place your hands on your breasts with your fingers spread and your nipples in your palms. Squeeze and release your fingers as you massage the circumference of your breasts.

Stop smoking. Smoking seems to be related to breast pain and the formation of cysts.

Herbal help:

Ease with evening primrose. "Though there is no scientific explanation of it, taking evening primrose oil relieves breast pain in about 30% of the women I see," says Dr. Michele A. Gadd, MD, a participating surgeon at Massachusetts General Hospital. Health food stores sell evening primrose oil in tablet form. Take three tablets nightly before bed when you experience breast discomfort, she says.

Try these herbal teas. Corn silk, buchu and uva ursi teas—available at most health food stores—are three very mild diuretics that seem to relieve breast tenderness in some women, says Dr. Yankauskas. By flushing fluid from your system, diuretics can help reduce breast swelling.

Ease with ayueveda. At night, apply a paste made from 1/2 teaspoon of yellow turmeric and 1 teaspoon of warm castor oil to the area of the breast where the cysts are, says Vasant Lad, B.A.M.S., M.A.Sc., director of the Ayurvedic Institute in New Mexico. He adds this caution: Turmeric can stain skin and clothes, so cover the paste with something that you won't mind staining. Discolouration should wash off your skin in about two weeks, he adds.

Try pain-relieving tea. In *Herbal Healing for Women*, herbalist Rosemary Gladstar, author of several other herb books, offers this recipe for Immune Cleanser Tea, which she recommends as part of an overall health care program to treat fibrocystic breasts. You can find all of the ingredients-freshly dried herbs and powders- in most health food stores or by mail order. Gladstar says to mix the ingredients in these proportions: one part yellow dock root, three parts dandelion root, two parts burdock root, one part ginger powder, one part dong quai, one part astragalus, one part licorice root, one part chaste berry and four parts pau d'arco. To make the tea, says Gladstar, use four to six tablespoons of this combination per quart of water. Simmer over low heat in a tightly covered pot for 20 minutes, then turn off the heat and let the herbs sit in the covered pot for another 20 minutes. Strain the tea so that no dried herb remains and let the tea cool to a drinkable temperature. Gladstar suggests drinking three to four cups of the tea daily for five days, then going off it for two days. Continue this treatment for a maximum of three months, she says.

Broken Nails

The pain: Since nails are dead tissue, it's the skin around and underneath them that hurts when they're broken, brittle or problematic.

The cause: A hangnail forms when a small piece of the cuticle (the skin around the nail) dries up, dies and peels off. Brittle nails occur because as you age, nail cells and the "mortar" that holds them together gradually break down, says Paul Kechijian, MD, a dermatologist. "A lack of moisture doesn't cause the problem but it can worsen an already brittle condition," says Dr. Kechijian. If your toenail is black and elevated, it's probably because blood has pooled underneath the nail, usually due to injury or improper footwear.

See your doctor if:
...after two weeks of applying moisturiser you haven't seen any improvement, and they still bother you, you may want to see a doctor, says Dr. Kechijian. "If they either hurt or affect the everyday functions of your hands, then it's time to consult a dermatologist."
...pain doesn't feel as if it's coming from the skin of a toe but from inside the toe. You can fracture the bones in your toe but not realise it and only treat the toenail injury.
...you have diabetes or a history of gout.
...an ingrown nail yields pus, reddish streaks on the toe, or is accompanied by fever or a great deal of swelling.

Quick relief:
Handle a hangnail. If you get a hangnail, don't pick at it or try to bite it off. It can actually become infected. To remove a hangnail the right way, use this three-step technique. Start by softening. Never cut off a hangnail while it's dry. Instead, soften it by soaking it in warm water and olive oil. Clip it cleanly. Use nail scissors or nail clippers to remove the hangnail. Cut it as short as you can without damageing the skin around it. You don't want to leave a stub that you can nibble on or play with. Apply the finishing touches. After clipping the hangnail, massage the skin around your nail with moisturiser, cover it with an adhesive bandage, and leave it alone.
Cure a cuticle. To repair damaged cuticles and keep them problem-free,

add these steps to your nail-care routine. First, soak them. Before you do anything to your cuticles, soften them in warm sudsy water for several minutes. This prevents drying and cracking. Then give them a gentle push. Wrap the tip of an orange stick in cotton gauze. Then use the stick to gently push back each cuticle. Finish with petroleum jelly. After pushing back your cuticles, massage them with a thin layer of petroleum jelly to seal in moisture This will help keep your cuticles soft and healthy.

Fix a split. To salvage a split or broken nail, apply a very small amount of nail glue to the tear. Reinforce the tear by covering it with a small piece of tissue from a tea bag. Let the glue dry completely, then use a fine buffer to even out the nail surface. (Be sure to leave the tissue in place.) Finally, apply a top coat over the tissue.

Drain a damaged toenail. To fix it (and take away the pain), thoroughly heat one end of an unfolded paper clip with a match or lighter, says Edward Beckett, D.P.M., a podiatrist. "While the tip of the paper clip is still hot, put it through the nail plate," Dr. Beckett explains. "This will melt the nail so that the fluid will escape." Keep the drainage hole in the nail clog-free (that means no ointment or bandages) in case more liquid wants to ooze out. And don't burn your fingers with the heated paper clip.

Take off a toenail. This is pretty serious business, but if your toenail is about to fall off, the best thing to do is take charge and care for it yourself rather than wait for your sock or something to catch on it and painfully tear the nail from it's attachments, says Richard Braver, D.P.M., a sports podiatrist. You'll want to clean the nail with soap and water, then clip it as close as possible to the underlying skin, says Dr. Braver. "Don't do this unless the toenail is very loose and about to come off anyway," Dr. Braver says. "Put some antibiotic cream on the skin and nail and bandage it fairly snugly." Keep a close eye on it, too. If the toe becomes red and swollen, exudes pus, or remains painful after a few days, see your podiatrist for treatment of a probable infection.

If you notice an off-yellow or red watery drainage from the nail bed (not yellowish-green pus), then you should soak your foot in warm water with a few capfuls of Betadine antibiotic solution. Add a few tablespoons of Epsom salts to promote drainage. Soak for 10 minutes twice a day. Regardless of whether you soak, apply a small amount of antibiotic cream to the toe and change the bandages twice daily for three weeks. If, after this time, the nail is still loose or you notice fluid under the nail, see your podiatrist.

Ongoing care:

Lift an ingrown toenail. Once a nail has penetrated the skin you need to encourage it to grow outward. Soak the toe in warm water (with a teaspoon of salt) for 10-15 minutes. then put a wisp of cotton under the side of the nail that's ingrowing. The cotton will help lift the nail off the skin as it grows out.

Soak with salt. To cleanse the area around a damaged toe nail and prevent an infection, soak your foot in a saltwater solution, made with one teaspoon of table salt added to a quart of warm water, says Dr. Beckett. Do this a couple times a day for three or four days. This is a general approach to promote drainage of an infected toe. It also adds a soothing effect on the irritated area.

Nutritional remedies:

Try fish. Eat more coldwater fish such as salmon, mackerel and herring, advises Julian Whitaker, MD, founder and president of the Whitaker Wellness Centre in Newport Beach, California. "It's rich in omega-6 fatty acids, which can strengthen nails."

Helpful vitamins and supplements:

Horse around with biotin. Years ago, researchers found that the B vitamin biotin increased the toughness of horses' hooves. Doctors saw the positive results in horses and concluded that biotin might have the same effect on human nails. To get biotin in your diet, fill your glass with milk and your plate with servings of corn, barley, cauliflower, and legumes such as peanuts and soybeans. But you'll have to take biotin supplements to get the amount you need for brittle nails, says C. Ralph Daniel III, MD, clinical professor of dermatology. Take 300 micrograms four times a day with food for four to six months. This should provide the necessary amount of biotin and could increase your nail thickness over a six-month period.

Take your quercetin. Quercetin is a bioflavonoid, or plant compound, that is sold as a dietary supplement in tablet form. "Quercetin controls the body's response of excessive inflammation," explains Nancy Dunne-Boggs, a doctor of naturopathy. "I usually tell people to take 300 milligrams three times a day after they sustain an injury." You can find quercetin supplements in drugstores and health food stores. You'll only need this for a few days or up to two weeks.

Get supplement support. Strong nails require adequate vitamin intake, says Richard K. Scher, MD, a nail specialist and professor of dermatology. Be sure that your vitamin supplements include minerals, especially zinc and iron.

Everyday prevention:

Reach for hand cream. Apply a moisturising hand cream to your nails and hands frequently. The cream traps the moisture in your nails and keeps them from drying out, says Dr. Kechijian. "This is a wise step for any person who constantly wets and dries their hands during the course of a day." Nails expand when they absorb water, then contract like an accordion when they dry, so he suggests applying a hand cream immediately after you dry your hands. Any over-the-counter cream should do the trick. Whatever hand cream you pick, buy several small tubes of it and leave them all over the place—your pocketbook, your desk drawer, beside the kitchen sink. That way, you'll always have some on hand.

Make bedtime a formal affair. Before going to bed, coat your nails and hands with a thick layer of petroleum jelly. Then slip on a pair of white cotton gloves to protect your hands overnight. You'll love the way this treatment makes your nails look. This is especially helpful in winter, when hands and nails dry out quickly.

Keep them short and sweet. If you're bothered by brittle nails, Dr. Kechijian advises that you trim them shorter. Shorter nails are much less likely to be injured or get caught on something and tear. To keep nails strong, they should be cut straight across and rounded slightly at the edges. Use sharp nail scissors or clippers. He also recommends cutting your nails after washing, when they're softer, less brittle, and less likely to break. File away any rough edges by stroking the nail file in one direction—not back and forth.

Avoid cutting corners. When trimming your nails, leave them square at the corners. This maximises nail strength and helps prevent ingrown nails.

File away flaws. Keep an emery board in your purse or desk drawer. At the first sign of a nick or chip, use the board to smooth out the unevenness and prevent further damage. Always file in the same direction; don't wield the board like a saw.

Glove 'em or leave 'em. If washing dishes is one of your daily chores, Dr. Daniel suggests investing in several pairs of vinyl gloves with cotton liners. The vinyl outside keeps the water off your nails, while the cotton liner absorbs sweat so that your nails won't get wet inside the gloves.

Watch your washing. Good hygiene is certainly important, but if you're prone to brittle nails, don't wash and dry your hands anymore than you have to, says Dr. Daniel. Although you'd think wetting your hands would keep them moist, frequent washing and drying of hands actually strips away the moisture in and around your nails. That may also cause them to dry out and become brittle.

Go acetate, not acetone. Take a look at the ingredients list of your nail polish remover. It should be made with acetate, not acetone, Dr. Daniel says. "Acetone nail polish removers are stronger, but they can take much-needed moisture out of your nails and can perhaps lead to the nails becoming more brittle. I recommend nail polish removers with acetate because they are less likely to dry out a person's nails," he says. Or eschew nail polish altogether because the process of removing the polish dries out and damages the nail, suggests Dr. Kechijian. "Just leave them alone, buffing them lightly for a slight sheen and a more finished look."

Find some real tools. "Your nails aren't screwdrivers, and they aren't scrapers," says Dr. Scher. "A lot of the problems I see are from people abusing their nails by using them as tools."

Invest in your cuticles. Nail damage is often self-inflicted. "Nail biting is a big problem," Dr. Scher says. "Besides causing infection, it can cause permanent injury." His tip for keeping yourself from snacking on your fingernails is to treat yourself to a manicure, with all the extras. "If you spend good money getting your nails done, you are less likely to chew them up," he says.

Have bad taste. Sabotage the taste of your fingernails, says Dr. Kechijian. How? Try one of those bitter-tasting nail products that are designed to discourage nail biting. They are available at any drugstore. Trying to bite your nails after putting this stuff on your nails will inspire an instant "yecch."

If the shoe fits, wear it. There are ways to be kind to your toenails, too. "Make sure that your footwear fits properly," Dr. Scher says. If your shoes are too tight, it can lead to nail fungus and to ingrown toenails to boot. If you are a runner, buy new running shoes every several months, he advises. "Those cruddy old shoes can harbour fungus over time."

Kick your shoes off. "I don't care what kind of shoes you wear, they are going to make your feet sweat," Dr. Kechijian says. He advises going around as much as you can in stocking feet in your home.

Wear protective shoes. They're called work boots for a reason. If you're doing work, wear the right boots. "You need to protect your feet the same way you protect your skin and eyes," Dr. Beckett says. "If you're carrying something heavy, then put on a good pair of boots. Sandals aren't going to protect your toes if you drop something." While we're on the subject of sandals, it's a good idea to wear them if you're going to be anywhere close to rocks in water. "Waterproof sandals can really protect a guy who's trying to walk through a stream," Dr. Beckett says. The point is that you not go barefoot if there's a chance you'll be walking across anything hot (pavement), sharp (rocks and glass), slippery (rocks in water), or uneven. Wear sandals at the poolside or in the gym shower, todiminish your chances of picking up or spreading a fungus that may damage your nails and feet.

Herbal Help:

Soak in horsetail. This herb looks like the tassel on a mare's nether parts. High in silica, horsetail lends strength to weak, lacklustre fingernails, says Shatoiya de la Tour, herbalist and founder of Dry Creek Herb Farm and Learning Centre in California.

Combine 1/2 teaspoon of dried horsetail, available in health food stores and through mail order with 1 teaspoon of comfrey in a cup of boiling water. Comfrey has been used traditionally by herbal healers to soothe and heal wounded skin, so this herb can help soothe dry, cracked skin around your nails. Steep the herbs for 15 to 20 minutes and let cool to a comfortable temperature. Then soak your nails in the mixture for 5 to 10 minutes several times a week, de la Tour suggests. You can also make the soak using 1 teaspoon of horsetail and 1 teaspoon of dill, which contains calcium, she says.

Brush with comfrey. You can also soak your nails in a horsetail tea bath and then brush your cuticles with a comfrey paste, suggests Kathlyn Quatrochi, N.D., a naturopathic physician and herbalist and author of *The Skin Care Book: Simple Herbal Recipes.* Instead of adding the comfrey to the tea, mix it with enough water to make a paste and then brush it on your cuticles with an old nail polish brush. To soften cuticles, rub in a light application of olive oil after the horsetail and comfrey treatments, Dr. Quatrochi recommends.

Lubricate with camomile and oil. If your nails are dry and split easily, rub them with camomile-infused olive oil, de la Tour suggests. "This

---

How to give a healthy manicure

Some manicures—French manicures or sculpted nails, for example—are designed to make your nails look great. Others are designed to make your nails look great and healthy. Here's the best way to buff and shine your nails to perfect health, according to Ida Orengo, MD, an associate professor of dermatology.

First, place your hands in a small dish of warm water mixed with mild detergent for five minutes to remove dirt and bacteria. "This will get your nails fresh and clean and avoid the possibility of pushing any bacteria under your cuticles while giving yourself a manicure," says Dr. Orengo. Dry your hands gently with a soft clean towel.

While they're still soft, gently cut or clip your nails to about 1/4 inch in length. Hard, dry nails can crack or split when you cut them. One-quarter inch is the perfect length for strong nails. Anything longer can break, split, and chip more easily.

• With an orange stick wrapped in cotton, gently push back your cuticles. Cuticles should never be cut, says Dr. Orengo, because they protect your nails against bacterial and fungal infections.

• File your nails with an emery board. This also needs to be done while they're soft and pliable. Otherwise, they could split. File in one direction, from side to centre, until they are squared off at the top. Filing in a back-and-forth motion can weaken and damage the nail, says Dr. Orengo. Filing nails to a point will also weaken your nails and cause them to break easily.

• Rub your nails with a nail moisturising lotion. The lotion will hydrate your nails and prevent them from drying and cracking. "Rub the lotion liberally into your hands and nails," says Dr. Orengo. Wipe off the excess. Wait two or three minutes for the moisturiser to soak into your nails.

• Before applying colour, brush on a clear pre-coat polish. The clear polish will prevent your nails from turning yellow.

To prevent your nails from drying out, remove polish with a non-acetone remover no more than once a week, says Dr. Orengo.

soothes and moisturises," she says.

Try a soothing herbal salve. To ease dryness, cracked skin, and minor infections that can occur when the skin around your nails is damaged and vulnerable, herbalists suggest hand-and-nail relief salve, infused with horsetail, comfrey, and usnea, de la Tour says. Begin by infusing your base oil with the three herbs. Rub it into your fingers at night, and you'll really start to feel the difference," de la Tour says. The comfrey soothes, the horsetail strengthens, and the usnea helps fight infection (all three herbs are available by mail). "A lot of nurses, who have their hands in water all day, love this formula," she notes.

Massage with herb-enriched castor oil. For dry, ripped cuticles, rub a drop of castor oil into the cuticle of each nail, suggests beauty expert Stephanie Tourles, a licensed aesthetician and author of *The Herbal Body Book.* "Castor oil is thick and has lots of vitamin E, so it's like food for the cuticle skin. And, it makes the nails shiny," she says. You could also add a drop or two of carrot seed, lavender, or sandalwood essential oils to a two-ounce bottle of castor oil for an herbal nail treatment, she says.

Offer 'em olive oil. Immerse your fingertips in a half-cup of warmed olive oil and soak for 15 to 30 minutes. The oil helps rehydrate brittle nails.

Break open the bath beads. As an alternative to olive oil, break open three or four bath-oil capsules and empty their contents into a half-cup of warm water. Soak your fingertips in the diluted bath oil for five minutes. Use this treatment once a day.

Other alternatives:

Believe the hypericum. If you drop something on your toe, try hypericum, a homeopathic remedy specifically recommended for nerve-rich areas of the body, such as fingers and toes. "Take a low potency of 30C every few hours as needed for the pain," says Dr. Dunne-Boggs. "It should be apparent within six doses or so that the hypericum is working. You probably won't need to take this for more than two or three days." Follow label directions for dosage information.

Try yoga. Brittle nails are sometimes the result of bad digestion and may be helped with a daily exercise sometimes called the stomach lift, says Stephen A. Nezeenon, MD, yoga teacher and staff physician at the Himalayan International Institute of Yoga Science and Philosophy. Start by standing with your feet about two feet apart. Keep your back straight and bend forward slightly at the waist. Place your left palm on your left thigh, just above the knee, and your right palm in the same place on your right thigh. Breathe out all the way, then bend your neck forward sot hat your chin tucks into your throat. Without breathing, suck in your stomach muscles as if you were trying to touch your belly button to your backbone. Hold for as long as possible, then relax and breathe. Stand up straight. Repeat the exercise three times. (Don't do the exercise during menstruation, or pregnancy, after surgery, if you're bleeding or if you have heart disease or high blood pressure.)

Bruises

The pain: A tender, discoloured area that occurs on the skin at the site of an injury.

The cause: Because of a fall or a bump, the blood vessels underneath the skin rupture, leaking blood out into the surrounding tissues. The blood then discolours the skin on top of the injury. Bruises become more common with age because collagen—the connective tissue that cushions skin—breaks down, leaving underlying blood vessels more vulnerable. Long-term sun damage can also make skin more susceptible to bruising.

See a doctor if:

...you have bruises that appear without any seeming cause. Sometimes bruises are indications of serious illnesses such as blood disorders, says Mitchell Kaminski Jr., MD, a clinical professor of surgery.
...you suddenly start to bruise easily and frequently. Easy bruising could be a sign of a blood disorder. In such a case, you should consult a doctor, says Karl Kramer, MD, a clinical professor of dermatology.
...The bruise occurs at a joint and is accompanied by swelling.
...the bruise occurs above the ear on the side of your head, which is an area that is susceptible to fractures.
...the bruising is accompanied by a fever.

Medication:

Besides aspirin (see below), there are several medications that can contribute to excessive bruising, says Arthur K. Balin, MD a dermatologist and cosmetic surgeon and co-author of *The Life of the Skin*. These include:

Anticoagulants like heparin (Heparin Flush or Mueriparin) and warfarin (Coumadin or Marevan).

Nonsteroidal anti-inflammatory drugs, such as ibuprofen

Certain antibacterials, including nitrofurantoin (Macrodantin)

Certain heart drugs, such as verapamil (Isoptin or Berkatens)

Check with your doctor to see if a medication you may be taking is contributing to weakened blood vessels, excessive bleeding, or bruising.

Quick relief:

Make nice with Rice. Keep the acronym 'RICE' in mind, and follow the instructions it gives if you have a severe bruise, says Dr. Jenny Sutcliffe, in London.

- **Rest** – take the weight off the injured part of the body.
- **Ice** – wrap the area in an ice pack to reduce the internal bleeding—never put ice directly on to the skin as it may cause a burn, so wrap it in a towel first; if no ice is available, a packet of frozen peas or corn (again, wrapped) is an ideal substitute. Leave on for 10 minutes, and repeat the application four times a day for the first 48 hours—after that, the bleeding should have stopped.
- **Compress** – wrap a bandage around the area to prevent or reduce any localised swelling.
- **Elevate** – raise the bruised area so that it is higher than the heart to reduce any swelling; you may have to lie down to do this.

If the bruise is a minor one, and there is no localised swelling, ice may be all that you need. Apply ice as soon as possible after the injury occurs. Wrap the ice pack in a towel to keep it from contacting your skin directly and keep it in place for about 15 minutes. Then let the skin warm before reapplying the ice. You can ice the bruise four or five times the first day, then after 24 hours switch to heat to improve circulation to the bruised area. Gently but securely wrap the bruise with an elastic bandage. Then elevate the limb as much as possible for the first 24 hours. The pressure and elevation will help stop the blood from flowing into the tissues and minimise the size of the bruise.

Give it a little squeeze. By pushing down with a small amount of pressure on the injured area, you can cut off some of the flow from the busted blood vessels. Apply the pressure as soon as possible after the injury. The less blood that spills internally, the less bruising will develop, says Vail Reese, MD, a dermatologist.

Heat it up. After using ice for the first 24 hours, switch to heat, says J. Greg Brady, D.O., a dermatologist. The heat increases the circulation to the bruised area, helping the scavenger cells to reabsorb the blood that has leaked from the broken vessels into the skin. Apply a heating pad or a warm compress for 20 minutes a few times a day.

Swap heat and cold. When you bump your shin, the best way to reduce the swelling is to apply a little hydrotherapy. Start with some ice wrapped in a washcloth immediately after the injury, says Dr. Thomas Kruzel a naturopathic physician. Leave the cold on for 10 to 15 minutes. You can repeat the treatment every two to four hours, or as needed for pain and swelling, he says.

After the swelling has gone down, alternate cold and hot compresses. For the hot part, soak a washcloth with hot tap water and hold it against the bruise for about three minutes. Switch to a wet washcloth wrapped around ice for a minute or so, and then return to the hot. Always start with the hot and end with the cold, alternating that process as many as three to five times. Wait for a few hours and repeat, says Dr. Kruzel. "Generally, I have the person do it one or two times daily," he says. "Basically, what you're doing is stimulating the flow of blood around the bruise, which helps carry away debris and damaged tissue," Dr. Kruzel says. "It also brings in a lot of white blood cells, which promotes healing."

Nutritional remedies:

Reach for the citrus. Vitamin C and substances called bioflavonoids that are in oranges and other citrus fruits strengthen capillary walls. As the blood vessels get stronger, they're less prone to leakage so there's less bruising, advises James Duke, Ph.D., botanical consultant, author of *The Green Pharmacy*. Also, he says that both vitamin C and bioflavonoids promote more rapid healing of capillaries after they are damaged. To help prevent bruises, make sure you eat some citrus fruit every day. You can also try daily application of vitamin C creams or lotions (available at chemists or from a dermatologist.)

Helpful vitamins and supplements:

Try a multivitamin. If bruises show up frequently, without much apparent cause, maybe you're just not getting enough vitamin C from your diet, Dr. Kaminski. If so, be sure you get a supplement, he advises. "I recommend that people take a multivitamin to ensure that they're getting the basic requirements for the vitamins they need."

Try some special K. A deficiency of vitamin K can prevent normal blood clotting, says Dr. Kaminski, and you need some clotting action to help prevent bruising. "Some people who bruise excessively and have a lot of broken blood vessels below the skin should eat more vegetables rich in vitamin K," he says. Vitamin K is abundant in leafy greens and members of the cabbage family, such as broccoli, brussels sprouts, cabbage, and spinach, among others. "You might consider a supplement of K as well." Bruise-diminishing creams containing vitamin K can help resolve bruises faster by providing the vitamin to the site of the injury.

Everyday prevention:

Go easy on the aspirin. If you're taking aspirin for any reason, it could be contributing to the number of bruises you're getting, says Dr. Balin. "There is some evidence that an adult aspirin, which is 325 milligrams, will thin the blood too much and cause blood to leak through the vessels. Among other things, that will lead to more bruises. It's good to take aspirin but only the smaller dose."

If you're taking aspirin to help reduce your risk of heart attack, as some doctors advise, you shouldn't stop taking it without talking to a physician. But your doctor might recommend another solution, switching to baby aspirin, which has only 81 milligrams. That much aspirin will not cause the same problems as the stronger, adult dose, so it's safer and more appropriate for daily consumption, recommends Dr. Balin.

Protect your vulnerable spots. Be sure to wear protective clothing, especially over those areas where you tend to repeatedly bruise yourself, suggests Dr. Balin. Wear long sleeves and long pants, sweaters that fall below your waist and cover your hips, and shoes that protect your feet. If you repeatedly bruise your thighs or forearms, ask your pharmacist about a protective pad that you can easily slip on to guard that area.

Bruise-proof your home. "A lot of bumps and bruises are caused because we didn't see something, or we bump into the same object over and over again," says Dr. Balin. The solution: "Make sure that you have good lighting in all your rooms and make your environment as uncluttered as possible."

Pad yourself up. If your sport or activity recommends using padding or protective gear, use it. A little bit of padding can go a long way to prevent a bruise after a fall or impact, says Dr. Brady.

Be careful out there. One of the only surefire ways to prevent bruising is to use caution and common sense. Bumping into cabinets, walking into furniture, dropping a can on your foot are all things that cause bruising— and things you avoid if you pay attention, says Dr. Brady.

Herbal Help:

Apply arnica, pronto. A traditional bruise buster and the first choice of many herbalists for soothing black-and-blue spots, arnica has been shown by researchers to contain a substance called helenalin, which has anti-inflammatory actions. Commission E, the expert panel that judges the safety and effectiveness of herbal medicines for the German government, concurs that this herb is helpful for treating bruises. "Arnica cream or tablets are very effective," says Dr Stephen G Motto, a musculo-skeletal physician with a speciality in sports medicine at London Bridge Hospital.

Applied to unbroken skin at the point of impact, arnica can lessen or even help avoid the discoloration and swelling of a bruise, says Lisa Murray-Doran, N.D., a naturopathic doctor and instructor at the Canadian College of Naturopathic Medicine in Toronto. "Important advice to remember about this powerful herb is that arnica is toxic if taken internally or if absorbed into the bloodstream by contact with scratched, cut, bleeding, or otherwise broken skin," she says. "So use it only on unbroken skin." Also, people with very sensitive skin should not use arnica because the oils can be irritating. (Don't confuse the herb with homeopathic remedies using arnica, which are extremely dilute and therefore safe.)

If you've banged your shin, fallen, or otherwise set the scene for a painful, purple shiner, apply arnica cream, salve, or a compress to the spot, Dr. Murray-Doran suggests. To make a compress, add 60 drops of arnica tincture to a cup of warm water. Soak a cloth in it, then lay it on your skin. Hold the compress in place with a dry cloth tied over it, she says. "Leave it in place for 20 minutes to an hour, until the wet cloth dries," Dr. Murray-Doran suggests. "If you do this soon enough after getting bumped, you may not see a bruise at all."

You can also use arnica gel, says herbalist Sharleen Andrews-Miller, a faculty member at the National College of Naturopathic Medicine in Oregon. **Use an arnica compress and ice**. You can also alternate between an arnica compress and an ice pack on bruised skin, suggests Leslie Gardner, an herbalist. You can make a compress by steeping the fresh herb in hot water, straining it, and then soaking the cloth. "I would alternate the two for one to four hours, then rub arnica cream or oil into the bruised area," she says.

Make a poultice with comfrey or calendula. Concoct an herbal poultice by rehydrating a tablespoon of dried herbs in an equal amount of warm water or by crushing fresh comfrey leaves or calendula petals, Dr. Murray-Doran suggests.

Comfrey, a traditional skin remedy dating back to ancient Greece, contains a substance called allantoin, which prompts tissue repair even below the surface of the skin, and rosmarinic acid, which reduces swelling. While herbalists caution against taking comfrey internally without guidance due to the plant's concentration of potentially dangerous pyrrolizidine alkaloids, applying comfrey externally to a bruise does not pose a threat, Dr. Murray-Doran says.

Calendula's sunny yellow and orange flowers have a long-standing reputation as antiseptic wound healers for bruises and other skin ailments. This herb has potent abilities to repair damage to the skin caused by sunburn, according to herbalists.

"Apply this poultice directly to bruised skin and hold it in place with an adhesive strip, or use gauze and tape for a larger area. Leave it in place for three to four hours, and you should see swelling, pain, and discoloration reduced. Or, if you apply the poultice as soon as you're injured, it may keep the area from looking and feeling bruised," advises Dr. Murray-Doran.

Sprinkle on some parsley. Crush some fresh parsley leaves, then spread them directly on the bruise, advises James Duke, Ph.D. a former ethnobotanist with the U.S. Department of Agriculture who specialises in medicinal plants. Parsley can promote healing and clear up black-and-blue marks within a day or so, he says. Hold the leaves in place by covering them with an adhesive bandage or with gauze and tape.

Try parsley cubes. Parsley has a traditional reputation for dispelling black-and-blue marks. Ice can prevent swelling. Combine the two in parsley-packed ice cubes and you have an instant bruise remedy that you can stock ahead of time in your freezer, says herbalist Sharleen Andrews-Miller.

"Just whirl a handful of parsley and about 1/4 cup of water in a blender or food processor until it looks like slush. Then fill ice cube trays half-full," she suggests. "Apply to bruised spots as needed, wrapped in gauze or thin cloth. Parsley ice cubes also work well for cooling minor burns." Discard them after use.

"As a bonus, you can grab a parsley cube out of the freezer when you're cooking and you need a little parsley in a soup or sauce," adds Andrews-Miller.

Banish bruises with bilberry. The bilberry herb helps heal the broken capillaries that caused the bruise, says Michael Carlston, MD, at the University of California, School of Medicine. You can find bilberry capsules in health food stores or even your local drugstore, Dr. Carlston says. Take a 60-milligram bilberry capsule three or four times on the day you get your bruise.

Pump up your capillaries. Grape seed extract contains bioflavonoids, which strengthen capillaries, making them less likely to break under pressure, says Kenneth Singleton, MD, a physician. Take 20 to 50 milligrams of grape seed extract, Dr. Singleton suggests.

Soothe with St. John's wort. There has been some scientific verification that this herb is useful for treating bruises. Try steeping one to two teaspoons of dried herb in vegetable oil for a few days. Then use the oil to treat bruises.

Heal with hazel. The astringency of the leaves and bark of witch hazel made it a popular early American remedy for all sorts of skin conditions, from bruises to varicose veins. Witch hazel water is available at chemists.

Get help from Helichrysm. Treat bruises with compresses soaked in cool water that has been spiked with four drops of the essential oil helichrysum (also known as immortelle or everlast), recommends aromatic consultant John Steele. "Helichrysum reduces swelling, controls bleeding under the skin and has an anti-inflammatory properties," says Steele. Lavender oil can be substituted for the helichrysm. Use the compress once or twice a day, leaving them in place for about ten minutes each time. For severe bruises, apply several drops of undiluted helichrysum directly to the bruises several times a day, he suggests.

Hands-on help:

Rub the right way. Simply 'rubbing it better' can work, says Dr David Bowsher, MA, MD, PhD, FRCP (Edinburgh), research director of the Pain Research Institute in Liverpool. "Rub the affected joint with the hands, using olive oil so that you don't chap the skin," he says. The sensation created by the rubbing hands can block pain messages, in the same way that TENS (transcutaneous electrical nerve stimulation) machines can send blocking sensations to the spinal cord.

Bunions

The pain: A painful, red, swollen protrusion that juts out from the base of the big toe.

The cause: A bunion is a troublesome growth of bone on the outside of the big toe. Pain comes from walking improperly or because your shoe is pressing against that out-of-place bone. If you're under 30, chances are your bunions are inherited and they're difficult to get rid of. Poor-fitting shoes don't cause bunions, but can exacerbate the problem.

See a doctor if:
...your bunions hurt every day, even with property fitting shoes.
...the pain limits your activities.
...your big toe is hitting or hiding under your second toe, or you can't bend your big toe.
...your bunion is paired with a callus on the inside of your big toe or on the ball of your foot. A callus indicates that your body weight is not being properly transferred to your other joints, a condition that can be remedied with orthotics.

Medical treatment:
Podiatrists can prescribe orthotic devises for people who are bunion-prone that can help prevent bunions from developing. Surgery, a long-term solution, takes only 30-40 minutes. Generally you'll be walking within a day or two.

Quick relief:
Relax a bunion's tender spot. Put the tip of your middle finger on the underside of the ball of the big toe that has the bunion. Then place the thumb of that hand on the top of the big toe and gently push and turn the big toe down and under the foot and toward the little toe. Hold that position for at least 90 seconds, then slowly release the toe, repeating several times to help relieve the pain.
Soak your feet. A 10-minute warm water soak will give quick, temporary relief from all kinds of foot ailments, bunions included. Also, you can speed up healing of mild bunions with whirlpool baths and ultrasound.
Ice up. If your bunion feels hot and swollen, it may be inflamed. Cool it

down by applying a cloth-covered ice pack, suggests Marika Molnar, P.T, director of West Side Dance Physical Therapy in New York City. "I like to use a Ziploc-type resealable plastic bag half-filled with water and crushed ice and wrapped in a damp cloth," she says. Apply for 10 or 15 minutes, then remove for a few minutes to let your foot warm up before applying again. (If you have circulation problems in your feet or diabetes, you're better off avoiding ice for any foot problems.)

Try a shot of hot, then cold. Use contrast baths to get circulation going again and to relieve bunion pain. Sit on the edge of the bathtub with the affected foot under the faucet. Let hot water flow over it for 3 minutes, then cold water for 1 minute, then hot for 3 minutes, and cold for 1 minute. Then repeat one more time. Instead, you may begin with cold water for 3 minutes, followed by hot for 1 minute, repeating the procedure two more times. You may also soak the foot in alternate pans of hot and cold water.

Nutritional remedies:

Try pineapple. Naturopaths suggest taking bromelain, a protein-dissolving (proteolytic) enzyme found in pineapple, for inflammatory joint problems such as bunions. If you don't like the taste, you can buy it as a supplement. Naturopath Michael Murray, N.D., co-author of *Encyclopedia of Natural Medicine* and several other scholarly books on nutritional and naturopathic healing, recommends taking 250 to 750 milligrams three times a day. (In human studies, doses up to 2,000 milligrams have caused no side effects.)

Everyday prevention:

Cover bunions with doughnut pads. A doughnut pad (sometimes labelled a bunion cushion) has a hole cut in the middle to prevent putting pressure on the swollen area. Available at most chemists, some bunion pads have adhesive on the back, while others may need to be adhered with first-aid tape. Position the opening of the pad over the part of your bunion that sticks out the most, says Steven Subotnick, a podiatrist and author of *Sports and Exercise Injuries.*

Stomp on pain. Nonsteroidal anti-inflammatory medications such as ibuprofen or Advil can relieve the pain and swelling of most types of foot pain. Follow package directions. This is a temporary fix, however. You don't want to stay on over-the-counter painkillers for more than a few weeks, advises Tzvi Bar-David, D.P.M., a podiatrist. So make sure to try other strategies to relieve your specific foot problem.

Slip on some skin. Moleskin, that is, and place it over the corn or bunion to protect the area. You'll find it at most pharmacies and grocery stores.

Soften your steps. A soft orthotic device, available at most pharmacies or from a podiatrist, can help absorb shock and take the pressure off sore spots.

Go barefoot. To prevent bunion pain, go without shoes as much as possible. Go shoeless or wear sandals or open-toed shoes as much as possible.

Shoe shopping for bunion sufferers

Wear the right shoes. Soft shoes can immediately ease the pain, especially if they're extra wide around the toes. Consider talking to a podiatrist about orthopedic or moulded shoes, a sometimes costly but helpful option. Never wear ill-fitting shoes (see below).

Measure your foot. Experts advise selecting footwear that gives plenty of space. "You must get the pressure off your bunions with properly fitted shoes," says Cheryl Weiner, D.P.M., a podiatrist.

To do that, always get your foot measured when you buy shoes, says Nancy Elftman, a certified orthotist/pedorthist (a professional shoe fitter). Make sure that the width of your foot is measured at its widest point-from your big toe across to your baby toe while you're standing barefoot or in socks.

Look for a full or softly rounded toe box. The toe box is the front of the shoe where the toes sit. The toes of any shoes you wear should be round or square, not pointy. Certain sport-shoe makers sell models with lots of toe room.

Stick with flats. Heels shift your weight forward to the ball of your foot, which is something that you don't want if you have bunions, says Kathleen Stone, D.P.M., a podiatrist. "You want no more than a one-half-inch heel to distribute your body weight evenly across your foot."

Get arch support. This also helps distribute your body weight evenly across your entire foot surface, says Dr. Stone. Running shoes usually fit the bill.

Stretch your shoes. Consider having a cobbler stretch your shoes over the bunion area. This can help ease the painful pressure.

Heat up. Applying a heating pad to bunions on a regular basis helps increase blood flow, which breaks up the inflammation.

Exercise your toes. Work the muscles that control the side-to-side movement of your big toe with the following exercise, says Molnar.

Sit with your feet flat and straight out in front of you. Try to move your big toes toward each other, then bring them back. If you can't manage this at first, use your hand to help move your toes. "The muscle that you are using is under the inside anklebone, about one inch down. You can feel a little bulge at this spot as you contract the muscles."

"This exercise helps properly align the joint by rebalancing muscles and stretching contracted tendons in your foot," Molnar says. "Unless your joint is very deteriorated, it will help keep your bunion from getting worse." She suggests that when you're sitting, try to do five or six repetitions few hours. "This is a difficult exercise to do," she says. Keep at it however, and it will get easier.

Herbal help:

Cure with calendula. Treat with non-prescription calendula ointment, a natural antiseptic and anti-inflammatory. You can spread the ointment directly on the injured area—even the open blister—as often as you like, says Stephen Messer, N.D., a naturopathic physician.

Counter with capsacian. Capsacian, the hot ingredient in red pepper, is also medically "hot" as a pain reliever for inflammatory conditions. When applied to the skin at the site of pain, capsacian blocks certain pain nerves by depleting them of substance P, one of the compounds responsible for producing pain. Many studies show that creams containing 0.025 percent capsacian relieve all sorts of pain after a few weeks of treatment. Capsacian creams are available over-the-counter. Or bite off one end of a hot pepper and chew it, and rub the other end directly on the bunion! If you use a cream, be sure to wash your hands thoroughly afterward so that you don't get it in your eyes. Also, since some people are quite sensitive to this compound, you should test it on a small area of skin before using it on a larger area. If it seems to irritate your skin, discontinue use.

Tame the pain with turmeric. Research suggests that like red pepper, turmeric depletes nerve endings of substance P. Applying about a teaspoon of grated fresh turmeric directly to the bunion twice a day could conceivably be helpful. Other studies show that when ingested, the compound curcumin in turmeric has potent anti-inflammatory effects, another reason that it might help relieve bunion pain. The standard dose of curcumin is 400 milligrams three times a day, which is the equivalent of about six to eight teaspoons of turmeric. That's way more turmeric than you'll want to use in a curry. To get this herb's anti-inflammatory benefits, you'll have to use capsules.

Get help from willow. Willow is herbal aspirin, thanks to the compound salicin that it contains. A closely related compound, salicylic acid, is a callus remover and wart treatment and also shows up in many over-the-counter preparations for treating bunions and corns. Salicylates are absorbed through the skin. Try applying fresh willow by wrapping the inner bark around the bunion, or adding some dried bark to your daily herbal teas. If you're allergic to aspirin, however, you probably shouldn't take aspirin-like herbs, either.

Get aid from arnica. The flowers of this plant, also known as mountain daisy, are useful for treating muscle and joint complaints, according to Commission E, the body of experts that makes herbal recommendations to the German government. It doesn't take much extrapolation to speculate that this herb might also help deal with bunions. For a tea, use one to two teaspoons of dried herb per cup of boiling water and steep for ten minutes. Don't drink more than two cups a day for more than three days. For longer-term use, go with an arnica ointment, which is what homeopaths recommend for all sorts of muscle, joint and sports injuries. Many health food stores and pharmacies now carry arnica ointments. Follow the package directions.

Cool it with camomile. Essential oils of camomile, has been suggested by aromatherapists for treating bursitis and could conceivably be useful for bunions. It has well-established anti-inflammatory activity that could help keep bunions under control. After you've drunk your camomile tea, apply the spent tea bag directly to the bunion.

If you have hay fever, however, you should use camomile products cautiously. Camomile is a member of theragweed family, and in some people, it might trigger allergic reactions. The first time you try it, watch your reaction. If it seems to help, go ahead and use it. But if it seems to cause or aggravate itching or irritation, discontinue use.

Ease with Clove. Clove oil is almost pure eugenol, a potent anaesthetic widely used by dentists for treating toothache. You might try clove oil by placing a few drops on a cotton bandage and applying it directly to the bunion once or twice a day. If it irritates your skin, discontinue use.

Go for ginger. In addition to having some proteolytic activity, spicy ginger is also a pain-relieving anti-inflammatory that might help control the discomfort of bunions, according to Indian researchers. They gave three to seven grams (1½ to 3½ teaspoons) of powdered ginger a day to 28 people with painful and inflamed joints. More than 75 percent experienced noticeable relief from pain and swelling. After up to 30 months, none reported adverse effects from this dosage of ginger. For bunions, try drinking ginger tea made with one teaspoon of grated fresh ginger per cup of boiling water. You can apply rated ginger directly to the bunion once or twice a day as well.

Soothe with Sundew. This herb has a long folk reputation as a treatment for bunions, corns and warts. About 15 years ago, scientists learned why: It has proteolytic activity. To use this herb, crush the fresh plant and apply it directly to the bunion once or twice a day for up to a week.

Burns

The pain: First-degree burns, like sunburns and scalds, are painful and red, but the skin surface is unbroken. They usually heal on their own in a week or two.

Second-degree burns ooze, blister, and are painful. If the burn is confined to a small area, smaller than a silver dollar, you can treat it at home. Expect it to take two to three weeks to heal.

Third-degree burns leave skin charred that can turn white or cream-coloured. They can be caused by fire, chemicals, electricity, or any prolonged contact with hot surfaces. Oddly, these serious burns may not hurt, often because nerve endings are damaged. But that's all the more reason why you need to seek immediate medical help.

The cause: Fire and a hot stove aren't the only things that can char your skin. Exposure to electricity, chemicals, and radiation can all burn you. Even tap water can reach 140°F at times, causing a third-degree burn within five seconds.

See a doctor if:
...you have a severe second degree burn (severe blistering) or a third degree burn.
...the burn covers more than 10 to 20 percent of the body.
...the face, hands, or genital area has been burned.
...you have suffered chemical or electrical burns
...the burn becomes infected or you start to develop chills and a fever. Signs of infection usually occur two or three days later and include increased redness or pain, swelling, pus, and red streaks spreading from the burn up the extremities.

Remedies:
Cool it fast. As soon as you can, immerse the burned area in cool water and keep it there for 5 to 10 minutes, says Randolph Wong, MD, a plastic and reconstructive surgeon and director of the burn unit at Straub Clinic and Hospital in Honolulu. Cool water stops the burning process and helps ease pain. Don't use ice to cool a burn, though. That's too cold and could further injure already-damaged skin. If you're not near water, use whatever

is convenient to cool a burn quickly—even a glass of milk, says D'Anne Kleinsmith, MD, a dermatologist.

Cool with a compress. To further reduce pain, apply a washcloth or towel soaked in cool, not icy, water on and off for several hours, says Evelyn Placek, MD, dermatologist and doctor of internal medicine.

Add some milk. If you are soaking the burn in cool water, add some milk as well. The cool water helps get rid of the pain, and the lactic acid and sugar in the milk make the skin feel more comfortable, explains Melvin Elson, MD a dermatologist.

Get help from hydrotherapy. For minor (first-degree) burns, hold the area under cold water until the pain subsides, suggests Charles Thomas, Ph.D., a physical therapist and co-author of *Hydrotherapy: Simple Treatments for Common Ailments*. Then, he says, switch to slightly warmer water (a little cooler than body temperature) and keep the burned area in the water until there's no pain when you take it out of the water. After this treatment, apply a little aloe vera gel, suggests Dr. Thomas.

Elevate the burn. One way to get the sting out of a fresh burn is to position yourself so the burn remains at the level of your heart. That helps prevent swelling.

Sprinkle sugar on a singed tongue. It eases the pain on one of life's little annoyances.

Suck on a lozenge to relieve mouth burns. If hot food burns your palate, cough lozenges containing benzocaine may lessen the pain. If they don't help, ask you dentist or doctor for a lidocaine anaesthetic mouthwash.

Deflame the pain. If you take an anti-inflammatory medication within an hour of getting the burn, you'll not only ease the pain but you also might actually prevent the burn from getting worse, says Dr. Placek. Aspirin or ibuprofen works best. Dr. Placek recommends taking two 200-milligram tablets or capsules of ibuprofen every six hours for one to two days to reduce inflammation and swelling and to help decrease the severity of the wound. Do not use this type of medication, she cautions, if you have a stomach ulcer. Or try 650 to 1,000 milligrams of aspirin every six hours, 325 to 650 milligrams every four hours, or 325 to 500 milligrams every three hours, recommends W. Steven Pray, Ph.D., R.Ph., professor of nonprescription drug products at Southwestern Oklahoma State University.

Ongoing care:

Use antibacterial ointments. Over-the-counter salves like Neosporin or Bacitracin (Cicatrin) will help kill germs and prevent infection, says Dr. Wong. Sealing the wound before it heals with greasy folk remedies such as butter or Vaseline can keep nerve endings from drying out, he says, but they do little to control bacteria that can get into a wound after a burn.

Bandage the burn. For small burns, place an adhesive strip over the antibacterial ointment, large enough to avoid the adhesive sticking to the traumatised skin, explains Dr. Wong. For larger burns, you'll need a sterile piece of gauze dressing over the injured area, held down with medical adhesive tape, being certain that it is loose enough to allow for some swelling and loose movement without compromising blood flow.

Change and clean daily. If your burn is blistered or open, you should bandage it with dry, sterile gauze. Take off the gauze bandage at least once a day, and gently clean the burn area with antibacterial soap and water, says Karl Kramer, MD a dermatologist. Reapply ointment such as Polysporin or Polyfax, and then cover the wound with fresh gauze. "As long as it looks better every day, then you are probably doing all right," Dr. Kramer says. You may use the ointment over a small blistered area, but burns with blistering over an area larger than a silver dollar need to be seen by a doctor, he adds.

Keep it moist. Once the wound has healed over, keep it supple with a thin layer of moisturising lotion. This will help restore elasticity to the skin and reduce dryness, itching, and scaling, according to Dr. Wong. Fragrance-free lotions are best, but anything that traps moisture will be effective, says Dr. Wong, including vegetable shortening. However, don't use lanolin, he says, because it can cause a burning sensation.

Leave blisters intact. Blisters provide a natural protective layer for the burned tissue. "You should leave blisters alone because they function as a nice, sterile dressing. As long as that skin is intact, there's no avenue for bacteria to get in," says Jedd Roe, MD, assistant professor of emergency medicine at the University of Colorado School of Medicine.

Clean open blisters. Treat erupted blisters with a mixture of one tablespoon of white vinegar and one pint of water. Ideally, you should let blisters heal by themselves, but if they do break open, this is the remedy to try, says Dr. Elson. Soak the blistered area in this mixture for 15 minutes, three or four times a day, he suggests. You can use a washcloth or compress. "This solution fights bacteria, infections, and inflammation," he says. "It should dry up the blister in a day. "See a doctor if is the blister fluid is white or yellow since those colours are signs of infection.

Protect fresh skin. Once the skin heals, apply moisturisers or sunscreens daily. Over-the-counter products can help prevent scarring, according to Dr. Wong. Even the healed skin tends to be dry and fragile for the first year because burns often damage oil and sweat glands, he adds. He recommends moisturising sunscreens that have a base of aloe.

Dab on Preparation H. The popular haemorrhoid treatment can shave 1-3 days off the typical 7-15 day burn healing time. Preparation H contains a live yeast derivative, which has been found to speed wound healing. Dab a little H on the burn and cover with a bandage or other sterile dressing. Change the dressing daily and check to make sure an infection doesn't develop.

Avoid putting butter or petroleum jelly on burns. While these products may feel gentle, they are risky because they spark bacteria growth that could lead to infection, warns John P. Heggers, Ph.D., professor of surgery, microbiology, and immunology. "Butter contains salt, which draws all the water out of the cell tissues and causes them to collapse. Petroleum jelly prevents the tissue from breathing and eventually kills the tissue," he explains.

Nutritional remedies:
Drink up. "Blistering sunburns and excessive burns drain the body of fluid," says Don W. Printz, MD a dermatologist. Drink at least eight, eight-ounce glasses of water each day to keep yourself well-hydrated.

Eat extra. Beef up your daily caloric intake to enhance tissue healing. Eating extra helpings of carbohydrates, protein, and even fat gives your body more energy for healing burned areas, which is especially necessary if you are burned over a large part of your body, says Dr. Wong.

Helpful vitamins and supplements:
Think zinc. To encourage healing from within, Dr. Wong suggests taking 220 milligrams of zinc sulphate in pill form once or twice a day until the burn dries up, unless you develop some gastrointestinal upset, then discontinue its use immediately. This mineral helps the regeneration of new skin, he says, especially when taken with 10,000 units of vitamin A or 10,000 units of beta-carotene. (Check with your doctor before taking zinc.)

Ease the pain with E. Use vitamin E cream at any time during the healing process to prevent scarring. Or open a vitamin E capsule and spread the oil over the burn. Burns cause the body to produce more free radicals, unstable molecules that damage healthy cells. Vitamin E is a powerful antioxidant that promotes healing by destroying free radicals.

Soothe it with C. Take 5,000 to 10,000 milligrams daily of vitamin C with bioflavonoids and 50,000 IU (international units) of vitamin A daily. Do this for about two weeks- no longer- to promote faster healing.

Add some A. "Any healing tissue can benefit from 10,000 international units of vitamin A twice daily, says Elson Haas, MD, author of *Staying Healthy with Nutrition*. He recommends continuing for a full three weeks after you get the burn, even if it heals sooner, so your skin has the vitamins it needs to rebuild properly.

Everyday prevention:
Walk away from the grill. When your propane grill doesn't light right away, shut off the gas and take a walk before you try again, says Ian Cummings, MD, director of emergency services at the Day Kimball Hospital in Putnam, Connecticut. The gas is heavier than air, so it sits at the bottom of the grill. If it doesn't light right away, and you keep the gas on, the gas collects to the point of a minor explosion when you finally get it to light. "A lot of guys try to light up a propane grill and it blows up in their face," Dr. Cummings says.

Use lighter fluid, not gasoline. Getting charcoal to fire up can be a frustrating experience, but don't get carried away in your quest for a fast barbecue. Only use lighter fluid to light the grill, Dr. Cummings says. Gasoline might give you a quick light, but it will also probably give you a good burn and a trip to a hospital.

Buy a grease fire extinguisher. Many people burn themselves trying to put out grease and oil fires in the kitchen. "Don't put water on it, for God's sake," Dr. Cummings pleads. Buy a fire extinguisher made especially for grease fires and place it in an easy-to-reach location in the kitchen. They're available at hardware and home supply stores. You should also have a fire extinguisher in your workshop area, in your garage, and near wood-burning stoves, adds Dr. Cummings.

Don't be a flame magnet. Something as innocent as putting a teakettle on the stove can have serious consequences if you're wearing a housecoat with dangling sleeves, which can easily catch fire. Don't wear loose-fitting clothing when you're cooking, especially garments with wide, dangling sleeves. Look for flame-retardant fabrics and avoid clothes made of cotton, cotton/polyester blends, rayon, and acrylic, which ignite easily and burn quickly.

Herbal help:

Buy an aloe plant. "Every kitchen ought to have an aloe vera plant," says Michael Carlston, MD, assistant clinical professor in the department of family and community medicine at the University of California. Aloe cools the burn and helps the healing process. If you have an aloe plant, break off a leaf and rub the gel found inside it on the burn. Or use an over-the-counter aloe vera cream found at most chemists. Just avoid using creams that contain alcohol, as they will irritate the skin, adds Dr. Carlston.

Place a potato. Place a quarter-inch-thick slice of raw potato directly on the minor burn area. "Raw potatoes hold in a lot of moisture and have enzymes called proteases that are used by the skin for healing," explains Mark Stengler, N.D., a naturopathic physician, and author of *The Natural Physician.* He recommends using a fresh potato slice twice a day on the site for at least three days to take away redness and swelling.

Treat from the kitchen. Make a garlic-and-onion paste and place it directly on the burn. These plants possess antiseptic properties, says James A. Duke, Ph.D., a botanical consultant, who specialises in medicinal plants, and author of *The Green Pharmacy.* Chop up onions and garlic, then mash them with a spoon to make the paste, he advises. You can spread this paste directly on any burn from a first-degree up to a mild second-degree and leave it on for four hours or so. (A mild second-degree burn will appear red, swollen, and blistery, and you will feel some pain.) If the garlic causes further skin discomfort, use the onion alone, says Dr. Duke.

Apply an herbal compress. "Once you're beyond the initial cooling-down, you can apply an herbal compress that will help healing begin and protect the burn from infection," says Sharol Tilgner, N.D., a naturopathic physician. Combine 1 teaspoon each of calendula, St. John's wort, echinacea, and Oregon grape root tinctures in ¼ cup of very cold water. Soak a clean cloth in the mixture and apply it to the burn, Dr. Tilgner suggests. You can apply this compress a few times a day, she adds. Traditional skin healers, these herbs have all demonstrated antibacterial or immune-stimulating activity in laboratory studies.

Rub on a calendula-and-comfrey salve. Once a minor burn is healing, a calendula-and-comfrey salve will help the skin heal with less scarring, says Lisa Murray-Doran, N.D., a naturopathic doctor and instructor at the Canadian College of Naturopathic Medicine in Toronto. Both herbs have traditional reputations as skin menders. Comfrey contains a substance called allantoin that prompts rapid tissue repair, and researchers suspect that compounds in calendula called triterpenes prompt the growth of new cells. But do not use comfrey on deep burns or on burns that show signs of infection, such as redness, puffiness, or oozing, Dr. Murray-Doran cautions. Comfrey promotes such quick cell regeneration that the surface of the burn could heal, leaving infected or damaged skin underneath.

Try St. John's Wort. In one study, the blood red oil made from this herb's small yellow blossoms healed first-degree burns in 48 hours and mended second-degree burns three times faster than conventional treatments did, with less scarring. "The oil also eases the pain that can come with nerve damage in a burn," notes Dr. Murray-Doran. To make your own St. John's wort oil, put I cup of fresh yellow flowers in a quart jar and cover with olive oil. Close with a tight-fitting lid. Place the jar in a sunny window or a warm spot and shake it daily. The oil will turn red. After two to three weeks, strain out the flowers and store the oil in a dark, cool place. To use the oil, thoroughly cool the burned area of skin with cold water, dry the area carefully, and dab on the oil. Reapply two to three times a day, as needed.

Lay on some lavender. In the 1920s, the founder of modern aromatherapy, French chemist Rene-Maurice Gattefosse, discovered the burn-healing power of lavender quite by accident. After burning his hand in a laboratory accident, he quickly dunked it in pure lavender oil and was surprised by how quickly the skin healed. Use a few drops of undiluted lavender directly on the burn, recommends aromatherapist Michael Scholes.

Take the sting out with honey. Using raw honey, available in natural food stores as opposed to processed in the supermarket, can be spectacularly effective against burns when applied as a lotion. Recent Chinese research shows honey has soothing, antiseptic properties that help speed healing, according to Andrew T. Weil, MD, a clinical professor of internal medicine.

Get aid from ayurveda. Add a pinch of turmeric to fresh aloe vera gel (available in most health food stores) and apply the paste to the burned area, then cover the area with gauze, says Vasant Lad, B.A.M.S., M.A.Sc., director of the Ayurvedic Institute in Albuquerque New Mexico. Wash off and reapply the paste two to four times a day, covering the area each time, until the burn heals. Turmeric can stain the skin, says Dr. Lad, but any discoloration should wash off in about two weeks. Dr. Lad also suggests using fresh cilantro juice on a burn. To make the juice, he says, put cilantro leaves and water in a blender, using enough of each ingredient to make a puree that will cover the burned area. Dr. Lad suggests applying this mixture two teaspoons at a time, three times a day, directly to the burned skin, covering the area with gauze. Continue the treatment as necessary, he says.

Seek echinacea. Few people know that echinacea is a gentle antiseptic that helps prevent infection at the burn site—apply a few drops of the tincture directly to the burn. Taking a teaspoon or two orally will beef up your immune system, helping it protect you from infection.

Place some plantain. It's one of the most popular folk herbal remedies for burns in the United States. Juice from fresh plantain leaves can be applied directly to mild burns.

Bursitis

The pain: Swelling and redness in and around the joints, accompanied by chronic, dull, throbbing pain that radiates out from the joint. Often occurs after a sudden activity or overuse of a group of muscles and tendons.

The cause: "Bursitis and tendonitis are different problems, but are both caused by the same things," says David Richards, MD, an orthopedic surgeon. "Either you have a chronic case of bursitis or tendonitis caused by the cumulative effect of doing the same thing over and over again—such as turning wrenches on an assembly line eight hours per day for 18 years. Or you have an acute case of bursitis or tendonitis caused a weekend of moving furniture or digging and planting a garden." With seniors, the wear and tear on a body that accumulates with age is the primary factor. It also takes longer to recover from injuries as we get older, so it's easier to develop acute attacks. "With tendonitis, you get an inflammation that develops in your tendons, which connect muscle to bone," says Dr. Richards. "And it can be quite painful." Bursitis is equally painful, but originates from different origins. It's caused by an inflammation of a bursa, a fluid-filled sac surrounding joints or tendons. Normally, a bursa reduces friction by cushioning muscles or tendons and bones that constantly move back and forth across each other.

See a doctor if:
...the pain from your bursitis or tendonitis worsens after three to four days, or if it doesn't subside at all after proper rest and other home remedies. Besides ruling out serious injury, your doctor can prescribe medications and exercises that can alleviate pain and still give you some degree of mobility.

Quick relief:
Give it a rest. This might sound obvious, but because bursitis and tendonitis are often triggered by using a body part in a fashion it's not used to, rest is one of the first steps on the road to recovery. "Complete rest is necessary in order for the pain to subside," says Keith Jones, the head trainer for the Houston Rockets basketball team. Whatever activity triggered the bout of bursitis or tendonitis, avoid it for three to six weeks,

if possible. Even multimillion dollar athletes take a break when they have bursitis and tendonitis—you should too.

Try some ice. In addition to rest, Jones recommends putting ice wrapped in a thin towel on the area that ails you. "If you suffer from bursitis or tendonitis, make sure you apply ice to the sore area for 20 minutes at least three times per day," says Jones. "The combination of the rest and the ice should pay noticeable dividends within days."

Give it an ice massage. Tendonitis and bursitis pain generally is localised, so there's no need slap a big bag of ice over a large area. Instead, fill a paper cup with water, freeze it, peel off the upper edge to expose the ice, and then massage the ice up and down the tender area, says Jon Kluge, physical therapist, certified athletic trainer, and director of a Sports Injury Centre. Massage for 8 to 10 minutes until the skin is just reddened and numb to the touch.

Beat the heat. If you're suffering from bursitis or tendonitis, avoid the urge to apply a heating pad to the affected joint until the inflammation subsides, says William Pesanelli, a physical therapist. "It's like pouring lighter fluid on an already existing fire," cautions Pesanelli. "If you're suffering from bursitis or tendonitis, the tissues in the sore area are already inflamed and will feel warmer to touch than the rest of your body, so adding heat will only make matters worse." Instead, you'll find more relief by using ice until the inflammation is gone.

Elevate your injury. If the inflammation is in the knee, foot or ankle, then Jones recommends you elevate the affected area above your heart level. "If you put two or three pillows below your sore ankle to prop it up, then it often can help reduce the swelling," Jones says. However, if you have a history of impaired circulation in the injured area, don't elevate it above your heart level because limiting blood flow to an area of the body that has impaired circulation can be dangerous.

Ongoing care:

Treat the inflammation. Taking an anti-inflammatory for a week to 10 days, such as two to three ibuprofen three to four times per day, depending on your weight, should help ease the pain and swelling that comes with either bursitis or tendonitis, says Dale L. Anderson, MD, the author of *Muscle Pain Relief in 90 Seconds.* If the symptoms persist, a doctor might prescribe a different anti-inflammatory drug. All anti-inflammatory drugs should be taken with food or milk because they can cause your stomach to get upset if taken on an empty stomach, says Dr. Anderson. Because anti-inflammatory medicines like aspirin and ibuprofen may aggravate certain conditions, ask your doctor for another battle plan if you have ulcers or an inflamed bowel disorder, advises Dr. Anderson. Also, if you're planning to have surgery and take an anti-inflammatory, make sure to stop a week before your operation because these drugs can thin your blood, which can complicate surgery.

Rub a tendon. Tendonitis responds especially well to massage, says Den E. Benjamin, Ph.D., a muscular therapist. Friction massage is especially effective, according to Dr. Benjamin. "Rub the tendons very gently and you'll slowly wear down the scar tissue in the tendon itself," he notes. Such a massage usually takes a massage therapist 10-15 minutes.

Nutritional Remedies:

Pine for pineapple. This tasty fruit contains enzymes that break down protein. One of these enzymes, bromelain, is particularly important because it has anti-inflammatory properties. Pineapple reduces swelling, bruising and pain and speeds the healing of joint and tendon injuries. Many athletes believe that pineapple helps heal sprains and tendonitis. Some eat lots of pineapple before and after strenuous workouts to help protect their tendons, as tendonitis is a major problem for them. The bromelain content of pineapple is not all that high, but it probably can't hurt to add fresh pineapple and pineapple juice to your menu while you're getting over an episode of tendonitis or bursitis. Papaya contains enzymes similar to those in pineapple, so you might want to add some of this fresh fruit to your menu as well.

Helpful vitamins and supplements:

Make for the manganese. When bursitis strikes, you can have chronic inflammation that forms waste products (oxidants) in the body, says Alison Lee, MD, a pain-management specialist and acupuncturist with Barefoot Doctors, an acupuncture and natural-medicine resource centre in Michigan. She recommends taking a manganese supplement of 50 to 100 milligrams per day in divided doses to help build up the body's antioxidant-fighting properties. Take this amount for one to two weeks, then cut back to 15 to 30 milligrams of manganese per day for up to a month if your pain persists. But after that, it's time to go back to an everyday-size dose of 2.5 to 5 milligrams of manganese per day, Dr. Lee says.

Everyday prevention:

Limber up. To prevent bursitis and tendonitis, take time to stretch first, says Pesanelli. For example, if you are about to perform a task that your body is not used to, warm up that area of the body first. "Tendonitis or bursitis is often triggered when someone does something that their body's not used to," says Pesanelli. "If you've been playing pinochle all winter and then want to go out and garden for three hours on the first warm spring day, make sure to do some slow warm-up activities first, then a few gentle stretches to prepare for the activity," says Pesanelli." And don't go out and do three hours worth of activity if you've been inactive for a while. You need to gradually work up to that level of activity." To get some idea of what your body can handle (before you find out the hard way), it's a good idea to sign up for a stretching class.

Learn your lesson. If something causes you to have an acute attack of bursitis or tendonitis, make a mental note of the trigger and try to avoid it next time, says Dr. Richards. "If you don't figure out the trigger, then it will happen again." If you can't completely avoid the activity that triggered the first attack, try not to do it as often and make sure you warm up properly before doing it, says Pesanelli. "If you have to lift something pretty heavy, then make sure to move around first to prepare the body before performing the task. A few simple minutes of light and gentle stretching and exercise before the fact can help you avoid days or weeks of aggravation."

Wrap it up. If you need to continue to perform an activity that might cause a reoccurrence of the tendonitis in your knees, put on a knee sleeve before you do anything else, says Jones. Available at chemists and many sports stores, the sleeve is a flexible, cylindrical bandage that you can pull into place over your knee. "The knee sleeve serves two important purposes," says Jones. "First, it keeps the area warm, which helps maintain flexibility. And second, it keeps the joint from being bounced around, which can cause another flare-up of the tendonitis." Similar devices are available at drug stores for your ankle, elbow and wrists.

Ease back into activity. After you've been treated for bursitis or tendonitis, don't jump head-first into the activities you were doing before the attack. "You must ease yourself back into action after you start to feel better. Otherwise, it is a vicious cycle," cautions Dr. Richards. "You'll suffer an attack of bursitis, feel better and then be in pain again quickly if you don't slowly ease your way back into things."

Change slowly. Don't go suddenly from running one mile a day to running three. Increase your level of activity gradually, says John P. DiFiori, MD, a sports medicine specialist. "Allow your body to become accustomed to the new demands. That will be very helpful in preventing bursitis and tendonitis."

Pay attention to pain. If you begin to feel even some slight tenderness or soreness in a shoulder, elbow, or knee (the three most common sites for bursitis and tendonitis), don't ignore it, says Dr. DiFiori. People who try to work through pain often end up with chronic cases of bursitis or tendonitis. Instead, reduce your activity and apply ice to the area.

Double-check your equipment. Sports equipment that is not fitted properly for you can cause bursitis or tendonitis, says Dr. DiFiori. If the grip on a tennis racquet is too big, for example, you could develop a problem in your elbow. Check with a coach or pro to make sure that your equipment is well-suited.

Take a break. "Incorporate rest into your work and training program," says Dr. DiFiori. "If you are sitting at a computer and typing all the time, take periodic breaks." How often? "Take a five-minute break every hour," says David Jones, MD, medical director of the Spine and Sport Medical Centre in Orange, Texas.

Stand up straight. Poor posture can be a contributor to bursitis or tendonitis in the shoulders, says Dr. DiFiori. Pay attention to your posture and be sure to incorporate your abdominals and upper back into your flexibility and strength-training program. A physical therapist or trainer can be very helpful in providing specific posture-training programs.

Easing the pain with exercise:

Keep active. To prevent injuries such as bursitis and tendonitis, get yourself on an exercise program, suggests Pesanelli. If you can get out for a brisk walk or swim three times or more per week all year round, you'll be able to keep your heart, lungs and muscles in good condition. Many senior centres also offer exercise programs specifically tailored to older adults. Just be sure to consult with your physician first before embarking on an exercise program, says Pesanelli.

Stretch out tendonitis. Tendonitis is usually the result of tension in the muscles attached to a particular tendon, so you have to eliminate the tension in the muscle in order to relieve the pain in the tendon, says James Waslaski, a sports massage therapist and author of *International Advancements in Event and Clinical Sports Massage.* For example, he says, try stretching your calf muscles if you have tendonitis in your Achilles tendon. Icing the inflamed and tight tendon will help the symptoms, but you need to stretch regularly to address the underlying cause, he says.

Try some shoulder soothers. Step one for dealing with bursitis is to not exercise. If you have a flare-up, the only exercise you should do is lift an ice pack onto the sore spot. Once the pain and swelling subside, you should do some mild stretching exercises, says Dan Hamner, MD, a physiatrist and sports medicine specialist.

"With bursitis, you have to be careful and hold back a bit on activity," he says. "But if you totally rest an extremity for too long, you'll lose strength and range of motion. This is particularly true for the shoulder." For shoulder bursitis, Dr. Hamner offers the following easy movements to restore range of motion and keep the swelling down. Before all of these exercises, he recommends doing five minutes of ice treatment (simply wrap some ice in a towel and hold it on the painful area). He also suggests controlled, slow movements for best results.

Shoulder soother #1: Stand and bend forward at the waist at a 45-degree angle.

Let both arms hang loosely straight down, parallel to your legs, and bend your knees slightly to keep pressure off your back.

Move one arm clockwise in a small circle and in 10 rotations increase the size of the circle from about a foot to about three feet in diameter, allowing your entire arm, from your shoulder to your hand, to rotate.

Wind down in another 10 rotations back to the smallest circle.

Then try the rotations counterclockwise, using the same arm movement.

Repeat the sequence on the other side. Try this exercise three to five times a day.

For variety—and only if your shoulders can tolerate it—try this exercise with a one- or two-pound weight in each hand, says Dr. Hamner.

Shoulder soother #2: Stand with your feet shoulder-width apart and your arms at your sides.

Raise your injured arm, with your elbow locked and the palm of your hand facing forward, above your head about 10 degrees short of vertical, as if you were raising your hand in class.

At the same time, extend your other arm, with your elbow locked and the palm of your hand facing your leg, behind you about 10 degrees. Hold this stretch for one to two seconds.

In a controlled manner, gently swing your injured arm down and back and your other arm forward and up. Each arm should mirror the previous position of the opposite arm.

Repeat 10 times, alternating arms.

"Doing these motions slowly should help bring relief to the bursae," says Dr. Hamner.

For shoulder tendonitis: A door frame can be a true ally against shoulder tendonitis, either as a good preventive measure or whenever pain strikes, says Dr. Hamner. He recommends doing at least four stretches twice a day. "We would be in great shape if we got into the habit of doing stretches every day. Just look at our cats and how often they stretch," he says.

Step inside a door opening.

Place your palms and forearms flat on the jamb on each side of the door frame, with your hands slightly above shoulder level.

Gently lean your upper body forward through the doorway while your lower arms bear the weight. You should feel a stretch in both shoulders.

Hold the stretch for at least six seconds.

Help your hips. The hips are another common spot for bursitis, says Dr. Hamner. Here's a stretch to ease the pain. Ice the spot for five minutes before giving this a try.

Lie flat on your back with your knees bent and your feet flat on the floor.

Using your abdominal and quadriceps (front of thigh) muscles, and your hands if you need to, raise your legs.

In a slow, controlled movement, bring your knees toward your chest as far as you can.

Hold the stretch for two to three seconds.

Relax and slowly lower your legs back to the original position.

Repeat this stretch 10 times.

Ease Achilles pain. The Achilles tendon, the thick band that attaches your calf muscles to your heel bone, often becomes irritated. According to doctors, these exercises will help ease the pain and repair the tendon.

Achilles exercise #1: The first exercise, a stair stretch, is fairly vigorous, but the Achilles is a tough, long tendon, and it takes a fair amount of effort to overcome tightness, according to says John Cianca, MD, an assistant professor of physical medicine and rehabilitation. Stand on a step with your heels hanging over the edge. To bolster your balance, hold the railing.

Gradually drop your heels until you feel a stretch, but not pain. Try to hold the stretch for 20 to 30 seconds.

Then step off and let your feet rest on the floor in a neutral position. Repeat this exercise two more times, says Dr. Cianca.

Achilles exercise #2: Pretend to write the letters of the alphabet with your feet. Include letters that involve a lot of pointing and flexing, recommends Dr. Hamner. (If you're not much for letters, try making foot circles—25 one way and 25 the other.)

Aid your elbows. For elbow tendonitis relief, you'll need support from a sturdy tabletop, suggests Carl Fried, P.T., a physical therapist.

Sit facing the long end of a narrow table.

Stretch the painful arm across to the far side of the table so that your wrist hangs completely over the edge and your fingers are extended. Keep your arm straight, with your elbow locked and your palm facing down.

Grasp the back of that hand with your other hand and slowly try to bend the wrist down as far as possible.

Hold for 10 seconds and then release.

Repeat these steps up to 10 times twice a day.

Or try a variation on this exercise. Head for the refrigerator or pantry and grab a can that fits your grip. Put your arm in the same position along the edge of the tabletop—palm down and wrist over the edge—but hold the can in your hand. Gently move your wrist up and down 25 times. Pause for a few seconds and do 25 more. Try this twice a day, says Fried.

Knead your knees. To relieve tendonitis in your knees, Dr. Hamner recommends doing what he calls cross-friction finger massage.

Sit in a chair.

If your right knee is red and swollen, cup your right hand across the front of that knee so that your index finger is on top of the painful area and lying across the tendon running down the front of the knee.

Place your middle finger on top of your index finger.

Press down and gently massage the painful spot, working your fingers firmly for five to seven minutes. This could be painful at first, but it should ease up. If your fingers get tired, knead the spot with your thumb.

Be flexible. "Well-stretched, flexible muscles may help prevent bursitis or tendonitis," says Dr. DiFiori. He advises stretching all the extremities and the trunk once or twice a day. Because different activities place demands on different parts of the musculoskeletal system, it may be helpful to discuss the ideal flexibility program for your activity with a physician or certified personal trainer. It is important to avoid overstretching and to stretch at the right time.

Try this sequence, Dr. DiFiori suggests. Warm up a bit with a little walking or light jogging. Then, stretch a little. Only after that should you start your activity. You should also stretch immediately after any exercise, with a more-moderate-to-full stretch at that point. That greatly improves flexibility. Hold each stretch from 15 to 30 seconds. Stretch gradually—no bouncing. And repeat each stretch three to four times.

Get strong. "Developing muscular strength helps prevent bursitis and tendonitis," says Dr. DiFiori. That is why he recommends strength training, working out with weights at least twice a week.

Focus on large muscle groups: the abdominals and lower back, the biceps and the triceps in your arms, the chest and the upper back, the quadriceps and the hamstrings in your thighs, and the calves. Use a weight that you can lift comfortably at least 8 to 12 times. Do two sets, with 8 to 12 repetitions in each set. Your physician or personal trainer can suggest specific exercises for your activity.

Warning: Don't overdo strength training. You can actually develop bursitis or tendonitis if you use weights that are too heavy and lift them too many times or lift with improper technique.

Herbal help:

Soothe with Willow and other natural pain relievers. Willow bark is herbal aspirin. So are meadowsweet and wintergreen. They all contain salicylates, natural precursors of aspirin. To make a tea, try using one to two teaspoons of dried herb per cup of water and boiling it for about 20 minutes. Have a cup two or three times a day. Or try a teaspoon of tincture of any of these herbs three times a day. Remember, though, that if you're allergic to aspirin, you probably shouldn't take aspirin-like herbs, either.

Ease with Echinacea. This herb, also called coneflower, is good for connective tissue injuries such as tennis elbow, skier's knee and jogger's ankle, according to Michael Moore, author of *Medicinal Plants of the Desert and Canyon West* and one of the nation's leading herbalists. All of these injuries are, in fact, types of tendonitis. He recommends taking up to a half-ounce of echinacea tincture daily until the swelling and pain are reduced. That's a lot of tincture, but echinacea is not hazardous (although it may cause your tongue to tingle or become numb), so it's probably worth a try.

Have some horsetail. This herb is one of nature's richest sources of the element silicon, and some say that it is in a form that is especially easy for your body to use. A number of studies show that silicon plays an important role in the health and resilience of both cartilage and connective tissues such as tendons. (Cartilage forms a significant portion of joints.) This herb should be taken with the guidance of a holistic practitioner. You can make a tea by putting five teaspoons of dried horsetail, one teaspoon of sugar and one quart of water in a pot. Bring it to a boil, then reduce the heat and let it simmer for about three hours. Strain the tea and let it cool before drinking it.

Lick it with licorice. Licorice can be every bit as effective a treatment for bursitis and tendonitis as the commonly prescribed drug hydrocortisone, according to Daniel Mowrey, Ph.D., author of *The Scientific Validation of*

Herbal Medicine and Herbal Tonic Therapies. Plus, the herb has none of the usual side effects, such as weight gain, indigestion, insomnia and lowered resistance to infection. that are associated with cortisone and hydrocortisone. (While licorice and its extracts are safe for normal use in moderate amounts—up to about three cups of tea a day—long-term use or ingestion of larger amounts can produce headache, lethargy, sodium and water retention, excessive loss of potassium and high blood pressure.)

Try turmeric. Joseph Pizzorno, N.D.. president of Bastyr University in Seattle, and naturopath Michael Murray, N.D.. co-authors of *A Textbook of Natural Medicine,* are just two of the herbal scholars who note that curcumin, a compound abundant in turmeric. has proved as effective as cortisone in the treatment of some kinds of inflammation. They suggest taking both 250 to 500 milligrams of curcumin and 250 milligrams of bromelain three times a day, between meals.

Treat your joints gingerly. A gentle way to combat inflammation from chronic tendonitis and bursitis is to drink a tea made of ginger and sarsaparilla root, says David Winston, professional and founding member of the American Herbalists Guild and a clinical herbalist. "Ginger and sarsaparilla are both good systemic anti-inflammatory herbs," says Winston. "They're a good combination for chronic inflammation." For each eight-once glass of tea, you'll need about one teaspoon of the dried ground-up herbs, says Winston. Mix two parts sarsaparilla to one part ginger, and steep for about 45 minutes. Drink three cups a day for several weeks, says Winston. Don't use dried ginger without medical supervision if you have gallstones.

Calf Pain

The pain: Calf pain may be sudden and sharp or a dull, throbbing ache. It may be accompanied by swelling and discoloration.

The cause: Sore calves can be triggered by foot problems-such as high arches or flat feet, by ill-fitting shoes. Or the pain may be the result of a muscle tear, a partial rupture of the Achilles tendon, or the tendon inflammation called tendonitis. There are also more serious medical conditions that can cause calf pain, such as phlebitis (inflammation of a vein) and intermittent claudication (in which arteries have become narrowed, resulting in an insufficient blood supply).

See a doctor if...
...your calf pain doesn't subside within a couple of days.
...you notice any tender lumps beneath the skin.
...walking a few blocks causes excruciating calf pain that stops when you sit. The pain could be caused by something minor, like fallen arches. But it could also be a symptom of either phlebitis or intermittent claudication, says John Cianca, M.D., an assistant professor of physical medicine and rehabilitation. These are both serious conditions that affect your circulation.

Quick relief:
RICE to the occasion. RICE means rest, ice, compression, and elevation. Rest an injured calf for the first day or two, ice the area for no more than 20 minutes at a time every 2 to 3 hours as needed, compress the leg with an elastic bandage, and elevate the leg above the level of your heart, if possible. You can apply moist heat (such as a hot-water bottle) to the injury after the first 72 hours, says Allen Selner, D.P.M., a podiatrist. "Moist heat is more effective than dry heat," he says.
Rub and wrap. Once the swelling recedes, rub your injured calf with a pain-relieving balm (such as BenGay, Radian-B or Deep Heat) and wrap it in a plastic wrap, says Dr. Selner. Then top that wrap with an elastic bandage. "This will help to retain the heat and relax the calf muscle so that it doesn't cramp up," he says. You can wear the combination wrap as long as it is comfortable.

Reach over the counter. To reduce the pain and inflammation of an injured calf, try an over-the-counter nonsteroidal anti-inflammatory drug (NSAID) such as ibuprofen, says Brent S. E. Rich, M.D., staff physician at Arizona Orthopedic and Sports Medicine Specialists. If you still need pain medication after a week, see a doctor.

Everyday prevention:
Wear lifts. If your calf pain is caused by an injury, "take pressure off your heel," says Myles J. Schneider, D.P.M., a podiatrist, and co-author of *The Athlete's Health Care Book.* Heel lifts (available at athletic shoe stores) can help ease the strain on tendons and muscles, says Dr. Selner. To make heel lifts, "cut two 1/4 inch-thick pieces of cork and place them in your shoes."
Don't push it. Avoid any activity that puts undue stress on your calves-such as walking uphill or cycling-until your calf is completely healed, says Dr. John Cianca.
Stop smoking. People who have intermittent claudication should kick the habit, says Robert Ginsburg, M.D., director of the Cardiovascular Intervention Unit at the University of Colorado Health Science Centre. Smoking is a leading contributor to the atherosclerosis that decreases blood flow, he says.
Apply heat. A warm, not hot, heating pad or blanket can alleviate superficial pain from thrombophlebitis, says Dr. Ginsburg. (Don't use heat on a recent injury, however. It will make the swelling worse and interfere with healing.)
Step into support hose. Department store hosiery can constrict your circulation, but compression support stockings prescribed by a physician can greatly improve blood flow and relieve pain from venous insufficiency, says Richard F. Kempczinski, M.D., a vascular surgeon.
Consider surgery. Stripping and removing damaged veins can relieve severe venous insufficiency, says Dr. Ginsburg. Anticoagulants can also be helpful, he says. Pain and severe arterial insufficiencies may require such procedures as a balloon angioplasty or bypass surgery.

Easing the pain with exercise:
Pain-Preventing Exercises
Stretching and strengthening the muscles in your calves can help prevent pain in the future, says Dr. Rich. Here's a simple routine to try. Just be sure to warm up your calf muscles, advises William S. Case, a physical therapist. He suggests doing these exercises after you take a hot shower.

Stand facing a wall and place your palms flat against the wall. Shift your stance to place one foot behind the other. Keep your back heel down and the toes of that foot turned slightly inward as you bend your front knee. Now lean into the wall, pressing it with your palms. Hold the stretch for 30 seconds. "This is a very good exercise for calf pain when there is no swelling," says Stephen G. Motto, DM, a musculo-skeletal physician with a speciality in sports medicine at London Bridge Hospital.

"Remember to keep the heel of the backwards-extending leg on the floor."

Sit on the floor with your legs straight in front of you, toes pointing upward. If you can reach your toes, grab them with your fingers and pull them toward you, stretching the calf. If you can't reach your toes comfortably, wrap a towel around your foot and pull on both ends to get the same effect. Hold for 30 seconds.

Sit in a chair and raise and lower your heels. Or raise yourself up and down on your tiptoes, holding onto a table for support. Do one set of each exercise, starting with 20 repetitions and building up to 40 repetitions, says Case. But if you start to feel pain in your calves, stop and rest. "Don't exercise more than you're ready for," he says. "You may do more damage."

Strengthening your shins may also reduce calf pain, adds Dr. Selner. Put 2 pounds of rice in a stocking and drape the stocking over your toes. Sitting in a chair with your knees bent and your feet on the floor, lean forward and pull your toes toward your shins. "This exercise strengthens the toe extensor muscle, so you put less pressure on the calf," he says.

Hoof it till it hurts. Though walking brings on intermittent claudication, a walking program is the first step in treating it. "You should walk until you reach your level of pain tolerance," says surgeon Joseph M. Giordano, M.D.

Squelch Cramps with Sensible Shoes

If your calf pain isn't the result of an injury, revamping your footwear may relieve the soreness', experts say. These shoe-shopping strategies can help.

Pamper your calves. Wear running shoes as often as possible, advises Dr. Selner. "If you have to wear dress shoes at work, change into them when you get to the office."

Toss those spikes. If you wear high heels, stop, recommends Dr. Selner. "Wear heels no higher than 1½ inches high." But if you're used to wearing very high heels, don't suddenly switch to flats: "The sudden change can trigger calf pain," he says.

Check your shoes' shocks. Replace worn shoes, says Dr. Schneider. "Losing the shock absorption in your shoes can lead to calf pain," he says. Once you lose ⅛ inch of tread, get new shoes or have the soles replaced.

Wear inner soles. These products, which are available in the foot-care section of any chemist, can increase your shoes' shock absorption by 30 percent, says Dr. Selner.

Try arch supports. When you wear arch supports inside your shoes, they help correct mechanical imbalances that affect the way you walk. These imbalances may throw off your gait and put extra pressure on your calves, says Dr. Schneider.

"When you reach the point where you can't stand the pain anymore, stop. Push yourself a little more each day, keep increasing the distance, and gradually the condition will become less prevalent."

Hands-on help:

Rub the right way. "When muscle fibres in the calf muscles tear, it is important to massage them and stretch them to prevent any adhesions from developing or to break them down once they have formed," says Jenny Sutcliffe, PhD, DPP, MBBS, MCSP, former Senior Lecturer in Paediatric Neurology, Great Ormond Street Hospital, London, and author of *The Reader's Digest Body Maintenance Manual.* Use circular movements of your thumb to rub deep into the flesh of the sore area. Then try standing on a step resting only on the ball of the affected foot– you may need to hold on to the banister for balance. Rise up so that you are on tiptoe, then lower yourself so that your heel is below the level of the stair. "Stop when you feel any pain, but practice the exercise as often as you can," says Dr. Sutcliffe. The pain will disappear as the calf muscles are stretched.

Add some oil. Use your favourite massage oil to give the rub some extra oomph. "Massage is very effective, especially with arnica, lavender oil and other balms, which both heal and relax," says Dr. Motto.

Carpel Tunnel Syndrome

The pain: The first symptoms of CTS aren't that far removed from the sensation you get in your foot when it "falls asleep." You may experience tingling, numbness, or pain in the hand and fingers, especially in the thumb and first two fingers. The more you use your hand, the more it will hurt. As the condition progresses, your hand can become so weak that you can't even grip a glass.

The cause: The median nerve that runs to your thumb and first two fingers is constricted when your body's tendons and tissues swell and press against it. The nerve and the nine tendons that move your fingers are encased in a sheath called the synovium, making a sausage-like bundle that passes through the bony, hourglass-shaped passageway on the underside of the wrist that's known as the carpal tunnel.

When you're doing things like typing or bowling, the repetitive motions of your hand and wrist can cause the tendons and synovium to become inflamed and swollen. Often, carpal tunnel syndrome is caused by repetitive strain injury, which is the result of over-and-over-again wrist or finger motion, especially if it's combined with gripping vibrating tools or using instruments that put pressure at the base of the palm. People who type or sew or hammer or paint for many hours every day often get the tendon swelling that causes the nerve pain. Even slight swelling in the wrist area can press the nerve enough to short-circuit the signal. Women, especially pregnant women, are more prone to CTS than men. Regardless of your sex, however, you're at greater risk for CTS if you're overweight and if you don't exercise very much. Women's risk is also increased by taking oral contraceptives and during menopause.

See a doctor if:

...you have any or all of these symptoms: numbness in your hands that wakes you at night; clumsiness and a tendency to drop things; tingling and numbness in the thumbs, index fingers, or long fingers during work or at night. Without prevention or treatment, the problem nearly always gets worse, says Houshang Seradge, MD, an orthopaedic surgeon. Ignore the problem too long and you may have trouble telling warm from hot with your hand, have difficulty buttoning your shirts, or

when reaching in your pocket feeling for change, be unable to distinguish between a dime or a quarter, says Dr. Seradge. "The hand essentially becomes dull, blind, and weak," Dr. Seradge adds. Surgery may relieve the pressure. In advanced cases, however, the nerve damage can be permanent.

Quick relief:

Make nice with ice. For acute pain, or within one to three days of the onset of pair, apply ice to the painful area for 15 ' to 20 minutes, five to six times throughout the day. Cold treatments help reduce inflammation and swelling, explains David Ross, D.C., a chiropractor. Remember to wrap the ice in a towel before putting it on your skin, to protect your skin from the extreme cold. And use common sense: If your pain gets worse, stop the ice applications arid try something else.

Ease with heat. For chronic pain, or pain that persists for more than three days, lay a hot pack or hot-water bottle over the affected area six to seven times a day for no more than 15 to 20 minutes at a time. Heat relaxes and soothes deep-seated aches and increases blood flow to speed healing, according to Dr. Ross. Be careful not to overheat your body or fall asleep on the pad. A heating pad could also be used, but since hot packs and hot water bottles lose heat over time, they are safer.

Practice acupressure. "Acupressure works by activating the pituitary gland to release endorphins, which are strong, painkilling, opiate-like chemicals," explains says David Nickel, O.MD, a doctor of Oriental medicine in Santa Monica, California, and author of *Acupressure for Athletes*. If both wrists are affected, begin by treating the most sensitive side first. If most of the pain is on your left side, for example, place the thumb of your right hand on the inside of your left wrist crease or a few inches above, toward the elbow. Then place your right index finger on the back of your left wrist, opposite your right thumb. Probe for the most sensitive area, then apply firm pressure to both sides of your wrist, alternating five seconds on and five seconds off. At the same time, gently move your left hand from side to side. To increase the pain-reducing effect, exhale or blow through your mouth when you apply pressure. Continue the on-and-off applications for one minute. Repeat on the opposite wrist, if necessary.

When used correctly, this acupressure technique significantly reduces pain within minutes, says Dr. Nickel. You can expect to feel tenderness, soreness, or an aching sensation in your wrist, under the thumb or finger, during treatment. But if the pain is worse after using this technique, apply less pressure or discontinue treatment.

Bring down the swelling. To help ease the pressure in your inflamed wrist, you can take over-the-counter anti-inflammatory like aspirin or ibuprofen. Dr. Seradge suggests taking two 200-milligram tablets three times a day with meals. You can increase this to twelve 200-milligram tablets per day, but you should check with your doctor first.

Nutritional remedies:

Have a carpal-soothing salad. Many foods contain natural anti-inflammatory chemicals, called proteolytic enzymes, that may help relieve the pain and swelling of carpal tunnel syndrome. In his book *The Green Pharmacy*, James A. Duke, Ph.D., the world's foremost authority on healing herbs, recommends eating his Proteolytic CTS Fruit Salad made of pineapple, papaya, and grated ginger. Liberally spice your other food with sage and cumin, and you will have added even more natural anti-inflammatory and pain-relieving chemicals to your diet.

Add some oil. You can also soothe the inflamed nerve and tissues with flaxseed oil, a supplement rich in omega-3 essential fatty acids, says Ellen Potthoff, D.C., N.D., a chiropractor and naturopathic physician. Any type of inflammation responds well to essential fatty acids because no matter where it hurts, they interrupt the process of inflammation early.

You should feel better in two to four weeks if you start taking one tablespoon of flaxseed oil every day, says Dr. Potthoff. Because the oil turns rancid quickly when exposed to heat or light, buy a product that is packaged in a dark plastic bottle, then store it in your refrigerator. Also, look for a date on the packageing. Taste is another way to tell if you're getting good-quality flaxseed oil. "It should have a really nice nutty flavour and a dark amber colour," says Dr. Potthoff.

Helpful vitamins and supplements:

Try B6. Vitamin B6 seems to help relieve the symptoms of CTS, says Jill

---

Pain-Fighting Toys and Games

"In carpal tunnel syndrome, it is important to have some wrist extension, wrist flexion, and side-to-side movement," says Dan Hamner, MD, a physiatrist and sports medicine specialist. He offers these gentle—even playful—exercises.

Do the Slinky shimmy. Remember that coiled toy from your childhood that gave such delight as it slinked down your stairway? Well, that toy of yesteryear can be an exercise tool for today, says Dr. Hamner. Simply cradle the ends in the open palms of both hands and gently move your wrists up and down as you flop the Slinky from hand to hand.

Deal yourself a great hand. You don't have to be Amarillo Slim to ease carpal tunnel pain, says Dr. Hamner. The simple act of card shuffling is an ideal exercise to work the wrist muscles from side to side. When your bridge club meets, volunteer to be the steady dealer.

Do the yo-yo. The up-and-down glide of a yo-yo is a great exercise to flex and extend the wrists, says Dr. Hamner. Advanced yo-yo performers can try the cradle and walk-the-dog moves.

Stansbury, N.D., a naturopathic doctor.

While doctors aren't sure why this supplementation works, some speculate that CTS is actually caused by a deficiency. Although you can get B6 pretty readily from everyday foods like potatoes, brown rice, bananas, green vegetables, and chicken breast, the average diet doesn't usually provide the Daily Value of two milligrams.

Also, the content of your diet doesn't really tell the whole story when it comes to CTS. Low levels can be caused by other factors, says Dr. Stansbury. "Some people may just need more of this vitamin because they use more up," she says. "And stress is one factor that can increase your need for B6 as well as other B vitamins."

Researchers hit on the link between low levels of this vitamin and CTS in the late 1970s. One early study found that 22 of 23 people who took B6 for 12 weeks got complete relief from pain and tingling in their hands. How this happens is still a bit of a mystery, says Dr. Stansbury. The problem is that B6 has so many roles in the body that doctors have had difficulty pinpointing any one key action that could have a direct effect on the carpal tunnel area. Like other B vitamins, B6 works with enzymes, the chemicals that spark reactions in your body. It is an essential part of many chemical reactions involved in the body's production of energy, protein, and fats. "It gets around," says Dr. Stansbury. While that emphasises the fact that we really need this vitamin, however, it doesn't say anything about the direct role that it plays in helping to relieve CTS. B6 seems to work best on mild to moderate cases of CTS, says Thomas Kruzel, N.D., a naturopathic doctor. To end the tingling, take 50 milligrams of B6 each day, he suggests, and give it time to work. It usually takes 12 weeks to get the full benefit.

You can boost the healing power of B6 by taking at least 10 milligrams of riboflavin (sometimes called vitamin B2) along with it, says Dr. Kruzel. The riboflavin seems to improve the effect by converting B6 to a more active form that is essential to more than 60 chemical reactions in your body.

Buy bromelain. Bromelain, an enzyme found in pineapple, is nature's anti-inflammatory medicine. This hungry enzyme can take a bite out of pain and swelling and help you heal faster, says Dr. Kruzel. Just be sure you don't blunt its effect by taking it with meals: If you do, all of its enzymatic energy goes into digestion. If you take it between meals, however, it goes to work digesting the products of inflammation.

When you have swelling and pain in the tendons of the wrist (or any body part), a substance called fibrin is produced and deposited around the tendons. Like a tight shoe that gives you blisters, the fibrin puts more pressure on the already crowded tendons and results in even more inflammation. Bromelain helps stop that cycle. Its action breaks down the fibrin and then eats it up.

When the tingling pain of CTS strikes, take two 500-milligram tablets or capsules of bromelain between meals two or three times a day, says Dr. Kruzel. Bromelain is measured in milk-clotting units (mcu) or gelatin-dissolving units (gdu). The higher the number, the greater its potency. Look for a supplement with a strength between 1,800 and 2,400 mcu or 1,080 and 1,440 gdu per capsule. Bromelain may cause nausea, vomiting, diarrhoea, skin rash, and heavy menstrual bleeding. Do not use it if you are allergic to pineapple.

Beat it with bioflavonoids. You might also consider adding bioflavonoids to your supplement arsenal, suggests Dr. Potthoff. Rich in powerful antioxidants, bioflavonoids are used to treat injuries because they relieve pain and promote healing, she says. She recommends taking 1,000 milligrams of a broad-range bioflavonoid supplement that contains citrus bioflavonoids and quercetin three times a day.

Everyday prevention:

Sharpen your knives. Simple household chores such as cutting meat or clipping hedges can cause pain for those with carpal tunnel syndrome. Keeping your tools sharp or well lubricated reduces the amount of pressure needed to use them.

Take a break. Ease off on the work a little bit. It's pretty simple advice, but hard to do when your job requires that you keep slicing and dicing that chicken coming down the assembly line, or slapping away at that keyboard. If you can't stop what you're doing entirely, then cut back when you can and take frequent, short breaks, says Mark Bracker, MD, clinical professor of sports medicine. And when you go home, don't launch into another hand-intensive activity like painting your garage.

Work at right angles. We've become a nation of desk jockeys and computer geeks, which puts us more at risk for carpal tunnel because of the intensive hand work. But often, all it takes is a simple change of posture or better ergonomics at our "workstations" to relieve the symptoms, says Dr. Seradge. You should sit in a 90-90-90 position, meaning your elbows, back, and knees should be at 90 degrees. That position evenly distributes body weight and makes you sit up straight, he adds. And it keeps your wrists straight.

See eye-to-eye. Keep your monitor at eye level, says Dr. Seradge. It'll help ensure that you maintain a good working posture.

Mickey with your mouse. Put your mouse in a position where you don't have to reach. Or trade in that mouse for an alternative, like a touch pad or track ball, suggests Dr. Seradge.

Go ergo. "There are a lot of good ergonomic products and advice out there. I would experiment and see what helps you," says Dr. Seradge. A simple example of one is using a wrist pad on your keyboard to alleviate pressure on the carpal tunnel. A rolled towel or a strip of hard sponge under your wrist can work well. There is no need for expensive commercial equipment.

Sleep with a splint. Carpal tunnel frequently wakes you up at night with pain and tingling sensations. That's because in sleep, you often fold your wrist and put pressure on the already inflamed nerves and tendons. Try sleeping with a wrist brace or wear one during the day to limit your hand movement and hold your wrist in a "neutral" position. You can find the braces at most drugstores.

Splint carefully. Resist the temptation to self-prescribe a splint for carpal tunnel syndrome or another repetitive strain injury. If you think you need one, consult your doctor. Wearing a splint improperly can aggravate your injury and slow the healing process, says Dr. Ross. If your doctor prescribes a splint, wear it only as prescribed and discontinue its use as soon as you can. Overuse of a splint can make you dependent on it, causing your muscles to atrophy. "Splints are meant to act as extra ligament support while you are healing, not to replace your own strength. You wouldn't want to wear a cast forever, would you?" asks Dr. Ross.

Lose weight. Being overweight can aggravate repetitive strain injuries, says Margaret Cullen, a registered occupational therapist, and certified hand therapist. When you are overweight and sedentary, there's a greater chance that less oxygenated blood and nutrients will be delivered to your tissues. If your muscles don't receive the food and oxygen they need to function correctly, they tire quickly. Extra pounds also add to the weight that the muscles must support to move your hand and arm.

Get your blood moving. Aerobic exercise increases the flow of oxygenated blood to your hands while removing the waste products from inflammation, says Cullen. Exercise also releases endorphins, your body's natural mood-enhancers. Aim for 30 to 40 minutes of aerobic exercise at least three times a week.

Don't smoke. Smoking can make repetitive strain injuries such as carpal tunnel syndrome worse. Nicotine constricts your blood vessels and replaces oxygen with carbon monoxide, explains Cullen. So the blood flow to your tissues is reduced.

Stretch the point. Workers who use their hands intensively on the job should do this three-minute stretching routine every hour, or at least once after the lunch break, says Dr. Seradge, developer of the routine: Start with your right hand, hold each position for a count of 10, and let your motions flow from one position to the next. Remember to keep breathing normally as you do these. Stop if you feel pain. Stand with your arms relaxed at your side, feet shoulder-width apart. Bring your right arm up straight in front of you to shoulder level with your palm facing up. Spread your fingers and bend your wrist down until your fingers point toward the floor. Then, bring your hand up and make a fist. Keeping your arm straight, flex your wrist toward yourself. Bend your arm at the elbow and pull your fist toward your shoulder. Keeping that position, rotate your arm out to the side from the shoulder and turn your head to look at your fist. With your arm still out to the side, straighten your arm, and—with your palm facing up—extend your fingers and bend your wrist down until your fingers point to the floor. Turn your head slowly to look over the opposite shoulder. Repeat the sequence with your left hand.

"That gets those muscles, nerves and tendons ready," Dr. Seradge adds. "If you're having symptoms of carpal tunnel, you should see a physician and do this routine every hour or so."

For a free copy of Dr. Seradge's complete exercise program, send a stamped (single first-class stamp), self-addressed envelope to Houshang Seradge, MD, Director, The Hand Institute, The Orthopedic and Reconstructive Research Foundation, 1044 Southwest 44th Street, Oklahoma City, OK 73109. The Foundation also has a videotape with exercises and ergonomic tips. For more information, write to Dr. Seradge.

Prevent a comeback. After your symptoms are under control, exercise can help prevent the return of carpal tunnel pain. The key is to use gentle strengthening movements and to vary the motions, say doctors and physical therapists. Here are a few simple exercises that you can do while watching television or even relaxing in a bathtub:

Mimic a mime. For this wrist exercise, stand facing a wall. Extend your arms out at shoulder level directly in front of you with your palms facing the wall. Without touching the wall, pretend that you are a mime stuck in an enclosed box and trying to find an exit. Slowly move your palms and shoulders up as you reach for the imaginary ceiling, says Dan Hamner, MD, a physiatrist and sports medicine specialist.

Try pretend window washing. While standing or sitting, extend your arms in front of you and gently move your hands clockwise as if you were rubbing smudges off a window. Then change directions and move counterclockwise, says Dr. Hamner.

Offer some high-pressure prayer. Put your hands together as though to pray, then press the palms together. This helps to stretch the wrist muscles, says Susan Isernhagen, P.T., a physical therapist. Hold the pressure for a count of five and relax. As a variation, keep your fingertips touching as you move your palms apart.

Play sweatless tennis. There's no need for a racquet or net for this strengthening exercise offered by Dr. Hamner. Simply extend your arms straight out in front of you with your palms up and hold a tennis ball in each hand. Squeeze the ball, then relax. Do this 10 times, shake out your hands, and repeat.

Reach for new heights. Here is an exercise to get the fluid out of your wrists and fight the numbness, tingling, and jabbing pain it causes by pressing against the median nerve, says Dr. Hamner. While watching television in your favourite chair, rest your hands and elbows on top of the backrest so that your hands are behind your head—and most important, above the level of your heart. Hold that pose during an entire commercial and gradually build your way up to a half-hour sitcom.

Be kind at the keyboard. "We often put ourselves in a head-forward, limb-forward posture at a computer keyboard, and that puts strain on the neck,

Ergonomic computer use

Perching in front of a computer all day could qualify you as a prime candidate for repetitive strain injury. In fact, reported cases of repetitive strain injury have increased sixfold in the past decade, making it the unofficial health complaint of the modern age. You can help protect yourself if you set up your workstation this way:

Your head is directly over your shoulders, about an arm's-length from the screen. You should be looking straight ahead at the monitor.

Your neck is stretched upward and relaxed.

Your shoulders are pulled down and relaxed.

Your elbows are at your sides, bent at about a 90-degree angle.

Your wrists are straight and level. Avoid resting them on the keyboard.

Your fingers are in straight lines with your forearms, gently curving onto the keyboard.

Your knees are slightly lower than your hips.

Your feet are flat on the floor.

Your chair is inclined slightly forward.

Your keyboard is flat, at or just below elbow level.

---

shoulders, elbows, arms, wrists, and fingers," says Robert Markison, MD, a hand surgeon. He offers this fight-back survival guide:

Maintain proper posture. Keep your head resting on the centre between your shoulders and avoid leaning forward.

Avoid extreme wrist positions by keeping your wrists almost straight on the keyboard, not below it or arched upward.

When typing, move your hands over to reach the keys on the edges to type the letters Q, A, Z, and punctuation symbols. Avoid straining your tendons by stretching the little finger out.

Don't pound the keyboard like a jackhammer. Try a kinder, gentler touch.

Alternate tapping the spacebar with your right and left thumbs to avoid overusing one thumb.

"Play" the keyboard as you would play a piano, moving your arms as well as your wrists. Rest on the wrist pad only when you are not typing. Also, check your grip on your mouse. It should be comfortable and relaxed rather than tight, with your wrist parallel to the ground, not tipped up or back. Position the mouse near the keyboard and the keyboard at a level where your elbows are at about a 90-degree angle. Placement is important because repeatedly reaching for the mouse can hurt your elbows and shoulders over time. If using the mouse continues to bother you, replace it with a trackball or another type of pointing device.

Every 30 minutes or so, stop typing or working the mouse and stand up and stretch.

Vary your routine. Alternate tasks whenever possible to avoid sequences of activities that use the same muscles and tendons. For example, if you spend most of your day in front of a computer or doing intensive filing or photocopying, break up this time with meetings or a walk down the hall. "This forces you to move and stretch your body," notes Ira Janowitz, P.T., a certified professional ergonomist. The human body is designed for movement, not for sitting still longer than an hour at a time."

Sit right. Sit so that you maintain the normal curvature of your spine in your lower back and neck. Slouching damages the disks and ligaments in your spine, according to Dr. Ross. Over time, your spine weakens, and your spinal nerves and associated soft tissues may become damaged.

Choose tools that fit your hands. From staplers to wrenches to wire cutters, many gadgets are too big or too heavy for some peoples' grips. "Just as you try on shoes for size, you should try out tools before buying them," says Janowitz.

Check your chair. If you sit for long periods of time, make sure that you have a chair that is properly proportioned for your body. Furniture is not one-size-fits-all. A chair with a too-deep seat presses against your calves, obstructing your blood flow, says Janowitz. A chair with a too-small seat, on the other hand, presses against the backs of your thighs, impeding circulation there. When you are sitting, your knees should bend at close to a 90-degree angle, and your feet should be flat on the ground. The back of the chair should firmly hold you upright and not allow you to slouch back as the day wears on and you get tired. And don't forget to get up and stretch every 20 to 30 minutes, advises Dr. Ross.

Use a friendly phone. If your job requires moderate to heavy phone use, wear a headset. Refrain from pinning the receiver between your shoulder and chin, which could leave you with a pain in the neck—literally.

Make arrangements. Rearrange your work areas to reduce repetitive reaching. At home, for example, store the dishes you use every day on cupboard shelves between waist- and shoulder-height so that you can easily retrieve them. 11, same rule applies at work: Keep the supplies that you use most often at your fingertips.

Practice yoga. Certain forms of hatha yoga can help a woman develop an awareness of her body's messages, including pain, according to Marian Garfinkel, Ph.D., a health educator and certified senior yoga teacher. "The more aware you are of your body, the more you may be able to treat and prevent injuries, including repetitive strain injuries," explains Dr. Garfinkel. Yoga helps put you in tune with your posture and how you use your arms and legs. "Yoga can't cure a repetitive strain injury on its own. But it can help when used in combination with other therapies, like acupuncture," says Dr. Garfinkel.

Herbal help:

Soothe with St. John's Wort. Widely known for its ability to treat depression, St. John's-wort also helps nerves recover when they are damaged, inflamed, or strained, says Dr. Stansbury. Thousands of years before doctors coined the term carpal tunnel syndrome, the relaxing herb was used to heal nerve pain and tingling, she says.

For the squeezed median nerve, St. John's-wort helps in two ways. Its sedative effect helps to reduce pain, while its anti-inflammatory activity can help shrink swollen tendons. Don't expect the kind of quick pain relief that comes from popping a pharmaceutical like aspirin or ibuprofen, though; St. John's-wort typically takes a few weeks to start working.

Start out with 200 milligrams of extract standardised to 0.3 percent hypericin three times a day, says Dr. Stansbury. You should start to see some improvement in about two weeks. If you don't, take a little more, she says—300 to 400 milligrams three times a day.

While St. John's-wort is generally very safe, some people who take high doses find that they're more sensitive to sunlight. The dose that can cause this sensitivity is highly variable, says Dr. Stansbury, so if you are fair-skinned, avoid excessive sun exposure. St. John's-wort should only be taken with a doctor's supervision, and do not take it without medical approval if you are taking antidepressants.

Try turmeric. Turmeric is an herb that contains a powerful anti-inflammatory chemical called curcumin. The herb has traditionally been used in India's Ayurvedic medicine to treat pain and inflammation.

The effect of turmeric has been compared to that of cortisone, the pharmaceutical sometimes used to treat CTS symptoms. Although turmeric's pain-fighting power is not as strong as cortisone's, the herb is a lot easier on your system, says Dr. Kruzel.

Like bromelain, turmeric promotes the breakdown of fibrin. For some relief, opt for capsules of the standardised extract. Unlike the turmeric on your spice shelf, the capsules contain 95 percent pure curcumin. Dr. Kruzel gives people with CTS 250 to 500 milligrams of curcumin a day. Keep taking this dose until the inflammation has been reduced, he advises, then take half that dose for one to two weeks until your symptoms are gone. If the symptoms return, repeat with the high dose and return to the lower dose again after they improve. Do not use turmeric supplements without talking to your doctor.

Rub it in. You can make your own pain-relieving lotion by adding several teaspoons of ground red pepper to a quarter-cup of skin lotion, suggests Dr. Duke. Ground red pepper contains several compounds that ease pain and inflammation. He also suggests adding several drops of lavender oil— another natural anti-inflammatory that has a relaxing scent—to the lotion. He cautions that some people may be sensitive to the chemicals in ground red pepper, so test the lotion first on a small area and stop using it if it irritates your skin.

Work with willow. Willow bark, the original source of aspirin, contains chemicals (salicylates) that both relieve pain and reduce inflammation. You might also try other herbs rich in salicylates, notably meadowsweet and wintergreen. With any of these herbs, try steeping one to two teaspoons of dried, powdered bark or five teaspoons of fresh bark for ten minutes or so, then strain out the plant material. You can add lemonade to mask the bitter taste and drink two to three cups of tea a day. Remember, though, that if you're allergic to aspirin, you probably shouldn't take aspirin-like herbs, either.

Cure with camomile. Camomile tea is best known as a tasty way to calm jangled nerves. But its active compounds (bisabolol, chamazulene and cyclicethers) also have potent anti-inflammatory action. Camomile is widely used in Europe for many inflammatory diseases.

Get comfort from comfrey. Pharmacognosist (natural product pharmacist) Albert Leung, Ph.D., and noted herbalist and photographer Steven Foster, in their excellent *Encyclopaedia of Common Natural Ingredients*, explain that applying comfrey to the skin can help relieve pain, swelling and inflammation. This has been confirmed through studies using laboratory animals. The active compounds are allantoin and rosmaranic acid. Comfrey has gotten a lot of bad press in recent years because it also contains pyrrolizidine alkaloids, compounds that may cause liver damage when the herb is ingested. But there's no evidence that comfrey is risky when applied to the skin. Add a few teaspoons of dried, powdered comfrey to the recipe mentioned above for red pepper or to any favorite skin cream.

Soothe with cumin. Cumin is used liberally in Mexican foods. "My former U.S. Department of Agriculture colleague, molecular biologist Stephen Beckstrom-Stemberg, Ph.D., and I once studied the properties of this spice and discovered three pain-relieving compounds, seven that are anti-inflammatory and four that combat swelling," says Dr. Duke. "If I had CTS, I'd use lots of cumin on food and add it to my curried rice."

Chafing

The pain: Red, raw, itchy area where skin rubs against skin or against something abrasive.

The cause: The friction of rubbing rips skin cells from the surface. This itches. So we scratch, ripping off more skin cells and further inflaming the area. As we make our way down to raw, bloody skin, the bacteria, yeast, and fungi that naturally live on our skin's surface literally make their way under our skin, causing infection.

See a doctor if:

...the affected area begins to ooze or weep, or if you have severe pain.

...you follow these tips and don't see relief within a couple of weeks, or if the chafed area gets worse.

Quick relief:

Hit the showers. Bacteria, yeast, and fungi love to set up camp on raw, sweaty skin. So if you return from a long run or some other athletic excursion and find yourself chafed to the quick, then jump in the shower. The water will wash the wound. And your antibacterial soap will send germs packing, says Richard A. Miller, D.O., an avid runner and dermatologist.

Soften after your shower. If your skin is raw but not bloody, rub in a moisturiser after bathing. The moisturiser will trap the water on your skin, preventing the evaporation of moisture and further drying of your skin, says Daniel Groisser, MD, a dermatologist. Also, moisturiser will help reduce the itchy feeling that results from chafing, keeping you from scratching and worsening the chafed area. Dr. Groisser recommends using Curel moisturiser for your body, Eucerin Light on your face, and Cetaphil (Eucerin or Aysain) as a wash instead of soap. Use as needed and as directed on the package.

Cream yourself. If you've rubbed yourself bloody, apply an over-the-counter antibiotic ointment such as Polysporin (Polyfax) once you've washed and dried your raw skin, Dr. Miller.

Cover it up. If you are bleeding somewhat heavily, place a non-stick bandage (such as Telfa Pads or Boots Melolin Dressing) over the wound, says Dr. Miller. You can secure the bandage with netting (such as Gauztape or Ace Wraps), available at most chemists or medical supply stores. If you use a regular adhesive bandage or tape, you may further irritate the wound when you remove the covering. Change your bandage once a day.

Ongoing care:

Air it out. Chafed skin will heal faster if it's left uncovered and allowed to breathe. It it's not possible during the day, make sure your sleepwear is loose and comfortable so you skin can get some "airtime" while you doze.

Don't forget skin folds. Applying an over-the-counter cream like Micatin (Mycil), mixed with a 1 percent hydrocortisone cream, in between skin folds can also help overweight people cure chafing. Skin folds are prime areas for chafing because they're moist and there's a lot of friction from movement.

Rinse, then rinse again. After you bathe or shower, rinse your body thoroughly so that no soap remains on your skin, says Mary Lupo, MD, a dermatologist. Soap residues can compound chafing by irritating the skin, and they can disrupt your body's natural moisture barriers that normally shield you from at least some of the friction generated by skin-to-skin rubbing.

Don't be rash. Your shower and antibiotic ointment should take care of bacteria. But if you notice a bumpy rash forming on or near the chafed area, you may have developed a yeast or fungal infection. This usually happens on the inner thigh and groin, says Dr. Miller. You can combat such infections by using an over-the-counter anti-yeast or antifungal medication, such as Lotrimin AF (Canesten) cream or powder or Micatin (Mycil) cream, twice a day for two to three weeks. If you sweat a lot, stick to powders instead of creams. If the rash persists or gets worse, see a doctor for a prescription ointment or pill.

Zap it with zinc. "Zinc oxide, the white paste that lifeguards put on their noses, is wonderful for treating chafing-it's simple and inexpensive," says dermatologist John F. Romano. "Just apply a thin layer on the area where you tend to chafe. If you have trouble removing the zinc oxide because that area is hairy, apply a little olive oil or mineral oil and wipe it off."

Everyday prevention:

Take a powder. Dust areas that are prone to chafing with baby powder, suggests Jerome Z. Litt, MD, a dermatologist. "Powder adds some slip to the skin and helps prevent rubbing," he says. "It also absorbs moisture." Cornstarch is often used for this purpose.

Wear chafe-proof clothes. Such clothing either prevents skin from rubbing against skin or clothing from rubbing against skin, says Dr. Miller. And you don't have to spend a lot of money to get some. For instance, if your nipples tend to chafe from running, cut two holes in the front of your shirt. If your thighs usually chafe, wear tight shorts beyond your mid thigh.

If your inner arms chafe, wear a T-shirt instead of a jersey. If your groin gets chafed, wear loose-fitting underwear and pants, says Dr. Groisser.

Smear on petroleum jelly. Another simple and inexpensive remedy is petroleum jelly. "It's best to apply the jelly before you exercise," says D'anne Kleinsmith, MD, a cosmetic dermatologist. The petroleum jelly protects the area from friction. And there might be some areas that need special attention. "Runners frequently complain that their nipples get chafed by a shirt in the up-and-down motion. I advise my patients to spread some petroleum jelly over their nipples before running," says Dr. Kleinsmith. For even more protection, cover each nipple with a small adhesive bandage.

Put away the panty hose. Women who are prone to chafing should definitely avoid wearing panty hose, according to Dr. Kleinsmith. "Panty hose don't allow the skin in your upper thighs to breathe," she says.

Switch to boxers. Men who get chafing around the waist, crotch and upper thighs might want to try wearing boxer shorts. Tighter-fitting jockey underwear is more likely to cause chafing around the waist and thighs.

Wash before you wear. Be sure to wash any new clothes before you wear them, says Richard H. Strauss, MD, a sports medicine doctor. Washing sometimes softens fabric enough to lessen abrasion. It also removes dyes and sizing (chemicals used to add crispness and lustre to new clothes) that can irritate skin in some people, says Dr. Romano. Washing is especially important when you wear dyed exercise clothes, Dr. Romano points out. The skin absorbs dye as you sweat-and that's something you want to avoid.

Wrap it Up. People who are overweight or who have big thighs are more likely to have chafing, but there's a way to find relief. Wrap elastic bandages around the portions of the legs that rub, suggests Tom Barringer, MD, a family physician who is a fitness runner. For any vigorous exercise, wrap elastic bandages around each thigh or wear cycling style shorts, which come down farther on the thigh and are tighter than regular shorts. That will shield the skin on the inside of your thighs. But be sure the elastic bandage is secure, so it does not move across the skin.

Turn on your hair dryer. "Once you're out of the shower, put your hair dryer on a low setting and dry all areas prone to chafing and yeast," says Deborah S. Sarnoff, MD, a dermatologist. "Be meticulous in drying," adds Dr. Lupo. "Lift your belly if it hangs down a bit and dry the skin underneath. Lift your breasts as well. And pay particular attention to your thighs."

Use tampons, not pads. Since sanitary napkins prevent the free flow of air and cause a build-up of moisture where crotch and thigh meet, use tampons instead, suggests Dr. Sarnoff. If you can't use tampons, make sure that you change your sanitary napkin frequently and sprinkle a little ZeaSORB powder over fresh napkins.

Lose weight. If you're significantly overweight, the best way to prevent chafing is to lose excess pounds, says Dr. Sarnoff. Then you're much less likely to have sagging skin that can rub against the rest of your body.

Herbal help:

Oil your skin. The Australian tea tree makes an oil that can speed healing and protect your chafed skin from infection. You don't have to travel to Australia and chop down a tree. Just go to your local health food store and buy a bottle of tea tree oil. Soak a cotton ball in water, apply just a few drops of the oil to the cotton ball, and then press the cotton ball into the chafed area several times a day until your skin heals, says Eve Campanelli, Ph.D., a holistic family practitioner. Some people with very sensitive skin may experience an irritation or allergic reaction to tea tree oil. If you have sensitive skin, be sure to do a patch test before using the oil: Place a drop of the oil on a patch of clean skin on your arm, wait 24 hours, and if you don't experience any irritation, then the oil is safe to use.

Concoct your own skin-saver. You can make a soothing ointment by mixing an ounce of vitamin E cream or olive oil, which is naturally high in vitamin E, with 5 drops each of lavender and geranium essential oils, 15 drops each of bee propolis and poplar bud tinctures, and a quarter-teaspoon of a low-alcohol calendula tincture. Apply the mixture to the chafed area three times daily. The ointment is safe, even on sensitive skin, says Pamela Taylor, a doctor of naturopathy. Ingredients such as vitamin E help soothe skin and promote healing, while others such as bee propolis— a natural antibiotic substance made by bees to protect their hives—fight infection. Most of these ingredients can be found at your local health food store. Poplar bud tincture is often sold as Balm of Gilead. If you can't find it, substitute 15 drops of tincture of comfrey (its use should be limited to 4 to 6 weeks' daily application) or double the amount of calendula tincture to a half-teaspoon, Dr. Taylor recommends.

Chapped Lips and Skin

The pain: Flaked, cracked, peeling skin.

The cause: When skin cells dry out, they shrink, weakening the barrier that keeps outside elements like bacteria from getting through. Cold, dry weather is a common cause of chapped skin, but indoors heated air can also rob your skin of its moisture. Lips are particularly susceptible because they lack the natural oils that the rest of our skin employs to stay supple. They also lack melanin, the pigment that protects us from the sun and turns us tanned.

See a doctor if:

...you have persistent dryness, redness, or scaling. It could be a sign of premalignant activity, says Alexander H. Murray, MD, head of the division of dermatology at Dalhousie University Faculty of Medicine in Halifax, Nova Scotia. It looks like a bad case of chapping, but if it resists healing and hangs around more than a couple of weeks, get yourself checked by a doctor. Plus, if your lips crack and get infected when they're chapped, a doctor can prescribe antibiotics to get you back in shape.

Nutritional remedies:

Drink up. Whether the furnace is cranked up at work on a wintry day, or you're hiking on a sun-baked trail over the weekend, you need to drink liquids, says Diana Bihova, MD, a dermatologist and author of *Beauty from the Inside Out.*

Say yes to yoghurt. If the corners of your mouth have become red, chapped and cracked, your problem may be an overgrowth of yeast (a fungus organism), caused perhaps by antibiotics or stress, says Lenore S. Kakita, MD, a dermatologist. If you have a cold, or if saliva slips into the corners of your mouth when you're asleep, yeast can break down that sensitive skin. Head to the supermarket for liquid acidophilus yoghurt, and swish it in your mouth several times a day, Dr. Kakita advises. Conditions such as diabetes may even be the culprit, so if the condition is consistent or severe, see your physician. An antifungus preparation or oral medication may be needed.

Helpful vitamins and supplements:

Get needed vitamins. A lack of B-complex vitamins and iron can play a part in the scaling of lips and cracking corners of the mouth. Use a multivitamin to make sure you're getting enough.

Everyday prevention:

Call in the balm squad. Using lip balm regularly is the best way to keep lips moist and prevent chapped lips, says Sylvia Brice, MD, a dermatologist. "All lip balms, no matter what their ingredients, are basically a way to replace or add to the normal, moisture-retaining barrier of the skin," she explains. How often should you use lip balm to prevent your lips from chapping? It depends on where you live and the time of year. "I live in Denver," says Dr. Brice. "It's very dry, it's cold in the winter, and there is lots of sun. A person living here should use lip balm on a daily basis, applying it a couple of times a day." If your neck of the woods is less dry, less cold, or less sunny, you may be able to use lip balm less frequently.

Choose a product with sunscreen. The lips take a solar beating just like other areas of the face that are exposed to sunlight, but they typically don't get protection from sunscreen, says Richard Odom, MD, a dermatologist. That is why he suggests using a lip balm with a sun-blocking ingredient. But he adds this caution: Some people are sensitive to sunscreen, and their lips can become chapped because they are using it on their lips. If you notice any itching or redness, go back to a lip balm without the extra protection.

Turn to old faithful. Who can imagine the uses that the old standby, Vaseline, has seen? It has never been better than as a treatment for chapped lips, says Dr. Alexander H. Murray. Apply as needed to your parched lips, and give dryness the kiss-off.

Tap into hydro power. Hydrocortisone in a 1 percent balm comes in a little tube available over the counter at any chemist and most supermarkets. It promotes healing and can stave off infections in cracked lips, says Abraham R. Freilich, MD, a dermatologist. Apply to your lips a couple of times a day when you have chapped lips.

Hit the kitchen. If you don't have anything else in the house, use Crisco. That will moisturise your lips," says Judy Johnson, R.N., a nurse in a dermatology office in Alaska. Dunk your finger into that familiar blue can or box and slide a thin coating on your parched puss. You don't have to be brand-conscious either, she says. Any vegetable shortening you have will do just as well. Not only will you get some instant relief but also you'll be able to grease up the cookie sheet in a whole new way.

Use the stick, not the lick. Yes, licking your lips moisturises them, but only for a few seconds. The new coating of water on your lips evaporates immediately, and that makes your pucker even more parched. Not only that, but your saliva has digestive enzymes in it, which irritate your lips. "Licking your lips causes chapped lips," says Dr. Brice. But for many people, trying to stop lip-licking is about as easy as trying to stop blinking.

Make an herbal lip balm

You can make a basic protective and moisturising herbal lip balm in just a half-hour, says Shatoiya de la Tour, herbalist and founder of Dry Creek Herb Farm and Learning Centre in California. Here's her formula, which can be customised by adding essential oils or tints as needed.

De la Tour recommends using olive oil, almond oil, or a mixture of the two, but you can experiment with other oils to find one you like best. And for storage, "you can buy little jars and lip-balm tins from catalogues, or you can save jars," de la Tour says. "I love little pimiento jars—they're just the right size." If stored away from extreme heat, balms can last for years, but if you detect a rancid odour, the balm has gone bad.

Before you start, assemble all of your materials so that you can work quickly:

Oil
A small saucepan
Beeswax (available by mail)
A measuring teaspoon
Measuring cups
Small jars with tight-fitting lids

Warm the oil. First, put the teaspoon in the freezer to chill. Then gently warm 1 cup of oil in a saucepan over very low heat. While the oil warms, put 1¼ ounces of beeswax into a glass measuring cup and melt on low heat in the oven for about 20 minutes.

Add wax. Pour the melted beeswax into the warm oil. Test the consistency by dipping the frozen spoon into the warm mixture, then putting it back in the freezer for about 30 seconds. When you remove the spoon from the freezer, rub your finger through the balm. It should be soft enough to apply to your lips but not runny "If the balm is too soft, add more beeswax," says de la Tour. "If it's too hard, add more oil. You can customise the mixture by adding more beeswax or oil to create a softer balm for home use or a harder balm that won't melt so easily for travel." At this point, you can add essential oils or other custom ingredients to the basic lip balm, depending on your needs.

She suggests carrying lip balm with you wherever you go and using it every time you feel like licking your lips. Dr. Brice says that lipstick can function just like a lip balm with sunscreen. Lipstick is based in a fatty ingredient, so it provides a barrier to keep moisture in. "And since most lipsticks are opaque, they protect you from the sun," she says. "It is probably the only makeup that is good for your skin."

Bathe sparingly. If chapped skin is a problem on the body, bathe only on

Pour and store. Finally, while the balm is still a warm liquid, spoon it into clean jars. Lay wax paper over the tops of the open jars while the balm cools to keep it clean. Cap the jars after the balm has completely hardened.

Other options:

Before beginning the recipe, infuse your chosen base oil with an herb to add scent and healing power to your balm. Lavender, calendula, plantain, nettle, camomile, and comfrey are all good choices that soothe and promote healing.

Short on time? Adding 1 drop of essential oil to a cup of the plain base oil is a shortcut that lends aroma and healing qualities to your balm. Try peppermint, lavender, camomile, or rose.

If you tend to get fever blisters or sun blisters on your lips, make a protective balm. Start with a ready-made infused oil from a catalog or health food store, or make your own. Replace 1/4 to 1/2 cup of the base oil with oil infused with St.-John's-wort, which has antiviral properties. Then infuse the new oil with usnea, a bacteria-fighting lichen.

To add a rainbow of hues to your next pot of lip-shiner, use the techniques that follow.

For a reddish tint: Steep a teaspoon of alkanet in the base oil for your lip balm for 10 minutes, strain the oil, then proceed with the recipe, suggests de la Tour. "This root adds a slight red colour," she says. "It's a nice touch." Look for alkanet at health food stores or in mail-order catalogues.

For a custom colour: Warm 2 ounces of castor oil in a small saucepan and stir in half a tube of your favourite colour of moisturising lipstick until it melts. Stir thoroughly and pour it into a small wide-mouth glass or plastic jar. Add the colour as desired to the basic lip balm recipe. "That way, you get exactly the lip gloss colour you're looking for," she says.

---

alternate days. You'll cut down on contact with soap and water, which strip away the skin's natural protective oils. Bathe in tepid water and avoid bubble bath. Bath oils will help your skin retain moisture. Afterwards, apply an oil-based lotion or petroleum jelly while you're still damp.

Wash only when needed. To help chapped hands heal, limit hand washing to after using the bathroom and before handling food. When washing dishes, wear rubber gloves with cotton gloves inside them.

Thumb your nose at it. If you're stuck at the top of the ski hill and feel your lips withering, use your head. Or nose. Run your finger over the side of your nose or forehead and borrow some skin oil. Transplant it to your lips. "If you have oily skin, that will work in the short term," says Johnson.

Humidify while you sleep. During the winter, dry indoor air can turn your lips into little Saharas. To help counter the problem, Dr. Brice says to use a humidifier in your bedroom. Keep it on while you sleep, she advises.

Be careful of oral hygiene products. A skin sensitivity or allergy to products like mouthwash or toothpaste can cause chapped lips, says Dr. Odom. If you have recently switched brands and notice that your lips are itchy, swollen, or have a rash, stop using the new product.

Change toothpaste. Certain toothpaste can promote chapping in some sensitive people, Dr. Freilich says. The flavouring agents seem to be the main culprit. He suggests brushing with just water or with baking soda when your lips are chapped.

Try Aquaphor or Atrixo which are available at most chemists. "It's like a heavy-duty Vaseline," says Johnson. It stays on longer than Vaseline, she adds, but is extra greasy. Use it when you need relief. Just be sure to warn your woman before you plant one on her.

Herbal help:

Oil your lips. Add two drops of camomile oil and two drops of geranium oil to two teaspoons of aloe vera gel. Apply to lips.

Rushed? Reach for castor oil. If you have absolutely no time to whip up lip balm, go for castor oil, suggests Stephanie Tourles, a licensed aesthetician, and author of *The Herbal Body Book*. "Get a little bottle at the chemists," she says. "Its really, really thick and costs very little money. When I want a lip treatment with staying power, I use castor oil. It coats your lips with a thick lacquer of shine." If your lips are really chapped and sore, add tea tree or eucalyptus essential oil. "Use 10 drops of essential oil in a 2-ounce bottle of castor oil," Tourles says. "Both are very soothing and healing."

Childbirth Pain

The pain: It's not hard to figure out where labour it got its name. Birthing a baby is hard labour—literally. And there's no way around it: From the first contractions to the final pushes that send your baby into the world, delivery usually hurts. Natural remedies can help ease the pain and prepare your body for the work ahead so that you stay more comfortable.

Medication: The most common medical option for pain relief during childbirth is the epidural. In an epidural, doctors inject a small amount of a numbing drug near the spine. "Epidurals can provide virtually complete relief from labour pain," says Mark Norris, MD, a professor of anaesthesiology, obstetrics, and gynecology. Serious side effects are rare. Moreover, the pain medications used today allow a woman to avoid the pain while still being alert and "present" during the delivery.

You should know, however, that some doctors believe that epidurals slow labour and increase the risk of caesarean delivery. Dr. Norris admits that anaesthesia during delivery remains controversial. Your best bet is to "discuss your options with your obstetrician and anaesthesiologist well before you go into labour," he says.

Preparing for the big event:

Attend childbirth education classes. "The more you know about childbirth, the less you will fear the experience," says Carrie Klima, R.N., a certified nurse-midwife and assistant professor at the Yale University School of Nursing. "Fear can make you anxious, and anxiety can make you more sensitive to pain and less able to control it." Don't wait until the last three months of your pregnancy to enrol in a class. The earlier you start, the more time you have to practice the skills that you will need during labour. You may want to attend a few different types of classes to compare their philosophies and methods.

Encourage your husband to attend classes with you. These days, hospital allows husbands to stick around for the duration of the childbirth process. You are both better off if he has at least some knowledge what to expect. Most childbirth education classes include husbands.

Relax. Learning relaxation techniques such as deep breathing also seems to help lessen childbirth pain. Studies show that pregnant women who practice these techniques for 30 minutes during the day have quicker, easier labours, according to Nancy Marshutz, R.N., a nurse-midwife. You can choose from various techniques, such as progressive relaxation, which releases the tension muscle by muscle, according to Wendy Hoffman, a certified childbirth educator and labour assistant.

Studies have shown that it takes about three months of practice to become proficient in a particular relaxation technique, so start your training early. A good childbirth education class should teach you a number of relaxation techniques. "You may need just one to get you through labour and delivery, or you may need to switch from one to another as the process becomes more intense," notes Hoffman.

Consider a Midwife. Women who opt for natural childbirth often choose to deliver with the help of a certified nurse-midwife. Certified nurse-midwives use a variety of natural methods to help a woman manage childbirth pain, such as visualisation, self-hypnosis, massage, and soothing lighting and music. "If a birth proceeds normally, most women don't need pain medication," contends Marshutz. "But if they do, there is always the option of going to hospital." If you opt for natural childbirth, however, you should know that anaesthesia may be required if you need a caesarean section.

Consider hiring a certified labour assistant. This person stays with you throughout your entire labour. Like a midwife, she can help you (and your husband) with all sorts of pain-relieving tactics: getting you into a comfortable position, giving you a massage, and coaching you through your relaxation techniques. Labour assistants are certified by a number of organisations.

Do Kegel exercises. To strengthen and tone muscles used during childbirth, this routine works your pelvic-floor muscles, which support the pelvic organs. The key to performing Kegels correctly is squeezing the muscles as though you were trying to stop the flow of urine. Hold for a count of 10, then release. Do 20 repetitions, five times a day. You can do them anywhere—at your desk or in the car while waiting for the traffic light to change, for example. Although these directions may seem simple, some women find that learning proper technique from a trained health professional helps. Ask your obstetrician or midwife for a referral.

Accept pain as part of childbirth. "Pain is totally subjective," notes Debra Grubb, MD, director of the Natural Choice Birth Centre in California. "A woman who views labour as hurtful or even life-threatening will experience a lot more pain than a woman who welcomes labour as the final step toward having the baby that she has waited so long for. It really comes down to trusting the process. Childbirth has evolved over millions of generations, and it works."

Relief during labour:
Move around rather than lying down. Take a walk, practice your

squats-do whatever feels right for you at the moment. "Labour is a dynamic process, explains Dr. Grubb. "Your baby is trying to manoeuver into the birth canal. By changing positions frequently, you give your baby a number of opportunities to find his way out, however he fits best." Also, research has shown that staying mobile decreases the length of labour and makes it more comfortable for the mother.

Vary your positions. Changing positions frequently during labour may distract you somewhat from the pain and may even relieve some discomfort. Shifting positions (such as from lying on your back to squatting), for instance, may improve the alignment of the foetus in relation to the birth canal. This can help reduce pain and encourage the baby's descent in preparation for childbirth.

Add some heat. Warm compresses are really helpful. A warm washcloth placed on your lower abdomen right above your pubic bone, either during or between contractions, is fine.

Avoid lying flat on your back. It is the worst position that you can be in when you are in labour. "It shifts the weight of your uterus, impedes blood flow to the uterus and your baby, and limits your baby's ability to rotate into the proper position for delivery," according to Klima. It's better to lie on your side, sit up, or walk around.

Take a warm shower or sit in a warm bath. Being surrounded with and supported by water helps relax tense muscles, explains Klima. This, in turn, lowers your perception of pain and encourages relaxation. Some birthing centres and hospitals have tubs in which you can sit during labour. And some even perform deliveries right in the water.

Try accupressure. Using your thumbs, apply pressure to the left and right sides of your sacrum (the triangular bone at the base of your spine). This acupressure technique works especially well if you are having back labour, in which pain settles into your lower back, says Ming Ming Molony, O.MD, a licensed acupuncturist and doctor of Oriental medicine in private practice. You will know when you have hit the right points. They will feel tender at first, but as you press them, the pain win ease up. You can apply pressure as long as it feels good or helps the pain. If you have difficulty reaching your back, ask your husband or labour assistant to lend a hand.

Focus on relaxation. Natural breathing will follow. "You instinctively know how to breathe during labour, and you are going to do it right no matter how you are trained," says Dr. Grubb. "Just be aware that your breathing pattern is going to change and that you shouldn't try to fight it."

Practice guided imagery. This mind-body exercise supports childbirth by helping you to relax, relieving pain, and creating a positive emotional environment, explains Carl Jones, a certified childbirth educator and author of *Mind over Labour and Childbirth Choices Today.* Like other relaxation techniques, guided imagery works best if you learn and practice it before you go into labour.

One exercise, called opening flower, can help you relax as your cervix during the early stages of labour. To try it, simply create a mental picture of a flower bud slowly opening into full bloom, coaxed along by the sun's rays.

Another exercise, called radiant breath, is especially helpful during the final stages of labour, when contractions are coming fast and furious. As the name suggests, you "see" your breath as soft, radiant, and golden. With each inhalation, imagine your breath filling your womb with energy.

If you have difficulty conjuring either of these images, you may do better to visualise what is really happening, says Jones. "See your baby's head pushing through and widening the cervix, as though he were slipping on a turtleneck sweater," he suggests.

Listen to music. Any soft, harmonious composition can help you relax. And if you have played it for your baby in utero, the baby may respond to it, too, says David Chamberlain, Ph.D., president of the Association for Pre- and Perinatal Psychology and Health in San Diego. Keep in mind, though, that loud music with a strong beat seems to make babies move and kick a lot-not what you want during childbirth. In one study, babies preferred Mozart to rock'n'roll. Lullabies are always safe.

You can buy recordings of music created specifically to soothe you and your baby during labour. For information, write to Transitions Music at P.O. Box 8532, Atlanta, GA 30306.

Herbal help:

Herbs can play an important role in preparing a woman's body for the hard work of labour and delivery, says Mary Bove, N.D., a naturopathic doctor, midwife, and member of Britain's National Institute of Medical Herbalists. Afterward, botanical skin washes and a simple "recovery tea" can soothe stretched skin and help the uterus begin contracting.

Ask about mother's cordial. "There are specific herbs that herbalists, naturopaths, and herbally trained midwives recommend for birth preparation," Dr. Bove notes. "But they should only be used in the last month of pregnancy and under the supervision of a health-care professional." Dr. Bove suggests asking your caregiver about mother's cordial for birth preparation. "The herbs in this formula help the cervix soften and shorten so that it can dilate more easily," she notes. "It also helps prime the uterine muscle so it's ready to contract smoothly during labour and clamp down after birth to prevent haemorrhageing." If you are interested in trying this, speak to an herbally trained health practitioner. Do not take this without medical supervision because taking too much or using it too soon can cause premature labour.

Drink raspberry tea daily. Herbal experts call raspberry leaf the top pregnancy herb. Raspberry leaf is rich in vitamins and minerals and contains a substance that helps prepare the uterus for labour and birth," notes Aviva Romm, a certified professional midwife, and herbalist and is the author of *The Natural Pregnancy Book*. Drink a cup or two daily during

Episiotomy Pain

Sometimes, under the force of expelling a full-term baby, the tissues between the vulva and anus tear or the pelvic muscles weaken and lead to a bulge in the bladder or rectum. To prevent tearing in this tender area (called the perineum), physicians and midwives sometimes take pre-emptive action and make a neat, clean cut (an episiotomy) to enlarge the birth opening. The incision is stitched up after delivery.

If you've had an episiotomy or a natural tear during delivery, intercourse could be uncomfortable for as long as three to six months. Sitting, walking, and urinating can be painful for a few weeks.

You can take the following natural steps to encourage healing and reduce pain and swelling in this sensitive area. If the pain worsens or doesn't subside within two weeks, or if you experience sudden bleeding, your episiotomy may be infected. Call your doctor right away.

Chill out the swelling. To reduce inflammation, apply ice packs to the incision as needed for 15 to 20 minutes at a time for the first 12 hours after delivery. Look for cold packs that are about the size of sanitary pads and contain dry ice; they're sold at chemists and medical supply stores. When you crack the pack, it becomes cold. Remember to wrap it in a towel to prevent skin damage.

Take a sitz bath. Relaxing in a tub of water, either a shallow sitz bath or a deep regular bath, provides relief.

One study compared cold sitz baths with warm ones. The researcher found that the women who took cold soaks had less pain afterward because cold acts as an analgesic. But if warm water feels better to you, that's fine, too. Warmth increases circulation to the area and aids healing.

Wash with herbs. To soothe tenderness, relieve inflammation, aid healing, protect against bacteria, and improve circulation, try this herbal combination. Put one handful each of calendula flowers, comfrey root, yarrow flowers, and rosemary leaves into a pint of boiling water. Remove from the heat, cover, and steep for several minutes. Strain the liquid and transfer it to a plastic squirt bottle.

When the liquid has cooled to room temperature, use it to wash your vaginal area after you urinate. Or you can make a large batch and use it in a sitz bath. Simply pour the room-temperature liquid into a clean, shallow pan large enough to sit in, then do exactly that—sit in it for 10 to 15 minutes. You can store the solution in the refrigerator for two to three days. Let it warm to a comfortable temperature before using.

Try vitamin E. Vitamin E has skin-healing properties and is often prescribed to people who have undergone surgery. If you have had an episiotomy, wait a couple of weeks for the laceration to heal a little—that is, when the incision is knitting back together, no longer weeps any fluid, and shows no signs of infection. Then open a vitamin E capsule and apply the liquid to the area.

the second and third trimesters of pregnancy, Dr. Bove suggests. It helps the whole uterine muscle get co-ordinated so it can contract effectively during labour. To make raspberry-leaf tea, pour a cup of boiling water over 2 tablespoons of the herb and steep for 20 minutes. Labouratory studies show that raspberry leaf extracts nudge uterine contractions into a more regular rhythm. The effect may be due to an alkaloid that is found in high concentrations in raspberry leaves. As a bonus, raspberry can increase the flow of milk after childbirth.

Prepare your perineum with lavender, calendula, and oils. Some herbalists say that massageing the perineum (the area around the outside of the birth canal) with oil can help minimise tearing at birth. The same oils and herbs that make a good "belly balm" can help make your perineum supple and more stretchable during delivery. Dr. Bove suggests rubbing your perineum daily during late pregnancy with a teaspoon of the balm.

Ease labour pain with aromatherapy. During labour, lavender essential oil can help ease tension, while peppermint essential oil can ease any feelings of nausea that you may experience, Dr. Bove notes. "Put a few drops on a tissue and sniff as you need it," she suggests.

Rest more comfortably with passionflower. Take the edge off early labour pains and help yourself rest between contractions with passionflower tincture, Dr. Bove says. Research shows that passionflower, called a "rest-provoking agent" by herbal healers in the late nineteenth century, has sedative, anxiety-relieving properties in animal studies. "Passionflower is good during the early dilation stage," she notes. "It can help you stay calm, so you don't waste energy that you'll need for the birth." Take 30 drops of tincture in a little warm water. "If needed, take up to three doses 15 to 20 minutes apart, then wait four or five hours," Dr. Bove suggests.

Try Aviva's Pregnancy Tea This citrus-and-mint-flavoured beverage supplies a pregnant woman with fluid as well as small amounts of nutrients and herbal constituents that can help with birth and breastfeeding,

According to Romm, the raspberry leaves contain calcium and magnesium and help prepare the uterus for labour. Nettle, which contains vitamins and minerals, can help prevent haemorrhageing during delivery, and lemon balm, which adds a pleasant, citrus-mint flavour, has a calming influence. Oatstraw is also a nerve soother. Rose hips contain vitamin C and add a tart flavour and cranberry red colour to the tea. Alfalfa contains vitamins A,D, E, B6, and K as well as calcium, magnesium, and iron. Spearmint adds another minty note.

"Start drinking this tea in the second trimester, at about the 12th week of pregnancy," Romm suggests. "You can continue enjoying it throughout pregnancy, during labour, and after the baby is born, too. It helps with milk production."

"We keep a jar of it in the refrigerator, and everyone in my house drinks it," notes Romm, who has four children. "It tastes great hot or cold."

This combination is also good frozen. You can suck on ice pops made with it (just freeze it in small paper cups or use ice-pop moulds) during labour. Or drink it as a nutritive iced tea after labour, suggests Lisa Murray-Doran, N.D., a naturopathic doctor and instructor in obstetrics and gynaecology at the Canadian College of Naturopathic Medicine in Toronto.

Here's the recipe.

8   tablespoons raspberry leaf
8   tablespoons nettle
4   tablespoons oatstraw
2   tablespoons lemon balm
2   tablespoons rose hips
2   tablespoons spearmint leaf

Combine the herbs and store in a jar or airtight container. To prepare the tea, add 4 tablespoons of the herb blend to a quart jar, then fill the jar with boiling water. Cover and steep for at least 30 minutes. Strain, sweeten with honey if desired, and drink one to four cups a day, Romm suggests.

Cold Sores

The pain: A tingling sensation outside your mouth or above your lips is usually the telltale sign. Within two to three days, a painful, fluid-filled blister appears. It swells, ruptures, and oozes fluid that forms a yellow crust. Eventually, it peels off and reveals new skin underneath. The blister usually lasts 7 to 10 days.

The cause: What causes cold sores, commonly called fever blisters, is herpes simplex virus type 1 (HSV-1). About 90 percent of all people are infected with this virus. The infection usually takes place during childhood. In many cases, the person doing the infecting doesn't have an active cold sore, and the person being infected doesn't get one. In fact, in many people, the virus never produces an outbreak but simply hibernates in the nerves close to the lips. In approximately one-third of those who carry the virus, it crawls out of its cave 2 to 12 times a year and makes an unsightly, painful lip sore. Various factors can trigger an outbreak. Sickness is a common cause, tagging the condition with its two nonmedical names: cold sore and fever blister. Stress is often to blame, which is why cold sores have an uncanny ability to pop up exactly when you don't want them, like before an important date or job interview. Too much sunlight can often spark a sore. And so can direct trauma—for example, a shot of novocaine into nearby nerves.

See a doctor if:
...a mouth sore persists beyond 10 days with or without treatment time. Your doctor or dentist to determine if an underlying infection is causing the problem and can prescribe medication to solve the problem.
...you get four or more cold sores a year.
...you experience fever, swollen glands or flu-like symptoms with a cold sore.
...your cold sore is so painful that you have trouble eating or carrying our normal activities.

Medication:
If you know that you are prone to cold sores in some situations, your doctor might be able to help prevent that predictable outbreak. "I prescribe

acyclovir (Zovirax) to skiers who routinely get cold sores when they are in the mountains where the sun is more intense," says Sylvia Brice, MD, a dermatologist. "They can start taking the medication the day before they begin their ski trip, and it is very effective."

Acyclovir works by travelling directly to cells infected with the herpes virus and ordering the virus to calm down, to stop generating so many copies of itself. You can take the drug before events that you know typically trigger a sore: a day at the beach, a trip to the dentist, or a major stress. Or, says Dr. Brice, you can take the drug immediately at the first sign of a cold sore, the tingling, itching sensation that is all-too-familiar to those who have frequent outbreaks. In either case, you don't have to make an appointment every time you want to prevent an impending sore. Your doctor can write you a prescription for a supply that is sufficient for self-treatment.

Never use a topical steroid on a cold sore. Topical steroids can cause the herpes virus to spread.

Quick relief:

Dry it out. Soothe the sore area by applying a wet, warm face cloth over the area. Then, set your hair dryer on low and blow-dry the cloth. This will ease some of the pain.

Give it a frosty reception. If your lip starts tingling, put ice on it to slow the growth of the virus that causes cold sores. That should lessen the severity of an outbreak, Dr. Rodu says. Wrap an ice cube in a towel and apply it to the affected spot for 5 to 10 minutes, repeating about once an hour.

Lube up. Moisturising ointments such as petroleum jelly can soothe the pain and prevent cracking and bleeding skin, says Brad Rodu, D.D.S., a pathologist. Apply them as needed.

Paste it. Make a paste by mixing meat tenderizer with a few drops of water. For the first day, apply the paste to the cold sore every two to three hours and hold it on with a washcloth for 5-10 minutes. After the first day, reduce the treatment to three times daily. Repeat until the sore clears.

Get milk. A compress of whole milk placed directly on the cold sore can ease pain and speed the healing process. Allow the milk to sit at room temperature for 10-15 minutes before placing the compress on you skin. Be sure to rinse the skin afterwards. (Note: only whole milk, rather than skim or other kinds, has the extra protein needed for this remedy.)

Ongoing care:

Keep your hands off. People just don't realise how highly contagious cold sores are, says Geraldine Morrow, D.MD, past president of the American Dental Association, and a dentist in Anchorage, Alaska. "If you have a cold sore on your lip, don't pull it, don't stretch it, don't touch it." You could get "very, very painful" cold sores on your hands, especially if the fluids from the blister get under a hangnail, she says.

Sleep upright. If you have a cold sore, try propping a few pillows behind your head at bedtime, letting gravity help the blisters drain, recommends Lenore S. Kakita, MD, a dermatologist and an adviser to the American Academy of Dermatology. Otherwise, fluid may settle in your lip during the night.

Reschedule your dental appointment. The last thing that you want to do when you have a cold sore is "open wide," says Dr. Morrow. The movement will stretch your lips, aggravating your tender cold sore, and it could cause it to break open and spread.

Nutritional remedies:

Check your diet. To prevent cold sores, some naturopathic doctors advise that you eat more foods that are high in the amino acid lysine, such as yoghurt, chicken, fish, and vegetables. At the same time, they say, you should cut back on foods that are high in arginine, another amino acid. Foods that might be adding to your cold sore troubles include chocolate, nuts, seeds, and gelatin. Avoid spicy or acidic food during an outbreak, since they'll aggravate the sore and cause pain.

Defend with garlic. In test-tube studies, garlic has shown antiviral effects against herpes virus and many other viruses. Enjoy a few minced cloves tossed onto a plate of pasta, or add them to a mixed green salad.

Helpful vitamins and supplements:

Lick 'em with lysine. Lysine is an amino acid that inhibits the replication of herpes simplex. Research suggests that a diet high in lysine and low in arginine can prevent the virus from multiplying. Although it relies on arginine to thrive, the virus can't distinguish between lysine and arginine, so it's easily tricked into attaching itself to the lysine. But unlike arginine, lysine blocks the steps the virus must take to replicate. To keep lysine levels high, take 500 to 1,500 milligrams daily at the first sign of symptoms, says Jennifer Brett, N.D., a naturopathic doctor. Continue with that dosage until symptoms disappear. If you're having an outbreak, take 3,000 milligrams of lysine daily until the lesions disappear. Check with your doctor before you use this supplement, especially if you are pregnant or nursing.

Try vitamin C. Vitamin C with bioflavonoids should be your next line of defence. These supplements will boost your immune system by stimulating production of white blood cells, the infection fighters in your body. The blisters will heal faster as a result, says Dr. Brett.

Bioflavonoids, chemical compounds related to vitamin C, can help reduce the inflammation and pain that's associated with cold sores, says Dr. Brett. You can buy a formula that includes both bioflavonoids and C or take each as a separate supplement.

In one study, 20 people with cold sores took 600 milligrams of vitamin C and 600 milligrams of bioflavonoids three times a day for three days. Another 20 took 1,000 milligrams of C and 1,000 milligrams of bioflavonoids five times a day for the same amount of time. Ten participants received look-alike pills that didn't contain either of the active ingredients (placebos).

At the end of the study, researchers found that the vitamin C and bioflavonoids stopped the cold sores from blossoming into unsightly blisters. They also concluded that the therapy achieved the best results when people took the supplements at the first sign of symptoms.

This research also showed that taking the two together inhibits the progression of the virus. Those who were treated with 1,000-milligram doses had cold sores for a little more than 4 days. Those treated with placebos had sores for more than twice as long—at least 10 days.

To prevent cold sores, take 1,000 milligrams of vitamin C with bioflavonoids daily, Dr. Brett advises. To speed healing of existing sores, she recommends 3,000 milligrams of vitamin C daily in divided doses and 1,000 milligrams daily of quercetin, a commonly used bioflavonoid.

Zap 'em with zinc. Upping your intake of zinc can also reduce the frequency, duration, and severity of cold sore outbreaks. This mineral has been shown in test-tube studies to block the reproduction of the virus. It produces T lymphocyte cells, which are important body defences against viral infections.

During a cold sore outbreak, take 50 milligrams a day of zinc in divided doses with food, says Michael Traub, N.D., a naturopathic doctor. As a preventive, take 20 milligrams a day. Also, since zinc supplementation can lead to copper deficiency, you should take 1 to 2 milligrams of copper for every 25 milligrams of zinc you take, says Dr. Traub.

Everyday prevention:

Give it the brush-off. Switching to a new toothbrush at the right time may stop the spread of the virus in your mouth. A moist toothbrush can harbour the germs for up to seven days, spreading the virus to the lips and throughout the mouth each time you brush. Researchers say you should use three new toothbrushes during each outbreak. The first new brush should be opened during the tingly phase just before the blister appears. Get another new brush when the blister breaks. Get a third brush when the blister disappears.

Use clean cups. Be sure everyone has his or her own clean cup in the bathroom. Family members shouldn't share washcloths, towels or toothbrushes either, because this virus thrives for days on the dampness and can spread.

Play it safe in the sun. Sun exposure can trigger a cold sore outbreak. To prevent it, be sure to wear a lip balm that contains a sun protection factor of at least 15, Dr. Rodu suggests. Reapply it every hour as necessary. If you have an open cold sore, don't use the balm stick directly on your lips, or you'll spread the virus around, says Dr. Kakita. Instead, use a cotton swab to apply balm not only to your lips but also to the skin around the outside border.

Bundle up on blustery days. Cold, windy weather is a well-known trigger for cold sores. Always wear a ski mask, or cover your mouth with a scarf when the wind kicks up and temperatures tumble, Dr. Rodu advises.

Save your kisses for later. When you get a outbreak, avoid kissing and any direct contact with children—especially those under age 5, who are most susceptible to the herpes virus, Dr. Rodu says. Even after the scab has formed, you can still spread the virus, so wait a week or two after the scab comes off before resuming kissing or other mouth contact.

Avoid alcohol. It seems to evoke cold sores.

Herbal remedies:

Erase with echinacea. Medicinal herbs such as echinacea and St. John's-wort can also speed healing, lessen the severity, and shorten the duration of cold sores, says Dr. Traub. Echinacea, also known as purple coneflower, strengthens the immune system. It also increases the levels of a chemical called properdin, which activates the part of the immune system responsible for shoring up defence mechanisms against viruses and bacteria.

Dr. Traub recommends taking one 300-milligram capsule of echinacea four times a day during a cold sore outbreak. For prevention, take one 300-milligram capsule daily during times of stress or as soon as you feel a cold sore coming on, he says.

Wipe 'em out with wort. St. John's-wort has strong antiviral properties that may help to prevent the virus from replicating. In fact, this herb's antiviral activity is so significant that high concentrations of it have decreased HIV (the virus that causes AIDS) in a laboratory setting. The active ingredients that possess these antiviral properties are hypericin and pseudohypericin. During a cold sore outbreak, take one 300-milligram capsule of St. John's-wort daily, says Dr. Traub. Buy the standardised extract that contains 0.3 percent hypericin.

Have a tea party. Like some over-the-counter (OTC) drops, nonherbal tea contains tannic acid, too. The OTC medications are more effective, but you may want to try putting a wet tea bag on the sore for a few minutes every hour to provide temporary relief until you can get to the drugstore, Dr. Rodu says.

Soothe with lemon balm. Also known as melissa, lemon balm's demonstrated antiviral, anti-herpes properties seem to result from compounds in the herb, including tannins, that are known as polyphenols. The body's cells have receptors that viruses latch on to when they're trying to take over the cells. The polyphenol compounds have the ability to latch on to the cells' viral receptor sites. They take up those spaces and prevent the viruses from attaching to the cell, thus preventing the spread of infection. Mints, especially lemon balm, contain antioxidant vitamins and selenium, which strengthen the immune system. And all mints also contain at least four antiviral compounds that target the herpes virus. You can get results with herbal ointment containing lemon balm (widely available in Europe), or by using topical applications of lemon balm tea, which you can brew using two to four teaspoons of herb per cup of boiling water. Then apply with a cotton ball several times a day.

Try anti-herpes tea. In his book *The Green Pharmacy*, James Duke, Ph.D., recommends this " Happy Herpicide Tea," which is made from several herbs that are members of the mint family: hyssop, lemon balm, oregano, rosemary sage, self-heal and thyme.

To make the tea, fill a saucepan half full of water. Bring the water to a boil, then add fresh lemon balm leaves until the pan is about three-quarters full. If you don't have access to fresh leaves, you can use about a quarter-cup of dried lemon balm. (This is an usually high amount of herb for brewing a tea, but you really need a lot of it to get the antiviral action that you want.) To the lemon balm and water, add two parts each of dried oregano and self-heal and one part each of hyssop, rosemary, sage and thyme. Aside from the lemon balm. the actual amounts of the other herbs don't make much difference. Just make sure you use twice as much of the oregano and self-heal as you do of the others. Finally, toss in a little licorice root to sweeten the tea and steep it for 20 minutes. This mixture contains a dozen compounds that are active against herpes.

Add a dash of red pepper. The hot ingredient in red pepper is capsaicin. Tests on laboratory animals show that capsaicin can prevent outbreaks of herpes in the eye for up to two months. You wouldn't want to sprinkle cayenne on a cold sore. But why not season your Happy Herpicide Tea with hot-pepper sauce? Although you drink it rather than dab it on, you'll still benefit from the active ingredients.

Add essential oils. Aromatherapists note that combinations of essential oils, such as lemon and geranium or eucalyptus and bergamot, can be helpful against herpes if applied at the first sign of an outbreak. Some aromatherapists say that rose oil and lemon balm oil have contributed, in some cases, to complete remission of H. simplex lesions, sometimes after only one application. You can apply any of these oils topically using a cotton ball. Warning: essential oils are highly concentrated plant extracts. Make sure you never ingest them. Small qualities of some oils can be fatal.

Colic

The pain: When a pediatrician says a baby has colic, he's using a term that describes frequent attacks of abdominal pain that may originate in the infant's intestines. Though a baby with colic may cry to the point of exhaustion, the pain may be as upsetting to parents as to the child.

The cause: The cause of colic is not definitely known, but sometimes the attacks are associated with hunger or swallowing air. Occasionally the attacks end when the baby passes wind or has a bowel movement. Colic tends to be worst when a child is three weeks to three months old. It usually ends spontaneously, without any special help from parents, within five months.

Call the doctor immediately if:
...Your baby cries constantly for more than 3 hours and can't be consoled.
...The crying seems like a painful cry.
...New symptoms appear beyond the crying.
...The infant's behavior seems different than his normal behavior.
...You are feeling so tired and frustrated that you think you might hurt the baby.

Remedies:
Try a hum drum. Try anything that creates a low-level humming in the background: Running a vacuum cleaner, a dishwasher or another appliance can help calm colic.

Get a fish tank. "Some parents got an aquarium filter and put it in their baby's room," says pediatrician Ronald G. Barr, MD, director of Child Development at Montreal Childrens Hospital in Quebec. "The sound of the bubbles going through the filter helped quiet their colicky baby."

Put baby next to the washer. "For years, parents have been taking their colicky babies for a drive to soothe them—and it really works," adds Dr. Barr. But he points out that any movement that's soothing can help. So here's a variation. Put your baby in his infant seat, fasten him securely, and place the seat next to the washing machine or dryer while it's in operation, suggests Helen Neville, R.N., a pediatric nurse at Kaiser Permanente Hospital in California. For this to work, the seat must be touching the appliance, so the baby can feel the vibrations.

Use some pressure tactics. Take a hot water bottle and place it in the baby's crib. Then put a towel over the bottle and place the baby so that his head and feet drape over the bottle and his belly is on it. For some babies, "the warmth and pressure of the hot water bottle appear to help a lot," says pediatrician Birt Harvey, MD.

Schedule baby's playtime. Keeping a log of your child's episodes will help you recognize the times when baby is more agitated. "You can schedule specific playtimes to keep the baby happy, so he'll be less likely to have crying fits," says Becky Luttkus, head instructor at the National Academy of Nannies of Denver. "Keeping a calendar can also help you discover a pattern as well as aid your physician with data he might need," says Dr. Barr.

Give plenty of TLC. Snuggling is good medicine for crying babies, whether the sobs are caused by colic or something else. "Anything you can do to keep the baby calm and happy certainly helps," says Dr. Barr, who has studied the effects of snuggling on crying infants. One of the best ways to soothe your child is to pick him up, hold him and cuddle him.

Consider feeding. In the past, some doctors have suggested that babies should not be fed during a colic attack. But a growing number of doctors believe that food is the best thing for a colicky baby. "There's a lot of debate, but I think you should feel free to feed the baby as frequently as you wish," says pediatrician Dr. Barr, "When a baby is fed, he's not crying because he's eating, and in cultures where babies are fed three or four times an hour, there is little colic. So I suggest trying to feed your baby during a colic attack."

Go with ginger ale. Ginger ale can coax wind from a colicky baby, just as it does in adults, says William J. Fanizzi, MD, a pediatrician, who's treated over 100,000 children during his 35-year career. But be careful how much you give an infant. "What does ginger ale do? You drink some ginger ale, and you burp a little bit—especially if it's bubbly," he explains. And when you burp, the ginger ale and some of the wind that's stuck in the stomach will come out, and you'll feel better. It's the same thing with kids. But I wouldn't advise giving ginger ale to a colicky kid more than a few times— they can get accustomed to the sweetness, and we don't want that." Try pouring about two ounces into a baby bottle and swishing it around until the fizz is nearly gone.

Feed with fennel. Fennel tea is a favorite colic remedy in Germany, says Varro E. Tyler, Ph.D., author of *The Honest Herbal.* "They've been using it for years," he says. Fennel not only helps expel wind but also has been found to have a calming effect, he says. Try using a cup of bottled water heated on the stove, mixing in a teaspoon of fennel seeds and a quarter teaspoon of raw sugar. After letting the mixture cool, strain out the seeds and pour it into the child's bottle.

Colitis

The pain: If you have ulcerative colitis, you'll know it. Symptoms include diarrhoea, bloody stools, cramps and abdominal pain, prompted by inflammation and sores in the large intestine.

The cause: Colitis is one of a group of conditions known collectively as inflammatory bowel disease. Ulcerative colitis causes open sores in the large intestine and almost always results in bloody, watery stools. Plain colitis, which is less severe, doesn't involve ulcers and tends to be confined to the upper part of the large intestine.

See a doctor if:
...you have frequent bouts of diarrhoea, bloody stools, cramps and abdominal pain. Your doctor can confirm the diagnosis and prescribe the proper course of treatment.
...you have known Crohn's disease or ulcerative colitis, and initial medication and dietary changes don't help during a flare-up.

Medication:
In ulcerative colitis, daily use of the prescription drugs sulfasalazine and 5-aminosalicylic acid components have been shown to prevent flare-ups. If you take sulfasalazine, you should also take a daily one-milligram supplement of folic acid.

Nutritional remedies:
Eat sparingly. Diarrhoea and cramps make it hard to tolerate any food at all when you're having an attack, says Sheila Crowe, MD, a gastroenterologist. To keep pain to a minimum, "eat very plain food, such as applesauce or boiled, skinless chicken or soft, cooked carrots—and not much of them," says Dr. Crowe.
For now, cut out the fibre. While your colitis is active, stick to bland, low-fibre, low-fat foods such as plain toast and gelatin, so that you won't irritate your colon, says Barbara Frank, MD, a gastroenterologist.
Pass up the popcorn. Seeds, nuts and popcorn irritate the bowel and, worse, impede its functioning during an attack, says Dr. Crowe.
If it hurts your stomach, stay away. There's no telling what might

worsen the pain—for some it may be spicy foods, for someone else, acidic foods or a seemingly innocuous spoonful of cereal, or any food imaginable. "If you feel worse after eating any type of food at all, don't eat it during an attack," advises Dr. Crowe.

Super nourish yourself. "During colitis flare-ups, you may feel too rotten to eat well, so it's important to eat a high-quality diet the rest of the time," says Joel Mason, MD, a nutritionist and gastroenterologist."You want to build an adequate store of nutrients in your body."

Drink deeply. If you have diarrhoea (and you probably do), you may get dehydrated. To replace lost fluid, try to drink at least ten glasses of water or juice a day during an attack, says Dr. Crowe.

Be your own diet detective. Since each individual case of colitis is so different, you need to be on the lookout for specific foods that your body may not tolerate well, says Stephen McClave, MD, a gastroenterologist. If a specific food causes trouble on multiple occasions, avoid it. But if it happens only once, retest. If you find that cabbage makes your symptoms worse, for example, don't avoid all leafy vegetables.

Try pectin protection. Fibre may be an important dietary help for colitis sufferers, says Danny Jacobs, MD, a surgeon and assistant professor of surgery at Harvard Medical School. And pectin, the soluble fibre found in apples and other fruits and vegetables, is particularly pleasing to the colon. "Apples are a marvelous source of pectin," he says, "and as long as you don't eat the seeds (or peels), there's no limit to how many you can consume."

Fix friendly fruits. James Scala, Ph.D., a nutritional biochemist offers these suggestions for taking the trouble out of fruit by reducing the amount of fibre. Be sure to peel all fruits (even grapes!), he advises. And if you're eating a citrus fruit, cut it into sections, removing all white, fibrous material. Dr. Scala also recommends eating canned fruit that's preserved in juice rather than sugary syrup. And be sure to avoid dried fruit.

Lighten up on lactose. Inability to digest lactose, the sugar in milk, can be a factor in colitis, says Dr. McClave. "A lot of us teeter on the edge of milk intolerance, and a bowel disease like colitis can tip the balance." By avoiding all milk products, you may be able to reduce your symptoms.

Avoid crunchy veggies. You need to take the crunch out of carrots, asparagus, zucchini, squash and other popular vegetables, says Dr. Scala. The best way is to cook them until they are very tender, he says. Pressure cooking is especially effective.

Cook with onion. "In my database, the top compound with anti-inflammatory bowel disease effects is quercitin, and the best source of this compound is onion skins," says James A. Duke, Ph.D., author of *The Green Pharmacy*. He suggests putting the whole onion, skin and all, into soups and stews while cooking. Remove the parchment like skin at the last moment before serving. Naturalists suggest taking 400 milligrams of quercitin, available at health food stores, about 20 minutes before each meal.

Tell it to Dear Diary. Recording your foods, moods and flare-ups can help, says Dr. Scala. "Keep track not just of what you ate or drank but also where, when, why and how you felt at the time. If you can relate the onset of a flare-up to a food or an emotional experience, you'll be able to manage your illness more effectively in the future."

Helpful vitamins and supplements:

Supplement your strategy. Since colitis can attack your nutritional status, multivitamin/mineral supplements are important, says Dr. Scala. "Take a multivitamin/mineral supplement that provides twice the Recommended Dietary Allowance of key nutrients," he recommends. "For the small price, it's worth it."

Fuel yourself with folate. People with ulcerative colitis should consider taking a daily multivitamin/mineral supplement that contains at least 400 micrograms of folate, recommends Dr. Mason. This is particularly true for those individuals who use sulfasalazine (Azulfidine or Salazopyrin), the most commonly prescribed drug for controlling colitis. The drug tends to inhibit your body's ability to use this B vitamin, he says. If more than 400 micrograms of folate is taken per day, however, it should be done under the supervision of a physician.

Everyday prevention:

De-stress for less distress. After food intolerance, emotional stress is the biggest challenge for colitis sufferers, says Dr. Scala. To reduce stress, he calls for "a regular exercise program. Exercise will dissipate the effects of stress better than anything." In addition, Dr. Scala recommends stress counseling. A psychologist or therapist can teach you relaxation techniques like progressive relaxation or meditation.

Check your medicine chest. Ulcerative colitis patients need to be cautious about using nonsteroidal anti-inflammatory drugs, warns Gary R. Gibson, MD, assistant professor of medicine at Northeastern Ohio University College of Medicine. Over-the-counter ibuprofen (Advil), aspirin and a dozen prescription drugs can erode the lining of the small intestine and colon. Be sure to check with your doctor before taking any of these medication.

Herbal help:

Try psyllium. Metamucil is a commercial fibre product that is basically ground psyllium seeds and husks with some flavouring added. Metamucil works as a laxative because in the intestine, the mucilage in psyllium seeds absorbs water and swells to many times its original size. It adds bulk to stool and helps stimulate the muscle contractions we experience as "the urge." Psyllium's ability to absorb fluids also makes it useful for treating diarrhoea, a common colitis symptom. In addition, as it travels through the digestive tract, psyllium exerts a soothing effect, which may help relieve the cramping of colitis. If you use psyllium, make sure that you also drink plenty of fluids. Also watch how you react to it if you have allergies. If allergic symptoms develop after you take it once, don't use it again.

Take some tea. Commission E, the body of experts that advises the German government about herbs, suggests using astringent herbs containing tannin, such as tea, for relieving gastrointestinal distress. Besides plain beverage tea, several common herbs are rich in tannin, including bayberry, bugleweed, billberry, black walnut, English walnut, carob and raspberry.

Ease with valerian. An Italian study suggests that valerian is a useful addition to other medicines that relieve spasms in smooth muscles such as the intestine. Valerian also helps relieve stress, which apparently contributes to inflammatory bowel disease.

Try essential oils. Aromatherapists recommend massage with a few drops of any of the following essential oils diluted in a few tablespoons of vegetable oil: basil, bergamot, camomile, cinnamon, garlic, geranium, hyssop, lavender, lemongrass, rosemary, thyme and ylang-ylang. Massage is relaxing, and using essential oils makes it even more relaxing. Relaxation helps relieve the stress of having inflammatory bowel disease. (Remember that essential oils are for external use only.)

Other herbs can help. Herbalists recommend camomile, peppermint and wild yam to help relieve muscle spasms, including those of the intestine. Noted British herbalist David Hoffmann, author of *The Herbal Handbook*, suggests treating with a combination herbal cocktail of two parts bayberry and one part each of camomile, mugwort, peppermint, valerian and wild yam. Herbal pharmacologist Daniel Mower, Ph.D., author of *The Scientific Validation of Herbal Medicine and Herbal Tonic Therapies*, recommends several herbs for treating ulcerative colitis and Crohn's disease, including fenugreek, gentian, Inger, goldenseal, licorice root, myrrh gum and papaya leaf.

Constipation

The pain: Difficult or infrequent bowel movements.

The cause: For food to be properly digested, it needs to encounter a number of chemicals as it works its way toward the colon. Among them are beneficial bacteria, stomach acid, pancreatic enzymes, and the yellowish substance called bile that comes from the liver. If these partners have done their work, food wastes are almost in the form of a stool by the time they reach your colon. There, your colon muscles quickly contract to move the waste to your rectum, which signals the brain to get you to a bathroom. But sometimes this digestive trip gets off track, and your colon holds on to waste.

When those stools remain in the colon for more than a few hours, they start to dehydrate and harden from lack of fluids. Occasionally, they develop rough edges that can cause microscopic tears in your rectum. That explains why bowel movements can be painful for someone who has been constipated: When you flex the muscles to move your bowels, the hard stools start scraping away at tender internal tissues. If you have trouble moving your bowels in more than one out of four attempts, you're probably constipated, says Christopher Lahr, MD. director of Complete Colon Care in South Carolina, and the author of *Shining Light on Constipation.*

See a doctor if:
...constipation is accompanied by abdominal pain, especially far removed from the bowel or anus, such as the right upper quadrant of your abdomen under your rib cage.
...you see blood in the stool.
...you've experienced fever or fatigue for more than a week or weight change.
...you've gone more than two weeks without a bowel movement.
"Don't use any treatment for more than a few weeks before seeing your doctor," adds Sam Sugar, M.D., a doctor in Illinois. Physicians want to know about changes in bowel habits.

Medication:

The medications you take to treat an existing condition may occasionally cause constipation. Pain medications, especially narcotics like codeine and morphine (Duramorph), can induce the gut to slow down its normal functioning, says Dr. Lahr.

Here are other drugs that could lead to constipation:

Over-the-counter (OTC) antacids, for example aluminium hydroxide (Alu-Cap) and calcium carbonate (Tums)

Antidyskinetics, which are prescribed to treat Parkinson's disease, for example benztropine (Cogentin) and trihexyphenidyl (Artane)

Tricyclic antidepressants, for example amitriptyline (Elavil).

Lithium (Lithane), which is prescribed for manic-depressive illness.

Calcium channel blockers, especially verapamil (Isoptin or Berkatens) used to control high blood pressure.

OTC diarrhoea products such as loperamine (Imodium A-D).

OTC and prescription iron supplements for example ferrous fumarate (Femiron or Pregaday).

If you're taking these medicines under a doctor's direction, don't stop without checking with your doctor first. Just let your doctor know that you're having a problem with constipation—and maybe she can recommend some substitutes.

Quick relief:

Have some honey. Stir two teaspoons of honey into a 10-ounce glass of warm water. Drink this lubricating liquid on an empty stomach and you'll be relieved within a half-hour, says Maoshing Ni, Ph.D., a doctor of Oriental medicine and licensed acupuncturist. Dr. Ni recommends repeating this treatment as needed up to three times a day.

Flush it. An enema may also induce defecation within 30 minutes. Use a single pint of water or salt water, doctors suggest. Avoid over-the-counter enemas containing soapsuds, sodium phosphate, or biphosphate, each of which can irritate and even damage the bowels. An oil-retention enema may be helpful in loosening a hard stool and is available in disposable bottles at your local drugstore. Follow package directions.

Use a footstool. "If you're constipated, propping your feet up on a stool with your knees bent while you sit on the toilet will straighten the angle of your bowel and help you pass stool more quickly," says Jacqueline Wolf, MD a gastroenterologist.

Mow to go. "Mowing the lawn or running a vacuum cleaner can both help relieve constipation," says Joyann Kroser, MD a gastroenterologist. Just walking around tends to loosen things up. For a more aerobic remedy, take that old Schwinn for a spin around the neighbourhood.

Take a dose of encouragement—but not too often. Popular stool-moving remedies such as enemas, stool softeners, and castor oil have all shown positive effects. They mildly irritate the colon into action and slow down water absorption from the gut. Don't use any of these habitually, though, says Dr. Sugar. Used long term, these powerful remedies can damage your colon.

Nutritional remedies:

Breakfast with bran. Bran, the high-fibre portion of grains, is a constipation-prevention all-star. Study after study has shown that it is the most effective fibre you can eat to keep your body regular. "If you are really serious about preventing constipation, eat a cereal every day that is 100 percent bran," says Harris R. Clearfield, MD a gastroenterologist. But go slowly, he suggests. Start by topping your regular cereal with a small amount of bran cereal and then gradually change the ratio of the cereals until you have a full serving of the bran.

Flavor your health with fruit. Add a topping of sliced fruit to your bran cereal, Dr. Clearfield suggests. "People have more frequent bowel movements during the summer simply because they are eating more fruit," says Dr. Schuster. Most fruits will help to some degree, but the best is famous for what it does: prunes have a renowned laxative effect on the digestive system.

Add fibre. The root of the word constipation means "to press or crowd together." Think of the freeway at rush hour with cars just inching along. Your listless gastrointestinal tract, if constipated, moves slower, unless you help it out. The best way to do this is to consume more fibre. Both soluble and insoluble fibre play a role in preventing constipation. Soluble fibre, which dissolves easily in water, takes on a soft texture in the intestines helping prevent dry, hard stools. Insoluble fibre passes almost unchanged through the intestines and adds bulk to the stool. "Try to get from 25 to 40 grams of fibre in your diet a day," says Dr. Lahr. High-fibre foods include beans, whole grains like buckwheat, bran cereals such as All-Bran, fresh fruits like avocados, and vegetables such as artichokes.

Go slow. Adding too much fibre too quickly to your diet may solve your constipation but replace it with wind, bloating, and diarrhoea. But you can avoid these side effects by introducing it slowly. Each week, increase your daily intake by no more than 5 grams, the amount of fibre in 1 cup of cooked carrots, suggests Dr. Lahr.

Wash it down. While fibre provides the bulkiness of fecal matter, it alone cannot ensure adequate passage of stools through the body. To complete the job, the bowel needs water. Without it, stools dry out and become difficult to pass. "The simplest way to influence your BM ability is to increase your intake of water," says Dr. Sugar. To maintain good bowel movements, he advises drinking six to eight glasses of water a day.

Watch out for water robbers. Coffee, tea and alcohol are all diuretics that can leave you somewhat dehydrated. Since you need fluids in your system to aid bowel movements, you're more likely to have constipation if you drink these beverages. When you do have them, go for moderation and help compensate by drinking plenty of water.

Don't skip meals. Often women—especially dieting women—get constipated because they eat only one large meal a day, says Joanne A. P. Wilson, MD, a gastroenterologist. "Eating stimulates the reflex that causes stuff to move forward in the gut. Women who diet often eat fewer meals to cut calories. That decreases movement through the gut." When nothing moves, you can't pass stool. Breakfast is particularly important, because that's what starts your digestive juices flowing every day.

Start the day piping-hot. Can't go to the bathroom in the morning without having a cup of coffee first? Join the unconstipated crowd. "A hot drink in the morning—tea, coffee, or even hot water—stimulates what is called the gastro-colic reflex, which often causes a bowel movement," says Dr. Clearfield. He recommends drinking a hot beverage when you get up or having it with breakfast.

Have a flaxseed-and-oatmeal breakfast. Heat one teaspoon of ground flaxseed in a quart of water, bring it to a boil, and simmer 15 minutes. Then add rolled oats to the water, following the directions on the box, and continue cooking until the oatmeal is cooked. This healthy breakfast soothes irritated intestines and may help unblock bowel movements, says David Molony, Ph.D., a licensed acupuncturist.

Try hot broth (or other natural laxatives). "If you have mild discomfort from constipation because you're travelling and can't get to the gym or eat your fruits and vegetables, try a glycerine suppository, milk of magnesia or prune juice," says Dr. Wilson. "Sometimes even a warm cup of broth will help your bowels move more quickly."

Avoid milk and cheese. If you have a problem with constipation, try avoiding milk products temporarily. Both milk and cheese contain casein, and insoluble protein that tends to plug up the intestinal tract.

Add some apple juice. Apple juice works wonders because it contains sorbitol, a natural sugar with laxative properties. So a glass a day might be just what you need to get things working again.

Swallow some seeds. The lubricating effect of pine nuts, flaxseed, and sesame seeds can all help ease a mild case of constipation, says Dr. Ni. Eating a whole handful of any of these, now available in many grocery stores, should do the trick. Dr. Ni recommends eating a handful once a day, chewing them well, and drinking a glass of water afterward.

Helpful vitamins and supplements:

Try C & M. The nutrients vitamin C and magnesium can help keep you regular, says Jullian Whitaker, MD founder and president of the Whitaker Wellness Centre in California. "In fact, in Germany, they actually sell powdered vitamin C as a laxative," he says. His advice: Take at least 500 milligrams of vitamin C and 400 milligrams of magnesium in supplement form every day to prevent constipation. When constipation occurs, he says to increase the dosages for both nutrients by 100-milligram increments each day until you get relief, up to a maximum of 5,000 milligrams of vitamin C and 1,000 milligrams of magnesium. Go back to the preventive

Filling up on Fibre

You can help prevent constipation by making high-fibre food choices at breakfast, lunch and dinner. Five servings of fresh fruits or vegetables a day plus six servings of whole-grain breads, cereals or legumes will give you the 25 grams of fibre recommended by the National Cancer Institute. Here are some great sources of fibre.

FOOD	PORTION	FIBRE (G.)
General Mills Fibre One cereal	½ cup	13.0
Barley, pearled	½ cup	12.3
Pears, dried	5 halves	11.5
Health Valley Fruit & Fitness cereal	¾ cup	11.0
Kellogg's AU-Bran cereal	⅓ cup	10.0
Nabisco 100% Bran cereal	½ cup	10.0
Blackberries	1 cup	7.2
Chick-peas	½ cup	7.0
Kidney beans	½ cup	6.9
Lima beans	½ cup	6.8
Refried beans, canned	½ cup	6.7
Black beans	½ cup	6.1
Raspberries	1 cup	6.0
Whole-wheat spaghetti	1 cup	5.4
Figs, dried	3 (about 2 oz.)	5.2
Lentils	½ cup	5.2
Succotash	½ cup	5.2
Post Raisin Bran cereal	¾ cup	5.0
Guava	1	4.9
Navy beans	½ cup	4.9
Artichoke hearts	½ cup	4.4
Pear	1	4.3
Oatmeal	½ cup	3.9
Raisins	½ cup	3.9
Wheat germ, toasted	¼ cup	3.7
Brussels sprouts	½ cup	3.4
Sweet potato	1	3.4
Orange	1	3.0
Apple	1	3.0

dosages once the problem has cleared, he says. If you develop diarrhoea, he adds, decrease the amount of vitamin C to 500 milligrams.

Buy bulk. For those people who want a simple, reliable daily dose of fibre, try a supplement (also called a bulk agent), such as Metamucil, Konsyl, FibreCon, or Citrucel (Fybogel or Celevac), recommends gastroenterologist Marvin M. Schuster. Mix the supplement in a glass of water or juice to help it work more effectively and take it with a meal. Start with one dose and increase to three times a day as needed. The supplement forms larger softer stools by combining with food. If you take it right before bedtime—as you would an over-the-counter laxative—it won't work nearly as well. He also says to check with your doctor about any medications you are taking that the supplement might block from being absorbed. If that is the case, take the medication about an hour before you take the supplement.

Add a little more. For his part, Dr. Lahr observes that underdosing on fibre additives could be a problem for many consumers. "The label recommends 1 tablespoon one to three times a day," he says. He agrees with the amount but has found that the dose is often more effective if taken all at once. "I have come upon this through trial and error over 10 years with thousands of patients. Start at the recommended level, but work up to 3 heaping tablespoons of the additives once a day. That will dramatically improve most people's bowel regularity," he observes. Just be sure that you have one 10-ounce glass of water when you take those 3 tablespoons.

Try milk of magnesia or magnesium citrate. Both of these laxatives will jump-start your digestive tract and induce a bowel movement anywhere from 30 minutes to 3 hours after you take them. They work by drawing fluid into the bowels and triggering the release of bowel-activating hormones. Neither, doctors warn, should be used on a regular basis, and they should not be used at all by people with kidney problems. Both should be taken with "an adequate amount of water," which is usually doctor-talk for one to two 8-ounce glasses of water.

Everyday prevention:

Move around. Sitting around directly affects the colon by making its work more sluggish. "We generally recommend just walking," Dr. Lahr explains. "Try to walk up to three miles a day." He says that bedridden people, who are frequent constipation sufferers, should at least stand up as often as possible (if your doctor says that it is safe for you to do), letting sheer gravity aid the digestive process.

Go when you have to. On occasion, according to Dr. Lahr, people simply ignore the urge to defecate. This may happen for a variety of reasons, but a primary one has to do with habit. "Some people don't want to go anywhere other than their own home," he explains. While he sympathises with that desire, he warns that ignoring the urge to move the bowels could lead to constipation. So wherever you are, try to go to the bathroom when you get the urge.

Heed warning signs. According to Dr. Lahr, some people accept constipation as a fact of life, ignoring symptoms or habitually treating them with quick-acting laxatives. Either approach could have serious consequences. "Those over age 65 are at high risk for colon cancer," he says, "and constipation can be a sign of colon cancer." So keep your doctor informed about your bowel movement patterns—and give a call immediately if constipation is accompanied by abdominal pain or if you see blood in the stool.

Make a toilet date—and keep it. You wouldn't dream of leaving the house without doing your hair. So why not take the same care with your colon? Eating, especially in the morning, is a wake-up call to the bowel, says Dr. Wilson. Yet what people do is get up, race out of the house, stop on the way for breakfast and head to the office. That doesn't give your bowel a chance to respond. And public bathrooms are not usually conducive to quiet time, and this causes further and further delays. The answer? Schedule time at home in the morning. Usually, the bowel is ready to expel its contents about half an hour after the first meal.

Sit or get off the pot. Trying to force out hard, dry, recalcitrant stool won't relieve your constipation; it may lead to haemorrhoids and a protrusion of rectal tissue through your anus, also known as prolapse of the rectum, says Dr. Wilson. If you really can't go after 15 minutes, get off the pot and try again later.

Get into training. You can actually train your bowels to get on a regular schedule, says Vera Loening-Baucke, MD a paediatrician. Her advice: sit on the toilet for about ten minutes after the same meal every day. The key is to stay relaxed. Eventually, says Dr. Loening-Baucke, your body will catch on.

Easing the pain with exercise:

Find the pressure point. In the ancient disciplines of acupressure and acupuncture, the miracle point for relieving constipation is the "hegu," located in the web between the index finger and the thumb. About a thumb's width down from the web on either hand, squeeze the hegu with the thumb and index finger of your other hand. Breathe deeply and continue throughout the day as often as you think of it until you feel the urge to visit the bathroom, says Robert Rakowski, D.C., a chiropractic physician, acupuncturist, and clinic director of the Natural Medicine Centre in Houston.

Pump up to pump it out. Strength training has also been shown to speed up bowel transit times, according to a study supervised by Ben F. Hurley, Ph.D., director of an exercise science laboratory. The seven men in Dr. Hurley's study worked out on weight-training machines three times a week for 13 weeks. Their transit times improved by an average of 56 percent. One possible explanation is that exercise raises the level of a gastrointestinal hormone that helps speed up the movement of stool through the intestine and the bowel.

Steer clear of strenuous, heavy lifting. Gentle weight training is good, but don't push the limits. When you exert yourself at weight lifting, you might aggravate haemorrhoids by increasing the pressure on your rectal area, says Benjamin Krevsky, MD a gastroenterologist.

Sit up for soothing. It's possible that abdominal exercises that work the muscles closest to the intestinal tract can also unblock the dam, says Dr. Hurley. The following simple crunch is easy and effective. He recommends doing it at least three times a week:

Lie flat on your back with your knees bent at about a 45-degree angle and your hands crossed over your chest or cupped behind your ears, with your elbows out.

Position your feet together flat on the floor, about six inches from your buttocks. Keep your legs slightly apart.

Curl your upper torso up toward your knees, raising your shoulder blades as high off the floor as you can. Only your shoulders should lift, not your lower back.

Hold your torso up for a second, feeling your abdominal muscles contract.

Return to the starting position, then continue without relaxing between repetitions. Repeat about 30 times or until you feel fatigued.

Put some spine into it. The spinal twist, a yoga position, can relieve constipation, says Richard Miller, Ph.D., a clinical psychologist and co-founder of the International Association of Yoga Therapists in California. He recommends practising the pose every day if you are frequently constipated.

Sit up straight in a chair with your feet flat on the floor. Gently twist your torso to the right, then take two or three deep, even breaths with long exhalations while holding the position. Gently twist to the left and again take two or three deep breaths. Doing this once is fine, but to enhance the results, do it two or three times. This will help the stool move down toward the rectum, says Dr. Miller.

Shoulder the burden. A yoga position called the shoulder stand can increase peristalsis, the tiny contractions that force stool through the bowels, Dr. Miller says. Begin by lying on your back on the floor, perpendicular to a wall, with the top of your head close to the wall. Supporting your lower back with your hands, raise your legs and move them past your head so that they lightly touch the wall. Be sure to put the weight on your upper back and shoulders, not on your neck, Dr. Miller advises. Breathe evenly with long exhalations. Hold the pose for 30 seconds at first, then work up to one to three minutes.

Just breathe. Regular, deep breathing works the diaphragm and relieves constipation, says Dr. Miller. Here's how to do it.

Lie flat on your back with the hardcover edition of War and Peace, Webster's Dictionary or some other heavy book on your stomach at the navel. Move the book up and down with your breathing for about 10 minutes a day, says Dr. Miller. Try to replicate that deep belly breathing while standing (without the book, of course) and take long, slow

Be Selective about Laxatives

Many over-the-counter products are sold as laxatives, but not all laxatives are recommended by doctors. In fact, heavy use of some laxatives can be counterproductive and even risky, according to Ronald L.Hoffman, MD director of the Hoffman Centre for Holistic Medicine in New York City. Heavy use of some laxatives can give you diarrhoea, according to Dr. Hoffman. And many are habit-forming: If you always rely on a laxative to prompt bowel movements, your body may begin to need it to trigger the action. Laxatives containing castor oil can damage your intestinal lining, and those that have mineral oil can interfere with your ability to absorb certain vitamins and minerals, according to Dr. Hoffman.

Safest are the natural or vegetable laxative products, high-fibre bulking agents such as Metamucil, Citrucel or Perdiem (Celevac or Fibrebran) that are sold at most chemists. "If you can't tolerate a high-fibre diet, these bulking agents are very safe, helpful supplements," according to gastroenterologist Nicholas Talley, MD Ph.D., associate professor of medicine at the Mayo Clinic in Rochester, Minnesota.

Dr. Talley recommends taking the cautious approach with bulking agents. Follow the directions on the package, increasing the dosage slowly if needed.

exhalations. After you can do that, try it while sitting, he says. Your goal is to make a habit of that kind of deep breathing. Throughout the day, check yourself now and then to make sure that you're breathing deeply from your diaphragm rather than from your chest, says Dr. Miller.

Hands on help:

Rub it out. Massage the area around the belly button in a clockwise fashion to stimulate bowel movement, suggests Dr. Ni. Concentrating on the abdomen, repeat this circular motion 100 or more times until you feel the urge to go. Another useful massage technique that Dr. Rakowski recommends is actually a direct stimulation of the colon itself. The colon begins on your right side just above the hip bone and travels up the right side to about the rib cage, across the bottom of the rib cage to your left side, and, finally, down the left side to the hip bone. If you massage along this path, which follows the motion of flow inside your colon, you can stimulate bowel movement. Do this massage in one-minute intervals and repeat as needed until you feel relief.

Apply some pressure. When proper eating and exercise fail to relieve constipation, try these acupressure points to relax the abdomen, reduce discomfort and encourage regular bowel movements, says Michael Peed Gach, Ph.D., director of the Acupressure Institute in Berkeley, California, and author of *Acupressure's Potent Points*. While lying down comfortably, press CV 6, the Sea of Energy point, which is found three finger-widths below the navel. Close your eyes and breathe deeply as you use all of your fingertips to apply gradual pressure. Dr. Gach suggests pressing the point for two minutes. You can also press each LI 11 point, situated at the outer edge of the elbow crease, says Dr. Gach. He recommends holding one LI 11 point for a half minute, then switching to the other side. Repeat this remedy three times a day, he adds.

Try an aromatic rub. Try a gentle abdominal massage to stimulate elimination, says aromatherapist Judith Jackson in her book *Scentual Touch: A Personal Guide to Aromatherapy.* She says to add six drops each of rosemary and thyme essential oils to one ounce of a carrier oil such as olive or almond. (Carrier oils are available in most health food stores.) Massage the stomach area up the right side, across the top and down the left in a circular motion, she suggests.

Urge with your fingers. Overall, women report more constipation than men. Dr. Lahr says some women experience constipation because of a rectocele—a bulge of the lower rectum into, over, or behind the vagina, sometimes caused by a hysterectomy as the rectum falls into the place of the uterus. Rectoceles trap stool and make evacuation extremely difficult. However, a woman can insert a finger or thumb into the vagina to spur defecation. Pushing on the rectocele bulge through the wall of the vagina helps to push the stool out of the rectum. "There is nothing dangerous about using the fingers to aid defecation," he says. "We manage a lot of people with rectoceles. We just tell them, 'Put your finger in your vagina and empty the stool out.'"

Herbal help:

See about senna. Sometimes, if diet and lifestyle changes don't do the trick, as a last resort you can try senna, a strong-acting herb that stimulates peristalsis, the wavelike muscle action of the intestine, says Melissa Metcalfe, N.D., a naturopathic doctor. Its active ingredient, a chemical called anthraquinone, is responsible for this effect.

You might want to use senna as a one-time option, though, suggests Kristin Stiles, N.D., a naturopathic doctor at the Complementary Medicine and Healing Arts Centre in New York. It's not safe for long-term, chronic constipation. If you take senna repeatedly, your bowel may lose the ability to function on its own.

Dr. Metcalfe recommends that you purchase senna tea bags at a health food store and start off cautiously with one cup of senna tea—no more—each morning. "Senna is probably going to cause some cramping at first. It really increases peristalsis quickly, so you want to start off slowly with it," she cautions.

You can also make a tea with 1/4 teaspoon of powdered senna or put 15 drops of tincture into a cup of hot water. After you learn how strongly senna affects your system, you might try taking a 100-milligram capsule once a day for a few days—usually in the morning, suggests Dr. Metcalfe. If you can't find capsules of that dosage, simply open a larger capsule and use just some of the powdered senna.

This is a powerful herb that can produce cramping and fluid deficiencies. It can also interfere with the absorption of nutrients and essential substances called electrolytes; do not use it for more than 10 days, and do not take it with any other dietary supplements. If you are pregnant or nursing, do not use senna without discussing it with your doctor. It can cause diarrhoea in breastfed infants. Also, you should not use it for any period of time if you have haemorrhoids, abdominal pain of unknown origin, colitis, Crohn's disease, or irritable bowel syndrome.

Senna works well in combination with psyllium. In a short-term study at the University of Wisconsin-Madison, 42 people who had been having less than three bowel movements a week were given psyllium or psyllium with senna. Although both laxatives increased the frequency of bowel movements, those who took the combination had more moisture in their stools and experienced more relief.

Sip the rhubarb remedy. For a tastier way to get your fibre, cook up one of the favourite recipes of James A. Duke, Ph.D., master herbalist and retired ethnobotanist and toxicology specialist at the U.S. Department of Agriculture and author of *The Green Pharmacy.* Cook three stalks of rhubarb without the leaves. Puree with one cup of apple juice, a quarter of a peeled lemon, and one tablespoon of honey, then drink up. Try this remedy three times for one day. The rhubarb not only provides fibre but also contains a natural laxative. But don't overdo it, he warns. The drink has powerful laxative properties.

Go with garlic. Take two capsules of garlic (300 to 400 milligrams per capsule) twice a day with your largest meals. Garlic works to kill harmful bacteria harbouring in the colon, says Jennifer Brett, N.D., a naturopathic physician. Some bacteria can cause changes in stool consistency. Others release toxic by-products that can cause cramping of the large intestine. Garlic also increases bile flow into the intestines. Bile is a natural stool softener, and increasing the flow speeds up the rate of elimination of the bowel contents, she explains.

Eat a sprig of fennel with dinner. In some fine restaurants, a sprig of fennel is used as a garnish on plates of pasta. This herb, which grows wild in some parts of California, stimulates secretions to enhance bowel movements, says Dr. Molony. "It can really get things moving inside you." Check your produce aisle for this garnish, and have a sprig with your meal, he suggests. It is also good as a breath freshener after a meal, he adds.

Spike with bitters. Put 10 to 15 drops of Angostura bitters in two ounces of juice or water and drink this mixture before every meal. The gentian (an herb) in the bitters works best to stimulate bile secretion and bowel movement for people with chronic constipation, says David Winston, a founding and professional member of the American Herbalists Guild.

"Bitters must be tasted—not taken in capsule form—to work best," he adds. Angostura bitters can be purchased at grocery and liquor stores.

Start with flaxseed. Naturally high in fibre, flax contains acids that reduce inflammation of the mucous membranes in your intestines and balance hormones. Pour 2 tablespoons of seeds (available at health food stores) into an 8-ounce glass of room-temperature water and let stand for 15 minutes. (It's crucial that you take the flax with at least 8 ounces of water, otherwise it will cause obstruction in the digestive tract.) The flaxseed will become nice and squishy and gelatin-like. Drink a glass of the seed mixture at night. The next morning, don't just take a shower, grab a cup of coffee, and run out the door. You must allow adequate time for a bowel movement. You can also sprinkle a teaspoon to a tablespoon of ground flaxseed on hot cereal or on salads. Flax is very light-sensitive and becomes rancid quickly, so buy it in small amounts and try to use it within a few weeks, she suggests. Store flax in the refrigerator to prevent rancidity.

Consider psyllium. As an alternative to flaxseed, you can buy fibrous psyllium husks at supermarkets, chemists, or health food stores. Flax and psyllium husks are equally able to move stool along. Although some say that psyllium can make you feel bloated, it is more palatable than flaxseed. If you opt for psyllium, take 1 tablespoon of the powder every morning, and your stool will pass more readily.

Look to dandelion for relief. The bitterness of this weed can stimulate contractions of the colon and move stools along. Use between 1 and 3 dropperfuls of dandelion root tincture in 1/4 cup of water. (A dropperful is roughly 15 drops.) Then drink it slowly by holding each mouthful for about a minute. The bitter taste will stimulate bile flow. Drink it three times a day.

Reserve licorice tea for tough jobs. When all else falls, licorice will come to the rescue. Licorice root tea will loosen the bowels in obstinate constipation. If you consume licorice tea and prunes before going to bed, you will have no problem moving your bowels in the morning. To make the tea, boil a tablespoon of licorice root for 30 minutes in a cup of water. Strain the tea before drinking, and let it coot slightly.

Be cautious with certain herbs. Aloe, buckthorn, cascara sagrada, frangula and senna all contain powerful natural laxative chemicals called anthraquinones. "I suggest trying any of these anthraquinone herbs only as a last resort. You should try a high-fibre diet and other, gentler herbs before reaching for any of these. Any herb that contains anthraquinones can be unpleasantly powerful," says Dr. Duke in his book *The Green Pharmacy.* If you use buckthorn, cascara sagrada or frangula, which are all barks, insist on aged bark. The anthraquinones in fresh bark irritate the digestive tract and may cause bloody diarrhoea and vomiting. Anthraquinones laxatives should not be taken over long periods of time or during pregnancy or nursing. If you take these laxatives for long periods, you may become dependent on them.

Find some fenugreek. Like psyllium, fenugreek seeds contain fluid-absorbing mucilage. If you use fenugreek seeds, make sure you drink plenty of water to keep things moving along. And don't use more than two teaspoons at a time, as any more may cause abdominal distress.

Get help from homeopathy. If you have haemorrhoids and develop constipation along with a full feeling in your stomach or abdominal cramping that is temporarily relieved by passing gas, try Graphites, suggests Cynthia Mervis Watson, M. D. a family practice physician specialising in homeopathic and herbal therapies in California. If you alternate between feeling constipated and having diarrhoea and suspect that it may be caused by anxiety or medication, Watson suggests Nux vomica. And if your belly is bloated, your stools are hard and dry, you have a painful anus after defecating and you feet depressed and run-down, try Natrum muriaticum, she says. For each of these remedies Dr. Watson says to take either a 6X dose three or four times a day or one 30C dose once a day. Graphites, Nux vomica and Natrum muriaticum are available in health food stores.

Corns

The pain: If a corn or callus grows thick enough to press on nerves, it can hurt. "A large corn can be as irritating as a pebble in your shoe," says Kathleen Stone, D.P.M., a podiatrist. Corns and calluses are little pads of dead skin that build up after all those miles of fancy footwork. Painful and protuberant, these islands of dead skin are a signal from our feet that they have had enough. Corns develop on the toes only, while calluses show up on the heels or on the bottoms of the feet.

The cause: Corns and calluses form on parts of your feet where there is excessive friction due to underlying bony deformities. Extra layers of skin form in these areas, creating calluses on the bottom of your feet and corns on the top, says Ernest Levi, D.P.M., podiatrist in private practice in New York City.

See a doctor if:

...you continue to use home treatments but your corn or callus keeps getting worse. See a doctor to make sure you don't have an infection. A doctor can also shave that corn or callus for you. Also, if you have persistent calluses and corns, your foot doctor may talk to you about surgical options to correct your particular problem, says Dr. Levi.

...if you have numbness or reduced sensation in your feet. You may have a medical problem such as diabetes or poor circulation.

...you have diabetes or poor circulation in your feet. You should not try any home remedies without consulting with your doctor.

Quick relief:

Soak your feet in Epsom salts. To relieve pain, try soaking your feet in Epsom salts and warm water recommends Suzanne M. Levine, D.P.M., a podiatrist. Soaking twice a day, for ten minutes each time, should provide some relief

Soak, then rub. Soften corns or calluses by soaking your feet in plain lukewarm water for five or ten minutes. Then use a pumice stone or a synthetic abrasive pad, available at any chemists, to rub off dead skin a little at a time. "I recommend the new synthetic spongelike pumice pads, which contain abrasive material and can be wetted with water and liquid soap and used in the bath or shower," says Kathleen Stone, D.P.M., a podiatrist.

Oil 'em up. After soaking and rubbing, use a moisturising cream to help keep your feet soft, says Dr. Stone. "I like vitamin E cream or vitamin E oil (not vegetable oil), which penetrates the skin very nicely."

Get fitted. Corns and calluses are your first warning sign that your shoes don't fit properly, says Donna Astion, MD, foot and ankle specialist. Go to a shoe store that has professionals who will carefully measure your feet—both length and width—before you start trying on shoes. Avoid shoes that rub corns or calluses.

Cushion the worst offenders. To lessen pain from soft corns between your toes, work a tuft of lamb's wool between your toes, suggests Dr. Stone. Lamb's wool is available at your chemists.

Bag 'em with aspirin. One way to soften hard calluses is to crush five or six aspirin tablets into a powder, then add ½ teaspoon each of lemon juice and water, Apply this paste to all hard-skin areas. Wrap your entire foot with a warm towel, then cover with a plastic bag, suggests Dr. Levine. After sitting still for at least ten minutes, remove the coverings and file the callus with a pumice stone. Caution: Don't try this remedy if you are allergic or sensitive to aspirin.

Everyday prevention:

Size them up. Once we reach adulthood, we often forget all about shoe size and just assume it stays the same. Not so. "Many people wear shoes that are too narrow or too small," says Arnold Ravick, D.P.M., a podiatrist. "Most people don't have their feet measured after they stop growing and figure that they will be the same size all their lives," he says. "But as you age, your feet swell and spread, and the bones buckle." Feet can grow from one to three sizes during your lifetime, Dr. Ravick points out. And during pregnancy, feet may swell or expand by as much as a size by the last trimester. To make sure that your shoes fit, he suggests having your feet measured by a shoe salesclerk at a speciality shoe store. "You must get your feet accurately measured," he says. "Because if you wear shoes that fit poorly, you may get corns and calluses."

Respect your differences. Keep in mind that your left foot may not be precisely the same size as your right. Get both feet measured when you go to the shoe store. If there is a big difference in sizes, you may want to shop at a store that allows you to mix and match sizes, suggests Douglas Hale, D.P.M., a podiatrist. If the difference is a size or less, buy shoes that fit the larger foot and then apply heel pads and tongue pads to keep the smaller foot from slipping around.

Be anti-pronation. If a shoe salesclerk or a podiatrist has told you that your feet pronate, that means they roll inward when you walk. This may make you callus-prone. To prevent pronation, tell the salesclerk at the shoe store that you want an anti-pronation, extra-sturdy shoe, says Lawrence Z. Huppin, D.P.M., a podiatrist. These shoes have especially well-built heels and soles that don't bend easily.

Find the orthotics rack. If calluses have been giving you trouble for quite awhile, you're probably all too familiar with the pharmacy rack that has foot-care products. Dr. Astion suggests trying over-the-counter orthotics The orthotic fits into the inner sole of the shoe and helps redistribute the sole of your foot, which could take some of the pressure and friction off of the foot area that's getting beaten up. If those over-the-counter orthotics don't work, look in the phone book for an orthotist, who can get you a custom-made pair.

Use padding. On that pharmacy rack offering dozens of foot-care supplies, you'll find protective pads for your feet. The package directions will tell you what to do. Every morning before you put on your shoes, put the pads around those areas where you tend to form corns or calluses, says Dr. Levi. Traditionally, adhesive-backed felt, called moleskin, was used as a doughnut-type pad around corns and calluses to take pressure off them. The patents whom Dr. Stone treats seem to prefer a new synthetic material, Cushlin, available at most chemists in Dr. Scholl's products. The material is thin, soft, resilient and rubbery. It doesn't flatten out and holds up well. Cut sheets of the material to pad around, not over, your corn or callus.

Don't get the point. Many women's shoes and some boots for men and women are designed as if our feet were pointed. Instead, look for a rounded toebox in shoes. In general, try to exercise good judgement by selecting shoes that best fit the shape of your feet, says William H. Rutherford, D.P.M., a clinical instructor in podiatry.

Heave the heels. If you are a woman who is accustomed to high heels, it may be high time for a flatter-heel shopping spree. When you wear heels that are higher than 2 inches, you are putting too much pressure on the metatarsals, the bones directly beneath your toes. "You want to get the force off that area," says Dr. Huppin. Flat shoes are a much better bet.

Reach for the running shoes. Even if you are not a runner, many experts say that running shoes are the best all-around shoe for foot support because the heel is very thick and stable. "It is better than any other kind of athletic shoe," says Bruce Lebowitz, D.P.M., director of a podiatric clinic. If you can't wear them on the job, you can still wear them to and from work, at home, and at play. Your feet will thank you for it.

Lace it up. A corn is caused by your shoe rubbing against a toe, and the rubbing is far less abusive if you wear shoes with laces, says Dr. Hale. Because the laces make the shoe hug the foot, you feel less pressure on your toes than you feel from slip-on shoes.

Lace up to save your toes. If you have corns on top of your toes, Nancy Elftman, a certified orthotist/pedorthist (a professional shoe fitter), suggests lacing your sports shoes so that one lace goes from one bottom eyelet to the top eyelet on the opposite side. The other lace is alternated through the lace holes. Then, by pulling on the single lace, you can lift the toe box and give your toes more room. (This also helps if you have a long second toe.)

Support your arches. "People with high arches are particularly susceptible to corns," says dermatologist Joseph Bark, MD, Kentucky. How do you find out whether the shape of your arches is a contributing factor? "Check for corns on three pressure points on your feet that carry your weight: on the ball of the foot, right below the smallest toe and on your heel,"Dr. Bark suggests. If this is your problem, try store-bought arch supports.

Be a beachcomber. "Walking barefoot on the beach can get rid of your calluses," says Robert Diamond, D.P.M., a podiatrist. "The sand acts as a natural pumice stone and files them down."

Get them wet. To keep your feet soft, try this natural remedy. Buy a foot soak containing the herb calendula, available in many health food or chemists. Following package directions, mix the calendula with water and give your feet a good long soak. This herbal soak, done once a week or so, will loosen up dead skin and help new skin cells grow, says James J. Berryhill, Ph.D., naturopathic doctor.

Avoid medicated Corn Pads. One of the most popular store-bought remedies for corns is among the worst, says Dr. Diamond. "Medicated corn pads cause more problems than they're worth," says Dr. Diamond. "The medication is salicylic acid, which turns the corn white and blister-free, so it can peel off. But what happens frequently is that the acid is so strong it goes through the corn and eats at the toe, causing an ulcer in the toe."

Lay on low-cost lotion. There are many products that can help soften corns and calluses. Lotions and bath oils that contain lanolin, glycerin or urea are available at most chemists. "Fruit acid moisturisers such as LactiCare are also very effective when you apply them heavily," says Dr. Bark.

Herbal help:

Aid with ayurveda. Here's a remedy from Vasant Lad, B.A.M.S., M.A.Sc., director of the Ayurvedic Institute in New Mexico: First, clean the area with tree oil. Then apply a paste made by mixing 1 teaspoon of aloe vera gel with 1/2 teaspoon of turmeric. Once the paste is applied, cover the area with a bandage. The treatment works best at night when you're off your feet, according to Dr. Lad. (Since turmeric can stain skin and clothing, he suggests putting on old socks after you've applied this remedy. Any skin discoloration should wash off in about two weeks.)

In the morning, says Dr. Lad, remove the bandage and soak your foot in a bucket of warm water for ten minutes. Then rub mustard oil deeply into the corn or callus. Continue this treatment for several days, and eventually, the corn or callus will fall off, says Dr. Lad. Both tea tree oil and aloe vera gel are available in most health food stores. Mustard oil is available in Indian pharmacies and by mail order.

Try a rub-out recipe. To remove corns and calluses, try this home remedy suggested by Julian Whitaker, MD, founder and president of the Whitaker Wellness Centre in Newport Beach, California. "Mix one teaspoon of lemon juice, one teaspoon of dried camomile tea and one garlic clove that has

Pamper for prevention

Since corns and calluses are really nothing more than mounds of dead skin, doctors say it helps to keep your feet free of build-up. You can give yourself an excellent pedicure at home by following these steps from Douglas Hale, D.P.M., a podiatrist at the Foot and Ankle Centre of Washington in Seattle.
• First, you will need a water basin, footbath powder (available at any chemists), a towel, moisturising cream, a pumice stone, toenail clippers, and a nail file.
• Add the footbath powder to the basin and run warm, not hot, water into it. Soak your feet for 10 minutes.
 – Towel your feet dry. Gently clean any dirt underneath your toenails.
 – Rub the moisturiser on and give yourself a foot massage.
 – With a pumice stone (never use a knife or sharp object to cut dead skin), gently rub dead skin away.
 – Finish up by cutting your toenails straight across with clippers and filing away any rough edges.
Note: If you have diabetes, decreased sensitivity or decreased circulation, check with a podiatrist before you attempt this, says Cheryl Weiner, D.P.M., a podiatrist, and president of the American Association for Women Podiatrists.

been crushed. Rub this mixture directly on the corn one or more times a day." This kitchen-created remedy helps dissolve corns and calluses for quicker relief, says Dr. Whitaker. Dried camomile tea is available in most health food stores.

Seek homeopathic help. Try a 6C dose of one of the following remedies three times a day until you see improvement, says Chris Meletis, N.D., a naturopathic physician. According to Dr. Meletis, Ranunculus bulbosus works when you have hard skin that is very sensitive, often with burning and intense itching. For painful calluses on your toes and fingers that are worse on your right side, worse with heat and better with cold, he says to use Lycopodium. Ranunculus sceleratus may help if you have a piercing pain, with burning and soreness that are worse when you let your feet hang down, he says.

Fight with fig and pineapple. When King Solomon developed boils, his physicians applied figs; this is one of the very few descriptions of the medicinal use of herbs in the Bible. Figs contain protein-dissolving enzymes that help dissolve unwanted skin growths, including corns. Papaya and pineapple contain similar enzymes, and all three fruits have age-old reputations for reducing corns and warts. Open a fresh fig and tape the pulp to the corn overnight. Or cut a square of pineapple peel and tape the inner side to the corn overnight. The following morning, remove the herb and soak the foot in water. After an hour or so, try to remove the corn. It should come off fairly easily, but you can rub it gently with a pumice stone if necessary. Some stubborn cases. However may- require four to five overnight treatments. Folklore attests to fairly similar procedures using papaya.

Try willow or wintergreen. Willow contains aspirin-like compounds known as salicylates that relieve pain. But salicylates are also powerful acids that can help dissolve corns and warts. Just use this herb carefully, placing willow bark poultices directly on the corn itself: don't let the herb come in contact with the surrounding skin. Because they're acidic. salicylates may cause skin inflammation. Wintergreen is another good source of salicylates. Some herbalists recommend that you apply wintergreen oil to remove calluses, corns, cysts and warts. Again, to make sure you avoid irritation, apply the oil only to the corn itself and not to the surrounding skin. Remember to keep wintergreen oil or any product containing it out of the reach of children. The minty smell can be very tempting. but ingesting even small amounts can prove fatal to young children.

Celandine Corn Remover

Here's a gentle herbal remedy that you can make yourself for softening and removing corns. The herb celandine has a world-wide reputation as a corn remover.

> 6 cups water
> 1 teaspoon potassium chloride
> 4 ounces fresh celandine, chopped
> 1 cup glycerin

Put the water in a medium saucepan and add the potassium chloride. Heat and stir until the potassium chloride dissolves. Remove from the heat. add the celandine and let stand for 2 hours.

Return the pan to the heat and bring the mixture to a boil. Reduce the heat and simmer for 20 minutes.

Using a sieve or wire strainer, strain the liquid into a medium bowl. Discard the plant material.

Return the liquid to the pan and let it simmer until it is reduced to 1½ cups. Add the glycerin and continue simmering until the liquid is reduced to 2 cups. Strain the liquid, place it in a bottle and store it in cool place. Apply it to corns twice a day—for example, before you leave for work and before you go to bed.

Note: Potassium chloride is available at supermarkets as a commercial salt substitute.

Cracked Skin

The pain: Inflammation of the skin that can range from a mild discomfort to the really miserable skin bubbles that make you wonder whether you are about to boil over. When dermatitis develops to the stage where you can see cracking, crusting, and oozing, it is generally diagnosed as some kind of eczema.

Some people start getting skin outbreaks in childhood, with flare-ups that may continue off and on throughout their lives. Called atopic eczema, this rash is probably inherited from Mom, Dad, or other forebears who passed along the genes. The outbreaks can occur anywhere on the body, but the most common points of affliction are joint areas like the inside of the elbows or backs of the knees. Another type of rash, allergic contact dermatitis, shows up when you have touched something that causes the outbreak. A rash from poison ivy is the classic example of this variety.

The cause: Your skin naturally loses water to the environment through evaporation. "Your skin is a barrier between the water in your cells and the atmosphere. Some people are predisposed to dry skin because they have bad barrier function," explains dermatologist Robert Schosser, MD. In other words, you can get as wet as you want, but if your skin can't hold the moisture in, it will continue to be dry. The causes are just various, ranging from your own genetic makeup to food, air, sun, artificial products, natural substances, and just about everything else. A skin irritation also can be caused by something you have repeatedly come in contact with, such as metal, latex, or some other substance.

See a doctor if:
...if self-help hasn't worked within a week or two.

Nutritional remedies:
Eat healthy oils. Although most of us consume far too many saturated fats, few of us actually eat healthy oils, which would contribute to the overall health of our skin. "The oils in your diet are part of every cell membrane in your body," says Eugene Zampieron, a doctor of naturopathy. "Try to use flaxseed oil, avocado oil, or walnut oil in your diet. You'll notice a difference in the texture of your skin.

Everyday prevention:

Moisturise day and night. "You want to constantly keep moisturiser on the skin," says David E. Cohen, MD, clinical instructor of environmental sciences at the Columbia University School of Public Health. Rub it on your hands whenever they start to feel dry. Use a light, fragrance-free moisturizer during the day and use petroleum jelly before you go to bed at night, he advises. The best time to apply a moisturiser is in the morning right after your shower, he says. After you have patted yourself dry, "quickly apply the moisturiser while your skin is still hydrated with water." Even better is to moisturise a second time right before you go to bed. "When you put on the moisturiser at bedtime, you are less likely to rub or sweat it off, and it can really help your skin."

Chose the right moisturiser. Use a moisturiser that contains alpha hydroxy acids, says Dr. Schosser. Alpha hydroxy acids—which include glycolic, citric, and lactic acids—hold water in the skin. Dr. Schosser recommends Lac-Hydrin Five or AmLactin (Compeed), which are both available at most chemists. Use these twice a day, but not immediately after showering. They tend to sting and burn.

Get wet. The best time to use a moisturiser is just after you shower or bathe, because the skin is hydrated already, and you want to make sure that moisture stays in the skin. "The idea is to train your skin to hold moisture in without too much help," says Yohini Appa, Ph.D., director of research and development for the Neutrogena Corporation in Los Angeles. In fact, truly dry skin can become addicted to moisturiser, so remember that if your skin and moisturiser are working well together, twice a day (once in the morning and once at night) ought to be plenty. If you still feel dry during the day, try a more therapeutic moisturiser, Dr. Appa says.

Use a humidifier. If you live in a dry climate, or it's winter and the heating system in your home or office dries up the air, a humidifier will be a big help, says Dr. Schosser. With the air wet, your skin won't lose so much moisture through evaporation.

Give yourself a good soak. "The best way to treat very dry skin is to hydrate it every night," says Houston podiatrist William Van Pelt, D.P.M., former president of the American Academy of Podiatric Sports Medicine. "Each skin cell is like a little sponge, so each night before going to bed, I recommend soaking your feet or whatever part of your body is especially dry in warm water for about 20 minutes. During this soak, the skin cells will absorb water. Then pat yourself dry.

Cool it. People with dry skin know that excessive washing can make the problem worse. But water isn't the culprit; water temperature and bathing products that aggressively remove oil are. "Bathing can put water back into your skin, but if the water is too hot, it melts the protective skin lipids, which will then go down the drain," says Dr. Schosser. "So, soak in a tub for 20 to 30 minutes, but make the water warm, not hot. Afterward, put a capful of mineral oil on a wet washcloth and apply this to the areas that tend to be dry such as the arms, legs, and body (avoid the face, underarms, and groin) to keep that added water in. After that, you may also use a moisturizing cream like Eucerin original formula cream to your arms and legs."

Favour showers. People who are prone to eczema shouldn't take long baths, says Dr. Cohen. "You tend to relax in baths and sit in them a long time, and you get that crinkled, white skin. That's simply a sign that you have compromised your skin's barrier function by overhydrating. Your skin will actually be drier after you get out." Instead, take a brief, cool shower lasting three to five minutes. "That is the most moisturizing, protective way to bathe," he says.

Cleanse gently. If you need to use a deodorant soap, Dr. Schosser says, try a mild antibacterial in a moisturizing bar base.

Pick a sensitive soap. The best soaps to help prevent eczema are mildly moisturising rather than drying, says Dr. Cohen. He recommends soaps that are fragrance-free and for sensitive skin, like Dove, Purpose, Basis, and Aveeno. Glycerine-based soaps such as Neutrogena advertise themselves as "smell-good deodorant soaps," which are very drying and full of fragrances, according to Dr. Cohen.

Pat and moisturise. When you get out of the shower, pat rather than rub your skin with a towel. When you rub too hard, you may rub right down to the raw areas that are most likely to develop into patches of eczema. And after you have patted yourself dry, don't forget to apply moisturiser right away, says Dr. Cohen.

Avoid solvents. Approximately 65,000 different substances can cause contact irritant dermatitis, with the rash usually occurring after repeated exposures, says Dr. Cohen. But there is one category of irritants, called solvents, that cause most cases of this kind of dermatitis. Solvents include water, soapy solutions of any kind, plus alcohol, acetone, varnish, thinners, gasoline, and kerosene. Often, people are exposed to these solvents at work, and the rash shows up as a result of frequent daily contact.

Favour nitrile gloves. Nitrile gloves with cotton liners (available at medical supply stores) provide far more protection against many solvents than latex or vinyl gloves, says Dr. Cohen. If you are cleaning up with water and mild detergent, however, you can use everyday latex gloves with cotton liners. Avoid using plain latex gloves; rubber can be irritating to some people.

Salve up for the future. If you work with solvents, you should also moisturise your hands very frequently, ideally after every contact. If you notice a rash starting, you can usually prevent it from getting any worse by using an over-the-counter hydrocortisone ointment, following the directions on the product label. "These ointments can be very useful in aborting a minor attack and preventing it from becoming a major ongoing episode of eczema," says Dr. Cohen.

Wash not, itch not. Eczema on your hands is a painful affliction, particularly if the skin is sore and cracking, because you need to use your hands for so many things. "The vast majority of cases of hand eczema are caused by repetitive hand washing," says Dr. Cohen. Soap and water are very drying to the hands, and it is that lack of moisture on the skin that triggers the rash of hand eczema. So avoid washing your hands more often than necessary.

Don't get into scents. In moisturisers as well as soaps, fragrances can irritate sensitive skin and actually cause eczema, says Dr. Cohen. "Avoid moisturisers with fragrance, period," he says. Even if the label says "unscented," the product might have a masking fragrance. "The label should say 'fragrance-free,'" he says.

Reserve the preserves. As long as you are reading moisturiser labels, you may also want to avoid moisturisers with preservatives, Dr. Cohen warns. "Many of the preservatives have formaldehyde as a component, which can cause allergic eczema in some people."

Choose jelly. "The blander the moisturiser, the better off you are," says Dr. Cohen. His favourite is petroleum jelly. "It is an excellent barrier moisturiser, it is inexpensive, and it has virtually no chance of causing eczema." To avoid the greasy feeling of petroleum jelly, wait five minutes after you apply it to your skin, then remove the excess with an old cotton T-shirt. "Your skin won't feel greasy, and you will have given the moisturiser time to soak in," he says.

Ring off. Remove your rings before you wash your hands, Dr. Cohen says. Irritants, particularly soap, get trapped under the ring, and those irritants can stay on your finger for hours, triggering the eczema.

Buy weaves that breathe. Synthetic fabrics like polyester and permanent press fabrics have a formaldehyde-based substance in them to keep them wrinkle-free. "This is an allergen, and it can irritate eczema-prone skin," says Dr. Cohen. If your skin is reacting, try some other types of clothing. "Fabrics like non-permanent press cottons and silk are more breathable and tend to contain fewer chemicals," he says.

Beware barbs in sheep's clothing. "When you look at wool under a microscope, you see little fishhook-shaped barbs, which can irritate the skin of someone prone to eczema," says Dr. Cohen. When you scratch to relieve the irritation, you can end up with a new patch of eczema. If you want to wear wool clothes for warmth or fashion, have a tailor put in a silk lining or wear a silk shirt or camisole underneath your clothing, he says.

Wash out what you buy. Many manufacturers of clothing, bedding, towels, and other fabric items use a fabric finisher on their products that can cause allergic contact dermatitis, says Rhett Drugge, MD, a dermatologist, who is president and founder of the Internet Dermatology Society, and chief editor of the *Electronic Textbook of Dermatology*. To remove the finisher, run new clothes through the washing machine before you put them on, he advises.

Don't go soft. "I'm emphatically opposed to fabric softeners or dryer sheets for people who are prone to eczema," says Dr. Cohen. "They add a tremendous amount of unnecessary fragrances and irritant chemicals to your clothes."

Never mind the sweet smell of spring. Fragrance-free laundry detergents are always preferable, says Dr. Cohen. "It's nice to have your clothes smell like a spring day, but when you sweat, those fragrances leach out onto your skin and can trigger eczema."

Battle bacteria. Some people with eczema may find that antibacterial soaps help control the problem. Dr. Cohen recommends Lever 2000 and Dial, which he says are non-drying antibacterial soap bars.

Seek some sun. The ultraviolet light of the sun can help prevent or reduce the inflammation of eczema in about 90 percent of people who are prone to the problem. "Since a lot of eczema is on the arms and legs, wearing shorts and short-sleeved shirts in the summer can often help prevent or relieve flare-ups of eczema," says Dr. Cohen. But since too much sun will cause its own problems, make sure to use a sunscreen of at least SPF 15 and reapply often. (For about 10 percent of people, sunshine makes the rash worse, and they should cover up or stay out of the sun.)

Glue the cracks. Although it doesn't cure skin fissure, you can lessen the pain by apply Super Glue to the slits, says Rodney Basler, MD, a dermatologist. "A little dab of Super Glue takes the air away from the nerve endings and seals the slits." He says this procedure is perfectly safe on slit and minor paper cuts but shouldn't be tried on deep wounds.

Mind over malady:

Don't be furious. Your skin and your emotions are closely related, says Ted Grossbart, Ph.D., an instructor in the department of psychiatry at Harvard Medical School, and author of *Skin Deep: A Mind/Body Program for Healthy Skin.* "Stressful emotions and how you deal with them can play a large role in whether eczema is triggered or not. With eczema, one typical emotional trigger is anger," he says. One way to deal with that anger is to express it verbally rather than through your skin, he says. But if expressing your anger seems inappropriate, don't give up. "Simply admitting to yourself that you are angry can often prevent your eczema from getting worse."

Soothe yourself. Stressful emotions can make you want to scratch, which will just make your eczema worse and cause future flare-ups. But, says Dr. Grossbart, you can turn your scratching hand into a soothing hand. "First, you need to be clear about what kind of stressful events push your buttons and make you scratch more. Then, instead of scratching at those times, rest your hand lightly over your skin or on your skin. Over time, this light, loving, soothing touch actually will soothe; you will feel much less itchy." These techniques are most effective when used as part of an ongoing professionally guided program, Dr. Grossbart adds.

Denture Pain

The pain: Mouth or tongue pain associated with ill-fitting dentures.

The cause: Most people get used to dentures within a few weeks and no longer have sore spots as they the learn to use their dentures. Ongoing pain usually mean a denture plate isn't fitting right anymore and needs to be adjusted, relined or recast.

See a doctor if:
...your dentures don't fit as well as they once did.
...you notice a red inflammation on your gums under your dentures
...you have soft, white slightly raised sores on your tongue, gums, or on your cheeks.
...you have pain when you tighten your jaw or find it difficult to open your mouth.
...the teeth don't meet properly or are too long, resulting in problems closing you mouth.
...the dentures continually cut into your gums or cheeks.

Medication:
Any drug that dries out the mouth can contribute to denture pain, says Gretchen Gibson, D.D.S., a geriatric dentistry specialist. Without enough saliva, your dentures will rub against your gums and cause discomfort.

Medications like prazosin (Minipress or Hypovase) that are used to control high blood pressure and antidepressants like amitriptyline (Elavil) are among the common drugs prescribed to seniors that can dry out your mouth and lead to denture discomfort, Dr. Gibson says. Denture pain also may be a side effect of:

Diuretics such as chlorothiazide (Diuril) or furosemide (Lasix)

Nitroglycerin (Nitrostat) and other drugs used to control angina

Oxybutynin (Ditropan) and other drugs used to control urinary incontinence

Oral steroids like beclomethasone (Beclovent or Becotide) used for asthma

Quick relief:

Massage your gums. To relieve sore gums associated with new dentures, massage your gums several times a day, following this routine recommended by Richard Shepard, D.D.S., a dentist. Place your thumb and index finger over your gum, with your index finger on the outside. Massage each section of sore gum by squeezing and rubbing with your thumb and finger. This will promote circulation and give your gums a healthy firmness. Keep your gums clean by rinsing your mouth daily with a glass of warm water mixed with a teaspoon of salt.

Go over the counter. Rub your sore gums with an over-the-counter topical pain killer. But don't use the medication too long—it can irritate the tissue.

Everyday prevention:

Stick with what is comfortable. When you first get your dentures, continue eating what you have been eating until you get accustomed to them. "Many of my patients think, 'Boy, the first thing I'm going to do after I get my dentures is go out and eat a big, juicy steak.' That simply isn't a good idea," explains dentist Kenneth Shay, D.D.S. "Your mouth needs time to adjust to having two pieces of plastic inside of it. So continue eating what you were eating before you received your dentures until you feel comfortable and confident that you can chew your food well."

Steam your vegetables. "You tend to bite your cheek or tongue when you get a new set of dentures-particularly your first set," says Frank Wiebelt, D.D.S., chairman of the Department of Removable Prosthodontics at the College of Dentistry at the University of Oklahoma Health Sciences Centre. To avoid this, chew slowly. Also, stay away from raw vegetables or anything else that's crunchy or difficult to chew. "It's funny, because one of the first things my patients want to eat when they get new dentures is a steak and a salad, and both are among the most difficult things to eat," he says. "A steak is very tough. And believe it or not, lettuce is also difficult to chew. So eat your vegetables, but eat them steamed, and try to avoid anything that's tough for the first two weeks or so.

Avoid the pads. Don't rely on over-the-counter dental pads or liners to adjust your fit. They reduce the bite space—the distance between the upper and lower teeth—and put undue pressure on the jawbone.

Give your gums a rest. Don't leave your dentures in too long, especially when they are new, otherwise your gums will let you know they don't like it. If you develop sore gums, take your dentures out and set them aside for a few days while your gums heal. Then try using the dentures again, suggest Flora Parsa Stay, D.D.S., a dentist, and author of *The Complete Book of Dental Remedies.* Take your dentures out for at least six hours a day, either while you're sleeping or when you're at home doing household chores, Dr. Shay says.

Clean 'em right. Take your dentures out of your mouth before bed, brush them thoroughly with a denture cleanser, then place them in a glass of water overnight. Avoid using regular toothpastes because they are too abrasive for most dentures, according to Dr. Shay. These pastes can damage your dentures to the point that they don't fit properly, which will cause sore gums.

Don't be a Mr. Fix-It. Even if you are savvy enough to conquer leaky toilets, balky air conditioners, and funky flooring, don't attempt to adjust or repair your dentures on your own, Dr. Shay warns. The handyman approach can cause irreparable damage to your dentures and harm your health. Over-the-counter (OTC) adhesives (creams and powders), for instance, when used properly enhance the fit of dentures, but other OTC denture products such as home reliners usually cause irreparable damage to the dentures and should be avoided. Improperly repaired or relined dentures also irritate the gums and cause mouth sores. In extreme cases, dentures damaged in this way can traumatise the underlying tissue and actually accelerate the shrinkage of bone under the gums, Dr. Shay says, causing the dentures to be looser and function poorly. So leave any necessary adjustments or repairs to your dentist, he urges.

Read out loud. New dentures can make talking difficult for the first week or so. One of the best ways to overcome this problem is to read out loud, advises Jerry F. Taintor, D.D.S., an endodontist. As you're reading, listen to your pronunciation and your diction and correct what doesn't sound right.

"Keep in mind that you're probably more aware of any changes in speech than anyone else is. But any time you speak out loud—whether reading or just talking to yourself in the car-you help yourself accommodate more quickly,' says Dr. Wiebelt.

Videotape yourself. A videotape can help you, suggests George A. Murrell, D.D.S., a prosthodontist. A videotape allows you to see what others see when you're talking. And a dentist can use the pictures to determine any problems in jaw or lip movements.

Drink a lot of water. New denture wearers often suffer from either dry mouth or excessive saliva. Either way, frequent sips of water will solve the problem, says Dr. Wiebelt. "Excessive saliva results because the mouth can't tell the difference between the dentures and food in the early going. By sipping water, you wash away the excessive saliva that can cause a gagging or sick feeling." Sucking on hard candy or a lozenge also helps dry mouth, but sipping water is better, especially for people who are overweight, have diabetes or suffer from serious tooth decay.

Rule out allergies. Some people are allergic to dental cleansers and adhesives, Dr. Stay says. A few are even allergic to materials in the dentures themselves. In addition to a burning sensation in the mouth, these allergies can irritate the gums and cause mouth ulcers. If you suspect you have an allergy, ask your dentist about substitutes for the cleansers and adhesives you're using. Then try out the alternative products one by one and see whether the irritation subsides. If no change occurs after this elimination process, leave your dentures out and see what happens. If your dentures are causing the problem, you may need new dentures made with different materials, Dr. Stay says.

Herbal Help:

Douse the ache. Take out your dentures then rinse your mouth three times a day with a 1/2 cup of rinse made with goldenseal, a potent herbal remedy, to help soothe denture pain, Dr. Stay says. To prepare, add 1/2 tablespoon of dried goldenseal and 1/4 teaspoon of baking soda to 1/2 cup of warm water. Cool and strain before using. Goldenseal is available at most health food stores.

Reach for homeopathic relief. Take a 6X dose of arnica, a homeopathic remedy, three times a day, which may help subdue denture pain, says Richard D. Fischer, D.D.S., a dentist. Homeopathy is a form of medicine that relies on minute amounts of plants, minerals, and other substances to stimulate a person's natural defences and promote healing. Arnica is available at many health food stores. Check the label to make sure it's a 6X concentration: In homeopathy, a number followed by an X or C indicates the strength of the remedy.

Cleaning your dentures

The best way to clean dentures and keep your breath fresh is to brush your dentures nightly with regular hand soap and lukewarm water, using a soft-bristle toothbrush. "If you're going to use toothpaste, don't use any brand advertised as a whitener. Those toothpaste are too abrasive for the denture surface," says Frank Wiebelt, D.D.S., chairman of the Department of Removable Prosthodontics at the College of Dentistry at the University of Oklahoma Health Sciences Centre.

Other tips:

Wear your glasses. If you wear glasses for reading or close work, put them on when you're cleaning your dentures. And make sure you have plenty of light. Your eyesight and lighting conditions should be optimal for a good cleaning. Dentures won't be cleaned properly through 'feeling."

Clean dentures over a filled sink. That way, if you drop your dentures, the water will break the fall and prevent chipping. Alternatively, clean them over a thick towel.

Brush your gums and tongue. Even though you have dentures instead of a full set of teeth, brushing is important, because bacteria still invade the gums and tongue. Brush with a soft-bristle brush to remove bacteria and keep breath fresh. Toothpaste is optional. Rinse with salty water.

Seek an herbal solution. Dab a bit of aloe vera gel or eucalyptus oil on a cotton-tipped swab and apply directly to your gums where the dentures are causing pain, Dr. Stay suggests. These products, which are available at most health food stores, soothe and heal sore gums. You can use the gel or oil as needed, but for best results, avoid eating for at least one hour after applying these products.

Diverticulosis

The pain: Most people never know they have diverticuli (small multiple pouches that generally develop on the colon) until the one of the sacs becomes inflamed. By then, the disease may have progressed into diverticulitis, a more serious complication, accompanied by abdominal pain, usually around the left side of the lower abdomen. The pain may be accompanied by fever, nausea, vomiting, chills, and cramping.

The cause: A diverticulum is a grape-sized pouch, or sac, that protrudes from the wall of the colon (large intestine). Sacs occur in other places along the gastrointestinal tract as well, but rarely. The pouches are thought to arise from excess pressure build-up in the colon, usually due to a lack of fibre in the diet. Doctors often compare the condition to an inner tube poking through weak spots on a tire.

Typically with diverticulosis, diverticuli (small multiple pouches) appear. Once established on the colon, they're permanent. Most people never know they have the condition, says Michael Epstein, MD, founder of Digestive Disorders Associates.

Diverticulitis occurs, though, when the diverticuli trap bits of stool or undigested food and become inflamed. This inflammation causes abdominal pain, usually around the left side of the lower abdomen. If it becomes infected, the pain is accompanied by fever, nausea, vomiting, chills, and cramping. At this point, people often see their doctor, who diagnoses the disease. Fortunately, that transition from diverticulosis to diverticulitis may not occur—the statistical likelihood is 10 to 25 percent—and you can do things to improve your odds of never developing either affliction.

See a doctor if:
...you feel unexplained pain in the lower left part of the abdomen, says Peter McNally, D.O., gastroenterologist. The pain may be accompanied by a fever and sweating, especially during bowel movements. If you have these symptoms or if you notice bloody stool, "See your doctor that day," says Dr. McNally.

Medication:

Sometimes taking medicine is a catch-22. That's especially true if you have diverticulitis and taking a pain medication may make your situation worse. Sure, the pain may go away for a time, but the pain medication may make your already sluggish colon move even slower and make your diverticulitis worse, says W. Steven Pray, Ph.D., R.Ph.., professor of non-prescription drug products at Southwestern Oklahoma State University. Beware of constipation-causing pain medications, especially narcotics like codeine, which is found in products such as Tylenol with Codeine and morphine (Duramorph). Also, be sure to tell your doctor that you have diverticulitis before taking corticosteroids, for example, fludrocortisone (Florinef), cortisone (Cortone Acetate), and dexamethasone (Deltasone). These drugs can mask symptoms of diverticulitis and ulcers, says Dr. Pray.

Several drugs may even cause diverticulitis, warns Dr. Pray. Alert your doctor if you have diverticulosis or are at risk for it before taking donepezil (Aricept), which is used to treat Alzheimer's disease; risperidone (Risperdal), which is prescribed for psychotic disorders like schizophrenia; and sertraline (Zoloft or Lustral), which is used to treat depression.

If you already have diverticulitis, your doctor may have prescribed an antispasmodic such as hyoscyamine (Gastrosed or Buscopan). This powerful medication may interact with certain other medications. Be sure to tell your doctor if you are also taking any of the following:

Over-the-counter diarrhoea medicine containing kaolin and pectin (Kapectolin) or attapulgite (Kaopectate)

Antifungals such as ketoconazole (Nizoral), which are used to treat serious fungus infections

Tricyclic antidepressants such as amitriptyline (Elavil)

Over-the-counter and prescription potassium supplements, which may be used to treat high blood pressure, such as potassium chloride (Kay Ciel)

Nutritional remedies:

Fill up on fibre. "A high-fibre diet in combination with regular physical activity may be the most important preventive factors in reducing the risk of diverticular disease," says Walid H. Aldoori, MD, Sc.D., a nutrition and epidemiology specialist. "A healthy colon is a low-pressure colon," says Dr. Aldoori. "And to maintain this low pressure, you need a high-fibre diet. "Eating more dietary fibre—the indigestible portion of vegetables, fruits, grains, beans, and other plant foods—adds bulk to your stool, allowing the colon to exert a low, gentle pressure to move it along. In one of Dr. Aldoori's studies, the men who ate the most fibre (32 grams or more of fibre per day) had a 42 percent lower chance of getting diverticular disease than men who ate the least (13 grams).

Favour five servings. If it seems tough to track grams of fibre, get three to five daily servings of fruits and vegetables. "That will get you close to 30 or more grams of fibre per day," says Dr. Aldoori. And that's good news because in Dr. Aldoori's study it was the fibre from fruits and vegetables that proved the most protective against diverticulosis. Apples, peaches, bananas, nectarines, and fresh vegetables are fibre-rich.

Five servings may be more than you are used to. Many people who think that they are eating lots of fruits and vegetables are surprised when they actually start to keep track, says Gregory. "When we actually measure their fibre intake, it is often amazingly low." Gregory says that most of her patients get only 12 to 13 grams of fibre a day, the same amount as the folks in Dr. Aldoori's study who ended up with diverticulosis.

Choose the best bran. Wait a second, what happened to bran, the food that is practically synonymous with fibre? It is true that bran, the outer husk of grains, can be an important component of a high-fibre, diverticulosis-preventing diet, says Dr. Aldoori. But he cautions that too many people eat grains and cereals that are highly refined or processed. "Foods like white bread, pancakes, and rolls are generally not as useful as whole-grain products in preserving the integrity of the colon," he says. To get fibre from grains, says Gregory, choose a one-cup serving of a high-fibre cereal like raisin bran and then slice up a medium-size banana for a topping; the combo will net you 11 grams of fibre. And when you eat pasta—eat whole-wheat, rather than the refined-white kind.

Sprinkle on the bran. Wheat bran or oat bran, found in health food stores, are also good sources of fibre. But if you think that bran tastes like sawdust, disguise it by sprinkling it on top of a tossed salad or add it to a meat loaf or casserole.

Count the amount. To help you accurately measure your fibre intake, "go to a bookstore and purchase a book that helps you count your fibre intake," says Patricia Gregory, R.D., a dietician. To keep accurate count, start a food diary, recording your daily intake of fibre until you get in the higher-fibre habit.

Get fibrous slowly. To some people, eating more fibre to protect their intestines seems like a bad joke—with a punch line of flatulence, bloating, and abdominal cramps. But eating extra fibre doesn't have to mean digestive upset if you just increase your intake gradually. Up your average daily-fibre dose by 5 grams per week until—in about a month—you have reached 25 to 35 grams per day, suggests Gregory.

Raise your glass. Dr. Epstein says increasing water and fibre at the same time is a good idea. Lacking sufficient fibre, the bowel has to work harder to push the stool out. He advises drinking plenty of fluids, six to eight glasses daily, which just means a tall glass every couple of hours. Not sure you're getting enough water? Test yourself by examining your urine. "It should look light, not dark," says Dr. Epstein.

Juice up. Many people with intestinal problems are deficient in vitamin K, found in dark green lettuce and criciferous vegetables such as broccoli and kale, says Cherie Calbon, M.S., a certified nutritionist and co-author of *Juicing for Life.* She advises those with diverticualr disease to load up on beta-carotene, which is believed to help heal intestinal tissue. A juice that provides a healthy dose of both nutrients can be prepared by juicing three carrots, three celery ribs and one-fourth of a head of cabbage. Drink this blend once a day, she says.

Build a base at breakfast. Another good idea: Mix a tablespoon of powdered fibre with a glass of orange juice in the morning. "It's a real simple, healthy way to start the day," says Dr. McNally. Check your pharmacy shelves for powdered fibre that comes in different flavours, consistencies, and sizes like Metamucil and Citrucel (Fibogel or Celevac).

Subtract seeds. Doctors are currently debating the effects of seeds on diverticulosis. Some experts say seeds of all types can aggravate the condition and lead to diverticulitis. Dr. Epstein, for instance, tells people to at least cut back on seeds as well as corn, nuts, and popcorn.

Moderate the meat. Dr. Aldoori's study also found that men who ate beef, pork, or lamb as a main dish more than two times a week had over three times the risk of diverticulosis compared to men who ate meat meals less than once a month. Nobody knows why meat may increase your risk for the disease, though Dr. Aldoori theorises that it may trigger a type of bacterial activity in the intestines that weakens the walls of the colon. "You should reduce your meat intake," he says, "not only to help prevent diverticulosis but also to help prevent heart disease and many cancers."

Chew it out. Chew each bite of food at least 20 times. Chewing stimulates the gastrointestinal tract to produce the right enzymes to break down your food. "Besides, eating should be taken as an opportunity to relax and reward yourself, rather than another daily rushed obligation," explains Nancy Russell, MD, an internist. If you find yourself unable to slow your chops, put your fork or spoon down between mouthfuls.

Pick some prunes. Prunes combine lots of fibre with a sweet delicious taste. They've been a folk remedy for constipation for ages.

Cut out the java. Sometimes people drink a lot of coffee to try and get their stools to pass. That's the wrong approach. Steady high doses of coffee will harm, not help, your diverticulosis. Caffeine is a diuretic, and stools without water get hard, which is what causes pouches to form. Lots of caffeine can also cause the muscles in the colon to contract more, which prevents the stool from passing along. So if you have diverticulosis, switch to decaf—or at least cut down on the leaded stuff.

Take fast action. Consider going on a short, doctor-approved fast to help the digestive system get back on track. When people are hospitalised with serious diverticulitis attacks, they are put on liquid diets, which are, essentially, fasts. Applied to hundreds of conditions, fasting, when done correctly, enhances the body's natural tendencies to heal itself. It has been used since Socrates' time for health rejuvenation and spiritual growth. But it also has specific physiological benefits for repairing the colon, explains Joel Fuhrman, MD, and author of *Fasting and Eating for Health*. Avoiding food gives the colon an opportunity to rest. Fasting also changes the bacteria populating the gut, giving beneficial bacteria a chance to repopulate themselves, Dr. Fuhrman explains. Do a home fast only under the supervision of your doctor, he cautions.

Helpful vitamins and supplements:

Try a fibre supplement. Sometimes women with diverticulosis find that high-fibre foods make them feel even more crampy. If fruits, beans and vegetables are a problem for you, try a fibre supplement such as Metamucil or Fibercon (Fibogel or Celevac), says Linda Lee, MD, a gastroenterologist. Available in supermarkets and chemists, supplements can be taken in granular form (mixed in water or juice) or wafer form (washed down with at least eight ounces of water). Supplements soften and bulk up your stool, which should keep pouches from forming.

Go pro. Take one to two "probiotic" capsules with meals. A healthy bowel is populated by beneficial bacteria, or probiotics, that complete the digestion of proteins and carbohydrates while also keeping bad bacteria at bay. "When someone contracts diverticulitis, I usually figure that there is some sort of bacterial imbalance," says William D. Nelson, N.D., a naturopathic physician. He recommends the probiotics L-acidophilus and Bifidobacterium that are found in the refrigerated section of most health food stores. Look for a supplement that contains 1.5 billion micro-organisms per gram and that also contains "fructooligosaccharides," or FOS. This is food for the bacteria that helps them get established in your colon. Take one to two capsules with each meal for six months, or until your symptoms are resolved.

Get your B's. Take 100 milligrams of B-complex vitamins twice a day. The B vitamins are powerful nutrients for the colon and might also ease stress, says Dr. Russell. She also recommends, if possible, supplementing with 500 to 2,000 milligrams of vitamin C a day as well as 400 to 600 milligrams of vitamin E, and 10,000 to 15,000 milligrams of vitamin A. At least take a multivitamin, she adds.

Help your pancreas. Enlist five pancreatic enzymes to aid digestion. Look for a formula at the health food store that contains lipase to digest fat and oils, cellulase to digest fibre, amylase to digest starch and sugar, lactase to digest milk, and protease for protein, advises says Dr. Russell. Take according to package directions for as long as needed.

Easing the pain with exercise:

Get moving. Regular physical activity may be an important factor in preventing of symptomatic diverticular disease. In Dr. Aldoori's study on exercise, he concluded that men who exercised the least had the highest risk of developing the disease. (Those who had low levels of physical activity and low levels of fibre intake had the very highest risk of developing the disease—$2^{1}/_{2}$ times higher than men who got plenty of exercise and fibre.)

How does exercise protect the colon from diverticula? No one knows for sure. But there are some theories. Exercise speeds transit time—the time it takes for the stool to move through the intestines—which means that the colon may have to generate less pressure. Exercise delivers more blood flow to the muscles of the colon, which may keep them stronger. Whatever the reason, your next step is to get more fit, says Dr. Aldoori. Check with your doctor before you take up any new fitness program, and then get started.

Walk. Increased physical activity—any kind of increased physical activity—can lower the risk of diverticular disease. And that includes walking briskly three to five times a week, depending on your current level of fitness and age, says Dr. Aldoori.

Run. Dr. Aldoori's study also showed that those who participated in very vigorous exercise, like jogging or running, had the lowest risk of the disease. "The more you increase the level of physical exercise, the more benefits you will probably get," he says.

Choose another kind of exercise fun. The most important thing in regard to exercise and diverticular disease prevention is that you remain active, says Dr. Aldoori. Just moving about may get your digestion working and help prevent the disease. Stair climbing, rowing, callisthenics, bicycling, and racquet sports all lower the risk of getting diverticulosis if performed regularly.

Everyday prevention:

Use laxatives carefully. Bulk laxatives like Metamucil or Fybogel are safe for continual use, but stool softeners or stimulant laxatives or enemas should be reserved for only occasional use. Remember that some herbal or natural laxatives can be just as strong and irritating to the bowel as over-the-counter drugs. Check with your doctor.

Don't smoke. Smoking is terrible for your intestines. It decreases the blood supply, which can cause or increase cramps.

Breathe easy. Relieve tension by giving your breath attention. Negative emotional states result in negative effects on your bowels—spasms, too much stomach acid, and acid reflex, to name a few, says Dr. Fuhrman.

Bringing focus to your breath is a natural tranquiliser for the nervous system, explains Andrew Weil, MD, author of *Spontaneous Healing*. Try his simple relaxation technique:

Start seated with your back straight. Place the tip of your tongue just behind your upper front teeth and keep it there for the entire exercise. Making a "whoosh" sound, exhale completely through your mouth. Now inhale quietly through your nose to the count of four. Next, hold your breath for a count of seven. Exhale completely through your mouth making a "whoosh" sound to a count of eight. Repeat this cycle three more times for a total of four breaths. Do this at least two times a day, with progressively slower breathing counts. "Do it whenever you are aware of internal tension," says Dr. Weil.

Herbal help:

Ask for Robert. Relieve digestive inflammation with Roberts Complex. You can purchase this mix of healing plants at health food stores; follow the instructions on the label. "It's a classic remedy among naturopaths," says Dr. Nelson. Look for a brand that contains marsh mallow, slippery elm, goldenseal, echinacea, cabbage powder, and bromelain. Take the formula for three months, or until your symptoms are resolved.

Say hello to aloe. Have two teaspoons of aloe vera juice two times a day, straight or in tea or juice. Sold in health food stores, the juice of aloe is well-known for healing irritation of the gastrointestinal tract. It is also helpful as a mild laxative, explains Dr. Russell. If it becomes too much of a laxative, however, reduce the dosage to only one teaspoon before meals.

Go for ginkgo. Take 40 to 80 milligrams a day of ginkgo capsules. Be sure to get a variety containing 24 percent ginkgo flavone glycosides. Most people know ginkgo for improving memory and alertness. But since ginkgo helps microcirculation, it may help re-establish the tiny blood vessels in the gastrointestinal tract, explains Dr. Nelson. Take ginkgo all the while you are trying to heal your gastrointestinal tract, which is typically for six months.

Imbibe bitters. Stimulate digestion and relieve constipation with bitter herbs. Put 10 to 15 drops of Angostura bitters in a shot glass of your favourite tea or juice and drink it before meals, advises David Winston, an herbalist. Angostura bitters are made from the herb gentian and can be purchased at grocery and liquor stores. Eaten as salad or steamed, other bitters that are good to incorporate into your diet include dandelion, endive, raddicchio, and broccoli rabe. You may also like drinking chicory, a healthy coffee substitute.

Find some flax. Commission E, the German expert panel that passes on the safety and effectiveness and dosage of medicinal herbs for the German government, approves using one to three tablespoons of crushed flaxseed two or three times a day (with lots of water) to treat diverticulitis.

Seek out slippery elm. Dr. Weil suggests using slippery elm bark powder to treat diverticulitis. The fibrous bark contains large quantities of a gentle laxative that soothes the digestive tract while keeping things moving. The U.S. Food and Drug Administration has declared slippery elm to be a safe and effective digestive soother. Prepare it like oatmeal, adding hot milk or water to the powdered bark to make a cereal.

Soothe with camomile. British herbalist David Hoffman, author of *The Herbal Handbook*, suggests sipping on camomile tea throughout the day. This herb is particularly valuable in treating diverticulitis because its anti-inflammatoryaction soothes the entire digestive system, he says. Try making a tea with two teaspoons of dried camomile per cup of boiling water. Steep for five to ten minutes.

Go wild for yams. According to California herbalist Kathi Keville, wild yam helps relieve the pain and inflammation of diverticulitis. Her formula: two parts wild yam, (anti-inflammatory and antispasmodic), one part valerian (relaxing digestive tract soother), one part black haw (anti-spasmodic) and one part peppermint (anti-inflammatory and anti-spasmodic).Try a couple of tablespoons of this herb mixture brewed in a quart or so of water.

Dry Eyes

The pain: If you have dry eyes, you'll often feel like you've got an eyelash stuck in your eye. Your eyes may burn, redden, and itch. Sometimes your vision will blur.

The cause: Like your car's windshield, your eyes have a built in cleaning system designed to ensure better vision. To clean your windshield, you squirt fluid onto the glass and your wiper blades spread it around. To lubricate and clean your eyes, glands secrete tiny tears that get spread around by your eyelids when you blink. "Your eyes must constantly produce this tear fluid for you to feel comfortable and have clear vision," says Robert Cykiert, MD, an ophthalmologist. "Otherwise, they get dry and uncomfortable." Sometimes dry eyes are a chronic problem because the tear film has been damaged by a disease, such as Sjögren's syndrome, in which the tear gland is inflamed and there are fewer tears to replenish the film. And many women experience dry eyes as a result of the hormonal changes that may occur during pregnancy or menopause. But most people only experience the dry eyes every now and then, in response to some environmental factor, like low humidity or staring at a computer screen.

See a doctor if:
...you need to apply drops more than three to four drops of artificial tears, advises Dr. Robert Cykiert, MD. An ophthalmologist can insert plugs into the tiny hole in the corner of your eyelid. The plugs will prevent tears from draining into the back of your nose. This is a quick, reversible office procedure that takes just a few minutes. If you wear contact lenses, ask your doctor about getting refitted with a type that doesn't need as much moisture.
...if you have dizziness and double vision along with eyestrain.

Medication:
Any type of antihistamine—whether prescription or over the counter—can dry out your eyes, says ophthalmologist Larry R. Taub, MD. If you take antihistamines like Benadryl for allergies, consider cutting back your dosage (Motion sickness medications like Dramamine also contain antihistamines.) Or up your use of artificial tears, he says.

Other medications that may dry out your eyes include:

Some heart medications, for example, propranolol (Indcral or Angilol) used to treat high blood pressure may reduce tear production

Some antidepressants like amitriptyline (Elavil)

Over-the-counter decongestants used for nasal stuffiness, such as pseudo-ephedrine (Sudafed) or phenylpropanolamine (Tavist-D or Day Nurse)

Anticholinergics like dicyclomine (Bentyl or Merbentyl) used to treat intestinal or urinary problems

Remedies:

Buy tears. Sold over-the-counter, artificial tears can provide the lubricant you need. You have your choice of dozens of products. All have their merits. But not all may be right for you, says Dr. Larry R. Taub. So choose those most comfortable to you. Tears have the following differences:

Thick versus Watery. Thicker tears and ointments will stay on your eyes longer, but they can temporarily make your vision blurry. Ointments work best at night when it's impractical to keep getting up and applying tears. Dr. Taub that you use thicker tears during the day when thinner tears stop working their magic. You can tell if tears are thick or thin by checking the active ingredients. Thicker tears contain methylcellulose.

Preservatives versus No Preservatives. Preservative isn't necessarily a bad word. It makes your bottle of tears last longer. Tears without a preservative can only be used right after opening and then must be thrown away, which makes it more expensive. Some people, however, find tears containing preservatives to be irritating, says Dr. Taub. Use the kind with preservatives if you need only apply tears four to five times a day. If you need more frequent applications, switch to a brand that is labelled preservative-free.

Once you chose a type of ointment or drops, feel free to try different brands in that class. You may find that some work better for you than others.

Get rid of anti-redness drops. Stay away from eyedrops that are designed to ease red, bloodshot eyes, such as Visine, Murine or Optrex. They may make your eyes look better, but the ingredients in these drops can actually dry you out more than they help, says Paula Newsome, O.D., an optometrist

Stay away from irritants. Pollen, pollution, smoke and other airborne particles won't necessarily dry out your eyes. But they can make already dry eyes feel uncomfortable and red, explains Dr. Taub. So sit in the nonsmoking section at restaurants, run a filtered air conditioner during the summer, and wear the kind of sunglasses that wrap around your eyes in windy, dusty areas. Sunglasses will also keep the bright light from the sun from irritating your sensitive eyes.

Preserve your natural tears. Dry winter heat, a hair dryer in your face, or your car's air-conditioning vent, all can suck the moisture from your eyes. So keep that blast of air pointed in a different direction. And use a humidifier during winter months, says Dr. Taub. Such methods will keep you from robbing your eyes of their own moisture.

Apply a warm compress. Heat will stimulate your glands to produce more oil, which will keep your tears from evaporating as quickly, says James Gigantelli, MD, director of ophthalmic plastic and reconstructive surgery at the University of Missouri in Columbia. Fill a wash basin with hot tap water and immerse a washcloth. Apply the washcloth to your eyes for about 10 minutes twice a day.

Drink plenty of water. Guzzling down glass after glass of water won't solve your problems entirely. But it can aid you in your quest to keep your eyes moist, says Dr. Newsome. Aim for eight 8-ounce glasses per day.

Take reading breaks. When we read or work at a computer, we often forget to blink, which keeps the fluid we do have from getting spread out over our eyes, warns Dr. Cykiert. You can't consciously remember to blink. You'll drive yourself nuts. But you can take a break every 10 minutes or so. That way you'll naturally resort to your normal blink rate.

Try palming. Rub your hands together and get them a bit warm, then gently cover your closed eyes with your palms, says Jeffrey Anshel, O.D., an optometrist, and author of *Healthy Eyes—Better Vision.* "That'll let all the muscles around your eyes relax and keep your eyes from having to work," says Dr. Anshel. Breathe easily as you palm your eyes. Do this for about five minutes, and this should rest your eyes quite nicely, he says.

Take a deep wink. Take a deep breath while raising your shoulders and scrunching your eyes and fists closed as tightly as you can, then exhale and relax all of the muscles at once, recommends Anne Barber, O.D., an optometrist. This technique is called a deep wink. She says that by "tightening up the voluntary muscles (like your fists and shoulders) and letting them go, we frequently can trick the involuntary focus muscles to let go at the same time." This should help relax those overworked eye muscles.

Cool the fire. According to the principles of Ayurveda, a 5,000-year-old traditional form of medicine from India, your body is governed by five elements—space, air, earth, fire, and water. When one of these elements is not balanced, you get sick. The eyes are the seat of pitta, or fire, in the body, so eyestrain suggests a fire imbalance in the body. One thing that helps cool this fire is sandalwood oil, available in health food stores, says Pratima Raichur, a doctor of naturopathy, an Ayurvedic practitioner, and author of *Absolute Beauty.*

Add a drop of the oil to an ounce (two tablespoons) of water and stir. Soak two cotton pads in the diluted oil, squeeze out all the excess liquid, and put them over your closed eyes for about five minutes, Dr. Raichur says. This helps rebalance the heat element and alleviate the eyestrain.

Calm your mind, calm your eyes. You can relax your eyes through meditation anywhere, even in your office, by "sitting and closing your eyes, paying attention to your breath and how you're breathing," Dr. Raichur says. "And as we start paying attention, the breath starts slowing down. It relaxes by itself." This signals your mind to relax. "And when the mind is relaxed, the eyes become relaxed," she says.

Make the light right. "Lighting is probably the most overlooked and underemphasized aspect of office work," says Dr. Anshel. "The lighting is very critical because it causes glare. If it's not directed properly, it can cause poor vision, which can cause strain in itself. And without light, there's no sight." So turn off your computer monitor and check to see if there are any reflections of lightbulbs on the blank screen. If so, that could be causing your problem. Move the light or the computer so that there is no glare on the screen, he says.

Distance yourself. Keep at least 20 inches between yourself and the computer screen and ideally 26 inches or more, Dr. Anshel says. This "reduces the amount of focusing that people have to do on the screen." The closer you are, the more you need to focus, which is part of the problem with eyestrain.

Brighten up. Pay attention to the contrast between your office lighting and the computer screen, Dr. Anshel says. It's like when Mom told you not to watch TV in the dark because it was bad for your eyes. You shouldn't look at a dim computer screen in a brightly lit office. Your eyes will have to readjust from the room light to the monitor light, causing fatigue and strain, Dr. Anshel says. To remedy this, adjust the brightness control on your monitor if the screen seems dark, he says.

Get prepped for dry-eye situations. If you are about to be in a situation where you know you usually get dry eyes—when you are about to spend time in front of a computer, for instance—put in a drop before the activity. Or put in a drop at the first sign of discomfort.

Prepare for takeoff. The air in aeroplanes is uniquely drying and irritating, says Dan Nelson, MD, an ophthalmologist. First, the plane has probably just been cleaned, so the air is loaded with chemicals. Second, the air in the plane is pressurised at 5,000 feet, which means dry air. Third, that air is recirculated during the entire flight. "Many flight attendants have trouble with dry eyes," he says. Use eyedrops before you get on the plane and while flying, he suggests.

Keep your eyes moist on the road. "People often experience dry eyes in cars," says Dr. Nelson. Make sure that the vents aren't blowing in your eyes. Or sit in the back seat if you are not driving.

Block out wind and cold. Being outdoors in cold, dry, windy climates can steal moisture from your eyes, says Dr. Nelson. The best way to protect your eyes is with a pair of glasses. If regular sunglasses don't help, he says, try wraparound sunglasses with lenses that are close to your face. If wraparound glasses don't help, try moisture-chamber glasses. These have pieces of plastic film on the sides of the frames that form an enclosure around your eyes. They are available at your local optician, eyeglasses stores, and some outdoor and wilderness outfitters. And if they don't work, try wearing ski goggles, says Dr. Nelson. "The complete enclosure prevents evaporation and increases moisture. They keep the wind out, and they can be worn over other glasses."

Watch out for dry indoor air. Being indoors in winter can also take a toll on your eyes—the heating dries out the air. To prevent dry eyes, Dr. Nelson recommends using a vaporiser next to your bed while you are sleeping or in your office while you are working. "They tend to work better than humidifiers in really making the air wet."

Monitor your makeup. Perhaps your makeup or eye cream should take the blame for early-morning dry eyes. If you have dry eyes and routinely apply makeup or creams to the eye area, stop using them for a few days and see if your symptoms go away, Dr. Nelson suggests. And be sure to take off all of your eye makeup at bedtime. "Leaving your makeup on just exposes your eyes to irritating or drying chemicals."

Splash a little water in your eye. If closing your eyes for a few minutes doesn't relubricate them, step into the nearest washroom and splash water in your eyes, says Monica L. Monica, MD, Ph.D., an ophthalmologist and spokesperson for the American Academy of Ophthalmology. (If you wear contact lenses, skip this remedy. Otherwise, bacteria routinely present in water could interfere with your wetting solution or lodge under your lens and lead to infection.)

Moisten your eyes before blow-drying your hair. Do you use a hair dryer every morning? To keep from drying your eyes along with your tresses, use artificial tears before and after you blow-dry, says Dr. Monica. For extra measure, moisten your eyes halfway through, too.

Skip the alcohol. Drinking alcohol can leave your mouth parched. It can dry out your eyes, too. If you go out for a social drink, keeping alcohol to a minimum (or choosing a non-alcoholic beverage) is kinder to your eyes, says Dr. Monica.

Stay smoke-free. "Smoking is notorious" for causing dry eyes, says Dr. Monica. If you smoke, or if you live with someone who does, using artificial tears will keep your eyes moistened. Quitting, of course, solves the underlying problem.

Wear your lenses part-time. To ease the strain of dry eyes, "Remove your lenses at the end of the workday, just like you kick off your shoes," says Dr. Monica. If you have dry eyes, this might be a good idea whether you have daily-wear or extended-wear lenses.

Pretreat at bedtime. If you wake up with scratchy, burning eyes, use tear ointment such as Lacri-Lube before you go to bed, says Dr. Monica. It's thicker than artificial tears and available over the counter at your drugstore. It will help keep your eyes lubricated, but it's only for overnight use, because it blurs your vision.

Protect you eyes with sunglasses. Any kind of glasses are helpful, but the wraparound kind really work the best. Glacier glasses, which have leather shields on the sides, provide even better protection.

Wash your eyelids. About half of the people who suffer from dry eyes have "crusty" eyes when they wake up or at other times of the day. This condition, called blepharitis, is actually an inflammation of the glands and lash follicles along the margins of the eyelids. It's thought to be caused by a bacterial infection, and severe cases are treated with antibiotics. Saline solution, baby shampoo, even diluted dandruff shampoo (if you're careful not to get it into your eyes!) can all be used to clean eyelids, experts say.

Ear Pain

The pain: Your ear hurts—on the outside, from your ear canal out, or on the inside, behind your eardrum. The pain is dull and throbbing or so exquisitely sharp that it makes you whimper and fear to move your head. There may or may not be discharge, which can smell quite foul.

The cause: The microbes that cause earaches usually show up first as a respiratory infection in your nose or throat. All it takes is a little push—you blow your nose, you lie down—and the viruses or bacteria move into your eustachian tubes. These are tiny channels that connect your nasal passages to your inner ears. From there, it's a short trip to the middle ear and your eardrum, which is laced with sensitive nerve endings. The infection creates pus, which pushes against your eardrum, causing pain. It can even make the eardrum burst. Children get more earaches because they have more respiratory infections and because their eustachian tubes are immature and unable to handle even a small infection.

Other causes of earache include swimmer's ear, which can happen when excess water is trapped in the ear canal, and the changes in air pressure that occur during an aeroplane flight. Earaches can also be triggered by hair and other objects that get stuck in the ear.

See a doctor if:
...your pain lasts longer than 24 hours.
...you have truly severe pain, discharge, hearing loss, an earache accompanied by a fever of 102°F or above, or tenderness when you press the soft areas near your ear, around your jaw, or in the upper neck area.
...you feel acute pain during an aeroplane flight that doesn't go away immediately afterward, since that could be a sign of a perforated eardrum. For swimmers, see a doctor if you have persistent itching and discomfort from swimmer's ear that doesn't go away when you try home remedies.

Quick relief:
Warm up to olive oil. A few drops of olive oil or mineral oil can provide temporary relief, says Clough Shelton, MD, an associate clinical professor

of otolaryngology at the University of California, Los Angeles. Warm it up like a baby's bottle under hot tap water for a few minutes. Test the oil first (it should be about body temperature) and apply it with an ear dropper. Make sure to use only enough to coat the inner lining of the ear, he says.

Turn on the heat. You can try setting a heating pad on medium and placing it on top of the sore ear. Or you can turn a hair dryer on the lowest warm setting and direct the warm air down the ear canal, holding the dryer 6 to 12 inches from your ear. Do not use the hair dryer for more than three to five minutes. A hot waterbottle wrapped in a towel makes a comforting pillow for an aching ear. A warm compress—such as a towel rung out in hot water—provides effective warm, moist heat. Or try warming up an oven-safe plate and wrapping it in a towel.

Prop yourself up. You're better off sitting up in bed than lying flat on your back, says David Marty, MD, otolaryngologist and author of *The Ear Book*. Sitting up actually allows blood to drain away from the head so there's less congestion in the eustachian tube, he says. "That's why kids with an earache will quit crying when you pick them up and start crying again when you lay them down," he says. "It's not that they want to be held, it's just that they feel better with their heads up."

Try a vasoconstrictor. Over-the-counter nasal sprays like Neo-Synephrine contain the ingredient phenylephrine, which helps return your eustachian tube to normal functioning, says Charles P. Kimmelman, MD, professor of otolaryngology at Manhattan Eye, Ear and Throat Hospital. "The spray shrinks down the lining of the nose and hopefully the region around the entrance of the eustachian tubes, allowing the tube to function better. If the eustachian tube returns to normal, you'll feel better," he explains. Don't use phenylephrine-containing nosedrops for more than a few days, and make sure you don't exceed the daily dosage recommended on the label. Overuse of nasal sprays can actually make the problem worse.

Opt for a painkiller. Another possible temporary remedy for ear pain: an over-the-counter analgesic like Advil or Tylenol, says W. Steven Pray, Ph.D., a professor of pharmaceutics. "Just don't fall into the trap of taking an analgesic and thinking because your ear doesn't hurt anymore, you don't need an antibiotic," he says. "The analgesic doesn't kill the organisms—it just controls the pain."

Massage a little. Earache pain can be very sharp, so people tend to tense up, says Michael Wynne, Ph.D., an otolaryngologist. Relax that tension with a little light massage. Using your fingertips, apply gentle pressure and rub your jaw and neck with circular strokes for 5 to 10 minutes. Massaging the large muscle groups in the jaw and the back of the neck helps reduce tension and improves overall relaxation, thereby decreasing some of the discomfort, he says.

Nutritional remedies:

Reach for the hot sauce. "Food that is so spicy that it makes your nose run can ease earaches associated with congestion," says Evelyn Kluka, MD, pediatric otolaryngologist. "Try a good hot-and-sour soup.

Fill up on fluids. Drinking lots of water and juice not only helps soothe the symptoms, but repeated swallowing can also help clear your eustachian tubes, says Dr. Kimmelman, Chewing and yawning are also good for clearing your eustachian tubes, he says.

Watch your diet. "I advise people with ear infections to stop consuming dairy products, sugar, and coffee," says Amy Rothenberg, a doctor of naturopathy and editor of the *New England Journal of Homeopathy.* "These foods all seem to make the body work harder to heal."

Helpful vitamins and supplements:

Boost your daily intake of immunity-bolstering vitamins and minerals. Here are the four best to take.

Vitamin C: Up to 4,000 milligrams per day in divided doses

Vitamin A: 50,000 IU (international units) each day for two days, followed by 5,000 IU per day for up to four weeks

Zinc: Up to 100 milligrams per day

Copper: 4 milligrams per day

Everyday prevention:

Ask about antibiotics. Because a bacterial infection is one of the most common causes of earache, most doctors recommend taking antibiotics like Amoxil and Ceclor to beat the bug, stresses Dr. Pray.

Don't be a blowhard. If you have a cold, blow your nose slowly and gently. Blowing too hard can force bacteria-laden mucus into the middle ear, leading to an ear infection, warns Anne Simons, MD, a professor of family and community medicine.

Reduce nasal congestion. By keeping your sinuses clear, you help relieve pressure inside your eardrum and prevent blockages inside the eustachian tubes. Solutions for unclogging your nose include: using a plain saline nasal spray two or three times a day; eating spicy, peppery foods; and if necessary, using a decongestant like Sudafed, according to package instructions.

Quit abusing cotton swabs. Cotton-tipped swabs are fine for cleaning your outer ears, but when you start using them to clean out wax from inside your ear canal you might as well be sending out an engraved invitation to an ear infection. So don't. Not only can swabs break the inner ear's delicate skin and make way for infection, says Dr. Wynne, but also they can cause problems when they accidentally get shoved in too far or break off and damage an eardrum. And ear wax, believe it or not, is a first line of defence against infection and, therefore, ear pain. Too much aggressive ear wax removal and you have cleared the way for bacteria to

Jettison Aeroplane-Ear Pain

The ear pain we get when we are climbing or descending from eight miles above the earth isn't caused by infection. Our ears often ache when we are aloft because of unequal pressure on the inside of the eardrum and the outside. That stretches the eardrum inward and causes that sharp pain. Try these airborne ear-savers.

Clear the way before takeoff. Taking a simple over-the-counter decongestant 30 minutes before your next flight leaves the ground can put an end to air-travel-related earaches, say researchers. In a study of 190 fliers with recurrent ear pain, only 32 percent of the people who received a decongestant containing pseudoephedrine before takeoff had ear pain. Sixty-two percent of those in the no-decongestant group felt some pain and popping.

The decongestants work by opening up the eustachian tube, which prevents pressure (the source of the pain and popping) from building up inside your ears. The medicines also help decrease secretions that might block the tube, says study co-author Jeffrey Jones, MD, director of the department of emergency medicine at Butterworth Hospital in Grand Rapids, Michigan.

Be sure to take the decongestant before you fly, says Dr. Jones. It won't work as well if you take it after your earache gets started. Building on his earlier study, Dr. Jones also found that oral decongestants work better than nasal spray. One dose should last you all day, so you don't have to keep popping decongestants if your flight is delayed. The only side effect seen in the study was drowsiness.

One caution: Avoid pseudoephedrine if you have thyroid disease, heart disease, high blood pressure, diabetes, or an enlarged prostate.

Consider the Frenzel manoeuver. If you don't want to take decongestants—or you can't for health reasons—try the Frenzel method of

proceed unhindered to your inner ear.

Don a shower cap. If you have a ruptured eardrum, it's critical to keep your ears dry until the eardrum heals. Water can lead to continued infection. It's best not to swim at all if you have a ruptured eardrum, says Evany Zirul, D.O., a professor of clinical medicine. When you shower, wear a shower cap or stuff your ears with cotton balls slathered with petroleum jelly, or plastic earplugs, to keep water out of your ears.

Humidify your nose. "Use a plain saline nasal spray, available over the counter, several times a day when your nose is congested. It will reduce the congestion caused by a cold or allergies, thereby reducing your ear discomfort," says Dr. Kluka.

Breathe away an ache. According to Effie Chow, R.N., Ph.D., a certified clearing your ears instead, says Dr. Jones. Pinch your nose closed and push your tongue firmly against the back part of the roof of your mouth. That works a little air through your eustachian tube. This method works best for preventing the problem rather than treating it, says Dr. Jones, so you will want to start doing it as soon as the plane begins its descent.

Blow some bubbles. Another trick from the frequent-flyer crowd is to chew gum during air flights. You swallow more often when you chew gum, and swallowing makes the eustachian tube open and close faster, says Evany Zirul, D.O., professor of clinical medicine at the University of Health Sciences in Missouri.

Plug into earPlanes. Available at chemists, these earplugs contain a tiny valve that equalises the pressure in your ear over a much longer period of time than your actual descent in a plane would. Put them in before your flight and leave them in until after you have checked your baggage.

Don't pop under pressure. Don't try to clear your ears by holding your nose, closing your mouth, and then trying to build the pressure inside your eardrum. "This routine tries to force air through a tube that may already be blocked, and it can actually injure your ears," says Dr. Jones.

Give baby his bottle. To prevent a baby from developing an earache during takeoff or landing, give him a bottle to suck on as the plane climbs or descends. The sucking action can help clear his ears. For extra insurance, make sure that the baby is sitting upright during his feeding, says Dr. Jones.

Give the kids some suckers. Older children can suck on candy or lozenges during the flight—or give them gum if they are old enough (try this tip yourself, too). The idea is to keep them swallowing so that their ears stay clear. If they have complained about ear pain before, Dr. Jones says, you may want to give them a decongestant recommended by your pediatrician.

acupuncturist and Qigong master. Qigong's deep-breathing techniques are effective for earaches and other pain, because they oxygenate the body, strengthen the immune system and open blockages.

"Breathe in deeply from your diaphragm, not your chest, bringing air in through your nose," says Dr. Chow. "Imagine the area right behind your naval to your upper chest area as an accordion, and fill it with air through your nose. Keeping your lips closed, expand the accordion. Then exhale, collapsing the accordion, and allow the air to escape through your lips. Continue this exercise until you feel relaxed and the pain eases." Dr. Chow suggests that this breathing be done from time to time over a 24-hour period.

Say no to nickel. "Earrings containing nickel can cause allergic reactions in many women," says Hilary E. Baldwin, MD, a dermatologist. "And most jewellry contains nickel. Some women even have trouble with 14 karat gold, because it may contain trace amounts of nickel. So it's best to stick with sterling silver or hypoallergenic stainless-steel posts. In fact," she adds, "if your skin is sensitive, any part of the earring that touches your ear should be nickel-free."

Swab your earrings. To prevent infections, Dr. Baldwin advises women to keep earrings as clean as possible: Swab the posts or fasteners with a cotton ball soaked with rubbing alcohol before each wear.

Herbal help:

Use essential oils to prevent earache. Combine two or three drops of the essential oil of immortelle, also known as everlasting, with two or three drops of the essential oil of lavender or with one drop of the essential oil of damask rose and add them to an ounce of sweet almond or vegetable oil. Dip two cotton balls into the mixture, and gently place one in each ear, says Mark Stengler, N.D., a naturopathic physician and author of *The Natural Physician.* Then, spread some oil on your fingers and massage the ear and the skin around it, he says. These oils help prevent infection. Note: See your doctor before using an herbal ear preparation if you already have ear pain or if there is a discharge.

Ease with Ephedra. Also known as ma huang or Chinese ephedra, this herb contains two powerful decongestants, ephedrine and pseudo-ephedrine. They can help drain the fluid in the middle ear that is associated with middle ear infections. Pseudoephedrine is the active ingredient in many over-the-counter decongestants. One of these products, Sudafed, even takes its name from this compound. In a study of fliers with recurrent ear pain, 70 percent of those who took pseudoephedrine experienced relief. Be careful to stick to the recommended doses when using this herb. Adults shouldn't use more than one teaspoon of dried herb to make a tea or take more than one teaspoon of tincture. Although the herb can be taken up to three times a day, you should be cautious because ephedra is a stimulant and might cause insomnia or raise blood pressure. Some people have died from overdosing on this herb in an attempt to get high, and the U.S. Food and Drug Administration has taken steps to stop the sale of ephedrine supplements. Ephedra could be great for treating some children's problems, but because of the controversy surrounding it, you should consult your pediatrician before using it. Children should be given less than half of the amount appropriate for adults.

Get garlic. Like echinacea, garlic and its extracts have antibiotic and immune-boosting benefits. In studies, dripping garlic oil directly into the ear canal has been shown to treat fungal infections as well as or better than pharmaceutical drugs. Taken internally, garlic can help cure a middle ear infection. If you have an earache, add more garlic to your cooking. You might also try putting a few drops of garlic oil in the painful ear.

Go for goldenseal. This is another potent natural antibiotic. Some naturopaths suggest using a mixture of echinacea, goldenseal and licorice root (this just for flavour). You can make a tea using either a teaspoon of each herb or a dropperful of each tincture per cup of boiling water. Enjoy a cup three times a day.

Find forsythia, gentian and honeysuckle. All three of these herbs produce antibiotic activity. Practitioners of traditional Chinese medicine often prescribe them in powdered form, sprinkled on applesauce to treat children's ear infections. They are easily used to make tea.

Make a drinkable herbal juice. Mix 30 drops of echinacea and 30 drops of goldenseal tinctures in juice or water. Echinacea strengthens immunity by stimulating white blood cell production, while goldenseal harbours antibacterial compounds, says Michael Traub, N.D., a naturopathic physician. In addition, goldenseal has astringent properties: It helps dry up secretions and reduce inflammation, he says.

Make time for Mullein Mullein flowers have many fans. One British herbalist suggests putting mullein flower oil drops in the affected ear.

Make herbal ear drops. Dilute the essential oils of garlic and mullein by mixing three to five drops of each oil separately into one teaspoon of a carrier oil, such as jojoba, avocado, or apricot kernel. Place three drops of the garlic oil mixture and two drops of the mullein oil mixture directly in the aching ear. Do this three or four times a day until the pain subsides.

Numb pain with St. John's Wort. " To help soothe really sore ears, I recommend using St. John's wort oil," says Feather Jones director of the Rocky Mountain Centre for Botanical Studies in Colourado. "St. John's wort is a neural anti-inflammatory, so it is very effective in soothing inflammation around the nerves of the ear canal and stopping the pain. Plus, it's a good antiviral herb. The best way to use it is by mixing a solution of one-half St. John's wort and one-half mullein flower oil." As with other oils, add about three drops to the affected ear, cover with a cotton ball, and reapply every six to eight hours as necessary.

Enjoy peppermint. A number of herbalists suggest using mints, which are antiseptic, to relieve earache. Peppermint sounds most promising, because it contains menthol. Try using it as a tea.

Take teatree. Aromatherapists and many herbalists consider teatree oil a significant antiseptic when applied to the skin. Try mixing a few drops in vegetable oil to make eardrops. Just don't use the drops if there is a possibility that the eardrum has been perforated, and don't take teatree oil, or any essential oil, internally. The oils are extremely concentrated, and even small quantities of many of them can be poisonous. Just to be on the safe side, discontinue use if you experience any irritation.

Listen to homeopathy. If your ear pain is accompanied by great irritability and chills, Dr, Rothenberg suggests using Lepar sulphuricum. If it's teamed with a stuffy nose, excess saliva, and diarrhoea, select Mercurius vivus. If the pain has made you really irritable and pain radiates from your teeth to your ear, she recommends Chamomilla. With each of these remedies, select a 30X potency and take two or three pellets, advises Dr. Rothenberg. She recommends taking the remedy one time and only repeating it if you get better and then worse again. If it doesn't work, it means that you need a different remedy, Dr. Rothenberg says.

Beach swimmer's ear

Be careful with your cleaning. Cleaning your ears a day or so before a swim may actually rob your ears of the protection they need to prevent swimmer's ear, says Dr. Pray. "You need to keep the wax inside to protect and lubricate," he explains. "It's just as if you put wax on your finger and then put your finger in water—you know it's not going to get wet." When you do clean your ears, don't dig for wax; simply wipe the outer ear with a clean washcloth, he says.

Try alcohol. A drop or two of isopropyl alcohol in the ear may cause any water that remains in the ear to evaporate, says Dr. Pray.

Dry it out. Made with isopropyl alcohol and glycerin, Swim-Ear is one of several products on the market designed to evaporate any water that may remain in the ear, says Dr. Pray.

Try treating it with a mixture of vinegar and alcohol: Mix one-half ounce of distilled white vinegar with one-half ounce of rubbing alcohol and put three drops of the mixture in the affected ear three times daily until the pain subsides. The alcohol will help evaporate any remaining water drops, and vinegar kills lingering bacteria.

Blow-dry soggy ears. The key to avoiding swimmer's ear is to deprive bacteria and fungus of the moisture they need to thrive. So, after your next swim or shower, aim a blow-dryer into your ears, suggests Dr. Zirul. "But use a low setting so that you don't burn your ears, and keep the dryer 12 to 18 inches away from your ear," she says. Thirty seconds or so should be long enough to dry them.

Leave your wax be. No matter how desperate you are, do not use cotton swabs to remove earwax, advises Dr. Zirul. "Using cotton swabs can contribute to swimmer's ear by scratching the ear canal, giving the infection a place to start," she says.

Endometriosis

The pain: Abdominal or lower back pain experienced by women during bowel movements or intercourse, or intense cramps that occur during the menstrual period.

The cause: For unknown reasons, the tissue that normally lines a woman's uterus begins to migrate and grow in other areas within the abdomen while still behaving like uterine tissue. That means that other internal organs may have an island of tissue that swells and sheds blood every month. Since this blood can't exit the body via the normal route, it causes swelling and inflammation.

See a doctor if...
...you have severe pelvic pain before and during menstruation or experience heavy or irregular bleeding. You should also consult your doctor if you have painful bowel movements or urination, pain during intercourse, or lower back pain.
...your pelvic pain causes you to miss work or other-wise limits your activities.
...you suspect you have endometriosis. Endometriosis has been called "the great imitator" because its symptoms often mimic those of other ailments, such as irritable bowel syndrome, urinary tract infections, even tubal pregnancies. Because a doctor's diagnosis is needed to determine the cause of pain, be sure to consult your doctor before you try any kind of self-treatment, says Owen Montgomery, MD, an obstetrics/gynaecology specialist. Dr. Montgomery recommends keeping a calendar of symptoms to help the doctor determine whether you have endometriosis or a different ailment.

Medication:
A variety of surgical techniques, including excision and laser vaporisation, can be used to get rid of endometrial tissue. There are many options, but the condition is nearly impossible to cure.

The leading drug treatment for endometriosis, danazol, inhibits your body's ability to produce the hormones that fuel the growth of endometriosis tissue. Danazol is available by prescription only. You may see some results in a month, but it could take six months for the drug to take full effect. As with any drug, there can be side effects from danazol. One drug comparison trial showed that women in the danazol group had more complaints about weight gain, muscle pain, and depression than the women using a new drug called nafarelin. There were also some problems with liver enzymes and cholesterol counts.

Nafarelin is available in a new nasal spray called Synarel. It seems to control endometriosis without the weight gain, muscle aches, or cholesterol changes seen with danazol. It can, however, induce hot flashes and nasal irritation and is more likely to cause vaginal dryness than danazol.

Oral contraceptives interfere with the normal menstrual cycle, resulting in lighter flow and less cramping.

Quick relief:

Sit in a sitz. "Warming treatments are helpful, and so is aromatherapy," says Amanda McQuade Crawford, a professional member of the American Herbalists Guild (AHG), and member of Britain's National Institute of Medical Herbalists. Try adding three drops each of the pure essential oils of rose geranium, clary sage, and cypress to a nice hot sitz bath (several inches of water in the tub), she suggests.

Geranium is said to ease anxiety and depression, clary sage is used for easing pain and tension, and cypress is recommended for fatigue and mood swings, according to Valerie Ann Worwood, a British aromatherapist and author of *The Fragrant Mind*. You can also use the essential oils for aromatherapy inhalation, McQuade Crawford says.

Soak up some castor oil. "Castor oil packs are incredibly useful for just about anything that hurts," says Ellen Kamhi, R.N., Ph.D., an herbalist, and host of the syndicated radio show Natural Alternatives, "and I've seen cases of endometriosis respond phenomenally well." Here's what to do: Take a piece of undyed wool flannel and soak it in castor oil. Place the flannel over the area of the abdomen that's painful and cover with a piece of clear plastic, then with a towel, and finally with a heating pad or hot water bottle heated to a comfortably warm temperature. Leave the pack on for about an hour. "I believe the packs work by helping to shrink the misplaced endometrial tissue," says Dr. Kamhi.

Soothe with heat. Place a warm heating pad on your abdomen, says David Redwine, MD, director of the Endometriosis Institute in Bend, Oregon. "Keep the temperature comfortably warm, and use the pad as long as you need to," he says. (As extra insurance against burns, you should put a cloth between the pad and your skin.)

Take a painkiller. The pain of endometriosis can be severe, especially during menstruation, says Sue Ellen Carpenter, MD, an obstetrician and gynaecologist. Tiny endometrial growths called petechiae are very active in producing prostaglandins, substances linked to the symptoms. Over-the-counter nonsteroidal anti-inflammatory drugs such as ibuprofen can help by interfering with prostaglandin production. Just follow the package directions.

Nutritional remedies:

Get your diet in order. It's a good idea to cut down on foods that might be increasing your oestrogen levels, says Barbara Silbert, D.C., N.D., a chiropractor and naturopathic doctor. Foods that are high in saturated fat have a tendency to make oestrogen more available to the body. She also recommends cutting down on alcohol and getting your fill of foods made from soy, such as tofu, tempeh, miso, soy milk, and soy flour. You should also eat more fibre and exercise regularly, she says.

Eat for a stronger immune system. Just as diet influences the severity of other diseases, it may have a role in causing endometriosis pain. 'There are data suggesting an association of autoimmune disease with both the risk of developing endometriosis and the extent or severity of endometriosis," says Dan Martin, MD, and a reproductive surgeon. To build a stronger immune system, eat plenty of fresh fruits and vegetables that are rich in vitamins. Vitamin C is especially important, so fill up your plate with vegetables and fruits such as broccoli, red bell peppers, oranges, strawberries and cantaloupe-all high in vitamin C.

Grind up some flax. "Essential fatty acids (EFAs) are important for women who have endometriosis because they help control inflammation," says Kathleen Maier, a physician's assistant. "The easiest, least expensive way to add EFAs to your diet is to buy a pound of flaxseed at a health food store. Because flaxseed goes rancid quickly, store it in the freezer and grind up small batches at a time, using a coffee grinder," suggests Maier. "Use about a tablespoon a day, sprinkled over cereal or in soups or stews."

Cut back on caffeine. Instead, opt for fruit juice or herbal tea. If you reduce the caffeine level in your diet, you may find that the severity of your symptoms decreases. Caffeine is a stimulant. When you take a stimulant, any problem gets worse. It makes the whole system go into a hyper mode.

Don't forget fish. Rich in omega-3 fatty acids, fish such as mackerel, herring and sardines are also helpful, because they suppress prostaglandin production, suggests gynaecology and fertility specialist Camran Nezhat, MD. Prostaglandin is a hormone in the uterine lining that causes cramping.

Bring on the bioflavonoids. Found in citrus fruits, garlic, onions and all vegetables, bioflavonoids seem to reduce excessive bleeding by strengthening capillary walls. They may also help lower excessively high oestrogen levels. Supplements of bioflavanoids are available at health food stores. Try 1,000 mg daily.

Drink lots of water. Drink eight 8-ounce glasses of water a day. Water retention can increase endometriosis pain, and the more fluid you take in, the less likely you are to retain water.

Beat it with beans. Many in the natural medicine camp have embraced soy products for treating endometriosis and other ailments that are related to oestrogen. The soy supporters tout soybeans because they are high in two oestrogen-like plant compounds, genistein and daidzein. Both of these phytooestrogens prevent your body from taking up the more harmful forms of oestrogen circulating in your blood. They take the place of that oestrogen, binding to oestrogen receptor sites and preventing more harmful oestrogens from binding to the same receptors.

The soy supporters are right. Soy is high in genistein and daidzein, but lots of other beans are also quite high in genistein, which appears to be the more active of the two phytooestrogens. "I predict that in the near future, the scientists who have been claiming that soy is a unique source of genistein will stop doing so. I also predict that there will be more emphasis on bean sprouts," says James A. Duke, Ph.D., author of *The Green Pharmacy*. As beans germinate, their genistein content (and the total phytooestrogen content) increases.

Pinto beans have almost as much genistein and daidzein as soybeans. Also, consider that some beans that don't have as much daidzein as soybeans have quite a bit more genistein. These include yellow split peas, black turtle beans, lima beans, anasazi beans, red kidney beans and red lentils. Also quite high in genistein are black-eyed peas, mung beans, adzuki beans and fava beans. An analysis of scurfy peas showed that they have 50 times more genistein than soybeans.

" I'd suggest eating as many edible beans as possible as often as possible. Also use generous amounts of bean sprouts in your salads and be sure to eat lots of bean soups, and baked beans," says Dr. Duke.

Pick peanuts. When peanuts are analysed, it turns out that they contain many of the, same healthful substances as soybeans and other beans. There's an extra bonus to be had if you select Spanish peanuts. The papery red membrane around Spanish peanuts is the original source of oligomeric procyanidins (OPCs), substances that also may help control hormone-dependent cancers and possibly endometriosis.

Add alfalfa. Alfalfa sprouts contain phytooestrogens, so use them liberally on salads. Even if they don't relieve endometriosis symptoms, they are green vegetables, and eating more vegetables lowers cancer risk. If you have lupus or a family history of lupus, however, steer clear of alfalfa sprouts. There's some evidence that they may trigger lupus in sensitive individuals.

Eat regularly. Eating three meals a day will help maintain your blood sugar level, says Deborah A. Metzger, MD Ph.D., director of the Reproductive Medicine Institute of Connecticut in Hartford. "When blood sugar gets too low, there's a lack of energy, and it can make it harder to deal with pain," she says.

Helpful vitamins and supplements:

Flush out toxins with magnesium. The other strategy to take with endometriosis is to get your body working to flush out as much oestrogen as it can, says Jennifer Brett, N.D., a naturopathic doctor, In the case of endometriosis, oestrogen could be considered a toxin. Your body has too much of it, and it's causing harm, she adds. Having a body full of toxins is like having a full vacuum cleaner bag, observes Dr. Silbert. To empty the bag, you need to help the liver and kidneys function at peak capacity, since they're the organs that do most of the cleaning up and cleaning out. Supplements can help keep them working at their best. "Your body works a whole lot better when there aren't so many toxins clogging up the works," she says.

Magnesium is an all-purpose toxin flusher, says Dr. Silbert. One of its jobs is to transmit fluids to and from cells, your bloodstream and lymphatic system (whose primary job is immunity), and your tissues. In supplement form, 350 milligrams should be effective when taken in combination with other supplements that also help to flush out oestrogen and toxins, she says.

Get better with B6 & milk thistle. You may also want to consider taking vitamin B6 and the herb milk thistle. Both will help the liver break down and dispose of excess oestrogen, says Dr. Brett. Studies have shown that when you supplement with B vitamins, you also help relieve other ailments associated with having too much oestrogen, such as pre-menstrual tension (PMT).

Try taking 50 milligrams of vitamin B6 twice a day, says Dr. Silbert. Because some women's bodies have trouble metabolising this vitamin in its standard form, she recommends taking pyridoxal-5-phosphate (P5P). This is the activated form of vitamin B6 that everyone's body can handle; if you take 50 milligrams of P5P twice a day, you'll be getting the equivalent of the same dose of vitamin B6. When you're taking milk thistle, follow the dosage directions on the package, typically one or two 150-milligram capsules three times daily.

Look for lipotropic factors. Lipotropic factors are another supplement that will help your liver excrete toxins, says Dr. Silbert. The lipotropic factors choline (also called lecithin), inositol, and methionine enhance liver function and chemical reactions that promote detoxification. In general, they work to unclog the liver so it can do its job better, she says. Look for a product labeled lipotropic factors and select the one that contains the closest ratio of the three factors. Check the label for directions. A typical brand contains 1,000 milligrams of choline, 1,000 milligrams of inositol, and 300 milligrams of methionine, and calls for taking one tablet three times a day. To make sure your kidneys are doing their share of the work, drink plenty of water—at least eight, eight-ounce glasses every day, advises Dr. Brett.

Try natural progesterone. Massage 1/4, to 1/2 teaspoon of a nonprescription natural progesterone cream (such as ProGest) into the soft areas of your skin three times a day, alternating between your face, neck, inner thigh, inner arms, and breasts. Natural progesterone helps counteract the effects of excess oestrogen. If you have pain only after ovulation, start the cream just before you ovulate and continue through your period. Don't confuse natural progesterone cream with the yam-derived creams usually sold in health food stores. You'll want a product with a 3 percent formulation.

Everyday prevention:

Enact a tampon taboo. "Tampons are bleached white with chlorine, and so are most sanitary napkins," says McQuade Crawford. "Studies show that chlorinated compounds can cause a number of problems, such as endocrine system disruption, reproductive problems, infertility, and cancer. I tell women to avoid using tampons, at least until they have been free of the symptoms of endometriosis for at least six months," she advises. Unbleached, unscented, nondeodorant cotton pads are available at many natural food stores, she notes.

Say no to plastics. "When a woman with endometriosis comes in to see me, I always tell her to avoid using milk, juice, or bottled water that comes in plastic containers," says Maier, "and to look for glass bottles instead." Plastics are considered by herbalists to be endodisruptors, and it is suspected that the chemical additives in plastic containers can leach into liquids and foods.

Counter constipation. "If you're constipated and bloated, you're going to feel a lot worse," says Dr. Metzger, especially if the endometrial tissue has encroached into your bowel area. So be sure to eat plenty of vegetables and other high-fibre foods and drink lots of water to keep your bowels moving.

Change sexual positions. Painful sexual intercourse may be remedied by choosing a position in which the woman has greater control over penetration, says Dr. Metzger. "The missionary position is not the best for control. The female on top is better. The best thing to do is experiment to find the most comfortable position."

Exercise if at all possible. A program of regular exercise, three times a week for at least 30 minutes, can help relieve pain and menstrual cramps, says Dr. Carpenter. Exercise reduces menstrual flow and, therefore, the endometrial irritation and inflammation. It also increases your body's production of endorphins, natural pain-blocking substances released by the brain, says Dr. Metzger. Walking is a good basic exercise, says Dr. Metzger, though some women with endometriosis may find it too jarring. In that case, swimming or doing a routine of stretches are good ways to keep the juices flowing.

Keep a calendar of symptoms. If you know when endometriosis pain is likely to occur each month, you can plan around it.

Stop smoking. While there's no scientific proof, most experts suspect that smoking aggravates endometriosis symptoms and pain.

Herbal help:

Try an herbal trio. " In order to get endometriosis under control, you have to reduce the amount of oestrogen in your body," says Dr. Brett. The herbs red clover and black cohosh and genistein, a supplement derived from soybeans, can help your body excrete oestrogen, she notes.

These three supplements are phytooestrogens, or plant forms of oestrogen. They bind with oestrogen receptor sites, which are like dedicated landing sites on your cells. These sites would normally be occupied by your body's much stronger oestrogen, but when plant oestrogens start to hog the sites, your oestrogen has no place to go and ends up being excreted, says Dr. Brett. "That's exactly what you want to happen with endometriosis," she explains. If you reduce the amount of oestrogen circulating in your body, you'll probably also reduce the pain of endometriosis, she says.

If you take red clover or black cohosh, follow the directions on the package. Label directions on one brand of red clover supplements call for two 430-milligram capsules three times a day. A typical black cohosh brand recommends one 540-milligram capsule three times a day. Black cohosh is particularly effective at relieving cramps, notes Dr. Brett. You can get genistein by taking a supplement of mixed soy isoflavones and following the directions on the label. A typical dosage is one 540-milligram capsule a day.

Say yarrow. Not only will the herb yarrow help get your kidneys in prime working order, it may also ease the painful cramps that can accompany endometriosis. Yarrow has antispasmodic properties that help relax muscles that cramp or contract, so it can ease your uterine and abdominal muscles. Dr. Brett advises following directions on the package. A typical dose is two to three capsules of between 250 and 350 milligrams taken two times a day.

Ease with evening primrose. A natural anti-inflammatory, evening primrose oil can help reduce the pain of endometriosis, says Dr. Brett. It's especially helpful with cramping, she says. Traditionally, evening primrose oil has been used by herbalists and naturopathic doctors to help relieve symptoms of a wide range of women's ailments. Often recommended by naturopaths to relieve PMT and deal with menopausal discomforts, it can also work well if you're troubled by endometriosis. The oil has two components that seem to provide relief—gamma-linolenic acid (GLA) and tryptophan. Both of these substances promote good health in women. Evening primrose oil is also one of the best sources of phenylalanine, a natural pain reliever. Dr. Brett recommends taking oil that provides 250 to 300 milligrams of GLA daily.

Try this tea. "When I see a woman with severe endometriosis, one of the first things I do is try to ease her pain," says Maier. "This tea combines relaxing herbs like passionflower, damiana, and skullcap, which eases pain, with nourishing, mineral-rich alfalfa leaf, nettle, and red raspberry leaf, which balances hormones." Blend equal parts of each dried herb and infuse 1 tablespoon per 8-ounce cup of freshly boiled water; steep for a minimum of an hour in a covered container. "When dealing with nourishing

Herbal Formulas for Endometriosis

Herbal treatment is always best when it is tailored to hormonal shifts that occur at ovulation. These two herbal formulas combine specific herbs that perform specific functions in specific proportions, and they are taken at specific times. They were designed for women with endometriosis by Amanda McQuade Crawford, herbalist, and member of Britain's National Institute of Medical Herbalists. McQuade Crawford suggests that you try the remedies for up to three months. If you don't experience relief within that time, switch to conventional medicine.

Formula I: Pre-menstrual

This mixture uses tinctures of six herbs: chasteberry seed (to help normalise hormones), cramp bark (to ease muscle pain), yarrow flower (to tone the bowel wall and improve digestion), skullcap (to reduce tension and help ease pain), wild yam root (to ease depression and pain linked to hormonal changes), and cinnamon bark (to dilate blood vessels and improve circulation). You'll find these tinctures in health food stores. You'll also need a small funnel and a bottle large enough to hold the mixture—a little more than eight ounces.

1 oz. chasteberry seed tincture	2 oz. cramp bark tincture
2 oz. yarrow flower tincture	2 oz. skullcap tincture
1 oz. wild yam root tincture	2 tsp. cinnamon bark tincture

Using a funnel, pour the tinctures into the bottle. McQuade Crawford suggests taking teaspoon diluted in eight ounces of water, four times a day, from ovulation (about midcycle) through the end of your period.

Formula II: Postmenstrual

The second formula also uses chasteberry and wild yam root tinctures, combined with tinctures of five other herbs: blue cohosh root (to stimulate tissue health when there's scarring), sarsaparilla root (an immune-system tonic and hormone balancer), milk thistle seed (to aid hormone metabolism and enhance liver function), partridgeberry (to help shrink benign growths), and valerian root (the "queen" of herbal painkillers)

2 oz. chasteberry seed tincture	1 oz. blue cohosh root tincture
1 oz. sarsaparilla root tincture	2 oz. milk thistle seed tincture
1 oz. partridge berry tincture	2 oz. wild yam tincture
1 oz. (or more if needed for pain) valerian root tincture	

Combine the tinctures as instructed in the previous formula. McQuade Crawford suggests taking one teaspoon of this mixture diluted in eight ounces of water, four times a day, from the time your period ends until ovulation (about midcycle).

herbs, I prefer using a tablespoon. It will yield a stronger infusion than the usual teaspoon that is generally recommended," explains Maier. She suggests drinking a cup three times a day.

Blend an herbal pain eraser. To make a simple tincture formula that's very effective, Maier says, blend equal parts of cramp bark, kava-kava, California poppy, and passionflower tinctures in a four-ounce bottle. She recommends taking one teaspoon three times a day, or as needed for pain. Cramp bark and kava-kava help relax the muscles and ease pain; California poppy and passionflower relax the tension that contributes to muscle pain, says Maier.

Relieve body-bending cramps. "If your cramps are really excruciating, try this tincture formula," advises Dr. Kamhi. Use tinctures of Jamaican dogwood, kava-kava, white willow bark, and valerian. Dr. Kamhi recommends taking 10 drops of each tincture two hours before bedtime and again right before you go to bed. Valerian can act as a stimulant in some women, so omit it from the mixture if you react this way. Jamaican dogwood has traditionally been used for menstrual cramps and for insomnia due to nervous tension or muscle pain. Kava-kava is an antispasmodic, and white willow contains salicin, the compound from which aspirin was derived.

If you try this tincture formula, don't exceed the recommended dose and use only as needed, not on an ongoing basis. Use only before bedtime or when you'll be home all day, as it can make you drowsy. It should not be used when driving. This formula is not recommended during pregnancy or when breastfeeding, warns Dr. Kamhi.

Try a mushroom tonic. The stress of endometriosis can take its toll on other body functions, especially the adrenal glands, which produce and regulate hormones, notes Maier. "That kind of chronic stress can affect the immune system, so I use an immune-strengthening formula of reishi mushrooms and herbs added to a favourite soup," she says. If soup doesn't work for you, you can try combining an ounce each of astragalus, Siberian ginseng, and reishi mushroom tinctures and take a teaspoon three times a day, suggests Maier. Studies show that astragalus increases the body's antiviral compounds, Siberian ginseng stimulates the immune system and boosts energy, and reishi improves blood flow to the heart.

Try a vitamin cocktail. Some women benefit from the following daily supplement regimen, according to Susan Lark, MD, author of *Fibroid Tumours and Endometriosis:* between 400 and 2,000 international units (IU) of vitamin E (women with diabetes or high blood pressure should take only 100 IU); 3 milligrams (5,000 IU) of beta-carotene; 300 milligrams of vitamin B6 and 50 milligrams of B-complex vitamins; up to 4,000 milligrams of vitamin C; and 800 milligrams of bioflavanoids. The doses recommended for vitamin E, vitamin C, vitamin B, and the B-complex vitamins are high and should not be taken without the advice of a doctor.

Other alternatives:

Get help from homeopathy. If you are anxious and weepy and have pain in your ovaries that spreads down to your thighs, try a 6X dose of Lihum tigrum three times a day or a 30C dose once or twice a day until you feel better, suggests Cynthia Mervis Watson, MD, a family practice physician specializing in homeopathic and herbal therapies. She says that the same dosage of Sepia may help other women, particularly pale-skinned brunettes who have pre-menstrual tension, with outbursts of anger and pain during intercourse or menstruation. Belladonna, in a 6X dose three times a day or a 30C dose once or twice daily, may relieve endometriosis, says Dr. Watson, especially if you feel hot and flushed, feel restless and anxious, develop sudden pain during menstruation that spreads into your legs and have a blood flow that is bright red and profuse.

Opt for acupuncture. Acupuncture and electro-acupuncture may help ease the pain of endometriosis in minutes, and in some cases give permanent relief. In one study by researches at UCLA, daily treatments with electro-acupuncture provided long-term pain relief to several women who had already received medical treatment for the problem. Trigger point therapy (injections of saline solutions into tender spots, sometimes called Western acupuncture) may also help.

Try hands-on healing. Acupressure relieves pain in some women, says Susan Anderson, an endometriosis sufferer who is a member of the national board of the Endometriosis Association, a self-help group based in Milwaukee. When pain begins, press the area on the inside of your leg about two inches above your ankle bone. To locate that spot, press with your thumb until you locate an area that feels tender. Another spot where pressure can ease pain is the web of your hand, at the base where the bones of your thumb and index finger meet. "If it doesn't hurt when you press, then it's not the right spot. Know that it will hurt, but you need to keep pressing, and you should feel relief in the pelvic area," says Anderson.

Mind over malady:

Relax progressively. Chronic pain causes a release of stress hormones, which in turn increases pain sensitivity by reducing the production of endorphins, says Alison Milburn, Ph.D., a health psychologist who specialises in chronic pain. "The added complication is that people with chronic pain tend to position their bodies to try and compensate." They might sit differently or walk differently, and this sets up patterns of chronic muscular tension that can cause muscle spasms and such.

A technique called progressive muscle relaxation can help by systematically tensing and relaxing individual muscle groups in your body, Dr. Milburn says. Close your eyes, take a few deep breaths and tense the muscles in your face. Hold for a few seconds, then take a deep breath and release. Repeat this in your neck, shoulders, arms and down through your body. The whole process should take about ten minutes.

"Try to do it regularly, daily or even three or four times a day," Dr. Milburn says. "You don't want to do it only when the pain is bad. It's a skill that you need to practice regularly."

Meditate. Relaxing through meditation or visual imagery helps many women sleep better, reduces stress and helps women cope with the pain of their disease, says Paula Petersen, MD, Ph.D., an attending physician at Cedars-Sinai Medical Centre in Los Angeles. Try tapes on visual imagery, pain relief, meditation or deep relaxation and use them to take a break during the day, she says. If you have a private office at work where you can listen to the tape during your lunch break, "think about spending 15 to 20 minutes meditating, allowing the body to sort of reset itself so that you can cope with the rest of the day," she says. Those who can't take a break at work should find time when they first get home. They should "take 20 minutes, put their feet up, block out the rest of the world, take care of themselves and then move into whatever needs to be taken care of in the evening," says Petersen.

Eye Pain

The pain: A burning or stinging sensation in the eyes.

The cause: The eyes have been called the most sensitive organs in the human body. That's because they're honeycombed with pain receptors—extremely sensitive, finely tuned nerve endings that help protect these vital organs. This means that the slightest insult to the surface—a blast of cold, dry air or an inward-growing eyelash, for example—can stimulate these nerves, firing a pain signal to your brain. The result: Your eyes smart or feel scratchy. Other factors inside your body can also excite your eye's hyper-sensitive receptors. A sinus infection can inflame the adjacent muscles, for example, and trigger a throbbing, sometimes sharp, pain behind the eye socket. A simple act like rolling your eyes can hurt.

Ironically, keeping your eyes too still for too long can strain the muscles that move your eyes into their proper position. That's why you feel a dull ache around your eyes after staring at spreadsheets on your computer screen for hours or reading page after page of that three-inch-thick novel. If the reading light is dim or the overhead lighting is too harsh, your orbs may ache even more. In addition, wearing ill-fitting glasses or trying to see through outdated prescription lenses can also strain surrounding muscles. Sometimes, the pain you feel in your eyes originates elsewhere in your body. "What feels like eye pain is often actually a headache or pain in the facial muscles caused by tension," says Robert E. Kalina, MD, an ophthalmologist.

But if the pain is severe, your eyes are red and your vision's blurry, the likely culprit is uveitis—an inflammation involving the pigmented areas in the eye. It's often brought on by an infection elsewhere in the body. Severe pain with other symptoms—most notably nausea and haloes around lights—is a sign of glaucoma, a build-up of pressure around the eye that can lead to blindness if left untreated.

See a doctor if:
...you have persistent burning or stinging.
...you have a chemical burn
...you have something embedded in your eye.
...you've received a blow to the eye.

...you have a dull ache around your eyes that persists for more than two days.
...you have a sudden or piercing pain deep in your eyes.
...your eye pain is accompanied by a change in your vision, headaches, nausea or sensitivity to light.

Quick relief:

Blink. Blinking vigorously is likely to stop the smart of a mild eye burn, says Hunter Little, MD, an ophthalmologist.

Flush out chemicals, then rush to the doctor. Immediately flood the eye with water, using your fingers to keep the eye open as wide as possible. Hold your head under a faucet or garden hose or pour water into the eye (any clean container is okay in this case) for at least 15 minutes, continuously and gently. Roll the eyeball as much as possible to wash out the eye. Then seek medical help immediately. If it's a chemical burn, "speed is what counts," says Jason Slakter, MD, attending surgeon in the Department of Ophthalmology at the Manhattan Eye, Ear and Throat Hospital. If you take this swift action, the doctor may only need to apply a patch and prescribe antibiotic drops (to prevent infection), and your burned eye will heal on its own. More serious damage may require surgical repair.

Take two aspirin and relax. If you're experiencing a dull ache in or around your eyes, it may be headache-related. If so, one or two aspirin every six to eight hours should relieve the problem, says Dr. Kalina. If the pain is still there after two days, see your doctor.

Cool down sunburned orbs. Cover your eyes with a cool washcloth and take a pain reliever such as aspirin or ibuprofen, says Dr. Little. If the sting doesn't subside in a day or two, see the doctor.

Work it down—and out. If blinking doesn't work, you can use your eyelids to gently push the speck down and out, says Kathleen Lamping, MD, an ophthalmologist. Grasp the eyelashes of your upper lid between your fingers, then pull your upper lid over your lower lid. This allows your lower eyelashes to brush the speck off the inside of your upper lid. Then blink a few times. Sometimes this manoeuver moves the offending particle to the corner of your eye, says Dr. Lamping. If that happens, use the corner of a cloth handkerchief or moist tissue to draw it out. If you don't have a handkerchief or tissue, use your fingertip—gently.

Wearing contact lenses? Take them out. Once your eyes are irritated, contact lenses aggravate the situation. "The irritating item may be on your contact, not in your eye," says Dr. Lamping. "Remove your lens right away."

Try a cold compress. Allergies—to ragweed, makeup, pet dander or just about anything—can make your eyes itch. A cool compress will cut down the itch and soothe your eyes. Wet a washcloth or towel and place it on your closed eyes whenever they itch—for at least 2 minutes or as long as 20.

Apply cold, wet tea bags. "The tannic acid in tea bags (another form of

Get aid from shades

"Sunglasses that block out 99 percent or more of the UV rays should be standard outdoor wear, especially if you live, play or work near sand, snow or water," says Dr. Little. Long-term exposure to the sun's radiation may cause cataracts, retina damage or other eye problems.

Here are specific ways to protect yourself.

Wear them in the tropics and mountains. The UV rays are extra-intense and potentially more damageing at high elevations or near the equator.

Wear them when taking sun-sensitive drugs. Photosensitising drugs such as tetracycline that make your skin more sensitive to light can also make your eyes more sensitive to UV rays.

Wear them if you've had cataract surgery. Or make sure that your intraocular lens or post-surgery contact lenses are the UV-absorbent type.

Choose close-fitting wraparounds. Studies show that harmful UV damage can occur from rays that enter under, over and around the sides of ordinary frames.

Wear "amber-tinted" or "polarised" sunglasses for boating. Amber-tinted UV-absorbent lenses block the harmful "blue rays" of the sun. And polarised lenses cut reflected glare bouncing off pavement, water or snow. Both types are ideal for fishing or skiing, says Dr. Little.

Sport a wide-brimmed hat, too. This will help protect your face, lips and eyes from the sun's damageing rays, which can predispose you to skin cancer, wrinkles and age spots, says Dr. Little.

cold compress) will soothe and cool down the itch," says Wilma Bergfeld, MD, head of clinical research in the Department of Dermatology at the Cleveland Clinic Foundation. Wrap the tea bags with paper towels to avoid any staining of the eyelid.

Extinguish the fire in your eyes. The Indian medical discipline known as Ayurveda teaches that sickness arises from an imbalance in one of the five elements that make up the human body: space, air, fire, water, and earth. According to Ayurveda, eye irritation indicates an imbalance in the fire element. To restore balance, soak cotton pads in cold milk, squeeze out the excess, and place the pads over your closed eyes for about five minutes. Use this remedy once a day until your eyes feel better.

According to Pratima Raichur, a doctor of naturopathy, an Ayurvedic practitioner, and author of *Absolute Beauty*, to restore the balance, soak cotton pads in rose water, cold milk, fennel tea, or coriander tea; squeeze out the excess liquid; and then place them over your closed eyes for about 5 minutes once a day until your eyes feel better. Dr. Raichur stresses the importance of prevention when it comes to maintaining fire

Pinkeye

Also known as conjunctivitis, pinkeye involves the inflammation of the conjunctiva, the film that covers parts of your eye and inner eyelid. Besides leaving your eye swollen and sore, pinkeye sometimes produces a sticky discharge that leaves your eyelids "glued" together when you wake up in the morning.

Typically, pinkeye results from an allergy to pollen, pet dander, or certain chemicals or from a bacterial or viral infection. In fact, the same viruses that cause the common cold can also cause pinkeye. And like the common cold, infectious pinkeye is extremely contagious and easily spread by hand-to-eye contact.

How long pinkeye lingers depends on what type you have. Allergic pinkeye, for example, will stick around until you're no longer exposed to the allergen. Viral pinkeye almost always get better within 3 to 10 days, even if left untreated. Bacterial pinkeye, the most serious of the three, will continue to worsen and could even lead to loss of vision unless treated with antibiotic eye drops or ointment.

This is why seeing a doctor at the first sign of pinkeye is so important. She can decide whether you require a prescription or you can manage the condition with self-care alone. Then use these strategies to help relieve the immediate symptoms and prevent the spread of germs:

Remove your contacts. If you wear contacts, take them out at the first sign of redness and irritation. They'll trap the germs in your eyes. Wear eyeglasses until your symptoms subside.

Run hot and cold. Alternating hot and cold compresses stimulates circulation and draws infection-fighting white blood cells to your eyes. Soak a clean washcloth in very warm water, wring it out, and hold it against your eyes for a minute. Then soak the cloth in cold water, wring it out, and hold it against your eyes for a minute. Repeat this process two or three times.

Check out chickweed. The herb chickweed helps fight infection, yet it's mild enough to use on your eyes. Brew a pot of chickweed tea and let it cool until it is comfortable to the touch. Then dip a clean cloth into the tea and hold the cloth against the affected eye while it's closed. Continue re-wetting and reapplying the cloth for up to an hour. You can buy chickweed in some health food stores.

Leave your eyes au naturel. Avoid wearing eye makeup while you have infectious pinkeye. Replace your mascara and liner. If your mascara wand or liner becomes contaminated, you'll just keep transferring the virus or bacteria from one eye to the other.

balance in your body, and that means reducing the amount of hot and sour foods and drinks you consume. She recommends cutting down on alcohol, spices, coffee, and tobacco.

Everyday prevention:

Never stare directly at the sun. Not even if there's a solar eclipse, reminds Dr. Little. "Staring at the sun can burn your retina like sun directed through a magnifying glass burns paper," he says.

Try artificial tears. To control chronic burning from dry, indoor heating, for example, try a drop or two of lubricating artificial tears, says Kenneth Kauvar, MD, an ophthalmologist and author of *Eyes Only.* Tear products come in thick or thin viscosity, and the first drop may sting a bit, he says. The second drop is more soothing.

Apply lip balm on your brows. A waxy lip balm applied on the eyebrows or upper lids provides a waterproof barrier that blocks sunscreen from trickling into your eyes when you sweat, says David Harris, MD, a dermatologist. Avoid menthol types, he adds. The vapours can sting your eyes.

Wear cotton before you dye. A cotton headband absorbs dripping hair dye or permanent-wave solution.

Use grease shields on frying pans. This prevents accidental food splatters.

Spritz and sprint. Close your eyes before using hair spray, then leave the area quickly.

Aim nozzles that-a-way. Direct nozzles away from your face when using any household sprayers, toxic or otherwise. Always work in a well-ventilated room when using caustic household chemicals. And when you open a container filled with a caustic substance—or even one that can release volatile fumes, like ammonia—turn your head away.

Store goggles near the jumper cables. "Jump-starting a dead battery can release caustic battery acid fumes and splashes. That's why you should learn the correct way to handle a battery and put on eye goggles and gloves before you ever touch one," says Dr. Slakter.

Don watertight goggles before the plunge. They protect against chlorine-caused eye burns in swimming pools.

Don't let the drops drain away. If your doctor has prescribed medicated eye drops to relieve pain from infection or some other cause, you need to make sure the medicine stays in your eyes and doesn't roll down your cheeks, says Mitchell H. Friedlaender, MD, director of corneal services at the Scripps Clinic and Research Foundation in La Jolla, California, and co-author of *20/20: A Total Guide to Improving Your Vision and Preventing Eye Disease.* The correct way to apply eye drops: Tilt your head back and squeeze a drop or two inside your lower eyelid. Keep your eyes closed for a good two minutes. Or, you can use your finger and press in the inside corner of your eye. "This allows the drops to penetrate into the eye and prevents them from getting into the bloodstream," says Dr. Friedlaender.

Give your eyes a break. Taking a brief rest from prolonged reading or

Healing Sties

Each of your eyelids contains eyelash follicles. Sometimes one of these follicles becomes infected, perhaps because it's clogged with dandruff-like scales or you've used a germ-laden mascara brush. Eventually, a painful red lump with a white head of pus sprouts at the base of the eyelash. This is what's known as a sty.

If you have a persistent or recurrent sty, see your doctor. It could be a sign of diabetes or a cyst. Also see a doctor if your sty doesn't get better or gets worse after two days.

As with a pimple on your face, a sty should never be popped. It may rupture beneath the surface of the skin, aggravating the inflammation. Instead, heed this advice.

Hold a hot potato. Wrap a warm, damp washcloth around a hot baked potato (the cloth will retain the heat longer). Then hold the cloth against the affected, closed eye for five minutes. Repeat four times every day for two weeks. This will gently coax the sty to break open and heal.

Give your eyes a break. Stop wearing eye makeup until the sty heals. This means all eye makeup—mascara, eyeliner, and shadow. Otherwise, you may end up with several sties instead of one.

other close work may be enough to relieve eye strain, says Dr. Kauvar. Look up from the page or computer screen and gaze off into the distance every ten minutes or so. Or let your eyes unfocus every so often.

Do pencil push-ups. Simple eye exercises can limber up tired eye muscles that have been fixed on a computer screen for hours, according to James L. Cox, O.D., behavioural optometrist. Try focusing your eyes on a pencil as you slowly move it in toward your nose and then back out again. Repeat for a full minute every 20 minutes, says Dr. Cox.

Use soft overall lighting plus spotlights. Dim lighting or glare strains eyes as your muscles keep trying to move your eyes into a position to obtain the most light, says Dr. Kauvar. The best illumination, he says, is soft overall background lighting with a light aimed at what you're reading.

Take your specs in for a check-up. "Glasses that slide down your nose can make your eyes ache as the muscles on the side of your eyes try to move your eyes to compensate for an abnormal eye deviation," says Dr. Kauvar. Your glasses should fit properly, he says. An outdated eyeglass prescription can also strain your eyes. So be sure to have your eyes checked for any vision changes at least once a year.

Wear protective goggles for chores. As a regular form of exercise, mowing and weed whacking can keep you and your lawn in great shape. But stir up grass and dirt, and you're apt to get some in your eyes.

Easing Blepharitis

The morning alarm is ringing, but your eyes refuse to rise and shine. They're so swollen shut with sticky, crusty discharge, it feels like the sandman pasted your lids with glue.

"It can be alarming to have to pry open your eyes in the morning, but eye discharge is rarely harmful and is simply part of your body's natural defence system," says Walter I. Fried, MD, Ph.D., clinical assistant professor of ophthalmology at University of Health Sciences/Chicago Medical School.

In most cases, waking up with oozy, crusty, red-rimmed eyes means your eyes have been invaded by bacteria from contaminated eye makeup, for example, or from extra-oily skin. A bacterial invasion can lead to blepharitis, an inflammation at the base of the eyelashes that produces thick, yellowish pus filled with bacteria-fighting white blood cells.

A sticky, yellowish discharge that seals your eyes shut is also your body's natural response to pinkeye, a bacteria or virus-caused infection that attacks the transparent membrane covering the eyeball.

Another type of sticky discharge—thinner, clear and non-crusty—can mean you have a cold, an allergy to pollen, dried-out eyes from gusty winds or an eyelash touching your eyeball. "This sticky, watery discharge usually goes away once the irritating factors are removed," says Dr. Fried.

Blepharitis remedies:

Oozy eyelids that are also swollen means you have an infection that requires antibiotic eye drops and possibly oral antibiotics, too," says Dr. Fried. Here are more ways to deal with discharge.

Come unglued. If your eyes are glued shut, loosen the crusts with a warm, wrung-out washcloth.

Wash your lids. Next, dip a cottonball in a solution made with 1/2 teaspoon of salt dissolved in a teaspoon of warm water and rub it along the lash line. You can also apply a commercial eyelid scrub.

Get the oil out. If blepharitis is a problem, it helps to remove excess oil from your eyelids, says Dr. Friedlaender. To remove excess oil from eyelids, you may cleanse the lashes and lid margins with baby shampoo or another mild detergent. Also, gently massage the lids using a downward motion as if "squeezing toothpaste out of a tube," he says. Then massage the upper lid and pat off the oil with a tissue. Do this every night for a week or two. If you have chronic blepharitis, you should make cleaning and massageing your eyelids a regular habit "like brushing your teeth," says Dr. Friedlaender.

Protective goggles or safety glasses will eliminate that problem, says Dickie McMullan, MD, an ophthalmologist. They're a good idea when using or cleaning paint brushes and rollers, too.

Find something else to do with your hands. Try to resist rubbing your eyes or scratching an itch, says Monica Dweck, MD, an ophthalmologist who specialises in eyelid problems. If you claw at your eyelids, you'll only irritate them further. You may even scratch your cornea, which can lead to scarring or vision loss.

Use a tear ointment at bedtime. If your eyes still feel irritated, an over-the-counter tear ointment, such as Lacrilube, will help ease the scratchiness while you sleep, says Dr. Dweck. The ointments differ from artificial tears, because they last longer, lubricating your eyes. But they blur your vision and should only be used overnight.

Ponder the problem. Since relieving this pesky irritation is linked to the cause, you should "think over in the last day or so what you've done and see if there is any obvious cause for it," says Jeffrey Anshel, O.D., an optometrist. If you're allergic to cats and play with your girlfriend's kitty all afternoon, then it's a no-brainer where your puffy red eyes came from. Ditto for sleeping with your daily-wear contact lenses in. Once you have an idea of the cause, it's usually easy to pick the appropriate remedy.

Drop the drops. Think twice before you use eye drops for your bloodshot eyes. They reduce redness by constricting the swollen blood vessels that cause the bloodshot eyes. But Dr. Anshel says that your eyes can get addicted to the stuff and may cause the blood vessels in your eyes to actually get bigger over time. "So it actually makes the eye redder, requiring you to use more drops," he says. Pretty soon your eyes will be hooked, but you'll still have the problem.

Check your contacts. Often your eye will be red because a speck of pollen or dust is attached to your contact lens. Pop them out and make sure, says Dr. Anshel. Also, as contacts get older, they don't get oxygen to the eye as well as they used to, which forces your body to send over more blood. This, in turn, leads to red, puffy eyes. This could be a sign that you need a new pair, so see your optometrist or ophthalmologist.

Fight allergies. If you think your sore eyes are caused by allergies, try some antihistamine or anti-inflammatory drops. There are a number of these drops available without a prescription, including Naphcon A, says Carol L. Karp, MD, an ophthalmologist. Follow the directions on the label.

Don't share your washcloth. Viral or bacterial discharge is loaded with germs that can be passed on to others (or back to yourself), says Dr. Fried. Non-disposable objects—including your hands—that have touched your tears should be washed in hot water.

Give your old mascara the heave-ho. Contaminated cosmetics are prime suspects in eye infections. Toss any eye cosmetics that you used while you were infected and any that are more than six months old. Otherwise, you may be reapplying bacteria, says Dr. Fried.

Eyestrain

The pain: There are many different kinds of eyestrain, but the symptoms are similar for all. They include headaches, blurred vision, dryness, and overall discomfort.

The cause: Like other parts of your body, your eyes are susceptible to stress and overuse. When you focus intently, your brain sends constant messages to your optic nerve to stay alert and keep the object in focus. Heeding the call, your eye muscles work valiantly to maintain sharp images. But when they don't get relief, your eyesight can blur from the strain. Most often, you have eyestrain from doing a lot of close work, like reading or staring at a computer screen. This type of work requires two sets of muscles in your eye to work together. One set turns your two eyes toward each other to make one image, and the other set focuses on the object. Sometimes there's a lack of co-ordination between the two, and this results in eyestrain. Also, you might have presbyopia, a focusing problem that hits people in their late thirties or early forties and will require you to wear glasses for close work.

See a doctor if:

...the eyestrain is persistent. "You should be evaluated by an ophthalmologist," says Carol L. Karp, MD, an ophthalmologist.
...you have dizziness and double vision along with eyestrain. "You should see your optometrist or ophthalmologist," advises Jeffrey Anshel, O.D., an optometrist in Carlsbad, California, and author of *Healthy Eyes—Better Vision.*

Medication:

No medications will cause eyestrain specifically. But a few may make it harder to focus, which can cause eyestrain if you don't do something about it, says W. Steven Pray, Ph.D., R.Ph., professor of non-prescription drug products at Southwestern Oklahoma State University in Weatherford.

Common medications that may blur vision include:

The glaucoma medication acetazolamide (Diamox)

Antiarthritic and anti-inflammatory medications such as fenoprofen (Nalfon or Lederfen), ibuprofen, ketoprofen (Orudis KT), or naproxen (Aleve)

Antidepressants such as amitriptyline (Elavil) and imipramine (Tofranil or Marplan)

The antihypertension medication chlorthalidone (one of the ingredients of Combipres)

Psoriasis drug etretinate (Tegison)

Antibacterial and antibiotic agents such as sulfonamides (an ingredient in Bactrim DS) and tetracyclines (Doxycycline or Tetrachel)

Quick relief:

Look out. "When you start to feel eyestrain, look up and into the distance," says Dr. Karp, Sometimes your eye muscles will be fatigued from focusing on close objects, and looking away will allow them to relax.

Cry fake tears. Often while you're staring at something up close, the surface of your eyes can dry out and cause burning, Dr. Karp says. A preservative-free artificial tears solution like Refresh or Hypo Tears PF (available at your chemists) will lubricate your eyes and also help break up the spasm behind the eyestrain, relaxing the eyes, she says.

Use your palms. Rub your hands together and get them a bit warm, then gently cover your closed eyes with your palms, Dr. Anshel says. "That'll let all the muscles around your eyes relax and keep your eyes from having to work," says Dr. Anshel. Breathe easily as you palm your eyes. Do this for about five minutes, and this should rest your eyes quite nicely, he says.

Take a deep wink. Take a deep breath while raising your shoulders and scrunching your eyes and fists closed as tightly as you can, then exhale and relax all of the muscles at once, recommends Anne Barber, O.D., an optometrist. This technique is called a deep wink. She says that by "tightening up the voluntary muscles (like your fists and shoulders) and letting them go, we frequently can trick the involuntary focus muscles to let go at the same time." This should help relax those overworked eye muscles.

Apply moist compresses over your closed eyes. Twice a day, close your eyes, tilt back your head and place a warm washcloth over your eyelids for a few minutes. A cool compress made moist from raspberry-leaf tea also may bring relief. After removing the compress, gently massage your eyelids for 10 or 15 minutes. The warm moisture rejuvenates and relaxes your tired eyes and unclog pores. The compresses also help remove bacteria that build up on your face and eyelids during the day.

Close your eyes. Shutting your eyes for a few minutes—or even several seconds—will refocus them and ease the strain.

Nutritional remedies:

Eat an eyeful. Eat more fruits and vegetables, especially those rich in the antioxidant vitamin C, says Jay Cohen, O.D., an optometrist. "Getting more vitamin C is a good idea for overall eye health and particularly for eyestrain," he explains. "Vitamin C deficiency may make the eyes a little more sensitive, so you're more prone to eyestrain. You could probably get the vitamin C you need from fruits and vegetables, as opposed to a supplement."

Helpful vitamins and supplements:

Get your B's. Deficiencies in the B vitamins may lead to eyestrain, says Dr. Cohen. "A Japanese study found that people who get eyestrain from working on computers benefit from injections of vitamin B12," he says. In fact, he points out, one sign of a deficiency in the B vitamins is red, irritated eyes. While Dr. Cohen doesn't recommend taking large doses of any individual B vitamin, he does advise a B-complex supplement containing the RDA for the essential B vitamins.

Take 10,000 IU (international units) of vitamin A each day. Vitamin A has long been associated with eye health, and a deficiency has been shown to increase the likelihood of eye problems.

Everyday prevention:

Take a break from your close-up work. "It's not natural for our eyes to focus on a two-dimensional plane like a computer screen without straining," says Paul Planer, O.D., a behavioural optometrist (A behavioural optometrist approaches and treats the eye as part of the whole body system.) Whether you are gazing at a monitor or the pages of a book, look away every 15 minutes, he says. Close your eyes for 10 to 20 seconds while inhaling and exhaling deeply and slowly. Also, as part of your eye-relief break, stand up and do a body stretch. With that movement, you will relieve your eyes from their focusing work and get more blood and oxygen circulating, says Dr. Planer.

Blink frequently. "Blinking distributes new tears across the corners of your eyes, which keeps them healthy and moist," says Bob Lee, O.D., assistant professor of optometry and co-ordinator of computer vision services at Southern California College of Optometry. That action maintains optical clarity and reduces dry-eye complaints.

Shield your eyes from glaring light and change the blinking ones. If there is reflection from a monitor, it will hasten eyestrain, cautions Dr. Planer. Change the position of the monitor or use lower-intensity lighting. If fluorescent lights are blinking, change them soon to head off headaches and eyestrain, he advises.

Refocus. Every 15 minutes, focus on different objects at different distances. For computer users, it helps to look away from your computer screen and focus on an object that's farther away—a clock on the wall or cars passing outside the window, suggests Dr. Planer. "Also try to vary the distance of your computer screen—move back a few inches if you have movable keyboard," he says.

Hit pause. If you play video games, hit the pause button now and then. People often get blurry vision and fatigued eyes by over-focusing on the computer monitor during favourite video games, says Dr. Lee. To avoid that, hit the pause button, stand up, walk around, and focus on distance objects, he advises.

Consider a specialist. If you must do a lot of close-up work, consider going to a behavioural optometrist for a pair of prescription occupational glasses. With these specially fitted glasses, your lens is matched to the close-up task you are performing most often, says Dr. Planer. These lenses may also be tinted. "Typically, a light gray tint works best for computer work because it tends to make the letters on the computer screen come out a bit and offer more of a contrast," Dr. Planer says.

Make the light right. "Lighting is probably the most overlooked and under-emphasized aspect of office work," says Dr. Anshel. "The lighting is very critical because it causes glare. If it's not directed properly, it can cause poor vision, which can cause strain in itself. And without light, there's no sight." So turn off your computer monitor and check to see if there are any reflections of lightbulbs on the blank screen. If so, that could be causing your problem. Move the light or the computer so that there is no glare on the screen, he says.

Distance yourself. Keep at least 20 inches between yourself and the computer screen and ideally 26 inches or more, Dr. Anshel says. This "reduces the amount of focusing that people have to do on the screen." The closer you are, the more you need to focus, which is part of the problem with eyestrain.

Brighten up. Pay attention to the contrast between your office lighting and the computer screen, Dr. Anshel says. It's like when Mom told you not to watch TV in the dark because it was bad for your eyes. You shouldn't look at a dim computer screen in a brightly lit office. Your eyes will have to readjust from the room light to the monitor light, causing fatigue and strain, Dr. Anshel says. To remedy this, adjust the brightness control on your monitor if the screen seems dark, he says.

Make sure your glasses still work. Because your ability to focus continues to decrease with age, the glasses you wore 5 or 10 years ago may not be strong enough for you today. Most likely, you need glasses with a higher magnification. "People think that wearing glasses causes the eye to become weaker or more dependent on the glasses," says Robert Cykiert, MD, an ophthalmologist. But that's not the case. It's just that your focusing ability for close-up vision gets progressively worse as you age with or without glasses. "If you get the right glasses for your needs, you should never experience eyestrain." You can try finding reading glasses at your local chemist. But first you should see an ophthalmologist or optometrist for an exam to rule out eye disease. If your prescription is equal in both eyes and you don't have an astigmatism (an unequal curvature of the surfaces of the eye), you can try a pair of reading glasses sold in stores. Otherwise, your doctor can order prescription lenses for you to use at the distances prescribed. If your glasses are made for you to read at a computer's distance, for instance, and you wear those same glasses to read a book, you'll strain your eyes. People typically read at 14 inches but use a computer at 20 inches, says Dr. Cykiert.

Keep 'em moving. To avoid the dreaded computer "zombie" stare, pump some life into your eyes by moving them every 20 minutes, suggests Robert-Michael Kaplan, O.D., a behavioural optometrist, consultant in vision care in British Columbia. But you need something worthy of distraction. Dress up your monitor, Dr. Kaplan advises. Place brightly coloured round stickers on each of the four corners of the frame and another between each set of corners so that your monitor is bordered by three stickers on each side. Every 30 minutes, imagine that your eyes are like a bug that can hop from one sticker to the other. First move from the middle dot on the left side of your screen straight across to the middle dot on the right side. Next move from the middle dot on the top of your screen to the middle dot on bottom. Finish up with a diagonal move from the bottom right corner up to the top left corner of your screen. As your eyes dart to each sticker, breathe and enjoy the ride. The secret is to keep your eyes moving. As long as they are moving, they are under less strain and you won't be tempted to glare-stare at your computer screen. To keep this exercise interesting, try randomising the left-right, up-down, and diagonal eye movements, says Dr. Kaplan.

Book it ahead. If you're the type of reader who can become totally engrossed in the latest novel, there's a good chance that your eyes will stay glued to the page even after they start to ache and show signs of strain. Maybe what you need is a traffic cop inside your books. Use a bookmark as a stop sign, suggests Jacob Liberman, O.D., Ph.D., an optometrist. Write the words, "Put me 10 pages ahead" on the bookmark, and when you come to the marker, move it 10 pages ahead. Each time you reach the bookmark, that's your reminder to stop reading, blink several times, and rest your eyes by looking out the window or across the room. Pause for at least 30 seconds before you resume reading, suggests Dr. Liberman.

Tone down your attire. "Bright, white clothes will reflect off the screen and create glare that can tire your eyes," says Dickie McMullan, MD, an ophthalmologist. A white blouse or short may be the worst, but wearing it with a tan jacket or muted scarf reduces the glare.

Don sunglasses year-round. Whether you're swimming, skiing or just running errands, the sun's ultraviolet rays can make you squint, straining the facial muscles around your eyes. Buy yourself a good pair of sunglasses—ones specifically labelled as blocking out as much ultraviolet light as possible, says Charlotte Saxby, MD, an ophthalmologist.

Wear a wide-brimmed hat. The cool thing about baseball-style caps is that, along with sunglasses, their wide brims help shade your eyes, reducing glare and squinting, says Dr. McMullan. So if you have one, wear it—bill forward.

Exercise your eyes. To prevent eyestrain, try moving your eyes slowly and smoothly as far to the left as you can, then as far to the right as you can. Continue by looking up, then down, then at all four diagonals. Repeat the sequence three to five times, once or twice a day. You may feel a little pain at first—stop if it's too much. Or try watching a ping-pong match—it gives your eye muscles a good workout.

Read upright. "Don't read when you're lying down—especially on your side," says Susan C. Danberg, O.D., an optometrist. "When you're on your side, one eye is closer to the page than the other, so you get unequal focusing." Instead, hold the book parallel to your face. "If your head is tipped forward, for example, the book should be tipped slightly back," she advises.

Herbal help:

Take eyebright. During intense eye use, take this herb as a tea two or three times a day.

Get help from homeopathy. Take a 30C dose of the homeopathic remedy Ruta, also called Ruta graveolens, two times a day, when you are feeling symptoms of eyestrain. "Ruta is the number one homeopathic treatment for eyestrain because it relaxes the eye muscles with no side effects," says Mark Stengler, N.D., a naturopathic physician and author of *The Natural Physician.* Since Ruta pellets are pleasant tasting, you can let them dissolve in your mouth, he advises.

Hands-on help:

Orbit your orb. Using your thumb or forefinger, gently press the bone surrounding each eye socket. Start at the upper inner corner of your eye and move along the top of the bone toward the outer corner of your eye. Then move along the bottom of the bone toward your nose. Press each point along the way for 10 to 20 seconds.

Try acupressure. With both thumbs, press the B2 points, located on the upper ridges of your eye sockets close to the bridge of your nose, recommends Michael Reed Gach, Ph.D., director of the Acupressure Institute in Berkeley, California, and author of *Acupressure's Potent Points.* Press upward into the indentations of the eye sockets and hold for two minutes while you concentrate on slow, deep breathing, suggests Dr. Gach. He says to be sure to wash your hands carefully before putting them near your eyes.

Facial Pain

The pain: Pain in the face, ranging from a dull throbbing to sharp "lightning bolts" of pain.

The cause: Doctors know that pain in the face means that you probably have a problem somewhere else—like your head, jaw, neck or even your teeth. Finding the "where" can sometimes take a little detective work.

The face, head and neck have nerves that communicate together. If a nerve in your neck is pinched or irritated, the hurt can travel up that nerve and cause pain in your face, says Steven Mandel, MD, a neurologist.

Lots of conditions can cause facial pain. People who get migraines or cluster headaches can get it. Sinus, ear and eye infections can cause it. A toothache can make your face hurt. And arthritis in the neck can cause discomfort in the face. A controversial and hard-to-diagnose jaw condition called temporomandibular joint disorder (also known as TMD) can sometimes cause facial pain, although you're likely to experience other symptoms as well, such as a "clicking" sound in the jaw or headaches.

Sharp facial pain is the major symptom of a condition called tic douloureux also called trigeminal neuralgia), a disorder in which certain facial nerves misfire. In those who have the disease, it can be triggered by cold drafts, drinking cold liquids, washing the face, shaving, chewing or even talking.

Facial pain is also a rare but possible sign of a stroke, although you're likely to experience other symptoms as well, such as numbness or trouble with your vision.

See a doctor if:

...your pain lasts for more than a day or two. "Get professional help," advises Samuel Seltzer, D.D.S., an endodontologist.

...you have pain when you bend over, a feeling of "heaviness" in the face, nasal stuffiness, discoloured mucus, or postnasal drip.

...you have difficulty opening your mouth, pain when you compress your jaw, or clicking sounds when you open and close your mouth.

...you have weakness, numbness, or paralysis in your face, you're vomiting, or you're unable to turn your head. "Get to an emergency room immediately," says Ira Klemons, D.D.S., Ph.D., director of the Centre

for Head and Facial Pain.

...you have severe pain radiating from one bloodshot eye.
...you have continuous, throbbing pain on one side of your face that is worse at night or when you chew.
...you have sudden pain in both temples and you feel generally ill or your scalp is suddenly sensitive to touch.

Since facial pain is usually caused by an underlying problem, treating that problem—be it toothache, headache or TMD—will make the facial pain go away.

Medication. If you have tic douloureux, take medication for control. Doctors have found that the best way to control the pain of tic douloureux is through drug therapy. Anticonvulsants or similar medications, such as carbamazepine, that directly affect the nerves are often prescribed. Consider surgery when medications fail. A minor operation using a special needle inserted into the nerve through the cheek can stop the pain. The downside is that there is some loss of feeling in the area of the nerve.

Quick relief:
Make nice with ice. Massage the affected area with a cold pack or a plastic bag filled with ice cubes until the area is numb, suggests Leon Robb, MD, director of the Robb Pain Management Group in Los Angeles. "For pain in your forehead, apply the ice to the back of your neck, just below your skull," says Dr. Robb. "For pain across your face, apply the ice just above your 'jawbone." Lay a thin towel over the affected area so that the ice doesn't make direct contact with your skin. Limit your treatment sessions to no more than 10 minutes of every hour, Dr. Robb cautions. Leaving the ice on longer than that could make the pain worse.

Give peas a chance. If you don't have a cold pack handy or you are out of ice cubes, use a bag of frozen peas instead, suggests Steven Syrop, D.D.S., director of the TMD-facial pain program at Columbia University School of Dental and Oral Surgery in New York City. "The bag will adapt to the contours of your face," he notes.

Heal with heat. If muscle tightness is causing your discomfort, apply moist heat (such as a warm towel) to the painful area for about 15 minutes at a time, recommends Dr. Robb. You can do this five to six times a day.

Pick a painkiller. A nonsteroidal anti-inflammatory drug (NSAID) can provide relief, especially if you have trigeminal neuralgia. Try an over-the-counter medication such as aspirin or ibuprofen.

Cream it with pepper. For lingering, burning pain from a herpes zoster (shingles) infection of the face, try capsaicin cream (marketed as Zostrix or Axasin), made from hot peppers. Be careful to keep it out of your eyes.

Hands-on help:

Hit the spot. You can relieve a muscle spasm by applying gentle pressure in the area of the facial nerve, says Dr. Robb. The point is located at the jaw joint, Just in front of each ear and night below the cheekbone. You can feel it when you open and close your mouth. Steadily press the point on the affected side with your finger for I to 2 minutes, keeping your mouth closed, he says. Repeat as often as necessary.

Treat yourself to a mini-massage. Pain in your forehead may originate in the back of your neck, says Dr. Robb. "Massaging the back of your neck, just below your skull, may bring relief," he says.

Stave off stress. Stress doesn't cause facial pain, but it can make it worse. Consider leaning a relaxation technique that you can use during tense times such as meditation, visualisation, or yoga.

Get the point. Acupuncture is highly effective in easing facial pain, says Irwin Koff, MD, a general practitioner in Kahuku, Hawaii, who is certified in acupuncture. "The procedure has no side effects if it's performed properly," he notes. He suggests contacting a qualified acupuncturist in your area.

Fibromyalgia

The pain: Debilitating muscle aches, stiffness, and fatigue, sometimes accompanied by headaches and a case of the blues. "It spans the spectrum of pain from annoying to disabling," says James Stark, MD, a physiatrist.

The cause: Fibromyalgia is one of those mysterious ailments with no identifiable cause, vague symptoms, and no standard treatment. Some medical textbooks and dictionaries don't even list it as a disease or condition. Studies suggest that people are born with an inherited tendency toward fibromyalgia, and it may be brought on by physical or emotional trauma, stress, or exposure to environmental toxins, including tobacco smoke. This condition, as with all chronic pain, may also cause depression.

See a doctor:
...if you suspect that you have fibromyalgia. The classic symptoms are chronic pain, profound fatigue and general debilitation. Although there is no specific test for it, your doctor may be able rule out other causes with testing and determine whether you have fibromyalgia or if another disease or condition is causing your problem.

Quick relief:
Hop into hot water. Heat can soothe the pain of fibromyalgia. Try a long soak in a hot bath, or use a hot tub with a gently whirlpool if available.
Use a high-tech washcloth. Pick up a heat pack from your local chemist, soak it in hot water, wrap it in towels and put it on the area that hurts. The heat pack is made of a special material that holds water at an even temperature for an hour.

Nutritional remedies:
Put Fat on the Fire Reducing any kind of inflammation usually brings about some improvement, says Hope Fay, N.D., a naturopathic doctor. In fibromyalgia, there is clearly inflammation in the muscles and probably in the intestinal tract as well. You may be able to lessen inflammation throughout your body by reducing your consumption of meat and taking essential fatty acid supplements that do not contribute to inflammation, Dr. Fay says.

She suggests a 1,000-milligram capsule of evening primrose oil or one to two teaspoons of flaxseed oil three or four times a day. Some people do better if they start with small amounts and increase with time, says Dr. Fay. You can take these preparations at these doses for three to six months and then gradually begin to cut back, she advises.

Feed on flax. Consume a tablespoon ground flaxseed (available in health food stores) every day, recommends Jennifer Brett, N.D., a naturopathic doctor. Flaxseed contains the fatty acids found in flaxseed oil. These fatty acids can act as an anti-inflammatory. Flaxseed is also rich in a fibre called lignan. Flaxseed has a nutty flavour and tastes good sprinkled on hot cereal or added to rice or pasta. Just don't cook flaxseed—always add it after cooking the cereal, rice, or pasta, Dr. Brett says. The reason: The heat from cooking destroys the fatty acids.

Go fish. Eat at least two three-ounce servings of fatty fish such as mackerel, salmon, and tuna each week, recommends Dr. Brett. These types of fish are rich in omega-3 fatty acids, which have anti-inflammatory properties.

Helpful vitamins and supplements:

Get magnesium for your muscles. Many fibromyalgia patients seem to have low levels of magnesium, which may be a significant cause of their muscle pain, says Elizabeth Wotton, N.D., a naturopathic doctor. It isn't really known why some people lack magnesium. Perhaps they don't absorb it well or aren't getting enough in their diets. Whatever the reason for the shortage, the solution is to take a magnesium supplement. Doing so usually relaxes the muscles, allows blood to flow into the constricted areas, and flushes out the waste products of inflammation, says Dr. Wotton. Your doctor can do a white blood cell magnesium test to determine if you are lacking this mineral, she says. Another theory suggests that the muscle pain and soreness stem from a lack of adenosine triphosphate (ATP), the basic fuel source for muscle cells. A combination of magnesium and a substance called malic acid will increase the production of ATP. Look for a magnesium supplement that contains malic acid in health food stores, she says, and take 200 milligrams three times a day for four to six months.

Increase your vitamins and minerals. Malnourishment seems to be part of the problem for many fibromyalgia patients. Either their diets are quite poor, food allergies are involved, or the people just aren't extracting enough energy and nutrients from food, says Dr. Fay. She tells her patients to cut out coffee, sugar, and refined foods and start on healthier diets that include more fresh fruits and vegetables, more whole grains, and less red meat. Also, she suggests that they take multivitamin/mineral supplements that provide more than the recommended daily amounts. "You want to make sure that you're getting amounts of vitamins and minerals that are higher than the RDAs," she says.

Increase enzymes and stomach acid. Sometimes deficiencies are due to poor absorption of minerals and vitamins in the digestive tract. People with fibromyalgia often have low levels of stomach acid, which leads to an incomplete breakdown of food, says Dr. Fay. To increase stomach acid, Dr. Fay suggests taking two five-milligram capsules of a hydrochloric acid supplement with each meal. These supplements are available in health food stores, but before taking them, you should check with your doctor to determine if you indeed have a problem with low stomach acid.

"If you get any type of burning sensation, just back off the dose a little," she says. "I'd keep it up for several months, minimum. Eventually, your body should start producing more hydrochloric acid on its own." Using hydrochloric acid alone, without lifestyle and dietary changes, however, will not spur the gastrointestinal tract to make its own hydrochloric acid, explains Dr. Fay.

Plant the Good Bugs. Occasionally, digestion and absorption problems may be caused by an overgrowth of yeast (candida) in the gut, says Dr. Fay. Yeast is naturally present in the body in small numbers, but a poor diet, mercury dental fillings, or a course of antibiotic drugs can cause it to grow out of control, she explains. She suggests working with a naturopathic doctor or doctor of Oriental medicine to determine the exact nature of your condition.

Yeast can crowd out the good bugs such as acidophilus in your system and increase inflammation, aggravate food allergies, and interfere with the assimilation of minerals and vitamins, says Dr. Fay. Garlic and pau d'arco are two effective herbal treatments for killing yeast. Dr. Fay suggests taking two 250-milligram capsules of garlic three times a day with meals. Or you can take an extract of pau d'arco bark. The herb is available in 100-milligram tablets, and the typical dose is three a day. "It's really quite safe. It would be pretty hard to do yourself harm with it," Dr. Fay says. While you're killing the candida, you can recolonize your gut with acidophilus, the good bacteria that help maintain intestinal health, says Dr. Fay. She recommends taking one acidophilus tablet in the morning and another at night. "With my patients, I do the recolonizing for at least three to four months," she says. Be sure to check with your doctor before supplementing with acidophilus if you have any serious gastrointestinal problems that require medical attention.

Everyday prevention:

Breathe deep. Practice deep breathing for five minutes several times a day. "You want to slow your breathing, but not so much that you find yourself gasping for air," says Susan Middaugh, Ph.D., a research psychologist. She suggests aiming for eight breath cycles per minute. You should feel the area below cage expand as you inhale and contract as you exhale. "This technique, also called diaphragmatic breathing, relaxes tightened muscles, improves circulation to the muscles, and calms the central nervous system, says Dr. Middaugh.

Keep a food diary. Keep a food diary to pinpoint possible symptom-triggering foods. For two weeks, write down everything you eat and when as well as any symptoms you have. Then review your notes at the end of the two week, looking for foods that seem to instigate flare-ups. A food doesn't have to be "Junk" to cause symptoms. "It could be something that's perfectly healthy," Dr. Brett notes. Different foods bother different people, but according to Dr. Brett, the most common culprits are wheat, dairy, eggs, alcohol, soy, corn, shellfish, tomatoes, potatoes, eggplant, and peppers. These problem foods may intensify the pain or make it more frequent. Not everyone with fibromyalgia has food sensitivities. But those who do might notice hip and lower back pain and stiffness 12 to 24 hours after eating their trigger foods, Dr. Brett says. "Some people also complain of mental fogginess-they feel that they have hangovers, even though they have had nothing to drink," she adds.

Dine on barley. "Barley green can be helpful, because it acts as an anti-inflammatory agent when you have fibromyalgia," says Julian Whitaker, MD, founder and president of the Whitaker Wellness Centre in Newport Beach, California. "Try to have it once a day, just sprinkle it on your salad, or mix one to two tablets in water and drink it." Barley green is available in most health food stores.

Live for the moment. Fibromyalgia pain can be unbearable one moment, better the next. Take advantage of the good moments by doing spur-of-the-moment things. For example, instead of draining your energy by planning elaborate dinner parties weeks ahead, simply invite some friends over when you're having a good day.

Pace yourself. Keep a diary of your activities, then use it to try to spread those activities out. Look for patterns: for example, many women with fibromyalgia feel best between 10 am and 3 pm. Use those "windows" to do things like shopping, chores and career tasks.

Get some support. Minimise muscular strain by using back supports and arm rests when you can. Neck supports, particularly while sleeping, may also help.

Hug your dog or cat. A friendly head scratch or hug can make a dog drool in delight and a cat purr with pride. Pets help reduce pain, tension and stress, says Norman Harden, MD, director of the pain clinic at the Rehabilitation Institute of Chicago.

Easing the pain with exercise:

Stretch regularly. If you have fibromyalgia, begin and end your days with gentle muscle stretches and massages. They boost your body's supply of oxygen and enhance muscle tone and flexibility.

Stand in the doorway. The doorway stretch prepares your muscles for exertion, says Devin Starlanyl, MD, physician and author who has fibromyalgia.

Stand in the middle of a doorway facing forward, with your arms outstretched and your hands resting firmly on each side of the doorjamb at shoulder height.

Take a step forward and feel the stretch across your chest. Hold the stretch for 30 to 60 seconds.

Return to the starting position and move your hands farther down on the doorjamb. Again, take a step forward and stretch.

This is a good stretching exercise to do once or twice a day, Dr. Starlanyl says. She also advocates stretch breaks every one to two hours throughout the day. "You can do a variation of the doorway stretch—extend both arms above your head and reach up, trying to touch the top of a door. And an easy stretch for your calves while seated is to raise both feet off the floor while keeping your heels down," she suggests.

Play wall ball. Tennis ball acupressure, anyone? You don't need a racquet or a net to do this tennis ball exercise offered by Dr. Starlanyl.

First of all, identify the tender spots, or "trigger points," where the pain seems to originate. Place a tennis or lacrosse ball on that trigger point and apply pressure by leaning against a wall or lying on the floor with the ball between your body and the firm surface. When you compress the trigger point, liquids in that area are forced out. When the pressure is lifted, the blood and other body fluids rush back in and flush the area, bringing needed oxygen and nutrients to the tissues.

If the trigger point is under one buttock, for instance, here's how to apply pressure with a tennis ball.

Lie on your back with your knees bent and your feet flat on the floor. Your knees should not touch.

Raise your hips slightly and slide a tennis ball under one of them.

Move your hip down and rest on the ball for 30 to 60 seconds. You can expect to feel some pain, but you can control the pressure that you exert. If you roll it around, the pain should ease.

Exercise. Engage in some form of aerobic exercise for at least 30 minutes every day. "We don't know if lack of physical conditioning causes symptoms, but it certainly contributes to symptoms," says Dr. Harden. Regular low-impact aerobic exercise increases blood flow to the muscles and boosts endorphins, the body's natural pain fighters. In several studies, aerobic exercise has provided dramatic pain relief. If you haven't been physically active, you may need to start working out at a snail's pace. Try to increase the amount of time you spend exercising by no more than 5 minutes each week, suggests Dr. Harden.

Spin your wheels. Stationary cycling can reduce tenderness and promote sound sleep, says Dr. Stark. He urges people who have been inactive to gradually ease into a cycling or similar type of program after conferring with their doctors.

Rock away the pain. Never underestimate the aerobic benefits of your favourite living room rocker, says Dr. Stark. Maybe you can gently rock back and forth through your favourite half-hour sitcom. The rocking action activates leg muscles and lessens the effects of immobility, he says.

Stride often. A 20-minute walk, properly executed, can do wonders for fibromyalgia., says Dr. Starlanyl. She offers these walking tips.

Keep your head held over your shoulders for balance.

Shift your weight from your heels to the balls of your feet to your toes as you step forward.

Push off each step from your toes, using your calf muscles.

Move briskly, but be able to maintain a conversation without being short of breath.

Take up tai chi. This ancient Chinese martial art enhances mind-body connection, balance, and harmony, says Dr. Stark. Its slow, fluid, circular motions in graceful sequences strengthen muscles and improve co-ordination and balance. Think of it as a moving meditation, he adds.

Try warm-water exercise. Water at body temperature is best. Check with your local health clubs about special therapeutic "aquacize" programs held in heated pools.

Herbal help:

Aid with astralagus. For chronic conditions like fibromyalgia, many natural healers believe that the first step is to help the body help itself. That begins with nurturing and strengthening the immune system, says Dr. Wotton. Astragalus provides what is known as deep immune support. Studies show that it helps guard your body by increasing the activity of protective cells and raising the level of antibodies in your system. The exact mechanism isn't clear, but the herb seems to work within the bone marrow itself, where immune cells are manufactured. Dr. Wotton recommends taking one teaspoon of astragalus liquid extract three times a day. You can also take astragalus capsules. If the supplements are 500 milligrams, a typical dose would be one or two capsules three times a day with meals. "Astragalus begins to build up the immune system to provide support on a long-term basis. It's really good for this type of chronic condition because it gives you some stability," she says. "You should take it for at least four to six months."

Get a lift with ginseng. Deep weariness is one of fibromyalgia's most nagging symptoms; it's a weariness brought on by pain, stress, and lack of energy. To give her patients a lift, Dr. Wotton recommends ginseng. "It's a tonic herb that makes you feel less run-down," she says. Although ginseng has a reputation as an energy booster, it's not actually a stimulant but rather an adaptogenic herb. Its purpose is to help the body adapt to different conditions. In the case of stress and fatigue, the adrenal glands may be functioning erratically. If they are working too hard—pumping out too many hormones—ginseng will reduce this action. If they aren't functioning well and aren't releasing enough hormones, ginseng can stimulate them to produce more.

Fibromyalgia 101

Since fibromyalgia is so elusive and so difficult to identify, the U.S. Arthritis Foundation offers these helpful clues.

Fibromyalgia is a syndrome characterised by generalised muscle pain and fatigue. It does not affect the joints.

Pain may start in one part of the body and seem to gradually spread all over.

People describe fibromyalgia pain as burning, radiating, gnawing, sore, stiff, and achy.

People with fibromyalgia experience soreness and tenderness in at least 11 of 18 identified tender points on the body.

Nine out of 10 people with fibromyalgia experience fatigue caused by interrupted sleep.

No single lab test or x-ray can diagnose fibromyalgia.

The cause is unknown, but doctors say stress, physical injury, smoking, poor posture, and other factors may play a role.

"By supporting the adrenal glands, ginseng increases endurance and strengthens a person's ability to withstand stress," says Dr. Wotton. "In that way, it can boost energy and bolster the immune system, even though it doesn't have a direct effect on the immune system itself. People with fibromyalgia sometimes get in their situation because they don't let up and either can't or won't give themselves and their bodies a break. Finally their bodies just get worn down."

She recommends one to two teaspoons of the liquid extract twice a day or one 200-milligram capsule twice a day. But don't take ginseng after 2:00 p.m., she cautions, because it can keep you awake at night. It may also cause irritability if taken with caffeine or other stimulants.

Match the herb to the symptom, says Dr. Brett. She often prescribes the following herbal remedies to her patients. (All of the doses are for the tincture form of the herbs in amounts appropriate for a 150-pound woman. You can buy these herbs in health food stores.)

For aching joints and an upset stomach, take 30 drops of black cohosh three times a day.

For muscle cramps and tightness, take 10 to 20 drops of cramp bark two times a day.

For muscle spasms with fatigue and coughing, take 10 drops of skunk cabbage three times a day.

For muscle twitching and pain accompanied by insomnia, nervousness, and restlessness, take 10 to 30 drops of skullcap two times a day.

For muscle spasms accompanied by insomnia, depression, and distress, take 15 to 30 drops of valerian three times a day.

For spasmodic pain, nightmares, and swelling around the joints, take 10 to 30 drops of peony two times a day.

If you are already taking over-the-counter pain relievers as directed by your doctor, you should check with your doctor before switching to an herbal remedy, advises Dr. Brett. Also, women who are pregnant should consult with their doctors before taking any herbs.

In fact, Dr. Brett suggests that everyone consult an herbalist or a naturopathic doctor to make sure that they are taking the right herb for their symptoms.

Hands-on help:

Massage those aches. Researchers at the University of Miami recommend massages for people with fibromyalgia. In one study, 10 people with fibromyalgia received 30-minute massages twice a week for five weeks. They experienced decreased anxiety and less stress, pain, stiffness, and fatigue.

Follow your fibres. Use your fingertips to trace the path of muscles in the area where you hurt. Press deep into the tissue, but always follow the direction in which the muscle fibres travel.

Mind over malady:

Guide pain away. Visualise the muscle pain in physical terms such as a burning fire or a terrible monster gnawing on your bones. By mentally extinguishing the flames or taming the monster, you may be able to reduce pain, says Dr. Harden.

Relax progressively. Practice progressive muscle relaxation for 10 to 15 minutes twice a day, recommends Dr. Middaugh. This technique involves gently contracting and then relaxing every muscle in your body. Why contract already-tight muscles? "People often don't realise that their muscles are tight until they contract them," she explains. "By first contracting and then relaxing their muscles, people with fibromyalgia are able to relieve some of the tightness." To try progressive muscle relaxation, begin by clenching your fists gently until you can feel the muscles tensing, says Dr. Middaugh. Hold for three seconds, then release. Repeat, working your muscles in the following sequence: arms, shoulders, neck, face, abdomen, lower back, buttocks, thighs, calves, and feet. To maximise the benefits of progressive muscle relaxation, you may want to get some training in the technique. Dr. Middaugh recommends training sessions with a licensed psychologist, psychiatrist, or similar health professional.

Flu and Cold Pain

The pain: Various symptoms that accompany infection by cold or flu virus, including sore throat, cough, fever, aches and congestion. The biggest difference between a cold and a flu is that a cold isolates in your head and chest, while you feel the flu all over your body. "People can usually function with a cold, but it's hard to function properly when you have the flu," says David Rooney, MD, a family physician.

The cause: Although they share some common symptoms, the flu is not simply a more severe version of a cold. You "catch" a cold when you inhale virus-containing droplets expelled by someone else or rub your eyes or nose with contaminated fingers. The virus—rhinoviruses cause about half of all common colds; coronaviruses take credit for most of the rest—latches onto a mucous membrane in your nose, eyes, or throat. There are roughly 200 cold viruses, each with a slightly different effect on your body. But your body's response doesn't vary much between each virus, which is why they are all lumped together under one name: the common cold.

The flu, on the other hand, comes in three different strains: A (which has many subgroups), B, or C. Most of us catch the A strain. The flu incubates in the body for one to three days, but lasts for three to seven days. Like the common cold, influenza viruses are spread by sneezing and coughing.

To fight the viral invasion, your body unleashes the symptoms to get rid of the cold or flu virus. As miserable as they are, headache, fatigue, muscle aches, chills, sore throat, dry cough, and congestion all simply reflect that the body is doing its job. So the discomfort is not from the virus itself, but from your body's response to the infection.

See a doctor if :
... you can't swallow or eat or breathe, it is not just a cold. And if it hurts really bad in your head or chest, it is not just a cold. In such cases, see a doctor.
... your cold does not improve within 14 days.
... you have green or yellow phlegm.
... you have trouble breathing or eating.
... your temperature tops 102°F.

... any of your symptoms last more than five days.
... your cold or flu is accompanied by out-of-the ordinary
symptoms (chest pain, blood in the mucus from your nose, or if
your phlegm or mucus is green, brown, or bloody).

Medication:

Ask your doctor about amantadine or rimantadine. The antiviral
prescription drugs amantadine (Amantadine HCl or Symmetrel) and
rimantadine or amantadine (Flumadine) can shorten the duration of
influenza type A infection. They have also proved 70 to 90 percent effective
when used as a type A preventive. Most important, they can also prevent
you from developing serious and potentially life-threatening complications
such as pneumonia, Reye's syndrome, convulsions, and ear infections. So
be sure to ask your doctor about these antivirals if you are age 65 or older,
have heart, lung, or kidney disease, diabetes, or another high-risk medical
condition. The only drawback is that they are not effective against
influenza type B and must be taken within 48 hours of the flu onset.

Quick relief:

Relieve your pain. For the aches and pains and headache that
accompany a cold or fever, take acetaminophen or ibuprofen according to
the bottle's instructions.

Steam away congestion. Pour three cups of water into a pot and bring it
to a simmer. Remove the pot from the stove and set it where you can sit in
front of it, such as on your kitchen table. Lean over the pot and drape a
towel over your head. (Don't put your face too close to the steam, though,
or you may burn yourself.) Inhale the steam for five minutes. This should
help loosen the mucus in clogged nasal passages.

Take a break. If you're sick, your body is telling you that it needs rest,
says Thomas Kruzel, N.D., a naturopathic physician. Stay home, stay in
bed, get rest. Try to sleep at least eight hours during the night and get as
much rest as possible, even if you don't actually sleep, during the day, says
Don Beckstead, MD, a family physician. There's no better way to relax your
body and recoup some of the energy that will help you fight viral invaders.
If you have trouble getting to sleep because you're really congested, raise
your head with a few extra pillows to help you breathe more easily. Lying
on your back with your head elevated, you might prevent mucus from
draining down your throat and disrupting your breathing. As for when you
should sleep, "Your body will let you know when it's tired," says Dr.
Beckstead.

Fight that fever. When Victorian maidens were in danger of swooning,
someone invariably applied a cool compress. Should your brow become
feverish, try that maiden's cure. Wet a washcloth in cool water and wipe
down your face and neck, says Dr. Beckstead. As the water evaporates, it
takes some of the heat from your skin. If it makes you feel better, you can

leave the cloth on your forehead until it warms up, he says. Reapply a freshly cooled cloth as many times as you like. But if your temperature reaches 101°, acetaminophen is generally the drug of choice, advises Dr. Beckstead.

Gargle for a sore throat. A pinch of salt—a quarter teaspoon—in a cup of warm water makes a good gargle for relieving throat pain. Warm liquids and salt can help shrink and dry out mucous membranes.

Ongoing care:

Humidify your world. Humidifying a room can help lick a cold or the flu. The vapour emitted by a room humidifier moistens the mucous membranes in your throat and nose, so germs are more easily trapped and expelled. In addition, dry air is a great breeding ground for cold viruses. You can use a room humidifier (be sure to get one with a filter system and clean it regularly). You can also add moisture by leaving bathroom doors open during showers, keeping lots of houseplants and keeping open pots of water (especially near stoves and radiators).

Elevate your head. Propping your head on pillows when you lie down makes breathing easier, especially if you have postnasal drip.

Make your own nasal spray. A home-made saline solution can clear your nose of irritants such as dust, pollen, and pollution. To make the solution, add one-half teaspoon of salt and a pinch of baking soda to one cup of lukewarm water. Spritz the solution into your nose a few times, using a child-size bulb syringe. Then blow your nose.

Throw other sprays away. Over-the-counter nasal sprays and decongestants may provide quick relief, but they are really doing you more harm than good. Overuse can cause a rebound effect. In other words, once you stop using them, the stuffiness comes back worse than before. If you use nasal sprays, stop the treatment after three days. Don't use decongestants for more than seven days.

Be selective. If you look for those cold and flu remedies that promise to erase every symptom, even ones you aren't sure you have, think again. "I tell my patients to simply ease each symptom with one medication," says Dr. Rooney. "And there's no reason to buy a brand name instead of generic."

Dr. Rooney recommends the following: To relieve the pain of headaches or muscle aches, use ibuprofen (Advil, Motrin). Do not take ibuprofen if you are allergic to aspirin or if you've had a recent ulcer, Dr. Rooney warns. To fight phlegm, look for guaifenesin (found in cough syrups such as Robitussin). If you're congested but don't have a cough, use pseudoephedrine (Sudafed). And to suppress a cough that keeps you up at night, use dextromethorphan (Vicks 44D or Robitussin DM). Once again, you should feel free to use the generic equivalents.

Follow the package directions on all medications. The perfect accompaniment to these medications is water, which will help thin the mucus that's plugging you up, Dr. Rooney says.

Exercise or not? How to Tell

If you're sniffling, sneezing, coughing, and just plain tuckered out, you probably won't welcome the sight of a fitness trainer shouting, "Hup, hup, hup, hup, one, two three, four." But for some people with the all-too-common cold, a modest workout might be just the thing to kick the germs.

When can you hit the trail, and when should you hit the hay? To help guide your exercise decisions when you're under the weather, you should do a quick symptom check, suggests William A. Primos Jr., MD, who practices primary-care sports medicine. If your symptoms are above the neck, such as a stuffy or runny nose or a sore throat, exercising is probably all right, advises Dr. Primos. But start at half speed, he cautions. If after 10 minutes you feel okay, you can increase the intensity and finish your workout. But if you feel horrible after 10 minutes, stop.

When your symptoms are below the neck, avoid exercise completely, recommends Dr. Primos. Some common symptoms that fall into this category are muscle aches, a hacking cough, a fever of 100°F or higher, chills, diarrhoea, or vomiting. Many of these are indicators of flu, and if you work out in this condition, you're likely to feel even weaker and certainly become dehydrated. If after five or six days, your symptoms haven't improve or have worsened, you should see a doctor.

Take it slow when you start again. If you've had flu or the below-the-neck symptoms of a bad cold (like a hacking cough), you can resume exercising when those symptoms subside, advises Dr. Primos. But ease back into it, or you could end up sick again. For every day that you were sick, exercise at a lower intensity for two days upon your return. If you were sick for three days, for instance, take it easy for the first six days that you work out after your illness.

Go hot and cold. A basic principle of naturopathic medicine is to assist the body in its natural healing processes. In the case of a fever, Dr. Kruzel suggests that you take a hot shower, soak a T-shirt in cold water, wring out as much water as possible, put it on, put a dry wool or flannel shirt on over it, and go to bed. "The idea," he says, "is to shock the white blood cells in your system into movement so that they can help fight the infection. The body tries to warm up the cold shirt, and that gets your blood circulating. It works extremely well."

Mollify your muscles. If you don't have a fever, take a nice warm soak in the tub to help ease the tired, achy muscles that are especially prevalent with the flu, says Dr. Beckstead. Twenty to 30 minutes is all it takes to start feeling better. Plus, the steam might help open up a clogged nose.

Toss your toothbrush. The virus continues to linger on wet toothbrush bristles and you can are-infect yourself day after day. Throw away your toothbrush three days after the onset of the flu and use a new one.

Stop smoking. Besides draining your body of vitamin C and hurting your throat, smoking slows recuperation time and keeps your immunity lower.

Nutritional remedies:

Sip some soup. The benefits of this long-time folk remedy have been elucidated, thanks to the efforts of a few curious scientists. Researchers at Mount Sinai Medical Centre in Miami Beach found that hot chicken soup got nasal mucus flowing significantly better than a cup of cold water. Hot water also outperformed cold, but didn't do quite as well as chicken soup. Because drinking either water or soup through a straw was not as effective as sipping it from a cup, the researchers believe the effect may be due, at least in part, to nasal inhalation of water vapour. And in another study, researchers at the University of Nebraska in Omaha found that, in a test tube, chicken soup slowed the movement of neutrophils—immune cells activated by cold viruses. "When you have a cold, neutrophils normally migrate from the blood to the mucous membranes, stimulating such symptoms as inflammation and mucus secretion and perhaps fever and cough," says Stephen Rennard, MD, chief of pulmonary and critical care medicine at the university's Medical Centre. "Although we didn't test this in people, it's possible that eating chicken soup may provide some immune system benefits." Vegetarians take note: While plain chicken soup provides immune benefits, Dr. Rennard also discovered that the vegetables added to the broth provided additional anti-inflammatory action. "We used onions, sweet potatoes, carrots, turnips and parsnips and found that each of these vegetables alone affected immune cells' activity," he says.

Eat the stinking rose. Sure you could take garlic capsules, even the popular odour-free ones sold in stores. But because no one will want to get too close and risk catching your cold, why not try a little bit of garlic, straight, fresh, potent, and in a palatable form? Make it a final addition to your soup, suggests Elson Haas, MD, author of *Staying Healthy with Nutrition.* "When you put your bowl of soup on the table, you actually press a clove or two of fresh garlic right into your bowl so you're not cooking it at all, but it gets to be dispersed into the warm soup."

Drink, sip, and guzzle fluids. Drink as much clear liquid as you can—at least eight glasses a day—whether you feel thirsty or not. Hot liquids like herbal tea or chicken soup are best for several reasons: They diminish a virus's ability to replicate, they soothe the throat, they help keep virus-fighting mucus thin and flowing and the warmth helps decongest the nasal passages and lungs. Water is beneficial as well—you it to fight off the infection. Whatever fluid you drink, make sure it doesn't have caffeine in it. Steer clear of coffee and colas. They'll only dehydrate you more.

Eat foods that boost your immune system. Dark leafy green and deep-orange-coloured vegetables bolster the immune system so that you can fight off the infection, says Maureen Williams, N.D., a naturopathic physician. Shiitake mushrooms, beets, garlic, and onions are also immunity boosters, she says. "Also try miso soup, found in most health food stores. Miso replaces electrolytes lost through sweating and diarrhoea."

Avoid high-carbohydrate foods. Sugar and high-carbohydrate foods such as breads and pasta made with refined white flour, white rice, pretzels, and rice cakes weaken the immune system, says Dr. Williams. Sugar-laden fruit juices are just as guilty.

Skip caffeine and alcohol. When you have the flu, caffeine and alcohol "are rocket fuel for bacteria and fungi growth," says Keith Berndtson, MD, an integrative medicine specialist at American Whole Health Centres in Chicago. "They create sugar swings in the bloodstream that throw off your immune system response to infections."

Munch on mushrooms. Certain mushrooms hold an important place in the treatment of illness in both China and Japan, and people world-wide have taken an interest in the potential healing properties of these fungi, especially their ability to stimulate immune function. "Mushrooms contain an array of novel compounds not found elsewhere in nature," according to Andrew Weil, MD, author of *Natural Health, Natural Medicine.* "And let's not forget that antibiotics are derived from closely related organisms—moulds." Of the food mushrooms with medicinal value, the shiitake is the best known. This large, meaty mushroom is most likely to be available dry. Soaked, then cooked, it makes a tasty addition to stir-fries or stews and holds its own in a soup.

Eat light. "A cold is a sign that your body is going through a detoxification process," says Dr. Kruzel. "Viruses love to set up housekeeping in bodies that need detoxing, which is why you see so many people get sick after big holidays, like Christmas and New Year's." Dr. Kruzel recommends cutting back on food at the early signs of a cold or flu. "If you feel hungry, eat soups, salads, vegetables, and fruits and drink fruit juices," he says. "Let your body do the work it needs to do."

Heat up your meals. Hot pepper helps open clogged nasal passages by thinning mucus and making your nose run. Try sprinkling ground red pepper, red-pepper flakes, or hot-pepper sauce on your food.

Drink carrot juice. Put a few drops of vegetable oil in a glass of fresh carrot juice, then take frequent sips throughout the day. Carrots are loaded with vitamin A, which strengthens your respiratory system and can quiet your cough. The vegetable oil coats and soothes your throat.

Get going with grapefruit. Grapefruit is a great food for fighting a cold, says Paul Yanick, Ph.D., a research scientist. One reason is that it's high in vitamin C, according to Dr. Yanick. A lesser-known reason, he says, is that it helps detoxify the liver. "the liver is your front line to the immune system," he says. He recommends eating one or more grapefruit and their white bitter pule each day to prevent colds and build immunity.

Put down some pineapple juice. "Fresh pineapple juice is wonderful for colds," says Eve Campanelli, PhD, a holistic family practitioner. "It's less

How to deal with a fever

If an oral thermometer shows you have a fever of 100°F or more, shed extra blankets or clothing—getting rid of extra insulation speeds heat loss and lowers body temperature. Take a comfortable tub or sponge bath. Cold water constricts the blood vessels, triggers shivering and may actually raise your body temperature. Cold water can be torture to a person with a fever, so make the water comfortably tepid enough to gently cool the bather. Call the doctor if fever lasts two or three days or longer, or if it hits 103°F.

allergenic that citrus and less acidic, and it contains more vitamin C. It also breaks down mucus better. She recommends drinking four to six ounces of juice (diluted with the same amount of water) at least four times a day to treat a cold.

Ease with ayurveda. Both apple and dark grape juices may be beneficial to those fighting the flu, says John Peterson, MD, an Ayurvedic practitioner. Apple and dark grape juices have properties that work against congestion and runny noses, according to Dr. Peterson. And, he says, dark grape juice is rich in tannins, substances that have been shown to kill viruses under laboratory conditions. Do not blend the juices, but you may dilute them if they are two sweet. Drink them at room temperature and at any time other than meals. He also suggests pear, cranberry and pomegranate juices.

Do feed a flu. You need vitamins and minerals to mount an effective defence against a flu bug. Aim for well-balanced meals, or at least try some bland fruit such as mashed bananas or applesauce.

Warm up in the kitchen. To take the chills out of your cold, make a beeline to the kitchen and fix yourself a traditional herb-and-spice cold remedy. Combine 1 ounce (by weight) of sliced fresh ginger, one broken-up cinnamon stick, 1 teaspoon of coriander seeds, three cloves, one lemon slice, and 1 pint of water. He recommends simmering this combination for 15 minutes and straining. Then drink a hot cupful every two hours. Sweeten with organic honey to taste, he suggests.

Helpful vitamins and supplements:

Crush a cold with vitamin C. While it may not be a cure-all, research seems to indicate that vitamin C does bolster the body's immune function, says Dr. Haas. And at high doses, vitamin C seems to help stop viruses from growing. Take 250 milligrams six to eight times a day for up to a week, suggests Dr. Haas.

Suck on a zinc lozenge. Zinc has also shown some ability to lessen a cold's severity. Three or four times a day, suck on a zinc gluconate throat lozenge until it dissolves in your mouth. Or take up to 50 milligrams of zinc in supplement form at least once every day. Zinc can make you feel nauseous, so take it on a full stomach. Also, doses of zinc over 15 milligrams a day should be taken under medical supervision.

Get a shot. See a naturopath if you want to consider an intravenous shot of immune-bolstering vitamins and minerals. Called a Meyers cocktail, this nutrient-dense mix contains 500 milligrams of vitamin C, 250 to 500 milligrams of magnesium, 250 to 500 milligrams of calcium, and 50 to 100 milligrams of B-complex vitamins, says Keith Berndtson, MD, an integrative medicine specialist. "Because the vitamins and minerals are going straight into your bloodstream, they get pushed right into the cells much more efficiently than if you were to load up on these nutrients orally," says Dr. Berndtson. The immune system boost that you get from this treatment can last for several hours and even days.

Bolster with beta carotene. Take 200,000 IU (international units) of beta-carotene at the beginning stages of a cold. "It strengthens immunity and probably has some antiviral effects as well," says David Edelberg, MD, assistant professor of medicine at Rush Medical College in Chicago. Beta-carotene can also help prevent secondary infections associated with colds. After the first large dose, take 25,000 IU daily until symptoms resolve, Dr. Traub suggests.

Herbal help:

Add some echinacea. Otherwise known as the purple coneflower, echinacea is a North American plant whose roots were used by Native Americans and early settlers to treat colds and flu. There is some evidence that in the early stages of a cold, echinacea can help fight infection by supporting the body's immune function and increasing white blood cell counts, explains Dr. Haas. Most health food stores sell echinacea in a liquid form known as a tincture. Add one-half dropperful of tincture to a few ounces of water and drink it three times a day the first day you feel cold symptoms coming on. If you don't experience any side effects the first day, from the next day on, add one full dropperful of tincture to the water each time instead. Don't take echinacea if you have an autoimmune condition such as lupus, tuberculosis, or multiple sclerosis or if you're allergic to plants in the daisy family, such as camomile and marigold.

Follow the goldenseal rule. Another healing herb is goldenseal. It also supports the body's natural immune response, Dr. Haas states. Take one-half dropperful of the tincture in a few ounces of water three times a day during the first day of your cold. If you don't experience any side effects the first day, from the next day on, add one full dropperful of tincture to the water each time instead. Don't take goldenseal for more than three weeks, though, because it can irritate the liver, advises Dr. Haas.

Ease with eucalyptus. Inhale the steam from eucalyptus essential oil and water. The key to eucalyptus's healing power is a chemical called cineole, or eucalyptol, which aids in the loosening of mucus. Put 10 to 15 drops of eucalyptus oil in a pan of water, heat to boiling, and remove the pan from the stove. Covering your head with a towel and leaning over the pan, inhale the steam through your nostrils—and blow your nose frequently. Repeat the steam inhalation three or four times daily. Be careful not to let the steam burn your face or sinuses while taking this steam bath.

Try the homeopathic remedy Oscillococcinum. Oscillococcinum (pronounced AH-sill-oh-cock-SINE-um) is a pill you can take twice a day for three days, says Earl Mindell, Ph.D., professor of nutrition and author of *Earl Mindell's Supplement Bible.* Available at some chemists and health food stores, this remedy eliminates many cold symptoms and helps you get over your cold more quickly. "Place these tiny pills under your tongue, where they dissolve very rapidly," he suggests. "Before you know it, your body begins producing antibodies to fight the cold."

Try an aromatic mix. Combine 20 drops of eucalyptus, lavender and clary sage essential oils to your bath. This aromatherapy mixture can help you feel better by melting away the fatigue associated with cold symptoms, according to Michael Scholes, president of the Michael Scholes School of Aromatic Studies in Los Angeles. For a totally relaxing and aromatic experience, fill a tub with your favourite bubble bath, pour in the mixture of essential oils, and soak in the bath for 20 minutes or so. The combination will strengthen the immune system and strip away fatigue, he says.

Sip a cup of hot ginger tea to boost your immune system's fighting power. Ginger is chock full of antiviral compounds to help fight infection, reduce pain and fever, and suppress coughing. "Ginger heats up the body, making it very difficult for viruses to survive," says Ellen Evert Hopman, a master herbalist and author of *Tree Medicine, Tree Magic.* What's more, it is a natural expectorant and a mild sedative that will help you get some rest.

The following ginger tea recipe will scoot you along to a quicker recovery. Chop up a one-inch slice of fresh gingerroot into slivers. Place the ginger in a non-aluminium pot. Add two cups of water, cover the pot tightly. Simmer for 20 minutes, then strain the ginger tea into a cup. Squeeze in the juice of half a lemon. Add honey to taste.

"Drink no more than two cups a day," says Hopman. "Too much ginger can irritate the lungs and actually produce mucus."

Ask for astralagus. For thousands of years in China, the herb used to enhance immunity has been astragalus root. Considered a tonic that strengthens the body's resistance to disease, this potent herb can stimulate practically all processes of your immune system. It increases the number of stem cells in bone marrow and speeds their growth into active immune cells. Astragalus also may help boost levels of interferon, one of your body's potent fighters against viruses, says Chris Meletis, N.D., chief medical officer at the National College of Naturopathic Medicine in Oregon. A heightened level of interferon can help prevent or shorten the duration of colds and flu. Astragalus even galvanises the production of white blood

Flu shot facts

Get a shot every year. The flu vaccine is different every year. That is because flu viruses are constantly mutating, or changing, as they travel around the world infecting different populations. To battle the current year's version of the flu, experts at the World Health Organisation, the Centres for Disease Control and Prevention, and the Food and Drug Administration collect and analyse those mutations in laboratories in dozens of countries. They choose the three most likely viral suspects for the current year's vaccine and, almost invariably, their selection is accurate. Upon injection, your body reacts to their presence by creating specialised immune substances called antibodies. These antibodies will attack the live virus or viruses should they ever pay you a visit.

Some people experience side effects from a flu shot, but this is relatively uncommon, says Steven R. Mostow, MD, professor of medicine at the University of Colorado, chairman of the American Thoracic Society's committee on the prevention of pneumonia and influenza. "The chances of having a fever or feeling sick the next day is 1 percent or less," he says, which means that 99 out of 100 people won't get sick after the shot. About 20 percent of those who get the shot, however, will have "a very mild sore arm the next day, which will last for one to two days."

Get a shot if you are flying out of the country. There are a couple of reasons why this is a good idea, says Dr. Mostow. First, when it is summer in the England, it is winter—and flu season—in the Southern Hemisphere. Second, if you are travelling to a developing country, medical care might not be up to par, so being hospitalised with a bad case of the flu is the last thing that you want. Third, air travel itself puts you at high risk for a rendezvous with a flu virus because lots of people are in close proximity on a plane, and the cabin's air is being continually are-circulated. "If you are leaving the country by aeroplane, get a flu shot," he says.

Don't get a shot if you are allergic to eggs. The viruses for the vaccine are grown in a chicken's egg, so anybody who is allergic to eggs will also be allergic to the flu vaccine and shouldn't take it.

cells called macrophages, whose mission is to destroy invading viruses and bacteria. To stamp out a cold or flu in its earliest stages, take one 500-milligram capsule of astragalus four times a day until symptoms disappear, says Dr. Meletis . Then take one 500-milligram capsule twice a day for seven days to prevent a relapse.

Lick it with licorice. The sweet taste of licorice—the herb, not the candy—soothes the throat. And, according to studies, it suppresses the cough reflex. To make a tea, add one-half teaspoon of licorice root to one cup of freshly boiled water. Allow to steep for 10 minutes, then strain and allow to cool slightly before drinking. Don't take licorice more than three times a day or for more than two weeks, especially if your blood pressure tends to be high.

Ease with elderberry. When you have that even-my-hair-hurts, overall achy and feverish feeling that signals that it's not just a cold but the flu that's coming on, try a shot of elderberry, says Daniel Gagnon, executive director of the Botanical Research and Education Institute, and owner of Herbs, Etc., in Santa Fe, New Mexico. "If you take elderberry extract early enough, you may be able to head it off at the pass before it becomes a full-blown flu," he says. "Elderberry extract contains substances that break down an enzyme that the virus uses to penetrate your healthy cells and reproduce," he says. "It works within 24 to 48 hours after you take it." The best way to take elderberry is the fresh berry juice, he says. But that's very hard to find. "Instead, you can buy the alcohol-based extract and take 40 drops every four hours the first day you feel sick." Continue to take for three days, he says. You can dilute the extract (also called a tincture) in water, juice, or herbal tea.

Break up congestion with horseradish. Another timeless herbal remedy for respiratory ills is horseradish. And if you've ever inhaled its pungent vapours, it's easy to understand why, says Ed Smith, a herbalist. "Horseradish is very high in polysaccharides, which stimulate the immune system. It's also rich in aromatic sulfur compounds, which are what you need to kill viruses and bacteria. And there's no doubt that it's good for breaking up congestion," he says. "The best way to get horseradish into your system is just eat it. A teaspoonful on some crackers should help clear you right up."

Give it the slip with slippery elm. Native Americans used to make slippery elm into a throat-soothing beverage because it contains large amounts of mucilage, which also acts as an anti-tussive, or mild cough suppressant, says Varro E. Tyler, Ph.D., a pharmacist. Although you can drink slippery elm as a tea, he recommends taking slippery elm in throat lozenges instead, because they provide a steady stream of mucilage to the throat. You can buy slippery elm "cough drops" at most health food stores, he says.

Have a little horehound. "Horehound is a good antispasmodic as well as a decongestant, which makes it a good cough remedy," says Patricia Howell, a professional herbalist. To make horehound into a tea, steep 2 heaping teaspoons of the dried herb in 1 cup of boiling water. If you don't like the taste, which Howell says can be "disgustingly bitter," you can buy horehound hard candy, which is frequently used as a cough lozenge, says Dr. Tyler in *Herbs of Choice.* Or you can steep horehound overnight, strain out the herb, and simmer the liquid until it's reduced by half. Then stir in an equal amount of honey and sip, says Howell.

Clear up with elecampane root. Elecampane root is also useful when you have a congested cough, says Howell, because it helps expel mucus while also drying out mucous membranes. Plus, it contains mucilage, so it also has a relaxing effect on a sore, irritated throat. To make a medicinal tea, Howell recommends pouring a cup of cold water onto 1 teaspoon of the cut root in a saucepan. Simmer for about 20 minutes, strain, and drink it warm. Drink the tea three times a day while you have a cough. Just remember that elecampane is quite bitter, so add some honey to sweeten it a bit.

Ease it with elderflower. Elderflower is good for opening pores and inducing sweat to break a fever. Plus, the extract from these tiny flowers contains compounds that help break up and clear out excess mucus and inflammation that usually accompany fever due to colds and flu. To make a tea out of dried elderflowers, pour a cup of boiling water over 2 teaspoons of the herb and allow it to infuse, covered, for 15 to 20 minutes. Drink it three times a day as needed, says Winston. For extra effectiveness, you can also combine elderflower with peppermint or yarrow. Make the mix of herbs equivalent to 2 teaspoons, with elderflower as the largest portion, he says.

Everyday prevention:

Pump up your immune system. There's pretty good evidence that aerobic exercise does increase the effectiveness of the immune system. And you don't have to train for a triathlon for your workouts to be effective. You're so much less likely to get sick if you walk 5 days a week for 30 to 45 minutes.

Wash your hands. By wash, we mean soap and water around every part of your hands, including under your fingernails. "Viruses live on hands," says Dr. Rooney. "If you wash your hands frequently, then you'll be less likely to catch a bug." And if you're a parent who doesn't want to catch whatever virus is going around your kids' school, make sure that your children get in the habit of scrubbing up at an early age.

Boost your immune system. Cold and flu viruses are everywhere in the environment around us. The key to not succumbing is to keep your immune system functioning at peak condition. Experts recommend that you get sufficient amounts of vitamins E, C, B6, and B12; folic acid; and the mineral zinc in your daily diet.

Stay cool. Long-term stress can wear down your immune system, setting you up for a cold. In a study at Carnegie Mellon University in Pittsburgh and the University of Pittsburgh, researchers exposed 276 adults to cold viruses, quarantined them, then gave them personality tests. Periodic stressful events had relatively little impact upon disease, but those who had endured severe chronic stressors for at least two years were three times more likely to get sick.

Wash out your nasal passages. You can greatly reduce your chances of catching a cold if you do a yoga nasal wash called neti once a day, says Stephen A. Neezon, MD, yoga teacher and staff physician at the Himalayan International Institute of Yoga Science and Philosophy. Here's what Dr. Neezon recommends: Start by filling a four-ounce paper cup halfway with warm water, then add 1/2 teaspoon of salt. Put a small crease in the lip of the cup so that it forms a spout Slightly tilt your head back and to the left. Then slowly pour the water into your right nostril. The water will flow out of your left nostril or down the back of your throat if your nostril is clogged. Spit out the water if it goes down your throat, or wipe the water from you face with a hand towel if it flows out of you left nostril. Fill the cup again, then repeat the procedure on the other side, pouring the water into your left nostril and tilting your head back and to the right.

Don't hang out with the newly infected. People are most infectious during the first three days that they have a cold, so avoid them, says Jack Gwaltney, MD, one of the world's leading experts on colds.

Watch out for kid stuff. Children are the major reservoirs of cold viruses because a child's immature immune system can't repel them as easily. Grandparents with chronic diseases should be especially wary, says Dr. Gwaltney, because a problem like chronic obstructive lung disease or heart disease could be complicated by the cold virus. They should steer clear of grandkids when they have a new cold, he says.

Hands on help:

Rub your nose in it. Gently massage the area around your nose. This acupressure technique will help relieve congestion, says David Molony, Ph.D., a licensed acupuncturist. After you have massaged the nose area for about five minutes, move your fingers up to your scalp. Beginning one inch above your hairline, lightly massage your scalp for another five minutes. You can repeat these steps as often as you like to get relief, he says. You can also relieve congestion by massaging the webbed area between your thumb and index finger for five minutes, Dr. Molony says. Use either of these techniques as often as you like and for as long as you have cold symptoms. The effects of acupressure can last for a couple of hours, especially if you perform them right before bedtime, Dr. Molony says. You will encourage a good night's sleep, which is an essential part of getting yourself well.

Press the eye area. There's another pair of acupressure points to know about, especially if you're suffering from a stuffy nose. Place your index fingers directly underneath each cheekbone again, but this time, they should be under the centre of each eye rather than near the nostrils. Gently press and hold for two minutes.

Foot Pain

The pain: Foot pain. The pain may progress from a dull, intermittent heel ache to a sharp, persistent pain. Classically, it's worst in the morning with the first few steps you take.

The cause: Most foot pain, is either plantar fasciitis or fallen arches. Fascia is fibrous tissue that lies beneath the skin but over bone and muscle. Plantar means "under your foot." And—it means "inflammation." Put it all together and you get inflammation in the tissue on the underside of your foot that supports you when you stand (which is why you don't feel any pain when you're sitting down).

Fallen arches, as the name implies, is a change in the depth of the arch in your foot. "The 'fall' occurs not overnight but over time as we age, if the foot isn't properly supported by the shoes you wear," says Richard Braver, D.P.M., a sports podiatrist. A high arch can become a moderate arch, while a moderate arch can become flatter. Flat feet can bring on their own set of problems, as the arch stretches out more, causing strain (and pain) of the foot. Think "increase" when trying to figure out what has caused the sudden onset of plantar fasciitis, says Dr. Braver. You've probably either gained weight or increased the amount you exercise (especially walking or running). Or you haven't been wearing good supportive shoes, and that has weakened your arches. Wearing poorly fitted shoes can lead to multiple foot problems, including plantar fasciitis and fallen arches.

See a doctor if:

...you feel nausea. Nausea signifies a deep injury, such as a tendon or ligament tear.
...your foot is black and blue. If there's enough strain or energy to cause a rupture of small blood vessels, then there may have been enough pressure or strain to fracture a bone or tear a ligament.
...foot pain persists for more than two to three days.
...if you're elderly, you have diabetes, or you have circulatory problems

Quick relief:

Ice up. Put some ice on your feet for 15 to 20 minutes at a time, once or twice a day, advises Marjorie Menacker, D.P.M., a podiatrist. Do this for two or three days in a row to decrease any inflammation in your foot. If you use an ice bag, wrap it in a dish towel so that it does not come in direct contact with your skin. Or you can freeze water in a small paper cup and peel off the top edge to make a 1/2-inch ice cup. Then massage in circles over the painful area for 10 minutes, recommends Dr. Menacker. If your feet feel no better after a few days to a week of trying a combination of ice, stretches, and wearing shoes with good arch support, you should see a doctor, advises Dr. Menacker.

Stomp on pain. Nonsteroidal anti-inflammatory medications such as ibuprofen or Advil can relieve the pain and swelling of most types of foot pain. Follow package directions. This is a temporary fix, however. You don't want to stay on over-the-counter painkillers for more than a few weeks, advises Dr. Bar-David a podiatrist. So make sure to try other strategies to relieve your specific foot problem.

Give 'em a break. If you feet hurt, try to stay off them. Do a minimal amount of walking, or don't walk at all.

Soak in plain water. One of the best treatments is a nightly foot-soaking alternating between hot and cold water. Place your feet in cold water for five minutes, then immediately soak in hot water for five minutes, and so forth. This has a "massaging" effect that invigorates feet by opening and closing blood vessels.

Elevate your feet. When you put up your feet, fluids leave your feet and you reduce painful swelling and pressure.

Soak them. Treat your feet to a soak in Epsom salts and warm water. The soak can drain swollen tissues and help relieve pressure. Follow the directions on the package, which is usually, one tablespoon of Epsom salts dissolved in each quart of water.

Everyday prevention:

Insert relief. An orthotic is a moulded insert for your shoe that helps to support your foot. They're available at medical supply stores or through a podiatrist. "An orthotic should be your first line of defence against foot pain," says Dr. Braver. "If you have a flat foot or falling arches, look for a firm arch support. On the other hand, if you have a high arch or plantar fasciitis, find a more cushiony, yet supportive orthotic."

You might need to trim an orthotic down to size. "Stand on it to see if the arch in the orthotic matches up with the arch in your foot," instructs Dr. Braver. "Also, make sure that your shoe is deep enough to withstand the extra height of the orthotic. If it causes blisters, then you shouldn't use it." A guy who is very heavy (and therefore putting more weight on his feet) may need to use two inserts together or go to a podiatrist for a "custom" orthotic. The right orthotic will make the pain go away, Dr. Braver says.

Cushion that heel. Shop around for heel cups or ask a podiatrist about some cushioning that will make your heel feel better. With extra cushioning, your heels aren't jarred so much by everyday walking or running. And with the slight heel lift, your Achilles tendon has a chance to relax, which eases the pull on your plantar fascia, explains Tzvi Bar-David, D.P.M.

Switch to running or walking shoes. If your foot's natural padding has eroded over time, wear sneakers. They have extra cushioning in the heel, which helps make up for your somewhat-reduced, natural fat pads, says James Michelson, MD, an orthopaedic surgeon. Lace-up shoes also will put less stress on the front of your foot if you have pain there.

Lose weight. If you've gained weight over the years, common sense tells you the extra pounds are putting extra pressure on your feet. This can create heel or forefoot pain, warns Dr. Bar-David. The lighter your body, the less the foot pain.

Go for depth. If inserts and running shoes don't do the trick, go to a speciality orthopaedic shoe store and ask for shoes that provide extra depth. These will allow you to stick even more cushioned inserts into your shoe to absorb even more shock, according to Dr. Michelson.

Avoid high heels. If you're a woman, wearing high heels could contribute to arthritis and other foot pain. High heels also push all of the force of walking into the front of your foot, where things are tight and immovable. Switch to flats, says Dr. Michelson.

Get your feet measured. Shoes that are too tight will make your feet hurt even more. Most women wear their shoes two sizes too small, notes Dr. Michelson, and many haven't had their feet measured in at least five years. Since your feet grow as you age, the shoe that fit when you were 40 may be too small now. Have a clerk or a friend measure your feet for you while you are standing. And do this every time you buy a new pair of shoes, advises Dr. Michelson. Some other ways to make sure you get the right fit: Shop at the end of the day. Your feet swell over the course of the day and you'll want shoes that fit when your feet are at their largest.

Keep in mind that one foot might be larger than the other. When you're shoe shopping, always fit shoes to your largest foot. (Use cushioning, if necessary, to fill in the gaps in the larger shoe.)

Make sure there's at least one-half inch between your longest toe and the end of the shoe.

Fit shoes standing up rather than sitting down.

When trying on the shoes, walk in an area that's not padded or carpeted. Walk around for awhile, don't just take two or three steps.

Take a break from shoes. The human foot was designed to be bare. So kick off your shoes whenever you can.

Make a footprint. To determine what kind of arch you have, put your foot in water, then step on a piece of paper. This should give you a footprint. "If you can see a full footprint, then you have flat feet," explains Dr. Menacker. "If your print has two distinct areas at the toes and the heel, but no print in the middle, then you have a high arch. If, on the other hand, you can see your whole foot, but there's an indentation for the arch in the print, then you have a moderate arch." Knowing the shape of your foot will help you choose orthotics and, most important, is a good piece of information to give shoe salespeople, who will, hopefully, steer you to the right type of shoe and lacing technique for your foot shape.

Pull a switch. Switching shoes during the day disperses the pressure throughout your foot.

Rub it out. Stretch and massage your own feet before getting out of bed, says Dr. Menacker. This will ease the pain of plantar fasciitis, a pain felt in the arch and heel of the foot. It's the most common culprit of foot pain for men and strikes most often in the mornings, the first time your feet touch the ground. A general rule of thumb for stretching is to hold each stretch for 10 seconds and repeat each stretch 10 times. "While lying on your back in bed, move your ankles back and forth to stretch out your calf. Next, put the heel of one foot under the toes of the other and pull your toes back with your heel," explains Dr. Menacker. "Finally, rub each foot with your hands to warm it up, if needed."

Aid your Achilles. "Pain at the back of the heel is usually cause by a problem with the Achilles tendon, which joins the calf muscles to the calcaneus, or heel bone," says Dr Jenny Sutcliffe, of London. The cause may either be a complete rupture of the tendon, a partial tear of it, inflammation or a lack of flexibility in the tendon that stops it lengthening. Put some ice in a towel and wrap this ice pack around the tendon for 10 minutes to lessen the pain and reduce any inflammation. If you wear high heels during the day, stretch your Achilles tendons each evening by standing with the balls of your feet on a step and allowing your heels to drop down as far as possible below the level of the step for at least 10 minutes. "And before you put them on for the whole day, break in new shoes at home by wearing them for 10 minutes or so each day, gradually increasing the time until you can wear them comfortably for at least two hours," says Dr. Sutcliffe.

Try tape. "Taping the heel can help," says Dr. Stephen G. Motto, at London Bridge Hospital. Using two or three 6-inch strips of zinc oxide (sticky) tape, pull the tape into a U-shape along the line of the heel where the skin of the ankle meets the sole. "The object is to squeeze together the fleshy part of the heel so that it acts as a shock absorber," says Dr. Motto.

Easing the pain with exercise:

Change exercises. If you're a runner, get on a stationary bicycle to rev up your heart. Or start swimming, at least for awhile, says Andrea Cracchiolo III, MD, an orthopaedic surgeon. It might be best to give your feet a break for a few weeks and then start running a little bit at a time to see how much stress your feet can take, he says.

Stretch your Achilles tendon. A tight Achilles tendon can force the fascia and tendons underneath your foot to work harder to support you. To stretch and strengthen your Achilles, try a wall stretch. "Stand an arm's length away from a wall, with your toes pointed toward it," Dr. Menacker says. "Keep your palms against the wall. Your arms should be straight to start, then bend them as you lean into the wall with your chest. Your heels should remain on the ground as you lean into the wall. Hold for 10 seconds and repeat for one to two minutes." You should always warm up before you do any sort of stretch, Dr. Menacker adds. A good way to warm up your feet and legs is by rotating your ankles around a few times.

Vary your stretch times. The Achilles tendon stretches can help alleviate heel pain when it strikes, but you should also do them routinely. Be sure to stretch before and after exercising. Also, stretch before going to sleep and before getting out of bed in the morning. Though you might think your legs and feet are relaxed at night, most people sleep with their feet pointed, keeping the plantar fascia and the Achilles tight all night long, says Dr. Bar-David. So plantar fasciitis is often worst during the first few steps in the morning. By stretching before you rise, you can get your feet off to a good start.

Modify your exercise. If your feet hurt because you give them a regular pounding every time you take a brisk walk, change your routine, says Donna Astion, MD, associate chief of foot and ankle service for the Hospital for Joint Diseases, Orthopaedic Institute in New York City. For instance, try taking every other day off, alternating between weight-bearing activities such as running and nonweight-bearing activities such as cycling. If you run, alternate between hard tar roads and softer surfaces like trails.

Take the first step. Here is a do-anywhere stretch to combat heel pain. You can do it while brushing your teeth, washing dishes, or standing and watching television, notes Thomas Meade, MD, an orthopaedic surgeon. To give yourself those options, use a stepstool or nail together some 2x4's to make a portable step. You should feel a stretch in the calf and plantar fascia. Dr. Meade warns, though, that you shouldn't do this stretch if you feel pain.

Stand with your legs straight on the bottom step of a flight of stairs, holding on to the railing. Or use your portable step and a table for support.

Stand so that the ball of the afflicted foot is on the edge of the step. Put the other foot flat on the step.

Slowly drop your heel down until you feel a stretch in the back of your calf muscle.

Hold the stretch for at least 20 seconds. Repeat 8 to 12 times and then switch to the other foot.

Use a therapeutic towel. This exercise is designed to stretch inflamed plantar fascia tissue and relieve pressure on the nerves in the foot, says Dr. Meade. It can help relieve pain and in general tune up your feet to keep future discomfort away. "Let pain be your guide," he adds. "This should feel tight but not painful."

Rubbing the Right Way

A five-minute foot massage can sometimes relieve discomfort, as well as make you feel relaxed and rejuvenated, says Leonard A. Levy, D.P.M., professor of podiatric medicine and past president of the California College of Podiatric Medicine in San Francisco. He recommends following these steps.

Sit comfortably in a chair or on the floor.

Bring your right foot toward you, resting your right ankle on your left knee.

Starting at the heel, press and knead the bottom of the foot with your fingers. Move up the middle of your foot, then veer over to your big toe and work across your foot to the little toe.

Massage the pad under each toe.

Gently squeeze each toe with your thumb and forefinger, moving each toe from side to side and gently stretching each toe out.

Wrap your hands around your foot at the arch so that your thumbs are on top and your fingers on the bottom. Knead your instep with your thumbs.

Place the outer edge of your palm under the tips of your toes and gently pull back. As you flex your foot, hold for a few seconds, then let go and relax.

Gently press the Achilles tendon (on the back of your heel) between your thumb and forefinger. Run your fingers up the back of your heel, ending above the ankle.

Lie on your back with your legs straight.

Loop a towel around the ball of your sore foot and gently but firmly pull the towel toward you. You'll feel tension in the bottom of your foot.

Hold the stretch for 20 seconds. Repeat 10 times and then do the same with your other foot.

Do the golf ball massage. It's too rainy to play 18 holes? Or maybe your foot hurts too much? Try this sporting stretch suggested by Steven Lawrence, MD, an orthopaedic surgeon. It's great for people with plantar fasciitis, arch strain, and foot cramps. Simply place your foot on top of a golf ball on a flat surface, then roll the ball forward and backward across the underside of your foot for about two minutes. The ball provides a soothing, relaxing massage.

Take the towel challenge. Does your spouse simply drop the bath towel on the floor after showering? Turn this irritating habit into an exercise opportunity, suggests Dr. Meade. The goal here is to try to pick up the towel with your feet, or more precisely, with your toes. Start at the near end of the towel and curl it toward you, using only your toes to scrunch it forward. Then try to pick the towel up with your toes and deposit it in the hamper or laundry basket.

For foot-fortifying variety, see if you can pick up 20 marbles or pencils, one at a time, with your toes and deposit them into a bowl. This motion strengthens the small muscles in the foot, which helps fight toe cramps, says Dr. Meade.

Try some toe tugs. For relief from toe cramps, doctors suggest looping a thick rubber band around all of the toes on one foot. Spread your toes apart, feeling the resistance from the rubber band. Try to hold this position for 5 to 10 seconds. Repeat 10 times before you switch and attempt the toe stretch with the opposite foot.

For variety, try a toe-of-war by placing the rubber band around each of your big toes and pulling them away from each other. Be sure to keep your heels in place. Hold for 5 to 10 seconds and repeat 10 times.

Play footsie with an orange juice can. If the arch of your foot hurts, you may have a touch of plantar fasciitis, or inflammation in the plantar fascia—the tough, gristly sheet of connective tissue that stretches from your heel to your toes. To soothe it, take a seat and—barefooted—roll your arch over a can of frozen juice concentrate for five to ten minutes, suggests Marika Molnar, P.T., director of West Side Dance Physical Therapy in New York City. "The cold helps reduce inflammation, while the massage helps loosen the tense tissues." Mark the juice can, keep it separate from juice that you plan to drink and reuse it as needed.

Stretch like a dancer. For a super-duper stretch, give this dancer's technique a try, suggests Helen Drusine, a massage therapist who works with professional ballet and Broadway dancers in New York City. Kneel on the floor or on a rug, with the balls of your feet on the floor, tucking your spread-out toes under to stretch the arches of your feet. Sit back on your heels so that most of your body weight presses your toes against the floor. Do this for a few seconds, slowly increasing your time as it becomes more comfortable. Do not do this stretch, however, if you have sore tendons, says Phyllis Ragley, D.P.M., vice president of the American Academy of Podiatric Sports Medicine. Try a light massage of your feet and toes instead.

Do the follow-up stretch. Next, says Drusine, perform the same exercise with the tops of your feet flat on the floor. Again, do not do this exercise if you have sore tendons.

Loosen up your calf muscles. Tight calf muscles can hobble your feet, interfering with their ability to properly strike the ground and roll forward, says Dr. Ragley. That, in turn, can cause heel or arch pain as tissues in your feet are unduly stretched to make up for tight calves. To stretch your calf muscles, stand barefoot facing a wall, with your arms straight out in front of you and your palms flat against the wall. Keep your heels on the ground, tuck your buttocks so that your body remains straight (do not bend forward at your waist), bend your elbows and lean into the wall until your cheek touches the wall.

Hold the stretch for as long as you feel comfortable. Then repeat (five times to start), this time with your knees slightly bent. "This helps stretch the soleus—the small muscle that leads directly into the Achilles tendon," Dr. Ragley explains. It's best to stretch after you've warmed up a bit from easy walking or after a warm shower or bath.

Herbal Help:

Soak in a scent. Aromatherapists often recommend adding 10 drops each of juniper and lavender essential oils to 2 quarts of cold water, then soaking your feet for ten minutes.

Make ginger a habit. Ginger root is a great remedy for arthritis and other pain related to swelling because it's a natural anti-inflammatory, says Neal Barnard, MD, author of *Foods That Fight Pain.* Though you don't have to use a lot of it to get significant relief, you do have to take it regularly, he says. Buy fresh ginger root at the supermarket. Mince up one-half teaspoon to a teaspoon per day. Either put it in your food as a flavouring or mix it into some water and swallow it like a pill. Cloves, garlic, and turmeric, though less studied, have shown similar effects in some people, according to Dr. Barnard.

Get help from homeopathy. If you have puffy feet that burn or sting, Andrew Lockie, MD, in his book *The Family Guide to Homeopathy,* suggests taking a 6C dose of Apis three times a day. He says that a similar dose of Sulphur will help if you tend to feel hot most of the time and have burning feet that feel worse at night. If you have a burning sensation in your feet that feels worse when walking, Dr. Lockie recommends Graphite 6C three times a day.

Hands-on help:

Press the point. "Acupressure can be very useful for foot pain," says Dr. Motto. One powerful acupressure point lies in the web between the big toe and the one next to it. Taking this firmly between the thumb and forefinger, apply firm pressure for 30 seconds. Simple manipulation of the foot can also be helpful, Dr. Motto says. "While you are lying down, hold the top of the painful foot with one hand and turn it inwards and outwards."

Frostbite

The pain: Freezing skin, most commonly striking the ears, nose, hands, feet and toes. With first-degree frostbite, the mildest sort, the skin turns waxy white and is cold to the touch but not blistering. In the most serious cases, fourth degree, deep damage occurs. The flesh hardens and turns grey or blue and eventually all feeling is lost in the affected area. Such patients require hospitalisation and often lose body parts due to amputation.

The cause: Frostbite is what can happen when bitterly cold weather meets a body that s trying to stay warm. Attempting to warm the inner organs, your body cuts back on the circulation to your hands and feet. And if they receive less than their share of warm blood, these parts can freeze. Severe frostbite may cause permanent damage. How do you know that you're getting frostbite? Watch the skin, says Carol Frey, MD, chief of the Foot and Ankle Service and associate clinical professor of orthopedic surgery at the University of Southern California School of Medicine. There is no standard amount of time within which frostbite can occur, but the ice crystals that form on the skirts surface are the first sign.

See a doctor if:
...the pain continues for more than a few hours.
...dark blue or black areas appear under the skin, or blistering occurs.
...your skin begins to feel warm even though it is not defrosting,
...the skin turns red, pale or white.

Quick relief:
Don't rub. "The old adage about rubbing frostbitten areas with snow is false, though it's been perpetuated for years," explains W. Steven Pray, Ph.D., R.Ph., professor at the Southwestern Oklahoma State University School of Pharmacy. "The snow's coldness does not help raise the temperature of the affected area. In fact, any kind of rubbing, with hands or otherwise, only traumatizes it."
Get inside. When frostbite strikes, get out of the cold. If you feel tingling and burning after 20 minutes, your circulation is returning. If numbness remains, get medical help.

Stay put and stay warm. Once you find a warm place and can begin to thaw your frostbite, stay there. If you must leave and there is any chance that your frostbitten area will re-freeze, avoid thawing it. According to Dr. Frey, refreezing will cause tissue damage far worse than the original damage from frostbite. Treat your skin gently before and after it has thawed. Avoid hitting or applying pressure to the injured area. If your toes have just been warmed, try to avoid walking (or skiing or skating) for as long as possible. If the frostbite is severe, it's safer to leave it frozen and go to a hospital immediately so the area can be property thawed.

Thaw in the tub, not by the fire. Dr. Frey recommends a water bath about 10 F warmer than body temperature for thawing frostbite. A warm water bath in the range of 102 to 111 degrees is ideal. But avoid the intense, dry heat of a campfire, stove or heater, because you might burn frostbitten areas. (Frostbitten nerve endings don't send a signal to tell you when exposed skin in danger of becoming burned.) Keep the affected area submerged for 15-30 minutes, or until the tip of the affected area returns to a pinkish colour and stays pink when pulled out of the water. The skin should feel warm to the touch. Elevate your feet after they've thawed.

Cover your ears. "Overchilled and windburned ears are best treated by protection as soon as possible," says William Epstein, MD, a dermatologist. "In fact just covering your ear with your hand may be all you need."

Everyday prevention:

Avoid contact with metal. Everything from steel-tipped shoes to metal machine controls have caused otherwise prepared people to become frostbitten, according to Thomas Sinks, Ph.D., an epidemiologist with the Centres for Disease Control and Prevention in Atlanta. Take extra precautions when handling snow shovels and tools in cold weather: Wear gloves or mittens.

Warm up your central heater. When you get cold, "the blood has a tendency to leave the surface areas, such as the hands or feet, and go to more central areas," says Dr. Frey. "But by putting on a heavy jacket and keeping your core body temperature higher, sometimes you can decrease the incidence of frostbite." And as an extra precaution when driving during winter, always carry extra blankets and clothing in your car, just in case the car breaks down, suggests Dr. Sinks.

Don't drink alcohol. Although it may make you feel warmer, alcohol actually prevents the constriction of blood vessels, increasing heat loss. A swig of brandy won't warm your toes and fingertips. In fact, alcohol reduces shivering, which is the body's way of helping you stay warm, according to Murray Hamlet, D.V.M., of the U.S. Army Research Institute of Environmental Medicine.

Drink plenty of water. Hydration increases the blood's volume, which helps prevent frostbite. Drinking fluids such as herbal teas, hot cider or broth is a good idea. But you should avoid caffeinated beverages, which constrict blood vessels. Drink before leaving shelter, and take a Thermos with you while you are outdoors.

Don't light up. "When you light a cigarette, the blood flow in your hand shuts off," says Dr. Hamlet. Restricted blood flow is a major factor in frostbite, as the body loses its ability to warm itself.

Try to walk where the wind is blocked. The wind chill factor is just as important as the temperature, so limit the amount of time you stay in the wind.

Stay dry. Wearing water-repellent clothes and changing clothes when they become wet will help keep your body warm.

Generate your own body heat. If you have no other way to protect your skin, try curling up in a ball or placing your hands underneath your armpits.

Wear mittens. Because mittens enclose all the fingers in a single, well-sealed "air pocket," they protect better than gloves. The most effective mittens have inside liners that can be taken out and dried separately from the mittens. Or wear two pair for extra insulation.

Keep your skin dry. To avoid frostbite, make sure you don't get water, gas or other liquids on your skin in subfreezing weather, warns Dr. Sinks. Gasoline is especially risky, since it evaporates quickly, chilling the skin (a handy thing to remember if you use a self-service gas pump).

Bundle up. In extreme cold, cover all your body parts with a hat, scarf, face mask and gloves. Keep your torso well covered too. Makes sure your winter clothes fit right, and dress in layers.

Buy boots that breathe. Leather boots are best in the cold because they breathe. You have a tendency to perspire less than with an all-plastic boot. Remember to wear layers of socks—a silk liner and a wool or cotton sock.

Herbal Help:

Apply aloe vera. The clear, fresh gel from this plant's leaves has long been used as a soothing cover for burns. Aloe has also been used as a first-aid for frostbite. When aloe is applied, the blood vessels relax, helping to heal frostbitten skin. Simply apply fresh aloe vera gel or cream containing aloe vera a few times a day, leaving the skin uncovered.

Ask for Agaricus. "The most common homeopathic frostbite remedy is Agaricus. I've used it and I've found it quite helpful," says Judyth Reichenberg-Ullman, N.D., a naturopathic physician. She suggests taking a 30C dose once or twice a day to treat frostbite that causes red fingers or toes and itching or burning of the skin. If you don't see improvement in 48 hours, discontinue use and see your doctor.

Gallbladder Pain

The pain: Pain in the upper middle or right abdomen, moving around to the back; nausea, and vomiting

The cause: Whenever you eat a high-fat meal, your body has to secrete bile to help you digest the fat. Bile is manufactured in the liver and stored in the gallbladder. From there, it's dumped into the small intestine, where it goes to work, helping to break down the fat that comes from foods like steaks, ice cream, and potato chips. Gallstones form from excess cholesterol, the same notorious fat that has an evil reputation for clogging arteries, and some people are just more likely to get them than others. When gallstones are inside the gallbladder, they might not be at all painful. Sometimes they betray their presence by causing intestinal discomfort or nausea, but only a doctor, with the help of x-rays, can tell you whether those symptoms are being caused by stones.

Once the stones start to move, even if they're just tiny broken pieces, excruciating pain may be knocking at your door. When those little pieces move into the bile ducts—the exit ramps from the gallbladder and the liver—pain is not far behind. And they can be dangerous, too, causing jaundice or serious infection from blocked ducts. Doctors have found that women are more likely to get gallstones than men, particularly if they're pregnant, and both sexes are at higher risk if they're overweight. If you've had gallstones once, you're at risk of getting them again.

See a doctor if...
...you have had gallstones and you recognise some familiar symptoms returning.
...you have abdominal pain accompanied by vomiting, chills, fever, or jaundice (a yellowing of the eyes or skin).
...your urine suddenly turns yellow-brown.

Medication:
Thankfully, hardly any drugs can cause gallstones to develop or worsen. But gemfibrozil (Lopid), a drug prescribed to reduce triglyceride blood levels and raise high-density lipoprotein (HDL) cholesterol, has been linked to gallstone formation. If you've been using this drug, talk to your doctor

about this side effect. He may wish to prescribe an alternative.

Nutritional remedies:

Get better with beet greens. "I've had people get really effective relief from gallbladder pain with beet greens," says William Warnock, N.D., a naturopathic doctor. When steamed, beet greens are unusually high in minerals, vitamin A, and a substance called betaine. According to Dr. Warnock, betaine stimulates the production of bile and simultaneously thins it out. He also suggests that betaine causes the muscles surrounding the gallbladder and bile ducts to contract and move things along.

Fibre up. Getting more fibre into your diet is a simple way to decrease excess fat. Dietary fibre binds with bile salts, which are a primary part of bile, and cholesterol in the intestines and prevents both from being absorbed by the body. You can up your fibre intake by eating as many fruits and vegetables as possible, along with brand and whole grains like wheat, oats, and rye, says Kristin Stiles, N.D., a naturopathic doctor at the Complementary Medicine and Healing Arts Centre in Vestal, New York.

Fibre absorbs large amounts of water, and water-soaked fibre bulks up and softens the stool. A well-hydrated stool absorbs lots of wastes and by-products of digestion, such as fat. With less fat around, the process of gallstone formation may be interrupted.

The recommended daily amount of fibre is 25 to 30 grams, says Dr. Stiles. If you find that you can't eat enough high-fibre foods to achieve that level, an alternative is to try one of the fibre/nutritional supplements found in drugstores and health food stores. Dr. Stiles recommends a supplement that contains psyllium. She suggests stirring two tablespoons of the supplement into a glass of water and drinking it at breakfast each day.

Eat light. Since being overweight is a common risk factor for gallstones, do what you can to keep the weight off. Especially steer clear of large, fatty meals, says Mike Cantwell, MD, "Fat makes the gallbladder work harder, increasing the likelihood of gallstones."

Fill up on fish. "Scientists have discovered that Eskimo populations in Alaska who consume diets rich in marine fish oils have almost no gallstone disease," says Thomas H. Magnuson, MD, an expert in gallstone disease. He says that plenty of additional scientific evidence indicates that a diet rich in fish oils, either from fish or from fish-oil supplements, may help prevent cholesterol gallstones.

Focus on grains and beans. "Some studies have shown that vegetarians have a lower risk of developing gallstones, possibly because of the higher fibre content of a meatless, plant-based diet," says Melissa Palmer, MD, a gastroenterologist.

Drink up. Drinking plenty of water flushes the liver and dilutes bile secretions that lead to gallstones, says Agatha Thrash, MD, a medical pathologist. She suggests drinking 8 to 12 eight-ounce glasses of water a day.

Drink green. "Green juices are great for preventing a recurrence in anyone who has had gallstones," says Elaine Gillaspie, N.D., a naturopathic physician. Juices with spinach and parsley are rich in chlorophyll, a pigment that has a natural cleansing effect, according to Dr. Gillaspie. She suggests an eight-ounce blend of two ounces of green juice and two ounces of carrot juice, diluted with an equal amount of water.

Eat breakfast. People who skip breakfast are essentially undergoing a short-term fast, and fasting has been shown to increase the risk of gallbladder disease. In fact, don't skip any meals, and be sure to eat at regular intervals.

Helpful vitamins and supplements:

Consider fish-oil supplements. Could a diet rich in omega-3's prevent cholesterol stones in people? "Some studies show a dramatic effect, so it is a reasonable assumption," says Dr. Magnuson. To benefit from omega-3's, you don't have to live on tuna-noodle casserole and canned mackerel for the rest of your life (unless you want to). Dr. Magnuson says that daily supplements of omega-3 fatty acids can provide the same amount of omega-3's eaten by Eskimo populations. Most health food stores stock a variety of fish-oil supplements. He suggests following the dosages recommended on the label.

See if you're C-deficient. Ask your doctor if you may be deficient in vitamin C or hydrocholic acid (a component of stomach juice), advises Melvyn Werbach, MD, a physician who specialises in nutritional medicine, and the author of *Healing with Food*. "Studies indicate that animals with a high-cholesterol diet and vitamin C deficiency are prone to developing gallstones. Another study found that about half of all people with gallstones are deficient in hydrochloric acid."

Be sure about calcium and hormones. Studies suggest that taking extra calcium may increase their risk of forming gallstones. If gallstones run in your family, you should talk to you family physician before you do. Because hormones are also involved in gallstone formation, women should consult with their doctors about using oral contraceptives or hormone replacement therapy.

Everyday prevention:

Lose a little at a time. While it's important to avoid being overweight, don't embark on a crash diet to get there. Losing weight fast can actually increase your risk of developing gallstones, explains Dr. Cantwell. Yo-yo dieting (a cycle of quick weight loss followed by weight gain) is especially hard on the gallbladder. It creates a situation where the gallbladder sits unused for a time, then suddenly gets overused. This stop-start activity only increases the likelihood of gallstone formation. A slow, steady weight-loss program, which includes regular meals of low-fat foods and plenty of exercise is the way to go.

Put on your walking shoes. If you don't exercise regularly, you could be risking gallstones. Regular exercise steps up metabolism (the pace of energy-burning), notes Robert Charm, MD, a professor of gastroenterology and internal medicine at the University of California. "When metabolism is slow, small gallstones can develop. Even simple activities like stretching or walking helps gallbladder health."

Herbal help:

Make the bile flow with milk thistle. If you can just "keep the juices flowing," you may help prevent gallstone problems, herbalists believe. You can get some aid from herbs that have what are called cholertic properties, meaning the ability to increase the amount of bile the liver produces and also boost the flow of bile from the gallbladder. At the same time, herbalists believe that herbs with cholertic properties stimulate gallbladder contraction.

Milk thistle is one herb with these properties. "It gets things moving and helps flush out the small stones," says Dr. Stiles. It is also believed to help improve the digestion of fats, he adds.

Although some supplement formulas are made up of a number of cholertic herbs, Dr. Warnock favours milk thistle taken by itself. "What usually happens when you put a lot of herbs into one capsule is that you don't end up with high concentration of any of them," he says.

For the most effective concentration, you need a standardised extract of milk thistle that contains 80 percent silymarin, the herb's primary active ingredient, says Dr. Warnock. (A naturopathic doctor can recommend a more specific amount.)

"It may take three to six months before it has a beneficial effect," says Dr. Warnock. You should never take it during a gallstone attack, however, and if you already have gallstones that begin to cause persistent pain or a fever, you should see a doctor immediately, not wait months to find out whether the herb is effective.

Cure with celandine Celandine has traditionally been used for treating the liver, and with good reason. In one study, researchers gave tablets containing chelidonine, an active compound in celandine, to 60 people with symptoms of gallstones for six weeks. Doctors reported a significant reduction in symptoms. Chelidonine and other compounds in celandine reportedly soothe the smooth muscles of the biliary tract, improving bile flow and curbing upper abdominal distress.

Soothe with peppermint, spearmint and other mints. Mints have traditionally been used to treat gallstones. One stone-relieving mixture, a British over-the-counter "gallstone tea" preparation called Rowachol, contains chemicals from several members of the mint family. In one British study, this product helped a quarter of those who used it.

Treat with turmeric. Turmeric is useful for preventing and treating gallstones, according to Commission E. Turmeric contains curcumin, a compound that has been tested for its effect on gallstones. In one study, mice with experimentally induced gallstones were placed on special feed containing a modest amount of curcumin, and within five weeks their gallstone volume had dropped 45 percent. After ten weeks they had 80 percent fewer gallstones than untreated mice. Curcumin increases the solubility of bile, which helps prevent the formation of gallstones and helps eliminate any stones that have formed. "If I had gallstones, I would definitely cook lots of curries and go heavy on the turmeric," says James Duke, Ph.D., author of *The Green Pharmacy.*

Go for goldenrod. Goldenrod contains the compound leiocarposide, a potent diuretic that helps the body flush excess water. "Commission E endorses this herb for gallstones," says Dr. Duke. "I'd suggest trying it for up to a month if you're not in serious pain." The commission recommends making a tea using five teaspoons of chopped, dried flowering shoots per cup of boiling water. They recommend drinking three to four cups a day between meals.

Genital Herpes

The pain: Blisters erupting from reddened, sensitive skin on your genitals that burst and form tiny, painful ulcers emerge.

The cause: There are two main forms of herpes, a viral infection of the skin or mucous membranes. Herpes simplex type 1 primarily causes cold sores around the mouth and lips, but it can also affect the genitals. Herpes simplex type 2 is the predominant cause of genital herpes.

The herpes simplex virus is a sneaky little devil. Most of the time it lies dormant in the nerve cells near your spine. The moment it notices that your immune defences are down, it comes to life and makes a beeline for the skin's surface surrounding your genitals. There, the virus forms clusters of painful, fluid-filled blisters that can hang around for two weeks or more.

Once herpes moves in, it becomes a permanent unwanted guest. While a lucky 40 percent of people infected with this sexually transmitted disease (STD) never have another outbreak after their initial episode, the not-so-lucky majority may have five or more recurrences a year.

See a doctor if:
...you notice a blister that suddenly appears on your genitals or if you have sores that are causing severe pain.
...you have had an outbreak in the past and you feel tingling, itching, or tenderness at the site of a previous outbreak. If you act quickly you might be able to prevent an outbreak.

Medication:
Medical treatment is aimed at relieving symptoms. Your doctor will probably treat your initial outbreak and perhaps recurrent outbreaks as well with the antiviral drug acyclovir. Gradually, outbreaks often weaken and may disappear altogether.

Quick relief:
Bathe often. During an initial outbreak, take a warm shower or bath two or three times a day. Gently pat (don't rub) the infected area dry. (Vigorous rubbing could spread the infection).

Try cold or heat. An ice pack, an infrared heat lamp or a hair dryer set on a cool or warm setting can relieve pain. (Back off at the slightest feeling of irritation.)

Try colloidal silver. Apply colloidal silver directly to the sores, says Cynthia Watson, MD, a family practitioner. Available at health food stores, colloidal silver has antiviral and antibacterial action, she says. "When you use it, the lesions seem to dry up in a matter of days."

Apply a cold compress. Apply a piece of gauze or a washcloth soaked in cool water directly on the sores. Cool compresses can help heal the lesions by drying them up.

Take a non-prescription painkiller. Acetaminophen (paracetamol), ibuprofen or aspirin might help relieve blister pain, says Dr. Workowski. Follow the directions on the label.

Ongoing care:

Keep blisters clean and dry. "You don't want blisters to become super-infected from bacteria on surrounding skin," says Judith O'Donnell, MD, a medical specialist for the Sexually Transmitted Disease Control Program at the Philadelphia Department of Public Health. "Bathe or shower daily with a gentle soap and water, or just water alone."

Take an oatmeal bath. A warm bath helps relieve genital irritation, says Kimberly A. Workowski, MD, assistant professor of medicine in the Division of Infectious Diseases at Emory University in Atlanta. And if you have sores, it can also help relieve itching. Best of all is a soak in an oatmeal bath, she says. She recommends Aveeno bath treatment, available at your chemist. The product contains a finely powdered oatmeal called colloidal oatmeal that's very soothing to itching skin.

Wear loose-fitting clothes. Squeezing into panty hose, tight underwear or other form-fitting clothes will further irritate sensitive herpes sores, says Dr. Workowski. "You'll get chafing, which can be extremely painful." Opt for loose-fitting clothing until your sores heal. Avoid synthetic fabrics since they don't allow the skin to breathe as easily as natural fibres like cotton.

Don't glop. Avoid gooey ointments with bases like petroleum jelly. They keep the lesions from drying, so they last longer and shed the virus for longer.

Soothe with salves. Dab your sores with a drying agent such as calamine lotion.

Nutritional remedies:

Follow the lysine-arginine connection. Research shows that a diet high in the lysine and low in arginine can prevent the herpes virus from surfacing. The theory is that the virus needs arginine to reproduce itself, but since it can't tell the difference between lysine and arginine, it's easily tricked into latching on to the lysine to accomplish its dirty work. Rather than helping the virus, however, the lysine blocks the necessary steps that it must take to reactivate, says Thomas Kruzel, N.D., a naturopathic doctor.

In one study, people with genital herpes took 1,000 milligrams of lysine daily for six months while eliminating arginine-rich foods from their diet. At the end of the study, lysine was rated effective or very effective at preventing herpes outbreaks in 74 percent of those who took it. An ounce and a half of provolone cheese contains 1,110 milligrams of lysine; two eggs provide 900 milligrams. One broiled centre-cut pork loin chop provides almost 2,000 milligrams. High-arginine foods include chocolate, peas, nuts and beer. (You don't have to give up those food entirely, but you should balance them by eating other foods high in lysine.)

To keep lysine levels high, take 500 to 1,500 milligrams daily at the first sign of symptoms and continue until symptoms disappear, says Dr. Kruzel. If you're having an outbreak, take 9,000 milligrams daily until the lesions go away and for four to five days afterward.

Beans. A cup of black beans, lentils, soybeans or winged beans provides more than 2,500 milligrams of lysine. If you're making bean soup with these ingredients, spice it well with hot-pepper sauce for a little extra anti-herpes action.

Alter your diet. "For some people, changing the diet to make it more alkaline can help prevent herpes outbreaks and help get over them more quickly," says Elson Haas, MD, director of the Preventive Medical Centre of Marin in California. That means eating more fruits (with the exception of citrus fruits, which are too acidic), vegetables, sea vegetables such as kelp and seaweed, millet, seeds and herbs and less meats, fish, eggs milk products, breads and baked goods, nuts and alcohol, according to Dr. Haas.

Helpful vitamins and supplements:

Boost immunity with vitamin C. Since the herpes virus tends to resurface whenever your immunity is low, a vitamin that supports your immune system is a real ally in your battle with herpes. Vitamin C is such a vitamin. It can recharge your immune system by strengthening white blood cells that will fight off the virus. It can also help speed healing—and the faster you heal, the less pain and discomfort you'll experience from the lesions. According to Dr. Kowalsky, this vitamin can also prevent damage to healthy cells and boost interferon levels. "It's known that viruses deplete vitamin C residing in white blood cells, so we know that if you want your immune system to stay strong, you need to take extra vitamin C," says Susan Kowalsky, N.D., a naturopathic doctor. To prevent outbreaks, she recommends 1,000 to 3,000 milligrams daily in divided doses; she also suggests taking it with food to avoid stomach irritation. Cut back if you experience diarrhoea, since daily doses above 1,200 milligrams can cause this problem in some people.

Think Zinc for Relief. Like vitamin C, the mineral zinc can help rev up your immune system. Zinc helps boost production of T lymphocyte cells, which are important body defences against viral infections. "Zinc also disrupts the replication of the herpes virus by blocking it from going into its reproductive cycle," says Dr. Kruzel. He recommends taking 15 to 30 milligrams of zinc daily to prevent outbreaks. If you're having a recurrence, however, take 30 to 45 milligrams daily until the lesions clear up, adds Dr. Kowalsky. Don't exceed 20 milligrams of zinc a day, however, without first discussing it with your doctor, because excess zinc can suppress copper absorption and affect cholesterol levels.

Try an infection-fighting trio. Vitamin A, beta-carotene, and vitamin E all qualify as strong contenders in the fight against recurrent herpes infections.

Vitamin A arms your immune system with the ammunition it needs to battle the virus. It can alleviate symptoms of an impending outbreak and reduce the number of recurrences. If you're pregnant, however, you need to consult your doctor before taking vitamin A, says Dr. Kowalsky, and no one should take doses of vitamin A above 10,000 international units (IU) without a doctor's guidance.

A safer alternative is to take beta-carotene, according to Dr. Kowalsky. A precursor of vitamin A, beta-carotene is an antioxidant that increases antibody production and white blood cell activity, and since it converts to vitamin A in the body, you'll reap its medicinal benefits without the possible health risks.

"Beta-carotene encourages new cell growth and strengthens your cells' outer layers, so that the virus can't penetrate, duplicate itself, and spread like wildfire," says Dr. Kruzel.

When symptoms of a possible outbreak occur, take 60 milligrams (100,000 IU) of beta-carotene daily in divided doses to jump-start your immune system, says Dr. Kowalsky. Although you should also check with your doctor before taking this high daily dose, beta-carotene doesn't pose the same risks as vitamin A.

Vitamin E also protects your white blood cells from invading viruses and strengthens other aspects of your immune system. It can help speed the healing of the lesions as well, says Dr. Kowalsky. She recommends taking 400 IU a day during an outbreak and continuing after the symptoms are alleviated.

Everyday prevention:

Shun the sun. Exposure to ultraviolet light at the sight of infection is known to trigger recurrence—something to keep in mind if you're a hard-core naturist.

Keep your hands clean. Wash your hands thoroughly with soap whenever you touch the infected area. The virus can live on skin for 30 minutes and can easily spread by contact to other parts of your body, especially your face.

Abstain when necessary. Obviously, if you or your partner has active genital herpes, don't even think about having genital contact of any kind, even with a condom, until well after the outbreak has healed. Even then, experts recommend that you always use a latex male condom or a female condom with spermicide to guard against transmission. Using a condom during an outbreak is a bad idea because sores may occur in an area unprotected by the condom. (If you and your partner both have inactive herpes and want to have a baby, talk to your health-care practitioner about options for safe conception and delivery.)

Herbal help:

Try an herbal medicine chest. Two other medicinal herbs that can inhibit outbreaks of the herpes virus are echinacea and licorice.

Echinacea is a potent antiviral and antibacterial herb that strengthens your immune system. Take 500 milligrams of echinacea twice a day at the first sign of symptoms to help prevent an outbreak or to speed the healing of lesions if you're already having a recurrence, says Dr. Kruzel. Continue taking this dose until symptoms and lesions disappear, he says, although you should talk to your doctor if you need to take it for more than eight weeks.

Similar to echinacea, licorice turbocharges your immune system and builds your resistance to the herpes virus, says Dr. Kowalsky. Take 1,000 to 2,000 milligrams of powdered licorice root in capsule form three times a day during an outbreak or when symptoms arise, says Dr. Kowalsky. Be sure to talk to your doctor if you're taking these doses, though, since daily use of high doses for more than four to six weeks can cause symptoms such as headache and lethargy and may even lead to impaired heart or kidney function.

Try tea tree. Apply a single drop of tea tree oil directly to herpes lesions once a day after showering, recommends herbalist Jeanne Rose. "Tea tree oil is gentle to the skin and helps any kind of external sore heal faster," says Rose.

Let lemon balm help. Also known as melissa, lemon balm's demonstrated antiviral, anti-herpes properties seem to result from compounds in the herb, including tannins, that are known as polyphenols. Mints, especially lemon balm, contain antioxidant vitamins and selenium, which strengthen the immune system. (Antioxidants are chemicals that mop up free radicals, the naturally occurring oxygen molecules that damage the body's cells.) All mints also contain at least four antiviral compounds that target the herpes virus. Varro Tyler, Ph.D., a pharmacognosist says that you can get results by using topical applications of lemon balm tea, which you can brew using two to four teaspoons of herb per cup of boiling water. Then apply it with a cotton ball several times a day.

Meet the mint family. Lemon balm is not the only mint with antiviral, anti-herpes activity. There are a whole bunch of other herbs in the mint family that are almost as effective.

"Here's where I plug my Happy Herpicide Tea," says James Duke,

Ph.D., in his book *The Green Pharmacy*. It's made from several herbs that are members of the mint family: hyssop, lemon balm, oregano, rosemary, sage, self-heal and thyme.

To make Dr. Duke's tea, fill a saucepan half full of water. Bring the water to a boil, then add fresh lemon balm leaves until the pan is about three-quarters full. If you don't have access to fresh leaves, you can use about a quarter-cup of dried lemon balm. (This is an unusually high amount of herb for brewing a tea, but you really need a lot of it to get the antiviral action that you want.) To the lemon balm and water, add two parts each of dried oregano and self-heal and one part each of hyssop, rosemary, sage and thyme.

Aside from the lemon balm, the actual amounts of the other herbs don't make much difference; just make sure you use twice as much of the oregano and self-heal as you do of the others. Finally, toss in a little licorice root to sweeten the tea and steep it for 20 minutes. This mixture contains a dozen compounds that are active against herpes.

Soothe with St. John's-wort. One compound in St. John's-wort, hypericin, helps kill H. simplex and several other viruses. Although ointments containing hypericin are effective against herpes sores, you don't need to buy one. Try brewing a strong tea, and after it cools, dab it on with cotton balls.

Get garlic. In test-tube studies, garlic has shown viricidal effects against both types of herpes virus and many other viruses, including those that cause colds and flu. You can make garlic into a tea, but you will probably enjoy it a whole lot more if you just toss a few minced cloves onto a plate of pasta or add them to a mixed green salad.

Add essential oils. Aromatherapists note that combinations of essential oils, such as lemon and geranium or eucalyptus and bergamot, can be helpful against herpes if applied at the first sign of an outbreak. Some aromatherapists say that rose oil and lemon balm oil have contributed, in some cases, to complete remission of H. simplex lesions, sometimes after only one application. This approach seems worth a try. You can apply any of these oils topically using a cotton ball. Warning: Essential oils are highly concentrated plant extracts. Make sure you never ingest them unless they've been prescribed by a reputable herbalist or aromatherapist. Small quantities of some oils, on the order of a single teaspoon, can be fatal.

Try a drug-herb combo. Dr. Duke reports news of a surprising study by Japanese scientists. They combined the pharmaceutical anti-herpes drug, acyclovir (Zovirax), with any one of four tannin-rich herbal extracts: Japanese avens, Javanese sumac, cloves and chebula. The combination treatment worked significantly better than acyclovir alone or the herbs alone. Because acyclovir is a prescription drug, you'll have to ask your doctor about trying this one.

Drink healing beverages. Tea and the juices of apple, cranberry, grape, pear, prune and strawberry all seem to help kill viruses. Tannins are usually the active components in these juices. Pear juice, which is rich in anti-herpes caffeic acid, might be your best juice choice.

Make an antiviral lotion. Blend equal parts of lavender essential oil, an antiseptic that's effective for dry and weepy skin problems, and oil infused with lemon balm, which has been shown in studies to act against the herpes virus. Then apply a few dabs of this antiviral lotion on the affected area three times a day during herpes outbreaks for up to a week, recommends herbalist Aviva Romm. You can also add a dash or two of this formula to your bath, she suggests.

Gout

The pain: inflammation, swelling, and severe pain in a joint. About half of all gout cases flare up in the big toe. Other joints that gout frequents include the instep, ankle, and knee. It may be accompanied by chills, shivers, and a little fever.

The cause: Uric acid, a by-product of the waste that your kidneys usually flush out of the body, builds up in your system and settles into the lining surrounding a joint.

See a doctor if:

...you have symptoms of gout. Gout is strongly linked with certain more-serious problems like high blood pressure, diabetes, kidney stones, and high cholesterol. So when you're seeing the doctor for pain relief, you may also be checked out for these other problems.

Medication:

If you have gout, a rheumatologist can be your best ally says Jim O'Dell, MD, professor and chief of rheumatology at the University of Nebraska Medical Centre. Your doctor may prescribe a number of drugs for gout treatment. If your attacks are few and far between, your doctor will probably just suggest a prescription strength anti-inflammatory drug or colchicine to help resolve each attack, says Richard S. Panush, MD, chairman of the department of medicine at Saint Barnabas Medical Centre in New Jersey. If your attacks are more frequent, however, your doctor will try to lower the levels of uric acid in your blood with a prescription for allopurinol (Zyloprim or Zyloric) or probenecid (Benemid). "Gout is one of the most satisfying problems a rheumatologist encounters because it's so easy to manage with medications," says Dr. Panush.

"We have seen an increase in the prevalence of gout at the same time that we have seen an increase in the use of thiazide diuretics in the treatment of high blood pressure," says Ronenn Roubenoff, MD, nutrition specialist. If you have been diagnosed with high blood pressure and your doctor has prescribed a thiazide diuretic to control the problem, you should talk to your physician about switching you to another medication. "Nowadays, there are many other drugs to treat high blood pressure, including beta-blockers, calcium channel blockers, and ACE inhibitors," he says. If you are able to switch, you might avoid ever having a first attack, according to Dr. Roubenoff.

Quick relief:

Take a pill. Take a prescription-strength amount of ibuprofen, says Richard Brasington, MD, a rheumatologist. "That means 800 milligrams four times a day," Dr. Brasington says. You can try this for up to a week. "The pain and redness should ease within a few hours, and you'll be completely better in a couple of days." Some people should not take such high doses of ibuprofen, so check with your doctor first. If you are currently taking blood thinners or have a heart condition or kidney disease, avoid high doses of ibuprofen, Dr. Brasington cautions.

Try a different anti-inflammatory. If ibuprofen doesn't do the trick for you, try naproxen sodium (Aleve or Naprosyn). It also helps relieve the pain and swelling. Take up to five regular-strength tablets a day for up to a week, Dr. Brasington says. You should only take these higher doses if your doctor says that it's okay, he adds.

Apply ice. Wrap ice in a towel and place it on the painful joint for 20 minutes three times a day for several days, says Doyt Conn, MD, from the Arthritis Foundation of the U.S.

Nutritional remedies:

Get the good oils. Scientists have discovered that oils like flaxseed oil and fish oils are rich in EPA (also known as omega-3 fatty acid), which is valued for its anti-inflammatory effects. Foods rich in EPA include green leafy vegetables, seeds (especially flaxseed), nuts, and grains. Some of the best seafood sources of EPA are anchovies, bluefin tuna, mackerel, and all types of salmon except smoked. EPA is also available in pill and liquid form at health food stores. Avoid anchovies, herring and sardines.

Drink water. Dehydration can trigger a gout attack. Whenever you drink plenty of fluids, especially water, you're activating the flush-out process that helps get the uric acid into your kidneys and then out of your system, says Richard S. Panush, MD. Make sure to get eight or more tall glasses of water every day. An easy method is to carry around a water bottle and take frequent sips.

Choose cherries and blueberries. Eat more blueberries and cherries, because they're rich in substances that counteract purines, says Julian Whitaker, MD, founder and president of the Whitaker Wellness Centre in Newport Beach, California. He says that some gout patients report finding relief by eating from a handful to up to 1/2 pound of cherries each day. Or juice about four handfuls of cherries with 1/2 cup of strawberries.

Get juiced. Drinking a quart a day of sour cherry or bing cherry juice can help prevent attacks of gout, says Devra Krassner, a doctor of naturopathic medicine and homeopathy. "The flavonoids in dark cherry juices are useful in the treatment of gout," Dr. Krassner adds. "You can also eat a half-pound of fresh or canned cherries to accomplish the same effect."

Repudiate purine-rich foods. Foods rich in a substance called purine can elevate uric-acid levels. Fortunately, the foods you usually have to reject are also bad for your heart health so you have a twofold reason to shun them. Try to cut back on the following: organ meats, anchovies, consommé, gravies, herring, mussels, pork roast, poultry, roast beef, and sardines, suggests Dr. O'Dell. "Most people with gout eat a lot of meat, which is high in purines," Dr. Conn says

Quit drinking. "Alcohol reduces the body's ability to get rid of uric acid," Dr. Conn says. "It's very important to cut it out of your life to possibly get rid of gout long-term."

Maintain a healthy weight. If you are over your ideal weight, you'll have higher levels of uric acid in your blood that may lead to more frequent and intense gout attacks, says Dr. Panush. Being overweight can also put you at higher risk for heart problems. Slowly but surely, lose those pounds, and you'll stack the deck in favour of fewer gout attacks.

Avoid crash diets. Low-calorie crash diets—like dropping to 1,000 calories a day—can change your metabolism so that you produce more uric acid. "Quick weight loss can cause a person to have their first attack of gout," says Dr. Roubenoff. Losing your extra weight is smart; losing it fast is foolish. Don't go on a diet of less than 1,000 calories a day without discussing it with your doctor, he advises.

Helpful vitamins and supplements:

Double up. Bromelain, an enzyme found in pineapples, and quercetin, a bioflavanoid (a pigment in plants), are two natural remedies available in pill form at health food stores. "You should take 125 to 250 milligrams of each three times a day between meals when you experience a flare-up," says Dr. Krassner. "You can also add 1.8 grams of eicosapentaenoic acid (EPA) to this every day." EPA is a fatty acid found in marine foods.

Everyday prevention:

Avoid aspirin. Low doses of aspirin may increase blood uric acid. "If you're on low-dose aspirin therapy for heart disease, talk to your doctor about your risk of gout," advises Dr. Conn. "It isn't an automatic cause-and-effect relationship, but it's a possible side effect to keep in mind."

Keep your tootsies toasty. Since gout seems to have an affinity for chilly climes, "keeping the toes warm is very helpful for preventing gout," says Dr. Roubenoff. If you are walking outside on a cold day, make sure that your shoes are well-insulated.

Wear the right size. Injuring the joint of your big toe can increase uric acid levels, either causing a first attack of gout or subsequent attacks, says Dr. Roubenoff. And you are setting up your big toe for some brutal battering if you wear a shoe that is too tight. When you try on new shoes, make sure that your toes can move freely. You may also feel a kind of burning sensation on the bottom of your foot if the shoe doesn't fit right. And if you own shoes that pinch your toes, get the jump on gout by giving them away. **Avoid thin soles.** Walking in shoes with very thin soles can also traumatise the toe joint, says Dr. Roubenoff. To be certain the shoes you buy have thick enough padding, walk on noncarpeted areas when you are trying them on for the first time. The shoe should be comfortable and have a little cushioning when you push down with your toes.

Herbal help:

Soothe with celery seed. Celery seed is a natural diuretic and anti-inflammatory that's been used since ancient times for treating gout and arthritis as well as colds and flu. Its healing properties are derived primarily from the volatile oil, which acts as an antiseptic in the urinary system by helping to clean out the organs that carry urine. "It's a clearing kind of herb," says herbalist Betzy Bancroft, You can buy the extract in capsules or tablets that are standardised by the percentage of volatile oil they contain.

Try aromatherapy. To ease the pain of gout, make a massage oil with one ounce of olive oil and five drops of juniper oil, then massage into the joint several times a day, suggests herbalist Jeanne Rose. To soothe gout pain in the feet, try a cool footbath spiked with juniper and rosemary essential oils, suggests aromatherapist Judith Jackson, author of *Scentual Touch: A Personal Guide to Aromatherapy.* She says to add ten drops of each oil to two quarts of cold water.

Let homeopathy help. "Colchicum is the homeopathic equivalent of colchicine, the prescription medicine that many Western doctors prescribe," Dr. Krassner says. "It may alleviate the acute pain of gout. Take two or three pellets of the 12C or 30X potency two times a day until the pain subsides." If the pain continues for more than a week, a professional homeopath should be consulted. You can find this homeopathic remedy, which is specific to gout, in a well-stocked health food store. Apis, a homeopathic remedy made from bee venom, also is available at many health food stores. "Apis helps in conditions that mimic the symptoms of a bee sting, like swelling, stinging pain, and heat," Dr. Krassner explains. Take two or three pellets of a low potency, such as 12C or 30X, two or three times a day. If symptoms do not resolve in a week, a professional homeopath should be consulted, she adds.

Choose chiso. This aromatic, weedy mint, imported accidentally or intentionally from Asia decades ago, is a popular food and medicine in the Orient. Japanese researchers have touted compounds in chiso to relieve gout. It contains fairly high levels of four compounds known as xanthine oxidase (XO) inhibitors, which help prevent the synthesis of uric acid. You can a little chiso to your tea, just as the Japanese add it to their sushi.

Try turmeric. One compound in turmeric (curcumin) inhibits the synthesis of substances called prostaglandins in the body that are involved in pain. The mechanism is similar to the one involved in the pain-relieving action of aspirin and ibuprofen, only weaker. Still, at high doses, curcumin stimulates the adrenal glands to release the body's own cortisone, a potent reliever of inflammation and the pain it often causes. East Indians revere turmeric and use it liberally in curries. That's a particularly nice way to take your medicine—you can also make a tea using turmeric or simply take it in capsules.

Add avocado. "My Botanical friends in the Amazon believe that avocado is useful for treating gout. It reportedly lowers uric acid levels in the blood," says James A. Duke, Ph.D., author of *The Green Pharmacy*." "There's no scientific evidence that I'm aware of to support this assertion, but I have a lot of respect for the herbal wisdom of the Amazonian people, and avocados are certainly tasty." So here's a good reason to add an occasional avocado to your diet. Just don't go overboard, though, as avocados are high in calories.

Gum Pain

The pain: Red or reddish purple gums that are puffy, swollen, bleeding (or bleed easily), receded, and sore, especially when you brush your teeth.

The cause: Gingivitis the long-term outcome of food particles lingering in the crevices between the gums and teeth. Left alone, the food helps create an invisible slime on teeth called plaque. When calcified (hardened) plaque builds up around the bases of your teeth, this local irritant inflames gum tissue. While you won't notice gingivitis at its earliest stages, the action of bacteria fighting white blood cells and plaque may cause your gums to turn red and sore and even to bleed.

In the early stages, gingivitis is reversible as long as you conscientiously clean your teeth at home and visit your dentist a couple of times a year for professional cleanings. If left untreated, gingivitis can lead to periodontitis, an advanced stage of gum disease that's characterised by receding gums, pockets forming between the teeth and gums, infection, loss of bone, and, finally, tooth loss.

See a dentist if:

...your gums are sore and bleeding, bleed during tooth brushing and flossing, or they begin bleeding for no apparent reason. See your dentist any time your gums are red, discoloured or bleeding whether or not you feel pain.

...you have loose or separating teeth.

...you have red, swollen, or tender gums, or your gums have pulled away from your teeth.

...you have persistent bad breath.

...you notice pus between your teeth and gums, or a change in the way your teeth fit together when you bite.

...you notice a change in the fit of partial dentures.

...you have mouth sores that won't heal.

Quick relief:

Ice it down. Apply an ice pack wrapped in a towel to your cheek or lip near the area of pain.

Soothe with salt water. Mix a teaspoon of salt in one cup of warm water, swish the mixture between your teeth, and then spit. That will help soothe your irritated gums, giving you a measure of temporary relief until you reach your dentist and can be examined, says Judith Post, D.MD, a dentist.

Moisten your mouth. Suck on ice chips or a lemon drop if you're suffering from gum irritation due to dry mouth.

Try an anti-inflammatory. Any over-the-counter medicine that reduces pain and inflammation could do wonders for your sore gums. "We recommend anti-inflammatory products such as ibuprofen (Advil), says Samuel Low, D.D.S., a periodontologist. You can take aspirin if you don't have an adverse reaction to it. But don't apply the aspirin directly to the affected gum area. That's a folk remedy that will only create a chemical burn in the gum tissue.

Nutritional remedy:

Choose fibre over sugar. Eat lots of high-fibre foods, such as fruits and vegetables, and less sugar-laden fare, says Meena Shah, D.D.S. Dietary fibre acts as a cleaning agent for your teeth. Sugary foods such as cookies, cake, and candy and sticky foods like raisins increase plaque build-up on your teeth and breed bacteria, she says.

Get milk. Like bones in the rest of your body, your teeth and jawbone can get brittle and shrink, leaving you more susceptible to gingivitis and other dental problems. Calcium seems to help people with gingivitis, since it strengthens bones and teeth.

Be nutty about cheese. Eat a handful of peanuts or an ounce of aged Monterey Jack or cheddar cheese after a meal or sugary snack to neutralise acids in the mouth that damage teeth and gums.

Don't be too sweet. Limit your consumption of chocolate and other sweets, says Eric Z. Shapira, D.D.S., spokesman for the Academy of

---

Winning-smile fruit salad

Vitamin C helps to give your gums a healthy glow. This kiwifruit salad has more than a day's supply of vitamin C.

8 kiwifruits, peeled and sliced
2 cups seedless red grapes
1 can (15 ounces) mandarin orange slices, drained
1 cup non-fat vanilla yoghurt
1 tablespoon thawed frozen orange juice concentrate
1 tablespoon honey

In a large serving bowl, combine the kiwifruits, grapes and oranges. In a small bowl, whisk together the yoghurt, juice concentrate and honey. Spoon the sauce over the fruit. Makes 4 servings.

General Dentistry. Remember each time you eat sweets, harmful bacteria produce acids in your mouth for at least 20 minutes. It is this acid that causes tooth decay. Snack on foods like nuts, popcorn, raw fruits, vegetables, and sugar-free drinks that don't promote decay.

Bar the drinks. Alcohol dries out the mouth and increases the likelihood of gum disease and tooth loss, says Dr. Shapira. If you drink, cut back to no more than one 12-ounce beer, four-ounce glass of wine, or one-ounce of liquor a day, Dr. Shapira urges.

Make your mouth water. Foods with strong flavours or foods that contain a lot of fibre stimulate saliva production. Sugarless gum will help your mouth produce extra saliva, as will the action of a chewing an apple. Saliva is one of your best mouth cleansers. Since lots of drugs produce dry mouth as a side effect, ask your doctor about any medication you're taking regularly.

Avoid spicy foods. They'll only irritate your irritable gums.

Helpful vitamins and supplements:

Get extra C. Supplement with 1,000 milligrams of vitamin C three times a day until your gums heal. Vitamin C promotes healing of bleeding, unhealthy gums. Every day, open a vitamin C capsule (any strength) and sprinkle the contents on a soft toothbrush. Brush your gum line with this powder, then rinse.

Boost your bioflavonoid intake. As part of your daily vitamin C regimen, Liz Collins, N.D., a naturopathic doctor recommends taking bioflavonoids. Naturopathic doctors believe that these nutrients are very effective in reducing inflammation and repairing and healing connective gum tissue. They're strong antioxidants that can prevent damage from free radicals, the free-roaming, unstable molecules that harm cells, and they're known to boost the effectiveness of vitamin C. "You should always take bioflavonoids with vitamin C," says Dr. Collins. You can buy a vitamin C and bioflavonoid combination formula or take the bioflavonoids separately. Two of the most effective bioflavonoids are quercetin and grapeseed extract. Take 1,000 to 2,000 milligrams of quercetin or 100 to 200 milligrams of grapeseed extract daily, says Jennifer Brett, N.D., a naturopathic doctor.

Add folic acid. Several studies have shown that folic acid can reduce inflammation, bleeding, and plaque build-up on the teeth when taken in pill form or used as a mouthwash. Research has also shown that it can help treat periodontitis, the advanced stage of gum disease. "Folic acid is a B vitamin that keeps the cells in your mouth healthy. Your mouth contains some of the fastest-dividing cells in the body, and any cell that divides quickly needs folic acid to replicate properly," says Dr. Collins. Take 400 to 800 micrograms of folic acid daily to treat gingivitis, she says. You can also make a mouthwash, which some studies say is more effective. Twice a day, empty a folic acid capsule into four ounces of lukewarm water and stir. Swish the solution in your mouth for a couple of minutes, then swallow it, says Dr. Collins. Repeat until you've finished the liquid.

Perfect Flossing Technique

It's dental floss time. Here's a step-by-step strategy:

Break off 24-36 inches of floss and wind it around one of your middle fingers.

Wind the remaining floss around the same finger of the opposite hand. As you use the floss and notice it is shredding, unroll a little bit off one finger and roll it up on the other.

Pinch the floss between your thumbs and forefingers. Using a gentle rubbing motion, guide the floss between your teeth. Never snap the floss into the gums. Not only does it hurt, but it can cause unnecessary bleeding.

As the floss reaches your gum line, curve it into a C shape against one tooth. Carefully slide into the space between the gum and tooth.

Press the floss tightly against the tooth. Delicately rub the side of the tooth, moving the floss away from the gum with upward and downward motions. You're basically using it like you use a towel to dry your back.

Repeat the process on the rest of your teeth. Don't forget the back side of your last tooth.

Queue up to Q10. Coenzyme Q10, or coQ10, is a vitamin-like compound found in human tissue that stimulates the immune system. It's chemically similar to vitamin E and is a powerful antioxidant that helps treat gingivitis and maintain healthy gums and other tissues by increasing the flow of oxygen to cells. In fact, in Japan, coQ10 is widely used to treat gum disease. Food sources include salmon, sardines, beef, peanuts, and spinach.

When researchers reviewed seven studies that used coQ10, they found that 70 percent of the 332 people with periodontal disease who took supplements of the enzyme showed signs of improvement. In one of these studies, for example, the group taking coQ10 showed a reduction in inflammation, receding gums, and tooth mobility.

Dr. Brett recommends taking 150 to 200 milligrams of the enzyme daily if your gums are inflamed and bleeding. As soon as the bleeding stops and the inflammation goes down, you can stop taking it.

Everyday prevention:

Get to know your dentist. If you'd enjoy keeping your teeth as you get older, practising good dental hygiene consistently is a necessity. That includes visiting your dentist for regular checkups and cleanings. For most people, regular means twice a year, although patients who are prone to gum problems may need more frequent visits.

Brush properly to maintain a plaque-free mouth. Flossing and brushing are the two best ways to keep your teeth free of plaque film. Use

Brush up on your technique

Although you've been brushing for decades, here are a few reminders.

Use a soft-bristled brush unless directed otherwise by your dentist.

Look in a mirror while you brush. If you can see what you're doing, it will help you clean your teeth more effectively.

Place your toothbrush at a 45-degree angle against the gumline and massage in place in a circular motion.

Move the brush back and forth gently in short (toothwide) strokes, four or five times on the outer, inner, and chewing surfaces of all teeth.

For the inside surfaces of the front teeth, move up and down gently with the tip of the brush.

Brush your tongue and gums to scrape away any odour-causing bacteria that accumulate.

Replace your brush when the bristles become frayed, which is about every three to four months.

---

a soft-bristled brush twice a day, and floss at least daily to clean between your teeth. And don't forget inside surfaces of your teeth—that's where plaque deposits tend to build up.

Ease up. To avoid gum abrasion, brush your teeth gently, for a longer period of time. "Most people are impatient to get it over with, so they compensate by brushing too hard," says Eric Spieler, D.MD, a lecturer in dental medicine. "That does remove plaque, but it also removes skin." Dr. Spieler recommends brushing for at least two minutes, or however long it takes to cover all the surfaces of your teeth. One sign that you're brushing too aggressively, he adds, is if the bristles on your brush are splaying outward. Using a soft-bristle brush is also a good idea.

Brush with baking soda. Mix baking soda with enough hydrogen peroxide to form a paste. With your toothbrush, gently rub the mixture onto your gums. Leave it on for a few minutes, then rinse. Baking soda's gentle abrasive action will help whiten your smile by removing the day-to-day stains that accumulate on your teeth while helping prevent the formation of plaque which, when left untreated, can lead to gingivitis.

Nuke bacteria with a hydrogen bomb. Gargling once or twice a day with hydrogen peroxide can help disinfect irritated gums, Dr. Spieler says. Brush your teeth first to break up the plaque, then use the peroxide (just as it comes from the bottle; no dilution is necessary) to wash it away. Rinse a lot afterward, and be careful not to swallow.

Apply appliances. Anything that encourages people to spend more time cleaning their teeth is a plus, Dr. Post says. So it helps to maintain a well-stocked arsenal in the battle against plaque. Among her other weapons of choice beside soft toothbrushes and floss are dental irrigators (WaterPik is probably the best-known brand); rubber gum stimulators, which allow you to clean at the gum line; and interproximal brushes, which get in between the teeth and under bridges where there are larger spaces. Interproximal brushes are miniature-size toothbrushes with tiny bristles covering the round-headed brush. You can usually find them at chemists next to the regular toothbrushes. All take aim at those spots between the teeth where bacteria love to hide—the spots brushes often miss. Dr. Post is also enthusiastic about the electric toothbrush, which she says has helped many of her patients improve the health of their gums.

Get out and about. Without daily contact with others, the incentive to brush and floss your teeth can quickly fade. This is particularly true of seniors who have recently lost a spouse or moved to a new community, Dr. Russo says. Join a jewellery making, woodworking, or other hobby group. Get a part-time job. Volunteer at your church or synagogue. Dive into the outside world at least once a day, Dr. Russo urges. It will encourage you to maintain good oral hygiene.

Snub smoking. Smokers are five times more likely than non-smokers to have gum disease, according to the U.S. National Institute of Dental Research. Smoking causes bone loss that weakens a tooth's underlying support and promotes gum disease, says Elizabeth Krall, Ph.D., an epidemiologist. In addition, smoking and chewing tobacco stain your teeth. These stains are a perfect place for plaque to hitch a ride on a tooth,

Save that tooth!

If a tooth falls or is knocked out of your mouth, don't panic. A dentist might be able to reattach it—no matter your age, says Eric Z. Shapira, D.D.S., dentist in Half Moon Bay, California, and spokesman for the Academy of General Dentistry. "I've saved a tooth in an 86-year-old man who fell and hit his face. We put his tooth back in, splinted it to his other teeth, and the bone healed around it," Dr. Shapira says.

Here's what you can to do to increase the odds that your tooth can be salvaged:

Pick up and hold the exposed surface of the tooth, never its root. The root surface has fibres and live cells that should not be distributed or destroyed.

If the tooth is dirty, rinse it lightly under water, but do not scrub or handle it more than absolutely necessary. Don't wipe anything off of the root.

Place the tooth under your tongue or store it in a glass of cold milk while you're on your way to the dentist. Saliva or milk will help keep the tooth alive and healthy while you are getting to the dentist, Dr. Shapira says.

Get to a dentist immediately—within one-half hour —is critical. Time is vital when it comes to replanting and saving a tooth, Dr. Shapira says.

causing cavities and aggravating periodontal disease.

Don't play dentist. Some chemists sell over-the-counter devices that resemble scalers (instruments used by dentists and dental hygienists to remove tartar and other deposits from teeth). Although they may be tempting, leave them on the shelf, advises Heidi Hausauer, D.D.S. "I've had people come into the office who have used these over-the-counter dental instruments and chipped their front tooth with them. I've seen patients gouge roots and chip enamel off lower incisors," Dr. Hausauer says. "It's particularly unwise for an older person to use them because he or she probably doesn't have the proper training or dexterity to use these products well. They could take the device, inadvertently shove tartar further down under the gum, and cause a severe infection." Instead of trying to do extensive cleanings yourself, get regular dental checkups twice a year, she urges.

Protect during pregnancy. A woman's chances of developing gingivitis increase during pregnancy, says Dr. Hausauer. The teeth and gums are most vulnerable to problems during the trimester, so a woman should see her dentist as soon as she knows she's pregnant, and continue to brush and floss regularly. Experts believe the increased risk has something to do with hormone changes that occur during pregnancy.

Herbal help:

Have a cuppa camomile. Camomile tea is useful against gingivitis because it reduces inflammation and kills germs, says James A. Duke, Ph.D., a botanical consultant. Infuse 2 teaspoons of the herb in a cup of water that has reached a boil and steep for 5 to 10 minutes. Drink a cup after meals, Dr. Duke suggests.

Smile and say aloe. Rinse after every brushing (until your gums get better) with an aloe vera mouthwash that contains no alcohol. Aloe soothes and heals painful gums.

Get garlic. Take garlic supplements to help healing and prevent infection. Garlic has a natural antibiotic action, says Stephen R. Goldberg, D.D.S., a dentist. Considered the poor man's antibiotic, garlic has often been used to treat infection in Third World countries. "You could add raw garlic to your meals, but you would have to eat a huge amount to get the same effect," he says. Instead, just have some garlic supplements every day, following directions on the label.

Block bacteria with bloodroot. Try an over-the-counter herbal product to prevent plaque. The herb called bloodroot seems to have the amazing ability to prevent bacteria in the mouth from creating plaque, says James A. Duke, Ph.D., author of *The Green Pharmacy*. But you don't have to forage in the wild for this one. Sanguinarine—the active compound in bloodroot—is an ingredient in an over-the-counter mouthwash called Viadent.

Cure with calendula. Calendula, a type of marigold plant, has mucous-membrane-healing properties. It can also help stop bleeding gums in the case of gingivitis, says Dr. Goldberg. He recommends using a non-alcoholic calendula extract. Mix 10 drops of extract in 10 drops of water and use as a mouth rinse twice daily after brushing.

Sip a soothing tea. Add two tablespoons of the dried herb anise and two tablespoons of dried sage (both sold in health food stores) to one cup of freshly boiled water. Allow the herbs to steep for 10 minutes, then strain the tea and drink up. Repeat as needed to relieve sore gums. Anise and sage have been used for thousands of years to both freshen breath and soothe gum disease by killing off harmful bacteria.

Pack some peppermint. You can't count on the "peppermint" in toothpaste to be of any help in preventing gingivitis, as most products are artificially flavoured these days. But real peppermint fights the bacteria that cause tooth decay. You can make a tea using two teaspoons of crushed peppermint leaves per cup of boiling water. Steep for ten minutes, then sweeten it with licorice and drink the tea or use it as a mouthwash. You can also chew fresh mint leaves instead of sweetened mint candies and gums.

Steep some rhatany. Commission E approves of using rhatany bark to treat gingivitis. Like tea, this herb is rich in astringent, antiseptic tannin. To make a rhatany tea, steep a teaspoon of dried herb in a cup of boiling water. Drink it or use it as an astringent mouthwash.

Stick with stinging nettle. In addition to the magnesium in nettle greens, Russian studies show that nettle tea has antibacterial activity. Mouthwashes and toothpaste containing nettle reduce plaque and gingivitis. It's even more effective if you add juniper. Look for dental products containing these herbs at health food stores.

Take some teatree. Teatree oil is a significant antiseptic, and many herbalists regard it as their first-choice disinfectant for external use. But if you're using teatree to treat gingivitis and canker sores, make sure you don't swallow it. To combat gingivitis, add a couple of drops of teatree oil to a glass of water, then swish it in your mouth. As with any other essential oil, teatree should never be taken internally, as surprisingly small amounts—a teaspoon or so—can be fatal.

Chew on watercress. Southern Chinese chew watercress to treat sore gums. If you like the taste of watercress, you might try chewing it to treat gingivitis, says pharmacognosist (natural product pharmacist) Albert Leung, Ph.D., author of *Chinese Herbal Remedies*.

Herbalize your water jet. Your dentist may have already recommended the use of a dental hygiene device (such as Water Pik) that uses a high-speed water jet to help remove food particles and plaque. Susun S. Weed, an herbalist and herbal educator and author of the *Wise Woman* series of herbal health books, suggests taking its healing power even further. She adds two to four drops of tincture of bloodroot or echinacea to the water reservoir of her machine and then uses the device as directed.

Haemorrhoids

The pain: There are two types of haemorrhoids: internal and external. Internal haemorrhoids are inside the anus. Symptoms typically are blood covering a stool, on toilet paper, or in the toilet bowl. You can't see or feel them except in the case of a protruding or prolapsed haemorrhoid, which can push through the anal opening and cause a dull ache, itch, or bleed. External haemorrhoids may include painful swelling or a hard lump around the anus that occurs when a blood clot forms. If irritated, they can itch and bleed.

The cause: Haemorrhoids are similar to varicose veins, only in a less visible place—around your anus and lower rectum. "Everyone has haemorrhoids," says James Surrell, MD, a colorectal surgeon. "They're a normal part of the human anatomy. More than 75 percent of people will have problems with haemorrhoids sometime in their life. Such problems are brought about by constipation, excessive straining, rubbing, or cleaning around the anus; obesity; lifting heavy objects; and standing or sitting for long periods can cause flare-ups. There may also be a hereditary factor.

See a doctor if:

...you have symptoms of haemorrhoids. When it comes to symptoms you suspect are caused by haemorrhoids, it's better to be safe than sorry, says Juan Nogueras, MD, a colon and rectal surgeon. If you detect a lump, blood in your stools, or changes in your normal bowel movement pattern, see a doctor to have it checked out immediately, he says. It may be haemorrhoids, but also it could signify something more serious.

Medication:

The list of medications that cause constipation (and therefore aggravate any haemorrhoid problem) goes on for pages, says Dr. Nogueras. "Whenever you're prescribed a new medication, it's a good idea to ask your doctor if constipation is a side effect," says Dr. Nogueras. Once you know, you can either ask about alternative medications or prepare for the added pressure on your haemorrhoids. You should also watch out for multivitamins and supplements that are high in iron, he says. "Iron can cause significant constipation."

If your haemorrhoids are too large or painful to endure, your doctor may recommend that you have them removed. This may be done with a simple technique called banding, in which a rubber band is snapped around the base of the haemorrhoid, cutting off its blood supply. Within a week it will drop off, passing out of the body in the stool. A quicker approach is for the doctor to open up the haemorrhoid with a scalpel and remove the clot that's causing all the pain. For the most severe cases, your doctor may recommend having the entire haemorrhoid removed under general or spinal anaesthesia.

Quick relief:

Soak your bum. Taking warm baths of 10 to 15 minutes several times a day relaxes your sphincter muscle and allows protruding haemorrhoids to recede back into places less painful, says Lester Rosen, MD, professor of clinical surgery at Penn State University Hospital. Or take a sitz bath: fill your bathtub with three to four inches of warm water and sit in the water for 10 to 15 minutes. (Don't use Epsom salts—they just irritate your haemorrhoids.)

Cream it. Over-the-counter topical steroid creams containing cortisone can help relieve itching but should only be used for a few weeks, says Dr. Rosen. You can go back to using them several months to years later. They can thin the skin, making it more susceptible to cracking and bleeding if used excessively, he cautions. Petroleum jelly or zinc oxide paste can reduce the pain and swelling of haemorrhoids. After wiping, dab a small amount of the cream or paste on a cotton ball and apply to the anal area.

Cool it. Put a wet washcloth in the freezer until it freezes, then apply it to the anal area for 10 minutes. Repeat as often as necessary over the next 24 hours to relieve pain.

Get corny. Use a cotton ball to dab cornstarch onto protruding haemorrhoids two to three times a day. The cornstarch absorbs moisture and keeps the anal area dry, which prevent irritation.

Take a load off. Lie face down with a pillow under your stomach for 15 minutes two or three times a day to elevate your haemorrhoids higher than your heart. This helps to reduce blood flow to the anal area, which decreases swelling.

Nutritional remedies:

Eat more fibre. Fibre-rich foods such as fruits, vegetables, seeds, nuts, and legumes can soften stools and make them easier to pass, says Dr. Rosen. He recommends at least 20 grams of fibre a day. You'll get about 2 grams of fibre per serving from each of the above food groups, and an all-bran type cereal would account for another 5 to 10 grams, he says. Check the nutrients listing on the food package to get the exact amounts. Dr. Rosen suggests slowly building up your fibre intake. Too much too fast can cause bloating and cramps.

Be wary of dairy. Dairy products such as cheese, chocolate, ice cream, and milk can make you constipated, causing the straining on the toilet that aggravates haemorrhoids, says Dr. Rosen.

Stop spicing up your life. Eating foods high in strong spices like red pepper and mustard can cause your haemorrhoids to flare up, says Andrew T. Weil, MD Coffee, decaffeinated coffee, or alcohol can also make symptoms worse as can tobacco. If you can't eliminate these things completely, limit your use of them as much as possible, he suggests.

Look to the East. If you'd like to try an alternative remedy, two traditional Chinese medicine remedies correct the imbalances that may cause haemorrhoids, says Dr. Weil. Eat an orange three times a day, or eat two bananas as soon as you wake up in the morning. Continue the remedy until your haemorrhoid is gone, he says.

Helpful vitamins and supplements:

Consume fibre supplements. Over-the-counter fibre supplements and stool softeners containing psyllium and methylcellulose can be effective when taken with a meal, Dr. Rosen says. Two examples would be Metamucil (or Fybogel), which contains psyllium, and Citrucel or Celevac, which contains methylcellulose. Dr. Rosen recommends taking them with breakfast or lunch to relieve constipation and excessive straining, which can lead to haemorrhoids. Taking these kinds of supplements every day would be a good habit for anyone who has experienced constipation problems in the past, he advises.

Everyday prevention:

Drink more. Fluids help move what you've eaten through the digestive tract and soften stools, says Eric G. Weiss, MD, a colorectal surgeon. He recommends drinking eight to ten 10-ounce glasses of any alcohol-free and caffeine-free fluids a day to help you stay regular and avoid painful haemorrhoids. Beverages containing alcohol and caffeine act as diuretics, causing you to lose fluids.

Become more active. Regular exercise helps make for regular guys, Dr. Rosen says. So guys with haemorrhoids should walk a mile or two, bike, or do some kind of aerobic activity every day. "Walking and exercise will help tone the abdominal muscles," he says. "That usually makes for more-regular people."

Don't count. "People believe the fallacy that you need to have a bowel movement every day," says Dr. Weiss. "It's not true. Normal is three times per day to three times per week." You should determine what is normal for you, and only be concerned if there is deviation from it.

Take it easy on the toilet. If you're in the habit of reading for long periods on the can, stop. With your legs open and knees up, this position can cause slippage of haemorrhoids, says David Beck, MD, a colorectal surgeon. That's not all. "People who sit on the hopper and strain a lot and push and just can't go are better off getting off," says Dr. Rosen. "I think if you don't go within 10 minutes, you probably should leave and try again later."

Paper things over. Wiping the area with scented toilet paper can severely agitate haemorrhoids, says Dr. Nogueras, even if you're using the most expensive brand. Instead, stick with the plain stuff, with no chemical additives whatsoever. And for severe external haemorrhoids that are difficult to keep clean, wet the toilet paper with water beforehand to keep irritation to a minimum, he suggests. You can make things even more soothing by moistening the paper with witch hazel.

Have a pillow, not a doughnut. Many people with haemorrhoids favour inflatable doughnut cushions that enhance comfortable seating at home or the office. But they really don't help haemorrhoids, says Dr. Nogueras. "It just puts additional pressure on the anus by spreading and stretching the surrounding area of the buttocks" he says. "If you need additional cushioning, use a small pillow instead."

Herbal help:

Summon witch hazel. Soaking a piece of toilet paper or cotton in witch hazel and applying it to the affected area works for some people, Dr. Rosen says. "Some people say that it burns; others say that it's soothing," he says. "If they have very irritated haemorrhoids that are open and bleeding, witch hazel doesn't usually work well. With haemorrhoids that are pushing out and are a little irritated and itching, witch hazel works." As long as it soothes, you can apply it several times a day.

Say hello to aloe. Applying an aloe gel can supply haemorrhoid relief. Use a pure gel, with no additives. These can be found at most chemists. You can apply a small amount several times a day.

Help yourself to tincture of butternut. "The root bark of the butternut tree is an excellent stool softener," says Betzy Bancroft, a professional herbalist. "Try taking 20 to 30 drops of the butternut tincture three times a day for as long as the haemorrhoids are painful," she recommends. You can find the tincture in health food stores with well-stocked herbal medicine sections or in mail-order catalogues. If you are pregnant, check with your doctor before taking butternut.

De-itch with figwort. Figwort has been used as a haemorrhoid remedy at least since the sixteenth century, when British herbalist Nicholas Culpeper wrote, "The decoction of the herb dissolves clotted and congealed blood within the body...(including) the haemorrhoids, or pile." Fig was an old slang term for haemorrhoids, which is how the plant got its name," Bancroft says. "Take 20 to 30 drops of figwort tincture—available in health food stores— three times a day. It works slowly, so you may not see any improvement for several weeks, especially if your haemorrhoids are chronic."

Soothe with St. John's-wort. Saint-John's-wort can help relieve the itching and burning of haemorrhoids, says herbalist Rosemary Gladstar, author of *Herbal Healing for Women.* Most health food stores carry salves made with this herb; Gladstar says to follow the directions on the label of the product you choose.

Get help from homeopathy. Take a 10- to 15-minute sitz bath in warm water twice a day, then apply Aesculus and Hamamelis ointment after each bath, says Maesimund Panos, MD, a homeopathic physician and co-author of *Homeopathic Medicine at Home.* Dr. Panos says that this ointment helps relieve pain and swelling and can speed healing. Taking two tablets of Aesculus 6X three or four times daily may also be helpful in speeding healing, she says.

Try tea. A compress soaked in strong, cold black tea is very soothing to haemorrhoids, says Agatha Thrash, MD, a medical pathologist. She suggests holding the compress against the haemorrhoids for several minutes.

Horse around. Like witch hazel, horse chestnut salve has stringent properties that soothe and shrink swollen haemorrhoidal tissues. It's available at health food stores.

Plan on plantain. Plantain has a strong folk reputation as a haemorrhoid remedy. This herb contains allantoin, the same soothing compound found in comfrey. Try making a poultice and applying it to the afflicted area.

Sweep with butcher's broom. This woody herb has a long history as a treatment for venous problems like haemorrhoids and varicose veins. The plant contains chemicals called ruscogenins, which have anti-inflammatory and vasoconstricting properties. " I'd try five rounded teaspoons of root in a cup of boiling water for internal consumption; you can sweeten the tea with honey. And for topical application, I'd use a tincture of the herb made with alcohol," says James Duke, Ph.D., author of *The Green Pharmacy.*

Try these herbal combos. Herbal pharmacologist Daniel Mowrey, Ph.D., author of *The Scientific Validation of Herbal Medicine and Herbal Tonic Therapies,* suggests making a tea for topical application using alumroot (astringent), goldenseal (vasoconstricting), mullein (soothing), slippery elm bark (soothing) and witch hazel (astringent). You can use any amount of these ingredients. David Hoffmann, noted British herbalist and author of *The Herbal Handbook,* recommends using a topical salve made from calendula, camomile, yarrow, plantain and St. John's-wort after every bowel movement. Try mixing one teaspoon of each herb in powdered form with enough emollient oil (almond) to form a paste, then apply.

Mind over malady:

Use your imagination. In his book *Healing Visualisations,* New York City psychiatrist Gerald Epstein, MD, suggests you close your eyes, breathe out three times and imagine that your haemorrhoids are puckering up like an old purse. Picture them shrivelling and disappearing as the walls of the anus become pink and smooth. Dr. Epstein says to practice this imagery for one to two minutes of every waking hour, for up to 21 days, until the haemorrhoids fade.

Hangover

The pain: Headache, nausea, thirst, muscle aches and other symptoms of alcoholic overindulgence.

The cause: Surprisingly, little is known about hangover—either what precisely causes it or what makes it feel better. "It has not been well-studied, considering how common it is," says Alan Wartenberg, MD, director of the addiction-recovery program at Faulkner Hospital, in Boston. It appears, however, that alcohol causes your blood vessels to contract (headache), causes the build-up of poisons such as aldehydes and lactic acid in your cells (body aches), and dehydrates your entire system (thirst).

See a doctor if:

...you drink large amounts of alcohol and never get hungover. It may seem like a blessing, but "It's a sign of certain types of alcoholism," says Eric J. Devor, Ph.D., professor of psychiatry.

...your headache lasts for more than a day or nausea lingers for more than two days.

...your hangovers become more frequent or severe or begin to interfere with you work.

Quick relief:

Get a gentle analgesic. Take some acetaminophen or paracetamol (Tylenol or Panadol) on the morning after. It's the over-the-counter painkiller that is most gentle on your stomach, which already is inflamed from your overindulgence, says Dr. Wartenberg. He cautions, however, that habitual drinkers who take multiple doses of Tylenol can damage their livers. Acetaminophen should not be taken regularly in people drinking three or more standard drinks a day. A standard drink is one shot of 80-proof distilled spirits, 12 ounces of beer, or 6 ounces of wine.

Nutritional remedies:

Slurp some broth. Drink fluids that contain minerals and salts that provide relief from dehydration. A cup of bouillon, for example, will replace fluid and is easy on your churning stomach, says Frederick G. Freitag, D.O., a spokesperson for the U.S. National Headache Foundation.

Find some fructose. Fructose is fruit sugar. Korean scientists have suggested that fructose can speed up the body's metabolism of alcohol by about 25 percent. Cherries, grapes and apples are especially good sources. Or try putting some honey in your morning tea; it's more than 40 percent fructose. (Maybe that's why one old-time hangover remedy among bartenders is simply honey in hot water.) Not far behind honey are dates, with 30 percent fructose.

Fill up on fruit juice. Relief will come faster if you get juiced on tomato, orange or grapefruit juice. "A large glass of any of these helps in two ways: it's high in fructose and it's also high in vitamin C, which helps minimise the effects of alcohol," says Seymour Diamond, MD, director of the Diamond Headache Clinic in Chicago.

Forget the hair of the dog. You've probably heard of this hangover cure: the "hair of the dog "—drink in the morning whatever got you drunk the night before. Your stomach is already inflamed by imbibing too much, so drinking more of the same makes no sense, says Dr. Wartenberg. The hair-of-the-dog remedy may have a calming effect on drinkers who are physically dependent on alcohol suffering through withdrawal, but it only feeds their dependency, says Dr. Wartenberg. The best solution for hangovers, of course, is to not drink alcohol, or only do so in moderation

Drink water. It's a good idea to drink a lot of water while you're drinking alcohol to avoid the next-day dehydration that can make hangovers even worse. Continue to chug water the next day to fight dehydration. If you like, you can drink Gatorade or other sports drinks, which will replace depleted minerals as well as water.

Helpful vitamins and supplements:

Load up on C. Taking vitamin C before drinking has been shown to counteract some of the effects of alcohol in some people by speeding up alcohol clearance from the body.

Swallow some B. Some hangover symptoms may be due to the loss of B vitamins that occurs when drinking, Dr. Wartenberg says. Andrew Weil, MD, author of several books, including *Eight Weeks to Optimum Health*, recommends taking a B-complex vitamin supplement plus an extra 100 milligrams of thiamin.

Everyday prevention:

Avoid the dark. There is anecdotal evidence suggesting that drinking darker coloured alcoholic drinks the night before is more likely to bring you brain pain the next day, Dr. Wartenberg says. These drinks contain congeners, chemicals that add colour and flavour, which may promote a headache. Red wine also appears to be a high-risk drink for the hangover-prone. Clear liquors like vodka and gin are better bets, although they too can produce hangovers if abused.

Don't take aspirin before you imbibe. Despite popular opinion that taking aspirin before you drink will help minimise or avoid a hangover, just the opposite is true. Scientists at the Alcohol Research and Treatment Centre at the Veterans Administration Hospital in New York City found that taking aspirin before or during drinking increases blood alcohol concentration to induce a quicker and more severe state of intoxication.

Fill 'er up. Before you drink, eat a good meal. "Alcohol levels go up much faster on an empty stomach," Dr. Wartenberg says. "Food slows alcohol's absorption. The faster your level rises, the drunker you get." And the drunker you get, the worse you will feel in the morning. High-protein foods, such as cheese, stay in your digestive system longer and soak up more alcohol. But avoid pretzels and other salty snacks, since they make you thirstier, leading to more alcohol consumption.

Avoid the bubbles. Don't mix alcohol with carbonated beverages, because they increase the rate at which alcohol is absorbed.

Easing the pain with exercise:

Get moving. You may not feel like hard exercise if your head is about to explode, but sometimes a real physical challenge is just what you need to help with recovery. Any kind of heart-pounding, blood-pumping exercise can help carry unwanted alcohol from your body, says Dan Hamner, MD, a physiatrist and sports medicine specialist. "Try shadow boxing in front of a mirror for several minutes," he suggests. "That should get your heart rate up. You want to get that bad stuff out of you as fast as possible."

Crawl to a sauna. More perspiration means a faster farewell for the toxins. "Alcohol is total poison for every cell in the body. A steam room should help for a hangover," says Dr. Hamner. Even a half-hour in a steamed-up bathroom might help a bit.

Stretch those muscles. When we drink too much, lactic acid and other poisons such as aldehydes build up in our muscles. Why? Because the liver gets overloaded trying to deal with all the toxins and can't keep up.

"Lactic acid is what makes you ache. Under a microscope, this molecule is abrasive to the body," explains Dr. Hamner. Try this soothing stretch to combat achiness from a hangover. You can do these movements even before you get out of bed in the morning.

Lie flat on your back and stretch your hands and feet out. Reach for all four corners of the bed.

Point your toes and stretch out your fingers.

Slowly bring your left knee to your chest. Hold that pose for a few seconds and then slide your leg down.

Repeat with your right leg.

Herbal help:

Cure with cinchona. The bitter bark that gives tonic water its flavour and is the source of quinine is used as a hangover remedy in China. Other bitter herbs often recommended for hangover include dandelion, gentian, mugwort and angostura, which is the same herb used in Angostura Bitters, a favourite hangover remedy among bartenders. You can make an anti-hangover tea by adding a few drops of Angostura Bitters to a cup of boiling water. In fact, any of these herbs can be made into a very bitter tea. Try cutting the bitter flavour by adding the tasty herbs roselle and tamarind, both of which are also reputed to help banish hangover.

Try ayurveda. For hangovers, stir one teaspoon of lime juice and a pinch of cumin into one cup of fresh orange juice and drink, says Vasant Lad, B.A.M.S., M.A. Sc., director of the Ayurvedic Institute in Albuquerque, New Mexico.

Get help from homeopathy. Nux vomica is a homeopathic remedy for hangover that works for many people, says Mitchell Fletcher, MD, a family practice physician and homeopath. He suggests taking one 6C or 12C tablet every three to four hours as needed until you begin to feel better.

Headache

The pain: By far the most prevalent is the tension headache. Also called a muscle contraction headache, it can leave a dull, steady aching in your head, with feelings of tightness or pressure. Sometimes it creates a feeling of a constriction about the head, as if you are wearing a hat that is much too small. The pulsating throb of a migraine headache is less common, but more likely to send you to the doctor in quest of relief. Some migraines are preceded by an aura or warning. Nausea, vomiting, and sensitivity to light and sounds often are symptoms accompanying these pounding headaches, which can wipe you out for four hours to three days. Migraine headaches occur more often in women than men. Cluster headaches are a relatively rare but very distinct type of headache that mainly affects men. The headaches come in series. They are sudden, excruciating one-sided headaches that can run from 45 minutes to 2 hours. Along with the headache comes nasal congestion. Typically, one eyelid droops, and the eye on the painful side gets irritated and watery.

The cause: Tension headaches are often caused by tension, or as a result of other emotional states, such as anxiety, anger, and repressed hostility. Other causes include being confined to one uncomfortable position for a prolonged period, such as cramped driving or riding in a car, or doing the same repetitive task over and over again on a job. Eyestrain, fasting, and even fun things like eating ice cream and having sex can trigger a hurt in the head. If you are prone to tension headaches, chances are you were born with a slightly different brain chemistry than people who get don't get them as often. This short circuit, of sorts, causes imbalances in the chemical serotonin, which is a messenger that helps regulate the diameter of your blood vessels. Once the serotonin gets out of balance, the blood vessels in your brain become inflamed—and that's when you end up with a head that's throbbing with pain.

During a migraine, blood vessels surrounding the brain initially constrict, then dilate and swell, becoming inflamed. Why this happens isn't really known, but about 70 to 80 percent of migraine sufferers have a hereditary link. The headaches also can be triggered by a host of things, including change in sleep cycle, missing or postponing a meal, medications that cause a swelling of the blood vessels, excessive use of medications for migraine and other headaches, bright lights, sunlight, fluorescent lights, television and movie viewing, loud noise, and certain foods.

Researchers aren't exactly sure what causes cluster headaches. It may be blood vessels dilating, inflammation or pressure on the nerves behind the eye. Or the headaches could be triggered by a decrease in oxygen in the blood.

Medication:

"If you have tension headaches, avoid taking too much medication—e.g. aspirin or paracetamol—too often. Through what might be a 'rebound effect', this can actually give you chronic headaches," says Marcia Wilkinson, MA, DM, FRCP Honorary Medical Director, City of London Migraine Clinic (now retired) and author of a number of popular books on migraine/headaches. "When I asked such patients why they took so many tablets, they would say, 'Because I would get headaches.' But I would ask them if these headaches were any less bad than the ones they might have if they didn't take the tablets!"

Clinical research since the 1980s suggests that many people with daily headaches are indeed suffering from a rebound effect due to overuse of some medications, says Alan Rapoport, MD, director of The New England Centre for Headache. When there's a rebound effect, you are actually getting increased and consistent pain from painkiller or tranquillizing medications that are supposed to make pain go away.

The drug rebound headache can be caused by both prescription and over-the-counter painkillers (Fioricet, aspirin, acetaminophen), sedative and tranquillizer drugs, and ergotamine tartrate (Cafergot), used for migraine. Fortunately, the headache often improves dramatically or goes away entirely when these prescription and over-the-counter medications are gradually stopped, says Dr. Rapoport. Daily prescription medications (such as antidepressants, beta-blockers, and calcium channel blockers) used to prevent headache then become more effective, he says.

See a doctor if:

...your headache problem is new.
...the intensity, frequency, or duration has changed markedly within the last three months.
...numbness or weakness in any part of the body accompanies the headache.
...the headache began after some trauma to the head.
...you are older than age 60 and just started having headaches.
...you have other medical conditions, such as high blood pressure, cancer, or a history of cerebral aneurysm in your family.
...your headaches interfere with your work or family life.

Quick relief:

Heat your hand. Run comfortably hot water over your hand for 10 minutes as soon as you feel a headache coming on. The heat draws blood away from your head, making this remedy effective against both tension headaches and migraines.

Freeze the pain. Cold helps constrict expanded blood vessels and block pain messages to your brain. Wrap ice or an ice pack in a towel and apply for 10 minutes to the area of your head that hurts.

Breathe in a bag. When you experience auras before a headache—a warning such as seeing flashing lights, squiggly lines, or feeling a tingling in the arms and hands—immediately stick your face in a paper bag. By breathing for a few minutes into a bag, you re-breathe some of the air you exhaled, building up the carbon dioxide concentration in your blood, says Egilius Spierings, MD, Ph.D., a neurologist and headache specialist. This, in turn, helps fend off migraines.

Pull the shades. Since light aggravates migraine symptoms, lie down in a dark room, advises Glen Solomon, MD, a headache expert.

Buck it with ice. When you lie down, put an ice pack wrapped in a towel or a cold compress on your throbbing head until the pain subsides to soothe swollen, pulsing blood vessels, says Dr. Solomon.

Dip your hands. If for some reason you don't want to put a cold compress on your head to relieve the pain, soak one or both of your hands in ice water for only as long as you can tolerate it, advises Dr. Spierings While your hands are in the water, ball them into fists and open and close them repeatedly. It can have the same effect as a compress on your head. "The cold water stimulates the cold pressor response, causing your blood vessels (including those in your head) to narrow," explains Dr. Spierings.

Sleep off a migraine. "If you have a migraine attack, just stay put and don't fight it," says Dr. Wilkinson. The best thing to do is to go to sleep—sleep itself seems to relieve the condition. "We did some research at the City of London Clinic and found that those who slept deeply while lying down did far better than those who simply dozed while sitting up in a chair."

Nutritional remedies:

Take a whiff of apple. In one study of people with migraines, the scent of green apples made their migraine pain fade. The reason why is unclear. It could be that you focus on the scent instead of the pain, or the smell may actually reduce muscle contractions in your head and neck. Green apple scent has previously been shown to reduce anxiety, and women with migraines say that their headaches are worse when they're anxious. Other pleasant smells may bring the same relief. You can find fragrances at health food stores, some pharmacies, and bath stores.

Consider a coffee cure. Like ice, the caffeine in coffee constricts expanded blood vessels in the brain. But limit yourself to one five-ounce cup, which contains about 100 milligrams of caffeine. Too much coffee can aggravate a migraine.

Steer clear of trigger foods. You can minimise the frequency and severity of migraines just by avoiding the foods known to cause them. The most common offenders: anything that has been aged, fermented, marinated, or pickled like aged cheese, red wine, and pickled herring. Also bypass any foods that contain monosodium glutamate (MSG), nitrates, or nitrites such as canned soups and lunchmeats.

Eat well. Skipping meals is a common trigger of migraines, says Dr. Solomon. "One way to avoid this trigger is to eat smaller meals throughout the day or be sure to eat three meals," he says.

Slurp up some celery. Celery juice is rich in coumarins, substances that have a soothing effect on he vascular system and that may benefit those prone to migraines, says naturopathic physician Michael Murray, N.D., author of *The Complete Book of Juicing.* Fresh celery juice may be drunk alone or combined with other vegetable juices such as carrot, cucumber, parsley and spinach. Dr. Murray says to drink an eight-ounce glass of the juice twice a day as a preventive, in conjunction with proper medical treatment.

Dodge the triggers. One of the most common triggers, especially for migraines, is tyramine. Chocolate, red wine, and aged cheese all contain this chemical. It causes blood vessels to constrict only to rebound and dilate painfully later. Nitrites, found in cured or processed meats like turkey, ham, hot dogs, and bologna, can cause problems for some people. So can monosodium glutamate (MSG), which is found in meat tenderisers, canned and dry soups, and some Chinese restaurant food.

Don't be a fathead. A scientific study reported in the medical journal *Headache* suggests that if you cut back on fat, you may cut back on migraines, too. When 54 people with regular migraines went on reduced-fat diets for a full month, their headaches were less frequent, less intense, and shorter in duration. This study found success with cutbacks to an ultralow 20 grams of fat (about 10 percent of calories from fat) in people who had previously been eating 80 to 120 grams of fat per day.

Helpful vitamins and supplements:

Try riboflavin for migraines: The first supplement to try if you suffer from migraines is riboflavin (vitamin B2), says Fred Sheftell MD a psychiatrist, headache specialist and co-founder of the New England Centre for Headache in Connecticut. In superhigh doses this benign B vitamin can help ward off a migraine attack by helping the brain cells utilise energy. "Almost as a matter of routine, all of our patients are put on riboflavin. We start them on 200 milligrams for a week and then bring them up to 400 milligrams," Dr. Sheftell says. According to Dr. Sheftell, some people experience nausea when they take as much as 400 milligrams—but if that happens, just return to the 200 milligram dose. It may take some time to get relief, so stick with the supplements for two to three months before you decide whether it has any benefit, says Dr. Sheftell.

Add some magnesium. Another promising migraine fighter is magnesium. This mineral plays a key role in regulating blood vessel size and also regulating the rate at which cells burn energy. Researchers estimate that 50 percent of migraine sufferers are magnesium deficient, says Burton M. Altura, MD, a professor of physiology and medicine. Does this mean that you can pop a few magnesium tablets to get rid of a headache? Not quite. But the supplement may be useful in preventing migraine headaches.

"We believe everyone should be taking 500 to 600 milligrams of magnesium a day in a combination of both diet and supplements," says Dr. Altura. "If people would bring up their total consumption of magnesium, they could reduce the frequency of recurring migraine headaches." If you have heart or kidney problems, however, be sure to check with your doctor before taking supplemental magnesium.

Trouble is, magnesium supplements often cause diarrhoea, says Jacqueline Jacques N.D. a naturopathic physician and specialist in pain management. This all too common side effect is a sign that the supplement is not getting absorbed.

If you want to get the most benefit from a magnesium supplement and minimise the chance of diarrhoea, Dr. Jacques advises taking magnesium glycinate, instead of magnesium oxide or magnesium chloride. Magnesium glycinate is in a form that is readily absorbed.

Try E. Dr. Sheftell recommends that women take 400 IU (international units) of vitamin E the week before and the week after their periods since a change in hormone levels can trigger migraines and vitamin E helps mute the negative effects of hormonal changes. If you are considering taking amounts above 200 IU, discuss this with your doctor first.

Iron out the problem. Not getting enough iron in the diet can lead to anaemia, in which the body doesn't get enough oxygen. To compensate, blood vessels dilate to admit more blood, which can cause head pain. The daily value for iron is 18 mg; a large baked potato has 7 milligrams. Meats are even better sources.

Everyday prevention:
Sleep well. "Changes in sleep patterns, changing shifts, jet lag—any of those can trigger migraines," says Dr. Solomon. It's best to maintain a regular schedule and get up and go to bed at the same time every day, he adds.

Beware being a slugabed. "Don't sleep late on weekends," advises Dr. Solomon. After a week of daily stresses, it might seem like a reward to relax and sleep in. But giving yourself that let down after stress is a common trigger. Awaking late can also trigger a migraine for two other reasons, Dr. Solomon says. It is a change in your normal sleep pattern and may cause you to miss a meal—breakfast—which can both trigger a migraine.

Sit up straight. "Make sure that you're not hunched over a keyboard or reading in a funny position that would put a lot of pressure on your neck or shoulders," advises Joseph P. Primavera III, Ph.D., a psychologist.

Keep a diary. "If you think that you are plagued by headaches, try to demystify the situation by keeping a record of them," says Dr. Wilkinson, Write down when they happen and how bad they are: Are they a minor nuisance? Can you carry on with normal activities? Are they so debilitating that you can't function while they persist? It is also important to look for clues to what might bring on your headaches—that is, the precipitating factors. Before you had a headache, did you have an argument with your partner? Were your children acting up? Did you have a difficult time at work? By keeping a record like this, you may identify things that you can change or avoid in your life that will keep the headaches at bay. "You might

---

Fire up your finger

You can out muscle a migraine by merely using your index finger if you master the practice of finger-warming. But this is a mind-over-body exercise that takes some concentration and practice. For headache-free people, the temperature of the index finger is usually around 85°F. But for some reason, people with migraines usually have finger temperatures in the 70° range—a full 15 degrees or so below "normal." If you can raise your finger temperature to 96°, you can "burn off" a migraine, according to Dr. Cady. "About 50 percent of people can reduce the frequency of migraines by 50 percent using this type of temperature biofeedback," says Dr. Cady.

If you want to practice, find a quiet place at home where you can either sit or lie down. Make yourself comfortable, but don't cross your arms or legs, says Dr. Cady. Place an oral thermometer on the fleshiest part of your fingertip and secure it with tape. It should read below 95° when you start. Then:

Close your eyes.

Breathe in slowly, stretching your abdomen so that you suck in breath through your nose. Inhale to a count of four.

Hold your breath for another four seconds.

Exhale through your mouth as you count to eight.

When you breathe in, say to yourself, 'My hand...,' and as you exhale, say, '...is warm,' " says Dr. Cady. While you're doing this exercise, you should make sure that you clear your mind of interfering thoughts or worries and imagine that the sun is beaming heat into your finger. Continue this exercise for 20 to 30 minutes twice a day.

"The goal is to get the temperature to 96° at will," Dr. Cady says. "If they have open minds, most people can start to do this." If you do this twice a day to fend off migraines, within four or five days, you'll begin to see results, he says.

also find that you are not having as many headaches as you think you are; and, if nothing else, keeping a record may make you feel that you are actually doing something about the situation, rather than passively accepting your suffering," says Dr. Wilkinson.

Avoid a pain-pill plethora. Taking too many over-the-counter pain medications for headaches can cause "rebound" headaches. Even if you don't exceed the number of tablets or capsules on the label, they can occur after repeated doses, says Dr. Primavera. He says that three pills a day for a month—100 in all—can trigger rebound headaches. "If you find that you're taking daily analgesics and you're having a daily headache, you may want to check with your doctor as to whether you're heading in the right direction," says Dr. Primavera. That guideline includes any combination of pain relievers, he stresses. "Having aspirin one day, Advil another day, and Tylenol another is only fooling yourself," he says.

Know what to take. "If an attack still comes, take medication early," says J. N. Blau, MD, FRCP, FRCPath, Medical director, City of London Migraine Clinic. You should find out what suits you. "Simple remedies—aspirin, paracetamol, ibuprofen—can be surprisingly effective," says Dr. Blau. "You should also take an anti-emetic (which will help stop nausea and vomiting) such as Motilium (domperidone); drinking something can help, as can eating a little of a carbohydrate food (bread, rice, potatoes)."

Have a denture adjustment. If your bite isn't symmetrical because your dentures are out of alignment, it can cause headache pain by straining jaw and facial muscles, Dr. Kunkel says. "Many older people hate to spend money updating or fixing their dentures but it's really a small investment if it eliminates headaches and improves the quality of your life."

Say yes to sex. Your partner is in an amorous mood, but you feel a migraine coming on? This is no time to say no, urges Roger Cady, MD, director of the Headache Care Centre in Missouri. Satisfying lovemaking is an exercise that Dr. Cady recommends to stop a migraine dead in its tracks—and it might also conquer a tension headache. Enjoyable sex reduces stress and inspires a sense of well-being, he says. It also may elevate your levels of serotonin.

Dim your brights. Bright lights can cause migraine headaches, says Lawrence Robbins, MD, founder of the Robbins Headache Clinic in Northbrook, Illinois, and co-author of *Headache Help*, vouches for it. Since overhead fluorescent lights cause glare, try to use lamps with incandescent bulbs. If you have to contemplate a computer monitor all day long, use a glare screen. And if you wear glasses, choose the kind that darken automatically in bright light.

Ask for acupuncture. Improvement rates of 55-85% have been reported, according to Alexander Mauskop, MD, director of the Downstate Headache Centre in New York.

Get help from homeopathy: If you have an occasional mild headache, Andrew Lockie, MD, recommends the following remedies in his book *The*

Family Guide to Homeopathy. He suggests taking the remedy appropriate for your symptoms every 10 to 15 minutes for up to ten doses.

If the headache comes on suddenly, feels like a tight band is wrapped around your head and is worse in cold air and you feel apprehensive, Dr. Lockie says to try a 30C dose of Aconite. Take a 30C dose of Apis, he says, if your body feels bruised and tender and you have a stinging, stabbing or burning headache that feels worse in hot air. If you have a flushed face, dilated eyes and a throbbing headache that is worse in the hot sun, he recommends a 30C dose of Belladonna. And for a headache that feels like a nail is being driven into your skull, he says to take a 6C dose of Ignatia.

Ease the pain with exercise:

Get off your duff. Some find that exercising when they get a tension headache makes it disappear. Others says that it makes things worse. But if you work out regularly, you may get fewer headaches, says Dr. Primavera. There are several reasons for this. If you're in shape, you have less muscle fatigue and less of the headache-causing tightness in the neck and shoulders that accompanies it. Exercise builds up your cardiovascular system, which tends to slow your pulse. This, in turn, makes your body more resistant against stress, says Dr. Primavera. And being active has a positive effect on levels of serotonin, a neurotransmitter that improves your mood and helps you manage headaches, he says.

Get loose. Try muscle-relaxation therapy, in which you repeatedly tense a group of muscles then let them go. You can do anywhere from 4 to 18 muscle groups, Dr. Arena says. "At the time you do that, you focus in on the difference between the tense state and the relaxed state." Some people eventually advance to the point where they can reach this relaxed state by simply recalling the feeling they got from this exercise rather than actually doing it, making it a technique that can be employed anytime, anywhere, says Dr. Arena.

Hands on help: Use your index finger to apply pressure to the correct acupressure points. According to Dr. Jenny Sutcliffe, the best ones to use are found: between the eyebrows; on either side of the nostrils; on either side where the neck joins the shoulder at the back; in the web between the thumb and index finger; in the depression behind each eyebrow; and just below the base of the skull on either side of the spinal column. Apply firm pressure, but not so much as to cause any discomfort, for about 30 seconds. "Acupressure will not help the root cause of a headache, but it can relieve the pain—and can be performed anywhere, at any time," Dr. Sutcliffe says.

Rub out a tension headache. Feel behind your earlobes for the ridge of bone there and rub—on both sides of your head—for 10 minutes, says Dr. Sheftell, Then do the same with your temples, then the back of the neck. These are major tension spots where muscles tighten and cause headaches.

Give it a pinch. Right at the top of your earlobe, where the fleshy part of your ear meets the harder cartilage, hides the headache ear point for acupressure. Put the forefinger on this point and the thumb behind this ear point and squeeze. For best results, pinch hard enough to experience a "good" hurt—that hot stinging sensation. Squeeze the point firmly for five seconds, then let up for five seconds, says certified acupuncturist Dr. David Nickel. Keep with the five-second intervals for a full minute. Exhale through your mouth as you apply the pressure, and inhale through your nose as you ease off the pressure point. If you pinch correctly, expect to feel headache relief in less than one minute, Dr. Nickel says. If you experience no relief after several minutes, you may want to stop the acupressure and try again later when you might be less tired or hungry, he suggests. If you can't find the exact point, press all over your ear until you hit a tender spot, Dr. Nickel recommends.

Compress your brain. During a headache, you may feel like grabbing your head and squeezing out the pain. That just might help. Pressing against your skull activates several acupressure points that can alleviate headaches. Place your palms on the sides of your skull, says Dr. Michael Reed Gach of the Acupressure Institute. Then gently press inward toward the centre of your head. Press in gradually for several seconds and breathe deeply, he recommends. Keep doing this all around your skull, especially in areas where you feel the most pain.

Point and push. One finger-width above the middle of your eyebrows lies another headache acupressure point, Dr. Gach says. Unlike the firm direct pressure you apply on many acupressure points, be gentle with this one, he advises. Place the tips of your fingers lightly on the point and cover your eyes with your palms. Use a gentle touch instead of pressure and relax your neck, allowing your head to slump forward. "As you breathe deeply, imagine that you are emptying your mind and letting yourself relax," Dr. Gach says. Hold the point for a minute or two.

Grab a handful. This acupressure point is famous for headache relief. You'll find it in the webbing between the thumb and the index finger, at the highest spot of the muscle that protrudes when the thumb and index finger are brought together. Press that point firmly with your thumb on the top of your hand and your finger underneath. Direct the pressure underneath the bone that attaches to your index finger, Dr. Gach says. "This may hurt a bit, but it indicates that you are on the right point," he says. Hold the point for a minute or two on each hand.

Grab a golf ball. Take 30 seconds to roll a golf ball about 50 times along the length of the palmside of one thumb. Then switch thumbs and repeat. Use this technique once an hour while you have a tension headache. Practitioners of reflexology believe that stimulating this area of your thumb relieves muscular tension in your head.

Foods Most Likely to Trigger a Migraine Headache

Ripened cheeses such as Cheddar, Swiss, Stilton, Brie, and Camembert
  Chocolate
Sour cream—no more than a half-cup daily
Nuts and peanut butter
Foods containing monosodium glutamate (MSG) and soy sauce, meat
  tenderisers, and seasoned salt
Citrus fruits—no more than a half-cup daily
A lot of tea, coffee, or colas—no more than two cups daily
Pizza
Cured meats such as sausage, bologna, pepperoni, salami, summer sausage,
  and hot dogs
Alcoholic beverages

Herbal help:

Feed on Feverfew. Don't wait until you're hurting to take feverfew says Dr. Sheftell. This cousin to the dandelion and marigold has been used to prevent headaches of all kinds. But medical doctors took little notice of this folk remedy until 1985. That was the year when a British survey of 270 migraine sufferers found that 70 percent had fewer headaches and less pain when they ate feverfew leaves daily. "It's important to understand that when you use a remedy preventatively, it takes a fair amount of time to evaluate its effectiveness," says Dr. Sheftell. "You need to take 125 milligrams of feverfew everyday for about 6 to 8 weeks."

Try an herbal mix. When your head is in the vice-like grip of a tension headache, take small doses of an herbal supplement that includes a mix of valerian, passion flower and skullcap, says Priscilla Evans, N.D. a naturopathic physician. This trio of herbs can help relax muscles in your shoulders, neck and scalp. "Valerian, is great for relaxing the nervous system, relieving tension and general pain relieving. Passion flower and skullcap help to calm stress," she says.

If you anticipate a stressful period that could trigger a tension headache, these soothing herbs can help minimise the impact. Stick with the manufacturer's recommendations if you choose a ready-mixed supplement. A typical recommendation would be to take 225 milligrams with meals or water twice a day. If you're using a tincture that combines the three herbs, take 10 drops three to four times per day, says Dr. Evans.

Sip some rosemary. "A good herbal preventive for some vasoconstrictive migraines is rosemary," says Lisa Alschuler, N.D., a naturopathic physician. "Like ginkgo, it helps keep blood vessels dilated." Try sipping one cup of rosemary infusion daily. Use 1 teaspoon of herb per cup, Dr. Alschuler advises.

Grab ginkgo and go. As an alternative to the rosemary tea, try ginkgo. This herb improves blood supply to the brain, helps maintain vascular tone, and keeps the blood vessels from leaking inflammatory chemicals, according to herbalists. Therefore, it helps prevent the initial vasoconstriction and ischemia (blood deficiency) that can occur in classical migraines, says Tieraona Low Dog, MD, a physician. Ginkgolides, substances present in the plant, also block inflammation and allergic responses, which can contribute to headaches, she says. In one study, ginkgo reduced headaches in 80 percent of the people who took it, most of whom were having migraines regularly. They had tried everything possible for their headaches, but nothing worked until they tried ginkgo. For migraine prevention, Dr. Alschuler recommends gingko taken as standardised extract capsules, 40 milligrams per capsule. two or three times a day. Ginkgo has been shown to have potentially harmful interactions with some pharmaceutical drugs (MAO inhibitors), and should never be used with aspirin or other non-steroidal anti-inflammatory medicines.

Make ginger part of your plan. "Ginger inhibits a substance called thromboxane A2, which prevents the release of substances that make blood vessels dilate," says Dr. Low Dog. In other words, it can help keep blood flowing on an even keel, which is essential in migraine prevention. Ginger is tasty and versatile: To prevent migraines, you can grate fresh ginger into juice, nosh on Japanese pickled ginger (available at health food stores), use fresh or powdered ginger when you cook, or nibble a piece or two of crystallised ginger candy every day, suggests Dr. Low Dog.

Mind over malady:

Seek out the classics. Mozart's music may be able to send your headache away, says Don Campbell of the Mozart Effect Resource Centre. Campbell tells the story of a woman with severe headaches who was desperate for relief. At the instruction of a music therapist, she began listening to Mozart's Symphony no. 39 in E-flat and Symphony no. 12 in A Major. After listening to the music for awhile, her headaches went away, he says. "For stress-related headaches, music is a great complementary therapy, when used as an adjunct to your traditional headache remedies." Experiment to find music that is soothing to you. The music should be soft, quiet, and melodious, he adds.

Turn down the bass. Maybe you love to crank up the bass on your stereo system. If you are, that's not helping your headache at all. Your head is doing enough throbbing without you adding a pounding beat. "A strong pounding beat will exaggerate and amplify a headache because it will literally cause your heart to pump harder, thereby pumping more blood into the brain, making your headache worse," says Dr. Steven Halpern of Inner Peace Music. Lay off the bass and listen to some softer, slower soothing music, he advises.

Heartburn

The pain: It's a burning, painful feeling that occurs behind your breastbone, usually an hour or two after eating. It can be felt as high up as in the jaws and the back of the throat, resulting in hoarseness, and can even radiate into the arms and back.

The cause: The flame to blame is stomach acid, which enters into the oesophagus via the lower oesophageal sphincter at the top of the stomach. When things go awry, this muscular valve—which normally opens and shuts to let food pass—can reopen, allowing acid to shoot upward. Some contributing factors are high-fat and spicy foods, including chocolate, peppermint, and garlic; certain medications, such as aspirin; smoking; beverages that contain carbonation, caffeine, or alcohol; and hiatal hernia. Other possible causes include stress, age, and poor digestion.

You may also have chronic heartburn because you've been infected with Helicobacter pylori, the same bacteria that contribute to stomach ulcers. People are also more prone to heartburn if they take medications that affect the muscles of the oesophagus or have a physical condition, such as a hiatal hernia, that is a contributing factor. Whatever the source of the problem, the mucous membranes of your oesophagus are probably inflamed and irritated, says Melissa Metcalfe, N.D., a naturopathic doctor.

See a doctor if:

...your heartburn occurs three or four times a week. Occasional heartburn is not serious. However, chronic, severe heartburn is a symptom of a reflux problem, meaning that stomach acid is regularly flowing upward, often due to a faulty oesophageal sphincter. Reflux can result in complications such as bleeding, shortness of breath, difficulty swallowing, and even weight loss. Self-treating this condition long-term also can mask more serious problems, namely, cancer of the oesophagus, says Norman J. Goldberg, MD, professor of medicine at the University of California.

...you have risk factors for a heart attack, like obesity, a family history of heart problems high blood pressure or diabetes. Your doctor will want to be sure your symptoms aren't caused by heart disease.

...you have unusual pain around the heart or pain accompanied by

nausea, vomiting, weakness breathlessness, fainting or sweating. You may be having a heart attack. Head to the emergency room if you're unsure.

Medication: A number of medications can kick your stomach's acid production into high gear. These include aspirin, other nonsteroidal anti-inflammatory painkillers, certain heart and blood pressure medications and asthma medication. If you suffer from recurring heartburn, make a list of all prescription and over-the-counter drugs you are currently taking and show it to your doctor.

Quick relief:

Chew some gum. Chewing gum can provide quick, temporary relief of heartburn, says Dr. Goldberg. Chewing gum causes you to create saliva. And saliva is alkaline-based, which neutralises acid. In addition, saliva contains a hormone called epidermal growth factor, which helps heal the oesophageal lining. So you decrease acid and patch up the damage. Just steer clear of peppermint-flavoured gum. Peppermint will make heartburn worse because it lowers the pressure in the lower oesophageal sphincter and allows acid reflux into the oesophagus, explains Dr. Goldberg. Chocolate and alcohol have the same effect, he adds.

Pop an antacid. Yes, it's painfully obvious, but taking an antacid makes sense because it contains chemicals that neutralise acid instantaneously, says Edwin J. Zarling, MD, an associate professor of medicine. Chilled liquid antacids are best for a soothing, throat-coating result.

Be aware, however, that the four types of antacids (grouped by active ingredients) have their own unique side effects, says Dr. Goldberg. Magnesium salts are more likely to cause diarrhoea and should not be taken by people with kidney disease. Aluminium salts can trigger constipation and can weaken bones with overuse. Calcium salts such as Tums can lead to kidney stones if taken long-term. And some sodium salts that contain aspirin, can cause stomach irritation.

Quench the fire. Drinking an eight-ounce glass of water may bring temporary relief, Dr. Goldberg says. "Water can wash acid back down the oesophagus and dilute the acid in the stomach," he explains. But since water absorbs quickly in the stomach, don't expect this relief to last long. This is best used to buy yourself some time until the antacid kicks in.

Loosen up. Relief may be as easy as loosening your belt a notch. Wearing pants that are too tight can create the abdominal pressure that can aggravate your heartburn, says M. Michael Wolfe, MD, a gastroenterologist. When you exercise, for instance, you might want to trade in your tight-fitting spandex pants for a pair of looser-fitting sweats.

Nutritional remedies:

Pick up a papaya. The tropical fruit contains papain, an enzyme that soothes the stomach. If fresh papaya isn't available, try chewable papaya tablets, available at health food stores.

Don't be fooled by milk. The worst thing you can do for heartburn is drink a glass of milk before bedtime, Dr. Goldberg says. Sure, milk neutralises acid when you take it, but during the night, it produces more acid. "So you wake up two to three hours after you go to bed with intense heartburn from that glass of milk," he says.

Sip soy. Unlike cow's milk, soy milk can soothe heartburn without making it worse hours later, says Steven Bailey, a naturopathic doctor. Mix 2 tablespoons chlorophyll (found at health food stores) with ½ cup soy milk, and drink it slowly. You can do this two to four times a day for up to two weeks, says Dr. Bailey. If you haven't gotten relief from your heartburn after those two weeks, you should see a doctor, he advises. And if you're allergic to soy, you should not try this remedy, he adds.

Helpful vitamins and supplements:

Go for glutamine. Another healing substance for damaged mucous membranes is glutamine, an amino acid that's available as a nutritional supplement. Dr. Metcalfe frequently recommends it for gastrointestinal disorders whenever inflammation is a problem.

Glutamine encourages the turnover or disposal of damaged cells, and it increases the production of new cells along the gastrointestinal walls, says Dr. Metcalfe. It's also a potent antioxidant, helping to protect cells from the damage caused by free-roaming, unstable molecules called free radicals. All of these actions equate with faster healing, she says. "I tell people to take one 500-milligram capsule four times a day until they are feeling better," says Dr. Metcalfe. "Usually, that's about a month."

Everyday prevention:

Lie on the left. If you must lie down after a big meal, try lying on your left side. Researcher speculate that lying on the right side puts the junction of the stomach and oesophagus lower than the gastric pool in the stomach, making it easier for acid to seep into the oesophagus.

Outsmart gravity. If you must lie down within several hours of eating, raise the head of your bed. Prop six-inch blocks under the headboard bed legs or place a foam, triangular-shape wedge under your shoulders, says Philip Katz, MD, director of the Comprehensive Chest Pain and Swallowing Centre at Allegheny University. But don't use pillows to prop yourself up. "Often, people end up with the pillows under their heads, not their shoulders. So they don't get the elevation they need," Dr. Katz says. If sleeping in chairs has become a habit to get relief at night, he warns, it's time to see your doctor.

Eat light. A very full stomach increases incidence of heartburn, probably by forcing the lower oesophageal sphincter open, Dr. Katz says. So keep portions small. In fact, you shouldn't eat anything within two to three hours of going to sleep.

Tune out stress. So many people eat in front of the TV or discuss problems at the dinner table, creating a nervous stomach and, as a result, heartburn, says Dr. Bailey. To control your postmeal outcome, declare dinnertime a stress-free zone by eating slowly in a pleasant atmosphere and listening to relaxing music, he suggests.

Eat slowly. If you eat more slowly, you are likely to eat less. To reduce the gulp factor, get a pair of chopsticks. Unless you're an accomplished user, they'll slow you down. Plus, your new skill will impress your friends the next time you go for Chinese food.

Chew completely. When your stomach receives partially chewed food, it has to secrete more acid to break it up for digestion. If you become a master masticator, you cut the acid level.

Eat no chocolate, drink no brews. The road to heartburn is almost always paved with alcohol, chocolate, fatty foods, mint and coffee (even decaffeinated coffees contain irritants that can affect your stomach and oesophagus), says gastroenterologist Grace Elta, MD. All are capable of weakening the lower oesophageal sphincter.

Pregnant? Skip spicy seasonings. Spicy seasonings are hard to digest, says Jennifer Niebyl, MD, obstetrics and gynaecology specialist. And when you're pregnant, the increase in the hormone progesterone slows down your digestion so much that it takes longer to digest a meal. The harder food is to digest, the more likely you are to get heartburn. "So eat bland foods such as rice and bananas and avoid cayenne and other types of chilli peppers," she says. If you're not a pregnant woman, don't worry about spices—the acid in you stomach is much more powerful than anything you can put into it.

Cool the fire with carbo's. Another strategy for stopping heartburn is to eat pasta, rice, potatoes or other foods high in complex carbohydrates, which absorb acid in the stomach.

Quit smoking. In case you needed another reason to avoid cigarettes, keep in mind that smoking inhibits saliva, stimulates stomach acid and relaxes the protective muscle between the oesophagus and stomach.

Herbal help:

Calm with DGL. An excellent herb to soothe those oesophageal tissues is deglycyrrhizinated licorice, or DGL, according to Dr. Metcalfe. For one thing, DGL has antispasmodic action, which means that it helps to control various muscle actions that can affect your digestive tract. The herb also helps reduce acid reflux by calming a cramping stomach, she says.

The primary medicinal benefit of DGL, however, is its ability to increase and build up the protective substances that line the digestive tract. By stimulating the body's natural defence mechanisms, licorice helps prevent the formation of ulcers and lesions due to the irritating acid, says Dr. Metcalfe. It's also a powerful, localised anti-inflammatory.

"It's the first thing I recommend to people—it's a great initial treatment," says Dr. Metcalfe. The typical dose is two 250-milligram capsules taken 20 minutes before mealtime.

Rather than swallowing the DGL with water, Dr. Metcalfe suggests that you suck on the capsules and let them dissolve slowly in your mouth. You can also get DGL in chewable tablets, which dissolve as you chew them. "You want the licorice to coat the inside of your throat and oesophagus to cover those inflamed and irritated tissues," she says.

Use it for four weeks and then assess if it's working, she suggests. If it is, your throat should feel less irritated. If not, see your health-care practitioner.

Gulp some ginger. "When people are travelling and have problems with heartburn, I tell them stop at a supermarket and buy some ginger," says Pamela Taylor, N.D., a naturopathic doctor. You can get either fresh ginger-root in the produce section or the powdered form that's sold as a spice.

Ginger works as an antispasmodic, relaxing the smooth muscle along the walls of the oesophagus, says Dr. Taylor. "If your digestion is working better, you're less likely to get that reflux, or backwash, of stomach acid," she says. "Ginger is an excellent tonic for the whole gastrointestinal tract.

If you're using ginger to prevent heartburn, take it 20 minutes before a meal. You can take it as a capsule, make a tea from the fresh root or the powder, or eat candied or pickled ginger as it comes from the jar. Ginger tincture is also available.

Get homeopathic help. If you have heartburn associated with heaviness after meals, excess wind and a bitter taste in your mouth, try Nux vomica 30C every couple of hours until you feel better, says Chris Melctis, N.D., a naturopathic physician. If food feels stuck behind your breastbone, your tongue is coated and you crave starch foods, try Pulsatilla 30C every two hours, he says. If your heartburn is accompanied by nervousness, tension and pain in the upper abdomen, he suggests Natrum muriaticum 30C every two hours. If you tend to eat to fast and have gurgling and bloating after the meal, he suggests Zinc metallicum 30C every hour or two.

Try an herbal trio. Take marsh mallow root, plantain or slippery elm immediately after each meal. All are available in tablet or tea form. These herbs are demulcents, which means that they coat mucous membranes. This lessens the corrosive effects of stomach acid and promotes healing.

Heel Spurs

The pain: Pain located in the heel of the foot. Pain from heel spurs often hurts when you first get up in the morning, but then eases during the day.

The cause: Heel spurs are bony protrusions on the bottom of the foot, caused by continuous pulling of the ligament that runs across the sole. Runners and others who are hard on their feet are very likely to get them especially if their feet turn in (pronation) when they run. (That excess movement just adds to the ligament pulling.) Those with high arches are also more likely to develop spurs.

See a doctor if:

...you think you may have a spur. "A lot of people think that because they have heel pain, it's a spur," says Terry Spilken, D.P.M., a podiatrist at the New York College of Podiatric Medicine. "But we also have to rule out other conditions such as arthritis and bursitis. The only way to properly diagnose a heel spur is with an x-ray."
...you have persistent pain and swelling, or discolouration.
...you have difficulty standing on the heel
...you experience any significant change in feeling or function
...you have tenderness when you squeeze the heel from the sides.

Easy Remedies:

Try aspirin, acetaminophen or paracetamol. An over-the-counter analgesic, such as aspirin, acetaminophen or paracetamol can alleviate acute pain.
Rest. Even a couple of days of limited movement will help reduce the inflammation around a bone spur.
Don't walk au naturel. "Walking barefoot is the worst thing you can do if you have heel spurs," says William Van Pelt, D.P.M., a podiatrist in Houston and former president of the American Academy of Podiatric Sports Medicine. "Walking barefoot stretches out the ligament on the bottom of the foot even farther, and being barefoot results in a less stable walk."
Wear the footgear of a cowboy. Instead, you should wear a shoe with a 3/4 to 1 1/2-inch heel, like a cowboy boot. That's because the heel shifts weight forward, taking some pressure off the heel.

Enlist sponge rubber support. Over-the-counter arch supports and heel cups, which are sold at chemists and sporting goods stores, help those with heel spurs in two ways: "They support the arch, which controls excess foot rolling or movement, and they help elevate the heel a bit, which takes some of the pressure off the spur," says Dr. Van Pelt. He recommends that you first try a pair of sponge rubber arch supports. If they don't bring relief, try a heel cup.

Give yourself a massage. "A regular massage of your entire foot, and particularly the heel, also helps a lot," says Dr. Spilken. The best way to do the massage? "Rub across the aching area with your thumb in order to get more pressure."

Apply ice for pain. When your heel spur is acting up, apply an ice pack wrapped in a towel to stop the pain, advises Dr. Spilken. Keep it under ice for ten minutes, then remove the pack for another ten. Repeat this procedure several times, or until the throbbing subsides.

Use heat for maintenance. Doctors recommend applying heat on a daily basis in order to bring more blood to the area and break up inflammation. A 15-or 20-minute session with a heating pad is usually enough.

Stretch your calf. Stretching your heel cord or Achilles tendon at the back of the foot can reduce or relieve heel pain, says Michael Steinbaum, D.P.M., a podiatrist. To stretch, stand about three feet from a wall and place your hands on the wall. Then lean towards the wall, bringing one leg forward and bending at the elbows. Your back leg should remain straight, with the heel on the floor. Hold for 20 to 30 seconds. You should feel a gentle stretch in the calf muscles on your back leg. Then switch legs.

Hiccups

The pain: Quick but not necessarily painful contractions of the diaphragm, the dome-shaped muscle between your stomach and your lungs, forcing you to inhale suddenly making the characteristic "hic" sound.

The cause: Hiccups may be the result of overeating, swallowing too much air or drinking carbonated beverages, all of which distend your stomach and irritate your diaphragm. This seems to stimulate the nerves—especially the vagus nerve—that run between the diaphragm and some sort of "hiccup centre" in the brain. Activated, these nerves instruct the diaphragm to contract quickly.

See a doctor if:
...hiccups last several days without improvement.
...you have bouts of hiccups several times a day or several days a week..
...you also have chest pain, heartburn or difficulty swallowing.

Quick relief:
Drink up. Drink something non-carbonated and non-alcoholic as shortly after the hiccups start as possible. Drink as quickly as you can. Some find this remedy works best if they plug both ears with their fingers and drink through a straw. Bartenders suggest guzzling a glass of water with a metal spoon in it.

Hear no evil. If there's nothing handy to drink, try simply plugging your ears with your fingers for about 20 seconds. This remedy has been reported in the medical journal *Lancet*.

Take a deep breath, bear down, and push. Pretend you're going to have a bowel movement. This stimulates the vagus nerve, which connects the diaphragm to the brain. (You may want to hover near a toilet when trying this.)

Rub your eyes. Again, it's a vagus-nerve stimulator.

Puff out your stomach. Change your breathing pattern, suggests Greg Grillone, MD, assistant professor of otolaryngology, head and neck surgery, at Boston University School of Medicine. Inhale slowly and deeply, expanding your diaphragm so that your stomach pushes out. Then exhale slowly and completely, contracting your diaphragm so that your stomach flattens.

Drink upside down. Bend your head over a glass of water and sip from the far side of the glass.

Squeeze it. Try pulling your knees up to your chest and compressing your chest.

Hold it. Your breath, that is. Hold it as long as you can.

Touch your throat. It's another way to stimulate the vagus nerve. Stick your fingers in the back of your throat and wiggle them. A variation is to use a cotton swab instead of you fingers (be careful not to swallow the swab) or lift the uvula (that little "punching bag" that hangs at the back of you throat) with a spoon. Another variation is to tickle the roof your mouth with the swab.

Yank your tongue. Grab your tongue and pull firmly. This also stimulates the vagus nerve. Sometimes just sticking your tongue out will do the trick.

Breathe in a bag. When you breathe into a paper bag, you end up inhaling a fair amount of carbon dioxide along with your customary oxygen. High CO_2 in your blood will trigger deep breathing, which may stop hiccups. Don't overdo it—try it sitting down, and stop if you start feeling light headed or notice tingling in your lips or fingers.

Get alarmed. When someone scares you, you hold your breath momentarily, forcing your diaphragm to go rigid and perhaps short-circuiting hiccups.

Nutritional remedies:

Swallow some sugar. Anywhere from a teaspoon to a tablespoon of sugar swallowed dry seems to help some people. (Hard candy can be a substitute if there's no sugar around.) The opposite approach—a spoonful of pickle juice, lemon juice, vinegar or another sour or bitter substance—is also a popular remedy. Strong tastes of either kind seem to shock the diaphragm's nerves out of their spasm.

Everyday Prevention:

Put your fork in first gear. Eating too fast causes you to swallow air, which may irritate the diaphragm, the all-encompassing umbrella of muscle that is under the lungs and above the cavity that houses your stomach, intestines, and other organs. When the diaphragm gets irritated, it goes into a spasm, which sets off the hiccups. The slower you eat, the less likely hiccuping will occur. "Slow down at meals by chewing thoroughly and carefully," says Jack A. DiPalma, MD, a gastroenterologist.

Constrain your sipping. Another way to break the back of hiccups is with a straw. If you have had frequent, long bouts of hiccups and you want to make sure it doesn't happen again, take along extra straws wherever you go and always use one when you drink cold beverages. A straw helps because it limits the amount of air you swallow.

Hold the bubbles. Soda and beer can spark a bout of hiccups because the carbonation sets off those unwanted diaphragm spasms. "Carbonated beverages that are cold are the worst," says Dr. DiPalma. So if you need a soda now and then, let it warm up a bit. And skip the ice.

Go for "just right." Any food or drink that is too hot or too cold can set off a bout of hiccups because foods at extreme temperatures stimulate irritation. For smoother, hic-free dining, let that piping-hot casserole down a few minutes.

Don't plump up. Overeating may cause a bout of hiccups by irritating the diaphragm. Never eat to the point where you feel too full, says Dr. DiPalma.

Be a teetotaller. Cartoon characters like Andy Capp always go "hic" when they are drunk. In real life, some people start hiccuping at the first sip of alcohol. "If you find that you have bouts of hiccups when you drink that are protracted, I would recommend abstinence from alcohol," says Dr. DiPalma.

Keep your lungs open. Smoking can cause hiccups if you are prone to them because it causes you to swallow air, and nicotine is an irritant which lowers the pressure of the esophageal sphincter. The esophageal sphincter is the muscle, linking the oesophagus to the stomach, that keeps stomach acid from coming back up into the oesophagus. It is not the prime reason to stop smoking, of course, but certainly a side benefit of stopping.

Check your meds. If you have started to take a new medicine and notice that you are hiccuping a lot more, you may be suffering from a minor-league side effect. If you think a medication is making you hiccup, ask your doctor about prescribing an alternative.

Hands-on help:

Press the point. Pressing firmly against the following acupressure points may stop the hics: in the indentation behind each earlobe, at the base of the throat in the centre of the collarbone, on the centre of the breastbone three thumb-widths up from the base of the bone, or the middle joint of your pinkie finger.

Mind over malady:

Tease your brain. There's some evidence that intensely focusing on a task is an effective remedy. Try to list the names of ten bald men, or try to remember the last time you saw a white horse.

Follow the sign. Close your eyes and picture a neon sign, like a theatre marquee, with the word "Think" blinking on and off. Concentrate on the sign and make it blink as intensely as possible, and your hiccups may vanish, says Dennis Gersten, MD, a San Diego psychiatrist and publisher of *Atlantis*, a bimonthly imagery newsletter, who first used this remedy when he was a child. "The technique has never failed me in my entire life," he says.

Hip Pain

The pain: Pain at the hip joint.

The cause: The origin of pain in the hip area is often complex. Its most common cause is osteoarthritis, the wearing down of the cartilage cushion between the ball and socket of the joint. But hip pain is sometimes caused by strained (or pulled) muscles. It can also stem from malfunctioning tendons in nearby parts of the body—the lower back, the buttocks, and the upper legs. A bad fall or a blow to the knee can cause the hip joint to dislocate. To complicate matters, most of your body's large muscle groups span your hips. That means the pain you feel may come not from the hip joints but from the spine, lower back, buttocks, or some other location.

See a doctor if:
...the hip pain is severe.
...the pain intensifies during or after exercise.
...the pain radiates from the buttock area down to the leg.
...the pain persists and is not relieved with rest, ice, or over-the-counter pain relievers.
...the pain keeps you up at night.
...the pain keeps you from bearing weight on the hip.
...the pain persists or gets worse after an injury, even a minor one.
...you also have open sores on your feet, or leg pain.

Quick relief:
Go polar. Ice is the first line of defence against hip pain, says John Cianca, MD, an assistant professor of physical medicine and rehabilitation. His suggestion is to "crush some ice and place it in a resealable storage bag, so it has a greater surface area. Lay a thin towel over your hip, then apply the ice at the site of pain for 15 minutes." If your pain is acute—caused by an injury, for example—you may need to reapply the ice as often as once every hour, Dr. Cianca says. But for chronic pain such as arthritis, once or twice a day may be enough.
Change the temperature. After 48 hours of cold treatment, start using heat instead, says Ramon Jimenez, MD, chief of staff at O'Connor Hospital in California, and president of the California Orthopedic Association. A

heating pad on a low to medium setting will do. "But don't fall asleep on it," he warns. You can also try soaking in a hot tub if you have access to one. "Keep the water in the 90 degree range," Dr. Jimenez advises. "Ideally, the water temperature shouldn't exceed your body temperature.

Smooth on a deep-heating ointment. Both the ointment itself and the soothing rub will ease tight hip muscles. Try Ben-Gay, Flex-all 454, Eucalyptamint, Radian-B or Deep Heat, available at chemists. Never use menthol-containing ointments with a heating pad, however, as serious burns may result.

Take a tablet. An over-the-counter pain reliever such as ibuprofen, acetaminophen or paracetamol can help a hurting hip, Dr. Jimenez says. "But if the dosage recommended on the label doesn't do the trick, alert your doctor," Dr. Cianca adds. "Something more serious may be going on."

Everyday prevention:

Be reasonable. Don't place too many demands on an aching hip, Dr. Jimenez cautions. In general, he says, stay away from any activity that aggravates your pain. You may have to drive to work instead of walking, or take the elevator instead of bounding up three flights of stairs—at least for the time being.

Get some support. "If you can't walk without limping, then use crutches or a cane," advises William S. Case, president of Case Physical Therapy in Houston. When you try to avoid bearing weight on your sore hip, you can easily strain muscles and tendons in other areas.

If you opt for a cane, Dr. Jimenez reminds you to use proper technique: Carry the cane in the hand opposite the injured hip. Move it forward at the same time you step out with the injured hip, so you're bearing weight on both the good hip and the cane. Then step out with your "good" hip. And be sure the cane's the right size, suggests Earl Marmar, MD, an orthopedic surgeon. "If Grandpa's cane from Ireland is the wrong size for you, it will increase your hip pain," he says. Ask your doctor to refer you to a medical supply store where you can be properly measured.

Be patient. If you have an injury, it's going to take a while for your hip to heal, especially if you have injured a muscle. "If you pull a hamstring muscle (located in the back of either thigh), it can take 6 to 10 weeks to get better," Dr. Jimenez notes.

Ready, set ... slow. Once you have recovered enough to bear weight on your hip, make a gradual return to your usual routine. "Give yourself time," advises Phillip A. Bauman, MD, clinical instructor in orthopedic surgery. "Don't fall into the trap of doing too much too soon."

Sleep in comfort. Avoid lying on the painful hip. And for softer support, use a foam egg crate mattress over your regular mattress.

Walk in the right shoes. Buy running shoes for walking—not walking or aerobic or cross-training shoes. Running shoes are extra light and specially designed to increase stability of the foot, says Bill Arnold, MD, rheumatologist.

Lose some weight. It's easy to overlook as a cause, but excess body weight can greatly increase hip pain, says Dr. Marmar. Every time you take a step, two to three times your body weight goes through the hip in terms of the pressure exerted on the joint," he explains. "Each pound lost represents two to three pounds less pressure on your hip."

Pinpoint your pain. If you do go to your doctor for hip pain, be prepared to talk about exactly where it hurts and when. Tell your doctor what kind of pain you're experiencing—whether it's dull or sharp, whether it comes or goes, whether it hurts more when you're moving or still, and what kinds of movements seem to make it worse.

Examine your architecture. If a curved spine or slightly shorter leg has altered your gait, you may be unaware of it. Here's a home test from Sidney Block, MD, a rheumatologist: Stand undressed with your back to a mirror and a hand mirror angled over your shoulder so you can see yourself from the rear. Or ask a family member to look at you from the rear. If the height of your knees seems unequal, if your pelvis seems titled downward in one direction or if your back looks curved, you may have discovered the problem.

Fortunately, your gait is correctable-usually quite easily. You may need a prescription shoe lift or just an over-the-counter lift inside one shoe, Dr. Block says. If the difficulty is severe, your doctor will refer you to an orthopedist or orthotist (a physical therapist who specialises in braces, special shoes and other appliances).

Easing the pain with exercise:

Make a marriage proposal. The position for this hip flexor stretch, recommended by Thomas Meade, MD, an orthopedic surgeon looks as if you're about to "pop the question" to your sweetheart. Stretching—elongating the muscles—helps relax muscles and improve flexibility.

Kneel on your left knee. Bend your right knee and keep your right foot flat on the floor in front of your body. Put your hands on your hips or rest your right hand on your right knee and let the other hang by your side. Tighten your abdominal muscles and lean slightly forward without arching your back. You should feel a stretch in the front of your left thigh. Hold for 20 seconds. Repeat three more times and then switch legs.

Push away. For variety, try this other stretching exercise recommended by Dr. Meade to relax and improve flexibility in your hip rotator muscles.

Lie on your back with your knees bent and your feet flat on the floor. To keep your neck from arching, place a pillow under your head.

Place your left ankle on top of your right knee. Keep your lower back flat on the floor as you use your left hand to gently push your left knee down toward the floor. You should feel the stretch in the buttocks area. Hold this stretch for 20 seconds, then repeat three times. Switch legs and repeat.

Kick a game-winning field goal. To strengthen the flexor muscles in front of your hip as well as the thigh, hamstring, and buttock muscles, try a little slo-mo air football, says Dr. Ciccotti.

Stand next to a countertop or sturdy railing and hold on with your left hand. Keeping your supporting left leg straight and your foot flat on the floor, raise your right leg as high as you can in front of your body. Hold that pose for no longer than a second before letting your leg fall and slowly swing behind your body as far as possible without straining. Hold the position for no more than a second, then swing back to the starting position, as if you were kicking a football in slow motion. Try 10 swings before switching to the left leg. By trying to raise your leg higher on each end of the swing, you can increase your range of motion, says Dr. Ciccotti.

Squat down. This do-anywhere exercise helps strengthen the front hip, front thigh, and buttocks muscles, says Dr. Meade. Stand with both feet flat on the floor hip-width apart. Cross your arms over your chest and face straight ahead, then slowly squat until your thighs are parallel to the floor. Try to keep your torso straight and your knees directly over your toes. Hold the squat for a couple of seconds and then stand up. Try 10 squats twice a day.

Try water wading. To strengthen arthritic hips without jarring pain from pavement, Dr. Jane Katz recommends walking chest-high in some H2O. Start off slowly by marching in place, raising your knees high as if you were leading the high school band onto the football field at halftime. Slowly pick up speed throughout your workout. Do this for one minute and follow it with a minute of rest, then do another minute of stepping followed by rest. Over time, work up to three minutes of continuous exercise.

Strike a pose. Yoga can also enhance hip flexibility, says Arthur H. Brownstein, MD, a physician. He recommends this simple pose: Sit on the floor and place the soles of your feet together. Pull your feet in, as close to the groin as comfortable. Then let gravity pull your knees toward the floor. If this position is uncomfortable at first, he suggests modifying it slightly by bending only one leg at a time and keeping the other leg extended. Hold the pose for 15 seconds. Repeat three times.

Hands on help:

Press the point. Using your index and middle fingers of each hand, press on either side of your tailbone, about where the crease in your buttocks begins. These points can relieve hip pain.

Hives

The pain: Red, intensely itchy bumps, which may also burn or sting.

The cause: Hives form when a trigger—often something you're allergic to, but not always—sends a flood of immune substances known as mast cells coursing through your blood vessels, squirting an inflammatory substance called histamine into your cells. Histamine makes blood vessels leak fluid, forming the red, itchy bump that you see and feel as a hive. Medications are the number one cause of hives. According to the American Academy of Allergy, Asthma, and Immunology, food is often a trigger. Even exercise or a hot shower can bring on a case of hives. Usually hives go away within a few days to a few weeks, but occasionally, a person will continue to have hives for many years.

Medication: If you're allergic to it, almost any prescription or over-the-counter medication can trigger hives, says Jonathan Weiss, MD, a dermatologist. If an outbreak occurs, cast a suspicious eye on any new drugs that you've just started taking.

See a doctor if:
...you get hives in your mouth or throat. Call an emergency number immediately. For people who have severe hives, most doctors will prescribe medication to have on hand for emergencies.
...you have hives that last longer than six weeks or cause intense discomfort.

Quick relief:
Alleviate with an antihistamine. An over-the-counter antihistamine, can reduce the itch and inflammation of hives and keep them from getting worse, says Dr. Weiss. If this method does not control symptoms, a visit to your dermatologist or primary care physician is necessary. He recommends 25 milligrams of Benadryl up to four times per day. Since Benadryl tends to make you sleepy, Dr. Weiss suggests taking a dose at bedtime so you can get the medication's full therapeutic effects without daytime drowsiness.
Keep cool. Heat of any kind makes hives worse. So until your hives subside, you'll be more comfortable if you keep as cool as possible, says

Helen Hollingsworth, MD, associate professor of medicine at Boston University School of Medicine

But stay comfortably warm. Some people break out in hives when any part of their bodies—skin, mouth or throat—is exposed to a sudden drop in temperature of 30 degrees F or more. You can test yourself by putting an ice cube on your forearm for 15 to 20 minutes, then remove it. If cold is a trigger, the hive will pop 10-15 minutes after you have removed the cube. People for whom cold is a trigger should not eat ice-cold food or drinks. The soft tissue of their throats can swell and block their airways. And they should never jump into a cold swimming pool. The sudden release of histamine from contact with the cold water can be so severe it can also cause anaphylactic shock, a body-wide swelling that can also lead to asphyxiation.

Chill the area. If you get hives from cold weather or cold water, you'll want to skip this next tip. But for most hive sufferers, ice and cold compresses are about the best thing you can put on your hives, says Paul Greenberger, MD, professor of medicine in the Division of Allergy and Immunology at Northwestern University Medical School.

Moisturise your skin. Dry skin tends to cause itching, which can irritate hives and make them worse. If your skin tends to be dry, apply a moisturiser to the area around the hives, says Dr. Hollingsworth.

Soak in an oatmeal bath. To relieve the itchiness of hives, add Aveeno brand colloidal oatmeal (an over-the-counter bath powder available at your local chemist) to a tub full of lukewarm water. It stays suspended in water, so it won't clog your drain. Soak for 10-15 minutes. Avoid using hot water, since it might make hives worse.

Add something alkaline. "Anything that's alkaline usually helps relieve the itch," says Leonard Grayson, MD, an allergist and dermatologist. So try dabbing milk of magnesia on your hives. "It's thinner than calamine lotion, so I think it works better," he says.

Helpful vitamins and supplements:

Try vitamin C and quercitin. If hives linger or return, supplement your diet with 1,000 milligrams of vitamin C, three times a day. Or, if you suspect that the hives are triggered by food, take 250 milligrams of quercitin (often combined with vitamin C in capsules) 20 minutes before each meal. Its antihistamine action may help reduce the hives.

Everyday prevention:

Track the cause. The best long-term treatment for hives is to find and remove the cause of these annoying, itchy bumps, says Dr. Greenberger. But this isn't always an easy task. Since so many different things can trigger hives, Dr. Greenberger suggests compiling a list of every medication and food item you've swallowed in the four hours before an outbreak. Jot down any temperature extremes, anything that may have put physical pressure on your body (like a tight waistband), and note whether or not you exercised.

Rule it out. Once you think you've spotted a cause, try to eliminate it. If you're not sure what caused your hives after you have tried to eliminate it, you should see a doctor, recommends Dr. Greenberger. If you think a type of food is the culprit, stop eating it and see if the hives clear. Herbs and food additives may also bring on hives, so unless you're sure you won't have a reaction to them, make sure that they are on your suspect list. Once you've pinpointed the offending food, you should refrain from eating even a small portion, says Dr. Greenberger. A tiny amount can cause a flare-up. If the hives started just after taking a new medication, talk to your doctor about a substitute. You may be able to determine the cause this way and put an end to the misery, says Dr. Greenberger.

Watch your diet. Be cautious about eating tomato sauce, citrus, strawberries, and shellfish while you have hives, advises Dr. Hollingsworth. No one knows why, but these foods frequently aggravate hives. Cow's milk, eggs, fish, shellfish, peanuts, soy protein, legumes, wheat, and tree nuts such as walnuts and hazelnuts can worsen hives, too, says Dr. Greenberger.

Wear the right clothes. Pressure generated by tight shoes and tight clothes are known to cause hives and that pressure may aggravate and worsen a case of hives that's already going. So be particularly careful to wear loose clothing and properly fitted shoes when you have hives, warns Dr. Hollingsworth. Wash new clothes before you wear them to avoid hive-causing chemicals in fabrics. Use mild, unscented detergents to wash clothes, and don't use softener sheets in the dryer.

Block the sun. People with hives triggered by the ultraviolet radiation of sunlight should be certain to always wear a sunscreen. Wearing the right sunscreen to block your trigger (UVA, UVB or both—your dermatologist can test you) may prevent these hives from appearing.

Herbal Remedies:

Seek out stinging nettle. This plant that will produce a hive if its hairs inject their histamine into you. But Andrew Weil, MD, an herb advocate and author of *Natural Health, Natural Medicine,* suggests using freeze-dried nettle leaf extract to treat hives and allergies. This might sound illogical, but the plant apparently doesn't contain enough histamine to be a problem when it's taken orally, and it does contain substances that help heal hives. Stinging nettle is sold in capsules in health food stores. Dr. Weil suggests taking one or two every two to four hours, as needed.

Pick up some parsley. One scientific study showed that parsley inhibits the secretion of histamine. If you have hives, try juicing some parsley and adding it to some other vegetable juice, such as carrot or tomato, to make it more palatable.

Get aid from amaranth. A tea made with amaranth seeds makes a good wash for hives, eczema and psoriasis, according to the widely travelled medical anthropologist John Heinerman, Ph.D., author of *Heinerman's*

Encyclopedia of Fruits, Vegetables and Herbs and many other books relating to healing with herbs and foods. To make this tea, add two teaspoons of amaranth seeds to three cups of boiling water and let it steep for 10 to 20 minutes.

Get better with ginger. When Canadian herbalist Terry Willard, president of the Canadian Association of Herbal Practitioners and author of *Textbook of Modem Herbology*, developed hives as a result of a food allergy, he simmered a half-pound of ginger in a gallon of water in a big pot for five minutes and added the resulting brew to a hot bath. After steeping himself for a while, he sponged off with camomile tea (one teaspoon in one cup of boiling water). "It worked every time," he says.

Add assorted essential oils. Aromatherapists suggest using camomile oil to treat hives: Place a drop or two directly on your hives and massage it in. Speaking of essential oils, the oils of caraway, clove and lemon balm (also known as melissa) are all antihistaminic, according to pharmacognosist (natural product pharmacist) Albert Leung, Ph.D. Mixing a few drops of each of these into a couple of ounces of vegetable oil will result in a soothing ointment that might help relieve itching. Just remember not to ingest essential oils, as even a small amount may be toxic.

Soothe with mint. Cornmint or peppermint, taken as a tea or wash, might help in treating hives. Menthol, one of the ingredients in mints, has been shown to have itch-relieving action.

Hot Flushes

The pain: Menopause-associate sensations of heat, which can range from brilliant red blushes to night sweats that bounce you out of bed.

The cause: We don't really know what causes hot flushes (sometimes called hot flashes), but we do know that as many as 65 to 80 percent of women will experience them at some point during their transition to menopause. One theory implicates an instability in the way the body regulates heat when your hormone balance is in flux. Another suggests that hormonal changes irritate blood vessels and nerves, causing the blood vessels to overdilate and produce a hot feeling. Whatever the cause, they're unpredictable and uncomfortable.

See a doctor if:
...your hot flushes become so frequent or severe that they disrupt your daily routine.
...night sweats continue for several weeks and you are having trouble sleeping as a result.

Quick relief:
Practice deep breathing. In one study, women who had been having 20 or more hot flushes a day reduced that number by half with the help of deep breathing. This technique seems to short-circuit the arousal of the central nervous system that normally occurs in the initial stages of a hot flash. When you feel a hot flash creeping up on you, prepare for deep breathing by sitting up straight and loosening your belt or waistband if it feels tight. Be in by exhaling through your nose longer than you normally would. Then inhale through your nose slowly and deeply, filling your lungs from the bottom up while keeping your belly relaxed. When your chest is fully expanded, exhale slowly and deeply, as if sighing. Continue this pattern of inhaling and exhaling until the hot flash subsides.
Keep ice handy. Keep a carafe of ice water on your night table, and when night sweats strike, sip as needed.

Nutritional remedies:
Fill up on phytoestrogens. The right diet is the starting point for all

women approaching menopause. "Along with a good exercise plan, the correct diet may be all that some women, who have minor menopausal symptoms and low risk factors for heart disease and osteoporosis, need to take," says Tori Hudson, N.D., professor at the National College of Naturopathic Medicine. Your diet should be very low in animal fat and high in good sources of phytoestrogens, says Dr. Hudson. Foods high in phytoestrogens include soy products (look for soy foods that are made from soy flour and whole soy rather than those made from isolated soy proteins), nuts, whole grains, apples, alfalfa, flaxseed, and rye. In addition, foods from the Umbelliferous family, such as celery, parsley, and especially fennel, contain active phytoestrogens, says Dr. Hudson. A diet high in phytoestrogens is thought to be the reason that hot flushes and other menopausal symptoms rarely occur among women who eat mostly vegetarian diets, especially when they eat a lot of soy products, she explains.

Watch out for spices. Monitor your reaction to garlic, ginger, ground red pepper, onions, and highly acidic produce such as citrus fruits and tomatoes. These foods may fuel your hot-flush fire, according to Judyth Reichenberg-Ullman, N.D., a naturopathic doctor. If you tend to experience hot flushes after eating one of these foods, eliminate the food from your diet for a week or so and note if your symptoms improve.

Steer clear of sweets. Eating sugar boosts your metabolism, and in turn, generates heat.

Ask for decaf. Stick with decaffeinated beverages. Researchers cannot yet explain why, but coffee, tea, and chocolate can trigger hot flushes in some women, notes Pamela Schwingl, Ph.D., an epidemiologist.

Avoid alcoholic beverages. Alcohol causes you to flush even when you aren't in a state of hormonal upheaval. It can certainly fan the flame of hot flushes. In a study at the University of North Carolina at Chapel Hill, women who had at least one alcoholic beverage a week were about 13 percent more likely to experience hot flushes than women who never drank. "Alcohol consumption proved to be one of the strongest lifestyle risk factors for hot flushes," according to Dr. Schwingl, the study's main author.

Helpful vitamins and supplements:

Ease with E. If a woman is beginning to have hot flushes, Dr. Hudson recommends 400 to 800 international units (IU) of vitamin E daily. (If you are considering taking more than 600 IU, discuss it with your doctor first.)

Cure with cream. Apply a cream containing natural progesterone to your skin. A cream delivers the hormone directly to your bloodstream so that it takes effect more quickly, according to Marcus Laux, N.D., a naturopathic doctor in California, and co-author of *Natural Woman, Natural Menopause*. Clinical evidence suggests that the cream may help reduce hot flushes by balancing a woman's hormonal makeup, he explains. Also, your body can convert progesterone to oestrogen or other sex hormones as needed, whenever it runs low on these substances.

Buy a product that contains a minimum of 400 milligrams of progesterone per ounce and apply one-half teaspoon two times per day, morning and night, until your hot flushes decrease, recommends Dr. Laux. At that point, reduce your dosage to one-quarter teaspoon two times a day. Then once your hot flushes are under control, cut your dosage again to one-quarter to one-half teaspoon per day. Rub the cream into your wrist, neck, chest, breasts, abdomen, and/or inner thighs (make sure that your skin is clean first).

While you can buy progesterone cream over the counter, Dr. Laux recommends consulting your doctor first to find out if progesterone cream is appropriate for you and to get a prescription for the proper strength. These products are not appropriate for women who have had cancer or who are at high risk for the disease, he adds.

Beware of the so-called wild yam progesterone creams, however. A laboratory analysis found that most of these products actually contain very little to none of the hormone, notes Dr. Laux. He recommends avoiding them completely.

Everyday prevention:

Give up smoking. Smoking depletes your body's level of the hormone oestrogen, making you more susceptible to hot flushes, notes Dr. Schwingl. In addition, some studies have shown that women who smoke go through menopause one to two years earlier than women who don't.

Turn down the heat. If you can, adjust the temperature of the room you are in to 60 degrees F. Simplistic as it may seem, turning down the heat or cranking up the air conditioning is solid advice. "Anything that raises body temperature even a tiny bit, such as being in a too-hot room, can aggravate a hot flush," says Robert Freedman, Ph.D., director of the Behavioural Medicine. Also, avoid dramatic temperature changes—wait a few minutes in a semi-cool lobby before entering an air-conditioned or heated room, for example. At night, sleep with a fan operating by your bed, even in winter, and use light blankets only.

Dress in layers. This way, you can slip off clothes as your body temperature rises so that you stay comfortable. Instead of a bulky turtleneck sweater, for instance, wear a cardigan or vest over a blouse.

Hit the tub. Before going to bed, draw a comfortably warm-not hot-bath. Then soak in it long enough for the water to cool, which should take about 20 minutes. This bedtime ritual may interrupt a pattern of night sweats (nocturnal hot flushes) so that they occur less frequently and are less severe, according to Helen Healy, N.D., a naturopathic doctor.

Easing the pain with exercise:

Get moving: "I recommend that a woman approaching menopause and beyond take up a good, weight-bearing, aerobic exercise that she really enjoys," says Dr. Hudson. Walking, jogging, aerobics classes, or tennis will all do the trick. Your goal here is to exercise for 30 to 60 minutes at least every other day, she says. If you're new to exercise or it's been years since you exercised regularly, get medical clearance before you work out, especially if you're over the age of 40. Results of a Swedish study showed that regular physical exercise definitely lowers the frequency and severity of hot flushes. The women in the study who had no hot flushes were those who spent an average of 3½ hours per week exercising. In contrast, women who exercised less were more likely to have hot flushes.

Herbal Help:

Turn down the heat with motherwort and black cohosh. "I like to start with the simplest things first," says Patricia Howell, a professional herbalist. "I mix 2 parts of motherwort tincture with 1 part black cohosh tincture." (Black cohosh isn't a hormone per se, but it normalises hormonal fluctuations prior to menopause, she says.) Start with ¼ teaspoon of the formula, mixed into a little water or a cup of tea, three times a day. Herbalists sometimes recommend increasing the dosage to ½ teaspoon three times a day. But Howell cautions that at high doses, black cohosh makes some women nauseated. If that happens, take it less often. Science supports motherwort's traditional use as a heart strengthener due to its ability to lower blood pressure, which may be why it's considered a hot flash helper. Motherwort also has sedative qualities to ease the insomnia that troubles many menopausal women, notes Rosemary Gladstar, author of *Herbal Healing for Women*.

Try an herbal trio. "My own standard recommendation for hot flushes and other symptoms of menopause is a trio of traditional herbs," says Andrew Weil, MD, author of *Spontaneous Healing*. Dr. Weil recommends taking one dropperful each of tinctures of dang gui, chasteberry, and damiana once a day at midday. Continue taking the herbs until your hot flushes cease, then taper off gradually. Damiana is a nervous system tonic, said to ease depression and anxiety. Chasteberry may counteract effectiveness of birth control pills. Don't use dang gui while menstruating, spotting, or bleeding heavily, because it can increase blood loss.

Cool down with violet. Violets can also cool hot flushes, says herbalist, Susan S. Weed. Eat the fresh leaves in your salad. Or brew a strong tea by steeping once ounce (by weight) of dried violet leaves (found at many herb stores) in a quart of boiling water overnight. Strain, refrigerate and drink within 48 hours. She suggests drinking at least a cup a day.

Follow sage advice. Garden sage is famed for the way it reduces or even eliminates night sweats. It acts fast, within a few hours, and a single cup of infusion can stave off the sweats for up to two days, says Weed. What's more, you probably have a bottle of sage sitting on your spice rack. Just make sure it's still nice and aromatic before you use it medicinally. To make a sage infusion, put 4 heaping tablespoons of dried sage in a cup of hot water. Cover tightly and steep for 4 hours or more.

Seek out herbal soothers. Try an herbal preparation specifically formulated for hot flushes or menopause. Such a product may include a combination of a few or many herbs, such as chasteberry, black cohosh, dong quai, panax ginseng (sometimes called Asian ginseng), and licorice root. These herbs complement and balance each other, increasing the effectiveness of the product and minimising its side effects, says James E. Williams, O.MD, a doctor of Oriental medicine. He suggests consulting a doctor who is knowledgeable about herbs so that she can recommend a good product and explain how to use it effectively and safely. If you choose a product on your own, be sure to follow the dosage recommendations on the label. You will find these herbal blends in health food stores. Note: if the product contains licorice root, limit your intake of the herb to five grams (less than one-quarter ounce) a day. Larger doses can produce side effects such as high blood pressure, headache, and lethargy. If you use dong quai, avoid exposure to the sun. Some people become photosensitive when they use dong quai and develop a rash or sunburn easily.

Mind over malady:

Combine deep breathing with visualisation. Using the two techniques together may enhance their chill factor, so they stop a hot flush more quickly, says Carol Snarr, R.N., a psychophysiological therapist (one who teaches biofeedback and other mind/body skills). Try this visualisation when you feel a hot flush coming on, suggests Snarr. Begin by assigning your hot flush a colour, such as red. As you exhale, envision the colour leaving your body, releasing the heat, and sending it away from you. Then as you inhale, see your breath as blue or another cool colour. Allow the colour to bathe your body, soothing your chest, your neck, and your head. When you feel that the hot flush has passed, you can end your visualisation by imagining yourself as you would like to feel cool and refreshed.

Cool your head. Some brain research has shown that hot flushes are stimulated by a brain chemical known as norepinephrine, which influences the temperature-regulating centre in the brain, says Sadja Greenwood, MD, a professor of gynaecology. "This may explain why daily stress reduction practices such as meditation, deep breathing and yoga, which result in lower levels of norepinephrine, help some women reduce their hot flushes," she says. In one study, menopausal women with frequent hot flushes were trained to slowly breathe in and out six to eight times for two minutes. These women has fewer hot flushes than women trained to use either muscle relaxation or biofeedback.

Ingrown Hair

The pain: Hair that becomes embedded in the skin, causing irritation, inflammation and scarring.

The cause: An ingrown hair occurs in one of two ways. When you shave too close, you can nick the top of the hair follicle and cause it to become partially obstructed. That forces the hair inside to grow at an angle. Eventually, instead of growing straight up through the follicle, the hair pierces the side of the follicle and buries itself in your skin. Your skin reacts by setting up an inflammation that appears as a tiny red bump. An ingrown hair can also occur when an individual hair grows straight up and out of a follicle, then curls back down and enters the skin. People who have thick, curly hair are particularly prone to that type of ingrown hair, but it can happen to anyone who shaves, plucks or uses wax to remove unwanted hair.

See a doctor if:
...an ingrown hair becomes infected.

Everyday prevention:
Rough up your skin. "One of the best ways to prevent the hairs from embedding in your skin is to take a dry washcloth and rub it over your skin before you shave," advises David Feingold, MD, a dermatologist. "That way you'll help loosen embedded hairs from their follicles for a less irritating shave."

Don't double up. Using twin-track razors can give you a double dose of agony. That's because the first blade pulls the hair while the second cuts it below skin level, often at a sharp angle that can embed back into your skin. Jerome Z. Litt, MD, a professor of dermatology, says you're better off using a single-track razor and settling for a less close shave. Pivoting-head razors cause less friction (and irritation) and do a better job than fixed-head types, adds John F. Romano, MD, a dermatologist.

Change your routine. Sometimes you can lessen ingrown hair pain simply by changing your shaving direction. "I try to get my patients to shave with the grain, whereas most people go against the grain," says Dr. Feingold. While you're at it, you may also want to change your choice of shaving gear. "If you now shave with a blade, try an electric razor. If you now use electric, go manual."

Play Sherlock Holmes. "Make a regular routine of examining your face very carefully with a magnifying glass, to look for hairs that are caught in the follicle," says Dr. Feingold. These troublemakers should then be removed with tweezers that have been sterilised in rubbing alcohol.

Stop shaving. Shaving puts hairs under tension and cuts them at an angle, making them prone to becoming embedded in the skin, and makes curly hair curl more tightly. Backing off from the razor, even for a few days, can bring relief.

Use an antibacterial bar. To help clear up inflammation, wash the ingrown hair area twice a day with an antibacterial soap of 10% benzoyl peroxide found at your local chemist.

Change your blade. If ingrown hairs are inflamed and infected, change your razor blade each time you shave until the ingrown hair is gone. Otherwise, you can reinfect yourself.

Moisturise. Try to protect your hair follicles by keeping a barrier of mixture between you and the razor blade. You can use the expensive foams and gels if you like, but a mild soap will also do the job.

Drop acid. The key, says Nicholas V. Perricone, MD, a professor of dermatology, is glycolic acid, one of the alpha hydroxy acids often found in anti-ageing cream and other skin treatments. Find a cream or lotion with 10-20 percent glycolic acid at your local chemist. Apply it twice every day as part of your daily routine, says Dr. Perricone. Be sure to apply it right after shaving. "Within a very short time, you'll start getting relief from the bumps," he says.

Ingrown Toenail

The pain: Pain, swelling and redness caused by the sharp end of a toenail growing into the flesh of the toe (usually the big toe).

The cause: You inherit the tendency for your nails to curl or become "dome shaped." This tendency causes the nail to curl down at the corners, then dig and grow into your skin. Other causes are poorly fitting shoes and improper toenail trimming.

See a doctor if:

...your nail is inflamed and pain increases steadily. See a podiatrist as soon as possible. A foot infection can spread quickly from an ingrown nail.

...you have any swelling or discharge in the area.

...you have poor circulation and decreased feeling in your feet due to diabetes. It's especially important that you get treated by a doctor before you try any home remedies, advises Kathleen Stone, D.P.M., a podiatrist.

Quick relief:

Put your toe on the rocks. Application of an ice cube or ice bag to the toe can relieve pain.

Soak your foot. When you have an ingrown nail, the area around it is likely to become inflamed, and that inflammation only makes the condition worse. If you can reduce the swelling, your symptoms will improve, says Loretta Chou, MD, an orthopedic surgery specialist. To tackle the inflammation, put some hot water in a bucket and soak your foot for 20 minutes. To help prevent infection, add a small amount of mild soap to the water, suggests Dr. Chou. Or use Epsom salts, following the directions on the package. Test the water with your hand to make sure it's not too hot. You can repeat the soak once or twice a day as needed to bring down the inflammation, says Dr. Chou.

Opt for oil. "Rub baby oil or olive oil on the side of the nail," says Phyllis Ragley, D.P.M., president of the American Academy of Podiatric Sportsmedicine. "It keeps the skin soft, so there is less pressure and discomfort. Also the skin can more easily accommodate the nail."

Everyday prevention:

Use antibiotic ointment. Ingrown nails easily become infected. Use an over-the-counter antibiotic ointment such as Neosporin or Polysporin (Polyfax). Smear on the ointment after your bath or shower, and be sure to do it again after you've soaked your foot, advises Dr. Chou.

Trim right. When you cut your nail, don't round the edges or you'll just encourage the skin to be become irritated. Instead, trim your nails straight across when you use a clipper. It's fine to file down the edges slightly to keep them from being so sharp but don't curve them, explains Dr. Chou.

Soak, then trim. Before cutting with a good-quality long-handled scissors or nail clippers, soak your foot in warm water to soften the nail and lessen your pain, says Frederick Hass, MD, author of *The Foot Book*. There are products that are made to soften ingrown nails, but read the label before using them. Some cannot be used by people with conditions such as diabetes or impaired circulation.

Don't cut a V. The old wive's tale that you can treat an ingrown nail by cutting a V-shaped wedge out of its centre is incorrect. It won't prevent an ingrown nail and chances are the only thing you'll do is hurt yourself.

Wear sandals. Open-toed shoes will keep the pressure off your toes and allow your foot to heal faster. And since the toes are open, there's no chance you'll accidentally jam your toes into the front of the shoe when you're walking downhill, says Dr. Chou. If you can prevent your toe from being injured, you'll be less likely to develop an ingrown nail, according to Dr. Chou.

Buy shoes that fit. If your shoes are too tight, you'll have more pressure on your nails, says Dr. Chou. Women, especially, are likely to wear shoes that are too small, partly because manufacturers pay more attention to style than to the actual shape of the foot. Since your feet tend to become longer and wider with age, you should get your feet measured each time you buy shoes. And when you select the pair you want, press the toe of the shoe to make sure that there's at least a finger's width from your longest toe to the end of the toe box.

Choose stockings with care. Make sure your socks or stockings aren't too tight, says Dr. Stone. This can be a contributing factor as you age. If too tight, they can cause the thickened nail to be pushed into the skin.

Ease the pressure. Roll a piece of cotton to twice the thickness of a candlewick and place it between the skin and the ingrown nail tip. Place iodine on the cotton and wrap your toe with gauze and tape. Add a drop of iodine daily and change the cotton once a week. This technique stops the ingrown nail from piercing the flesh as it grows out from the skin, says dermatologist Harold Fishman, MD, He recommends that if the pain does not lessen in a few days, you see your doctor.

Intercourse Pain

The pain: Sudden, intense pain experienced by a woman during intercourse.

The cause: The physical causes of intercourse pain fall into two general categories, according to Emanuel Fliegelman, D.O., a professor of obstetrics and gynaecology. If it hurts when the penis is inserted, the vaginal opening is probably inflamed, too dry, or too narrow. If the pain occurs after insertion, it could indicate a bladder or pelvic infection.

For some women, though, intercourse pain stems not from a physical problem but from emotional distress. They may fear sexual contact or harbour deep-seated anger toward their partners.

See a doctor if:
...you have recurrent pain with intercourse. "In general, women don't feel comfortable talking about it," notes Donald DeWitt, MD, clinical professor of family medicine. "They'd rather suffer in silence than open up, even to their partners." Unfortunately, this could have serious consequences, especially if your pain is produced by a condition such as endometriosis (which is an overgrowth of the tissue that lines the uterus).
...your pain is deep within the pelvis, severe or accompanied by a low-grade fever.
...the pain is accompanied by vaginal discharge, itching or dryness.
...your vaginal discharge has an unusual colour or odour.
...your pain persists for some time after intercourse.

Quick relief:
Maximise moisture. If your pain results from vaginal dryness, experts recommend using a lubricating product. But steer clear of petroleum jelly, Dr. Fliegelman cautions: "It's too sticky and gooey."

Nutritional remedies:
Drink fluids and eat bran. During sex, the wall of the vagina can get pinched between the man's thrusting penis and a stool sitting in the colon. If you are constipated a lot and it causes painful sex, try increasing the

amount of fluids you drink, says Jo Kessler, a licensed nurse-practitioner and certified sex therapist. And add bulk to your diet with fresh fruits, whole grains, vegetables or some form of bran. "When you clear up the constipation problem, then you don't have firm stool in the colon for the penis to thrust against," she says. With fluids, aim for six to eight glasses a day. If you're having trouble getting to the water fountain, try a sports fluid bottle, says Kessler. Many of them hold 16 ounces, and you can fill it up three or four time a day. "Have one at breakfast, one at midmorning, one at lunch, one at dinner and one at bedtime," she says.

Helpful vitamins and supplements:

Ease the way with vitamin E. Applying vitamin E to the vagina can help heal dry, irritated tissue, according to Cynthia M.Watson, MD, a family practitioner and author of *Love Potions.* She suggests either pricking a vitamin E capsule and squeezing out the oil or using the vitamin in liquid form (it's available at health food stores and chemists). Repeat the treatment several times a week. Note: Vitamin E is not a lubricant and should not be used during intercourse, Dr. Watson advises.

Ease the pain with exercise:

Put the squeeze on pain. Consciously working the pubococcygeal (PC) muscle, located at the bottom of the pelvis between the anus and the genitals, can teach you to relax the muscle during intercourse, says Felice Dunas, Ph.D., a licensed acupuncturist and author of *Passion Play.* This helps make penetration less painful. "You hold in urine by contracting the PC muscle," Dr. Dunas says. "So practice squeezing the muscle three times whenever you urinate. You should squeeze hard enough to stop the flow of urine." She also suggests exercising the muscle before you go to sleep: Squeeze it as tight as you can, hold for a count of 5 to 10, then relax. Repeat a total of three times.

Everyday Prevention:

Got a new prescription. Taking low-dose birth control pills for a long period of time may cause the vaginal tissue to become thinner, setting the stage for intercourse pain, says David Redwine, MD, director of the Endometriosis Institute in Bend, Oregon. You may want to talk to your doctor about changing your prescription, he suggests.

Stay healthy. Since painful intercourse can be caused by medical problems, including endometriosis and fibroids, it's important to have a gynaecological exam annually, experts say. Yeast infections and STDs can cause pain as well, so protect yourself. Keep the vaginal area clean, use condoms to prevent sexually transmitted diseases and get immediate treatment for vaginal irritations and Infections.

Don't force it. "I talk to women about how not to have intercourse when they don't want to," says Kessler. There are other ways to be sexual. You can still have sex without putting the penis in the vagina. Talk about various options with your partner before you get in a romantic situation.

Take it slow after pregnancy. Scar tissue left behind after an episiotomy can cause discomfort, so use lots of lubrication, says Susan E. Hetherington, Dr.PH., a certified nurse-midwife and sex therapist. She suggests that your partner put a dab of water-soluble lubricant on his finger, then, with your assistance, gently place that finger in the vagina. You should bear down, as if going to the bathroom, and that will release the muscle that stimulates the vaginal opening. This allows his finger to slip in more. Gentle touching will relax the vagina. Then, with proper lubrication, the penis will slide in. It should be a slow process with no deep thrusting initially, she says.

Keep a diary. If you are experiencing pain with sex, keep a record of what kind of pain you have and when, says Kessler. Keep track for two to three months and look to see whether the discomfort occurs on entry or with deep thrusting, whether it only occurs while intercourse is going on or if it continues after the penis is withdrawn, whether the pain always occurs at the same time of the month and whether it happens with every position or only with one. And if a woman has multiple partners, she needs to pay attention to whether she has the pain with all partners or just one, says Kessler.

Find the right doctor. "The main thing is to know that if it hurts, that's a signal that you need to do something about it. I always want them to get a medical exam as soon as possible," says Kessler. It's important to find a doctor who understands the problem, too. Some will do a pelvic exam and say they don't see anything, leaving the woman with the impression that it's all in her head. "Women need to keep seeking an answer. If one doctor says, I don't see anything and offers no other options, be persistent and get a second opinion.," Kessler says.

Get help for vaginismus. Doctors do have a technique—called vaginal dilation—for helping women with vaginismus (a condition in which the opening of the vagina closes, making penetration painful or impossible). With supervision, women first learn techniques to help them relax. Then, starting with a dilator about the size of the small finger, they learn to penetrate the vagina. Slowly, at a pace at which they are comfortable, they work their way up to a dilator that has a circumference equal to that of their partner's penis. When women start the process, they're often anxious and scared, says Kessler. "Once they realize they won't have to jam something into the vagina and won't have to progress any faster than they are ready to, they relax, and that brings relief and results," she says.

Prevent bladder infection. If burning sensation occur during intercourse and urination, it's very possible that you have a urinary tract infection. Once your doctor has examined you, diagnosed a urinary infection and prescribed appropriate treatment, the most important part—preventing repeat infections—is up to you. "Urinate at regular intervals of no less than every three to four hours," says Jack Lapides, MD, a urologist. Otherwise your bladder may stretch, retain urine, become inflamed and be invaded by bacteria.

Mind over malady:

Wait until you're ready. "A woman should be highly stimulated before penetration occurs," according to Dr. Dunas. This has two benefits, she says: It ensures that the vagina is sufficiently lubricated, and it lengthens the vagina to accommodate deep thrusting.

Explore your options. If one sexual position seems to cause you pain, then you and your partner should experiment to find something more comfortable. For example, if you have a problem with deep penetration, Dr. Dunas suggests trying a position that lengthens the vagina somewhat. Lying on your back with your legs straight out rather than up may help, she says.

Be honest. Talking about a sexual problem with your partner is seldom easy, Dr. Fliegelman says. But if you let your partner know what hurts, you open the door to a frank and honest discussion and the two of you may come up with a solution together.

Nurture your relationship. Negative feelings about your relationship or your partner can affect your sex life, experts say. Deal with problems as they come along, instead of letting them accumulate. Talk to your partner using "I" statements such as "I'm having a problem with ... " instead of "you" phrases like "You always . . . which can place blame and cause bigger rifts. Try writing about your anger as a way to express and defuse it, says Kessler.

When He Has Pain

Women experience intercourse pain far more frequently than men do. But that doesn't mean that men are immune. The skin of the penis can get irritated from too much friction within the vagina. The urethra (the tube that carries urine from the bladder) or prostate can become inflamed, making ejaculation painful. Or the head of the penis can feel sore, the result of infection with the human papillomavirus.

Perhaps the most serious intercourse-related condition that affects men is priapism-basically, an erection that won't let up. Don't think for a minute that this is a good thing: Priapism hurts like crazy, and experts warn that it can lead to permanent problems if it's left untreated.

Any one of these conditions will probably cause you enough discomfort to send you to your doctor-and that's exactly what you should do, experts say.

Intermittent Claudication

The pain: A deep, painful cramp that feels like its at the bottom of the calf muscle, right next to the bone.

The cause: Sometimes described as a "heart attack of the lower leg," intermittent claudication is caused by poor circulation in the legs, usually because the blood vessels are narrowed and choked with cholesterol and other fatty materials. It occurs when the calf muscles are crying out for more blood and the oxygen that comes with it.

See a doctor if:
...you have symptoms of claudication. Intermittent claudication is a symptom of underlying artery disease, and if not managed properly, it can lead to serious problems.

Quick relief:
Stop moving. Resting for a few moments will bring instant relief, as it reduces the oxygen demand of you leg muscles.

Nutritional remedies:
Fill up on foods with folate. High levels of the body chemical homocysteine are a risk factor in intermittent claudication, says William Hiatt, MD, a professor of vascular medicine. And when you increase the level of the B vitamin folate in your diet, you can lower homocysteine levels. Good food sources of folate include beans, broccoli, spinach, orange juice and fortified cereals.

Cut cholesterol and triglycerides. "Try to raise high-density lipoprotein (HDL) cholesterol and lower triglycerides," says Dr. Hiatt. HDL cholesterol is the "good" kind that helps usher "bad," artery-clogging low-density lipoprotein (LDL) cholesterol out of the body. (Triglycerides are a blood fat with the same mean streak as LDL.) The best way to affect both of these blood fats at once is to lose weight if you are overweight. "Even losing as little as 5 to 10 pounds will significantly lower them," says Dr. Hiatt.

Feed on fish. Besides being low in fat and high in nutrition, fish helps boost your levels of HDL cholesterol. Tuna, sardines, salmon, herring and mackerel are excellent choices.

Drink only now and then. Alcohol initially dilates blood vessels, which helps increase blood flow, but then has a rebound effect and constricts them. An occasional glass of beer or wine is fine, but if you have intermittent claudication, it's not a good idea to drink regularly.

Everyday prevention:

Stop smoking. Smoking is the number one risk factor for claudication. "Patients who claudicate are almost universally cigarette smokers," says Robert Ginsburg, MD, director of the Centre for Advanced Cardiovascular Therapy in California. "I don't think I've ever seen a claudication patient in my life who did not smoke at some time. The most crucial thing is for them stop smoking. It helps dramatically."

Ask about aspirin. Aspirin may help some people. "We recommend that our patients take one aspirin tablet a day," Dr. Ginsburg says.

Easing the pain with exercise:

Stop and start again. If your doctor's given you the green light to exercise, you may find that leg pain strikes while you're walking. When that happens, slow down until the pain diminishes and then continue your walk at your original rate. "When you start feeling the muscle cramps, try to walk a short distance before you stop to rest," says Dan Hammer, MD, a physiatrist and sports medicine specialist. "The objective is to extend the distance you walk. If you always try to increase the distance, you may be able to walk a few hundred yards farther each week." Walking is an effective remedy because the activity triggers the opening of formerly dormant blood vessels to take over the job of the clogged ones. It also teaches the muscles to get along with less oxygen.

Head for the hills. Dr. Hammer suggests that you vary your walking routine to include hills as well as flat terrain. "By varying walking surfaces, you stimulate the formation of new vessels that help blood bypass the blockages," he says. If the pain worsens when you walk uphill, check with your doctor about other possible conditions, such as arthritis of the spine.

Trek on a treadmill. Walking on a shock-absorbing treadmill and climbing on a stair machine can add variety to your workouts, especially during inclement weather, says Dr. Hammer.

Head for the dance floor. You can two-step to keep the pain away by doing the polka, tango, waltz or even country line dancing, says Dr. Hammer. "Dancing is a great exercise for this because it requires you to use your calf muscles more," he says. "If you can, try to go up on you toes every now and then. It will give you a little extra calf work."

Walk in the water. If your calves are really screaming in pain, a few laps of water walking may be in order, says Dr. Hammer. "I recommend that some people try walking waist-deep in a pool with a water vest on for as long as they can tolerate," he says.

Ban the heat. Because the blood flow in the legs is restricted, people who suffer from intermittent claudication often suffer from cold feet, too. If you're among them, don't warm your feed with a heating pad or hot water bottle. "You need increased blood flow to help dissipate the heat," says Jess R. Young, MD, a vascular medicine specialist. "If blood flow is limited, however; it can't get down to where you're putting the heat, and you'll burn the skin." Instead, warm you tootsies with loose wool stockings or socks.

Herbal help:

Get better with garlic. In one study, a large number of people with intermittent claudication were given 800 milligrams of garlic a day. On average, they walked noticeably better by their fifth week of taking the herb. "Garlic is a terrific herb for treating any cardiovascular problem," says James A. Duke, Ph.D., author of *The Green Pharmacy.* He suggests eating at least one raw clove a day. "I suggest chopping a clove and tossing it into a salad or sprinkling it over a pasta dish," he adds.

Grab some ginkgo. "Ginkgo is the premier plant medicine for intermittent claudication," says Dr. Duke. "It improves blood flow through the legs just as it does through the heart and brain by opening the arteries." Nine excellent studies shows that 40 milligrams of ginkgo extract twice a day provide better relief that the standard medicine prescribed for intermittent claudication, according to Dr. Duke. He suggests purchasing standardized ginkgo extract, available at many health food stores and pharmacies.

Go for ginger. In various studies, ginger has been shown to be almost as effective, or as effective, as aspirin and garlic in preventing the blood clots that trigger heart attack. Similar clotting in the leg can trigger intermittent claudication pain. "If I had this condition, I'd eat a lot of ginger," says Dr. Duke.

Pass the purslane. Saturated fat is a major culprit in causing any form of cardiovascular disease, including intermittent claudication. The beneficial oils known as omega-3 fatty acids help prevent cardiovascular disease, and purslane is our best leafy source of omega-3's. It's also extremely well endowed with antioxidants, substances that mop up free radicals, highly reactive oxygen molecules that damage the body's cells and contribute to heart disease. Purslane is a delicious vegetable. You can steam the leaves and eat them like spinach, or add them raw to salads and soups.

Irritable Bowel Syndrome

The pain: Alternating constipation and diarrhoea, bloating, unformed stools, wind, and sometimes, cramps followed by an urgent need to have a bowel movement.

The cause: IBS is not a disease, and rarely is there any inflammation of the bowel. Doctors who have studied the problem say that it's probably related to stress and food intolerance. "In my practice, I find there are two kinds of people who get IBS. First are people who are go-getters and really stressed out; they are hard-wired for stress to stimulate their colons. And then there are the folks who have an intolerance to certain foods," says Leon Hecht, N.D., a naturopathic physician.

See your doctor if:

...your bowel habits suddenly change.
...you're suffering from abdominal pain or vomiting.
...you have diarrhoea for more than a day or two.
...you experience rectal bleeding.
...you have IBS symptoms that don't clear up after a day or so.

Nutritional Remedies:

Eat slowly. If you're always first at your table to finish a meal, chances are you're also first in line to use the lavatory while the plates are being cleared away. Eating slowly may help you stop abnormal colon contractions from starting.

Hydrate. To start, you need to get enough water, and that may be a good bit more than you're accustomed to drinking. Some people with IBS have small, hard stools that are difficult to pass. By drinking water, they can add soft bulk to the stool and ease its passage through the bowel, says Melissa Metcalfe, N.D., a naturopathic doctor. "You should drink eight 12-ounce glasses of water a day, and more if you're an active person," says Dr. Metcalfe.

Fill up on fibre. While you're emptying your water bottle, also increase the amount of fibre in your diet, Dr. Metcalfe advises. Fibre absorbs water and helps move food and waste through the gastrointestinal tract more quickly. Some excellent sources of fibre are foods like prunes, apples, oat bran, and carrots. Boost your fibre intake to 25 to 35 grams of fibre a day.

Be a diet detective. Food intolerance is often a contributing factor to IBS, but the reactions can happen hours after a meal, so people don't always connect what they ate with how they feel, says Dr. Hecht. Many naturopathic doctors suggest that their patients try to find out what's causing the problem by a process of elimination. This is called, logically, an elimination diet. The first step is to cut out the foods that are most likely to be irritants. Many people, for example, have adverse reactions to sugar, wheat, and corn. Milk and other dairy products are also common culprits. Chocolate may also be a problem, and a high-carbohydrate diet is involved in 30 to 50 percent of Dr. Hecht's cases. Sometimes, blood testing or allergy testing can provide clues as well, he notes.

For many people, refined sugar is the culprit, says Dr. Hecht, because it is like a fertiliser for yeast bacteria. Although yeast is always present in the body, dietary sugar can lead to an overgrowth of yeast in the intestinal tract, and this can result in wind, bloating, and pain and trigger cramps and symptoms of IBS.

Decaffeinate your life. "Caffeine is a major bowel stimulant; it makes material move through the bowel too soon," says Ernestine Hambrick, MD, a colon and rectal surgeon. But just cutting out coffee isn't enough. Chocolate, tea and soda also contain caffeine, so eliminate them from your diet, too.

Steer clear of wheat and dairy. Many people with IBS are sensitive to wheat as well as milk and milk products, says Jacqueline Wolf, MD, a gastroenterologist. If you have this sensitivity and eat prepared foods, you may not realise that wheat or dairy products are among the ingredients unless you read the label. So read before you ingest.

Ban gassy foods. "People with IBS are sensitive to any amount of wind," says Jorge Herrera, MD, spokesperson for the American Gastroenterological Society. "And even normal amounts of wind will cause them to have cramps and bloating because wind tends to get trapped in pockets of the intestine, which causes distension, which, in turn, causes pain." Foods to avoid include: beans, cabbage and other green leafy vegetables, dairy products and processed foods containing milk. If you can't avoid them, try over-the-counter antiwind products that destroy wind in the upper intestine, says Dr. Herrera.

Juice up. If eating whole fibre-rich vegetables makes your IBS symptoms intolerable, try their juices for a week or two. Four ounces of carrot, celery, or parsley juice at lunch and dinner provides all the vitamins and minerals you need without aggravating your bowel, says Eve Campanelli, Ph.D., a practitioner of holistic medicine. You can buy these juices ready-made at the grocery store, or you can make your own concoctions at home with a juicer.

Eat lean. Since any form of fat is the strongest food stimulus of intestinal contractions, keep your diet as lean as possible, doctors suggest. Trim fat from meat, switch to low-fat cheeses and avoid fried foods.

Eat small. Large meals have been found to trigger both cramping and diarrhoea. So try eating smaller meals, more often.

Go soft on hard foods. Be wary of chunky, sharp-edged foods, such as nuts. Hard foods like nuts and seeds are more irritating than softer foods.

Skip dessert. Sugars and artificial sweeteners such as sorbitol are hard to digest and can irritate the bowels. So if you suffer from IBS, avoid sugar-free chewing gum and candy. If your sweet tooth is acting up, eat fruit.

Eat your meals at the same time every day. If you are like most people, a hectic daily routine dictates when—or maybe even if—you have your mealtimes. Eating "on the fly" throws off your body's circadian rhythms (its internal clock), so it doesn't know when to void. This can lead to constipation or to cycles of constipation and diarrhoea, both of which are characteristic of IBS. Establishing regular mealtimes, on the other hand, cues your body to void at certain times of the day. Choose times that work for you and stick with them.

Helpful vitamins and supplements:

Watch your B's. Medication prescribed for IBS can increase your needs for B vitamins. Check with your doctor and take a multivitamin/mineral supplement that includes all the B vitamins.

Choose activated charcoal. The active ingredients in charcoal tablets prowl the lower bowel for wind, soaking it up on contact, says Dr. Herrera. Be aware, however, that taking charcoal tablets can turn your stool black, he says. It's nothing to worry about, but it can certainly give you a start if you're already worried about the health of your colon. Note: While activated charcoal does absorb some wind, it also absorbs medications. Don't take it if you're taking other drugs.

Pick up some pectin. Pectin, another source of high fibre, is found in fruits such as papayas, oranges and grapefruit or in apple pectin—a granular natural supplement found in most health food stores, says Dr. Wolf. You can sprinkle apple pectin on your food or dissolve it in liquid.

Feed on fish and flaxseed oil. Scientists have discovered that oils like flaxseed oil and fish oils are rich in the omega-3 fatty acid called EPA, which is valued for its anti-inflammatory effects. Try taking two tablespoons of flaxseed oil every day. It's all right to slurp it right from the spoon, but the oil is pretty tasteless. Instead, just add the two tablespoons of oil to your morning cereal. You can even make a salad dressing out of flaxseed oil. Or take two or three fish oil capsules once a day before a meal.

Seek out psyllium. In a study published in a British medical journal aptly named Gut, 80 patients with irritable bowel syndrome were given either a supplement containing psyllium or a harmless, inactive substitute that looked and tasted like the supplement (a placebo). More than 80 percent of the group taking psyllium experienced relief from their constipation, while those in the placebo group noticed no change. Dr. Metcalfe recommends taking two tablespoons daily—in two separate doses—of a fibre/nutritional supplement that contains psyllium husks. Fibre supplements like Metamucil (Fybogel) come in a wide range of textures, and some are flavoured to make them more palatable. Take them before meals, or take one tablespoon in the morning and another before you go to bed. Just make sure you mix each tablespoon dose with at least two eight-ounce glasses of water, says Dr. Metcalfe.

Find friendly bacteria. If bad bacteria in your intestinal tract start to crowd out the good bacteria, any problems that you have with food sensitivities or with indigestion may be intensified. One way to combat the problem is to repopulate the gut with good bacteria. Usually, that means that you need to take acidophilus, says Michael Gazsi, N.D., a naturopathic doctor. Acidophilus supplements come in various dosages, depending on the manufacturer, says Dr. Gazsi. Your best bet is to follow the directions the label of the supplement and then observe any changes in your condition. A typical dosage is one capsule with a meal twice daily. "If the bowel continues to feel really irritated, I'd back off the dosage a bit or try a different brand," says Dr. Gazsi.

"Unfortunately, there's not a lot of quality control with some of these supplements. There's no way of knowing if you're getting enough or too many of the bacteria. You just have to see how you're reacting and adjust accordingly." Eventually, the good bacteria should re-establish themselves, and you can forgo the acidophilus supplement. If you want to continue taking it, it's all right to do so. "It's one of those things you can take indefinitely," says Dr. Gazsi.

Bring in the enzymes. Bacteria aren't the only players in digestion. You also need plenty of digestive enzymes, specialised proteins that break down the food chemically and make it available for use by the body. If enzymes don't do their work properly or are in short supply in the gastrointestinal tract, food passes undigested through the small intestine. As that undigested food reaches the bowel, it may be attacked and consumed by bad bacteria, which in turn causes wind and bloating. If you're having an irritable bowel problem partly because you lack enough digestive enzymes, you may benefit from taking a supplement to make up the shortage, says Dr. Gazsi. There are several types on the market. Look for a product that contains plant-derived enzymes and follow the dosage recommendations on the bottle.

Another way to get your enzymes is to eat more fresh, uncooked vegetables and fruit. You don't get the enzymes from canned, processed, and cooked food, since many of the natural plant enzymes are destroyed in cooking and processing, according to Dr. Gazsi. "You don't want to each too much raw food all at once, though," he says. "Some people try to change their diet too quickly and may make their irritable bowel even worse."

Everyday prevention:

Use laxatives sparingly. If you wake up with painful constipation or diarrhoea, and you're about to get on an aeroplane or attend an important event, it's okay to take a chemically based laxative or anti-diarrhoeal medication, says Dr. Hambrick. Just don't make it a habit. "You end up with a yo-yo effect that doesn't touch the underlying syndrome," says Dr. Hambrick. You'll go from constipation to diarrhoea and back and perhaps even develop a lazy colon that no longer works on its own.

Easing the pain with exercise:

Sit up and see if your colon takes notice. Hit the deck and reel off some sit-ups for temporary relief. This exercise can stop your bowel spasms pronto and may start normal contractions in your intestine.

Make the right moves. "Exercise contributes mightily to the normal function of the colon; it moves things along," says Dr. Hambrick. Do whatever you like—swim, run, walk—any kind of aerobic exercise, at least three times a week, and four or five times if you can. It needn't be strenuous—an after-dinner stroll might be just the ticket. "Some people say that they need to walk every day in order to have a bowel movement," says Eileen Marie Wright, MD, a physician. "The bowels do require some movement, but not heavy exertion. A daily 15- to 20-minute walk can make the difference for you."

Lift weights. Strength training three days a week cut the amount of time it took for food to pass through the bowel by about 56%, according to a 13-week joint study conducted by researchers at Johns Hopkins University and the University of Maryland.

Herbal help:

Calm the colon with peppermint. Irritable bowel syndrome isn't just irritating; it can be downright painful. When you're having an attack, you can calm your aching colon by taking peppermint oil extract, an herbal medicine long used for digestive problems, says Dr. Hecht. Also, to decrease the severity of your IBS symptoms, you should take it every day. Peppermint oil extract relaxes the smooth muscles that line the intestines and other internal organs. The herb also calms overactive peristalsis, the muscular contraction that moves food through the gastrointestinal tract, and relieves cramping. It also helps you belch and relieve wind build-up, according to Dr. Hecht. To get the medicine to the intestines where you need it, look for a peppermint oil capsule or pill that's enteric coated. The coating protects the extract from the acid of the stomach and enables it to release its therapeutic benefits in the colon, explains Dr. Hecht. He suggests a supplement that contains 0.2 millilitres of peppermint oil extract. "Take one capsule between meals three times a day," he says, but he advises that you not take the capsule immediately after a meal. "The peppermint oil sits on top of food in your stomach, and it may cause you to burp and regurgitate some of the food." You may also have some discomfort if you take too much peppermint oil, since it can cause some burning at the anus. "If that happens, just back off on the dosage and take less," suggests Dr. Hecht.

Drink ginger tea. Ginger's ability to ease nausea and other digestive problems is well-known. The herb can be a powerful friend to people with IBS because it also relieves wind and spasms. Chop a one-inch section of fresh gingerroot and let it steep in boiling water for five minutes before straining. Fill an insulated container with the tea and take small sips of it throughout the day. "This is very soothing," says Myron B. Lezak, MD, a gastroenterologist. He also likes a tea made from equal parts fennel seeds, dried camomile, and dried peppermint. Prepare this the same way as the ginger tea.

Fight cramps with cramp bark. During a flare-up, take one to three capsules of the herb cramp bark 15 minutes before each meal. When your symptoms subside, cut your dosage to one or two capsules only before your largest meal. Cramp bark relaxes tension in your bowels and allows stools to pass without spasms, explains Dr. Campanelli. You can buy cramp bark capsules in health food stores. How many capsules you need depends on your height and weight, she says. A woman who is five feet, four inches tall and weighs 120 pounds should take one capsule, while a woman who is six feet tall and weighs 200 pounds should take two or three. Each company dilutes its product differently, so be sure to follow the dosage directions on the package.

Mind over malady:

De-stress. Stress aggravates the symptoms of IBS. To calm down your colon, try to find a relaxation method that works for you, whether it's listening to a relaxation tape, meditating, more active relaxation techniques like yoga or tai chi, or just taking time for yourself, says Robyn Karlstadt, MD, a gastroenterologist. "Unplug yourself for 20 minutes a day."

Stay calm. "When the attack starts, it's good to take a deep breath, try to control yourself and realise this isn't going to snowball into an incredible situation," says Dr. Herrera. "You can control it. Just do whatever you're supposed to do and think about something else. A lot of people get too agitated, too excited, too preoccupied when the symptoms start, and it just feeds on itself. That's why they get into these one- or two-day-long episodes where they are incapacitated. It's uncomfortable, but it's not going to kill you or even get any worse."

Change your image: In one study of the effect of imagery on IBS, 20 out of 33 patients who tried it showed improvement in just seven weeks. Most impressive, 11 lost nearly all their symptoms. As always, for imagery to work you need to relax. When you're relaxed, place a hand on your abdomen and focus on feeling all warm and relaxed in that area. Then envision a calm river and visualise your own gastrointestinal tract functioning smoothly and steadily like that river.

Kidney Stones

The pain: Severe pain, usually between your ribs and hip, sometimes accompanied by blood in the urine and fever. The pain of passing a stone has been compared to the pain of childbirth.

The cause: Some people have a tendency to excrete high levels of calcium oxalate and calcium phosphate. If all goes well, you get rid of these calcium salts every time you urinate. Sometimes, however, the salts precipitate out and hang around the kidneys like bad leftovers. Eighty percent of all kidney stones are composed of these calcium salts. The sharp-edged crystals may grow and scrape like a dagger against the lining of a kidney or the ureter, the tube connecting the bladder with a kidney, causing mind-boggling pain. Men are more likely than women to get calcium stones, and genes play a role as well. Because of that genetic factor, if your parents or grandparents had kidney stones, you're at higher risk for getting them yourself.

See a doctor if:
...you have symptoms of kidney stones, such as pain or blood in the urine. The stones can't be ignored, and there's no way to can treat them yourself.
...you experience pain in the groin, lower back or testicles.
...you feel a need to urinate constantly.

Quick relief:
Turn on the heat. Immerse yourself in a hot bath or apply a heating pad to relieve some of the pain.

Nutritional remedies:
Eat carefully. Diet is important if you're trying to avoid kidney stones. Stay away from foods such as spinach, beans, parsley, tea, coffee, and dark green vegetables. Although many of these items are normally thought of as healthy foods, they are rich in oxalates, says Anne McClenon, N.D., a naturopathic doctor. If you have a problem turning oxalates into a form that your body can use, they remain in your urine. "They may precipitate as a stone," she says.

Drink up. Water, that is. It's a simple bit of advice, but it makes a lot of sense when you consider that stones come from dissolved solids, says Leon Hecht, N.D. It's similar to the rationale behind adding more and more water to soup that's too salty. The objective is to keep the saltwater solution in the kidneys extremely diluted so that a concentration of stone-forming salts doesn't get stuck there. Water causes the concentration of chemicals in the urine to decrease, making them more soluble and less likely to form stones. Drink at least 8 to 10 full 12-ounce glasses of water each day. Not juice or soda or milk—just water, says Dr. Hecht. (Salt and sugar can raise the level of calcium in your urine.) "You should drink enough so that you're urinating every couple of hours," he adds.

Cut back on meat. Studies show that diets high in animal protein increase the chance of forming stones. Most people who develop stones eat too much meat. How much meat is too much? Your daily total of meat should be no more than two three-ounce portions, or about 70 grams of protein. Measured by size, each portion should be no larger than a deck of playing cards.

Chalk up the brocc. Broccoli is rich in vitamin A, a nutrient that can help keep the urinary tract lining healthy and discourage the production of kidney stones. Other vitamin-A-rich foods include dried apricots, cantaloupe, carrots, Brussels sprouts, and sweet potatoes.

Shake off the salt. Eating salt starts a chain reaction that ends with more calcium being excreted. The result could be greater likelihood of who are at risk, says Brian L. Morgan, Ph.D., a research scientist. Table salt is out, as are high-salt luncheon meats, processed cheeses, snack foods, and foods packed in brine.

Bring on the rice bran. From Japan comes a natural healing idea whose time has come. In one study, patients with a history of kidney stone problems were given two tablespoons of rice bran twice daily after meals. Of 61 patients, 52 had no recurrence. The researchers believe that a substance in rice bran seems to reduce the intestinal absorption of calcium, thereby reducing your chances of getting a kidney stone.

Seek out citrates. Consider making a handful of dried apricots or a baked potato a regular part of your anti-stone diet. Along with a variety of fruits and vegetables, these foods are somewhat alkaline, which helps neutralise stoneforming acids in the body. Here's how it works. Alkaline foods increase the level of a mineral called citrate in the urine, and citrate, explains Lisa Ruml, MD, an assistant professor of medicine, helps block the formation of stones. To raise your levels of citrate, Dr. Ruml says, you need to get more fruits and vegetables into your diet. "Many of the foods that are high in citrates, like citrus fruits and vegetables, are also good sources of potassium," she says. Another way to increase your levels of stone-dissolving citrates is to drink more orange juice. In a study at the University of Texas Southwestern Medical Centre, men with histories of kidney stones were given either three glasses of orange juice a day or potassium-citrate supplements. The researchers found that the juice was almost as effective as the supplements. "We recommend drinking at least a litre (a little more than 32 ounces) a day if you have stones, because of its content of potassium and citrate," says Dr. Ruml.

Cut down on caffeine and alcohol. Keep caffeine use, especially coffee, at moderate levels. Caffeine increases urinary calcium, which ups the risk of having a kidney stone. As for alcohol, people who are prone to kidney stones consume almost twice as much alcohol as people who aren't.

Crave cranberries. For those prone to kidney stones, cranberry is the juice of choice, says naturopathic physician Michael Murray, N.D., author of *The Complete Book of Juicing*. He explains that cranberry juice reduces the amount of calcium in your urine. He recommends two eight-ounce glasses daily as a preventative.

Peel some bananas. Potassium, a nutrient found in fruits, like bananas, cantaloupe and apricots, and in vegetables, like lima beans and potatoes, has been linked with a lower incidence of kidney stones.

Cut the fat. "When dietary fat isn't fully absorbed from the gut, it can contribute to the formation of kidney stones by binding with calcium," says Melvyn Werbach, MD, a physician who specialised in nutritional medicine and the author of *Healing with Food*.

Consider calcium. Not long ago, doctors told people with kidney stones to restrict their calcium intake. But a Harvard study of nearly 46,000 men found that those who ate the most calcium were actually the least likely to form stones. In another Harvard study, women who consumed at least 1,100 milligrams of dietary calcium a day had one-third the risk of developing kidney stones compared with those who consumed less than 500 milligrams a day. Your doctor may recommend including a high-calcium food, such as a glass of milk, with every meal.

Helpful vitamins and supplements:

Stonewall with magnesium. Having high levels of calcium oxalate and calcium phosphate in your urine isn't a problem as long at you excrete those salts. For that to happen efficiently, they need to hook up with other essential chemicals in the urine. Otherwise, they'll clump together, form crystals, and precipitate out like sugar settling to the bottom of a glass of iced tea. That's where magnesium comes in. It binds with the calcium salts so they stay dissolved in the urine. Magnesium is a regulator of calcium, says Michael Gazsi, N.D., a naturopathic. "You excrete it rather than having it settle out in the kidney," he explains. "If you keep the magnesium ratio in the urine high, there's less chance of forming a stone." If you have a predisposition to calcium stones, Dr. Gazsi suggests that you take 500 to 1,000 milligrams of magnesium a day. "It's the single best thing you can do to prevent these types of stones," he says.

Boost protection with B6 For added insurance, you can take a vitamin B6 supplement, since B6 reduces the production of calcium oxalates, says Dr. Hecht. This vitamin does more than reduce the amount of calcium

Negate the oxylate

Doctors say you can minimise your chances of getting a calcium oxalate stone by avoiding or cutting down on your intake of oxalate-rich foods. These include:

baked beans	green, wax and dry beans, beets
blackberries	blueberries
celery	chocolate and cocoa
eggplant	grapes
collard, mustard, and dandelion greens	kale
lemon peel	okra
parsley	green peppers
raspberries	soybean curd
spinach	strawberries
tangerines	tofu
tea	watercress
wheat germ	

that's dissolved in your urine, however. It also prevents calcium in the urine from sticking together and forming a stone. Dr. Hecht recommends taking 25 to 50 milligrams of vitamin B6 daily along with a magnesium supplement. "Magnesium alone decreases the likelihood of kidney stones, but when you put it with vitamin B6, it has an even greater effect," he says.

Keep Your Cs Low. Vitamin C is good for protecting your cells and boosting immunity, but high doses can be a problem for people with a tendency toward kidney stones, says Dr. McClenon. That's because one by-product of vitamin C is oxalate. While this doesn't mean that you should avoid vitamin C entirely, it's probably a good idea to limit your dosage to no more than 2,000 milligrams a day, says Dr. McClenon.

Easing the pain with exercise:

Get into action. Regular exercise helps put calcium back into your bones, where it's most needed. People who are inactive tend to accumulate calcium in the blood stream. A daily workout for at least 30 continuous minutes is advised. (Remember to drink fluids before, during and after exercising, and to drink past the point at which your thirst is quenched.

Mind over malady:

Use your imagination. No, your kidney stones are not caused by stress, but tension can make things worse. What you can do to help yourself is imagine your stones vacating the premises. Do this exercise three times daily-in the early morning, at twilight, and at bedtime, says Gerald Epstein,

MD, author of *Healing Visualisations: Creating Health through Imagery.* Sit on a chair with your feet flat on the floor, your hands and elbows resting comfortably on its arms, and your back straight. Do this for 1 to 2 minutes each time. Tell yourself that a flock of birds is going to eliminate your kidney stones for you (Yes, birds!).

Close your eyes and breathe in and out slowly three times. See, sense, and feel the presence of your kidney stone lodged in your kidney. (If you don't know what a kidney looks like, thumb through an anatomy book or encyclopedia until you find a drawing of one.) Investigate it from every angle.

Now breathe out once. Imagine a flock of golden birds with golden beaks descending into your kidney. See them pecking away at the stone and removing it. They chip away—you see and sense that—until it's completely eroded. Then they fly away.

Breathe in and out again. See, sense, and feel a light sunshower coming from above, washing through your body and flushing the kidney to take away any residue of the stone that remains. Sense the flow of urine-containing long strands of residue-going down through your urethra and out of your body, to be buried deep in the earth.

Know that your stones have been eliminated. Breathe in and out and open your eyes.

Do this exercise for 21 days or until your stone disappears.

Knee Pain

The pain: Pain at the knee or kneecap.

The cause: Knee pain can attack from several angles. Arthritis is one common cause. If you're significantly overweight, you can put additional wear and tear on your knees. If you're sedentary and don't exercise, the muscles and ligaments in our knees can atrophy and weaken before their time.

"As we get older, we often run into problems with cartilage tears in the knees. After we've been on our feet for so many years, the cartilage may get brittle and tear even without a specific injury," says Terry Nelson, MD, an orthopedist,

See a doctor if:
...you have pain around the kneecap that occurs for the first time when you are climbing or coming down stairs and persists for two or more days.
...you have kneecap pain that occurs for the first time after sitting for a long time and persists for two or more days.
...you have pain that does not respond to the RICE (rest, ice, compression, and elevation) technique or a painkiller.
...your knee is swelling, especially after an injury.

Quick relief:
Know when to fold. If you get a sudden twinge in your knee that makes it "lock up," restricting full motion, get off your feet, says Andy Clary, head trainer for the University of Miami football team in Florida. You may be able to move again cautiously after a few minutes. But begin gently: Don't resume heavy or strenuous activity, Clary advises.

Press on some ice. For any knee pain, applying ice will help force your body to flush the knee with blood and oxygen, elements vital for repair. Ice also acts as an anaesthetic to soothe the ache, says Patrice Morency, a sports injury management specialist, who works with Olympic hopefuls.

Use an ice pack or ice cubes inside a plastic bag. Just make sure the ice pack is wrapped in a towel, so it doesn't come in direct contact with your skin. Apply ice to the sore knee no longer than 20 minutes every hour, says Morency.

Treat injuries with RICE. RICE is an acronym for rest, ice, compression, elevation. Give the knee some rest, ice it for 15 minutes at a time several times a day, compress the knee by wrapping it snugly in an elastic bandage and elevate the knee with pillows to drain fluids from the joint.

Warm your wobbly knees. Cold is fine for injuries after they first occur, but most lingering pain responds to moist warmth, says Edward J. Resnick, MD, a professor of orthopedic surgery. He recommends a warm, moist towel, a hot-water bottle, a moist heating pad, a warm bath or a whirlpool.

Try an anti-inflammatory. You can calm inflammation and soreness with over-the-counter remedies that contain the anti-inflammatory ingredient ibuprofen, according to Paul Raether, MD, a marathoner who is a physical medicine specialist.

Taken as directed, ibuprofen is also a painkiller, so it's important not to be lulled into a false sense of security when the pain eases. When you resume your activity, try it when you're not taking an anti-inflammatory, so you can feel the pain if your knee sends out warning signals.

Everyday prevention:

Lighten up. "To prevent knee pain from osteoarthritis or injury, the first thing that you have to do is lose weight," says James M. Fox, MD, an orthopedic surgeon and knee specialist and author of *Save Your Knees.* The reason, of course, is that more weight means increased pressure and stress on that weight-bearing joint. "If you throw a bag of sand in the trunk of your car for weight traction during the winter but then drive around with it all year, your tires will wear abnormally. If you weigh 10 extra pounds, you carry that extra weight around with you all the time, and your knees will wear abnormally. Those 10 additional pounds put 60 pounds per square inch of extra pressure on your knees every time you take a step."

Throw in the towel. If you're going to be hiking near a stream or other cold waterway, carry a small towel or facecloth with you. When you stop to take a break, plunge the cloth into the cold water, wring it out, and wrap it around your knee.

Unbrace yourself. Wearing a knee brace may be a short-term solution after a particularly painful bout of knee pain. But try to go without that brace as soon as possible to prevent becoming psychologically attached, suggests Dr. Raether.

Avoid the knee bashers. Some activities, such as running and hiking over hilly terrain, put a greater demand on the kneecap than others. "These force the kneecap strongly against the end of the thigh bone," says Dr. Raether. If you're having knee pain, minimise those activities until you've had time to strengthen your leg muscles, he says.

Check out new workouts. Knee problems often occur when someone starts a workout program without first understanding how to properly perform exercises or an activity.

Break up long drives. Your knees can really get stiff from being held in the same position during a long drive. If you have cruise control, use it, and stretch out your knees. If you don't try to shift positions from time to time and take a break from driving once an hour.

Sit right. When it comes to knee pain, it's not only how long you sit but also the way you sit that can cause problems, says Ed Lakowski, MD, co-director of the Sportsmedicine Centre at the Mayo Clinic in Minnesota. In particular, be wary of any position in which your knees are very flexed. "If you have to sit for a long time, find a way to straighten your leg to disengage the knee cap from its groove and relive the pressure," he advises.

Don't lock up. Locking your knees puts unwelcome pressure on an already-aching joint, says Paul Lotke, MD, a professor of orthopedic surgery. "Try bending your knees just a little when you stand," he suggests. "At first you'll feel as though you're squatting, even if you've moved only a fraction of an inch. But if you look at yourself in a mirror, you won't even notice it. The more you do it, the easier it will become."

Lose the limp. If you can't walk without limping, you should use crutches or a cane. Otherwise you're increasing the workload for muscles and tendons elsewhere in your body, and that can cause problems.

Ease back in. Once your knee is feeling better, return to your daily routine gradually. You should experience no pain at all when going about your daily tasks before you try to do something more stressful, like play a sport. When you feel as if you're ready to do something more stressful, disontinue any painkillers you may have been taking. That way you'll know if you're overdoing it.

Easing the pain with exercise:

Hoof it. "Millions of people experience knee pain or knee injuries,' says Dr. Fox. "Most of these pains, sprains, and strains could have been avoided with weight loss and proper muscular conditioning." That's because the muscles guide the knee joint like reins guide a horse, says Dr. Fox. If the muscles aren't strong enough, the joint is wobbling all over the place and is more likely to be injured. Stronger leg muscles will also help prevent the pain of osteoarthritis of the knee, says Arthur Brownstein, MD, a clinical instructor of medicine. "Ninety-eight percent of the pain in any arthritic joint is caused by weak muscles, tendons, and ligaments around the joint," he says. "Stronger muscles prevent pain by taking pressure off the joint."

"The best way to strengthen the hamstrings, quadriceps, and calf muscles is by walking," says Dr. Fox. He recommends doing it regularly for 30 to 40 minutes, three or four days a week, alternating with jogging or bike riding if you want to. It is a good idea to check with your doctor before starting any new exercise program.

Walk every mountain. Tired of walking a flat terrain all the time? Set your sights higher and try hill walking, suggests Dr. Brownstein. "You will really start to feel your quadriceps and hamstrings build in their strength and endurance once you start to walk up and down hills."

Just shoe me. If you exercise regularly but find that knee pain is starting to creep in, take a good look at your fitness shoes, says Dr. Fox. "The right fitness shoe keeps the knee stable and reduces impact both of which are key to avoiding injury. Running shoes, for example, aren't meant for walking. They have a different tread and cushioning than is necessary for that activity."

To find the best fitness shoe, Dr. Fox recommends shopping at a shoe store that deals with many different types of fitness and sports activities and that carries lots of different brands. 'Asking friends is a great way to get good advice about where to shop for fitness shoes," he adds. And if a friend has a favourite salesclerk at the store, get the name, too.

Hold up the wall. There's a long section of connective tissue that runs all the way from your hip down to your calf. It frequently gets tight, causing pain in the knee. This stretch will help ease the pain and keep that tissue toned, says Michael Ciccotti, MD, orthopedic surgeon and a team physician for the U.S. Women's National Soccer Team.

Stand at arm's length from a wall with your left side toward it.

Place your left palm against the wall at shoulder level.

Keeping both feet flat on the floor, cross your right leg over your left leg and lean your hip gently toward the wall.

Hold for about 30 seconds and then uncross your legs.

Switch sides and repeat. Try this stretch at least twice a day.

Grab an ankle. Strong, flexible quadriceps (the muscles at the fronts of your thighs) can help stabilise the kneecap, says Thomas Meade, MD, orthopedic surgeon. He offers this easy quad stretch:

Stand with your back straight and your feet shoulder-width apart. Place your left hand on a tabletop or a chair for support. Pull your right foot straight up behind you, grabbing your ankle in your right hand. Keep your knee pointed toward the floor. As you pull your foot back and up, you should feel a stretch in your thigh muscles. Hold the stretch for at least 20 seconds and then relax. Try five, then switch legs and repeat.

Get on your bike. The stationary bike parked in your bedroom or living room can be a real knee pleaser, says Kim Fagan, MD, a sports medicine physician. Working out on the bike can soothe an arthritic knee or most other types of chronic knee pain. To ensure a successful ride, Dr. Fagan recommends raising the seat as high as you can while still being able to reach the pedals and keeping the resistance level at a minimum. You should flex your knees as little as possible while riding.

Start with a 5-minute ride and gradually build up to 20 minutes, Dr. Fagan suggests. "Initially, you are using the cycle to increase range of motion and strengthen the knee. Once you build the time up, this also becomes a cardiovascular exercise," she says.

Ham it up. Give equal time to stretching the hamstring muscles located on the backs of your thighs, adds Dr. Meade, which also help stabilise your knees.

Stand and prop your right foot on the seat of a chair. Keep your leg straight and lock your knee. Bend your left leg slightly .

Place both hands on your right thigh just above the knee.

With your back straight, lean forward from the hip until you feel a stretch in the back of your thigh.

Hold for 20 seconds and then relax. Try five of these stretches and then switch to the other leg and repeat.

Take a 10-second pose. This isometric exercise can reduce pain and improve the ability of the muscles to absorb shock and cushion the knee joints, says Dr. Fagan.

While sitting or standing, straighten your leg completely, flex your foot back, and tense the quadriceps muscle around your knee joint. Hold for 10 seconds before letting it go. Try five squeezes.

"Ten seconds of this exercise five times a day will significantly strengthen the knee muscles and reduce pain and fatigue," says Dr. Fagan.

Sit and lift. This strengthening exercise doesn't look dramatic, but it will help tone your knee muscles, says Dr. Meade.

Sit on the floor with both legs straight out in front of you.

Knee care for runners

"When you run, for example, you're reproducing three times your body weight on ankles and knees," says Dennis Phelps, athletic trainer with the Athletic Rehab Care clinic in California. Yet most people, especially weekend athletes, runners, and aerobic dancers, take their knees for granted, rendering them very susceptible to injury. Abuse your knees and you'll know it!

Cut your aerobics class in half. Phelps treats a lot of people who plunge back into exercise full force before an injury is completely healed, delaying the healing process and risking reinjury. "If you insist on testing your knee, take it easy," Phelps says. "If you're itching to get back to aerobics, take half the class instead of a full hour, to see how it feels. If you feel pain, you know you're not ready. Stop and apply ice."

Stick close to home. By the same token, rehabilitated runners who've been nursing a knee injury should run on a track or around their neighbourhood so they don't get stranded in the middle of nowhere, crippled with pain. "Mark off a half-mile length, then run back and forth, so if you develop pain, you don't have to hobble a couple of miles to get home," Phelps recommends.

Run indoors. If your knees have been through the mill, consider using a treadmill—no hills, no potholes, no surprises, no pain. If you've had any kind of knee trouble, you should run on as flat a surface as possible.

Put a pillow under your right knee, but keep it straight.

Bend your left knee and place your left foot flat on the floor.

Place both hands, palms down, behind you. With the toes of your right foot pointed up, slowly and steadily try to push your right thigh down toward the floor. Hold for five seconds. Raise your right heel a few inches and bend your toes toward your body. Hold for five seconds.

Try 10 raises with your right leg, then move the pillow under your left knee and do 10 more with the left leg.

Strike a yoga pose. While strengthening the muscles around your knees, you also have to keep those muscles flexible. The most effective technique to do this is "a simple yoga stretch called the pelvic pose," says Dr. Brownstein. In fact, the pelvic pose is so powerful a pain-stopper that it can also heal knee pain. "I've prescribed it for people with advanced osteo-arthritis who were scheduled to have knee replacement surgery, and they have been able to regain full function with no pain."

To do the pelvic pose, kneel on a mat or carpeted floor with your heels beneath your buttocks. The tops of your toes should be flat on the floor, and your arms should hang freely from your sides. If you find that there is too much pressure on your ankles, roll up a towel and put it between the ankle joint and the mat or carpet. You can take this position anytime and hold it for as long as it is comfortable, Dr. Brownstein advises. 'When you are going through your mail, instead of sitting at the couch and bending over a coffee table, do the pelvic pose and read the mail in that position. Do it when you are folding laundry, watching television, or reading. It is the best way to prevent knee pain."

Don't pose in pain. If you already have some knee pain and you want to keep it from getting worse, you can still do the pelvic pose, but a modified version. When you start out, kneel upright near a sofa or bed, resting your arms on the mattress or sofa back for support. Put a stack of pillows or folded blankets on your calves behind your knees. "Slowly lower your body onto that stack," advises Dr. Brownstein. If the pain starts, just back off a little bit to a spot where it is no longer painful and rest in that position, supported by the stack. Now breathe deeply, slowly, and gently to bring oxygen into the muscle cells that you are stretching.

Repeat this modified pelvic pose and hold for as long as it is comfortable. Try to work up to 10 to 15 minutes, three to five times a day, suggests Dr. Brownstein. With each repetition, remove more and more of the stack so that you can put more weight on your legs. "Eventually, you will be able to come down all the way without pain so that you can take all of your upper body weight on your lower legs," he says. 'This will help your knees to heal."

Stand like a warrior. This yoga pose, called the warrior posture, is recommended by experts to strengthen the muscles around the knees and create flexibility in the muscles. Stand with your feet parallel about four feet apart (about even with your wrists when your arms are outstretched).

Then, turn your left foot slightly in and turn your right leg and foot out about 90 degrees. You'll wind up in a pose similar to a lunging fencer's. Keep your chest facing straight ahead wile you turn your head and look out over your right knee. Stretch your arms out to your sides and bend your right knee. Look over your right knee to make sure that it is in line with our right foot and vertical over your ankle. Hold that pose for 20 to 45 seconds. Repeat it three items on each leg.

Get some kicks. If you are sitting in an office chair all day, there is a good chance that your knee joints aren't being effectively lubricated, says Richard Braver, D.R.M., a sports podiatrist. To prevent getting knee pain when you are in this plight, he recommends an easy 10 second exercise called the quad pump. This exercise tightens up the quadriceps, the front thigh muscles just above your knees. Here is how it is done.

You can do the quad pump while seated in your chair. Just extend your legs so that your heels are resting on the floor, then tighten your quadriceps. Hold the contraction for two seconds, then release. Repeat this five times, relax, then do a second set.

"Basically, these pumps cause the cartilage to secrete a fluid that bathes the Joint in nutrients," says Dr. Braver. You can do this exercise whenever your knees feels stiff, he says, after sitting in a car, in a movie theatre, or in a long meeting.

Herbal help:

Make a beeline to bromelain. Made from pineapple, bromelain is touted as a natural anti-inflammatory that is thought to speed healing, according to Morency. It is sold in tablet form in some health food stores. "I've used it personally and know that it works," says Morency. According to the directions, you can take up to three tablets a day until the knee pain subsides. Then start to resume your activities with caution. (The only drawback is that bromelain can cause dermatitis in some people, so you should stop taking it if your skin begins to feel itchy)

Rub on some relief. "Ever since a bad skiing accident, I've had bad knees," says Jeanne Rose, a practicing herbalist and aromatherapist. Her solution: one drop of basil essential oil and one drop of sage, with eight drops of carrier oil, rubbed on her knees as an anaesthetic. "It works. I don't feel pain at all. So now I can lift weights to help make my knees stronger. It's really amazing."

Laryngitis

The pain: Inflammation of the vocal cords, causing extreme hoarseness or voice loss.

The cause: Some diseases that can affect voices are Parkinson's disease and diabetes. But for most people, laryngitis has common-sense causes. If you get a simple viral infection such as a cold, it can affect the larynx (voice box). If you let loose with a holler at your daughter's soccer game, your vocal cords may get the sensation that you're out to beat them. And then there are people who chronically abuse their voices because they overuse them professionally as do some teachers, singers, or lawyers.

A surprisingly common cause of laryngitis that is not as well known is gastrointestinal reflux (heartburn), which happens more frequently as you age. Reflux occurs when some contents of your stomach—including very harsh digestive acids—back up into your oesophagus. The acids from the stomach cause irritation and laryngitis.

See a doctor if:
...you've been having laryngitis for more than two weeks.
...you have laryngitis but can't remember when you had a cold or any other obvious reason for the problem. Hoarseness can be a symptom of laryngeal cancer, especially if you have a history of smoking or drinking.
...you suspect the cause of your laryngitis may be heartburn, especially if it's accompanied by coughing, throat clearing, or difficulty swallowing.
...you cough up blood or hear severe wheezing or other noises when your breathe.
...voice loss is accompanied by pain so bad that you have trouble swallowing.

Medication:
Many types of drugs can affect the voice and cause hoarseness. The most common are steroids. Many steroids can start to atrophy the vocal cords' mucous membrane, affecting the quality of the voice. But be sure you don't give up these drugs without your doctor's consent.

Quick relief:

Keep mum. Getting through a day without talking can be difficult. But when you have laryngitis what you need is a respite for your larynx and vocal cords, states Marshall Postman, MD, an allergist. "If you had tendonitis you would try not to use the joint that tendon was affecting, so with laryngitis really the best thing is to get vocal rest," Dr. Postman advises.

Don't even whisper. People think that whispering doesn't count as talking. But whispering is very straining and in no way saves the voice, warns Florence B. Blager, Ph.D. a professor of otolaryngology. When you whisper, the larynx tightens with a great deal of effort as your breath comes through a very constricted laryngeal area. This causes strain, and the louder you try to whisper, the greater the constriction, and the more the strain on the vocal cords.

Get steamed. Warm, moist air soothes the vocal cords. So turn on your shower as hot as possible and wait for your bathroom to turn into a steam room. Hang around outside the shower in the bathroom for five minutes a few times a day as you inhale the steam, says Jonas T Johnson, MD, a professor of otolaryngology. And use a humidifier when sleeping at night.

Get boiled. Using the power of humidity is also a good way to keep the airways moist and the secretions moving, says Anne L. Davis, MD, a professor of clinical medicine. You can give yourself a humidity treatment with simple kitchen equipment. Heat a large open pan of water until it's boiling and remove it from the stove. While it's still busily steaming, take it to the table, drape a towel over your head, and hang your head over the pot and inhale deeply. Keep your eyes closed and don't get so close that you burn your skin. Steam for between 5 to 15 minutes.

Shut your mouth. "The best thing is to close your mouth and breathe through your nose," says Robert J. Feder, MD, an otolaryngologist. Mouth breathing dries your vocal cords, which increases hoarseness.

Ongoing care:

Write it down. Carry a pad and pen or pencil with you, so you can still communicate, Dr. Blager says.

Avoid irritating environments. Don't go to places where smoke or fumes you inhale might irritate the larynx further, Dr. Blager recommends.

Don't gargle. A good gargle may seem like an obvious remedy, but it will actually do more harm than good. "Gargling doesn't seem to reach down into the larynx where the irritated or inflamed tissue is," says Dr. Feder. "More important, if you make noise as you gargle, the vibration can actually harm inflamed vocal cords."

Avoid aspirin. If you've lost you voice because you were yelling too loudly, you've probably ruptured a capillary. So stay away from aspirin, advises Laurence Levine, D.D.S., MD, a clinical professor of otolaryngology. Aspirin increases clotting time, which can impede the healing process.

See a speech therapist. People who are constantly hoarse with chronic laryngitis, or people who have screamer's nodes or singer's nodes (small calluses on the vocal chords), may improve with two to three months of speech therapy, Dr. Feder says.

Speak like Pavarotti. If you have to talk, don't try to project a whisper or yell. You'll eventually lose your voice entirely. Instead, speak the same way professionals learn to sing. Stand up straight, breathe into the small of your back, and speak as you exhale. Don't talk too fast or try to fit in too many words in one breath, says Susan Miller, Ph.D., an assistant professor of otolaryngology.

Nutritional remedies:

Liquefy your larynx. A phrase used among voice doctors and professional singers is "pee pale," says Gregory Grillone, MD, otolaryngologist and director of the Voice Center at Boston Medical Centre. Singers know that if their urine is not clear like water, they're not drinking enough water. And drinking enough water is a major part of good vocal hygiene. Drinking water keeps the secretions in the throat thin and mobile as well as helping the whole body with the healing process. So polish off at least 8 eight-ounce glasses of water a day.

Guard against reflux producers. Avoid alcohol, tobacco, caffeine, and mint or menthol, which all stimulate gastric acid and encourage reflux, says Dr. Grillone. Stay away from carbonated beverages, because the carbonation bloats your stomach, and as it does, it puts pressure on the valve between the stomach and oesophagus that is supposed to keep reflux from occurring.

Eat early and often. Severe heartburn involving acid reflux stomach acid that creeps up into the oesophagus and throat-can cause persistent laryngitis. You can reduce reflux by eating smaller, more frequent meals instead of a few larger meals; by waiting three hours after eating before laying down; and by raising the head of your bed about six inches higher than the foot, says Dr. Johnson.

Go for a soothing feeling. Suck on a hard candy or drink warm lemon and honey. These remedies can soothe a raw throat, Dr. Davis suggests.

Choose suckers wisely. Avoid mint and menthol products, which are too drying, says Dr. Feder. Stick with honey or fruit-flavoured soft cough drops, or hard candy. (Cough drops are basically just candy—they don't have any healing effect.)

Avoid milk, chocolate, and nuts. All three can thicken mucus, making you clear your throat more often, which closes the vocal folds forcefully. This can eventually make you hoarse, says Dr. Miller. If you notice yourself clearing your throat often, perform a personal experiment. Start cutting back on those foods and increase water to see if your mucus thins out.

Calm it with honey. A teaspoon of honey swallowed slowly may bathe your vocal cords in a soothing liquid, suggests Eric G. Anderson, MD, a family physician.

Try a soothing brew. Squeeze the juice from one to two fresh lemons, then mix it with a tablespoon of honey and a pitch of ground red pepper. Take a small sip of this mixture every few hours throughout the day, says Lisa Meserole, R.D., N.D., a naturopathic doctor.

Helpful vitamins and supplements:

Go from A to zinc. "People with laryngitis can get relief by sucking on zinc lozenges and taking up to 5,000 international units of vitamin A and 5,000 milligrams of vitamin C each day," says Elson Haas, MD, author of *Staying Healthy with Nutrition.* He advises continuing these levels of supplementation until your symptoms clear up and never exceeding 100 milligrams of zinc each day.

Everyday prevention:

Be smart about cheering the home team. Dr. Blager has studied the strain and damage cheerleaders can cause to their voices. "You overuse the cords, and, yes, you can ruin the vocal cords forever," Dr. Blager says. She advises people not to shout themselves hoarse at a sporting event. If you want to cheer for your team, give the voice some support. "Roll up your program and use it as a megaphone, so you get a lot of intensity increase without shouting. It lets you feel you're really contributing," Dr. Blager says.

Put your voice in the right place. With an illness such as flu, a person can become tired and weak, and breath can become shallow. When this happens, it takes effort to keep the voice forward. Even after the illness is gone, the shallow breathing pattern can remain, causing people to speak from deep in the throat, Dr. Blager says. That can cause hoarseness after just a couple of weeks. It may be necessary to relearn how to breathe and get the voice forward again, Dr. Blager says. Focus on breathing from the abdomen, not the chest, and focus the voice in the front of the face, not in the throat.

Strengthen your voice. One way to strengthen your voice, Dr. Blager suggests, is to practice extending your exhale up to 15 to 20 seconds. Two or three times a day, make a conscious effort to breathe out steadily on an "s" sound, while you time yourself or silently count the seconds. And concentrate on talking while you exhale. This helps you avoid speaking after all the breath is exhaled, which can result in strain on the throat.

Sing in the shower. Humming and singing in the shower focus your voice away from your throat and assure correct breathing. So humming and singing train you to put the least amount of stress on your larynx when talking, saving your voice in the long run, says Dr. Miller. Doing so in the shower makes you breathe in lots of warm, moist air, which also thins out mucus.

Leave the grunting to your ancestors. Grunting while straining to benchpress your weight or whack a hard-to-reach tennis ball can strain your throat and vocal cords, making your voice hoarse. Instead, breathe out slowly and steadily, says Dr. Miller.

Watch what you inhale. Any form of smoke will irritate your throat. So steer clear of smoke-filled bars, diners, and clubs, says Dr. Johnson. Obviously, if you're the one smoking, now is a good time to kick your cigarette habit.

Stop clearing your throat. Habitually rumbling your throat can irritate the voice box. "It's a mannerism that certainly could cause trouble," says Dr. Anderson. To break this habit, take a sip of water whenever you feel the urge to do it.

Get a grip on postnasal drip. Nasal congestion caused by flu, colds and allergies can ooze down into the throat and irritate the vocal cords, says Bruce Campbell, MD, an otolaryngologist. Break up any mucus with an over-the-counter expectorant that contains guaifenesin, like Robitussin-PE.

Herbal help:

Try some tea. Teas of horehound, mullein, and English plantain can help with laryngitis, according to James A. Duke, Ph.D., an authority on healing herbs and author of *The Green Pharmacy.* To make horehound tea, put one to two teaspoons of the dried herb in one cup of boiling water and let it steep for 10 minutes, or until cool. For mullein tea, steep one to two teaspoons of the dry herb in a cup of boiling water for 10 minutes; and for plantain tea, steep one teaspoon of the dry herb in one cup of boiling water until cool. Dr. Duke suggests drinking one to three cups of tea a day. You can find these in health food stores.

Get help from homeopathy. If you suddenly develop laryngitis along with a bright red, dry throat but you don't want water or other fluids, try a 30C dose of Belladonna every two hours, says Chris Meletis, N.D., a naturopathic physician. If your condition persists for more than two days, or if you notice white spots on the back of your throat, see your medical doctor or homeopath.

Try mallows. The mallows, including marsh mallow, the herbal forerunner of our pillowy candy treat, have been used for thousands of years as throat soothers. They are useful in treating laryngitis, cold,, coughs, sore throat and bronchitis. Mallows contain a special gelatinous fibre, mucilage, that soothes mucous membranes and helps protect them from bacteria and inflammation. Commission E approves mallows for throat pain, inflammation and irritation.

Ease with echinacea. Echinacea, also known as coneflower, is useful for relieving or treating laryngitis, according to Commission E. Echinacea also enhances immune function, which should help the body fight any virus that's causing the laryngitis.

Ease with elecampane. Elecampane is an antiseptic expectorant that is useful in treating laryngitis. Noted British herbalist David Hoffman, author of *The Herbal Handbook,* suggests a three-herb combo tea made with equal parts of elecampane, horehound and mullein. You might try one teaspoon of each per cup of boiling water and steep for ten minutes. Other elecampane fans suggest pouring one cup of cold water over one teaspoon of shredded elecampane and steeping it for ten hours. You can drink the tea three times daily.

Try ivy. Ivy is an old folk remedy for whooping cough. Commission E suggests taking a pinch of dried ivy (0.3 gram) to relieve inflammatory conditions of the respiratory tract, including laryngitis. Ivy has expectorant action and it helps minimise bronchial secretions that can cause cough and throat irritation.

Tie on some knotgrass. Commission E approves making a tea with two to three teaspoons of dried knotgrass per cup of boiling water to treat sore throat and laryngitis.

Pick some primrose. Commission E suggests using one to two teaspoons of dried primrose flowers or one teaspoon of the plant's dried root as a respiratory remedy for laryngitis, bronchitis, colds and coughs. (Note that this recommendation is for primrose, not evening primrose.)

Let sundew do it. If your laryngitis is due to a hacking cough, sundew is worth trying. It contains a cough suppressant compound (carboxy-oxy-napthoquinone), which is comparable to codeine, and other constituents that calm the muscle spasms that can trigger coughing. German studies of sundew as a treatment for laryngitis, sore throat and bronchitis show good results in more than 90 percent of users, with no significant side effects. One of the compounds in sundew, plumbagin, inhibits several types of bacteria that cause laryngitis.

Leg Cramps

The pain: A sharp, painful contraction or spasm of a muscle or group of muscles, which markedly limits use. It comes on suddenly and lasts from a few seconds to several hours.

The cause: Muscle cramps normally occur during hot weather, intense exercise when you're really perspiring, or both. The number one cause is dehydration, says Mary Kintz, an orthopedic physical therapist.

Your body needs fluids and electrolytes, substances that enable cells to communicate with one another, to carry out its biochemical reactions. When that communication breaks down, your muscles can become spastic—in other words, go into contraction and not let go, explains Kintz.

Muscles may also cramp when they are extremely fatigued from being overworked, says Kintz. These cramps often occur hours after an activity, when you're relaxing in front of the TV or falling off to sleep in bed.

See a doctor if:

...the contraction lasts for more than a day, makes it impossible to assume a normal posture or to walk, or occurs as often as two or three times per week.

Quick relief:

Pull the other way. The best way to stop a cramp is by reciprocal inhibition, says James Waslaski, a sports massage therapist.. Don't worry; it's not as complicated as it sounds. If the cramp is in the calf, contract the opposite muscle—in this case the tibialis anterior, located in the front of the lower leg—against resistance, advises Waslaski. Actively pull the toes toward your shin, which sends a message to your brain telling the opposing muscle to relax. Once the cramp stops, you should stretch the muscle that was cramping. Always choose stretches that work the opposite muscles as well, he says.

Smother inflammation. If you get leg cramps at night after exercise, you may have inflammation of your muscles and tendons. Make sure that your diet is rich in antioxidants (brilliantly coloured fruits and vegetables) and try taking one of the nonsteroidal anti-inflammatory drugs, like ibuprofen, a couple of hours before bedtime, recommends Dr. Ullis. "About 200 milligrams should be enough to decrease the inflammatory response," he says.

Cool it. If you get a cramp during exercise, it may be related to trauma and small tears in the muscle. Stop exercising immediately and apply ice wrapped in a towel, gently compressing the cramped area to keep down the swelling from injury, says Karlis Ullis, MD, a clinical medicine professor. Put the ice on for 10 to 12 minutes, remove when the area feels cold to touch but is not painfully cold, and repeat as needed, Dr. Ullis says. "You can also wet an elastic bandage with cold water and wrap that around the area," he says. "The quicker you can get the area cold, the better."

Take a stand. What sounds simple is also effective. The next time a night-time cramp sets your calf throbbing, get out of bed and stand tall. Raise your hands straight over your head and hold this pose for at least 10 seconds. It's a mini-stretch that reverses the direction of the muscle contraction.

Find cold ground. "The way to relieve an attack is to stand barefooted on a cold floor—a tiled bathroom floor, for example—with your knees slightly bent," says Jenny Sutcliffe, PhD, DPP, MBBS, MCSP, former Senior Lecturer in Paediatric Neurology, Great Ormond Street Hospital, London, chartered physiotherapist and author of *The Reader's Digest Body Maintenance Manual*. Pull your toes gently up towards you. Then knead the cramped muscle between the palms of your hands as if it were dough—or, even better, persuade your partner to do it.

Grab a towel or a T-shirt. If leg cramps have wakened you before, be as prepared as the Boy Scouts for the next assault. Keep a bath towel, a T-shirt, or a piece of rope within reach of your bedside. When a muscle cramp hits at 3:00 A.M., loop the cloth or rope around the arch of your foot. You can lie on your back or your side, but keep the cramped leg straight and bend your other knee slightly Slowly pull both ends of the towel or rope toward your chest, tugging the top of your foot toward your shinbone. Hold that stretch for 20 to 30 seconds and repeat a few times until the cramp vanishes into the night.

Massage the muscle. One effective cramp buster is a five-minute massage on the calf muscle. "Work the calf muscle up and down with the heel of your hand for about five minutes or until it feels good," says John Cianca, MD, at Baylor College of Medicine in Houston.

Take a slow stroll. You can also try to walk off the calf cramp. With each step forward, gently stretch your toes up toward your shin to lengthen the cramped calf muscle.

Roll in the relief. When a cramp puts your foot in a spasm, hobble over to the kitchen for relief. Kick off your shoe and grab a wooden rolling pin from the drawer. (An empty soda or wine bottle, tennis ball, or golf ball will also do the trick.) Plant the arch of your cramping foot on top of the rolling pin and hold onto a chair or table for stability. Slowly move the bottom of your foot back and forth over the rolling pin for a few minutes. Most of your weight should be on your good foot, but try putting some weight on the painful foot. "You're helping to get the muscles more relaxed," says Leonard A. Levy, D.P.M., a professor of podiatric medicine.

Avoid heat. Many muscle aches are best treated with a warm compress or heating pad, but heat treatment is not recommended initially for leg cramps. Applying warmth can cause swelling or bring more blood to the muscle, increasing the likelihood of calcification (in which blood gets trapped in the muscle and hardens).

Let gravity help. As with any type of leg cramp, encouraging blood flow away from the limbs and towards the heart can bring quicker relief. Elevate the area you're rubbing so gravity works with you.

Nutritional remedies:

Eat your vegetables. "Frequent leg cramps are usually a sign of an electrolyte deficiency, and I believe the answer is to increase your intake of calcium and magnesium," says Michael A. Klaper, MD, a nutritional medicine specialist. That means eating your vegetables, he says, particularly dark green leafy ones such as spinach and kale, which are good sources of both calcium and magnesium. Besides vegetables, good food sources of calcium include low-fat dairy products and sardines with bones. Good sources of magnesium include nuts, bean and whole grains.

Drink up. Lack of hydration is easy to correct. Drink plenty of water and sports drinks before and during exercise, Kintz says. "Water is okay if the exercise lasts less than 60 minutes. But if you're working out longer or working out in the heat, you may need to replace some electrolytes. That's when you want to switch to some of the sports drinks like Gatorade," Kintz says. Optimally, you want to drink about 64 ounces of fluid every day, and at least half of that fluid should be water—not juice or coffee. If you're cramping at night, make sure that you drink a few 8-ounce glasses of water during the late afternoon and around dinnertime.

Swig some salt. "Excessive sweating or a bout of diarrhoea can deplete the body's salt content and cause muscle cramps," says Dr. Sutcliffe. So, if you tend to have cramps, drink lots of water with half a teaspoon of salt mixed into it after strenuous exercise or a bout of diarrhoea. "Another way of preventing cramps from occurring is to make sure that you warm up before taking exercise and warm down after it, to make sure that the large muscle groups are well stretched," says Dr. Sutcliffe.

Helpful vitamins and supplements:

Supplement your minerals. The mineral deficiencies most often related to muscle cramping are magnesium and calcium. Both are important for proper muscle metabolism, says Alison Lee, MD, a pain-management specialist and acupuncturist. If you're eating a healthy balanced diet and still cramping at night, try taking a calcium-magnesium supplement. Given typical dietary practices, you're probably not getting the entire 1,000 milligrams of calcium per day that your body requires. Dr. Lee recommends filling in the gap with the proper dose of a supplement. Evaluate your diet, she says, and estimate how much calcium you're lacking. If you have thyroid problems or cancer, ask your doctor before taking calcium supplements, Dr. Lee says. Take most of the dose before bed, says Dr. Lee. Look for a supplement that comes in a ratio of two parts calcium to one part magnesium.

Take vitamin E. For frequent night-time leg cramps, a vitamin supplement may prevent recurrences. "If you get a charley horse at night, usually while you're lying in bed, then it may be a circulatory problem, which can be cured by taking a vitamin E supplement," says Steven Subotnick, D.P.M, a sports podiatrist, and author of *Sports Exercise and Injuries*. He suggests that women going through menopause try taking 1,200 international units of vitamin E every day for two weeks to end the problem. Other people should try 600 IU a day. In either case, decrease vitamin E intake to 400 IU daily after two weeks. Prolonged high dosages of vitamin E are not recommended.

Everyday prevention:

Sleep loose. If you've been exercising during the day, make sure that you stretch before you go to bed at night, says Dr. Lee. A slow, light, full-body stretch routine that takes 10 minutes or so is usually sufficient, although you may want to do a little extra stretching in the areas where you tend to tighten up, she says. "You can combine a good stretching routine with a hot bath or shower to really relax those muscles," Dr. Lee says.

Soak before sleeping. Treat yourself to a 10-minute relaxing soak in a warm tub before heading for bed. It will soothe your mind and calm your calves as well, says Dan Hamner, MD, a physiatrist and sports medicine specialist. As added insurance, try doing foot circles in the tub. While you're still seated in a comfortable position, pivot your ankles. Do 10 circles clockwise and then 10 counterclockwise with each foot. The warm water will increase blood flow and help the muscles relax, he explains.

Let your sheets breathe. Mom may have been a stickler about tucking your bedsheets tightly, but loose sheets are actually healthier for your toes and legs, say doctors. Dr. Hamner explains that sleeping on your back under tightly tucked sheets can leave your toes flexed toward the tops of your feet. You may get cramps in the arches of your feet while sleeping in this position, he says. So pull the top sheet out from under the mattress and give yourself some slack before you go to sleep.

Quell with Q-Vel. This is an over-the-counter quinine caplet designed to relieve night-time leg cramps. Quinine has been used to prevent and relieve nocturnal leg cramps since the 1930s. Fifty years later, doctors at the University of Utah School of Medicine decided to run a scientific test on the drug. They recruited eight men and women between the ages of 47 and 81 (the most susceptible age for nocturnal leg cramps) who'd been suffering cramps on the average of two nights a week for a year or more. When they took quinine, they experienced fewer, less severe cramps. What's more, when they took a placebo (inactive pills), the cramps lasted longer-anywhere from 6 minutes to more than 4 hours. But when they took quinine, the cramps either disappeared completely or didn't last long—14 minutes at the, most.

Try Benadryl. This over-the-counter antihistamine seems to prevent leg cramps in some people. Using Benadryl hasn't been proven effective in scientific tests, but a lot of patients and doctors find it works.

Easing the pain with exercise:

Build a better calf. "It is now thought that most cramps are caused by fatigue in the muscle," says Stephen G. Motto, DM, musculo-skeletal physician with a speciality in sports medicine at London Bridge Hospital. "So if you are plagued by leg cramps, your best bet is to get fitter by doing more walking or doing calf raisers." Standing an arm's length from a wall, extend the leg with the painful calf backwards. Place both hands on the wall and lean forward, keeping the heel of the backwards-extending leg on the floor and so stretching the calf muscle.

Pedal off the pain. A good cramp fighter is that trusty stationary bicycle that you keep in your bedroom or recreation room, says Dr. Levy. Five to 10 minutes of steady pedalling at the lowest resistance setting may improve the circulation to the calf area and untie that muscle knot. Adding a regular cycling routine—even 15 minutes' worth—to your day may also help keep future cramps away, advises Dr. Levy.

Do some lifts. Try the following two exercises the next time your toes or feet get crabby, says Dr. Hamner. First, stand so that the weight of your body is on your heels and your toes are slightly off the floor, supporting yourself by holding onto a chair or table. Maintain that pose for at least five seconds, feeling the stretch in your ankle and calf. Lower your toes until they're flat on the floor, rest for a few seconds, then repeat the toe lift. Next, lift your heels off the floor while your toes stay planted. Hold for five seconds, then relax for a few seconds.

Herbal help:

Have a kava. An effective herbal remedy for cramps and spasms is kava, available at most health food stores as a ground-up herb in capsule form, says David Winston, professional and founding member of the American Herbalists Guild and a clinical herbalist. "It's a powerful antispasmodic, especially good for people who get cramps at night in their feet and lower legs," says Winston.

Look for kava in a standardised extract (capsule) or a tincture. For the capsules, follow the directions on the bottle. he says. If you prefer a tincture, take 4 millilitres (or about 80 drops) three times a day. If you're sensitive to sedative-type drugs, however, be careful with kava. Because of the herb's anti-anxiety, mellowing actions, don't drive, operate heavy equipment, or drink alcoholic beverages when taking kava, warns Winston. And avoid kava if you're taking benzodiazepines (like Valium), he adds.

Ease with essential oil. "Lavender is the Swiss army knife of aromatic oils," says aroma consultant John Steele. He packs the versatile oil on long road trip to treat "driver's leg," that painful cramp in the calf that comes from hours of braking and accelerating. To use, he suggests massaging four or five drops directly on the affected area. "It works every time," says Steele. Tarragon and camomile essential oils are also effective for leg cramps, he says.

Get help from homeopathy. Gelsemium 6C is the remedy of choice if you have a burning sensation in your legs, feel better with movement and have fatigue after the slightest exercise, says Chris Meletis, N.D., a naturopathic physician. If you have twitching in your legs, with cramps localized in the calves and soles of your feet. Dr. Meletis says to try Cuprum metallicuni 6C. He suggests a6C dose of Veratrum album if the cramps are localized in your calves. you feel relief with massage and the pain is worse when walking, especially if your legs feel cold and look bluish. Take the remedy of choice two or three times a day until the cramps subsides, he says.

Use your mind

As you massage your leg's contracted muscle, you can further speed relief by using mental imagery. "If you measure a leg cramp-and we can do this in the lab-the instruments detect a shower of nerve impulses triggering repetitive, sustained muscle contractions," says peripheral vascular specialist Dr. Stanley Silverberg. If you can mentally visualise the muscle relaxing or the nerve impulses slowing, you may get rid of the cramp a lot faster.

Using Dr. Silverberg's description of a shower of nerve impulses, develop your own scenario. You can, for example, picture a narrow pathway running from your brain to your cramping leg. The pathway is crowded with messengers, each running toward the contracted muscle, each carrying a long spear. As they approach the muscle, they toss their spears at it, causing it to spasm with pain.

Now imagine that you have erected a stone wall across the pathway, a wall so high that no messenger can breach it. Picture the protective wall. No sharp lance can go over or through it.

Your muscle, now safe, begins to relax. Feel it become warm as you massage it. Feel the knotted fibres loosen and spread. Feel the relief.

Leg Pain

The pain: Pain in the leg.

The cause: Injury or overuse. The legs are also hot spots for various types of painful disease of the veins or arteries. It's also possible for leg pains to originate somewhere other than in the leg. This is called referred pain.

See a doctor if:
...the pain lasts more than three days.
...you also experience numbness, coldness or weakness in you legs
...pain occurs in both the upper and lower leg.
...you notice bluish skin coloration, ulceration or tender lumps below the skin.
...you sustain an injury that produces swelling or discoloration or you suspect bone damage from the injury.
...you have an overuse injury that does not improve after three weeks.

Quick relief:
Chill out with ice. Several days of ice-pack applications is perfect for relieving pain from an injury, says Lyle Micheli, MD, an associate clinical professor of orthopaedic surgery at Harvard Medical School. Wrap ice cubes in a towel and apply them to the painful area for 15 minutes at a time whenever you need relief. Just make sure the pain is from an injury Ice can aggravate the pain associated with vascular disease, says Robert Ginsburg, MD, director of a Cardiovascular Intervention Unit

Try compression. An elastic bandage will relieve pain and swelling from a quad or hamstring pull, says Dr. Micheli. (The quadriceps and hamstrings are muscles at the front and back of the thighs.) For relief from painful thrombophlebitis, compression support stockings do a fine job, says Dr. Ginsburg. These are prescription stockings designed for vascular pain relief. Knee-high support hose from a department store can actually constrict blood flow and increase pain, he says.

Get a leg up. Elevating an injured leg drains the fluids that cause painful swelling, says Dr. Micheli. It can also provide fast relief for the dull, aching heaviness of thrombophlebitis.

Warm away vascular pain. A warm, not hot, heating pad, blanket or other warming device provides fast, soothing relief for thrombophlebitis, says Dr. Ginsburg. Don't use heat on the first three days following an injury, however. It could make swelling worse.

Everyday prevention:
Be attentive to your symptoms. Try to identify what makes you, pain worse and what may make it better. Pay particular attention to the kinds of activities that affect the intensity or duration of your pain, advises Michael F. Nolan, Ph.D., a physical therapist. If constant or repetitive motion is part of your job, consider taking frequent rest breaks.

Be heart smart. "The same lifestyle changes that can prevent a heart attack can reduce vascular leg pain," says Dr. Ginsburg. "Give up smoking, stop eating fatty, cholesterol-laden foods and shed some pounds. A regular exercise program, especially a walking program, will re-establish quality blood flow throughout the leg."

Empty your pockets. Sitting on your wallet can bring on sciatica, says Stephen Mandel, MD, a clinical professor of neurology. Wearing tight belts and tight pants can also irritate nerves. So pick your pockets and trade in your designer jeans for a pair of comfortable chinos.

Use padding. Cushioned seats or knee pads can lessen the severity of hard surfaces and prevent sciatica and nerve compression, says Dr. Mandel.

Easing the pain with exercise:
Work your abs. Sit-ups and other stomach-strengthening exercises call relieve strain in the lower back, thus reducing referred leg pain, says Dr. Nolan.

Hands-on help:
Press this point. Pressing both thumbs at a point called the Supporting Mountain, located in the centre of the base of your calf, eases leg cramps in your calf and can help fight knee pain, lower-back pain and swelling in the feet.

Herbal help:
Soak away the ache. A soothing aromatherapy soak can help ease the pain of a sprained ankle, and it smells heavenly, too. Add 5 drops of sandalwood oil, 5 drops of lemon oil, and 2 tablespoons of witch hazel to a basin of warm water. Soak the sprained area until the water cools. "Citron, a substance in the lemon oil, helps relieve pain, and the sandalwood promotes circulation to the area, which speeds healing," says Douglas Schar, a practising medical herbalist in London, editor of the *British Journal of Phytotherapy*, and author of *Backyard Medicine Chest*.

Sip some "herbal aspirin." "White willow bark is herbal aspirin," says Schar. It contains salicin, which is the natural version of salicylic acid, the active ingredient in aspirin. It also contains tannins, which help reduce swelling. So if bottled painkillers make you queasy, brew up some white willow bark tea. To make it, steep 1 teaspoon of white willow bark in a cup of boiling water for 15 minutes, then strain. Drink one cup three times a day until the pain and swelling subside.

Heal with a special kind of ginseng. Drinking tea made with a certain type of ginseng, Panax notoginseng, "is a fabulous treatment for strains," says Schar. In fact, Asian practitioners have long used this herb, also known as san qi ginseng, to treat sprains, strains, and bruises. To make a tea, boil 1 teaspoon of the herb in a cup of boiling water for 30 minutes. Drink one cup three times a day.

It's thought that substances called ginsenosides give san qi its healing power, but exactly how or why they work isn't known. Different ginsenosides are found in different varieties of ginseng. This type of ginseng (which should not be confused with more common ginseng species in the Panax genus) is hard to find, but it is available through some mail-order catalogues.

Comfort with comfrey. Comfrey, also known as bruisewort, is a traditional herbal remedy for joint pain and bruises. This comfrey poultice is an effective treatment for sprains, says Dr. Song, director of the Northeast School of Botanical Medicine in New York. Chop a few handfuls of fresh comfrey and place it in a pot. Cover the herb with water and cook until tender. Let the mixture cool. When it's comfortably warm, strain off the water, place the herb directly on the sprain, and wrap the injury with an elastic bandage. When the comfrey cools, unwrap the bandage, rewarm the comfrey, and repeat. Apply this poultice two or three times a day until the pain and swelling improve.

Herbalists and scientists attribute comfrey's anti-inflammatory powers to a substance called allantoin. Tests in animals have shown that another substance in comfrey, rosmarinic acid, also reduces swelling.

Rub on an ancient remedy. Consider seeking out an even stronger herb-based remedy, called Shang Shi Zhi Tong Gao (translation: "attack and stop pain plaster"). This remedy includes clove oil, which contains the painkiller eugenol, and menthol, which eases pain and reduces swelling. The ingredients also promote the flow of blood and chi (qi) to the injury, says Eugene Zampieron, N.D., a naturopathic doctor, and co-author of *The Definitive Guide to Arthritis*.

"It's a very effective remedy for sprains and strains," says Dr. Zampieron. Simply place the self-adhesive plaster directly over the injured area and leave it on for a day or so. (It's waterproof, so it won't come off in the shower.) Shang Shi Zhi Tong Gao is available in Chinese herb shops.

Try Tiger Balm. If you don't have any Shang Shi Zhi on hand or can't find it easily, try Tiger Balm, another old Chinese remedy that contains menthol and clove oils. It's not as strong, say Dr. Zampieron, but it's easier to find at health food stores.

Morning Sickness

The pain: Queasiness and nausea that tends to occur during the seventh and fourteenth week of pregnancy. Not all pregnant women get it, and it can occur at any time of day

The cause: Doctors know that it's caused by the hormone oestrogen that's rushed into peak production during your eight or ninth week of pregnancy. It's usually considered a good sign since studies show that women with morning sickness are less likely to miscarry or deliver prematurely.

See a doctor if:

...you are losing weight. Normally weight gain during pregnancy continues even if you aren't keeping all your meals down.

...you feed dehydrated or you are not urinating.

...you can't keep anything down, including water or juice, over a period of four to six hours.

Nutritional remedies:

Keep crackers handy. The best way to beat morning sickness is to keep saltine-type crackers at your bedside and eat a few before you even get out of bed in the morning, says Jennifer Niebyl, MD, a professor of obstetrics and gynaecology.

Wash them down with juice. Next to the crackers keep a chilled container of juice or water, says Dr Niebyl. Fluids keep you from becoming dehydrated, which can make matters worse.

Eat this way. Eat five or six frequent meals that combine carbohydrates and proteins, says Barbara Silbert, D.C., N.D., a chiropractor and naturo-pathic doctor.

For breakfast, for example, she recommends crackers or toast—plain, unsugared carbohydrates—rather than a sugar-laden doughnut. Combine your plain carbs with protein such as cheese, peanut butter, or yoghurt. She also recommends kefir (a type of liquid yoghurt usually found in health food stores). "The key here is to always have easily digestible food in your stomach," she says.

Chew on it. Chewing gum might also help quell feelings of nausea, says

Willow Moore, a chiropractor and naturopathic doctor.

Try watermelon. If you can't keep juice or water down, eat a few chunks of ice-cold watermelon, suggests Miriam Erick, R.D., senior perinatal nutritionist, where she works with women hospitalised for severe morning sickness, and author of *Take Two Crackers and Call Me in the Morning!* Eat small, frequent meals. It's easier for your stomach to digest just a few bites at a time, and you'll be less likely to get nauseated. Make sure you don't overeat. Eat just enough to satisfy your hunger, because more could just make you feel worse. Save part of your lunch for the middle of the afternoon and part of dinner for a bedtime snack, says Dr. Niebyl. And take snacks along when you're away from home.

Act on your cravings. "Ask yourself what you would have if you could eat anything in the world," suggests Erick. What appeals to you,, Something salty? Sweet? Soft and chewy? Crisp and crunchy? Then eat whatever food satisfies your craving. If you want it, eat it, because in 30 minutes you could want something different. The exceptions include sweets and other foods with "empty" calories, which can upset your stomach and trigger nausea. And doctors strongly recommend that you avoid caffeine, artificial sweeteners and fried foods.

Lift an hourly glass. Getting extra liquids is important if you've been vomiting, so drink several ounces of clear broth, water, fruit juice or flat ginger ale or cola every hour or so. When you feel queasy, a cup of raspberry leaf camomile or lemon balm herbal tea can help soothe your stomach. "At the chemists you can buy a high-carbohydrate non-prescription drink that helps: it's called Emetrol. It helps calm the emetic centre, the portion of your brain that controls nausea," says Jack Galloway, MD, clinical professor of obstetrics and gynaecology. And sports drinks like Gatorade are also recommended, because they replace electrolytes—substances that regulate the body's electrochemical balance—that are lost when you vomit.

Helpful vitamins and supplements:

Don't be sick, B6. Studies from as early as the 1940s suggest that vitamin B6 provides effective morning sickness relief. In studies since then, researchers have found that pregnant women who take between 10 and 25 milligrams every eight hours get varying degrees of relief from their morning sickness.

Try taking 50 milligrams of B6 twice a day, says Dr. Silbert. "I think the activated form of vitamin B6, called P5P, is more easily absorbed and works best," she says. Dr. Silbert advises taking the supplement first thing in the morning. Depending on your morning sickness, you may want to take it even before you get out of bed. Then take a second dose around lunchtime, she advises. You should feel relief after the first few doses.

It might seem logical to take the vitamin as a preventive before you go to bed, but Dr. Silbert warns against it. "Enough of my patients have complained of having nightmares when they took a dose of B6 before going to bed," she says. "Just to be on the safe side, get your two doses in before the sun goes down." Some women's nausea is so bad that they can't keep the capsule down. Such women may need a vitamin B6 injection. The injection has to be given by a doctor, of course, but you may not have to go back repeatedly. One injection is usually enough to get things under control enough so that you can start taking the supplement orally.

Easing the pain with exercise:

Walk away from your problems. Stress makes morning sickness worse, which is one reason why so many working women suffer from morning sickness. "The boss is yelling at them, people calling in are yelling, and when they go home, their husbands yell at them, too," says Dr. Galloway. "You can bet they'll feel nauseated." But whether or not you have to report to a boss at the office or a grump-prone spouse at home, lots of walking is recommended as a stress reliever.

Many experts recommend walking for morning sickness and throughout pregnancy—especially if you've previously been sedentary. "Start at 10 minutes, but if your legs hurt, skip a day," says Dr. Galloway. "Work up to 45 minutes a day, five days a week." Light weight lifting also helps stress, but be careful to not hold your breath while pumping iron.

Herbal help:

Try the ginger cure. Ginger is another great nausea fighter. One study showed that 940 milligrams (about 1/2 teaspoon) of ginger worked as well for relieving motion sickness as the over-the-counter remedy dimenhydrinate (Dramamine). The results of a British study suggest that ginger works as well as drugs when relieving the nausea and vomiting sometimes induced by general anaesthesia and showed that it didn't have as many side effects as anti-nausea drugs.

One theory is that ginger works to prevent the gastrointestinal tract from relaying messages to the brain that trigger nausea and vomiting. Whatever the reason, it's worth a try. While ginger ale or ginger tea might help, the most effective form of ginger is the powder in a supplement capsule, says Dr. Silbert. Follow the dosage directions on the bottle.

Chew on anise. Herbalists have found that the volatile oils in anise seeds calm the stomach and relieve nausea, says Mary Bove, a naturopathic physician and a licensed midwife. Ask your obstetrician if it's okay to chew a few.

Sip raspberry-leaf tea. Try some raspberry tea as soon as you get out of bed. Herbalists say that the tea—or sucking on ice cubes made from the tea—helps relieve early-morning digestive distress.

Try some morning mint tea. Peppermint or spearmint infusions, sipped first thing in the morning, are effective against nausea, says Susan S. Weed, herbalist and author of the *Wise Woman* herbal series. To make an infusion, pour one quart boiling water over one ounce dried mint leaves in a quart glass jar. Cover tightly and allow the mint leaves to steep overnight, or for at least four hours. Refrigerate. If kept refrigerated, the tea will last for up to a week. If you wish, you can strain the leaves out or reheat the tea before drinking it. Many women keep the infusion by their bedside at room temperature and sip it as needed.

Try some peach and feel peachy. The Chinese use the leaves and Europeans use the bark of the peach tree to make a tea for morning sickness. The leaves contain the compound benzaldehyde, which should be of some help in relieving this condition. If you opt for bark, don't use more than a teaspoon.

Hands-on help:

Relieve the pressure with acupressure. While a daily all-over body massage might sound ideal, Wataru Ohashi, founder of the Ohashi Institute in New York City, recommends this quick technique that he claims will cure or reduce morning sickness.

Ask for your partner's help with this. Either sit or lie down on your side, with your partner behind you. He should press his thumb down your back, first following the groove between your left shoulder blade and your spine, then keeping up the thumb pressure around the perimeter of your shoulder blade, moving out toward your side. Keep the pressure on for five to seven seconds at intervals along this path. The pressure should be comfortable. If you feel a sore spot, ask your partner to keep his thumb there, giving that spot extra attention. Do the massage three times. Repeat the procedure down the right side. "If you stimulate the external, you can eliminate the internal discomfort," says Ohashi, who believes the trigger points you use in this exercise affect the stomach and the hormonal system.

Press your point. An acupressure point in your wrist can help relieve nausea, according to Elaine Stillerman, a licensed massage therapist on the staff of the Swedish Institute of Massage in New York City and author of *Mother-Massage*. The point 'is on the underside of your forearm, about 1 1/2 inches away from your wrist, dead centre between the ligaments. Press it with the pad of your thumb and hold for a count of ten. Breathe normally and repeat three to five times or until the nausea subsides.

Join the band. Developed for motion sickness and available at chemists, Sea Bands apply constant pressure to acupressure points for nausea, says Stillerman. Or you can try Stillerman's do-it-yourself-version: Affix a dried bean like a kidney bean over the point with an adhesive bandage and wear it overnight.

Motion Sickness

The pain: Queasiness, nausea, dizziness and vomiting that occurs when in motion in a car, on an aeroplane or train or on a ship or boat.

The cause: Motion sickness most often occurs whenever your brain gets different messages from different senses. Say that you're sitting in the backseat of a car with your gaze fixed just outside the window, watching the telephone poles flashing by. Your eyes tell your brain that you're moving fast. But since you're not being jostled around much inside the car, your inner ear, which keeps track of how your body moves in space, tells your brain that you're more or less immobile. The conflicting messages touch off motion sickness, explains Kenneth L. Koch, MD, professor of medicine. Your brain interprets the mixed messages as a danger signal. "The nausea, sweating, and headaches are your body's way of telling you to get out of there," says Dr. Koch.

See a doctor if:
...you're pregnant, have been travelling and have three to five episodes of vomiting.
...you still feel sick two or three days after the trip is over.

Medication:
Dramamine, Bonine, Marezine (Sea Legs or Cyclizine) and other over-the-counter motion sickness drugs are most effective when taken at least an hour before your journey.

But beware—all of these medications can make you drowsy, and blurred vision and dry mouth are additional side effects of the patch. If drowsiness is a worry for you, says Dr. Koch, try Marezine. He says it makes you less groggy than Dramamine does, and "it lasts up to six hours." Pregnant women should check with their doctors before using the patch or any motion sickness drugs.

Quick relief:
Look to the future. Looking at the horizon, when you're aboard ship or focusing a considerable distance down the road when you're travelling in the car is another key anti-motion sickness move, says Dr. Koch. When you

focus on things nearby, such as the waves dashing against the stem or the telephone poles whipping by, your eyes are inundated with evidence that you're moving fast, so they bombard your brain with "We're moving" messages. If you stare at the relatively unchanging horizon, your eyes will pick up fewer "We're moving" signs and transmit fewer signals to your brain.

Hold still. Keeping your head movement to a minimum helps fight motion sickness. If you want to look at something, keep your head still and move your eyes.

Hit the deck. If you're feeling queasy aboard ship, it will help to get out of the cabin and up on deck, says Don Nohr, captain of the Cypre Prince, a fishing boat that plies the choppy waters off British Columbia. The cabin is the wrong place to be because you can't see where you're going down there. In the cabin, your eyes tell your brain, "We're standing still," while your inner ear, registering your body's up-and-down, wave-induced movement, tells your brain, "We're moving." So get back up on deck so that the messages your brain gets from your eyes jibe with what its sensing from your inner ear. By the same token, if you're travelling by car over somewhat bumpy terrain (the kind that signals your inner ear that your body's in motion), moving from the backseat to the front and looking out the window can help alleviate carsickness.

Nutritional remedies:

Eat lightly. Steer clear of spicy or greasy foods before a trip, but don't go hungry. A small, easily digestible meal—try bread, crackers, cereal or granola bars—will keep your stomach occupied with normal digestion without burdening it with foods that may irritate or, like fatty items, take longer to digest

Everyday prevention:

Sit where it's still. The most stable areas are amidships in a boat or in the front seat of a car. On a train, face forward and sit near a window. On a bus, sit up front so you can see the road and anticipate curves and bumps. On an aeroplane, ask for a seat over the wing on the right side of the aeroplane. (Most flight patterns turn left.)

Don't read. Reading in a moving vehicle sends your brain the very mixed signals that cause nausea: Your eyes track across the printed words, while your inner ear detects every swerve of the car. Look out the window and let someone else read the map. But keep your mind busy—listening to music, doing problems in your head or other diversionary tactics take the punch out of motion sickness. Or take the wheel—people who get motion sickness rarely get it when they drive.

Keep busy. You may be able to keep seasickness at bay simply by not giving yourself time to think about it. If you stay very active on a big cruise ship, for example, your brain can override what's going on in you stomach.

Breathe freely. Avoid food odours and smoke-filled spaces. "Get cool air," says Dr. Koch. "Nobody knows quite why, but it seems to help."

Herbal help:

Get help from homeopathy. For motion sickness that's more dizziness than nausea, try Cocculus at 6°C or 12°C, suggests Michael Carlston, MD If the nausea outweighs the dizziness, use Tabacum, he says. Follow the directions on the label.

Try ginger. Some medical studies show ginger is better than Dramamine or other drugs at keeping motion sickness at bay. Start with two 900-milligram capsules of ground ginger root 15 to 20 minutes before a trip, says researcher Daniel Mowrey, Ph.D., director of the American Phytotherapy Research Laboratory. Take more whenever feelings of nausea arise. How much at one time is the right dose? "You know you've had enough when you can taste ginger at the back of your throat," Dr. Mowrey says. He says it works for up to 60 percent of people with motion sickness. "It's worth a try; ginger cannot hurt you," he adds.

Exercises that Prevent Seasickness

To keep yourself shipshape during your next cruise, try these exercises that may relieve dizziness or other symptoms of seasickness. If you practice them before the cruise, you may help train your body and your brain not to become dizzy. If you do them during or after the cruise, they may help re-establish you sense of balance.

Nod your head. Slowly, then quickly, bend your head forward, then backward, with your eyes open, 20 times. Turn your head from one side to the other slowly, the quickly, 20 times. As dizziness subsides, repeat with you eyes closed.

Shrug it off. While sitting, shrug your shoulders 20 times. Turn both shoulders to the right, then to the left, 20 times. Now bend forward and pick up an object from the ground, then sit back. Repeat 20 times.

Stand up, sit down. Change position from sitting to standing and back to sitting again 20 times. First do this routine with your eyes open, then repeat your eyes closed. (Open them if you feel yourself loosing balance.) Now throw a small ball from hand to hand above eye level.

Keep on moving. Walk across the room with your eyes open. Then closed 10 times. Walk up and down a slope with your eyes open, then closed, 20 times. Repeat on a flight of stairs, holding on to a railing.

Mouth Ulcers

The pain: Painful ulcers around the lips, gums or tongue. The pain can make talking, eating or even sleeping difficult. Mouth ulcers are recurrent by definition. These painful critters, also called recurrent aphthous ulcers, are yellowish grey or white with red borders. They're tiny, round, and appear individually or in bunches. They're not contagious and normally heal within 7 to 14 days

The cause: Stress, heredity, and certain foods such as chocolate, nuts, tomatoes, green peppers, strawberries, oranges, and other citrus fruits are top mouth ulcer triggers. Sharp-edged corn chips and pretzels are just as guilty. They can irritate and injure your mouth's lining and produce an ulcer, says Terry D. Rees, D.D.S., a periodontist. Studies show that vitamin and mineral deficiencies in B6, B12, folate, iron, and zinc are linked to the nasty sores. In rare cases inflammatory bowel disorders such as colitis, celiac, and Crohn's disease are the culprits.

See a doctor if:
...the sores recur more than once a month, show up in bunches, appear very large, or last longer than 14 days. Your doctor can determine whether you really have mouth ulcers or something more serious. "If your sore isn't painful, looks like a white or red and white patch or a lump, and it doesn't seem to heal, it may be the first sign of mouth cancer," says Sol Silverman, D.D.S., a professor of oral medicine.
...the sores are accompanied by fever, nausea, or swollen neck glands.

Quick relief:
Swish some salt water. Place one teaspoon of table salt in four ounces of warm water. Swish the solution in your mouth for 20 to 30 seconds and then spit it out. Salt water will keep your mouth clean and helps soothe the pain, says Terry D. Rees, D.D.S.

Gargle with antacids. Grab some Mylanta, Maalox, or milk of magnesia from your medicine cabinet. Chew the tablet or, if you have the liquid form, shake the bottle, take a swig, and swish it around in your mouth. Just don't swallow it. "The thick, milky solution coats the mouth ulcer and helps protect it from irritation and abrasion," says Ara DerMarderosian, Ph.D., a professor of pharmacognosy.

Coat with milk. If eating becomes impossible, rinse your mouth with a bit of milk before eating. The milk will coat the sore and make a supper possible.

Numb the pain. If your mouth ulcer is full-blown, dab on a topical anaesthetic gel or cream designed for oral use containing benzocaine. Zilactin-B and Orajel (Bonjela) are good choices to buy at the chemists. Use the anaesthetic before meals and more often, if necessary, for comfort. But you probably should not apply it more than three or four times a day. "They won't make your mouth ulcer go away any faster, but they'll quell the pain instantly," Dr. Rees says. Chemists also sell oral pastes that stick to the sore and act as a protective bandage.

Take time for tea. Ordinary tea helps ease the burning and itching . Soak a handkerchief or piece of gauze in cool tea and hold it to your sore for a few minutes until the discomfort subsides. Or use a cool, wet tea bag. Make sure it's a regular tea, not herbal tea, because it's the black tea's tannic acid that does the trick.

Rinse them away. As a first line of treatment, William H. Binnie, D.D.S., a professor of diagnostic sciences, suggests daily use of a prescription antiseptic mouthwash called Peridex. "Some patients get good control of mouth ulcers by this one method," he says. But he adds that people with mouth ulcers should avoid most mouthwashes because they contain too much alcohol and because they sting.

Nutritional remedies:

Watch out for hard food like potato crisps and pretzels. Eating too fast can also be risky, says Jonathan Ship, D.MD, an associate professor of oral medicine.

Spot your sensitivities. Many experts think that a small percentage of people with the problem are hypersensitive to various foods, which trigger the ulcers. "For example, my wife gets mouth ulcers if she eats strawberries or walnuts," says Dr. Ship. Other common triggering foods include tomatoes, chocolate, cereals, cheese, cow's milk, and citrus fruit, says Dr. Binnie. "If you see a repeating pattern where you eat a certain food and mouth ulcers occur, stop eating that food for a while and see how you do," says Stephen Sonis, D.MD, a professor of oral medicine.

Dine on daily yoghurt. "Eat at least four tablespoons of unflavoured yoghurt every day and you'll prevent mouth ulcers," says Jerome Z. Litt, MD, an assistant clinical professor of dermatology. He adds that it's unclear why the yoghurt works, but for some people it can be very effective.

Fill up on folate. "Frequent mouth ulcers can signal that you're not getting enough iron or folate," says Cherie Calbom, M.S., a certified nutritionist, and co-author of *Juicing for Life*. She recommends a daily dose of her nutrient rich folic acid special juice: Bunch up two kale leaves and a small handful each of parsley and spinach. Process the greens with four or five carrots, using the carrots to push the greens through the juicer. "This is also a good source of beta-carotene, which has been shown to heal mouth sores," she says.

Helpful vitamins and supplements:

Try A High-Potency Multivitamin. Studies show that deficiencies of vitamins B6 and B12, folic acid, and iron are prevalent among people with mouth ulcers. When the deficiencies are corrected, the sores often show improvement or complete remission. "Evidence of a vitamin deficiency often shows up inside your mouth and throat because of the rapid cell turnover rate that's characteristic of the mucus membranes," says Jennifer Brett, N.D., a naturopathic doctor. "Low levels of the B vitamins can cause swelling of the tongue and mouth ulcers. If you're not getting enough zinc, you won't heal as quickly from small injuries like biting the inside of your mouth. And without enough folic acid and iron, you won't maintain the necessary rapid cell division that you need to keep the lining of your mouth healthy," says Dr. Brett. A high-potency multivitamin purchased at a health food store should give you the nutrients that are necessary to prevent recurring mouth ulcers, says Dr. Brett. Take 500 to 1,000 micrograms of vitamin B12, 10 milligrams of iron, 800 micrograms of folic acid, and 15 to 20 milligrams of zinc, says Dr. Brett. If your multivitamin doesn't include all you need, simply add separate supplements to make up the difference.

Load up on vitamin C. Take 500 to 1,000 milligrams of vitamin C with bioflavonoids twice a day in pill form for five to seven days, says Craig Zunka, D.D.S., past president of the Holistic Dental Association in Front Royal, Virginia. "You'll notice that your mouth ulcer recurrences will drop dramatically," Dr. Zunka says. "If this doesn't work, up the dosage. But don't exceed 3,000 milligrams in a day. Megadoses of vitamin C can cause diarrhoea in some people," Dr. Zunka adds. In fact, taking more than 1,200 milligrams of vitamin C daily may be enough to cause diarrhoea in some people.

Try Thiamine. Other research shows that a deficiency of thiamin can lead to recurrent mouth ulcers. In a study, researchers determined levels of a thiamin-dependent enzyme in 120 people. Forty-nine of the 70 participants with recurrent mouth ulcers had low levels of the enzyme compared to only 2 among the 50 in the group without ulcers.

Go for vitamin E. Instead of swallowing the gelcap, crack it open and rub the oil on the ulcer, says Dr. Zunka. You can use plain vitamin E liquid for convenience. Four times a day, just saturate a cotton ball and dab it on the sore. "This will cut healing time by 40 percent," says Dr. Zunka.

Pop some lysine. Lysine is an amino acid supplement that works wonders for some guys. Take a 500-milligram tablet one to three times a day to prevent the mouth ulcers, says Dr. Zunka. "Some people just need to take the lysine when they begin to get a mouth ulcer," he says. If you're one of those guys, taking lysine for five to seven days should help it clear up fast. If you get mouth ulcers often, taking one or two tablets daily can stop them from starting, adds Dr. Zunka.

Everyday prevention:

Watch your mouth. If you cut, scrape, or injure the soft tissue inside your mouth, that damage could lead to mouth ulcers, according to Dr. Binnie.

Tell your dentist to take it easy. Some people experience mouth ulcers after dental work, says Dr. Ship.

Change your toothbrush. If you keep getting mouth ulcers, bacteria living in your toothbrush may be responsible. Change your toothbrush once a month.

Brush gently. If mouth ulcers always appear in the same spot inside your cheek or below your teeth, you may be brushing too vigorously.

Use a dab to deter it. To prevent a painful sore from getting a mouth-hold, ask your dentist about using Lidex, a prescription corticosteroid gel. "As soon as you feel a prickling or tingling sensation, put a thin smear of gel on that area," Dr. Binnie advises patients who use the gel. And you can use it a dozen times a day if you need to, he adds. "You can usually stop the ulcer from developing." Even if the gel doesn't stop the mouth ulcer, it can reduce or prevent pain, he says.

Nip it with a styptic pencil. This shaving-cut standby has been found by many mouth ulcer sufferers to stop the development of a new, still-tiny ulcer into a big, painful one. The active ingredient is the astringent alum, which dries out the sore. The trick is to catch the sore early. Dab it with a styptic pencil, it may save you a week or so of pain.

Manage your stress. If you are frequently getting mouth ulcers, the most important factor to deal with may be yourself, says Dr. Binnie, a professor of dentistry. The type of person who gets mouth ulcers tends to be an anxious, high-strung, and perfectionist person," says Dr. Binnie. "People who are really cool and laid back and don't have many cares rarely have the problem."

But even uptight folks don't get mouth ulcers all the time, Dr. Binnie says. They usually get them when they are about to undergo a specific stress, like a job interview, an exam, or a speech. In fact, Dr. Binnie's research shows that 54 percent of mouth ulcer patients said that a stressful incident was the most common factor associated with an on-slaught of mouth ulcers. "One way to prevent mouth ulcers is to learn to live with the stress in your life," says Jonathan Ship, D.MD, an associate professor of oral medicine. Meditation, yoga, or regular exercise are just some of the methods that may help you deal with stress.

Say so long to SLS. Studies suggest that the foaming agent sodium lauryl sulfate (SLS), found in toothpaste, may cause mouth ulcers. Study participants who brushed with an SLS-free paste for three months reduced mouth ulcer outbreaks by 70 percent. So find a paste without SLS, recommends Dr. Rees. You can start with Biotene, available at chemists.

Try triclosan. Switch to a toothpaste containing triclosan, an analgesic and anti-inflammatory agent that may reduce mouth ulcer recurrences, says Dr. Rees. Colgate Total is one product to try.

Zap 'em with licorice. The kind of licorice that stops mouth ulcers is a far cry from the black, stringy stuff that kids love to gnaw on. What you want is deglycyrrhizinated licorice or DGL. "DGL has anti-inflammatory properties. It speeds the healing process and soothes the discomfort of mouth ulcers," says Michael Traub, N.D., a naturopathic doctor.

In one study, 20 people with recurrent mouth ulcers used a DGL mouthwash. Fifteen people experienced at least a 50 percent improvement within one day and were completely healed by the third day. Among those who recovered was one patient who had had recurrent mouth ulcers for over 10 years. He had several sores on his tongue and lips, inside his cheek, on his soft palate, and in the back of his throat. By the seventh day after he started using the DGL solution, he was completely free of sores.

To begin the healing process, take two 200-milligram tablets 20 minutes before meals, says Dr. Traub, or chew one or two DGL tablets two or three times a day. While chewing, use your tongue to position the tablet residue on the sore to promote even speedier healing. Take DGL until the sore heals, he adds. In addition, you can empty the powder from a capsule into 1/2 cup of lukewarm water, dissolve the DGL, and swish the solution around in your mouth, says Dr. Traub. Repeat this at least two or three times a day until the sore has healed.

Wash it away. Wash out your mouth with goldenseal. Prepare a tea to be used as a mouthwash by using two teaspoons of the herb (available at health food stores) and one cup of water. Rinse with the tea three or four times a day. The mouthwash will ease the pain and speed healing, says Varro E. Tyler, Ph.D., distinguished professor emeritus of pharmacognosy.

Soothe it with calendula. Calendula as a tincture—a solution of the herb steeped in drinkable alcohol or a similar substance—is sold at some health food stores. Buy the water-based or glycerin-based variety; the alcohol-based tincture will sting, says Dr. Zunka. Smear the liquid right on the mouth ulcer or dilute it with water to use as a mouth rinse. To dilute, use 25 drops of calendula and four ounces of water. "Within 30 seconds, your pain will subside and healing will begin," says Dr. Zunka.

Ease the pain with echinacea. Add a dropful or two of echinacea tincture to a glass of water and rinse your mouth two or three times a day, herbalists suggest.

Grab some grapefruit. Eating fresh grapefruit may be torture if you have a mouth ulcer, but grapefruit extract may actually help. Natural grapefruit extract works wonders for bacterial infections of the mouth such as mouth ulcers, says Claudine Wingo, R.N., a member of the National Herbalists Association of Australia. Dab some right on the sore a few times a day or add five drops to a glass of water and swish the solution around in your mouth three times a day, she suggests. "It's very bitter," she says, "but it really works." Grapefruit seed extract is available in health food stores.

Treat it with tea tree. Apply one drop of tea tree oil directly to the sore to help guard against further infection. Be careful here: This is a strong essential oil, so no more than one drop, and let it sit on the sore and dissipate in your mouth, as opposed to quickly swallowing.

Soothe with a poultice. Antiseptic and anti-inflammatory herbs can be very helpful in calming a raging mouth ulcer, says Michael Lipelt, N.D., D.D.S., a naturopathic physician, biological dentist, and licensed acupuncturist. If you make a poultice with the herbs and apply it to the sore, long-term contact with those herbs can have a healing effect.

For the poultice, Dr. Lipelt recommends mixing five teaspoons each of goldenseal, myrrh, echinacea, clove buds, and white willow bark. Finally, add 2 to 4 drops of clove oil. If you are using powdered herbs, also add 5 to 10 drops of vegetable glycerin. Make enough to fill about 20 poultices, each about half the size of a tea bag—that will be about a week's supply. Empty a tea bag, then cut it in half, or use a square of clean gauze about the same size, and place a teaspoon of the herb mixture inside each piece. Tie with thread or string to make a small poultice.

If using fresh herbs soak the poultice in warm water for five minutes. Then gently squeeze out the excess water and insert the poultice between your cheek and gum, directly over the sore. For dried herbs, skip the soaking and squeezing and simply put the poultice between your cheek and gum, your saliva will do all the soaking necessary. A dried-herb poultice should be kept in place for 20 to 30 minutes, fresh-herb poultices, 10 to 20 minutes. You can repeat this up to three times a day for 7 to 10 days , using a fresh poultice each time.

Heal with myrrh. Myrrh is more than just a folk remedy for mouth ulcers. Germany's Commission E, the body of scientists that provides advice on herbal matters, has endorsed powdered myrrh for the treatment of mild inflammations of the mouth and throat because it contains high amounts of tannins. Tannin, the common name for tannic acid, is a constituent of many plants arid gives foods an astringent taste. An antiseptic with broad-spectrum antibacterial and antiviral action, it's especially helpful for treating mouth sores, which could be caused by a bacterium, a fungus, a virus or an allergy. To use powdered myrrh, just open a capsule (available at health food stores) and dab a little directly on the sore.

Cure with cankerroot. This plant got its name because of its traditional use as a treatment for mouth ulcers. American Indians and early settlers alike used cankerroot as a tea to treat both sore throat and mouth ulcers. Penobscot Indians chewed raw root for mouth ulcers and fever blisters. The plant, which is also known as goldthread, shares many of the active ingredients and healing properties of the more familiar goldenseal, barberry and Oregon grape.

Go for goldenseal. This herb was an American Indian favourite for treating all sorts of wounds. When scientists looked at this herb, they found that the Indians were on to something. It turns out that goldenseal contains astringent, antiseptic chemicals that help treat wounds and infections. To make a mouth ulcer mouthwash, use two teaspoons of dried goldenseal per cup of boiling water and steep until cool. Use it as a mouth rinse three or four times a day. Barberry and Oregon grape have similar constituents and healing effects.

Soothe with sage Although it is not among the richest sources of tannin, many herbalists suggest making a strong sage tea to treat inflammations of the mouth and throat. To make this tea, use two teaspoons of dried herb per cup of boiling water. Let it steep until cool and then gargle with it. You should not drink too much of this tea. Sage contains a fair amount of thujone, a compound that in very high doses may cause convulsions. Although sage is an excellent healing herb, sage is just one of those things—like aspirin—that is good in small amounts and not so good in large amounts.

Muscle Soreness

The pain: Stiff, aching muscles, usually following extreme exertion or activity.

The cause: The culprit, is lactic acid. As it builds up in muscles, especially muscles that aren't getting enough oxygen, lactic acid creates the soreness that we associate with over-exertion. If your body's in good working order, however, it quickly purges this excess waste product, usually within an hour.

Soreness that comes a day or two after you exercise has a different source. The delayed ache is caused by tiny tears in the muscle that become inflamed. Fitness experts call it delayed-onset muscle soreness, but you probably know it as plain old pain. It's a signal from your body to slow down and take a rest. It's also part of the recovery process that actually results in stronger muscles.

See a doctor if:
...pain persists for longer than a week.
...the pain is acute. If the pain is sharp or stabbing, you might have a muscle tear or joint injury.
...you also have a fever.

Quick relief:
Go hot and cold. Once the damage is done, says Jacob Schor, N.D., a naturopathic doctor, you can treat the muscle with alternating hot and cold packs after the first 24 hours. The contrast in temperatures works like a pump to increase the flow of oxygen and nutrients in the muscle. It also provides a flushing action to remove the tiny fragments of protein generated by the torn muscle.

Put your muscles on RICE. Even athletes follow RICE (rest, ice, compression, elevation), especially following the first day of practice, according to Robert Nirschl, MD, a professor of orthopedic surgery. When muscle pain from overuse strikes, rest your sore muscles at least 48 hours so they can begin to repair. During rest time apply ice, which works to constrict blood vessels, dull the pain and relax muscle fibres. Wrap some ice cubes in a thin cloth and apply the pack to the sore area for 20 minutes at a time. If the sore muscles are in your arm or leg, you can control swelling by compressing the affected area with a not-too-tight elastic bandage. Then elevate the limb above the heart. Lie down and prop it up on some pillows.

Melt the pain away. If your muscles aren't swollen, you can't beat a warm bath for soothing lingering soreness or stiffness. If you can't slip into a bath, use a heating pad on the muscle for 15 minutes. Steam baths or saunas also seem to penetrate and soothe long-standing achiness.

Drop a balm. Those tingly, icy-hot sports liniments containing menthol, such as Ben-Gay, may cause warming just below the skin. Just don't use them under heating pads or elastic wraps.

Ask for acetaminophen. Other over-the-counter (OTC) medications will probably reduce pain, but acetaminophen (paracetomol) is the best choice for muscle pain, says Dr. Evans. Why? Other possible painkillers on the pharmacy shelf—aspirin, ibuprofen, ketoprofen, and naproxen—all share a single drawback. These nonsteroidal anti-inflammatory drugs (NSAIDs) block your body's production of chemicals that cause swelling and pain, but in so doing, they interfere with your body's muscle-repair process.

Acetaminophen, on the other hand, blocks pain impulses within the brain itself, allowing the muscle-repair process to proceed normally, says Dr. Evans. It's also the pain reliever that causes the least amount of side effects when taken in normal amounts. Just make sure to follow the directions on the label, and never take more than 12 of the 325-milligram pills in a single day.

Nutritional remedies:

Eat an orange after exercise. Vitamin C after heavy exercise may reduce day-after swelling and pain, reports Dr. Clarkson. When your muscles are damaged by overuse, she says, they produce free radicals, the wide-ranging, highly charged atoms that can damage tissue and age your cells. Antioxidants such as vitamin C may absorb the free radicals before they can cause too many problems, according to Dr. Clarkson. So make sure you're getting the Daily Value (60 milligrams a day) of vitamin C, from fruits like oranges.

Flush yourself. Muscles need water, especially when they're being put through some serious paces. "Muscles are about 75% water," says Wayne Wescott, Ph.D., a strength training consultant. "So during training, the most important thing a person can do is to stay hydrated." He recommends downing a couple of glasses of water before and after a workout, and ad-libbing a cup or two during a workout if possible. And avoid diuretic beverages such as coffee, tea and alcohol when exerting yourself.

Helpful vitamins and supplements:

Take C and E and say ahhh. Because your muscles produce more free radicals when you exercise, you should take supplements of vitamins C and E, says Mark Stengler, N.D., a naturopathic doctor and author of *The Natural Physician: Your Health Guide for Common Ailments.* A healthy supply of these nutrients will help minimise the pain the day after your workout and will speed the healing process as your body rebuilds its muscle tissue. Vitamin C is also needed to help make collagen, the "glue" that holds muscle cells together. Following an injury, even a minor one like a sore muscle, the body needs to make more collagen to repair the damaged tissue. Vitamin E helps reduce muscle soreness, prevent cellular damage, and repair muscle tissue. To get your dose of pain prevention, take 2,000 milligrams of vitamin C in divided doses each day, along with 400 international units of vitamin E, says Dr. Stengler.

Block pain with bromelain. Even before your muscles seize up, you can get a jump on the healing process with bromelain, an enzyme derived from pineapple, says Dr. Schor. "If I know I'm going to be sore tomorrow—that I'm not going to want to get out of bed in the morning—I take bromelain." Like the clean-up crew the morning after a big bash, bromelain goes in and picks up all the debris floating around your damaged muscle. When you overwork a muscle enough to cause pain, bits of muscle fibre actually break off. These tiny scraps of protein may clog the muscle and cause pain and inflammation. The body has to clean house. Because it's an enzyme, bromelain helps by breaking down these proteins and digesting them. Once the waste products are eliminated, pain and stiffness go away, says Dr. Schor.

To speed up your own repair work, take 500 milligrams of bromelain three times a day between meals until the pain goes away, says Dr. Schor. If you take it with meals, bromelain's protein-digesting powers will work on your food, not on the muscle debris that's prompting your pain and inflammation. Be sure to check the product label to make sure that it specifies a strength of 1,200 to 1,800 milk-clotting units (mcu). "When it's not on the label, it makes me suspicious," cautions Dr. Schor. "The company may not know what it's doing, or it may have a very weak product and not want anyone to know."

Everyday prevention:

Start up slowly. The easiest way to avoid severe muscle pain after exercise is to start slowly any time you try a new activity, says Dr. Evans. Even if it's an activity you're used to, start slowly if you haven't done it in awhile, he adds. "Muscle soreness occurs primarily when you force your body to do something it's not accustomed to doing," he says. "If you know you're going to be playing tennis a week from now, do some jogging and light exercises a few days beforehand."

Follow the 10-percent rule. One of the best ways not to overexert yourself is to obey what's called the 10-percent rule, says Dr. Clarkson. Quite simply, it means that you never increase the difficulty of your workout more than 10 percent from week to week. "Because muscle pain usually hits 24 hours after exercising, it's easy to do a lot of damage to your muscles without realising it at the time," she says. "This rule prevents you from doing that." How does this translate into your regular exercise routine? Easily. For example, if you take 30-minute power walks three times a week, try to add three extra minutes, but go no further until you're used to the new time frame.

Plan ahead. "If you are going to indulge in physical activity when you are not really fit, and so muscle soreness is a very likely consequence, take an anti-inflammatory such as ibuprofen before rather than afterwards," says Stephen G. Motto, DM, with a speciality in sports medicine at London Bridge Hospital. "This will help prevent the soreness and much more effective than taking it after the fact," he says.

Easing the pain with exercise:

Get ready with a home stretch. When you stretch before exercising, you warm up your muscles, which may help prevent the tiny muscle tears that lead to morning-after pain, says Dr. Clarkson. Before your next round of vigorous activity, perform this all-around stretching routine, suggests Barbara Sanders, Ph.D., a physical therapy specialist. Keep in mind, these stretches should be slow and gradual, not bouncy. Don't try to complete any stretch that causes pain.

Shoulder rolls. Stand straight with your head high, your chin in, and arms at your sides. Rotate your shoulders up, back, down, then forward. Repeat five times.

Side bends. Stand with your right arm above your head, your left arm across in front of your stomach, knees bent slightly, and your feet about shoulder-width apart. Lean to the left as far as you comfortably can. Hold for five seconds, stand up straight again, then repeat. Now reverse the arm positions and follow the same process, leaning to the right.

Hip stretch. Lie on your back with your lower back snugly resting against the floor. Keeping the left leg extended, clasp the right leg with your right hand under the knee and bring it to your chest, letting the knee bend double. Hold for five seconds, release the leg, straighten it, and lower it to the floor. Repeat once, then do the same stretch with the left leg and left hand.

Hamstring stretch. Sit on the floor with your right leg relaxed, right knee bent so that the foot is flat on the floor. Extend the left leg straight in front of you. Now reach for the toes of the left leg with the fingertips of both your hands, feeling the stretch in that hamstring (the long muscle on the back of your thigh). If you can't reach the toes, grab onto your ankles. Stretch for 20 seconds, relax, and then do it again. Now change the position to extend your right leg and repeat the stretch.

Calf and Achilles tendon stretch. Stand three or four feet from a wall and lean into it, supporting yourself with your hands at roughly shoulder level on the wall. Bring your right leg forward, bending at the knee. As you lean forward, keep the left leg straight and left foot flat on the floor while pressing the right knee toward the wall until you feel a comfortable stretch in the straight leg. (Don't arch your back.) Hold for 20 seconds, then repeat with your left leg forward, knee bent, and your right leg extended behind.

Shoulder stretch. Stand straight with your arms extending straight behind your lower back. Grab your left wrist with your right hand and slowly pull both arms back from the spine as far as possible without causing pain, all the time, staying as upright as possible. Keep your neck straight, not arched. Maintain the stretch for a few seconds, relax, then repeat with your left hand grabbing the right wrist.

Watch for swelling. "If you develop muscle soreness, you should carry on exercising as long as the muscle doesn't swell," says Dr. Motto. "If it does, apply ice to the muscle, raise the relevant part and rest for three or four days. If the swelling and soreness doesn't disappear, go to the doctor."

Herbal help:

Go for ginger. For all-over muscle pain, take ginger, says Dr. Schor. "It's kind of like a home-style ibuprofen," he says. Ginger is well-known for its anti-inflammatory properties. Like bromelain, it also contains an enzyme that can break down protein, says Dr. Schor. In ginger, this enzyme is zingibain. Ginger has more, including various antioxidants, which help neutralise the free-roaming, unstable molecules called free radicals that play a role in causing inflammation. As a supplement, you can take ginger in tincture or capsule form. If you're in acute pain, take six 500-milligram capsules of the concentrated extract per day, says Dr. Schor.

Arm yourself with arnica. A popular remedy for relieving muscle soreness is homeopathic arnica pills, available from most health food stores, says herbalist David Winston. Winston recommends taking 3OX strength at the recommended dosage on the bottle for a few days or until the soreness dissipates. If you know that you're going to be exerting yourself and you anticipate soreness, you can begin taking arnica a few days ahead of time, Winston says.

Hands on help:

Get the massage. "Massage increases the blood supply to the area being treated," explains Dr. Jenny Sutcliffe, of London. "This speeds up the process by which the waste products that cause muscle soreness – lactic acid, carbon dioxide and urea – are eliminated from the muscles fibres, since these are carried away in blood and lymph." So take a warm bath to relax, and then massage the affected area. "Use an aromatherapy oil, such as marjoram, to maximise the benefits," says Dr. Sutcliffe.

Give yourself a hand. You can try Korean hand massage, a form of reflexology, to relieve muscle soreness anywhere in the body, says Alison Lee, MD, a pain-management specialist and acupuncturist. This medicinal practice looks at the hand as representative of the entire body: the top of the middle finger being your head; the ring and forefinger representing the arms; thumb and pinkie, the legs; the palm, the remainder of your body; and the front and back of the hand representing the front or back of the body, respectively. Pick out the place on your hand that roughly corresponds to the painful area on your body, and then stimulate that portion with a toothpick, suggests Dr. Lee. You hone in by probing the area for an especially tender spot, she says. "That corresponds to where your pain is," she says. "When you have the spot, press on it gently for a few minutes."

Nappy Rash

The pain: Nappy rash starts out as red, irritated skin, but it can turn nasty, causing the skin to break down if it's not treated promptly.

The cause: It occurs when a baby's tender bottom remains in contact with urine or feces for too long.

Quick relief:
Blow-dry that bottom. Keeping the infected area clean and dry promotes healing, but a towel can be too abrasive for the baby's battered bottom. "You can dry the baby just as effectively using a hair dryer set on the low (or cool) setting'. Use the dryer for about three minutes," says Becky Luttkus, head instructor at the National Academy of Nannies in Denver.

Add fresh air. What's rarer than dandelions in December? A newborn nudist with nappy rash. Fresh air and sunshine help heal nappy rash, while wet nappies encased in plastic pants set the stage for a full-blown case, experts say. A number of experts recommend laying the baby on a nappy and letting its bottom air-dry for a time before renappying. "We call this an air bath, and babies just love it," says suggests Luttkus. "It really is a good way to prevent or cure nappy rash, and it even helps to clear up yeast infections, which are often the cause of stubborn cases of nappy rash." To prevent baby's skin from becoming so dry that it cracks, smooth on a bit of moisturiser or nappy rash cream before airing, suggests says Alfred T. Lane, MD, a dermatologist. "You want the skin to retain some moisture, but you don't want it exposed to excess moisture," he explains.

Everyday prevention:
Use "gel" disposable nappies. If you go the disposable route, choose nappies with the newer absorbent gelling material. "These nappies pull wetness away from the skin better than other types of nappies, and they also keep the skin's pH level more acidic, resulting in less nappy rash," says Dr. Lane. Most major brands of disposable nappies have this gelling material.

Rinse cloth nappies with vinegar. If you have reusable cloth nappies, rinse them in vinegar during the wash to change the pH and help reduce nappy rash. "Just add 1/4 cup of plain white kitchen vinegar to each load of nappies during the final rinse cycle of your wash," suggests Luttkus. Also, don't use fabric softeners when washing nappies, because the softeners put a coating on the nappies that keeps them from absorbing as well, adds Luttkus.

Apply warm cornstarch. Store-bought "baby" (talcum) powders do nothing to treat nappy rash, according to studies by British researchers. "What may be tried instead is to take cornstarch, spread it out across a baking pan and warm it in an oven at 150 degrees for about ten minutes, so it's really dry. Test the temperature first. Then lightly dust it onto the baby's bottom," suggests Birt Harvey, MD, professor of pediatrics at Stanford University School of Medicine. The cornstarch is as "smooth" as baby powder, yet it is less expensive and appears to be more effective.

Don't fasten nappies. "Probably the best thing you can do is leave nappies off as much as possible, so the skin can air out. But since that isn't always advisable, try to place the nappy under the baby when he's lying on his stomach. You can do this during naps and other times when he's still," says Dr. Harvey.

Use paper instead of plastic. If your baby has excess leakage-which can contribute to nappy rash—place a paper towel between his skin and the nappy, advises Luttkus. The paper towel helps stop leakage, but without blocking air circulation. The disadvantage of a plastic nappy cover is that it seals in the moisture.

Breastfeed your baby. Numerous studies show that babies who are initially breastfed have a much lower incidence and severity of nappy rash than infants fed baby formula. In fact, the effects due to dietary influences are evident even after the infants are weaned, says John L. Hammons, Ph.D., a staff chemist at Procter & Gamble Company in Cincinnati who conducted one such study.

Wipe out soap and baby wipes. Two of the most widely used products to clean baby bottoms and protect them from nappy rash cause the biggest pains in that area-both literally and figuratively. "Commercially sold baby wipes contain alcohol, which aggravates nappy rash and causes a lot of pain," says Luttkus, head instructor at the National Academy of Nannies in Denver. "Besides the pain they cause, some wipes actually promote nappy rash because of chemicals they contain." Soap is another no-no for those with nappy rash. It is too harsh on the sensitive skin and also causes pain in the area. "Instead, you should rinse off the baby's bottom with plain, cool water," adds Luttkus. "Baths should be free of soap if your baby has a problem with nappy rash."

Go easy on ointments. Ointments that shield a baby's petal-soft skin from urine and feces can help clear up a case of nappy rash, but experts caution that they are to a substitute for promptly changing a soiled nappy. Creams you'll want to avoid using on nappy rash are those that contain steroids. Used regularly, these creams can inhibit tissue growth, which can increase the likelihood of skin irritation and other problems, Dr. Lane explains.

Neck Pain

The pain: Aching, painful neck and shoulder muscles.

The cause: Poor posture, tight muscles, muscle tension and back and other injuries can cause neck pain. Diseases such as rheumatoid arthritis, firbromyalgia and degenerated or herniated disks can also lead to neck pain. Physical changes that come with ageing can also cause neck pain: as time passes, the disks between the spinal vertebrae start to dry up and shrink. This can caused pinched nerves.

See a doctor if:
...you have neck pain that persists, even when you change position.
...you have dizziness, pain shooting down your arms or hands, or numbness or tingling in your fingers or arms.
...you have sudden or significant muscle weakness, such as the inability to lift your legs or extend your arms.
...you have a feeling of pain when you move your jaw and that pain is near your jaw, which may be a sign of an abscess or infection.
...you have onset of fever with a new onset of neck pain and stiffness, which could be symptoms of meningitis
...your range of motion is so limited that you can't perform important tasks such as driving a car.
...pain continues for more than two weeks.

Quick relief:
Apply heat or cold. You can apply a warm water bottle or an ice pack to relieve your neck pain, states Mary Ann Keenan, MD, director of Neuro-Orthopedics at Albert Einstein Medical Centre in Philadelphia. It's really your preference. "They both work the same way by increasing the circulation to the area."

Rest it and support it. The best immediate measure to take when you have neck sprain or strain is to rest your neck and support it with a collar. But use the collar only for a short period of time or only at night.

Nutritional remedies:
Drink a flood of fluids. "Well-hydrated muscles fatigue less quickly than

muscles that are poorly hydrated," says Karl B. Fields, MD, professor of family medicine. He encourages good fluid intake. "Water is used to transport minerals and electrolytes, which help with muscle contractions," he says. But remember that fluids with caffeine, like coffee and soda, are not helpful because they don't hydrate you very well. Choose water, sports drinks, or juices instead.

Everyday prevention:

Give your neck a break. Whatever you're doing, whether it's sitting at a desk or working on a hobby, if you stay in one position for a long period of time, your neck can get stiff and pain can creep up on you. To prevent this, get a kitchen timer, says Dr. Keenan. Set it to go off every half hour or so to remind yourself to stand up, do a little stretch, and take a little break.

Stand and sit up straight. "When you're not using good posture—specifically, you're slumping—all of a sudden your muscles are having to work hard to hold that head up," says Karen Rucker, MD. But you can take some of the workload off of your neck. Whenever you're sitting or standing, make sure that your shoulders are over your hips and your ears are over your shoulders. Your head should never be tucked under, like a horse in a bridle. "Think about the top of your head," Dr. Rucker advises. "Try to visualise the top of your head trying to touch the ceiling. You will lengthen, elongate your neck and get as tall as possible."

Get a chair with a better back. The old clerical chair had nothing more than a seat cushion and an oval pad that you could position somewhere in the middle of your back. If you're still using one of those, retire it in favour of a chair with a back that goes up to shoulder level. With the high-backed chair, your head, neck, and back are kept vertical, and you can lean your head back periodically to give your neck a chance to relax, says Don Chaffin, Ph.D.

Talk on a speakerphone. Wedging a phone in the crook between your tilted head and your shoulder can strain the neck. Even phones with headrests can cause pain, Dr. Keenan says. If you have long phone conversations, use a headset or speakerphone. You'll find both at electronics stores or office supply stores.

Buy an athletic bra. If you're a woman with a large bosom, you may not be getting enough support from your bra, and that can surely cause neck, back, and shoulder pain. Try an athletic or jogging bra, Dr. Keenan recommends, because they give more support and have wider straps. Athletic bras are designed so weight is distributed more evenly.

Use a fanny pack. Carrying a weighty shoulder-strap purse can put strain on your neck, Dr. Keenan says. A better option would be to switch to a fanny pack, which fits around your waist and doesn't put any strain on your neck at all. You can change to a hand-held purse for more dressy occasions.

Sleep with your neck in line. If you have an old pillow that's become droopy through years of use, throw it out, advises Dr. Keenan. It's time to get a good supportive pillow, she says. You want one that will keep your head in straight alignment with the midback, the line from the centre of your head down the back to the crease in your buttocks, and your spine when you lie on your back or side. Although pillows have firmness labels that can help, your best bet is to try them out before buying. Throw one on a bed display and lie down on it. Keep testing until you find the right one.

Set up your computer correctly. If you use or own a computer, make sure it's set up correctly, says Dr. Chaffin. Place the monitor at a distance comfortable for reading and at a level where your head is not bent forward or tilted back. Some experts suggest placing the monitor so you are looking at it straight ahead. The keyboard should be positioned so your elbows are at your sides, bent at about a 90-degree angle with your wrists straight and level.

Sleep right. That's on your side or back, supporting your neck with a collar or firm roll. The people in a study in Northern Ireland who had the best recovery rates for acute neck sprain were advised not to use too many pillows in bed, but to support the neck with a collar or by firmly rolling a hand towel and placing the roll inside the bottom edge of the pillow case.

Save high heels for special occasions. Few women make a connection between footwear and neck pain. High heels knock your spine out of alignment, which also makes your neck jut forward. Try to save high heels for special occasions and wear low-heeled shoes or flats most of the time.

Tilt your chair back. Often neck pain is caused by jutting your head forward. Solution: bring your reading material to you. When you read or watch television, recline your chair so that your head is supported by the back of the chair or a wall.

Get a copy holder. A copy holder attached to the monitor at eye level will allow your to read documents without straining your neck.

Trade up to a down pillow. To keep from waking up with a stiff neck, choose a pillow made of down or other pliant material or one of the orthopedic pillows instead of solid foam rubber.

Remember your headrest. Not enough people use the headrests in their cars, says Edward J. Resnick, MD, professor of orthopedic surgery. To get the best protection, make sure that the middle of your headrest is adjusted so that it's comfortably supporting the middle of the back of your head.

Avoid the draft. Cold air blowing from an air-conditioning vent or open car window can cause your neck muscles to contract. That creates tension in those muscles, and eventually pain.

Try a magnet. Magnets are reported to increase blood flow to the sore area and may have some effect on bone, muscle and tissue factors associated with healing. "Some people swear by them, and I think they can help," says Alison Lee, MD, a pain-management specialist and acupuncturist. Dr. Lee suggests that you place the magnets on the triggerpoints of the affected neck and shoulder muscles. To find the trigger point, feel you way along the muscle until you come of a particularly tender area. Don't use magnets if you have a pacemaker or other implanted device. Follow label directions.

Control that cough. Extreme movements during coughs and sneezes can injure your neck. Instead, cough or sneeze while maintaining good posture or even while tilting your head and neck slightly back.

Don't crack your neck. Cracking the neck to relieve pain isn't good, says Dr. Iglarsh. It can loosed up the neck joints, which will make them less stable and more prone to injury.

Stay away from sedatives. While you're sound asleep, your body turns continuously to make itself more comfortable, according to Dr. Halderman. Sedatives diminish this self-adjusting ability, so your body doesn't move around as much. As a result, you may stay in an awkward position for a long period of time—and wake up with an aching neck. The same thing happens when you have been drinking or you are exceptionally fatigued.

Easing the pain with exercise:

Get your neck stretched. If tension's causing your pain in the neck, you can relieve it with a little bit of stretching. "Just start by tilting your head from side to side, then rolling it around first to the right and then to the left," Dr. Keenan says. Next, take your hand, put it on top of your head, and help the stretch by pulling your head gently halfway down toward your shoulder on each side. Be sure to perform these stretches with slow, smooth movements. "Any quick stretch is more likely to tear a muscle or ligament. You need to do it more gradually," Dr. Keenan warns.

Try easy neck-exercises. While you're recuperating, follow this plan of gentle neck movements and posture corrections. This will shorten recovery time of acute neck sprains and reduce the likelihood of persistent symptoms. That's the finding of a Northern Ireland study of 247 people treated in emergency rooms for neck pain. The group who received instruction in home care suffered less severe neck pain and were much less likely to have persistent symptoms than those who rested their necks and relied on collars and those who received physiotherapy.

The theory behind the success of home care is that if you're given responsibility for your own treatment, you're more likely to become self-sufficient in managing episodes of minor discomfort. Learning what hurts and what feels good can prevent a vicious cycle-you have a muscle spasm, so you scrunch your neck one way and your shoulder another, and the resulting unnatural posture causes more spasms. Another plus seems to be that you become your own doctor instead of a victim of your symptoms.

Here are the essential components of this easy-to-do program. The exercises may hurt initially, but they won't harm your neck. Repeat the exercises as often as you like, the more the better. And be sure to start your day with these exercises to relieve any overnight neck stiffness.

Remain aware of your posture when you sit, Stand, read, and drive. Avoid slouching with your chin stuck out. Make sure your back is straight and your shoulders are braced.

Ten times each hour, draw yourself up straight arid tuck your chin in

Stretching for Full Mobility

A healthy neck is flexible enough to bend and twist easily in six directions: forward, backward, left, right, down toward the left shoulder, and down toward the right, says Kim Fagan, MD, a sports medicine physician. Here are some easy stretching exercises that will give you good range of neck motion and relieve tension-induced pain. They can be done either sitting or standing. Dr. Fagan recommends moving in slow, controlled motions to get the most out of these stretches. She cautions not to stretch to the point of pain.

Head up and down. Start with your head erect, facing an imaginary spot on the wall at eye level. Slowly tilt your head forward until your chin touches your chest, as if you were about to nod off during a boring movie. Hold that stretch for 5 to 10 seconds. Then slowly tilt your head backward as far as you comfortably can without feeling pain. Hold that tilt for 5 to 10 seconds. Think of this action as a slow motion nod of approval, says Dr. Fagan.

Do these head tilts twice a day, in the morning and evening. Start with 5 tilts and gradually build up to 15 per session.

Try the slow no-no. Start with your head facing forward, then slowly rotate it to the left facing forward as far as you can. Hold that pose for 5 to 10 seconds. Relax, then slowly turn your head to the right as far as you can. Hold for 5 to 10 seconds, then relax. Try to start with 5 rotations and gradually build up to 15 twice a day. As your neck muscles warm up, you should be able to turn farther to the left and right, says Dr. Fagan. This stretch not only helps relieve neck pain but also improves flexibility, making it easier to do things such as looking over your shoulder when you're backing out of the driveway.

Be a head rocker. Facing front, slowly tilt your head to the left, bringing your left ear toward your left shoulder. You should feel a warm stretch in your right neck muscles. Hold that stretch for 5 to 10 seconds, then relax and slowly tilt your head back to the right, bringing your right ear toward your right shoulder. Hold for 5 to 10 seconds. Start with 5 of these complete head tilts and build up to 15 twice a day, recommends Dr. Fagan. "You will actually feel a stretch, and as the muscles warm up, you should be able to get a better stretch with each one," says Dr. Fagan. "These stretches can help you deal with muscle pain and spasms." This stretch also helps relieve pain that comes from cradling a phone too long, she adds.

to assure yourself of correct posture.

Straighten your back, then try to touch each ear down on the corresponding shoulder. Then straighten up and try to look over one shoulder, then the other.

Stretch it. You bend your neck forward to read, write, do the dishes, sulk, drive. So much time spent in one position makes your neck muscles tighten and shorten, raising your risk of injury when you decide to look up at the stars. Compensate by lying on your back with your knees bent, flattening your neck to the floor by tucking in your chin without lifting your head. Hold for 5 to 10 seconds, repeating ten times. Turn your head slowly to either side while the chin is tucked.

Do safe sit-ups. If sit-ups are part of your fitness regimen, be sure that you are not putting extra strain on your neck. Sometimes, people yank their heads with their hands to help puff themselves up. This action can cause neck pain. Many experts suggest that instead of putting your hands behind your head when you are doing sit-ups, just cup your ears with your fingers. This will keep you from straining your neck.

Hands-on help:

Pull the trigger. If you carefully feel your sore neck, you'll find a spot of maximum tenderness called the trigger point. Pressure here may make the pain feel worse immediately, and may cause pain at points distant from the trigger point, but ultimately it will bring relief. Try pressing that sensitive spot for 1 to 2 minutes. The sensitivity you feel may stem from injury to the area, muscle fatigue, too much cold, chronic bad posture or emotional stress. These factors can cause the muscles to be easily irritated, overworked, and undersupplied with blood. The muscle fibres respond by banding together and tensing up. By restoring blood flow to the area, with its warmth, you can help "unstick" the muscle fibres and wash away the cellular wastes contributing to the pain. Apply heat and stretch gently afterward.

Make a good impression. Practitioners of acupressure say that you can ease your discomfort by applying pressure to two points on the back of your neck. The points are located two inches to either side of your spine, underneath the base of your skull. Using your thumbs, press the points simultaneously for one minute. Keep your eyes closed as you do it. To make it easier, you may want to sit and rest your elbows on a desk or table.

Mind over malady:

Use your imagination. Picture your neck pain as a ball that has a particular size, shape, colour and texture. It may be as small as a marble or as large as a basketball. Allow the ball to grow larger and larger. As it does, the pain may momentarily increase. Now let the ball shrink smaller than its original size, but don't let it disappear. As the intensity of the pain changes, allow the ball to change colour, too. Now imagine that the ball turns into a liquid that flows down your arm, drips on the floor and reforms into a ball. Now kick or throw the ball out into space. Watch it disappear. Most of your pain should be gone, says Dennis Gersten, MD, a psychiatrist and publisher of *Atlantis*, a bimonthly imagery newsletter. He suggests doing this imagery for ten minutes twice a day and whenever the pain flares up.

Paper Cuts

The pain: Small but deep incision caused by the edge of a piece of paper, usually on the fingertip.

The cause: Paper cuts can remain painful for days because every time you move your finger, the cut re-opens. Paper cuts tend to occur more often in the winter, when dry air and heat sap's the skin's natural moisture, leaving it dry, rigid and more vulnerable to a paper's sharp edge.

See a doctor if:

...the cut becomes red, swollen, inflamed, crusty or sore.

Quick relief:

Clean it. "Gently run warm water over your fingertip for a minute or so until it is totally clean, so that it doesn't become infected," says dermatologist Karen E. Burke, MD, Ph.D.

Soothe with salve. After cleaning the cut, apply a dab of antibacterial ointment, such as Bacitracin (Cicatrin), recommends Dr. Burke. The ointment will help kill germs, and it also moisturises the cut so it heals faster.

Cross it off. To close the gaping cut, gently push both edges together and apply a small strip of surgical tape-which sticks better than an adhesive bandage, according to Dr. Burke. "Position the tape perpendicular to the paper cut, so that the cut and the tape form an X. Then pull it tight across the cut, so that the skin will stay together and heal."

Coat it with zinc oxide. You know that white stuff that lifeguards put on the sides of their noses to protect them from the sun? It works for paper cuts, too, and you can buy it inexpensively at chemists. "Zinc oxide is a thick paste that seals out air and makes the cut more comfortable. And the zinc itself helps wounds heal more quickly," says dermatologist Sheryl Clark, M.D

Glue it together. It sounds crazy, but you might want to hold the cut together with Krazy Glue. "It stings when you first put it on, but it is not harmful," says Dr. Clark. "Just a little dab will do it. It helps seal out air, so that the paper cut is not painful while it heals." One caution, though. "It's rare, but some people are allergic to Krazy Glue," says Dr. Bergfeld. "So if your skin becomes red, inflamed, swollen or sore, discontinue it and see a doctor."

Feel serene with Vaseline. If you have no super-strength bonding glue or anti-bacterial ointment, apply some petroleum jelly (Vaseline) to the cut. "It acts as a coating that prevents air from getting to sensitive, exposed tissue," explains Rodney Basler, MD, a dermatologist.

Penile Pain

The pain: Pain at the penis, which may follow an impact or injury, or may be accompanied by prolonged swelling or erection.

The cause: An erect penis can collide with a woman's pelvic bone during intercourse, causing the fibrous penile tissue to rupture. (This is usually referred to as a fracture.) For the most part, though, penile pain signals an underlying health problem. Among the most common causes of penile pain is Peyronie's disease, in which the fibrous tissue within the penis thickens. "You'll feel knots developing on the surface of the penis, usually on the top part," says John J. Mulcahy, MD, Ph.D., a professor of urology. "You may also notice a curving, softening, or shortening of your erection." While the pain may subside on its own in time, Peyronie's disease should be treated by a physician, Dr. Mulcahy advises.

Prostatitis, an inflammation of the prostate gland, can also produce penile pain. "The pain radiates out the urethra (the tube that carries urine from the bladder), and you'll feel a burning sensation when you urinate or ejaculate," explains Stephen Jacobs, MD, a professor of urology. "But there's nothing wrong with the penis itself." More serious conditions such as prostate enlargement and prostate cancer seldom have penile pain as a symptom, he adds.

See a doctor if:
...you have intense or prolonged penile pain.
...you find it painful to urinate or you have any type of discharge, including blood.
...you have penile fracture. How do you know when you have one? "You'll hear a pop or snap, and the erection will go down," explains Dr. Mulcahy. A fracture requires surgery—but for it to be effective, it has to be done quickly.
...you have an erection that lasts longer than four hours or so. You may have priapism, a condition in which blood won't drain away from your penis. This painful condition can be caused by physical injury, disease, reaction to drugs or even self-injection treatments for impotence.
...you have redness or a rash on your penis that lasts longer than a week, or you have abrasions that ooze.

Quick relief:

Reach for a pain reliever. An over-the-counter painkiller may provide some relief, according to Dr. Mulcahy. "Depending on your degree of discomfort, aspirin or acetaminophen (paracetamol) may suffice," he suggests. "If neither works, then try ibuprofen."

Oil up. If your penis gets caught in your zipper, try a liberal application of mineral oil on both zipper and member. It might lubricate things enough for a painless extraction. Other options: unzip slowly, since a quick yank could prove disastrous. Break the zipper with a pair of wire snippers or pliers. The best idea may be to get to a doctor or emergency room. Unzipping the skin or trying to pry the zipper apart might only make things worse.

Helpful vitamins and supplements:

Ask about E. High doses of vitamin E have been proved to be helpful in some cases of Peyronie's disease, says E. Douglas Whitehead, MD, urologist and co-director of the Association for Male Sexual Dysfunction.

Everyday prevention:

Try something new. If intercourse aggravates your pain, experiment with different positions. "Work with your partner to find what is most comfortable for both of you," Dr. Mulcahy advises.

Just say no. With some conditions, you may need to avoid intercourse completely until you heal. "With an abrasion, for example, you don't want to do anything that tugs on the skin," Dr. Danoff says. "Just give it a rest." The same goes for Peyronie's disease, Dr. Mulcahy adds. "Getting an

---

Priapism, A Real Emergency!

Untreated, priapism can lead to permanent impotence. If you think you have it, you have 12-24 hours to act before permanent damage can occur. Don't take chances, get to an emergency room or call your urologist immediately. Once you've checked with a doctor, these suggestions may help:

Sit and soak. Sit in a warm bath and try to loosen up. This often relaxes the blood flow in the penis, permitting the organ to return to normal.

Try to climax. Try to ejaculate, whether through masturbation or with a partner. Letting nature take its course might ease a sudden case or priapism.

Quaff some cough syrup. Find a cold medicine that contains ephedrine or epinephrine, then follow the directions and take one adult dosage. Be sure to check with a doctor first, though. While the shrinkage of blood vessels caused by this medicine might help early in the game, in prolonged cases of priapism it could make things worse.

erection will make your pain worse—and having intercourse will make it worse still," he notes. "If you must have sex, be very gentle. The more aggressive you are, the more it's going to hurt."

Wear underwear. The easiest way to avoid entrapping your penis in a zipper is to make sure you have something between yourself and the zipper.

Watch the downstroke. Some researchers have found that unzipping may be just as hazardous to your health as zipping up.

Be protected. When participating in athletics, wear something padded in the crotch area. A jock strap won't protect you.

Phantom Limb Pain

The pain: Painful sensations felt by an amputee that seem to come from the missing limb. Phantom limb pain takes many forms. People who have experienced it describe the pain as burning, cramping, stabbing, shooting, aching, or throbbing. "Sometimes it feels like the limb is still there but in an abnormal position," says Marina Russman, MD, an anaesthesiologist and pain-management specialist. "For example, it feels like the missing hand is clenched in a fist, with the nails digging into the skin of the palm."

The cause: Experts cannot yet explain what causes phantom limb pain. Virtually every person who undergoes an amputation feels sensations that seem to come from the missing limb. It's disturbing at first, but patients tend to get used to it over time. The sensations usually go away completely within a year. But sometimes it can become chronic and increasingly severe.

See a doctor if:
...your pain does not improve with time, if it intensifies, or if it disrupts your daily activities or sleep, you should consult your doctor. "It's best to start treatment as soon as possible," says Dr. Russman. "The earlier the treatment, the better the prognosis."

Quick relief:
Get relief over the counter. For mild pain, over-the-counter drugs such as ibuprofen, aspirin, and acetaminophen (paracetamol) may help, Dr. Russman says. Ask your doctor or pharmacist to recommend an appropriate product. "If the medication doesn't work, or if your pain gets worse and you require a larger dose, let your doctor know," she advises.

Ongoing care:
Keep it under wraps. Many people say that it feels better to have the limb contained, even at night. There are several ways to do this, says Dr. Karen Andrews. You can wear a rigid cast that is designed to be pulled over the limb, a "stump sock" that provides compression, or an elastic bandage that is wound around the limb in a figure-eight pattern. "Ask your physician or a physical therapist to make a recommendation," Dr. Andrews suggests.

Are You Sure It's Phantom Limb Pain?

They produce very similar symptoms. But phantom limb pain and neuroma pain are quite different—and they require different courses of treatment.

"A neuroma results from the cutting or constant irritation of a nerve," says Karen Andrews, M.D "It causes tenderness and pain in the limb."

Whereas phantom limb pain usually develops shortly after surgery, neuroma pain is more likely to occur months after amputation. "If touching a specific area of the limb reproduces the pain, it's probably a neuroma," she explains. "It can be treated by burying the nerve deeper in the soft tissue."

Soothe with massage. "Rubbing the end of the limb can help relieve pain," Dr. Andrews says. She suggests gentle massage for 5 to 10 minutes, twice a day. "But don't be too rough in the area of the surgical incision," she cautions.

Train it. You may want to try rubbing the end of the limb with different fabrics so that it becomes accustomed to the sensations, Dr. Andrews says. Try bedsheets, towels, clothing, and other textures.

Use your imagination. A relaxation technique called imagery can help ease your discomfort, Dr. Andrews says. To begin, lie in bed or sit comfortably and close your eyes. Visualise an activity that you enjoyed before the amputation, she suggests. For example, if you have lost part of a leg, envision yourself riding a bicycle while pedalling with both feet or sitting at the edge of a lake and dangling the missing foot in the water. If you have lost an arm, you might imagine yourself swimming or tossing a ball. "Move the sound limb as if you were doing the activity, and visualize the motion of the missing limb," she advises.

Consult a professional. If you have not yet met with a physical therapist, you may want to consider doing so. A physical therapist can help rehabilitate your limb and teach you techniques for pain management, Dr. Russman says. Ask your doctor or nearby hospital for a referral.

Postoperative Pain

The pain: Pain after surgery.

The cause: it's not at all uncommon for people to say that they had less pain before surgery than they do after. With time they feel better-and you will, too. What's more, "the techniques available today can greatly minimise pain," according to James C. Erickson, MD, professor of anaesthesiology. "With some procedures, there doesn't have to be any pain at all." The severity of your postoperative pain depends on a number of factors, including the nature of your surgery, your physical and mental state, your previous experience with pain, and whether you develop any complications. Of course, the quality of the postoperative care you receive is important, too.

See a doctor if:
...you're having a significant amount of pain after surgery. "Speak up about it," urges Michael Ferrante, MD, at the University of Pennsylvania Medical Centre in Philadelphia. "It may not be possible to eliminate the pain entirely, but it can be made more tolerable."
...your pain gets worse over the course of a day or two
...you have fever, chills, or redness around the incision. All are possible indicators of an infection.
...you experience significant side effects from any pain medication that you may have been prescribed.

Quick relief:
Ease the ache with ice. Ice is a good local anaesthetic and can help reduce pain around your incision during the first 24 hours after surgery, according to Lee Swanstrom, MD He suggests putting crushed ice in a plastic bag, wrapping the bag in a towel, then laying the pack over your incision for as long as you are comfortable. "Don't use this treatment after the first 24 hours, though," he says. "It can delay wound healing." For the same reason, you should never put anything wet directly on a fresh incision.

Ongoing care:
Add some heat. After the first 24 hours, trade in your ice bag for a heating pad or hot-water bottle, Dr. Swanstrom suggests. "Heat keeps the muscles

around the incision from becoming stiff," he explains. Don't make the pad or bottle too hot, though-just around 100 degrees F. "And be careful not to fall asleep on it," he adds.

Got active as soon as possible. "It's wise to rest for the first day or two after surgery," Dr. Erickson says. "But then you should get up and do some easy walking and gentle exercise. If you stay in bed much longer than that, you'll have a lot more pain when you finally start moving around." Remaining inactive for an extended period of time also increases your risk of postoperative complications.

Lift your spirits. When you're recuperating from surgery, attitude counts, Dr. Swanstrom says. "Try to focus on the fact that every day you feel a little bit better," he urges. Of course, there may be times when you have more pain than you did the day before. "If you have an off-day, it's usually because you've overdone it," he says. "So ease up a bit—but also look at the overall trend toward improvement."

Medicate when necessary. If your doctor prescribed a painkiller before you left the hospital, take it only when you need to, Dr. Swanstrom says. "If you overuse the medication, you may experience side effects that can actually increase your pain," he explains. "For example, some drugs cause constipation-and when you have just had surgery, you don't want to be straining to move your bowels."

Time it right. While you don't want to overdo it with painkillers, you also don't want to put off taking them until you are doubled over in pain. "If you take your medication when the pain first starts, you may need only one pill," Dr. Swanstrom says. "But if you let your pain get really bad, you may have to take three pills-and you'll still be uncomfortable. It will take an hour or so for the drug to reach its full effectiveness." So when, exactly, should you take your medicine? "When you start noticing an ache or an unpleasant feeling," he advises.

Don't go cold turkey. If you are taking prescription narcotics for your pain, discontinue them as soon as you're able, Dr. Swanstrom says. But don't abruptly stop taking medication altogether, he cautions. Instead, switch to a nonsteroidal anti-inflammatory drug (NSAID) such as ibuprofen for a period of time.

Make a point of trying acupuncture. "Studies have shown that acupuncture can reduce your need for medication," says Felice Dunas, Ph.D., a licensed acupuncturist. "You can take smaller doses for a shorter period of time." Acupuncture also helps clear your body of anaesthesia, so you feel better sooner, she says. Make sure that you choose someone with the proper credentials.

Pre-menstrual Tension (PMT)

The pain: Mood swings, headaches, cramping, diarrhoea or constipation, acne, fatigue and other symptoms that make up pre-menstrual tension.

The cause: One possible cause of cramps and heavy bleeding during periods is an unbalanced ratio of oestrogen to progesterone, says Willow Moore, D.C., N.D., a chiropractor and naturopathic doctor. These are the two hormones that play the biggest part in regulating the female reproductive system. Usually, women who experience problems with their periods have too much oestrogen and not enough progesterone in the one to two weeks before their periods. This imbalance can set the stage for the painful cramping and heavy flow, along with other unwelcome symptoms such as headaches and mood swings.

See a doctor if:
...your cramps or blood flow are excessive enough to disrupt your life.
...you can't manage your children during that time of the month, or if you have blowups with your spouse.
...the symptoms interferes with your on-the-job performance or keep you from getting to work in the first place.

Quick relief:
Take ibuprofen for cramps and indigestion. Nonprescription ibuprofen (Advil, Nuprin, Neurofen) may help relieve your cramping uterus and aching legs, back, and head. Prostaglandins, hormonelike substances, are naturally high when you begin your period because their primary job is to help your uterus contract and expel menstrual fluid. However, women with cramps and aching legs, back, and head have abnormally high levels of these hormones, causing the uterus to contract harder and longer than normal and creating the pain. Ibuprofen and other prescription antiprostaglandin drugs help limit the production of prostaglandins.

Menstrual-related diarrhoea, nausea, and vomiting may also be brought on by high levels of prostaglandins, says Penny Wise Budoff, MD, of the Women's Medical Centre in New York. Her study showed that antiprostaglandin medications may ease these digestive upsets by limiting the manufacture of the culprit prostaglandins.

The dosage of ibuprofen is what you would normally take for pain relief: one or two tablets at the onset of symptoms. Take as often as directed until the symptoms go away. The tablets should be taken with milk or food. (People with ulcers or who are aspirin sensitive should not use ibuprofen.) Acetaminophen (paracetamol) won't do as good a job because it does not affect prostaglandins.

Take a mineral bath. Add 1 cup of salt and 1 cup of baking soda to a warm bath. Soak for 20 minutes. The added minerals make the water kinder to your skin, while the warmth increases your blood flow and relaxes your muscles, relieving cramps.

Go hot and cold. Water treatments can ease a variety of pre-menstrual symptoms, according to Tori Hudson, N.D., a naturopathic physician. To alleviate pre-menstrual headaches, Dr. Hudson recommends soaking your feet and ankles in a hot foot bath for 30 minutes while applying a cold cloth to the forehead and temples. "This treatment directs blood away from the head, which is good for the congestive headaches some women get before their periods," says Dr. Hudson. For pre-menstrual mood swings, Dr. Hudson recommends a neutral bath, an extended tub soak in water just slightly cooler than body temperature. (It's the temperature at which you start to feel chilly when a hot bath cools off, says Dr. Hudson.) She recommends soaking for about 20 minutes first thing in the morning, before bed or whenever you're feeling particularly frazzled, adding water as needed to maintain the temperature of the bath.

Nutritional remedies:

Shift your diet. To help defuse PMT symptoms, cut down on or steer clear of coffee, chocolate, soda, and sugar-laden foods, says Barbara Silbert, D.C., N.D. These types of foods can lead to cramps. Instead, experts recommend that you go for a diet that's full of fruits, vegetables and fibre. Foods that contain soy, such as tofu, miso, and soy milk can help your body deal with the hormonal shifts that occur during the menstrual cycle, says Samantha Brody, N.D., a naturopathic doctor specialising in women's health.

Manage your sweet tooth. Many women crave sweets pre-menstrually, but eating cookies, cake or candy will probably just add to the jitters by dramatically raising your blood sugar levels, says Yvonne S. Thornton, MD So when the urge strikes, bite into an apple instead of a candy bar.

Eat small, eat often. Smaller, more frequent meals keep your blood sugar levels steady, says Ellen Freeman, Ph.D., director of the University of Pennsylvania Medical Centre PMT Program. This keeps you calmer and also helps cut your craving for sweets.

Have some spaghetti. A PMT diet—heavy on complex carbohydrates such as spaghetti and whole-wheat bread—may help relieve food cravings and mood swings, says Dr. Freeman. Complex carbs play a part in increased levels of the brain chemical tryptophan, necessary for the production of serotonin, the brain chemical that is involved in mood. Judith Wurtman, Ph.D., a researcher at the Massachusetts Institute of Technology, has found that cereal and other high-carbohydrate foods actually relieve the psychological symptoms of tension, anxiety and mood swings that accompany PMT. She suggests having a heaping bowl of unsweetened cereal when you get hungry. (Reminder: Read the package label first, and choose a low-salt variety.) "It works like Valium," says Dr. Wurtman. In general, she has found, women who have PMT are more alert and happier when they eat high-carbohydrate foods rather than high-protein, low-carbohydrate foods.

Season sans salt. A low-salt diet can relieve pre-menstrual bloating, says Dr. Thornton. It may also help alleviate headaches and improve mental concentration, because women with PMT may have a degree of edema, or swelling, in their brains.

Pass on eggs and animal fats. Ararhidonic acid, a fatty acid plentiful in animal fats, can stimulate your body to produce a substance that causes cramping, says Guy Abraham, MD, a researcher who has conducted extensive research into PMT and menstrual discomfort.

Lay off spicy and greasy foods ten days before your period. That's the time when your progesterone levels are highest in your body, Dr. Abraham says. Progesterone is a hormone that, among other things, helps relax smooth muscles in the body, so your digestive organs may not be working their best then.

Helpful vitamins and supplements:

Call on calcium. Calcium works wonderfully to relieve some women's cramps. According to a study done at Metropolitan Hospital in New York City, 73 percent of women who took 1,000 milligrams of calcium a day for at least a month experienced fewer PMT symptoms than previously. The research suggests that the calcium helped reduce breast tenderness, headaches, and abdominal cramps. Researchers think these benefits stem from calcium's ability to relieve muscle contractions. A good daily dose is 1,000 milligrams, says Dr. Moore.

Make it magnesium. Like calcium, magnesium helps relieve muscle contractions, says Dr. Moore. Some studies have found lower levels of magnesium in women who have PMT and the cramping that's associated with this syndrome. Other studies suggest that increasing magnesium can ease or eliminate PMT symptoms. Taking 500 milligrams of magnesium a day may help ease the pain, says Dr. Brody. Too much magnesium, though, can cause diarrhoea. If that happens, reduce your intake to a level that your body can tolerate.

Be sure of B6. Vitamin B6 is a good supplement to take because it helps your body retain the cramp-relieving magnesium, but that's not the only reason you should consider vitamin B6. Some research suggests that vitamin B6 supplementation can also decrease cramps if you're deficient in it, says Dr. Silbert. Best of all, there's a little test that you can do to see if you may be lacking this vitamin, says Dr. Moore. Before you get out of bed, try to curl your fingers down to touch your palm where your fingers join. Your fingers should be as curled up as you can get them in this position, she says. If you can't bend your fingers enough to make them touch your palm, you should probably consider taking B6, she says. Taking 50 milligrams of B6 twice a day should help, says Dr. Silbert. " I recommend taking a dose with breakfast and another with lunch. Whatever you do, though, don't take it near bedtime. It seems to cause nightmares in some women," she says.

Many women's bodies have trouble converting this vitamin into a usable form, says Dr. Silbert, but there is a usable form called P5P, which is short for pyridoxal-5-phosphate. Because of possible conversion problems, Dr. Silbert often recommends taking 50 milligrams of P5P instead of straight B6.

Pump up the iron. Iron is probably the most important mineral you can take to help control menstrual blood loss, says Samantha Brody, N.D., a naturopathic doctor. Heavy menstrual flow can deplete your body's iron stores, and some researchers also believe that chronic iron deficiency may cause heavy bleeding. In one study, 75 percent of women who supplemented with iron had decreased menstrual blood flow compared with only about 33 percent in a group that took inactive substances (placebos). Thus, iron might just be the answer to your heavy bleeding problems. Do not take more than about 15 milligrams on your own, though, says Dr. Brody. You must be tested for iron deficiency before supplementing with higher doses.

Seek C and bet on bio-f's. Two other supplements for heavy bleeding are vitamin C and bioflavonoids, says Liz Collins, N.D., of The Natural Childbirth and Family Clinic in Oregon. Vitamin C can significantly increase iron absorption, so it goes in tandem with an iron supplement. But the combination of vitamin C and bioflavonoids is better yet, according to Dr. Collins. If you're prone to excessive menstrual bleeding, it might be the result of fragile blood vessels. Vitamin C and bioflavonoids may strengthen those blood vessels and make them less susceptible to damage. In one study, for example, 14 out of 16 women who supplemented with 200 milligrams of vitamin C three times a day along with bioflavonoids found relief from heavy bleeding.

Ease with E. Taking 150 to 200 international units of vitamin E premenstrually seems to help, says Karen J. Carlson, MD, an instructor at Harvard Medical School. This vitamin may have a powerful effect on the hormonal system, helping to relieve painful breast symptoms, anxiety and depression, says Guy Abraham, MD, former professor of obstetrics and gynaecologic endocrinology.

Feed on flax. Take one tablespoon ground flaxseed every day. Flaxseed contains essential fatty acids that help reduce pre-menstrual bloating and inflammation, says Mary Bove, N.D. You can buy flaxseed in your local health food store already ground, or you can grind it yourself with a coffee grinder and store it in the refrigerator. Try mixing it into recipes for baked goods or sprinkling it on cereal or yoghurt. Other sources of the essential fatty acids include fish oil, evening primrose oil and black currant seed oil, all found in most health food stores.

Everyday prevention:

Breathe deeply. Practice inhaling and exhaling slowly and deeply. Shallow breathing, which many of us do unconsciously, decreases your energy level and leaves you feeling tense, making menstrual pain even worse.

Read labels on pain relievers. Since caffeine can worsen PMT symptoms, you should make sure any pain relievers you take are caffeine-free. "You have to be a label reader," says Ellen Yankauskas, MD, director of the Women's Centre for Family Health in Atascadero, California. An over-the-counter pain reliever that contains caffeine can actually make your PMT symptoms worse.

Stay on the wagon. Alcohol is a depressant and diuretic that can worsen PMT headaches and fatigue and can accentuate depression, adds Dr. Yankauskas. For this reason, it's advisable to avoid drinking any alcoholic beverages, including wine or beer, when you've been having trouble with PMT, according to Dr. Yankauskas.

Snooze or lose. If you have PMT, avoid working at night or doing routine tasks that require staying up past your normal bedtime, says Katharina Dalton, MD, author of *PMT: The Essential Guide to Treatment Options*. The area of the brain called the hypothalamus that controls day/night rhythms is located next to the part of the brain that regulates menstrual hormones. Dr. Dalton's theory is that any disturbance in the day/night rhythm can interfere with your menstrual cycle and aggravate symptoms like irritability and fatigue. Dr. Bair adds that hormones are at their lowest at night, all the more reason to catch some Z's.

Easing the pain with exercise:

Exercise for endorphins. Aerobic exercise offers a heightened sense of well-being, because it stimulates your brain's production of the natural feel-good substances called endorphins. Exercising regularly is more important than exercising intensely, says Dr. Freeman. "You don't have to train like an Olympic athlete," she says. "Get out there three or four times a week for a half-hour walk or run."

Increasing your regular exercise levels during PMT can relieve many symptoms, says Dr. Thornton. If you normally walk for 30 minutes three times per week, do so for longer or add extra days when you're feeling pre-menstrual.

Sink into a yoga stretch. Kneel on the floor and sit on your heels. Bring your forehead to the floor and hold your arms against your body along the floor. Close your eyes. Hold this position for as long as it feels comfortable. About 3 minutes should take care of those cramps.

Do the sacral rock. Mary Pullig Schatz, MD, doctor, yoga instructor, and author of *Back to Health: A Doctor's Program for Back Care Using Yoga.* suggests certain simple-to-perform yoga poses as particularly good for menstrual cramps and lower back pain.

The "sacral rock" uses the floor to massage the painful muscles that are cramping and to stimulate acupressure points around your sacrum, the triangular-shaped bone at the base of your spine.

To perform the sacral rock, lie on your back with your knees bent and your feet parallel to each other on the floor, a few inches away from your buttocks. Place a folded pad behind your head and neck. Move your knees slowly to the left and back, then to the right and back. Repeat this at least ten times.

Then lie on your back and draw your knees up toward your chest. Support your legs by holding them behind the knees. Move your knees back and forth and from side to side, massaging your back muscles against the floor. Continue this gentle rocking motion for several minutes. To get up, roll all the way onto your side and push yourself up to a sitting position with your arms and hands. Getting up property is very important.

Herbal help:

Chase symptoms with chasteberry. In two surveys of doctors in Germany, chasteberry was rated as "very good" or "good" for treating PMT symptoms, from bloating and cramping to mood swings. Of the 1,500 women included in the studies, one-third reported having no PMT symptoms after being on chasteberry extract for an average of 166 days. Another 57 percent said they had significant improvement. Chasteberry seems to help by stimulating progesterone production. When that happens, your hormone levels start to stabilise and you begin to feel a whole lot better, says Lauri Aesoph, N.D., who specialises in the integration of natural and conventional therapies. Chasteberry comes in capsules; a normal dose is 175 to 225 milligrams a day. Be patient, though, advises Dr. Aesoph, since it may take about three months to work. If you are taking birth control pills, however, you should try a different remedy, since chasteberry may counteract the effectiveness of the pills.

Do some dong quai. Dong quai is an herb that's long been used in Chinese medicine for various women's ailments. One of its primary benefits is its ability to relieve cramps by helping the uterus relax. Dong quai can also help reduce menstrual blood flow, says Dr. Moore. Like chasteberry, it does this by helping to restore the balance between oestrogen and progesterone. Since high levels of oestrogen can cause many menstrual problems, dong quai often helps by decreasing the amount of oestrogen in your body, says Dr. Moore. Alternative practitioners believe that when your oestrogen levels are too high, the weaker form of plant oestrogen found in herbs such as dong quai takes up receptors that would normally be occupied by your body's much stronger oestrogen. When these sites are occupied by plant oestrogen, some of your body's oestrogen has nowhere to go, so it is excreted as waste. If you'd like to try dong quai, it's available in most health food stores. Just follow the dosage directions on the package you buy. (A typical dose might be one or two 550-milligram capsules twice a day.) Practitioners usually recommend taking it from 14 days after a period begins until the start of your next period. Do not take dong quai while menstruating, though, as it can increase blood loss.

Lick it with licorice. Like dong quai, licorice works to balance oestrogen, says Dr. Aesoph. It can also raise progesterone by inhibiting its breakdown, and it may help prevent bloating. If you want to try licorice, follow the directions on the package, says Dr. Aesoph. A typical dose for PMT is 250 to 500 milligrams once a day, beginning 14 days after the first day of your period and continuing until your next period begins—essentially the two weeks prior to the start of your period. Since licorice can have some side effects, however, check with your doctor before taking it..

Try a black cohosh cure. Black cohosh is another hormone-regulating herb that's often used for women's health problems, says Dr. Aesoph. In one study, researchers analysed the effects of a standardised black cohosh extract that's been used in Germany for more than 40 years. They found that it reduced depression, anxiety, and mood swings in women with PMT. If you decide to give black cohosh a try, follow the dosage directions on the package you buy, says Dr. Aesoph. A typical dose would be 20 milligrams in the morning and 20 milligrams in the evening.

Feel better with feverfew. Many antispasmodic and anti-inflammatory herbs are also used to relieve cramps, says Dr. Silbert. She often recommends feverfew. Some research suggests that this herb helps lessen pain by preventing the formation of prostaglandins, chemicals that are a critical part of the chain that creates the sensation of pain. If you want to give feverfew a try, it's best to take the amount indicated on the package on the days that you experience cramping, says Dr. Silbert. A typical dose is 125 milligrams three times a day.

Sip some raspberries. Raspberry leaf tea is an excellent antidote for menstrual cramps, say herbalists. Try one heaping teaspoon of dried leaves to a cup of boiling water. Steep for 3 to 5 minutes and enjoy.

Get help from homeopathy. Although PMT is usually treated on a personal, case-by-case basis by homeopaths, you might want to try one of the following 30C remedies before seeking professional help, writes Andrew Lockie, MD, in his book *The Family Guide to Homeopathy.* He suggests taking the remedy for the symptoms that most closely match yours every 12 hours for up to three days, beginning 24 hours before PMT usually starts in your cycle.

If your breasts are tender and your symptoms are worse in the

PMT Relief Menu

"What you eat has a direct impact on the amounts of hormones and brain chemicals, or neurotransmitters, in your system," explains David Edelberg, MD "These compounds help determine whether or not you experience PMT symptoms."

What's more, when you don't feed your body properly, it doesn't function properly, notes Mary Bove, N.D. PMT can be a symptom of poor nutrition.

The following one-day menu plan, which is based on guidelines provided by Dr. Bove, shows you what a day's worth of eating might be like for a woman who is trying to ease her symptoms. The five small meals supply a total of 2,200 calories-40 to 50 percent from complex carbohydrates, 30 percent from protein, and 20 percent from unsaturated fats. Red meat, caffeine, and fatty, sugary, and salty foods have all been eliminated.

This menu plan does come up short on certain nutrients, particularly calcium and iron. So if you decide to try it, you should take a multivitamin as well, says Dr. Bove. Try following a menu plan similar to this consistently for a few months to see if it helps reduce your symptoms.

BREAKFAST
Three-quarters cup whole-grain cereal (choose one that supplies three to five grams of fibre per serving) Four ounces skim milk
Fruit shake (blend two ounces tofu, one-half cup orange juice,
one-half cup pineapple juice, one-half small banana, and one-half cup fresh papaya)

MIDMORNING SNACK
One cup fresh strawberries with non-fat yoghurt and raw nuts; or one-half cup serving of steel-cut oatmeal

LUNCH
One cup pasta with one cup grilled or steamed mixed vegetables, one-half cup tofu, and one-half cup low-fat spaghetti sauce
One cup green vegetables (such as broccoli) or one cup salad with balsamic vinegar

AFTERNOON SNACK
One cup vegetarian lentil soup
Two ounces whole-grain roll or about two slices bread

DINNER
Eight ounces baked monkfish or other white fish with garlic, lemon juice, and a drizzle of olive oil
One cup whole-wheat couscous
Six ounces steamed green beans and red peppers
One-half cup non-fat sorbet

morning, try Lachesis, says Dr. Lockie. He recommends Calcarea if you crave eggs and sweets, have cold sweats and swollen and painful breasts and feel clumsy or tired. He says Nux vomica will help if you feel irritable, chilly and constipated, urinate frequently and crave sweet or fatty foods. If you are uninterested in sex, crave sweet or salty foods and feel irritable, weepy, chilly and emotionally detached, he says to try Sepia.

Hands-on help:

Buzz around in circles. Here's a massage technique that may help. Apply this gentle, vibrating stroke using your fingertips. Circle clockwise from the lower border of your ribcage down past your navel to the pubic hairline and back up the other side, around and around.

Find someone who kneads you. It's a natural tendency to want to rub sore, aching body parts. If you find yourself using your thumbs and fingers to dig into the muscles of your lower back, or pressing the palm of your hand on your lower belly, you've discovered one of the best hands on ways to relieve menstrual cramps. For an even more relaxing experience, have your husband or a friend massage you. Or better yet, get a professional massage. The person doing the massage should use warm oil to reduce friction, says Jocelyn Granger, a registered massage therapist.

Here are some strokes that Granger recommends.

Stand or kneel at the head of the person receiving the massage. Use the palms of your hands and your thumbs to do long strokes along the back toward you from about the middle of the buttocks to just below the shoulder blades. Keep your thumbs on either side of the spine, about 3 inches apart, and the fingers pointing upward and out. Make big ovals, returning to the buttocks by moving the hands along the sides of the body back up to the buttocks. As you feel the muscles relax, slowly apply more pressure on the back.

Remain in the same position and use the thumbs and heels of your hands to do deep circular friction right in the area of sacrum, the triangular bone at the bottom of the spine. Use plenty of oil. Slowly increase the pressure until you create warmth in the area.

Press the points. Acupressure can help relieve PMT and menstrual cramping. Place two fingers two finger-widths below your belly button. Press in as you breathe out, then relax the pressure as you inhale. For back pain, simultaneously press on both sides of your spine, just below the bottommost rib. Another point to try is located in the upper arch of each foot, one thumb-width from the ball of the foot. Firmly press one point with your thumb for one minute, then switch feet and press the other point.

Get reflexive. According to Terry Oleson, Ph.D., research shows that putting manual pressure to specific pressure points on the ear, hand or foot—a technique called reflexology—may relieve some of the symptoms experienced by women with PMT. Applying pressure to points on the upper half of the ear tends to relieve symptoms in the lower half of the body, while pressure to the lower half works on the upper half of the body and for headaches. You can try it on yourself, says Dr. Oleson. Gently pinch your ear between two fingers until you find a sensitive spot, he says. Once you find one, gently apply pressure with the two fingers for 30 to 60 seconds, then release and repeat up to three times if you like.

Mind over malady:

Pretend you're a belly dancer. Some people find that creating certain kinds of mental imagery eases pain and sometimes restores a body to normal. A few minutes of quiet time may allow you to come up with your own image, perhaps one of warmth, flowing, and calmness. If you draw a blank, you may want to try an image conjured up by a professional.

For menstrual cramps, try this colourful scene offered by Gerald Epstein, MD, author of *Healing Visualisation: Creating Health Through Imagery.* "Close your eyes and slowly breathe out and in three times. See, sense, and feel yourself to be a belly dancer, undulating back and forth, moving your pelvis in a rhythmical way. As you do so, see the menstrual blood flowing smoothly from you, and feel the muscles of the abdomen gently massaging the uterus. See yourself with transparent fingers gently massaging your uterus, knowing as you do so that the pain is disappearing."

Replay this mental image for 2 or 3 minutes every half hour until your cramps stop, Dr. Epstein recommends. The trick is to make the images so real you can smell the Oriental perfume, for example, and feel the silk veils caressing your skin.

Psoriasis

The pain: Psoriasis is an unsightly, chronic condition in which skin cells develop faster than normal and cluster on the surface of the skin. Psoriasis causes red, scaly patches of varying sizes, usually on the scalp and lower back and over the elbows, knees and knuckles. On the toenails and fingernails, it causes pitting and brownish discolouration, and sometimes it causes the nail to lift and crack. Psoriasis leaves no scars and usually itches only when it appears in body creases. In severe cases, it may cause scales, cracks and blisters on the palms of the hands and the soles of the feet. Psoriasis may also cause a rash on the genitals, profuse shedding of dead skin flakes and even (although rarely) arthritis involving the spine and large joints.

The cause: Although doctors aren't sure what leads to psoriasis, some researchers suspect that it is an inherited disorder in which the body's immune system attacks its own skin. When someone has psoriasis, his skin cells grow abnormally, and the rate of cell growth is much faster than normal, says Ross Bright, MD, medical director of the Psoriasis Medical Centre in Palo Alto, California. Doctors and researchers have not been able to explain what sets this process off, but there is evidence that it may be triggered by emotional stress, illness, or injury to the skin. There is no sure-fire way to prevent psoriasis. Once an itchy patch appears, it tends to spread-for a very simple reason: Scratching the itch can cause tiny wounds in the skin that lead to the development of new patches.

See a doctor if:
...you have severe psoriasis on your palms and soles, or it covers a lot of your body.
...you see blistering or pus-filled blisters or little white-heads that burst easily.
...your skin develops any sign of infection: yellow crusting, pus or honeycomb-shaped blotches of redness.
...you develop a rapidly spreading rash that covers most or all of your body.

Medication: If your psoriasis can't be controlled with moisturisers or coal-tar products, your doctor will probably prescribe either topical steroids or a calcipotriene ointment, which is made from a synthetic vitamin-D derivative. Another treatment—prescribed for about one-third of psoriasis patients—is ultraviolet light therapy. One form of UV therapy involves going into a light booth and being exposed—sometimes as briefly as a minute—to UVB rays, which are 1,000 times stronger than UVA's, the shorter tanning rays. UVBs actually turn off the skin's ability to reproduce cells. Another form of light therapy, PUVA exposes you to UVA rays. Before the light you'll be given psoralen, a light-sensitising drug.

Quick relief:

Head to the kitchen to soothe that itchin'. To soothe itching caused by dry skin and psoriasis, dissolve 1/3 cup of baking soda in a gallon of water. Soak a washcloth in the solution, wring it out, and then apply it to the itchy area. Or add a cup of apple cider kitchen vinegar to the water and apply that to the skin.

Go for oats. Oatmeal is a hallowed folk remedy for relief of itching. Some herbalists recommend using oatmeal-paste packs or oatmeal baths to treat psoriasis. Colloidal oatmeal bath products like Aveeno (Oilatum) are available at most chemists and include emollients which help get the scales off. You can scoop a few handfuls of oatmeal into a warm bath or put oatmeal in a piece of cheesecloth and tie it up to prevent the sticky oatmeal from clogging the drain.

Nutritional remedies:

Feed on fish. For a long time, researchers have suspected that eating certain types of fish can help ease psoriasis. A British study, for example, found that people with psoriasis who ate 6 ounces of fish such as salmon, mackerel and herring a day had improvement in symptoms in just six week. These and other cold-water fish contain a type of fat called omega 3-fatty acids, which appear to reduce the body's production of prostaglandins and leukotrienes, compounds that can cause skin inflammation. While eating fish certainly won't cure psoriasis, it may provide added relief when you're already receiving other psoriasis treatments. Salmon is a particularly good choice because it's high in omega-3's.

Ban the booze. Doctors are still trying to find out for sure why alcohol exacerbates psoriasis. They suspect that alcohol increases activity of a certain kind of white blood cell that's found in psoriasis patients but not in other people. (But it's also possible that drinkers are just more highly stressed and therefore more prone to psoriasis.)

Avoid certain foods. "Some anecdotal reports suggest patients do better when they reduce or eliminate tomatoes and tomato-based dishes—possibly because of high acidity levels," says David Kalin, N.D. "Also, some of my patients with psoriasis have noticed a decrease in plaques by avoiding or limiting their intake of pork products and other fatty meats as well as caffeine."

Everyday prevention:

Slick up your skin. Moisturise all of your skin, not just the affected part, twice a day, says Gerald Krueger, MD, professor of dermatology. He recommends using about an ounce of thinly applied petroleum jelly or other greasy over-the-counter skin lubricants like Cetaphil, Eucerin or Axsian cream. The moisturiser will help soothe the itch and prevent psoriasis from spreading, he says.

Oil up your bath. Besides using commercial lotions and creams, try adding baby oil or olive oil to your bath, says Jerome Z. Litt, MD, author of *Your Skin: From Acne to Zits*. A couple of capfuls may be enough to prevent new outbreaks and control existing ones, he says. Another alternative: Mix two teaspoons of olive oil in a large glass of milk and add that to your bath. But use extra care getting in and out of the tub and be sure to clean it well afterward because these oils can be extremely slippery, he cautions.

Moisturise after bathing. To get the most from your moisturiser, "Apply it within three minutes after leaving the shower or bathtub," advises Glennis McNeal, public information director at the Psoriasis Foundation. "We recommend that you pat yourself dry and apply the moisturiser liberally all over your body—not just on plaques. That's because even clear skin in people with psoriasis is drier than in people who don't have psoriasis. It's thought that little cracks on dry skin might encourage more psoriasis."

Be a lukewarm bather. Warm showers or baths are better than piping hot, because of the danger of overdrying the skin with hot water.

Be delicate with your derma. Your skin isn't an old cowhide, so don't treat it that way, advises Dr. Krueger. Resist the temptation to vigorously scrub with brushes and washcloths, which can damage your skin and aggravate psoriasis. Instead, use your bare hands to gently wash with warm water and a moisturising soap. Then pat yourself dry or leave your skin slightly damp and apply moisturiser. Also, avoid anything that traumatises the skin, from the rubbing of too-tight pants to scratches, bruises or sunburns. And never pick, rub or scratch psoriasis patches.

Check your medicine chest. A few frequently prescribed drugs for conditions such as arthritis, high blood pressure, and migraines can worsen psoriasis, Dr. Krueger says. If your psoriasis is flaring, ask your doctor if one of your medications could be behind it. Then ask your doctor about switching prescriptions.

Electrify your life. To avoid nicks and cuts that can spread psoriasis lesions on areas of the body where you shave, use an electric razor, suggests John Romano, MD

Soak up the sun. Many psoriasis patients are prescribed a specific regimen of ultraviolet light treatments. An easier and less expensive method is simply to hit the Great Outdoors. "We know that exposure to sunlight is extremely helpful for treating psoriasis," says Dr. Kalin. A moderate amount of sunlight enhances the production of vitamin D, which may be effective in controlling psoriasis. Be sure to regulate the time you spend gathering rays, since sunburn will make the psoriasis worse. Put sunscreen on all exposed areas except the psoriasis spots.

Treat with coal tar. Available in both over-the-counter and prescription strength, coal tar products are good for reducing not just the inflammation of psoriasis but its scaling and itching as well. They're available in ointments, creams, bath oils and even shampoos. Be careful: they stain fabrics.

Guard against infection and injury. "Infection may lead to an outbreak or worsen your condition, so it's important to try to avoid infectious disease, says Dr. Kalin. New lesions may also appear on injured skin, so try to avoid cuts and scrapes.

Take care of your nails. Nails can be trouble spots, so keep them cut short, don't poke things underneath to clean them and don't push or clip the cuticles too much, says Michelle Fiore, MD, a dermatologist. Stay away from false nails—they'll pull on your natural nail, and this aggravation can trigger an outbreak of psoriasis.

Fight the folds. Skin fold areas are potential trouble spots. Bacteria and yeast create by-products that can aggravate psoriasis. To keep skin-fold areas yeast-free, try over-the-counter preparations such as Lotrimin (Canesten), or use antibiotic soaps, cleansers or creams.

Go fragrance free. Wearing cosmetics or fragrance on your skin during light therapy may trigger irritation. Wait until treatments are done to use these products.

Herbal help:

Rely on red pepper. One herbal treatment that seems to help both dry skin and psoriasis is hot pepper, specifically one of the many creams containing 0.025 percent capsaicin. Capsaicin is the compound that makes hot peppers hot. Capsaicin creams such as Zostrix and Capzasin-P are sold as pain relievers, and they work. In one study, 98 people with psoriasis used a capsaicin cream, while 99 others treated their skin patches with an inactive cream (a placebo). The capsaicin group successfully reduced both scaling and redness, although the hot-pepper cream caused some burning, stinging and itching.

If you use a capsaicin cream, be sure to wash your hands thoroughly afterward so that you won't get it in your eyes. And, of course, if you ultimately get further irritation rather than relief from the cream, don't use it again.

Add avocado. Folk healers have long recommended rubbing mashed avocado on psoriasis patches. It's certainly cool and soothing.

Cure with camomile. Camomile preparations are widely used in Europe to treat psoriasis, eczema and dry, flaky skin. Naturopathic physicians maintain that applying this herb externally works better than commonly prescribed medications for treating psoriasis. Compounds known as flavonoids, which are found in camomile, have significant anti-inflammatory activity. You can buy commercial creams containing camomile at health food stores.

If you have hay fever, however, you should use camomile products cautiously. Camomile is a member of the ragweed family, and in some people, it might trigger allergic reactions. The first time you use it, watch your reaction. If it seems to help, you can continue to use it. But if it seems to make the itching worse, simply discontinue use.

Lick it with licorice. Naturopaths consider external applications of licorice to be equal or superior to hydrocortisone cream for treating psoriasis. They note that the compound glycyrrhetenic acid (GA), which is found in licorice, works rather like hydrocortisone in treating psoriasis, eczema and allergic dermatitis. Other scientists have shown that hydrocortisone works considerably better when used in combination with GA. If you'd like to give this herb a try, buy a licorice extract and apply it directly to the affected areas using a cotton ball or clean cloth.

Razor Burn

The pain: Cuts, abrasions and/or a red rash incurred while shaving with a razor.

The cause: "Razor burn is actually a skin irritation," says Evelyn Placek, MD "When you shave, you're basically peeling off part of your epidermis-the top layer of skin. The redness is a normal response to tissue injury. Blood flow increases to the area to heal the wound, and blood vessels dilated become red."

See a doctor if:
...it happens every time you shave. Razor burn can mimic the symptoms of other skin conditions, such as psoriasis, which require very specific treatments
...your skin becomes infected and crusty or if it is persistently red and scaly.

Quick relief:
Stem with a styptic pencil. If you have had previous bouts with razor burn, you may already know about the styptic pencil. Available at chemists, it is renowned for its ability to stem the flow of blood from those nasty nicks.

Put on the pressure. If you nick your skin, press directly on the cut with a piece of gauze or a clean cloth, advises Joseph A. Witkowski, MD, clinical professor of dermatology. Apply steady pressure for 10 to 15 minutes. "And don't peek," Dr. Witkowski cautions. "Every time you peek, you dislodge a clot, making the cut bleed again."

Add a dab of ointment. "If the nick is bad, apply antibiotic ointment to prevent infection," advises Jerome Z. Litt, MD, professor of dermatology.

Everyday prevention:
Choose the right tool. You should use a new, clean blade for every shave, Dr. Litt says. And if you're using double-track blades, you may want to consider switching to the single-track type. "The advent of double-track blades has produced more cases of razor burn," he contends. "They create irritation and sometimes follicle problems." He recommends Bic's Original

or Sensitive Shaver single-track disposable blades instead.

Get steamed. Men should wait until after their showers to shave, Dr. Litt says. The hot steam softens the whiskers, so the blade doesn't yank and pull so much.

Soften your bristles. "About 25 percent of men experience razor burn or other forms of shaving discomfort," says John McShefferty, Ph.D., president of the Gillette Research Institute. The reason? "Most of them don't take the time to properly soften their beards before shaving. You need about two to three minutes of soaking before you actually start shaving. The key, according to Dr. McShefferty, is to not dry your face after you wash or take a shower. "While your skin is still wet, apply a shaving gel or cream. Wait for a minute or two and then shave."

Lather up. Shaving cream is a must for men and women alike. "It keeps moisture in the hair follicles and makes the shave smoother," Dr. Litt says. Just make sure that you're not allergic to the product you're using, cautions David Margolis, MD, a dermatologist. "If you're sensitive to any of the ingredients, the shaving cream 'It'll make your skin red when you use it," he explains. To find out if you are allergic, put a little shaving cream on your arm and cover it with a bandage. Leave it on until the next day, then check for irritation. "If you are allergic, try a different brand-maybe one for sensitive skin or without fragrance," he says.

Check out a gel. You may want to switch from a cream to one of the highly lubricating gels on the market, Dr. Margolis says. "Generally, gel is more lubricating than foam," he notes.

Don't go against the grain. You can reduce your odds of razor burn by shaving in the same direction as your hair growth. "Don't use upward strokes on the cheeks or legs, and don't shave from side to side," Dr. Litt advises. You don't get quite as close a shave this way, but it trains the hairs to grow straight.

Follow directions. The natural growth of a beard may vary from one part of the face to another, Dr. Margolis says. "The hairs may not point in the same direction," he notes. "Let your beard grow for a few days and watch the patterns as the hairs come in."

Don't get too close. "If you try to shave very close-the way television commercials tell you to do-you'll only irritate your skin," says Dr. Margolis. His two rules of thumb: Never stretch your skin while you shave, and don't apply too much pressure with your razor. This is especially good advice for African-Americans, says Dr. Litt. "A black person's hair grows out in a curl," he explains. "If it's shaved too close, it will grow right back into the skin. This can lead to a follicle infection."

Delay your morning shave. If you reach for your razor the minute you wake up, you're probably walking around with an irritated face. When you sleep, body fluids tend to puff up the surface of your skin and hide the hairs, says Fred Wexler, director of shaving research for Schick. "If you shave right after you jump out of bed, the razor can't get as close to the hair follicle (the place where the hair comes out of the skin). It takes at least 20 minutes after you get out of bed for those fluids to disperse and for your skin to become taut again." If you're a morning exerciser, shave after your workout and shower, suggests Vexler. Your sweat is acidic and can irritate freshly shaved skin, so that burn will feel worse if you shave before you run or exercise.

Use short strokes. "When you use long strokes, you tend to press down harder and cause more friction—and friction causes razor burn," according to John F. Romano, MD "It's always better to use short strokes. You'll get just as good a shave, with a lot less irritation."

Make your mug moist. "Don't use colognes or commercial after-shave lotions, because they contain alcohol, which is drying and irritating to a freshly shaved face," says Dr. Romano. "You don't need an antiseptic on your face if you wash it regularly." McShefferty recommends applying an over-the-counter moisturiser, after shaving, to soften your skin. "Women tend to do this after shaving their but most men don't.

Beware of hydrocortisone creams. These over-the-counter medications for skin irritations are okay for occasional use and quick healing of nicks, cuts and other abrasions caused by shaving. But according to Dr. Romano, you should use them no more than twice a week. "Use them only when your skin is really bad," he says, "because eventually they can cause thinning of the skin."

Drop the soap. People with razor-sensitive skin should stick with a shaving cream that contains aloe or some other soothing ingredient, recommends Dr. Placek.

Switch to a hair-dissolver cream. If you know that you're prone to razor bumps, consider using a lotion depilatory, which dissolves hair. "These lotions may be a little smelly and messy, but they're less traumatic to the hair follicles than scraping a razor over them," says Dr. Placek.

Repetitive Strain Injury

The pain: Chronic pain, usually in the neck, shoulder, elbow, wrist or hand, brought on by repetitive actions usually related to on-the-job activities.

The cause: The "strain" part of repetitive strain injury comes from the muscles and tendons that become inflamed as the result of overuse. The most common RSI is carpal tunnel syndrome, in which the nerve that runs through a small tunnel of bone in the wrist is pressed and pained by the swelling of nearby tendons, causing tingling and numbness in the hand. But there are plenty of other spots for RSI: the elbow, the forearm, the thumb, the shoulder, the top side of the hand, the palm side of the any spot where the muscles of the hands and arms are used again and again.

See a doctor if:
...you have persistent pain but your symptoms subside when you stop the activity that's causing them.
...you have pain that radiates to other parts of your body.
...you have severe pain when you lie down (especially if it disrupts your sleep).
...you have numbness or tingling, along with pain.
you have clumsiness that you can't control, even when you fully concentrate on what you're doing.

Quick relief:
Do something different. If your job allows it, "break the monotony of repetitive tasks by moving around," suggests Joel Press, MD, a professor of clinical physical medicine and rehabilitation. "Set an alarm to ring every 30 to 45 minutes to remind you."

Everyday prevention:
Watch out for pain. Stay alert for the warning sign of temporary pain, says Robert E. Markison, MD, a hand surgeon. "If you have discomfort that lingers for more than half an hour after the task, you are probably doing too much," he says. If you take preventive measures early, you can head off RSI before it becomes a serious problem.

Practice posture prevention. Awkward positioning while you work can be a major factor in causing RSI, says Dr. Markison. The key to good posture, he says, is to bring the work to you rather than wrapping yourself around the work. If you are a computer operator, for example, sit upright, with limbs that are relaxed and flexible rather than strained and rigid.

To avoid postural errors, Dr. Markison says, watch out for these clues.

The tipped-forward bead. This can triple the force running through your spine and the muscles of your neck, compressing nerves and vessels in those areas, which can lead to problems in the arms and hands.

The extended arms. Don't put your limbs forward any farther than you have to. The farther away they are from your body, the more your circulation is reduced. Avoid the elbow extended, palm-down position when using a mouse.

Use a wrist rest. "If you type at the computer, always use a wrist pad to soften the stress on your wrists," says Mary Ann Keenan, MD, chairman of the Department of Orthopedic Surgery at the Albert Einstein Medical Center in Philadelphia. A wrist pad helps soften the blow of repetitive motion.

Sit properly. "Your wrists should be in a neutral position on the keyboard—that is, neither flexed up or down—with your elbows at a 90 degree angle," says Margot Miller, P.T., a physical therapist.

Bandage tennis elbow. So-called tennis elbow is actually a form of repetitive strain injury. "If you have tennis elbow, you can purchase a special pressure bandage from a chemist or medical supply store, which you can wear over your forearm to take the strain off," says Dr. Keenan.

Get lined up. If you use a computer, check the placement of your screen

---

Fight Back with Yoga

"For most people with an RSI, the top of the forearm is really tight and overused and the underside is underused," says Friend. For relief he recommends the yoga position called downward facing dog. "This posture creates the best skeletal alignment between the forearm and arm and between the shoulder and upper arm."

To do this pose, stand in front of a chair and put your palms flat on the front edge of the chair seat, placed about shoulder-width apart. Walk your legs backward until your arms are straightened and your feet are under your hips. Bend your knees and be sure to point your tailbone toward the ceiling, creating a gentle arch in the lower back. Pressing down on your hands, balance your weight evenly between your upper and tower body and pull your forearms and upper arms toward the chair, up away from the floor.

Keeping your hands flat on the seat of the chair, turn your shoulders out and away from your neck slightly. Take a deep breath, feel the stretch. Hold the pose for 15 to 30 seconds. Repeat three to ten times, says Friend.

Stretch

For a repetitive strain injury caused by doing activity improperly, moving your wrist the right way could be the cure, says Sharon Butler, author of *Conquering Carpal Tunnel Syndrome and Other Repetitive Strain Injuries*. The following stretches work the inside of the wrist, the base of the thumb and the muscles of the inside of the forearm.

Place your hands on your hips with your fingers pointing straight forward. Slowly roll your elbows forward to create a deeper bend in your wrists. You'll feel a sensation called the stretch point, the first sign that a stretch is taking place. Sometimes you'll even feel a light aching sensation, usually in the deeper muscles. Pause at each stretch point and wait until you feel the sensation fade. For variation, try pointing your fingers in a slightly downward direction and notice the difference in the sensations that you feet in your muscles.

To stretch the finger muscles and tendons, press your fingertips against the edge of a desk or table, bending at the base of your fingers and keeping your wrists straight. Press gently until you feet the stretch point and then hold that position until you feel a change in sensation. You can vary this exercise by doing it with your fingers spread apart.

and keyboard. "They should be in front of you rather than off to the side, which forces you to twist your body," says Dr. Press.

Check the height. The computer screen should be visible without any neck strain. "'Your eyes should gaze slightly downward, not up or way down," Dr. Press advises.

Please be seated—properly. The height of your chair is also important. "Your feet should be flat on the ground, and your thighs should be parallel to the ground," Dr. Press says.

Check your keyboard technique. "When you type, your forearms should be parallel to the floor, and your wrists should be in a neutral (straight) position," says Emil Pascarelli, MD, professor of clinical medicine and a repetitive strain injury specialist. "You should use your whole arm to move your hand over the keyboard rather than stretching your fingers to reach the keys." Also use light keystrokes and avoid leaning on the arms of the chair with your elbows while you type, Dr. Pascarelli says.

Hold the phone. You're almost guaranteed a repetitive strain injury if you always tuck the telephone receiver between your shoulder and your ear. "If you're on the phone for more than 20 minutes at a time, you should use a headset or a speakerphone instead," says Dr. Press.

Easing the pain with exercise:

Take 15 and stretch. Experts agree that breaks are a must, especially if you are doing data entry on a keyboard for hours a day, says Karen Allen, a senior physical therapist. Try every 15 minutes to take 1-minute mini-breaks, she says. You can do these while still seated at your desk.

During those mini-breaks, Allen recommends doing two easy stretches to help prevent RSI.

Stretch #1: Make a fist, then span or spread your fingers as far as possible. Relax. Repeat this three or four times.

Stretch #2: Hold your arms straight out in front of your body with your palms facing down. Bend your hands up, so that your palms face away from, you. Hold that stretch for five seconds. Then bend your hands down, so that your palms are facing toward you. Hold that stretch for five seconds. Repeat three or four times.

Be sure to leave your work space after every two hours of continuous computer use, says Allen. "For those breaks, give yourself 15 minutes to get away from your desk and move. Walk around a bit and shake out your hands," she advises.

Breathe away stress. Stress is another contributing factor to RSI, says Dr. Markison. To counter stress while at work, breathe more deeply. Just take a couple of deep breaths every now and then, he says. It is the simplest way to deal with stress in the workplace, and it helps restore blood flow to the hands.

He also suggests that people who must sit at keyboards entering written data speak the words in a whisper as they are typing. "If you look at people in high-speed, data-entry situations, their breathing is often shallow or halted. But when typists whisper the words as they are typed, they force themselves to breathe more deeply," he says.

Shrug off the pain. Shoulder shrugs can help protect your neck from repetitive strain injury, according to Dr. Robb. Simply shrug your shoulders, hold for 2 to 3 seconds, then relax. Do five to six repetitions every 2 to 3 hours. You may want to hold very light weights (no more than 1 pound) in your hands to build up your upper back muscles.

Arm yourself against harm. Your hands, wrists, and arms are the body parts most at risk for repetitive strain injury. To increase their strength and flexibility, Dr. Pascarelli recommends the following exercises.

1. Hold your left arm straight in front of you at shoulder level. (Maintain this position for all of the exercises.)

2. Place your right hand over the knuckles of your left hand and gently press downward, so the fingers of your left hand are pointing straight down and the palm is facing you. Hold for a count of 10. Repeat three times.

3. Make a fist with your left hand. Place your right hand over the knuckles of your left hand and gently press your fist downward. Hold for a count of 10. Repeat three times.

4. Position your left hand so that your palm is facing up. Then bend your wrist backward as far as you can so that your fingers are pointing

toward the floor. Place your right hand on the palm side of your left hand, over the knuckle joints, and gently pull your left hand back toward your body. Hold for a count of 10, then relax. Repeat three times.

5. Position your left hand so that your fingers are pointing upward and your palm is facing away from you, as though you were signaling someone to stop. Place your right hand on the palm side of your left hand, over the knuckle joints, and carefully press your left hand back toward you. Hold for a count of 10. Repeat three times.

6. Repeat the sequence with your right hand.

Dr. Pascarelli suggests repeating the entire series three to five times with each hand.

Hands-on help:

Massage with herbal infused oils. A mix of aromatherapy and massage can shorten RSI's stay. Try using herbal oils that contain either of the essential oils Roman camomile or a combination of rosemary and ginger for their anti-inflammatory and painkilling effects. Put some oil on your hand and work it into the affected area.

Restless Leg Syndrome

The pain: Sensations of jumpiness, itchiness, burning, aching, or twitching in the legs. This syndrome usually makes its presence known at night. "It's often an unrecognised cause of insomnia," say Jay Lombard, MD, co-author of *The Brain Wellness Plan.* You think that you "just can't sleep," but, in fact, what's keeping you awake is your legs.

The cause: Doctors aren't certain what causes RLS, but it may have a genetic link since the condition tends to run in families, says Ralph Pascualy, MD, medical director of the Sleep Disorders Centre at Providence Medical Centre. Some researchers also suspect RLS may be caused by low levels of dopamine, a neurotransmitter in the brain that helps regulate the body's nervous system.

See a doctor if:

...you have frequent "crawling" or other types of discomfort in your legs, occurring typically in the evening.
...you feel a overwhelming urge to move your legs or body to relieve the sensations.
...you find the symptoms get worse in the late afternoon and keep you awake until the wee hours of the morning.
...you notice the symptoms worsen when you sit or lie down.
...the discomfort interferes with sleep, your job or everyday activities.

Any drug that reduces or blocks activity of the brain chemical dopamine, responsible for the transmission of nerve impulses, can worsen the symptoms of restless legs syndrome, says Wayne Hening, MD, Ph.D., a research neurologist. In particular, be wary of prescription neuroleptic tranquillisers including haloperidol (Haldol) and chlorpromazine (Thorazine or Largactil). In addition, avoid: prescription antinausea medications containing metoclopramide (Reglan or Parmid), prescription tricyclic antidepressants such as amitriptylene (Elavil).

Quick relief:

Point your toes. If restless legs strike while you're sitting, point your toes and stretch your legs from foot to hip, says neurologist Sheryl Siegel, MD

Most people with restless legs try to resist the impulse to move their legs. But if you do, the urge to move will just build until nothing short of a day-long hike will satisfy the urge to move. Better to give in to the first impulse to move, she advises. You'll likely "travel" a shorter distance.

Get up. If restless legs strike after you have gone to bed, don't resist the urge to move, says Dr. Siegel. "Get out of bed and walk up and down the hall a couple of times or, if you have stairs, up and down the stairs."

Try hot or cold. Some people find that hot baths relieve restless legs, while others find that cold packs do the trick, says Sarah Stoltz, MD, a neurologist. She suggests that individuals experiment to see what works.

Massage your legs. "Rubbing your legs briskly, or running a vibrator over them, also brings relief for many people," says Ronald F. Pfeiffer, MD, a professor of neurology and pharmacology. Many experts believe massaging can shut off the pain impulses caused by restless legs. Doings stretches or wearing surgical socks may achieve the same result.

Nutritional remedies:
Don't eat dinner late. It may be the activity of the nervous system involved in digesting a big meal that triggers symptoms.

Helpful vitamins and supplements:
Try a mineral trio. A combined deficiency of three minerals could be responsible for the jumpiness of restless legs syndrome, according to Ross Hauser, MD "A lack of calcium, potassium, and magnesium can make the large muscles in the legs hyper-irritable," he says.

Calcium, magnesium, and potassium all have an effect on muscle contraction and relaxation. In addition, they help nerve transmission. Experts say that you can help your legs get some rest by making sure that you're getting enough of all three minerals. Dr. Hauser recommends between 800 and 1,000 milligrams of calcium, 300 milligrams of potassium, and 500 milligrams of magnesium once a day at bedtime.

When you're taking magnesium, you should be aware that supplements may cause diarrhoea in some people Also, if you have heart or kidney problems, be sure to check with your doctor before taking supplements.

Get help from 5-HTP. Have you ever noticed the little jerking movements that you or your partner make just as you're shifting into sleep? Those are outward signs that your brain is closing the gate on muscle movement for the night. If those muscles didn't voluntarily shut down, they'd go on obeying your brain impulses even in the midst of deep sleep. For people with restless legs syndrome, that gating mechanism may not be functioning at 100 percent efficiency, says Dr. Lombard. Some movement impulses are getting through, keeping your legs active all night long and leaving you exhausted come morning.

"An interesting supplement called 5-hydroxytryptophan (5-HTP) seems to work well," says Dr. Lombard. Experts believe that 5-HTP is used to make serotonin, a chemical messenger in the brain that can affect sleep quality. "The rationale behind using 5-HTP for restless legs is that raising serotonin levels will raise the gating effect," says Dr. Lombard. Essentially, it helps to separate mind from body, thus making it easier for your legs to lie still through the night.

Some people with restless legs who try 5-HTP notice a change for the better right away, but it might take from two weeks to a month for you to know whether or not it will work for you, says Dr. Lombard. Start with 100 milligrams about 20 minutes before bedtime, he suggests. You can increase the dose to 200 milligrams if you don't see results after the first few weeks, but don't go any higher, he advises. Higher doses can cause disturbing dreams and nightmares.

You shouldn't take 5-HTP for longer than three months without consulting a doctor. You should also avoid it if you are currently taking antidepressant or have taken them recently. The combined effects could cause a possibly fatal condition called a serotonergic reaction. Do not take supplements if you are pregnant or trying to conceive.

Focus on B vitamins and iron. Some scientists suspect that a deficiency of folate (a B vitamin) or iron-or both-may have something to do with the cause of restless legs. Dr. Stoltz says that it makes sense to make sure that your diet has rich sources of both. Legumes, oranges and orange juice, Brussels sprouts, spinach, asparagus and strawberries are good sources of folate. Steamed clams, lean beef, turkey, chicken, tofu, whole-grain bread and legumes provide a hefty serving of iron.

Quell with quinine. Taking two tablets nightly of Q-vel—an over-the-counter tablet that contains quinine and also vitamin E—seems to help settle restless legs.

Everyday prevention:

Maintain a regular bedtime. Fatigue aggravates RLS, says Dr. Hening. Getting all the shut-eye you can is important, particularly if you have a mild case of RLS that only flares up once or twice a month. Hit the sack at the same time each evening, he suggests. Even if you have to get up several times during the night to stretch your legs, a consistent bedtime should help you get an adequate amount of sleep. After all, adds Dr. Hening, a regular bedtime is known to generally promote better sleep and clinical experience has shown that waiting for fatigue to set in before going to bed may actually worsen the condition.

Splish and splash. Sitting in a warm bath or hot tub for 10 to 15 minutes just before bedtime sometimes helps relieve RLS, Dr. Hening says. If you have difficulty getting into a tub, stand in a shower and let the warm water gently pour over your back and legs.

Soak your feet. A cool-water soak just before bedtime is a good way to chill restless legs. "Many people soak their feet in cool water, and it seems to help somewhat, so I think it's worth trying," says Dr. Pfeiffer. Just don't overdo it—immersing your feet in ice or extremely cold water can cause nerve damage, so be sure to keep the water at least 50 degrees F.

Sleep in. If necessary, sleep in late, suggests Virginia N. Wilson, co-founder of the Restless Legs Syndrome Foundation and author of *Sleep Thief, Restless Legs Syndrome* a guide to coping with RLS. Because RLS is usually worse at night, many people who have it don't get to sleep until 3 or 4 a.m. So avoid early morning appointments because, odds are, you'll be groggy and irritable, she says.

Find an aisle land. Ask for an aisle seat in the back of the theatre when you attend a play or concert, Wilson suggests. If your legs begin to bother you, you will be able to stand up and walk around without blocking the view of other patrons. Likewise, ask for an aisle seat when making aeroplane reservations. Try booking a flight that has one or two stops before your destination so you can get off the plane and stretch your legs for a few minutes during each layover, Wilson says. Dr. Hening advises scheduling a morning flight when discomfort is less likely to occur. He also suggests talking to your doctor to see if medication will make the trip easier.

Avoid evening aerobic exercise. Although movement is important, try to schedule exercise that increases your heart rate for during the day rather than in the evening, says Dr. Siegel. Some people seem to experience restless legs more frequently after late exercise.

Stop smoking. "It's certainly worth trying," says Janet A. Mountifield, MD, a general practitioner who noticed that one of her patients was cured of restless legs syndrome after quitting a long-time smoking habit. One theory: smoking impairs blood flow to leg muscles.

Aid with aspirin. "It's unclear why it works, but taking two aspirin or Tylenol tablets at bedtime may help people with restless legs sleep better," says Thomas Meyer, MD

Herbal help:

Cure with kava. Some people with restless legs syndrome find relief with kava, an herbal remedy known for its antispasmodic properties, says David Winston, a clinical herbalist. Kava is available at most health food stores in two forms: as a standardised extract in capsule form, or as a tincture. If you use the tincture, take two to three millilitres three times a day. If using the capsule form, take one or two capsules (about 1,500 milligrams total) a day.

Stop it with skullcap. Skullcap is another effective herb used for treatment of restless legs as well as spasms, palsies and twitches. Buy it as a fresh tincture and take five millilitres (one teaspoon) two or three times a day as needed.

Saddle up with horse chestnut. Preparations of horse chestnut leaves, bark, and seeds are used in Europe for their good effect on vein health. There's reason to consider standardised extracts of this herb for the treatment of restless legs as well, according to Dr. Hauser. "Horse chestnut is unique in its ability to stabilise vascular membranes," he says. This may give restless legs the extra blood flow they need to prevent sensations of itchiness or burning.

Give this herbal remedy a try by taking 400 milligrams of standardised extract twice a day, says Dr. Hauser. Generally, people respond within a month, he adds. If your symptoms don't improve in that amount of time, stop taking it and see your doctor for an evaluation. **Horse chestnut is not for everyone.** It may interfere with the action of other drugs, especially blood thinners such as warfarin (Coumadin). It may also irritate the gastrointestinal tract. As with other herbs, you should not take it if you are pregnant or breastfeeding.

Mind over malady:

Zone out. Some people report that engaging in mentally absorbing games and activities like building jigsaw puzzles or solving logic problems stifles their attacks of RLS, Dr. Hening says. If you find an engaging hobby that requires intense concentration, it may help you control this condition, he says.

Relax. Once you've turned out the light and crawled between the sheets, try a relaxation exercise such as progressive muscle relaxation, says Dr. Siegel. "This is a two-step process: muscle relaxation followed by steady breathing." First, lie on your back with your arms at your sides and close your eyes. Take a deep breath and exhale. Then, tense and relax every muscle group you can identify, one at a time, starting with your toes and working all the way to your scalp. Then, start to count each inhalation and exhalation separately, so that on the first inhalation, you count "one," and on the first exhalation, you count "one" also. Count to eight, then start counting all over again. As thoughts or noises interrupt your breathing pattern, let them go and return to your counting and breathing. Do this for 5 to 20 minutes, depending on what you have time for.

Sciatica

The pain: Low back pain that radiates, producing shooting pain or numbness into your buttocks and down your leg, below your knee even into your foot and toes.

The cause: If all your nerves were a network of roads, the sciatic nerve would be a busy major motorway. All of the nerve impulses transmitted to and from the lower half of your body must pass through the sciatic nerve, the largest and longest in the body. From its roots in the spinal cord, the thick conduit branches through the buttocks and down the back of each leg to the foot. Pain that follows this route is called sciatica. Pressure on the nerve in the spinal area is normally the cause.

If you're under age 40 and you get sciatica, it's likely that one of those discs has slipped and is bulging between the vertebrae in your spine. Since the nerve runs alongside the spine, the off-kilter disc puts pressure on it.

If you're hit with sciatica when you're over 40, which is the age that it's most likely to occur, the cause is also disc-related, but in a somewhat different way. At that age, your discs are starting to become dehydrated. The shrinking discs can cause the spine to compress, increasing pressure on the nerve.

See a doctor if:
...you have shooting pains down your legs.
...back pain is accompanied by radiating, burning, or tingling, see your doctor.

Quick relief:
Get a chill. Apply ice where you feel sciatica pain to help reduce pain and swelling, says Sheila Reid, therapy co-ordinator at the Spine Institute of New England. To protect your skin, place a towel between your back and the ice pack. Ice may be used for 15 to 20 minutes every hour. Or, switch to the warmth of a heating pad, shower, or bath, she says. Heat relaxes muscles.

Reach over the counter. Non-prescription pain relievers such as acetaminophen (paracetamol), ibuprofen, or naproxen may help relieve temporary discomfort, says Steven Mandel, MD, clinical professor of neurology. But be sure to ask your physician first. Even over-the-counter medicines can have side effects.

Take a shower, then stretch. If a muscle strain, muscle spasm or other lower-back injury is responsible for sciatica, head for the shower, says Mary Ann Keenan, MD, chairman of the Department of Orthopedic Surgery at the Albert Einstein Medical Centre. Hold on to a grab bar or other sturdy structure so that you don't fall, then let the warm water run down over your body for five to ten minutes, with your back to the spray. As it does, gently lean forward from your waist until you reach a point just before it hurts. Hold that position for several seconds, says Dr. Keenan, then slowly straighten your body. Stand upright for a couple of seconds, then slowly lean back from the waist until you reach a point just before it hurts. Hold the position for several seconds, then slowly straighten once again.

Repeat the same gentle stretching movement to each side, says Dr. Keenan. By the time that you're finished, chances are good that you'll have quelled any muscle spasm that could be responsible for your pain. Don't linger too long in the shower, and don't soak in a hot tub or bath or use a heating pad for longer than 30 minutes, cautions Dr. Keenan. Too much heat can actually exacerbate your pain by increasing swelling.

Try a gel pack. To help reduce pain and inflammation, try applying a cold gel pack every few hours to whatever area hurts-your back, buttock or leg-for 10 to 15 minutes at a time, recommends Carol Hartigan, MD, a physiatrist who specialises in spine rehabilitation. Gel packs are available at chemists. (In a pinch, you can substitute a cold towel, soaked in ice water.)

Make a natural cushion. Buy a waist-cinching elastic back support from your local chemist or medical supply house, says Dr. Keenan. The cincher pushes in your abdomen, which makes an internal cushion of air that soothes and protects nerves around your spine.

Hit the tub. A shallow bath provides effective relief of sciatica pain, suggests Agatha Thrash, MD, a medical pathologist. Fill your bathtub with enough warm water, about body temperature, to cover you up to the waist, then soak for 20 minutes to two hours. Finish each bath with a shower that starts out with lukewarm water and ends with cool. If the pain is too intense to sit in a tub, Dr. Thrash recommends a hot shower. Stay in it for 20 minutes or so, holding the water in the tub, since it warms up the venous blood returning from the feet.

Nutritional remedies:

Helpful vitamins and supplements: Beat inflammation with bromelain and quercetin. Inflammation is a sign that your body is trying to repair itself from some type of trauma. With sciatica that trauma is caused by something pinching the nerve. The nerve reacts by producing pain, heat, swelling, redness or loss of function—the five hallmarks of the inflammatory response. The key to drug-free relief is to turn on your body's natural inflammation-fighting powers, explains David Perlmutter, MD, a neurologist, and author of *Lifeguide.* Bromelain, an enzyme found in pineapple, is the jack-of-all-trades when it comes to fighting inflammation. In a study of 146 boxers, researchers showed that bromelain significantly speeded up the healing process when the boxers were injured. Bromelain was given to 74 of the boxers four times a day, while the remaining 72 took an inactive substance (placebo). In 58 of the boxers taking bromelain, all signs of bruising disappeared in four days. In the group taking the placebos, only 10 healed completed in four days.

Quercetin, just one of more than 800 bioflavonoids that have been identified, works best with bromelain to block the inflammation process. Naturopathic doctors believe that bromelain helps your body absorb the quercetin, so they often prescribe the two together, says Dr. Silbert. Quercetin is rich in powerful antioxidants that stop the damaging effects of free radicals, free-roaming, unstable molecules that damage cells.

When the pain of sciatica strikes, take up to 1,000 milligrams of bromelain and 500 milligrams of quercetin four times a day between meals, says Barbara Silbert, D.C., N.D., a chiropractor and naturopathic doctor. The strength of a particular batch of bromelain is measured in milk clotting units (mcu). The higher the mcu number, the greater its strength. Look for a supplement with a strength between 1,800 and 2,400 mcu. Beware of bromelain supplements that merely list weight in milligrams; if the mcu measurement isn't listed on the label, you can assume that you are getting a cheap, ineffective preparation, cautions Jacob Schor, N.D., president of the Colorado Association of Naturopathic Doctors.

Strike oil. Any type of inflammation responds well to the essential fatty acids found in fish oil, flaxseed oil, and evening primrose oil. To reprogramme your pain process, take one tablespoon of flaxseed oil and 500 milligrams of black currant oil (or three capsules of evening primrose oil) every day, says Dr. Perlmutter. These two supplements are rich in omega-3 and omega-6 essential fatty acids that your body needs but cannot make. By adding them to your diet, you can stimulate your body to produce increased levels of good prostaglandins and reduce inflammation. If you want to use fish oil instead of flaxseed oil, take 1,000 milligrams two to four times a day, says Priscilla Evans, N.D.

Everyday prevention:

Please sit up. Prolonged sitting may aggravate your discomfort because it reverses the normal curve in your back, says John E. Thomassy, D.C. Sitting may compress discs and weaken low back ligaments and muscles. When you sit, maintain good posture. Don't slouch. Keep your knees level with your hips, feet flat on the floor, and back straight.

Get the angles right. If you are working at a desk or computer, adjust your chair so your elbows can be positioned at a 90-degree angle with your forearms parallel to the floor, advises Dr. Thomassy. Tuck a small pillow behind your back to help you sit up straight and promote the normal curves in the spine.

Break things up. Take frequent breaks when you're working, Reid says. Get up and walk around every half-hour. If you're travelling in a car, avoid prolonged time behind the wheel or even in the passenger seat. Make frequent rest stops at least every hour or so.

Step right down. Wear comfortable, low-heeled shoes, Dr. Thomassy urges. Heels that are higher than 1 to 1½ inches push your body weight forward and your spine out of alignment.

Get some Z. Try the Z position, suggests Augustus A. White III, MD, professor of Orthopedics Surgery at Harvard Medical School.

Lie on your back on a rug or exercise cushion with your knees bent and feet propped on a low table or chair. Your thighs should be nearly parallel to the floor. To get more comfortable, put a thin cushion under your buttocks and a pillow under your head. Then relax.

This relaxing position often provides quick relief, writes Dr. White.

Lift safely. Even if your back feels better after an episode of back pain, you'll need to lift correctly to prevent a relapse. "Lifting is when most people are injured," Dr. Thomassy says. Whether you're lifting a laundry basket or toolbox, make sure your feet are square to the object then crouch with your knees and hips bent and your back straight. Bring the object close to your body and when you rise, continue to keep your back straight.. If you have to twist, bend forward, or reach out for an object, take the time to get into the proper position before you try lifting. If that's not possible, get help.

Sleep sideways. If you want to minimise or stave off back pain and sciatica, don't sleep on your stomach, Dr. Thomassy cautions. Instead, lie on your side, curl your legs and slip a pillow between your knees. Or, go belly-up with a pillow or rolled towel under your knees. If you like to sleep with a pillow under your head, don't strain your neck with a big one. Instead, use a smaller one that keeps your head and neck in line with your upper back.

Get around. Stay as active as you can while you're recovering from sciatica, even if you only take short walks around the house, Reid says. After pain subsides, try gentle stretches and, later, mild aerobic exercise, Dr. Mandel suggests. Swimming and walking, for example, will help strengthen and condition your back and whole body. They may even make you less vulnerable to injury. "If people stretch and exercise," Dr. Mandel says, "they will reduce their chances of having back problems."

Possess good posture. Good posture means standing up straight, with your shoulders back and head directly over your body. To get a taste of perfect posture, try standing erect with your back against a wall. This is the position that can help prevent the pain of sciatica. Slouching puts more strain on your back than standing straight, says Bruce Dall, MD, an orthopedic spine surgeon. Standing, sitting, and walking tall takes pressure off your back, and it works more muscles of the body. "It's like exercising your back all day long."

Lift with your head, not your back. Here is where lots of people can do their spines a favour. Whenever you lift something that weighs more than a few pounds, keep the object close to your body so that you don't strain the disks in your spine, says Dr. Dall. For the same reason, never twist or turn your torso while you are lifting an object. If you have to change direction, turn with your feet and legs instead. If you have "' Pick tip a heavy item from the floor, make sure that you bend at the knees) not at the waist, he adds.

Sit less, sit smarter. "When you tell someone to avoid sitting, it sounds funny, but it is good advice," says Dr. Reilly. That is because sitting for more than two hours at a time puts a lot of stress on your spine. If you have to sit a lot to make your living, make an effort to get up and move around every hour or two, he says. When you do sit down, do it right. A firm chair is always preferred, says Dr. Reilly.

Favour flat feet. When you are sitting, try to avoid letting your feet fall on their sides into a V-shape, cautions Dr. Reilly. This foot position—what he calls duck feet—contributes to tight muscles in your back and buttocks. Instead, keep your feet flat on the floor.

Become an "arch"-ist. Maintain the arch in your back when you sit, says Dr. Dall. If you slump, the pressure on your disks goes sky-high. Putting a back support pillow or a rolled-up towel in the small of your back to help with your sitting posture. "I sometimes take a heavy pair of winter gloves and jam them down into the hollow of my back," says Dr. Dall, who suffers from sciatica himself.

Get down at the knees. Sit on the edge of your chair and lower your knees down below the edge of the seat. This will force you to balance yourself on the chair, which will maintain the arch in your back, says Dr. Dall.

Be careful in the driver's seat. Sitting for more than two hours at a time in the driver's seat can put your spine in a horrible position, especially if you overextend your right leg to step on the gas and the brake, says Dr. Reilly. Many car seats today are constructed so that the sides are higher than the middle of the seat. When you move over to the right to hit the gas and brake pedals, one part of your backside is put higher than the other, and stress on your back can occur, he says. Make a conscious effort to keep your rump in the centre of the seat, even if it means repositioning your seat from your favourite setting.

Lighten your load. Add this to your list of reasons for losing weight: Carrying around a lot of extra pounds will only load down your spine and make you more prone to degenerative changes of the spine associated with sciatica, says Dr. Reilly.

Pick your own pocket. A bulging billfold in your hip pocket can crimp your sciatic nerve, especially if you sit on the wallet for long periods of time, says Scott Haldeman, MD, D.C., Ph.D. He suggests that you put the wallet in a coat pocket or purse to make sure you don't put lopsided pressure on one buttock.

Give your calves a seat. Assuming a position with hip joints and knees bent is the best way to depress the sciatic nerve and avoid pain, says Dr. Haldeman. Here's a posture that should help: Lie on your back on the floor and place your lower legs on the seat of a chair for 10 or 15 minutes.

Don't cross your legs. Most people tend to cross the same leg all the time. That means you're always sitting on the same buttock, which puts a lot of pressure on the sciatic nerve on that side. Ideally you shouldn't cross your legs at all, But if you must, at least try to switch sides from time to time.

Sit for two. "Sciatica is not uncommon during pregnancy, and it is usually the result of the baby pushing against the sciatic nerve," says Jenny Sutcliffe, PhD, DPP, MBBS, MCSP, former Senior Lecturer in Paediatric Neurology, Great Ormond Street Hospital, London. She suggests you relieve the pain by lying on your back on a mat or carpet with your lower legs resting on the seat of a chair, a stool or a pile of cushions – so that your hip and knee joints are at right angles. "This position decreases the lumbar arch and relaxes the psoas and hamstring muscles," says Dr. Sutcliffe.

Check the clock. "If the pain is worse in the morning, this could indicate inflammation, so try an anti-inflammatory such as ibuprofen or a therapy such as acupressure or reflexology," says Stephen G Motto, DM, Dip Sports Med, musculo-skeletal physician with a speciality in sports medicine at London Bridge Hospital. "If the pain is worse after exercise, there could be a mechanical problem; try lying flat on your back with your knees bent, and do this as much as possible for a few days."

Easing the pain with exercise:

Stretch it out. For sciatica pain, try this stretch from Dr. White. Stand with your feet apart and hands on your buttocks. Push your hips forward and gently bend backward while looking up. Keep knees straight. Hold several seconds, relax, and repeat. You can do this several times a day, and it's especially helpful after sitting.

Find some fitness. "You have to exercise to keep your back healthy," says Dr. Dall. The better your muscle tone, the better the support for your back. Toned muscles will take a lot of the pressure off your spine, reducing your chances of getting sciatica.

Just be sure to start out slowly, especially if you are out of shape or are already prone to sciatica. "If you do things the wrong way or go out too hard too fast, you are vulnerable to injuring yourself and your back," says Dr. Reilly.

If you are unsure of how to begin a sound exercise plan, you would benefit from talking to a physician or physical therapist first, he adds. "Walking is the best general, all-around exercise for the back," says Dr. Dall. That is because it is low-impact and helps strengthen the spinal and abdominal muscles needed for back support.

Wearing supportive shoes is important whenever you walk. In addition, treadmills and well-paved level surfaces are recommended for beginners, says Dr. Reilly.

Get wet. To keep your back healthy and protect your sciatic nerve, go jump in the pool. "Swimming is very good exercise that can help keep muscles toned," says Dr. Reilly. Swim often-the more, the better if your back is in good shape.

If your back is already giving you some trouble, Dr. Dall recommends water physical therapy rather than swimming because some people tend to overarch their spines when they swim. For water physical therapy, you perform traditional exercises such as jogging or leg lifts in chest-high water. Because the water makes you buoyant, the spine isn't stressed by gravity.

Stretch for protection. "Stretching is key to any sciatica prevention program," says Dr. Reilly. Muscles tighten up when your body is left in a stationary position for too long, especially if you are seated. Doing some simple stretching exercises can help loosen up the muscles that surround the sciatic nerve, he says.

Here's one stretch that you can do for the sciatic region. Lie down on your back, grab one knee, and slowly bring it up and over toward the opposite shoulder, says Dr. Reilly. Hold that position for five seconds, then gently return to the lying position. Repeat the stretch with the other leg. As you get better at this exercise, you can increase the amount of time in the knee-holding position.

Lean towards yoga. Many of the stretches done in yoga can also help fend off sciatic problems. "It is a great way to stretch and put your spine through a safe range of motion," says Dr. Dall. "I've heard lots of people with sciatica say that yoga has helped them," Dr. Reilly concurs.

Build your back through your belly. "Healthy abdominal muscles make for a healthy back," says Dr. Reilly. The muscles in your stomach provide support for your spine. Patients with large guts and weak abdominal muscles often complain about back pain and sciatica flare-ups, he says. A gentle series of abdominal crunches done several times a week will help build those stomach muscles.

Dr. Reilly recommends partial sit-ups. Lie on your back with both knees bent, feet flat on the floor, and arms crossed and resting on your chest. Curl up, bringing your elbows toward your thighs, until your shoulders are slightly off the floor. Exhale while curling up and inhale while slowly lowering your shoulders to the floor again. Work up to a minimum of three sets of 15 repetitions, suggests Dr. Reilly.

Take a walk every hour. Taking a three-to-five-minute walk every hour will also speed healing, says Dr. Keenan.

Work the pelvis. Sit on the forward part of a chair with your feet flat on the floor and your back straight. Then follow these steps.

Slowly tilt your pelvis backward a bit so that your lower back is slightly rounded or flexed, and then return to the starting position.

Tilt your pelvis forward very slowly so that your lower back arches or extends a bit, and then return to the starting position.

Alternate between the two movements, tilting your pelvis forward so that your back arches or extends slightly and then slowly tilting your pelvis backward a bit so that your back rounds slightly. Then return to the starting position.

Tilt your pelvis toward your left knee so that your weight shifts to the forward part of your left buttock, and then return to the starting position. Repeat this with your pelvis tilting to your right knee.

Repeat each movement four to eight times before you move on to the next movement, reducing your effort with each repetition, Dr. Reese recommends.

Practice the cobra. Another good exercise for sciatica is called the cobra. Lie on your stomach with your hands flat on the floor, next to your armpits. Stretching your legs straight back, turn your thighs inward so that your heels move apart. Your buttocks will broaden, releasing tension in your lower back. Then draw your tailbone deeper into your buttocks, pressing your tower abdomen onto the floor. (Avoid clenching the muscles in your buttocks, which will pinch nerves further.) Holding your tower body in this position, lift your head and chest upward toward the ceiling. Keep your hipbones on the floor-don't push up with your arms. Hold this position for 30 seconds or so to really stretch your spine. "This will relieve the pain of sciatica in about 80% of cases," says Dr. Motto. But will make it worse in the remaining 20%. "If you are in the unfortunate 20%, this could mean that you have a significant problem and should go to see a specialist as soon as possible," Dr. Motto says.

Give your legs a lift. Try to keep pressure off the lumbar region of your spine, from which most sciatic pain radiates, says Dr. Haldeman. He suggests lying on your back with your lower legs resting on a chair or a low table (such as a coffee table). Your knees and hips should be bent at about 90-degree angles. Do this as needed for relief.

Herbal help:

Cure with curcumin. Several clinical studies show that curcumin has an anti-inflammatory action. Don't reach into your spice cupboard for relief, however. Instead, opt for capsules of standardised extract that contain 97 percent pure curcumin. When pain is acute, Dr. Evans advises people to take 250 to 500 milligrams three times a day. You shouldn't take turmeric as a remedy if you have severe stomach acid, ulcers, gallstones, or a bile duct obstruction.

Get very valerian. Sometimes pain and tingling can be due to muscle spasms in the piriformis muscle, a pear-shaped muscle in the buttocks that surrounds the sciatic nerve. Relaxing this muscle can help relieve pain, says Dr. Evans.

Naturopaths often use a mixture of soothing herbs such as valerian, passionflower, and kava kava to promote muscle relaxation. Although valerian has become a staple on chemist shelves, where it is sold as a sleep aid, its powers of reprieve go beyond sleep. "Valerian is also great for easing tension and for general pain relief," says Dr. Evans. It contains substances known as volatile oils that work together to make you sleepy as well as relaxing your muscles.

Sometimes, your sciatic nerve is in the grip of a spastic muscle, and that no-win tug of war is at the root of the pain. Your doctor will need to confirm if a spastic muscle is the source of your pain. If it is, taking 150 milligrams of valerian three times a day may help, says Dr. Evans.

Get help from hayseed. Many years ago, the European naturopath Parson Kneipp learned what people in the Alps did with the seed heads of the various grasses that they stored as hay to feed their animals through the winter. They swept up the hayseed and added it to baths, because they had discovered that this seed has the ability to soothe painful backs, joints and muscles. Kneipp popularised the use of hayseed for this purpose, and today many Europeans subscribe to Kneipp therapy, using hayseed that has been packaged in bath bags or prepared in the form of hot poultices.

The hot hayseed poultices used in Kneipp therapy have been approved by Commission E, the group of herbal medicine experts appointed by the German counterpart of the Food and Drug Administration to judge the safety and effectiveness of herbal therapies. According to Commission E, the poultices are effective for treating a range of rheumatic conditions as well as sciatica.

But how does hayseed work? It contains a good deal of a compound called coumarin, a camphorlike substance that boosts local blood flow when applied externally, according to Rudolph Fritz Weiss, MD, Germany's leading herbal physician. (Dr. Weiss's book, *Herbal Medicine*, is used in German medical schools.)

Strike back with stinging nettle. People have been flailing their bad backs with the stinging nettle plant since Roman times. This is a practice that involves taking sprigs of the fresh plant and slapping it against the painful area. Be warned, though: This practice stings like crazy. But that is part of the treatment. The sting is a counter-irritant, something that causes minor pain and in effect fools the nervous system into disregarding deeper pain. That's not all that stinging nettle does, however. Chemicals in the stingers that cause inflammation seem to trigger the release of the body's natural anti-inflammatory chemicals. So the body's own medicine helps get rid of the sciatic inflammation. Poultices made from stinging nettle are also good for sciatica, according to Dr. Weiss. (Remember that you need to wear gloves whenever you handle this plant to protect your palms from the stingers.)

Stop weeping with willow. Willow bark contains salicin, the herbal equivalent of aspirin. It can help relieve sciatic pain, and Commission E recognises it as an effective pain reliever for everything from headache to arthritis. The salicin content of willow varies from species to species. "I suggest starting with a low-dose tea made with a half-teaspoon of dried herb and working your way up to a dose that provides effective pain relief," says Dr. Duke. As with aspirin, long-term use of willow bark may cause stomach distress and even ulcers, so try sweetening willow bark tea with a little licorice, which has ulcer-preventing benefits. And if you're allergic to aspirin, you probably shouldn't take herbal aspirin, either.

Win relief with wintergreen. Wintergreen contains methyl salicylate, a close relative of the salicin in willow bark, and it's about equal in its ability to relieve pain. It has a long history of use both internally in tea and externally in baths and ointments for relieving painful conditions, among them sciatica and gout. Absorption through the skin may actually be more rapid than through the stomach.

Warning: You must keep products containing wintergreen oil or any product containing methyl salicylate out of the reach of children. The minty smell can be very tempting, but ingesting even small amounts can prove fatal to young children. You don't have to worry about wintergreen tea, but do take precautions with commercial pain-relief products intended for external use.

Mellow with country mallow. India's traditional Ayurvedic physicians have long used this herb to treat sciatica and other painful muscular and nervous system complaints. The reason appears to be its high concentration of ephedrine: It contains some 850 parts per million. The compound ephedrine is best known as a bronchial decongestant and stimulant, but it also is something of a muscle tonic, which is presumably why it helps relieve sciatica.

Pass the mustard. Ever hear of a mustard plaster? This home treatment has a long folk history of use as a treatment for both respiratory complaints and rheumatic problems like sciatica. Mustard is aromatic, which accounts for some of its use as a bronchial decongestant. But there's a different reason that it's used for sciatica, arthritis, lumbago, neuralgia and rheumatism. Mustard is a rubefacient counter-irritant, which means it causes a soothing feeling of warmth on the skin while its counter-irritant properties cause mild irritation, distracting the body from the deeper pain of sciatica. The combination of heat and counter-irritation has a pain-relieving effect.

Let St. John's wort work. "Try tablets of St John's wort (hypericum) for about a week; this is quite good for nerve pain," says Dr. Motto.

Hands-on help:

Do a butt press. You can ease sciatic pain by pressing on appropriate acupressure points, says acupressurist Michael Reed Gach, author of *The Bum Back Book*. First find the centre of the depression at the sides of the buttocks. Then press both sides simultaneously and hard, because the acupressure points lie deep below the skin, Gach says. Keep the pressure on for a count of 15, then release.

Rub the right way. Here is a massage for sciatica from Elaine Stillerman, L.M.T., a massage therapist. First, sit comfortably in a chair, on a bed or on a padded surface on the floor. Support your lower back with pillows or cushions. Rub massage cream between your hands, and with open palms, stroke from behind the knee to the hip for two to three minutes. Second, massage from the hip down to the back of the knee, moving your fingertips back and forth to apply friction. Follow the course of the sciatic nerve as you go down your leg, rubbing across the nerve. Third, using a loose fist, gently tap on the back of the thigh from the hip to the knee and back again. Continue doing this for 10 to 30 seconds.

If any of these strokes feels particularly comfortable, Stillerman suggests repeating it several times before continuing with the sequence. When you are finished, she says, rub an ice cube or put a cloth-covered ice pack on the painful area to soothe the nerve. You can do this massage every day, she adds. Besides helping to relieve existing pain, the massage may also prevent sciatica flare-ups, she explains.

Do not do this massage if the sciatic nerve is inflamed, according to Stillerman. She also cautions that pregnant women should use extremely gentle pressure; too much pressure could stimulate the saphenous nerve, which leads into the pelvic area, causing uterine contractions.

Shingles

The pain: Typically, during a shingles outbreak, you have tingling and pain around the torso, neck, or face. An oozing, blistering short-lived rash quickly turns to lesions, or small pus-filled blisters. Typically, the pain lasts from two to four weeks, but in some cases, it can last for months (a condition called postherpetic neuralgia). Burning and stabbing pain often precedes the rash by one to three days, so many people don't realise the two are connected. Other early symptoms may include a tingling, extreme sensitivity or dull ache on one side of the body, usually the trunk, buttocks, or thighs. You may have fever, headache, or other flu-like symptoms.

The cause: The same virus that causes chicken pox—the varicella-zoster virus—can continue to live an undercover existence in your nerve cells, and it may emerge later in your life. The second time around, though, you don't get the kid version of itchy, blotchy chicken pox. Instead, you get the adult version, shingles, which is characterised by searing pain and lesions that can leave a good-size scar.

It's hard to tell why the virus re-emerges in some people and not others and impossible to tell when it's going to crop up again. "The virus looks for the right opportunity when your antibody production is down," says William Warnock, N.D., a naturopathic doctor. "Stress is one of the biggest causes of reduced antibody production. When people become stressed, they don't eat right, they don't sleep well, and their immune systems just don't function as well."

See a doctor if:

...you have symptoms of shingles. With a prompt diagnosis, you have the advantage of an opportunity for early treatment.

...if shingles spread to your face. You want to make sure the illness doesn't affect your eyes—if that happens it could permanently damage your vision.

Medication:

Once it gets loose, there's no cure for the varicella-zoster virus, but there may be ways to slow it down or limit its damage during the outbreak. Medical doctors frequently prescribe an antiviral drug such as acyclovir

(Zovirax) or famciclovir (Famvir) to shorten the course of the infection. In order to hasten healing, treatment should be started within two to three days of the first appearance of the small blisters.

Quick relief:

Pull the reins on pain. With your physician's okay, reach for acetaminophen (paracetamol) or another mild over-the counter pain reliever such as ibuprofen, says Karl R. Beutner, MD, Ph.D. Your doctor can prescribe stronger medicine for more serious discomfort.

Stay dry. You can't do a lot to get rid of the shingles rash; it must run its course. But you can help dry the oozing blisters, says Dr. Beutner. Apply calamine lotion or a solution made from Domeboro tablets, both available at chemists. As the wet solutions evaporate from your skin, they also steal moisture from the blisters.

Pack some heat. If your pain remains after the rash, you can smooth a capsaicin cream on the affected area three or four times a day, Dr. Beutner says. But be sure you have no more rash. Capsaicin cream is made from the extract of cayenne pepper. "On an open rash, it really hurts," he says. Capsaicin cream usually begins to work within two to four weeks, but it must be applied three or four times a day, every day. If the product is not used in this way, pain may recur in a few days or weeks. When you first apply capsaicin cream, you may feel a burning sensation on your skin, which should subside within a few weeks.

Reach for the aspirin. When shingles pain strikes, desensitise yourself quickly with aspirin. A regular or extra-strength dose could deliver all the pain relief you need to get by while your body recovers. If you find aspirin isn't strong enough, tell your doctor. You may need another type of anti-inflammatory drug available by prescription only, to calm the affected nerve endings.

Try an aspirin paste. Post-herpetic nerve pain can linger after your herpes have healed. A small Boston University Medicine study conducted by neurologist Marilyn Kassiner, MD, found that four out of six patients suffering from post-herpetic neuralgia experienced significant relief 15 to 20 minutes after applying an aspirin paste the affected area. A fifth patient experienced some relief. All other treatments had failed for these people, who were in great pain.

This technique may work for you. To make the paste, crush an aspirin tablet and add it to 2 tablespoons of Vaseline Intensive Care lotion. Apply the paste where you need it three or four times a day. Don't try this remedy if you are allergic to aspirin. And if the treatment doesn't work within 15 to 20 minutes, it's not going to work at all for you.

Ice up. You can confuse painful nerve endings and ease the pain by putting a plastic bag full of ice over the area that hurts.

Go soak in vinegar. Soak a soft dish towel in slightly chilled apple cider vinegar and drape it over the affected area for 10 to 15 minutes.

Apply a cooling compress. "Soak some gauze or a washcloth in cool, clean water or a saline solution and put it directly on the blisters," suggests Clay J. Cockerell, MD, a professor of dermatology and pathology. The compress will dry out the blisters and speed the healing process, he explains, It will also help prevent secondary bacterial infection, which can lead to ulceration and scarring.

Strike gold with silver. Many doctors are recommending colloidal silver for shingles because it may have some antiviral and antibacterial action, says Cynthia M. Watson, MD, a family practitioner. "When it's applied directly to the blisters, they seem to dry up in a matter of days." Colloidal silver can be purchased in health food stores.

Take a bath. The itching associated with the blisters can be as maddening as the pain. You can relieve some of the itching and dry skin symptoms with an occasional colloidal oatmeal bath, such as Aveeno (Oilatum), an over-the-counter product, recommends Jessica Severson, MD, a clinical researcher in dermatology. For the consistency of the bath, follow the directions on the product. just don't bathe any more than you normally would, Dr. Severson cautions. The skin needs to be kept clean, but excess bathing could be irritating. "An oatmeal bath probably works best in the beginning and end stages of shingles. But if you have open sores, you may not want to put anything on them and risk irritation," Dr. Severson says.

Nutritional remedies:

Avoid arginine, load up on lysine. Varicella-zoster belongs to a larger family of herpes viruses, all of which share an important characteristic: They multiply with the help of the amino acid arginine and are inhibited by another amino acid called lysine. Lysine may work by blocking the virus's ability to absorb and use arginine. To keep shingles at bay, doctors advise, you should avoid arginine-rich foods such as chocolate, legumes, and nuts, especially peanuts, and eat more foods that are rich in lysine, such as fish, tofu, eggs, lean beef, and lean pork. You can also boost your lysine levels by taking a supplement. Dr. Warnock suggests taking 2,000 milligrams daily until the infection runs its course.

Beat the pain with a B Vitamin. Shingles is not just painful, it's intensely painful. Because your nerves carry the virus and the virus causes inflammation, having shingles is like having a raw wound inside your nervous system. Even a light touch can be painful, while something as innocuous as a tight shirt can give you a full day of misery.

Some people find shingles heals more quickly with vitamin B12 injections, says Anne McClenon, N.D. If the idea of an injection doesn't appeal to you, you can get B12 tablets to place under your tongue. Although some people have difficulty absorbing B12, most people can absorb at least some of the vitamin this way.

Vitamin B12 seems to maintain the fatty membranes that sheathe and insulate the nerves, says Dr. McClenon. There's also evidence that it reduces the inflammation of the nerve where the virus is causing pain, and it may even shorten the length of the illness.

"It definitely speeds healing," says Dr. McClenon, "and it may lessen the chance of a person getting the postherpetic neuralgic pain." She suggests taking a 2,000-microgram tablet of B12 each day during the course of the infection.

Everyday prevention:

Get into a lather. Wash your hands regularly, Dr. Beutner says, especially if you have an oozing rash from shingles. The blisters contain varicella virus, so you could unknowingly infect someone with chicken pox. You also can cover the blisters with an antibiotic ointment and wrap the area with gauze.

Take care of you. Because stress is a factor in developing shingles, relaxation is important. "Pace yourself," Dr. Beutner says. Stop and put your feet up or take an afternoon nap, especially if you don't feel well. "People should listen to their bodies and rest when they feel tired," he says. Since the pain of shingles can interrupt your normal night's sleep, try to make up for lost rest at other times during the day, Dr. Beutner says. Getting plenty of rest will keep you healthier overall and may help you mend more quickly.

Protect against secondary infection. Any open sore can get infected, which would only cause more problems. If you have open sores ore blisters caused by shingles, take action to prevent those secondary infections. Probably the easiest thing to do is to place an over-the-counter antibacterial ointment such as bacitracin (Cicatim) on the lesion. Hydrogen peroxide will also work. Don't overgoop your lesions, though, since they heal better when they're dry.

Take it easy. Treat your body gently during an outbreak. Do every thing you can to rest and avoid stressing the inflamed nerve route. That means don't exercise, don't try to work though the pain. Give the rash time to heal. Motion will increase inflammation of the nerve route and you could end up with persistent pain. So take it easy.

Wash up. Clean the affected area with soap and water, then apply 3 percent hydrogen peroxide, advises Leon Robb, MD Doing so will help prevent the sores from becoming infected.

Go under wraps. You can also protect the affected area by wrapping it with an elastic bandage, Dr. Cockerell says. This will prevent anything from touching or rubbing against the blistered skin. "Just be sure the bandage is tight," he cautions. "If it's loose, it will irritate the blisters." Be sure to place a nonadhesive gauze pad over the blisters before wrapping. If you can't wrap the affected area, Dr. Cockerell suggests coating gauze with petroleum jelly, then taping it over the blisters.

Don't share your pain. "Shingles is less infectious than chicken pox because the virus is not airborne," Dr. Cockerell explains. "Still, the virus can be transmitted by direct contact." When you have shingles, you should avoid contact with anyone who has not had chicken pox. "Wait until the blisters are crusted over, which usually takes four or five days," Dr. Cockerell says. If you do happen to infect someone, though, the person will develop chicken pox rather than shingles.

Wash gently. You should clean the blisters and any sores that may have opened by lightly sponging them with a mild soap and water one or two times a day, says Stephen Straus, MD, chief of the Laboratory of Clinical Investigation in the U.S. National Institutes of Health Allergy and Infectious Diseases. Wear clean, loose, cotton clothing so that you do not pinch or chafe the rash. Breathable clothing and airflow also keep the lesions dry, adds Dr. Straus.

Motion for the lotion. if dry skin is your problem, be certain to use a moisturising lotion frequently (especially after a bath), says Dr. Severson. Again, only apply the lotion when the sores aren't weeping. Most moisturisers are good, but keep away from any containing alpha hydroxy acids, which will sting any break in the skin, she adds.

Herbal help:

Boost your immunity with a&e. Herbalists believe that the most effective herbs are astragalus and echinacea. They work best if you take them as soon as you know you have an outbreak of the virus, says Dr. Warnock. Although you can take an herbal tincture, he recommends taking one 300-milligram capsule of standardised extract three times a day. If you use capsules of dried echinacea root, Dr. Warnock recommends 2,000 milligrams three times a day. Since echinacea is also safe at higher doses, you can take even more than the specified dose if you find it effective, says Dr. Warnock. "I'd do a high dose for a short period—just a few days. That's when it's most effective," he says.

While echinacea speeds white blood cells to the infection site, you can add astragalus to help with the healing process. This herb provides what is known as deep immune support, working within the bone marrow where immune cells are manufactured, says Dr. McClenon. She recommends taking one teaspoon of tincture three times a day. You can also take astragalus in capsule form.

"Astragalus provides immune support on a long-term basis. That's important because people who get shingles may have a weakened immune system that needs to be built up again," she says. "I'd recommend taking it for four to six months."

Lick it with licorice. Licorice also has strong antiviral properties. During the course of the infection, Dr. Warnock recommends taking a teaspoon of licorice root tincture twice a day or the same amount of standardised extract three times a day. Alternatively, you can take 500 milligrams of standardised extract in capsule form three times a day. If you take powdered licorice root in capsules, however, the dose should be 2,000 milligrams three times a day. Continue the treatment for two weeks after the lesions have healed, Dr. Warnock says.

Take licorice with caution, however, and don't take it at all if you are pregnant or nursing or if you have diabetes, high blood pressure, liver disorders, or kidney problems. In general, you shouldn't take high doses of licorice for more than four to six weeks unless you're under the supervision of a qualified health-care practitioner.

Limit the lesions. The skin outbreaks and pain of shingles can sometimes be eased with St. John's wort oil. Although naturopathic doctors find that St. John's wort oil applied to the unbroken skin acts as an anti-inflammatory, it also is used to relieve pain and strengthen nerves, says Dr. McClenon. "Thus, it's a good topical treatment for any kind of nerve pain. I would continue to use it for the residual pain that may linger after the outbreak."

Take tea topically. A strong tea made out of licorice, lemon balm, or both can be applied topically to the sore areas as an antiherpetic agent (shingles is a form of herpes), says David Winston, a clinical herbalist. To make the licorice application, add one teaspoon of dried licorice to eight ounces water, and simmer on the stove until the liquid reduces to half (four ounces). To make the lemon balm application, add eight ounces of boiling water to two teaspoons of the dried herb and steep, covered, for 20 minutes. These teas can be refrigerated and used the next day. Apply the herb teas with cotton balls, and let them dry on the skin. Try to remember to apply them two to four times a day, Winston advises.

Get homeopathic help. "The best homeopathic remedy for shingles is Ranunculus bulbosis, especially when the shingles are on the trunk of the body," says Stephen Messer, N.D., dean of the National Centre for Homeopathy's summer school. He recommends taking a 6C dose up to four times a day as needed for pain. You should notice improvement within a couple of days, Dr. Messner.

Say "aloe-ahhh." The thin milky liquid inside the leaves of the aloe vera plant may help soothe the blisters, Dr. Huemer says. If you have an aloe houseplant, cut a leaf and smooth the liquid over your skin. Or try an over-the-counter aloe lotion.

Lick it with lemon balm. Herbalists recommend many herbs that are members of the mint family, especially lemon balm, or melissa, to treat herpes. There's good reason for this. Lemon balm has been proven to have some effect on viruses of the herpes family. Varro Tyler, Ph.D., dean and professor emeritus of pharmacognosy (natural product pharmacy) at Purdue University, suggests using lemon balm to treat viral infections. One European anti-herpes product contains 700 milligrams of lemon balm leaf extract per gram of cream-based ointment. It has been shown to shorten the healing time of herpes sores by several days. You can achieve a similar effect, according to Dr. Tyler, from a tea made with two teaspoons of dried leaf per cup of boiling water. Apply the tea directly to the rash with a cotton pad several times daily.

Choose Chinese angelica. Also known as dong quai, this herb is revered in Asia as the best herb for menstrual problems and other women's health concerns. In addition, the Chinese have used the powdered root successfully to treat shingles. It can be used in tea or tincture. (Do not take this herb if you are pregnant, however.)

Use the power of passionflower. Passionflower is a mild tranquilliser, which is not a bad idea if you are being driven to distraction by the pain of shingles. But it also has reputed activity against postherpetic neuralgia. "I suggest adding some to a lemon balm—licorice tea," says Dr. Duke.

Try essential oils. If you enjoy aromatherapy, you might apply a few drops of essential oils that have been recommended for treating shingles. They include bergamot, camomile, eucalyptus, geranium, lavender, lemon and teatree oil. Since some full-strength essential oils can be irritating to the skin, dilute them by adding several drops to a couple of tablespoons of vegetable oil and apply them directly to painful areas. (Never ingest essential oils, as even a small amount can be toxic.)

Mind over malady:

See something completely different. When you're in pain, it's easy to wonder if it will ever go away, says Emmett Miller, MD, mind-body specialist. That can make your perception of the pain worse, he says. Dr. Miller teaches patients to use visualisation to see and feel their pain differently. First, take a deep breath and relax as you slowly let it out. Close your eyes and allow an image that represents your pain to arise in your mind. Is it hot or cold? Is it moving? What colour is it? Perhaps you see a twisting red-hot poker, Dr. Miller says.

Now, create a parallel image of something that would remove that object's harmful quality and put it to use. You might picture a fire hose extinguishing the hot poker, or an Eskimo with a bucket of snow, Dr. Miller says. If you can learn to transform your mental image of pain, he says, you may feel less affected by it physically.

Shinsplints

The pain: A dull ache that usually occurs in the inner front part of the lower leg.

The cause: Shinsplints are usually caused by exercise or other kinds of repetitive physical activity. Constant pounding—from running, playing tennis, or sometimes even walking in high heels—can irritate the tendons that link the leg muscles to the lower leg bones. The result can be shin pain and often swelling. Though beginning runners and joggers are most likely to get this overuse injury, you don't have to be a neophyte to get shinsplints. Anybody who does a sport that requires a fair amount of running (such as football or tennis) can get them, too, says Mark Veenstra, MD, an orthopedic surgeon.

See a doctor if...
...your pain lasts longer than two weeks.
...you have trouble bearing weight on the affected leg.
...your pain is accompanied by a bluish skin discolouration, ulceration or tender lumps beneath the skin.
...your pain recurs with only mild activity.

Quick relief:
Try RICE. Give rest, ice, compression and elevation a shot at relieving shinsplint pain. Ice is especially helpful.

Put it on ice. You can soothe sore shins by rubbing them for 20 minutes with ice that's been frozen in a paper cup, says Craig Hersh, MD Or fill an empty bread bag with ice, wrap it in a towel, and strap the bag to the front of your shin with an elastic bandage for 20 to 30 minutes, says James M. Lynch, MD, a team physician. If you apply ice quickly, it reduces inflammation and eases pain, says Dr. Lynch.

Make it hot. After three days of ice treatment, switch to heat, says William S. Case, president of Case Physical Therapy. "Apply moist heat—a bath, a shower or a moist heating pad will do—for 15 minutes once or twice a day," he advises. If you opt for a heating pad, first rub vinegar on your sore shin and then cover the area with plastic, suggests Arthur H. Brownstein, MD Then place the heating pad on top.

Pamper with a pain reliever. Any number of over-the-counter medications such as Advil and Nuprin contain the ingredient ibuprofen, which helps take the edge off pain, says Dr. Lynch. But aspirin and acetaminophen (Tylenol or Panadol) are also effective painkillers, he says. (Do not give aspirin to children because of the risk of Reye's syndrome.)

Helpful vitamins and supplements:

Block pain with bromelain. "Bromelain, an enzyme found in pineapple and papaya, works well for inflammatory conditions like shinsplints," says Cynthia M. Watson. You can by bromelain in pill form in health food stores.

Everyday prevention:

Let time heal all wounds. Exercise is a process of breaking down and building up muscle tissue, says Richard Simon, MD, an orthopedic surgeon. To avoid shinsplints, he suggests taking a day off between hard workouts, especially if you are a beginner.

Ease the pain with exercise:

Mix it up. If exercise is causing the shinsplints, varying your exercise routine can be the cure, says Melvin Williams, Ph.D. Just for starters, he notes, you should stop all high-impact, weight-bearing exercise. Tennis and jogging are definitely out for a while. You might even limit your walking if it aggravates the shinsplints.

Take some strides on the wet side. Dr. Williams has also felt the pain of shinsplints. When his shins start barking, he turns to water workouts as a low-impact alternative to running. "A lot of people tend to lay off exercise altogether when they get shinsplints," says Dr. Williams. "But I rest for a couple of days and then do alternate training like running in water." Water has a nice cushioning effect. Try running in your local pool or lake. It's probably best to run in place, but if the pool is big enough, jog slowly back and forth in the shallow end; waist- to chest-deep is best. If the lake is shallow enough and the bottom isn't too mucky, run up and down along the shore.

Wear flotation fashion. Dr. Williams suggests wearing a buoyancy vest while you take your wet run. This minimal life preserver helps keep you upright and further minimises impact to your shins.

Cycle for your shins. Bicycling is also good exercise alternative to ease your way back from shinsplints, says Dr. Williams. It involves far less trauma to your legs than the constant banging of running or other weight-bearing exercises. "Bicycling is non-weight-bearing," says Margaret Gutgesell, MD, Ph.D. "Just be sure to stay off hills and set the gears at the easiest level so there's no stress on the knees or ankles, and don't forget to set the bicycle seat at the correct height." You might also check other options, such as some of the newer stair-climbing machines that may reduce impact, says Dr. Williams. If you experience no pain when exercising, these may be good alternatives as well.

Get against the wall. Shinsplints can sometimes hang on for a while. Stretching before and after exercise is one good way to speed your recovery, says Dan Hamner, MD, a physiatrist and sports medicine specialist. As the pain recedes, try this calf muscle stretch suggested by Carl Fried, P.T., a physical therapist. "Every stretch should be a mild stretch," he recommends. "You should hold each one for at least 15 seconds to give your muscles time to get warm and loose."

Stand facing a wall with your right foot 12 inches from the wall and your left foot about 12 inches behind the right. Keep your arms straight and place your palms flat on the wall for support.

Bend your right leg at the knee, keeping your left leg straight.

Keeping both heels on the floor, bend your arms and lean your upper body forward into the wall, letting your full weight press against your hands. You should feel the stretch in the calf muscle of your left leg.

Hold the stretch for 15 to 20 seconds, then relax. Repeat two more times.

Change the position of your legs and stretch the other calf.

Pick up a pencil. Here's another playful exercise that may help ease the pain of shinsplints and prevent them from coming back, according to Steven Lawrence, MD, an orthopedic surgeon.

Take off your shoes and socks and sit in a comfortable chair.

Drop a pencil at your feet and try to pick it up with all the toes of one foot. Hold it for at least 10 seconds.

Drop the pencil and repeat the process five times with each foot.

Repeat twice a day.

Be a tortoise, not a hare. Many people get shinsplints when they suddenly decide to start working out and try to do too much too soon. If you are just taking up running or tennis, for example, be sure to start slowly. The best approach is to build up your muscle strength little by little. This will help avoid irritating the tissues around your shins. Take your workouts slow and steady, says Dr. Veenstra. If you are just taking up running, Dr. Veenstra recommends that you start out by walking the distance that you want to eventually run. Next, mix in a few short jogging spurts. Gradually make the jogging time last longer than the walking time, until you are running the whole distance. The entire process should take about a month or so, depending upon how far you set your first distance goal and the kind of shape you are in, he says.

Warm up. Avoiding tightness in your legs will help you avoid shinsplints, says Dr. Simon. Loosen up before you work out. Warm up your muscles with a short walk or light callisthenics, then do 5 to 10 minutes of stretching before you start running.

If the shoe fits, wear it. Investing in a good pair of athletic shoes is important to avoid shinsplints, says Dr. Veenstra. You will need a comfortable fit and plenty of shock absorption. You should replace old shoes when you can see about a quarter-inch of wear on the inside edge of the heel, he says.

Be sport-specific with your shoes. Get shoes specifically designed for the kind of exercise you do most often. Don't play tennis in running shoes or go running in tennis shoes, Dr. Veenstra advises.

Seek out a smart salesclerk. Next time you shop for athletic shoes, try to find a salesclerk who seems knowledgeable about the differences between athletic shoes. If you can't get advice that you trust at a store, ask a personal trainer or maybe the high-school athletic trainer for suggestions.

Avoid surface stress. Running on hard roads made of concrete or asphalt is harder on your shins than running on softer surfaces like grass, cushioned tracks, and gravel, says Dr. Veenstra. Even treadmills are better-cushioned than roadways, says Dr. Simon. If you do have to run on a road, be sure to switch directions now and then. Over time, the slant of the street can encourage shinsplints if one leg is a little higher and the other one is taking most of your weight.

Lighten your load. Being overweight puts more pressure on the connective tissues around the shins, says Dr. Simon. If you can shed pounds, you are less likely to get shinsplints.

Shorten your stride. Shortening your stride can help get rid of shinsplints. Try walking or running with a comfortable, shorter stride.

See if you're a P or an S. Because the way you run has a lot to do with how your shins feel, do some simple tests to determine whether you pronate or supinate.

Overpronators roll their ankles and feet inward while they run, inequitably transferring much of the pounding into the inner portion of their lower legs, says Paul Raether, MD, a marathoner and physical medicine specialist. Supinators, however, don't turn in their ankles when they run, directing damaging stress to the outside of the legs, he says.

One way to determine your footfall tendency: Step into the tub to get your feet wet, then stand on the dry floor and look at your footprints. (To make them easier to see, step on a couple of paper towels.) If you can see your arch, you are an overpronator; if you can't, you are an underpronator (supinator), says Dr. Raether.

Then pick the proper shoes. Choose carefully. "Some shoes on the market offer more control than others," says Stone. "If you pronate, you need what's called a board-lasted shoe." To tell if a shoe is board-lasted, pull out the insole-the extra strip of material that's inside the shoe. If there's no stitching between the insole and the bottom of the shoe, it's board-lasted, just what a pronator wants. If you're a supinator, you need the other kind of shoe: Look for an insole that is stitched or stitched and glued, says Stone.

Grab some low-cost orthotics. Specially moulded shoe inserts (orthotics) can often correct pronation, but they can cost a bundle. Here's an inexpensive alternative to try first: For a few dollars, get a pair of shoe inserts and slip them into your running shoes—they may be all you need, says Stone. If your shins are still in rough shape after using a cheap insert, see a podiatrist for the higher-priced model.

Walk before you run. It's always best to warm up the muscles of the lower legs before you go on a run, according to Stone. One way is to ride a stationary bike for ten minutes. Or take a brief walk before you break into a full-paced canter.

Pig out on hamstring stretches. Tight hamstrings—those tendons on the underside of your thighs-can literally knock you off your stride, says Stone. To keep hamstrings loose, she recommends the hurdler's stretch. After warming up, sit on the ground, extend your right leg forward, and place the bottom of your left foot on the inside of your right leg so that you're making a P with your legs. Slowly lean forward, reaching your hands to your right foot and keeping the small of your back down for a count of ten. Switch legs and repeat.

Strengthen those shins. Shin pain is often caused by weak lower leg muscles. To build those shin muscles, Stone suggests the following routine: Sit on a table with your legs hanging over the edge. Hook one ankle through the handle of a backpack that has a book in it. Without moving your upper leg, flex your foot upward for two to three seconds. Repeat 10 to 12 times. Then switch I feet and repeat. You can also strengthen your lower legs by performing basic lower leg exercises such as drawing each letter of the alphabet with the big toe of each foot in the air.

Give your calves a moving experience. Your calf muscles can use some attention, too: With your shoes off, stand erect. Slowly rise onto your toes and make like a ballerina for a count of three. Lower and repeat 12 to 15 times. If that's too easy an exercise for your calves, you can make it more challenging by performing the same exercise while standing on a step and allowing your calves to stretch over the edge of the step. Be sure to hang on to something, so you don't fall down the stairs.

Save your best stretch for last. Because research shows that your muscles are more elastic after they've been warmed up, a thorough stretch at the end of your workout will help eliminate any shin pain, says Stone. "The best time to work on flexibility problems that can cause shin splints is when you're finished exercising," she says. All exercises for hamstrings, tendons, shins and calves should be done after as well as before you begin your workout.

Herbal help:

Get some ginkgo. You can bring down the inflammation of chronic shinsplints and speed healing by taking ginkgo biloba, a common herbal treatment, says Alison Lee, MD, a pain-management specialist. Take 40 milligrams three times a day, says Dr. Lee. It may increase the effects of monamine oxidase inhibitor drugs, so talk to your doctor about using ginkgo if you are taking these.

Get homeopathic help. Try taking a 6C dose of Ruta graveolens three times a day until the discomfort begins to subside, says Stephen Messner, N.D.

Shoulder Pain

The pain: Shoulder pain comes in lots of shapes and sizes. Some folks ache in their upper backs and some in the front of their shoulders, along the line from the top of the breastbone to the armpit. Still others hurt along the top, from their necks to the curve of their shoulders. The kind of pain varies, too, from a dull ache to a sharp, stabbing pain. You may get symptoms that involve a steady aching pain, with intermittent bursts of sharper pain when you're in certain positions.

The cause: Most shoulder pain usually results from one of two causes: Muscles and tendons may be injured from prolonged overuse, as can happen when you paint or garden for too long. Or they can get pinched between bones or ligaments, a process called impingement that frequently results from activities that require power strokes or throwing, such as swimming, tennis or softball.

See a doctor if:
...pain, tightness, or limited range of motion in your shoulder interferes with everyday tasks such as combing your hair or fastening bra hooks and persists for more than five to seven days.
...your shoulder pain results from a fall or accident. See a doctor immediately to rule out a fracture.
...you experience extreme pain.
...you notice any swelling or redness.
...you have a fever or chills along with the pain.

Quick relief:
Stop what you're doing. If a particular activity has aggravated your shoulder, then give it up or at least cut back for the time being, experts say. "And avoid any movement that can make your pain worse—mainly reaching over or behind your head," advises Joel Press, MD, associate professor of clinical physical medicine and rehabilitation.

Act fast! "For those people who have overworked their elbow or shoulder and inflamed the joint, the first 48 hours afterward are critical," says William D. Stanish, MD, an associate professor of surgery at Dalhousie University in Halifax and director of the Orthopedic and Sports Medicine

Clinic in Nova Scotia. "Almost everyone may achieve relief in those first two days."

Rub it. Rubbing the pain can make it go away. It's a pain-control technique with solid scientific backing. "It's something that you can begin to do instantly to reduce the sensation of pain from something like a stiff shoulder, tendonitis, or bursitis," says Edward Resnick, MD, professor of orthopedic surgery. "Pain has to travel a fair distance from the injured area for us to perceive it," he explains. "When you rub the area that's injured, you're generating other impulses that will travel along the same pathways. These nonpainful impulses often interfere with the painful ones."

Freeze the flame with ice. Ice's cold competes with pain better than any other nondrug method, says Ronald Melzack, Ph.D., of McGill University, past president of the International Association for the Study of Pain. Freeze ice in a paper cup -that makes the ice a handy size to use. The most effective technique is to slowly rub the ice in circles on the spot that hurts. Within about 5 to 7 minutes, that spot will feel numb and your sensation of any pain will be greatly diminished. The intense stimulation that ice provides is an excellent way to 'close the gate' to the spinal pathway and inhibit painful information from reaching your brain." Use ice massage three or four times daily until you're fully recovered. If you don't improve, or if the pain gets worse, see a doctor.

Put the squeeze on pain. It's called compression. you may find that wrapping the aching area in an elastic bandage will reduce swelling and thus ease pain. Make sure the bandage is snug, but not so tight or applied for so long that it's uncomfortable or blocks the flow of healing blood. Watch for any swelling or discolouration anywhere on your arm. Take the bandage off when you give yourself an ice massage, and don't sleep with the bandage on.

Boost it up. Arms tend to hang down whenever they get the chance. They swing back and forth and blood can pool, both of which cause pain. Keeping the hurt area raised above the level of the heart, or in a sling to restrict motion, helps control swelling and pain.

Allow yourself a painkiller. No need to be a martyr: An anti-inflammatory such as aspirin, ibuprofen or ketoprofen (Orudis) taken several times a day according to package directions will ease the pain and swelling.

Use heat, but don't rely on it. Applying heat to a sore shoulder will help ease your pain, but it won't cure it. "A heating pad to shoulder pain is what a microwave oven is to a bad sandwich: The sandwich tastes better warm, but if you let it cool down again, it will taste just as bad as it did before you warmed it," says sports medicine specialist Charles Norelli, MD "In other words, you'll feel better while you have heat on your shoulder, but unless you fix the problem, you'll feel just as bad once you remove the heat."

Everyday prevention:

Rest ... kind of. Dr. Stanish advises that you avoid the offending activity for a full week. That doesn't mean become a couch potato. Do things that don't aggravate the injured arm or shoulder. If it hurts to raise your arm over your head, then don't, but use that arm below shoulder level. While you should take it easy, you don't want to completely immobilise an ailing shoulder, according to Phillip A. Bauman, MD, clinical instructor in orthopedic surgery. "The longer you limit your movement, the stiffer you become," he says. "That can lead to more pain, which causes you to limit your movement even more. Eventually, you could end up with frozen shoulder," a condition characterised by severe pain and stiffness.

Limit lifting. It's also a good idea to refrain from heavy lifting, while your shoulder is sore, says David Altchek, MD, a professor of orthopedic surgery. His rule of thumb: "Don't hoist anything heavier than a briefcase or a gallon of milk."

Tug your towel. After you step out of your morning shower and dry off, turn your towel into an exercise tool for your achy shoulders, suggests Thomas Meade, MD, an orthopedic surgeon.

Standing straight, hold one end of the towel with your right hand and let hang it down behind your back. Hold it so that your right fist is a few inches above your right shoulder Reach behind your back with your left hand and grasp the other end of the towel. With your right hand, try to raise the towel as high as you can while resisting the upward pull by bearing down with your left hand. Hold for 10 seconds, slowly lower your right hand, and relax. Try this stretch four more times, then repeat on the other side.

Hug yourself. You can warm your shoulder muscles with this body hug offered by Dr. Meade. He recommends doing this stretch twice a day to keep your shoulder muscles limber.

Stand straight and place your left forearm across your waist, with your left elbow bent at a 90-degree angle. Place your right forearm on top of your left so that your right hand cups your left elbow. Use your right hand to pull slowly and firmly on your left elbow for 20 to 30 seconds. Don't try to resist with your left arm. You should feel the muscles stretching in your shoulder and elbow joints. Switch arms and repeat.

Bring out the broom. There's no need for expensive gym equipment to keep your shoulders moving in all directions. Even a broom handle can help keep your shoulders supple.

Sit straight in a chair with both feet flat or, the floor. Hold the broom handle in both hands, palms down, in front of your waist with your arms straight. Slowly lift your arms and raise the handle as high as you can— ideally, over your head. (If you have tendonitis. don't go higher than your shoulders.) Count to 5 or 10 and then lower the broom handle back to waist level. Try at least 15 repetitions twice a day. "You should go to the point of feeling a little discomfort, but do not push it to the point of pain," advises Kim Fagan, MD, a sports medicine physician.

Soup up your shoulder. Shoulders need more strength training than most joints. "The shoulder's design is great for flexibility and range of motion, but it is lacking in stability," says Dr. Fagan. "For it to function properly, the surrounding muscles have to do their jobs well."

Grab a couple of cans of soup from the pantry and give yourself a workout before dinner.

Stand straight with your shoulders back. Your arms should be hanging at your sides with each hand holding a soup can.

Keeping your elbows straight and your palms facing the floor, slowly raise your arms to shoulder level. Hold for five seconds, then relax and slowly lower your arms. Repeat this lift four more times. Build up a little each day until you can hoist the cans 15 times per session.

Take cans in hand again. Before you put the soup away, try these moves, suggests Dr. Fagan. Hold one soup can with your arm hanging straight down at your side. Slowly and with controlled movements, swing the can back and forth like a pendulum. Be sure to keep your arm straight. For starters, try 25 swings with each arm three times a day. For variety, try making circular motions with the can. "The can-holding is a little resistance training for the rotator cuff," explains Dr. Fagan.

Shrug and strengthen. Don't expect Arnold Schwarzenegger deltoids, but here is a series of easy exercises to ensure healthier shoulders, recommended by Michael Ciccotti, MD, an orthopedic surgeon.

Stand straight with your arms at your sides. Lift your shoulders up for a count of two, then let them down on a count of two. Do 20 repetitions. Then try alternate left and right shoulder shrugs, repeating 20 times with each shoulder. Finish by moving both shoulders forward and then backward 20 times.

Swing a baby. After two days, when the pain is mostly gone, begin performing gentle "range-of-motion" exercises that put the joint through all its moves. The exercises help to prevent things from stiffening up and make sure that the injured area receives adequate blood flow in order for it to heal properly. Lean over and grasp the back of a chair with your uninjured arm, letting your tender arm hang down. Start swinging it slowly back and forth and side to side, until you get it going in circles. Do this for no more than 2 minutes at a time, several times a day; stop if it hurts too much.

Exercise after your workout. "Shoulder pain often results from repetitive motion-whether it's caused by your job or by playing a sport such as tennis or softball," says Robert Stephens, Ph.D., chairman of the Department of Anatomy and director of sports medicine at the University of Health Sciences College. "One of the best ways to remedy this problem, and help prevent it in the future, is to perform full range-of-motion stretching and strengthening exercises in order to compensate for these repetitive movements. For instance, if you have shoulder pain. after playing tennis, perform some gentle stretching exercises such as rotating your arm inward and outward and doing slow, full arm circles (like the backstroke and crawl stroke) in both directions. "Stretching the muscles associated with the movement that's causing you the pain may help prevent muscle imbalances and ease the tension on the joints," says Dr. Stephens.

Hoist some barbells. How do you "fix" shoulder pain? Besides practising full range-of-motion exercises, lifting weights often helps, adds Dr. Charles Norelli. "You want to strengthen rotator cuff muscles (behind the shoulder), and lifting weights is the best way to do that," he says. "Take a two- to six-pound barbell and lift it sideways, keeping your arm straight and your thumb pointing up. It's important to keep your thumb pointing up, because if it points down, you could be impinging your tendon."

Move it gently. Here are more range-of-motion exercises to try once your pain subsides. Lynn Van Ost, P.T., a clinical specialist, suggests these: Begin each exercise with your arm hanging down at your side. First, raise your arm straight in front of you until it is over your head (or go as far as you can without feeling any pain) and lower it back to the starting point. Then raise your arm out to the side and lower it. For the third exercise, keep your upper arm tucked against your body, but bend your elbow so that your forearm is in front of you. Rotate your forearm in toward your stomach and return to the starting position. Repeat the exercise again, rotating your arm away from you. Repeat each motion ten times before moving on to the next, and do the entire routine once or twice a day as long as you don't feet pain.

Find the cause

All shoulder pain might hurt like the dickens, but not all the pain comes from the same source. To determine the probable cause of your problem, sports medicine specialist Charles Norelli, MD, suggests you try these exercises.
'Hold your arm out and twist your wrist as though you were emptying a soda can, then raise your arm. If this causes pain, your problem is probably tendonitis," says Dr. Norelli.

"If the pain is in your right shoulder, grab your right elbow with your left hand and pull it across your body," advises Dr. Norelli. "If this causes pain, that might be an impingement sign-a signal that something in the bone or muscle is getting in the way." This problem may be remedied with specific range-of-motion exercises and light weight lifting.

Dr. Norelli points out that any severe shoulder pain requires professional medical attention. Heart attack pain, for example, can sometimes be transferred to the shoulder. While these quick "diagnostics' can give you a clue in many cases, if the pain is severe, be sure to see your doctor for a more thorough examination.

Side Stitches

The pain: A sharp pain under the rib cage that occurs while running or exercising.

The cause: Experts can't agree precisely on what causes them. Some say that side stitches are caused by cramps in the diaphragm, the sheet of muscles below your lungs that help you breathe. Others say that the cramp is actually in the abdominal muscles. And a few don't believe side stitches are caused by cramps at all. They suggest that side stitches may be caused by intestinal ischemia, reduced blood flow to the intestines during exercise, says Lewis Maharam, MD In fact, there may be more than one variety of what we call side stitches.

See a doctor if:
...if you get a stitch every time you exert yourself. A doctor can check your hydration and electrolyte status.

Quick relief:
Stretch it out. If you start to get a side stitch, you can still take measures to stop it. First stand up straight. If that doesn't help, bend so that you are slightly stretching the side with the stitch, says Stephen Nicholas, MD Still bending over, move around until you find a position that best relieves your pain. That kind of stretching helps put the muscle at rest.

Do some belly breathing. "It's the rapid panters-those breathing in a shallow, staccato fashion-that get into side-stitch trouble," says Dr. Nicholas. Instead, take long, deep breaths through both your nose and your mouth at the same time to get enough oxygen. If you do that, you won't have to pant. "The best track runners breathe this way, and they focus even more on deep, relaxed breathing to help stop a side stitch," Dr. Nicholas says.

Grunt and avoid it. This technique sounds primitive, but grunting at the first sign of a side stitch is a sure-fire remedy, says Owen Anderson, Ph.D., editor of *Running Research News.* "When your foot hits the ground and you make a forceful grunt, that helps you allow the diaphragm to be free and relaxed and release some of the tension." It's not necessary to grunt throughout the race, though—unless you want to frighten your fellow runners, says Dr. Anderson.

Go head over heels. Here's another quick fix for severe side stitches from Dr. Anderson: When you feel one coming on, stop running, lie down on your back, and pull your knees over your head. The pain should subside immediately (If it doesn't, call a doctor, says Dr. Anderson. This kind of pain can be a signal of a heart attack.)

Reach for the sky. Once you stop moving, raise your arms overhead, advises John Cianca, MD "This allows your chest to expand and contract more when you breathe," he explains. "It stretches the muscles, too."

Massage your gut. Take a deep breath while you're running and reach up, under your rib cage where the pain seems to be coming from, and rub the region, says James Walaski, sports massage therapist.

Moderate your pace. Slowing down or walking may keep your stitches from knocking you out of the race, says Dr. Anderson. "A lot of times, a runner who feels a stitch coming on can simply slow down a bit, try to relax and change breathing patterns. In five minutes, he won't even know he had that initial stitch." Once the pain subsides, gradually return to your original intensity.

Everyday prevention:

Warm up. Take time to warm up before your workout. Most side stitches occur within 10 to 15 minutes of beginning exercise. That is especially true if you run hard, which stresses the abdominal muscles. "Warming up properly allows the small blood vessels in your muscles to dilate, providing them with the blood they need to exert themselves," explains Alan Mikesky, Ph.D. "This benefits muscle in your body, including the muscles you use to breathe." Take a full 5 to 10 minutes to slowly step up your pace, and consider it time well-spent.

Know your stomach. A full stomach can cause a side stitch. If you have had a full meal, wait at least 2½ hours before you exercise. "Lighter foods like fruit tend to be handled pretty well by the digestive system, so you can eat those close to the time you start exercising, he says. Wait about 1 hour after eating bread, any other carbohydrate, or fruit.

Stay hydrated. Muscle spasms of all kinds are more likely if your body runs low on fluids, Dr. Mikesky says. Drink about 2 cups of water 45 minutes or so before you start to exercise. Then drink ½ to 1 full cup of water for every 20 minutes during exercise.

Tone your tummy. Stronger stomach muscles help support the internal organs thought to cause side stitches. One method to get them in shape is with stomach crunches. Lie on your back with your feet on the floor and your knees raised. Fold your hands on your chest. Gently lift your torso and back off the floor about three inches and gently exhale. Then inhale as you slowly lower yourself back down. Repeat 20 times.

Stay away from carbonated beverages. Some experts believe that one reason side stitches occur is because wind is trapped from bubbly drinks, says Susan Perry, a physical therapist specialising in sports medicine. As a result, it's best to avoid any carbonated drinks within a few hours of participating in the activity, she says.

Switch your speciality. If you've tried everything and painful side stitches continue when you run, you might consider riding a bike or walking to get your exercise. "There's much less jolting with biking and walking," explains Dr. Anderson.

Sinus Pain

The pain: Pressure and pain in the face, often accompanied by thick, discolored mucus, low-grade fever, cough or nasal obstruction.

The cause: Sinus problems arise when the sinus membranes swell, preventing the mucus from draining property. Mucus build-up leads to blockage and pressure. The result? Sinusitis, headaches, facial pain, difficulty breathing, and the need for multiple boxes of tissues. There are actually several different types of sinusitis. Acute sinusitis is a single episode of infection that usually lasts more than 10 days, which is longer than a. cold. In contrast, chronic sinusitis lasts for more than three months, although it may not be severe the whole time. Allergic sinusitis is the kind that affects people who have chronic allergies that open the way to sinus infection.

See a doctor if:
...you feel pain radiating from you nose to the blocked sinuses, either under the eyes or beneath the forehead.
...if your symptoms are accompanied by fever, a nasty taste in your mouth, or bad breath.
...your sinus pain doesn't improve after taking over-the counter medication for three to five days.
...you develop swollen eyelids and swelling along the sides of your nose.
...you have green or yellowish discharge, or blurred or double vision.

Quick relief:
Put your sinuses on the steam setting. Breathing in warm, steamy air is a great way to open up sinuses and get mucus flowing again, says Alexander C. Chester, MD "The incidence of sinusitis is greater in climates that have dry, cold winter months."
Hit the showers. If possible, leave the vent fan off while you take a warm shower. Spending some time in a steamy bathroom is an easy way to help your sinuses drain.
Get steamed. Anytime you're feeling clogged during the day, get a steaming beverage and practice this trick for instant relief. Put your nose

close to your cup of steaming coffee, tea, or soup, and cup your hand over it to direct the vapour up your nose. just be careful not to burn yourself.

Tent yourself. Fill your bathroom sink with hot water, place your head close enough to be able to breathe the vapour from the steam (but not so close that you burn yourself), and stretch a towel over your head and the sink bowl. The towel will trap the vapour and encase your head in a warm, mucus-loosening haven.

Take up the cloth. Lay a hot, wet washcloth over your eyes and cheekbones for fast relief. Wet the washcloth with hot tap water and wring it out, but make sure that the cloth isn't too hot because it could burn your skin. Rewet it every few minutes to keep it warm.

Drink chicken soup. The heat from the soup is mucus-thinning, and the garlic is too. For best results, drink chicken soup, or any other hot liquid, from a cup so the steam rises right up into your nasal passages.

Work it out. Even if you're tired and achy from sinusitis, a brisk walk or a light bike ride is wonderful for relieving sinus pain, says Dr. Chester. "In about three-quarters of people with sinus problems, aerobic exercise is a very effective decongestant." Exercise produces adrenaline (epinephrine), which shrinks blood vessels in your nose. When the swelling in your sinuses goes down, trapped mucus can flow freely. About 20 to 30 minutes of a light workout should help clear your cavities. Although a little exercise is good, however, it doesn't necessarily follow that more is better. if you're really feeling lousy, don't exercise strenuously or for too long, says Dr. Chester. And don't try an exercise cure if you have a fever to go with your sinusitis, he adds.

If you're going outside to exercise, try to avoid the things that trigger your sinusitis, says Dr. Chester. If you know that ragweed is your nemesis, for example, try exercising in the afternoon, when pollen counts are lower. Try fitting in your workout during your lunch break, for instance.

Pace it off. Relief may be as close as your front door. Whenever you feel especially stuffed up, put on your sneakers and head out for a leisurely stroll. "Exercising in the fresh air is great for relieving sinusitis pain," says Dr. Chester. Choose a fairly level course that will take you about 20 minutes to complete when you're going at a relaxed pace.

Hang down your head. An easy way to open clogged sinuses is to lie on your stomach on your bed with your arms stretched overhead and dangle your upper body over the side until the top of your head rests lightly on the floor, says Charles Gross, MD, professor of otolaryngology. In this position, gravity can help drain mucus from the maxillary sinuses, located behind your cheekbones. Hold this position for no more than five minutes.

For the most effective sinus relief when you are in this position, Dr. Gross recommends first spraying your nose with phenylephrine (NeoSynephrine or Alconefrin), an over-the-counter decongestant that will help open your nose, and waiting five minutes before giving yourself to gravity. You can practice this move every six hours as needed. If you try these decongestants, however, you shouldn't use them for more than three days to avoid the rebound effect, advises Dr. Gross.

Create a sinus-soothing steam. As with ordinary nasal congestion, breathing menthol, camphor or eucalyptus oil can help clear congested sinuses and relieve pain. Heat up some water on the stove until it's boiling, then pour it in a bowl and add a couple of drops of essential oil. Drape a towel over your head and, keeping a comfortable distance away, breathe in the steam from the bowl for about five minutes. Both the humidity of the steam and the action of the essential oil work to loosen mucus.

Nutritional remedies:

Don't share other's food. Don't swap food, utensils, or plates of other people, especially if they might have a cold, says Edmund Pribitkin, MD, an otolaryngologist. That little taste of whatever you are eating isn't worth a trip to the doctor's office for sinusitis treatment.

Fight with fluids. If you do have a cold, drink at least eight eight-ounce glasses of noncaffeinated, non-alcoholic fluids a day. Your best choice is water. "Hydration is a hallmark of sinus therapy," says Dr. Pribitkin. "If mucus can get thick, it can clog up sinus openings, and then it is a cesspool in there," says Dr. Mabry. As long as the liquids are flowing, there is less chance of the infection setting in.

Load up on fruits and vegetables. A healthy diet full of nutrient-packed produce will help keep your system sharp. A good multivitamin can fill in gaps in your healthy eating plan, says Dr. Mabry. A small preliminary study done in the Netherlands indicates that a food compound called glutathione may help in the fight against sinusitis. Found in fruits and vegetables such as watermelon, grapefruit, oranges, peaches, asparagus, potatoes, and broccoli, glutathione may help keep the lining of the respiratory tract healthy. It is far too early to recommend any specific amount of glutathione, says Dr. Gross, but eating a diet rich in fruits and vegetables is a good way to fortify your immune system so that you can better resist infections.

Eat spicy. Studies have shown that eating hot peppers or other spicy foods—many of which contain a fiery chemical known as capsaicin—will really turn on the nasal taps and get the mucus flowing.

Dodge dairy, caffeine and alcohol. Coffee, tea, cola and alcoholic beverages dehydrate you. Dairy products and chocolate thicken congestion.

Juice up. Both apple and dark grape juices may be beneficial to those with sinus problems, says John Peterson, MD He recommends drinking the juice at room temperature and apart from meals. You can dilute either juice with water if it seems too strong, he adds.

Helpful vitamins and supplements:

Think of zinc. Cold-Eeze cough drops, made with a special zinc compound, may be helpful in fighting viruses when you have a cold, says Dr. Pribitkin. They may also limit the length of a cold.

"C" your way clear. Guillermo Mendoza, MD, chief of allergy for Kaiser-Permanente in California, recommends a daily dose of vitamin C as a preventive against sinus pain. "If you are prone to sinus infection or you have chronic sinus problems, take 1,000 milligrams of timed-release vitamin C a day," he says.

Everyday prevention:

Sleep right. If only one nostril is clogged, you can open it if you sleep in the right position. If your left nostril is open, for example, lie on that side, says Dr. Chester. There are nerves in the chest wall that influence the blood flow to your nose, he says. By assuming this side-sleeping position, he says, you trigger the nerve reflexes that can open up the clogged nostril. By morning, there could be a new, well-rested, easier-breathing you.

Nap in a chair. Sinusitis can make you tired, but you should try not to sleep, or even lie down, more than usual. In fact, one study of patients with chronic sinusitis showed that lying down increased nasal congestion and made it 20 percent more difficult to breathe. Limit the time you spend lying in bed, says Dr. Chester. If you're feeling poorly, rest upright in a chair, he adds.

Scarf up for moisture. If it's chilly, use a scarf to cover your mouth and nose, Dr. Chester advises. This will help humidify the air and start the mucus running. Cram some tissues into your coat pocket—you'll need them.

Dodge the dry chill. During any season of the year, the best indoor environment for exercise is both humidified and well-ventilated with outside air. "It's best to avoid exercising in air-conditioned health clubs because the air is too dry and can make sinusitis worse," says Dr. Chester.

Wash your hands early and often. Viruses and bacteria can often hitch a ride to your sinuses on your hands. Go all day without washing your hands, and all you have to do to get infected is touch your mouth or nose. So wash your hands with soap and water to prevent transmission, says Richard Mabry, MD And make a point of washing your hands before you eat.

Be a fussy phone user. Use a public phone, and sinusitis germs can ambush you while you wait for the tone, Dr. Mabry warns. If you carry around a travel pack of moist alcohol wipes, you can discreetly rub down the mouthpiece of a public phone. If you borrow office equipment from someone-pens, calculators, or computer keyboards—give them a wipe-off (preferably with a sanitary wipe) before you start using them, he says.

Surrender the smokes. Smoking damages tiny hairlike projections in the sinuses called cilia that sweep mucus out, says Dr. Mabry. Without healthy cilia, your sinuses are much more likely to become dogged and infected. Smoking may also alter sinus secretions in a way that makes them less effective at clearing out the viruses and other particles that you breathe, says Dr. Pribitkin. Even second-hand smoke can make you more susceptible to sinusitis, says Dr. Mabry. So stay away from other people who smoke.

Attack allergy symptoms. Preventing allergic reactions—and with them, stuffy sinuses and nasal passages—can help prevent inflamed and infected sinuses, say Dr. Pribitkin. Many types of allergy shots and medications are available. Check with your allergist to see what is best for you.

Use the right stuff to unstuff. If you have an ordinary cold and want to cut your risk of getting sinusitis, try a mucus-thinning decongestant product, says Dr. Mabry. Steer clear of antihistamines, however, which dry up the sinuses and nose, leaving them open to infection. You can use a saline nasal spray, which will rinse the thick mucus from your sinuses but won't cause swelling of the nasal membranes or damage your cilia as some other products can, he says. Avoid nasal sprays other than the plain saline products, however, because, they can become addictive, says Dr. Pribitkin. If your allergies are causing stuffiness, ask your doctor about topical steroid nasal sprays. These sprays can help reduce the swelling around the opening of the sinuses, he says.

Get a shot. Flu shots can help reduce your risk for sinusitis. "They give your immune system a good kick in the pants," says Dr. Mabry. That way, your body is conquering germs before they can make you sick. Flu shots also help ward off sinusitis by immunising the body against flu viruses. Ask your doctor about seasonal flu immunisation.

Don't let stress get you. "Fifty years ago, research showed that stress causes the nose to stop up," says Dr. Mabry. Learning better ways to manage stress could help. A positive attitude has also been linked to a stronger immune system.

Crank up the humidifier. "I tell people to start using their humidifiers when they turn the heat on in their houses, and not to turn them off until the heat is turned off," says Dr. Mabry. A humidifier or vapouriser in, your home or office will help keep your nose and sinuses from drying out. Humidifiers need to be cleaned thoroughly, per the manufacturers' instructions, to keep moulds and other allergens from being sprayed into the air. if you have a cold-mist humidifier, you may need to clean it weekly with a solution of 1 part bleach to 10 parts water, he says.

Get into the clean-air act. "Sinusitis is much more common today than it was a few decades ago. I think it has to do with all the chemicals we have introduced into our environment says Kenneth F. Garay, MD, director of the Centre for Sinus and Nasal Disease in New York City. He notes that he sees more and more kids with this problem than he did 15 years ago, and they have more severe cases. Unfortunately, moving to a less-polluted area isn't an option for everyone. If you think that pollution may be irritating your sinuses enough to create a sinusitis risk, spend more time out of doors in the areas that have the cleanest air. If your local weather forecaster gives reports on the air quality, pay attention and try to limit your time out on exceptionally smoggy days.

Cover up. Chemicals and environmental factors at the workplace can contribute to sinus troubles, according to Dr. Pribitkin. Gypsum dust is a common problem for people who work in construction, for example. People exposed to such impurities may have to wear protective gear over the nose and mouth.

Breeze through. If you suspect that chemicals inside your home or office are irritating the lining in your nose and sinuses, you may want to open the windows regularly and air out the place. Invest in an air purifier, says Dr. Pribitkin, and discuss your concerns with an otolaryngologist.

Take care of those pearly whites. Dental abscesses can result in sinus infections if left untreated, says Dr. Pribitkin. That's just one more reason not to neglect your teeth.

Steep with a vapouriser. You can relieve stuffy sinuses as you steep at night by putting a few drops of the essential oil of eucalyptus, camphor or menthol into a steam humidifier set up by your bed.

Hold your head high. Elevating your head while you sleep promotes sinus drainage, experts say. Prop up your bedposts at the heat of your bed on books or bricks and see if it helps.

Be doubly clean. Use two-ply vacuum cleaner bags, suggests Dr. Mendoza. "They are stronger and less porous than regular bags, so they do not allow dirt and dust to filter through." When that happens, the particles can irritate your nasal passages and cause sinus pain.

Try a yoga rinse. You can help both prevent and treat sinus problems if you do a yoga nasal wash, called neti, once a day, says Stephen A. Nezezon, MD, yoga teacher and physician. Start by filling a four-ounce paper cup halfway with warm water, then add 1/2 teaspoon of salt. Put a small crease in the lip of the cup so that it forms a spout. Slightly tilt your head back and to the left. Then slowly pour the water into your right nostril. The water will flow out of your left nostril or down the back of your throat if your left nostril is clogged. Spit out the water if it goes down your throat, or wipe the water from your face with a hand towel if it flows out of your left nostril. Fill the cup again, then repeat the procedure on the other side, pouring the water into your left nostril and titling your head to the right so that the water flows out of your right nostril.

Easing the pain with exercise:

Cycle your sinuses clear. Dig your kid's bike out of the garage and take a spin around the neighbourhood. Put it into a low gear and pedal at a comfortable pace. The point here is to unblock your sinuses, not begin training for the Tour de France. "Your sinuses should open up shortly after beginning exercise," says Dr. Chester, so take some tissues along.

Ride inside. If you have a stationary bike and a humidifier, you can really unclog the works. Exercising in moist air will help loosen the mucus even more, says Dr. Chester.

Cold or Sinusitis? Here's How to Tell.

If you have sinusitis, you need to see a doctor right away. But how do you know if what you have is a sinus problem or a cold? Well, only a doctor can tell you for sure, but these signs can help you decide how to proceed, says Edmund Pribitkin, MD, an otolaryngologist.

SYMPTOM	COLD?	SINUSITIS?
Thin, clear, runny mucus	yes	no
Green or yellow mucus	no	yes
Facial pressure or pain	no	yes
Clears up in 10 days or less	yes	no
Fever	no	yes
Persistent cough in children	no	yes

Stay out of the water. You would think that swimming a few laps in your local pool would be a great sinus opener because you're exercising and breathing humid air at the same time. But as it turns out, even if water is good in the form of steam, it's bad in liquid form if you have sinusitis. Activities such as swimming, diving, and scuba diving can actually drive mucus farther back into your sinuses.

Be a spectator. Go watch a water polo or swim team compete. Just sitting in the humidified pool environment can make your nose run.

Keep fit. Regular exercise increases the blood supply to the sinuses, which can help keep them healthy and open. "Have you ever noticed that as your heart rate goes up, your nose runs, thereby cleaning the nose and sinuses? It is the same principle," says Dr. Gross. He emphasises that exercise is a preventive strategy, not a cure. if you have an existing sinus infection, don't go out and run a few miles or work out for an hour. Rest or engage in only light exercise, then once you are over a is bout of sinusitis, start a regular exercise plan to help ward off future episode

Wade, don't jump. Marriage, overseas investments, and water. These are three things you should never jump into feet first. But only the third has been linked to sinusitis.

'One thing I see here a few times a year are kids who go jump into a pool or lake feet first and drive contaminated water up into their sinuses," says Dr. Mabry. The unlucky swimmers get abscesses in their sinuses and a bad case of painful sinusitis. People are just not aware of the kind of force that drives water into the sinuses in situations like that, he says. Dr. Mabry suggests that you take the cautious approach and wade in, especially if you are not sure how clean the water is.

Clear your head with yoga. A legs-against-the-wall yoga pose can help clear your sinuses, says Larry Payne, Ph.D., director of the Samata Yoga Centre in Los Angeles and chairman of the International Association of Yoga Therapists.

Lie on your back with your buttocks pushed against the base of the wall. Raise your legs and hold them against the wall for 7 to 15 minutes, says Dr. Payne. "This changes blood flow within the body and changes the flow of your body's lymphatic fluids-the fluids that flow from the space between the body cells into the bloodstream. For the first few minutes, pressure in your sinuses will increase. But after awhile the mucus in your sinuses starts loosening."

Caution: If you have high blood pressure, stroke risk or glaucoma, you should not do this exercise, notes Dr. Payne.

Herbal help:

Root out sinus pain. "My favourite home remedy for sinusitis is to sniff horseradish," says Sanford Archer, MD, associate professor of otolaryngology. He recommends one or two quick sniffs of prepared hot horseradish two or three times a day. Stay four to six inches from the 'at because the strong smell can be very powerful, and avoid breathing into the jar, which could contaminate it for other family members, says Dr. Archer. It doesn't matter whether you use white or purple horseradish, but the white variety tends to be hotter.

Slurp goldenseal. Drink a cup of goldenseal tea twice a day for 14 to 21 days, suggests Scott Gerson, MD, an expert in Ayurvedic medicine. This herb is classified as an antimicrobial, meaning that it helps kill viruses and bacteria that can lead to infection. To make goldenseal tea, put one teaspoon of the loose herb 'in a tea ball and put the ball in an eight-ounce cup. Pour boiling water over the ball, let the tea steep for five to seven minutes, and drink. Buying a box of pre-packaged goldenseal tea bags is okay, too, says Dr. Gerson. They're available at many health food stores. But make sure to use the tea within four months because herbs' heating properties weaken with age. Goldenseal should not be used for longer than three weeks at a time, especially if you suffer from a chronic kidney disease. Otherwise, it is quite safe, says Dr. Gerson.

Get better with barley green. Barley green, which can be used in juices or simply sprinkled on salads as a topping, helps some people with sinus problems, says Julian Whitaker, MD, founder and president of the Whitaker Wellness Centre in Newport Beach, California. Barley green is available in most health food stores.

Soothe with eucalyptus and peppermint. Aromatherapists suggest rubbing diluted essential oils of eucalyptus or peppermint on the forehead and temples to relieve sinusitis. Mix a few drops of either or both oils into a couple of tablespoons of vegetable oil before applying it to your skin. You can also add a few drops of the essential oils to your bath. But use these oils sparingly, as too much can be overwhelmingly caustic. And never ingest them; even a small amount can be toxic.

If you don't have these herbal oils on hand, the bruised leaves work well. You can mash some leaves, moisten them with water and make them into a poultice. Either place it on your chest or stuff it into your nostrils (be careful not to push it in too deeply). "I'd also suggest drinking tea made with eucalyptus and any of the mints," says Dr. James Duke.

Say hello to oregano. Here's a member of the mint family that's simply loaded with antiseptic compounds. Oregano is useful as a hot tea (inhale the vapours as you drink) or in a massage lotion. You can add a few drops of the essential oil to any skin lotion or to vegetable oil.

Rub 'em open. Try massage to open blocked sinuses. With one hand over each eye, rub steadily on the bony ridge located right below and above your eyes. Then rub directly below your eyes and just above you teeth. This may chase pain away.

Skin Rashes

The pain: Rashes take many forms, but they're generally eruptions, or break-outs on the skin.

The cause: Lots of things cause rashes—plants, pets, jewellery, rubber, perfume, and fungi, to name a few. And if you've developed athlete's foot after using the shower at the local swim club, you know where the rash came from. Many times, however, a rash seems to appear out of nowhere. When the skin comes in contact with an allergic substance, the reaction is not immediate. A few days may pass before the rash takes hold—though once you have it, the rash can last a week or longer. One way to figure out the cause is to look at the location. If the rash is caused by an internal trigger, like food, medication, or virus, the rash will generally be more widespread and symmetrical. If something external caused the rash, like detergents, then it will be confined to areas of the skin that were exposed to the irritant, says Patricia Farris Walters, MD, clinical assistant professor of dermatology.

See a doctor if:
...your rash is accompanied by dizziness, nausea, headache or difficulty breathing. See your doctor right away to rule out a serious allergic reaction.
...you have a rash for longer than two or three days
...your rash burns, stings, turns raw or becomes blistered.
...you develop a roughly butterfly-shaped patchy red rash on your cheeks or over the bridge of your nose, or a red "bull's-eye rash" anywhere.

Medication:
If you are taking medication and develop a rash, call your doctor immediately, says Andrew P. Lazar, MD, associate professor of clinical dermatology. Some medications, including antibiotics such as tetracycline, can cause an allergic reaction in the form of serious rashes. Your doctor may recommend that you stop taking the drug or switch to something else. Other drugs that can cause rashes are:

All angiotensin-converting enzyme (ACE) inhibitors, such as captopril

(Capoten), that are prescribed for high blood pressure.

All antidepressants, for example, monoamine oxidase (MAO) inhibitors such as isocarboxazid (Parnate or Marplan).

Over-the-counter and prescription nonsteroidal anti-inflammatory drugs such as ibuprofen (Advil or Neurophen).

Quick relief:

Cool with creams. An over-the-counter corticosteroid cream may provide relief from itching, burning, and irritation, says Thomas Fisher, MD, a dermatologist. He says that application of 1 percent hydrocortisone applied thinly four times daily should provide some relief. Or try an antibiotic ointment containing polymyxin bacitracin twice daily with hydrocortisone, Dr. Fisher recommends. Avoid over-the-counter ointments with neomycin since it can cause allergic reactions.

Cool with a compress. If a rash starts oozing, Dr. Fisher recommends a cool compress with aluminium subacetate—Burrow's solution. You can make Burrow's solution from effervescent tablets that are sold in pharmacies as Domeboro. To make a compress, soak a clean handkerchief or piece of gauze in Burrow's solution, then place the damp cloth on the affected area for five minutes. Repeat this process four times, for a total 20-minute session. Do this 20 minute treatment three times daily. Follow each treatment with medicated cream.

Soak in soda. A half-cup of baking soda in a full bath makes a rash-relieving soak. "You could also make a paste from a spoonful of baking soda mixed with a bit of water and dab that on your rash to soothe your skin," says Dr. Walters.

Take an antihistamine. To reduce swelling and itching, take a non-prescription antihistamine, like diphenhydramine (Benadryl), at bedtime, suggests dermatologist Andrew P. Lazar, MD Benadryl may make you drowsy, which can be an added benefit if the itch has been keeping you awake at night, he says. Before taking an antihistamine, however, be sure to check for any interaction with your prescription drugs, cautions Dr. Lazar. Some antihistamines can speed up your heart rate. And if you have an enlarged prostate, an antihistamine might impede urination.

Soak in oatmeal. Use a colloidal oatmeal bath product in water as cold as you can tolerate to help calm your itchy skin, says Don W Printz, MD, president of the American Society of Dermatology. Soak for 5 to 10 minutes, he recommends.

Stick with it. Combining different anti-itch products can further irritate the skin, so once you've started using a particular cream, don't switch to another to see if you can get better results.

Fight fungus. Fungal rashes, such as athlete's foot, jock itch and yeast infections, may be treated with an over-the-counter antifungal cream, such as Lotrimin (Canestan). These conditions should be diagnosed by a doctor first, so you know exactly what it is you're treating.

Nutritional remedies:

Interview waiters. If you are allergic to a food, it's important that you avoid it. If you are allergic to peanuts, for instance, don't be timid about asking the waiter if the tandoori chicken is cooked in peanut oil.

Become food finicky. Sometimes an offending food can be a minor ingredient of processed frozen or canned foods. Read labels carefully. Look for dyes or preservatives like sulphates, says Jerome Z. Litt, MD

Get juiced. Both apple and dark grape juices may be beneficial to those with reddish skin rashes, says John Peterson, MD, an Ayurvedic practitioner. These sweet juices are used to "cool" many skin problems, according to Dr. Peterson. He recommends drinking the juices at about room temperature and apart from meals. If the juices seem too strong, he says, they can be diluted with water. He adds that papaya and pineapple juices may also be beneficial.

Helpful vitamins and supplements:

Take your Bs. B vitamins can revitalise flaky, itchy skin beset by a rash. B12, nourishes the skin and helps new skin cells form, says Kenneth Singleton MD Take 1,000 micrograms of a vitamin B12 supplement every day for two weeks, he says. Then cut back to 1,000 micrograms twice a week. You can continue taking this dosage indefinitely; even huge dosages are harmlessly excreted in your urine.

Oil up from the inside. A skin problem may signal an omega-3 fatty acid deficiency, says Dr. Singleton. Omega-3 fatty acids are healthy fats found in fish (like salmon, sardines, and tuna) and flaxseed. Ideally, you should get your omega-3's from eating fish three times a week. But if that's not appealing, Dr. Singleton recommends taking 3 to 6 grams of fish oil in a capsule every day. When the rash clears, cut back to 2 to 3 grams a day. You can safely continue taking this lower dose indefinitely, says Dr. Singleton. Or take a teaspoon of refrigerated flaxseed oil three times a day to replenish your omega-3 count and beat the rash. Both products can be found in health food stores.

Stock up on vitamins and minerals. Many rashes respond to increased intakes of zinc and vitamins A and C, nutrients that repair and build skin tissue, says Elson Haas, MD, director of the Preventive Medical Centre of Marin. He recommends 5,000 international units of vitamin A a day, along with 5,000 milligrams of vitamin C and up to 30 milligrams of zinc. He says to continue these levels of supplementation until the rash clears up.

Everyday prevention:

Cover with care. Ordinarily you leave a rash uncovered, says Dr. Walters, but if it's wet, oozing, and blistering, you may want to cover it with a light gauze bandage to prevent an infection.

Steer clear of irritants. Avoid the causes of your rash, and it stands to reason that you'll prevent future rashes, dermatologists remind us. If you discover that you're allergic to rubber, switch to vinyl gloves for washing the dishes. Some foot rashes are "shoe dermatitis" caused by leather tanned with chromates. If you often get rashes on your feet, shop for footwear that's been tanned with vegetable products instead, experts say. Since you can't tell by looking at the shoe what it's been tanned with, ask a salesperson at the shoe store.

Be a detective. Ask yourself some sleuthing questions. Have you recently eaten anything that is not a normal part of your diet? If the rash is on your face, have you changed your makeup recently? Or your soap? Or your perfume? Or hair spray? "If you suddenly get a rash, figure out what you have done differently in the last 24 to 36 hours," says Dr. Litt. "If the rash is on your body, were you wearing a new article of clothing? Have you changed your laundry detergent or fabric softener? By noting this information, you can help your doctor determine the cause of the rash." And once you have determined what's causing the rash, the simplest preventive is to stay away from whatever provokes it, he adds.

Read before you touch. The same advice applies for any products that you are in contact with regularly, such as paints, lotion, and detergents. If you are trying out a new soap, for instance, read the label carefully to make sure that it doesn't have the chemical that sets your skin screaming. It may be acetone, fragrances, lanolin, deodorants, vitamin E, turpentine, dye—and other things, says Dr. Litt.

Get fussy about contamination. Our immune systems are finely tuned, so it is important to avoid even incidental contact with an allergen. Avoid cutting boards or counters that could be tainted with rash-causing allergens contained in the soaps or detergents you used to clean it.

Glove up. If you are prone to rashes on your hands, wearing gloves while doing household cleaning or home improvements is wise. Dr. Litt recommends cotton liners inside rubber, plastic, or vinyl gloves. If you don't wear the cotton liners, sometimes the rubber or vinyl itself can cause a rash. Gloves that come with built-in liners don't offer enough protection, he says.

Coat your jewellery. Some people find that they have allergic reactions to jewellery, especially if it contains nickel. Try this trick, offered by Wilma F. Bergfeld, MD., head of clinical research in the department of dermatology at the Cleveland Clinic. "You can coat your jewellery with clear nail polish or polyethylene sprays so that the metal doesn't touch your skin." Though it wears off eventually and needs to be renewed, the coating won't harm the metal and it won't hurt gemstones either, if some of the polish or spray happens to get on them.

Slather your skin. Keeping your skin healthy means keeping it clean and moisturised. If your skin is damaged, red, or scaly, it is more prone to be injured or infected, according to Dr. Bergfeld. Use "bland" lubricants—ones that have no dyes, fragrances, or other additives that can irritate the skin. The lubricants will keep skin moist and supple, says Dr. Kakita. "frequent lubrication is helpful for dry skin. It is good to leave a little water on the skin after bathing, then lubricate. You can buy bland lubricants over the counter," she says. Many lotions and creams don't contain dyes, fragrances, and other elements that can irritate skin, she says.

Pamper your skin. Dry, irritated skin falls prey to rashes, says Vail Reese, MD Keep your skin smooth and moist by using a moisturising lotion every day. Apply the lotion after a shower but before you dry off. The water seals the lotion into the skin, keeping it moist for hours.

Shampoo your chest. Hairy men frequently develop rashes in the centre of their chests, Dr. Printz says. Out-of-place dandruff, just like the stuff on the top of your head, causes these rashes. Wash your chest with any dandruff shampoo to prevent this irritation, he recommends.

Don't let your laundry do you. If you often get rashes, it's a good idea to cut the number of chemicals you use in your laundry. Stick with one soap or detergent and forget all those softeners and perfumes. Or baby yourself by using laundry soaps that are recommended for washing nappies and infant wear. It might also help to run your clothes through the rinse cycle twice.

Herbal Help:

Soothe with salve. As an alternative to cortisone, Andrew Weil MD, suggests calendula cream, made from the petals of a marigold-like flower that is prized for its healing effect on skin. Calendula cream is available in health food stores.

Scratch the itch internally. The homeopathic remedy sulphur provides relief for people with eczema and can also aid people who have the itch of a basic rash, says Michael Carlston, MD Take one dose (usually two or three pellets) of a 30C potency sulphur product four times a day initially. Reduce the frequency of the dosage as the itching goes away, and stop when the rash is gone, Dr. Carlston suggests. You can buy sulphur in many health food stores.

Sore Throat

The pain: Throat pain, from a slight tickle to full-blown fiery inflammation.

The cause: Some sore throats are caused by physical irritants. But usually scratchy throats are the result of upper respiratory infections and postnasal drip. Any nasal airway blockage such as that caused by allergies-can lead to throat pain because the detour of breath from nose to mouth creates an irritated, dry climate inside your throat. "Your nose is designed to humidify, filter, and warm the air as you breathe in," says Deborah Loney, MD, an otolaryngologist. "But your mouth can't do any of this as effectively." Sometimes a sore throat can be the result of infection by bacteria or a virus.

See a doctor if:
...you have sore throat for ten days to two weeks.
...you have a sore throat and no other cold symptoms.
...the pain makes it difficult to swallow.
...the pain is accompanied by trouble breathing, or opening your mouth.
...the pain is accompanied by joint pain, earache, rash, fever over 101 degrees F, blood in the phlegm or saliva, persistent lump in the throat or hoarseness that lasts more than two weeks.

Quick relief:
Get steamed up. If you feel a scratchy throat coming on, try running hot water in the bathroom sink while you lean over it with a towel draped on top of your head, says Dr. Loney. Then inhale deeply through your mouth. Do this for five minutes and repeat the procedure a few times a day to help humidify your throat.

Swallow some ice. Crushed ice can cool the fire of your swallow.

Take a gargle. A warm saltwater gargle reduces painful swelling in minutes, says Eleanor Blaurock-Busch, Ph.D., director of Trace Minerals International. It also kills germs. Just add a teaspoon of salt to a cup of warm water, tip your head back, and gargle away. You can gargle as often as you want relief, she says.

Fight inflammation with ibuprofen. This non-prescription drug is as effective a pain reliever and inflammation fighter as its cousin, aspirin , but it may be easier on your stomach. Follow the directions and precautions on the bottle.

Try a saltwater squirt. Here's a twist on salt gargles: Fill a rubber ear syringe (the kind you'd use to clean a baby's ears and nose) with a pint of warm saltwater. Lean over a sink and squirt the warm water against the back of your throat. This irrigates your throat and is better than gargles, says Charles Gross, MD "A lot of pain in the throat is due to muscle spasm," he explains. "So this relaxes the muscle spasm. It also dilates the blood vessels, which brings in additional body-protective mechanisms. Particularly if you're taking antibiotics, it'll increase the concentration of antibiotics in this area."

Get a little lozenge. Non-prescription throat lozenges can cool a sore throat. These can numb the throat temporarily but don't change the course of the disorder much. In a pinch, sugarless hard candy can help.

Feast on a frozen treat. At last-here is a reason that you should eat dessert. Sucking on an ice pop can take the sting out of sore throat pain. It's cold, it's a fluid, and it tastes good besides.

Snort some salt. Plunging your nose into a saltwater solution and sniffing the fluid so it drips down the back of your throat may provide fast relief, says Eric G. Anderson, MD To make the solution, mix one level teaspoon of salt in a six-ounce glass of warm water. Bend over a sink, pour some of the water into your cupped hand and sniff up a small amount. Dr. Anderson recommends sniffing salt water three times a day for three days. Then taper off to once or twice a day until your throat starts feeling better.

Nutritional remedies:

Wash down trouble. Mucus can be fairly thick and irritating in the back of the throat, says Sanford Archer, MD Drinking a lot of fluids, preferably water, will help thin the mucus out and make it less abrasive. Eight to 10 eight-ounce glasses a day will do the trick, he says. But keep away from caffeine-containing drinks since they are diuretics that can actually cause you to lose more fluid and worsen your mucous problem.

Taste sweet relief. Putting a dab of honey on the back of your tongue will cause the thick, soothing liquid to glide across your irritated throat like a slow-moving waterfall, says Dr. Anderson.

Take some tea. Gargling with tea-brewed at double strength and allowed to cool to lukewarm temperature-once every 15 minutes will provide fast relief. "Tea contains tannic acid, which helps soothe the throat," says Hinda Greene, D.O., an internal medicine and emergency medicine physician. "It won't kill any germs, but it can help your throat feel better."

Go easy on the alcohol. If you're recovering from a sore throat, it's advisable to lay off of alcoholic beverages completely. It can exacerbate the soreness and the inflammation of the throat.

Have some tea, honey. Tea with honey is a traditional sore throat remedy. You can boost its therapeutic benefits with this spicy twist offered by Cynthia M. Watson, MD Stir into your tea 1 tablespoon of honey and the juice of half a lemon, then add ground red pepper to taste. "The pepper probably has a mild anaesthetic effect," she says. "It also stimulates the immune system."

Get some garlic. "When a sore throat is caused by a virus infection, as opposed to bacteria, eating garlic can bring quicker relief," says Yu-Yan Yeh, Ph.D., a researcher on the healing properties of garlic. "Garlic has been shown to have antiviral and antifungal activities."

Helpful vitamins and supplements:

Take a multi and maybe some C. "A good, balanced vitamin and mineral supplement is a healthy thing to take daily," says Dr. Archer. Some studies have indicated that you may reduce the chance of infection if you take 500 milligrams of vitamin C at regular intervals four times a day. "It can't hurt you at that dosage since vitamin C that isn't used by the body gets excreted through your urine," he says. "So if someone were constantly battling colds and wanted to try it, I'd say go ahead." Be aware that excess vitamin C may cause diarrhoea in some people.

Think zinc. Zinc lozenges can help the kind of sore throat that's associated with a cold. The zinc heads straight for the sore spot in your throat, says Dr. Blaurock-Busch. If you zap your sore throat with zinc every 2 to 3 hours, "You will feel soothing effects within a day," she says.

Everyday prevention:

Gain control of your allergies. You and your doctor should determine what medications work best to control the postnasal drip caused by your allergies, says Dr. Archer. If they are seasonal allergies brought on by pollen, maybe you just need to stay indoors with the air-conditioning on when the offensive pollen is really bad.

Be bold with moulds. If you are sensitive to moulds, installing allergy air filters on your furnace can help, provided they are cleaned regularly, says Dr. Archer. To help halt creeping versions of mould, repair all doorways and windowsills that leak water. And run a dehumidifier in moist places, such as the basement and any crawl spaces, he suggests. To prevent mould growth within the dehumidifier, remember to empty it frequently.

Do away with dust. People who are allergic to dust mites are in for a tough battle at home. Steam-cleaning your carpets and furniture every three months or so will reduce the dust collection. Get allergy covers for your mattress and pillows, says Dr. Archer, and use the hot-water setting when you launder your sheets and pillowcases. Wearing slippers around the house instead of going barefoot also helps since dust mites live off the skin scales that your feet shed.

Tumble dry your teddy bears. Stuffed animals can accumulate a lot of dust, too. Provided they don't have a lot of plastic parts, you can put yours

Work toward a Reflux Reduction

Sometimes a sore throat can be caused by gastroesophageal reflux disease (GERD), a condition where stomach contents, including the acid, splashes back up into the throat, says Dr. Archer. Caffeine, smoking, alcohol, and greasy or spicy foods can all aggravate the condition.

One way to prevent the backlash is to avoid eating anything one to two hours before you go to bed. When you do have a flare-up, liquid antacids work better than chewable ones, says Dr. Archer. Over-the-counter antacids contain about half the strength of their prescription cousins, he adds.

If reflux in bed is a problem, Dr. Archer recommends propping up the head of your bed about six inches by placing two cinder blocks under the legs at the headboard. This will keep stomach acid where it belongs. While you might expect a bunch of pillows to do the trick, Dr. Archer says that you need your whole bed raised. Pillows only raise up your head, without changing the angle from stomach to throat.

GERD can be a sign of a greater problem. If you have several sore throats a year that may be accompanied by heartburn, hoarseness, or regurgitation (a bad taste in the mouth), contact your physician.

in the dryer with the temperature set low for 20 minutes, says Dr. Archer. No need to wash—it is the heat that kills the dust mites.

Wash your pets. If you are allergic to dog or cat dander, you probably don't have to get rid of the family pet to prevent sore throats. "Washing your pet with shampoo and warm water twice a month will substantially reduce the amount of dander," says Dr. Archer.

Treat your toothbrush. If you share a bathroom with somebody who has a viral or bacterial infection, don't let them use your toothbrush, says Dr. Archer. It is an easy way to share the germs that can cause a sore throat. If all the family toothbrushes shack up in a communal holder, protect yourself by soaking your brush in some Listerine to kill the germs, he says. And be sure to throw out old, ratty toothbrushes as soon as they turn into has-beens (every three to six months, or as soon as the bristles begin to bend outward). If you keep them around, they can become breeding grounds for germs.

Crank up the humidifier. When your home heating system is on, it is possible for you to wake up in the morning with a sore throat, especially if you tend to breathe through your mouth when you sleep. Use a cool-mist humidifier in the living areas and bedrooms to help make the air inside your home less dry, says Dr. Loney. Just be sure that you clean it frequently since it can begin to harbour mould and create an irritating environment if you don't follow the cleaning directions on the humidifier.

Clean up your act. "Germs get passed around on people's hands easily," says Dr. Loney. Wash your hands frequently, especially before meals, to reduce the risk of getting an infected throat.

Come in out of the cold. Cold winter air may not feel like the desert, but it is just as dry as the Sahara. And when air is that dry, it parches your throat. In a humid, warm climate, you reduce your chance of getting a sore throat, notes Dr. Archer. If you live where winters are cold and dry, "at least try to limit the amount of cold air you expose your throat to," he says. Wrapping a scarf around your mouth when the temperature plummets may help.

Give it a rest. Colds and flu, which often bring sore throats, tend to stick around. That means your sore throat sticks around, too. Someone once said that to recover from a common flu takes the energy of a 40-mile hike with a 40-pound backpack," says Martin L. Rossman, MD So give you and your throat the day off. Better a day in bed than a week in misery.

Close your mouth. Breathing through your nose sends a stream of warmed, humidified air past your throat. Cooler, drier air from mouth breathing can be irritating.

Dodge the smoke. To avoid a sore throat in the future, don't smoke and don't expose yourself or your children to sidestream smoke. Smokers are more likely to have chronic throat irritation.

Warm your neck. Holding a hot-water bottle or warm (not hot) heating pad to your neck can further relieve the pain of a sore throat.

Elevate your bed. if you typically wake up with a sore throat—and it's not sore at other times of the day—you may be suffering from acid reflux, an upsurge of throat-searing stomach acid that occurs during sleep. Adjusting your bed frame so the head is elevated four to six inches higher than the foot will put gravity on your side and help keep the acid down, says Bruce Campbell, MD, an otolaryngologist.

Buy some houseplants. Keep plants in your rooms. The plants will absorb toxins that could irritate your throat.

Herbal help:

Gargle away infection. "If your throat is infected and mucusy, I recommend gargling with teas made from infection-fighting, inflammation-soothing herbs such as sage, thyme, goldenseal, echinacea, or myrrh," says herbalist Roy Upton. "The nice thing about using sage and thyme is that you can-take them right out of your kitchen spice rack, make them into tea, and gargle. You don't have to run out to the chemist." The other herbs can be found in health food stores. To make these kitchen-cabinet teas, just take a teaspoonful of the herb, add boiling water, let it infuse in a covered container for 10 minutes, and strain, says Upton. You can use the liquid as gargle as often as necessary.

"I also recommend adding some echinacea to the mix whenever you have an inflammatory condition" says herbalist Ed Smith, It stimulates your immune system so your body can get rid of the infection faster." For a sore throat, Smith recommends putting 30 to 40 drops of echinacea tincture into a glass of water and gargling with it several times a day.

Coat it with marshmallow. Mucilaginous herbs—herbs that reduce irritation and inflammation in the mucosal surfaces of the throat, bronchial tubes, and sinuses—are very soothing to a sort throat, says Feather Jones, director of the Rocky Mountain Centre for Botanical Studies. "Marshmallow is one of my favourites," she says.

Marshmallow root is 35 percent mucilage when it's dried. To draw out the plant's mucilage properties, make a cool marshmallow tea, suggests Jones. Boil 8 ounces of water, then turn off the heat and. add 1½ teaspoons of finely chopped marshmallow root. Put a lid on the pan and let stand for 30 minutes. Strain it and keep it in a covered glass container in the refrigerator. Sip it throughout the day, says Jones. Because bacteria like this rich mixture, experts advise that you make a fresh batch daily.

Suck some slippery elm. Another soothing treatment for a dry, scratchy sore throat is slippery elm in the form of a cough lozenge, says Upton. Slippery elm is also rich in soothing mucilage. It protects irritated mucous membranes, he says. Keep some lozenges in your pocket and take them as necessary.

Spice it. Sucking on a whole clove (the kind you use for baked ham) can quiet throat tickles.

Try aromatherapy. To speed the healing of a sore throat, aromatic consultant John Steele recommends applying a thin film of carrier oil externally over the throat area. Canola, sunflower, grapeseed and safflower are popular choices and are available in most health food stores. Apply seven drops of sandalwood essential oil over the carrier oil and rub gently into the skin, suggests Steele. "This treatment is soothing and smells wonderful, and the carrier oil prevents skin irritation," he explains. Or, he says, add two drops of tea tree, ginger, sandalwood or geranium essential oil to ½ ounce of warm water and gargle. Any of these essential oils can be taken with a spoonful of honey to coat the throat, says Steele.

Get ayurvedic aid. Stir ½ teaspoon of salt and 1 teaspoon of turmeric into a cup of hot water and gargle with this mixture before going to bed, says Vasant Lad, director of the Ayurvedic Institute in New Mexico. If your sore throat doesn't go away within a few days, see a doctor, he adds.

Get homeopathic help. To treat a bright red sore throat that develops suddenly on the right side of the throat, is sore to the touch and is accompanied by high fever and thirst, take a 6C or 12C dose of Belladonna and consult your doctor, says Mitchell Fleisher, MD If you feel irritable and the soreness begins on the right side and then moves to the left, and if your throat feels better after you drink warm beverages, Dr. Fleisher suggests a 6C or 12C dose of Lycopodium. If the soreness begins on the left side and moves to the right and is worse when you swallow saliva but better when you eat, he says to try a 6C or 12C dose of Lachesis. Take one of these

---

Soothe your sore throat with imagery

Simple remedies play their part in soothing a sore throat. But don't forget your mind-it's powerful medicine, says Dr. Martin Rossman, author of *Healing Yourself., A Step-by-Step Program for Better Health through Imagery* "For many people, visually imagining healing brings about symptomatic relief and sometimes helps bring about a cure," he says. Indeed, Dr. Rossman says, studies indicate you can improve your circulation just by concentrating on your blood flow. Endorphins, the body's natural painkillers, also respond to mind commands. Both are important in relieving all kinds of throat problems.

If you put your mind to work, you can ease a sore throat in as little as 15 minutes, Dr. Rossman says. "Choose your image. Focus your attention directly on where you have the pain. Imagine it in as much detail as you can."

Everyone imagines things differently, so let your mind go. And be thorough: Make your throat a real place. Give it textures, shapes, and colours. Hang some drapes if you want, or add a potted plant. Imagine it any way you want.

"I imagine a janitor with a bucket filled with a very smooth antiseptic solution," Dr. Rossman says. "He's wiping down the sides of my throat, every nook and cranny."

It's important that you find an image you like: You may prefer a more anatomical version, where your body fights the inflammation, or a more spiritual version, full of healing rays of white or golden light.

Imaging gets easier, and more effective, with practice, Dr. Rossman says. For a sore throat, repeat the exercise several times a day. If you don't notice improvement right away, don't get discouraged, he says. Keep practising. "It's inexpensive, it's entirely non-toxic, and it can't hurt."

---

remedies up to four times daily, says Dr. Fleisher, and if your throat doesn't feel better within 48 hours, see your medical doctor.

Ease with eucalyptus. Commission E, the body of experts that advises the German government about herbs, approves using eucalyptus to treat sore throat. Eucalyptus helps in two ways. The aromatic oil has a cooling effect on inflamed tissue, and the tannins in eucalyptus exert soothing astringent action as well. "I suggest using a few teaspoons of crushed leaf per cup of boiling water to make a soothing tea," says James A. Duke, Ph.D., author of *The Green Pharmacy*.

Lick it with licorice tea. Licorice has been revered as a sore throat treatment for centuries in both Europe and China. Commission E approves licorice for treating sore throat, and its effectiveness has been scientifically documented, according to pharmacognosist (natural product pharmacist)

Albert Leung, Ph.D. Dr. Leung recommends starting with three cups of water and five to seven teaspoons of root pieces. Put the herb in the water and bring it to a boil, then simmer until about half of the water has boiled away. Licorice not only soothes a sore throat, it also has an expectorant effect that can help treat colds and other respiratory conditions. (Like most non-nutritive sweeteners, licorice has an "off" taste that some people find less than appealing.)

Cool it with wintergreen. Wintergreen has a cooling, soothing flavour, and it contains methyl salicylate, an herbal form of aspirin that can help treat sore throat pain. Try it as a gargle for fast cooling of inflamed throat tissue and as a tea for pain relief. "I'd suggest putting 15 to 25 leaves in a cup of boiling water for both a gargle and a tea," says Dr. Duke. Don't give either aspirin or its natural herbal alternatives to children with sore throats. Also, if you are allergic to aspirin, you probably shouldn't take aspirin-like herbs, either.

Aid with agrimony (Agrimonia eupatoria). Commission E endorses using agrimony to soothe inflamed mucous membranes of the mouth and throat. Try a tea made with two to three teaspoons of dried herb per cup of boiling water.

Ask for anise. Anise tastes like licorice and is used as the flavouring agent in many "licorice" items. It's not as throat-soothing as real licorice, but Commission E suggests using it for respiratory problems, especially if you have a productive cough that produces phlegm. Anise helps break up bronchial congestion. You could make a tea by pouring a cup of boiling water over one to two teaspoons of crushed aniseed and steeping for 10 to 15 minutes. Strain the tea before drinking. The suggested dose is up to two cups a day.

Untie with knotgrass. Commission E approves using a tea made with two to three teaspoons of dried herb per cup of boiling water for treating sore throat and mild respiratory complaints. Knotgrass is astringent.

Make it myrrh. Here's another herb approved by Commission E as a treatment for sore throat. In Europe the tincture is added to water and used as a mouthwash and gargle.

Hands-on help:

Toe your throat. There's an acupressure point on your big toe that can help relieve sore throat pain. The point is on the underside of each toe—the area underneath where the toe curls.. To reach that area, lift your foot to the opposite toe with your thumb, or use both thumbs for extra pressure. You need a good deal of pressure so you really feel it, but don't press so hard that you're in pain. If it's hard to get the pressure in that point, use the eraser end of a pencil. Hold for up to five minutes.

Splinters

The pain: A sliver of a foreign object lodged in the skin.

The cause: Splinters can be caused by everything form stacking wood to sliding across along old park bench. They hurt because they're usually in your fingertips, where there are lots of nerve endings.

See a doctor if:
...the splinter is deeply embedded or occurs in a sensitive area such as the face or underneath a nail.
...a child has a splinter and is extremely afraid. A pediatrician may be able to give a local anaesthetic before removing the splinter.
...you can't remove a painful splinter on your own.
...you develop an infection. Redness or red streaks at the site of the splinter are warning signs.

Quick relief:
Let warm water do the work. Before you go probing for that splinter with a needle, give the affected area a good soak. "Often a 10- to 15-minute soak in warm water will cause the wood to swell, which causes the splinter to pop out on its own," says Marian H. Putnam, MD, a pediatrician.

Ice away the pain. If a warm soak doesn't do the trick, try putting an ice cube on the splinter. "Many people claim that it numbs the area, so it doesn't hurt as much when they try to remove the splinter," says Kathy Lillis, MD

Yank sooner rather than later. It's best to remove splinters sooner than later, says Howard Backer, MD, a physician who practices emergency sports and wilderness medicine. "If it's wood, you should remove it right away. If you don't, it will become infected; and then you'll need a doctor to drain the abscess and remove the sliver. And that's painful," explains Dr. Backer.

Get the right tweezers. If you must remove the splinter the old-fashioned way—by digging it out with a pair of tweezers—make sure you have the right tools for the job, says Dr. Lillis. "You should have tweezers with ridged edges, which are available at most chemist shops. And you can grip more easily if they have flat ends, as opposed to curved ones."

Cleanse those tweezers. Always wash tweezers in isopropyl rubbing alcohol before you use them, doctors say. You should then apply a liberal dose of hydrogen peroxide to the splinter itself . "The peroxide helps clean the wound to prevent any infection, and it can wash away any flecks of debris, so you'll have a cleaner removal," says Dr. Putnam.

Scrub up. Before you operate on yourself or anyone else to get a splinter out, wash your hands and the area around the imbedded splinter with soap and water, says Warren Bowman, MD That'll help prevent an infection that could be even worse than the pain of a splinter.

Use the right angle. Once you grab the splinter with tweezers or forceps, carefully pull it out at the same angle it went in. This will help avoid breaking the splinter off.

Don't slice and dice. Most slivers—at least one end anyway—lodge in the epidermis or outer layer of dead skin cells where it doesn't really hurt much to probe around. But don't get too carried away if you have a lance, says Carl Weil, an emergency medical technician and director of Wilderness Medicine Outfitters in Colorado. "You don't want to be slicing and dicing yourself. That will just make things worse," he says. The best strategy is to get at one end of the sliver, lift up, and pull with tweezers. If the splinter goes under the fingernail, you may have to cut a small V notch into the nail to get at the splinter. Then grasp one end of the splinter with tweezers and pull, Weil says.

Patch the hole. When you get the sliver out, clean the wound and the surrounding skin with hydrogen peroxide, a povidone-iodine solution such as Betadine, or just plain soap and water, says Dr. Bowman. Or you can use Hibiclens-a germicidal soap like the ones used in hospitals to prepare the skin for surgery, he says. All these products are available at chemists. After cleaning the area, flush it with clean water. "Then apply a small bead of antibiotic ointment and cover with a bandage," Dr. Bowman adds.

Pull it out with a poultice. Stuck with an impossible-to-remove splinter? Try this flax poultice, suggests Sharol Tilgner, N.D., a naturopathic physician, and herbalist. Grind a small amount of flaxseed in a food processor, mix in just enough water to form a pasted, and put it over the splinter. Bandage the area and let the poultice dry out completely. "Reapply a new poultice very day, covered with a new bandage," she suggests. "I've had luck using this to draw out glass and wood splinters. The longest I've had to use the flax continuously was for a week, but it worked. Flax seems to open the skin and suck out the splinter."

Give yourself a facial. If you have a few cactus plants on your windowsill, you've probably gotten a spine in your skin more than once. A mask of gel should help get it out. "Just spread the gel over the area. When it dries, you can peel it off like a sheet—and the cactus spine usually comes fight out," according to Dr. Putnam. In some cases, several applications of gel may be needed. A really stubborn spine may require tweezers to remove. While the mask technique works well for cactus needles, she adds that it may not remove other splinters as easily. (Glue, incidentally, is not a recommended method of removing cactus spines or splinters, according to Dr. Putnam.)

Sacrifice a plant. You can also make effective drawing poultices from the common houseplant aloe, says Weil. "Simply cut off part of a leaf of the plant, lay the cut edge over the splinter, tape it in place with an adhesive bandage and leave it there for several hours," says Weil. The aloe will help to draw the splinter out of the skin so that you can more easily remove it with a tweezers, he says. Some people are allergic to aloe, so before using it as a poultice, put some of the gel from the leaf on a small area of your skin and make sure that the area doesn't become red or irritated, says Weil.

Sprains

The pain: Swelling, pain and instability around a joint, usually after the joint has been subjected to excess pressure.

The cause: Strains (which affect muscles) and sprains (which affect joints) are embarrassingly common. With a strain, muscle tissue overstretches or tears outright, causing sharp pain followed by stiffness and tenderness. Strains usually affect the lower back and are often caused by lifting heavy objects incorrectly, such as by using your back instead of your legs, for example. A sprain, which forces a joint beyond its normal range of motion, is more serious. In a sprain, the ligaments—the tough bands of tissue that connect bones and hold joints in place stretch or tear. The result: swelling, pain, and bruising. Sprains commonly affect the ankle, knee, finger, wrist, and shoulder. Even though the injuries are different, basic care is the same, says Richard Parker, D.O., a staff physician with the San Diego Sports Medicine Centre.

See a doctor if:
...the pain or swelling is severe.
...there is looseness around the affected joint.

Quick relief:
Try some healthy RICE.
Rest it. If you've injured a foot, ankle, calf, or thigh parts of your body that help bear your weight—get off your feet immediately. Sit down, use crutches, do whatever it takes, Dr. Parker says. Rest for as long as it takes before you can walk in a relatively normal way. A significant limp can throw off your gait and lead to injuries in other areas of the body.
Ice it. After rest comes ice. You can use a bag of crushed ice, or if it's more convenient, use a bag of frozen peas or other small vegetables. Bang it on the counter to break the peas apart and it will conform to the contours of the injured area. First place a thin, damp dish towel over the injured limb to protect your skin. Then put the ice on, make it conform to the body part, and leave it on for no more than 20 minutes at a time. (Longer than that can cause frostbite Dr. Parker says.) You can help it conform by wrapping it with an elastic bandage. Ice the injury four to five time each day. Ice can

deaden the pain of a mild to moderate sprain, reduce inflammation, and increase deep circulation, which will help get nutrients to the injured areas, Parker says. (Don't use the RICE technique at all if you have Raynaud's disease, peripheral vascular disease, or hypersensitivity to cold.)

Compress it. Wrap on an elastic bandage to create 24-hour compression of the injured area, but don't make the bandage so tight that you've got a tourniquet. You also want to make sure that the bandage has enough elasticity to it. If you've used one bandage to help hold the ice in place, use a fresh one to maintain compression after you take the ice off. And replace the bandage every couple of days, Dr. Parker says. He advises you to buy a good name brand. "Some of the off-brands are pretty flimsy."

Elevate it. Propping your twisted knee up on a foot. stool or putting your sprained wrist in a sling helps reduce inflammation and pain.

Pop a pill. If the pain persists beyond the next two days or so, you can try an over-the-counter anti-inflammatory such as aspirin or ibuprofen or your doctor may prescribe an anti-inflammatory.

Nutritional remedies:

Eat pineapple. "You can speed recovery and get rid of any bruising from a sprain by eating a lot of pineapple, especially right after you injury," says Steven Subotnick, D.P.M., a sports podiatrist, and author of *Sports and Exercise Injuries*. "That's because pineapple has bromelain, an enzyme that helps heal bruises and speed healing. (Bromelain can cause dermatitis in some people, so take the pineapple off the menu if your skin begins to feel itchy.)

Everyday prevention:

Wear protection. For one to two weeks after the sprain, wear a protective bandage such as an Ace bandage around the sprain. After a few weeks, only wear the bandage when you play sports or put extra force on the injured joint. Keep that up for two to three months, says Andrea Sullivan, Ph.D., a doctor of naturopathy.

Stretch, then sweat. When you jump right into an athletic activity without warming up, your ligaments may just snap, says Michael Bemben, Ph.D. Begin with a slow five-minute jog, or ride your bike. Once you've increased your body temperature, take a few minutes to stretch your muscles. This makes them less likely to get injured.

Herbal help:

Soak away the ache. A soothing aromatherapy soak can help ease the pain of a sprained ankle, and it smells heavenly, too. Add 5 drops of sandalwood oil, 5 drops of lemon oil, and 2 tablespoons of witch hazel to a basin of warm water. Soak the sprained area until the water cools. "Citron, a substance in the lemon oil, helps relieve pain, and the sandalwood promotes circulation to the area, which speeds healing," says Douglas

Schar, a practising medical herbalist in London, editor of the *British Journal of Phytotherapy*, and author of *Backyard Medicine Chest*.

Sip some "herbal aspirin." "White willow bark is herbal aspirin," says Schar. It contains salicin, which is the natural version of salicylic acid, the active ingredient in aspirin. It also contains tannins, which help reduce swelling. So if bottled painkillers make you queasy, brew up some white willow bark tea. To make it, steep 1 teaspoon of white willow bark in a cup of boiling water for 15 minutes, then strain. Drink one cup three times a day until the pain and swelling subside.

Heal with a special kind of ginseng. Drinking tea made with a certain type of ginseng, Panax notoginseng, "is a fabulous treatment for strains," says Schar. In fact, Asian practitioners have long used this herb, also known as san qi ginseng, to treat sprains, strains, and bruises. To make a tea, steep 1 teaspoon of the herb in a cup of boiling water for 30 minutes. Drink one cup three times a day. It's thought that substances called ginsenosides give san qi its healing power, but exactly how or why they work isn't known. Different ginsenosides are found in different varieties of ginseng. This type of ginseng (which should not be confused with more common ginseng species in the Panax genus) is hard to find, but it is available through some mail-order catalogues.

Sip "sore muscle" tea. A tea made from poplar bark and cramp bark "can work wonders for sore muscles," says Schar. To brew up relief, add ½ teaspoon of poplar bark and 1 teaspoon of cramp bark to a cup of boiling water. Simmer for 10 minutes, then strain. Drink one cup of this mixture four times a day. This isn't the tastiest tea around, but it is good medicine, says Schar. Cramp bark contains scopoletin, which is thought to help fight pain, reduce swelling, and relax muscles, while poplar bark contains salicin, a natural painkiller. Cramp bark is sold through mail order. Poplar bark is difficult to find; try mail order sources or Internet herb sites.

Comfort with comfrey. Comfrey, also known as bruisewort, is a traditional herbal remedy for joint pain and bruises. Chop a few handfuls of fresh comfrey and place it in a pot. Cover the herb with water and cook until tender. Let the mixture cool. When it's comfortably warm, strain off the water, place the herb directly on the sprain, and wrap the injury with an elastic bandage. When the comfrey cools, unwrap the bandage, rewarm the comfrey, and repeat. Apply this poultice two or three times a day until the pain and swelling improve. Herbalists and scientists attribute comfrey's anti-inflammatory powers to a substance called allantoin. Tests in animals have shown that another substance in comfrey, rosmarinic acid, also reduces swelling.

Rub in relief. Substances in arnica called helenalins are believed to relieve pain and inflammation, while tannins in witch hazel bark relieve swelling and bruising. St. John's wort muffles or lessens pain signals to the brain and soothes the nerves irritated by inflamed muscles. A massage with oil containing all three combines the pain-relieving power of St. John's-wort with the anti-inflammatory qualities of arnica and witch hazel bark, Schar says.

To make the oil, mix 4 ounces of tincture (also called an extract) of St. John's-wort, 4 ounces of tincture of arnica flowers, and 1 ounce of tincture of witch hazel bark. Store the mixture in a glass jar. When you're ready to use it, blend 1 teaspoon of the mixture with 1 teaspoon of extra-virgin olive oil and massage into the affected area. Use the rub three times a day until the swelling and pain subside. (Don't use arnica on broken skin, however.)

Stings from Sea Creatures

The pain: Bites, stings or cuts caused by an encounter with a jellyfish, sea urchin or other ocean dweller. May be accompanied by severe burning, blistering, spots or red streaks at the site of contact.

The cause: Sea stingers such as jellyfish defend themselves by discharging venom from tiny poisonous cells, called nematocysts, which are found on the ends of their tentacles or spines. You can get stung just by brushing against portions of tentacles that have broken off and are floating in the water.

See a doctor if:

...you experience hives, nausea, vomiting or intense swelling or have trouble breathing.

...you have a fish-hook injury.

...you have trouble removing the tentacles from your skin or can't tolerate the pain.

...you have a deep, jagged wound, or a cut or sting that punctures your skin. You run the risk of getting an infection from bacteria that's in sea water, and the risk of getting tetanus.

Quick relief:

Take charge with a charge card. You can remove jellyfish tentacles with a credit card, and it won't even show up on your monthly bill. Jellyfish tentacles that get embedded in the skin deliver an attention-grabbing venom. Though painful, the venom is usually harmless (unless you swim in the South Pacific, where box jellyfish stings can be fatal). "You have to scrape them out, just as you would remove a bee stinger,' says Glenn G. Soppe, MD, a San Diego physician who lectures on aquatic bites and stings. "If you try to pull them out with your fingers, you'll inject more venom into your skin. If you have trouble scraping out the tentacles, put some baking soda or shaving cream on your skin to make it easier."

Try a little tenderness. It may sound as hard to swallow as a cut of gristly beef, but meat tenderisers help neutralise the venom of jellyfish and other sea life. "Most of these stings are protein in nature, and meat tenderiser is meant to degrade protein," explains Arthur Jacknowitz, PharMD, chairman of clinical pharmacy at West Virginia University School of Pharmacy. If you're swimming in an area where there are jellyfish, take along tenderiser (you can use it for that beachside barbecue, too). "Make a thick paste of meat tenderiser and salt water, and pat it on the skin in the first few minutes after being stung to get substantial relief," suggests Dr. Jacknowitz. When buying meat tenderiser, look for brands that contain either papain or bromelain, the active ingredients that dissolve jellyfish venom. (Bromelain can cause dermatitis in some people, however, so don't apply any more if the skin area begins to look red and inflamed.)

Revitalise with vinegar. Kitchen vinegar is also effective on jellyfish stings. Just make a 50–50 mixture of vinegar and salt water and apply it to the sting site, says Dr. Soppe. In a pinch, applying some diluted lime juice or ammonia may also work. To find vinegar in a hurry, check the nearest beachside French-fry stand.

Purify with peroxide. "Of course, the best remedy is a good defence. If you don't know what it is, don't touch it, and wear shoes while walking in tide pools," says Dr. Soppe. "But if you happen to cut yourself or get an abrasion from a piece of coral or a sea urchin, give the wound a thorough washing with hydrogen peroxide, followed by a good soaking in diluted vinegar."

Try a sticky solution. You can remove the fine, hard-to-get-to spicules of a sponge or coral by applying a piece of adhesive tape to the abrasion site and then removing it. When you pull off the tape, you pull up the tiny spicules. Then bathe the area with vinegar, suggests Constance L. Rosson, MD, who practices general medicine.

Get into hot water. "Stingray venom is heat-liable, meaning that heat degrades the protein that causes the pain. Your best bet is to simply soak the area for at least an hour in water that's as hot as you can stand without scalding yourself," says Dr. Soppe. Hot water from the tap is usually around 120'F, which is hot enough for this treatment. Since the fins of catfish and spines of starfish produce a similar type of venom, adds Dr. Rosson, the hot-water treatment is equally effective after an encounter with either of these sea creatures.

Wash in saltwater. If you've been stung by a jellyfish or any other stinging creature, wash off remaining pieces of tentacles by taking a dip in the ocean, suggests Saralyn R. Williams, MD, a toxicologist and emergency physician at the San Diego Regional Poison Centre. Just look out for more jellyfish before entering the water. The sooner you get the tentacles off your skin, the less damage they will do. And stay out of the pool. Don't rinse with fresh water or jump in a swimming pool, because fresh water shocks the venom cells into discharging more venom.

Remove jellyfish tentacles. Wearing rubber surgical gloves if possible, remove any large jellyfish tentacles left in your skin with tweezers. Whatever you do, don't pinch, rub or squeeze the tentacle pieces in your effort to remove them. Harsh handling will cause them to discharge more venom into your skin. If you can't remove all of the tentacles, get help from a doctor.

Hold still. Lie still and rest the stung area for about an hour, so that the venom won't spread to other parts of your body.

Stomach Pain

The pain: Any of a number of abdomen related pains—a dull ache, bloating, sharp cramps, acid pain, wind pain, or even pain related to diarrhoea or constipation.

The cause: The possible causes are diverse: stress, dyspepsia (more commonly called indigestion), heartburn, gallstones, ulcers, lactose intolerance, or irritable bowel syndrome. You might be overeating or not eating enough. You might have eaten food that was ill-prepared, spoiled, or that simply didn't agree with you. Muscle cramps can happen anywhere you have muscles, and that includes your stomach, where a cramp may be mistaken for a "generic" bellyache, indigestion, upset stomach or side stitch.

See a doctor if:
...a stomach-ache is so severe that you're doubled over, or if it is accompanied by nausea and vomiting that lasts longer than one or two days or keeps coming back.
...the ache is accompanied by a change in bowel habits, such as the onset of constipation or pencil-thin stools, diarrhoea that is persistent or getting increasingly worse and that is accompanied by fever, or if you find blood in your stool.
...you have a dull ache in your upper abdomen, your urine has become dark, and/or the whites of you eyes or your skin appears yellowish.
...a "stomach cramp" persists for more than 30 minutes, or if it seems to be increasing in intensity.
...the pain includes a feeling of pressure, nausea or vomiting, sweating, chest pain or trouble breathing. Heart attacks are often mistaken, early on, for attacks of indigestion Get to an emergency room fast!

Medication:
Tummy troubles are a side effect of many prescription drugs. If you experience stomach problems after taking your medication, talk to your doctor about prescribing a substitute. Here are some common stomach offenders.

Iron supplements taken to prevent or treat anaemia, such as ferrous sulphate.

Caffeine in any form, whether as coffee, caffeinated beverages, or as a stimulant.

Nonsteroidal anti-inflammatory agents used for sprains, strains, toothache, or cold and flu aches, including over-the-counter products such as aspirin, ibuprofen, and naproxen sodium.

Quick relief.

Give your belly a break. You can help your stomach recover from a bellyache by going on just liquids for the rest of the day, says Martin Brotman, MD, a gastroenterologist. Stick to clear liquids, such as chicken broth, flat ginger ale, broth, and water, and avoid carbonated or caffeinated beverages. Or don't eat anything for a while. "If you have a cramping pain, don't test it with food," says Roger Gebhard, MD "You want to avoid stimulating the gastrointestinal tract."

Loosen up. If you have a bloated, sore belly, make yourself more comfortable by wearing loose clothing. Loosen your belt. If you're wearing a tight shirt or pants, change into trousers, sweats, or pajama bottoms that have a bigger waistband, until your stomach settles down.

Warm your tummy. Turn a heating pad on low and place it on your abdomen until the pain subsides, says Dr. Brotman. "Warmth on the abdomen offers some comfort. If the pain continues for several hours and is new to you, notify your doctor."

Take time out. Soothe a sore stomach with rest. Put up your feet. Relax. "Close your eyes," suggests Dr. Gebhard. "Find in your memory a place you've been to. A place of beauty, maybe a lake or a campground or a beach. Go back to that spot in your mind. Sit on a rock. Listen to the natural sounds. Breathe naturally."

Take an antacid. "If the pain occurs when your stomach is empty, food can't be the cause," says Michael Oppenheim, MD, author of *The Complete Book of Better Digestion.* "Most likely, it's stomach acid-so taking an antacid is the answer." Almost any antacid can help neutralize stomach acid, but it can also have other effects on digestion, depending on the kind you choose. "The best thing to look for in an antacid is the amount of calcium or magnesium, it contains," says William B. Ruderman, MD "If you tend to have trouble with constipation, then pick a brand that lists magnesium first on the label. If you're more prone to diarrhoea, pick a brand listing calcium first." You should use these products for short-term relief but not over long periods of time, since they sometimes cause tolerance. Also, long-term use may mask a more serious problem.

Allay the acid. H2-blockers (histamine blockers), such as Tagamet HB 200, Zantac 75, or Pepcid AC, suppress acid at its source and prevent it from irritating the lining of the stomach. Use them to prevent an acid stomach if you know that you are going to be eating foods that have caused you heartburn in the past, particularly rich, spicy, or fatty foods, suggests Geoffrey C. Lamb, MD Follow label directions for recommended dosages. As with antacids, these are for short-term relief, not chronic pain.

Have a snack. A light snack can also absorb stomach acid if your stomach ache isn't the result of overeating. "A bland diet with soft foods is best-things such as bananas or crackers," says Dr. Ruderman. "Apple juice is an excellent choice. But stay away from overly sweet juices such as strawberry or raspberry as well as acidic beverages such as orange juice." He points out that the acidic drinks can actually aggravate stomach acid.

Drink to burp. If that stomach ache is the result of overeating, then a good burp is usually the quickest way to get relief. Adults may turn toward a product like Alka-Seltzer, but children usually prefer a better-tasting remedy. "My approach to treating mild stomach-ache is the same as what my mother did—with flat ginger ale or cola," says Perri Elizabeth Klass, MD, author of *Baby Doctor.* "The carbonation in the soda helps stir things up, so you burp and feel better. And I believe that if soda is a little flat, it has a slightly medicinal taste, which probably helps on a psychological level."

Find some fibre. Studies show that the incidence of stomach ache was halved among a group of children who ate high-fibre cookies at the first sign of stomach-ache. "Popcorn is also an effective source of fibre," says William Feldman, MD, in Toronto. "Eating prunes, and fruits in general, can help a lot," adds Dr. Klass.

Nutritional remedies:

Go through the process of elimination. Since your digestive processes get more finicky every year, that increases the likelihood that a certain food, beverage, or medication can often cause a stomach-ache. "Try eliminating different things, such as aspirin, to see if you feel better," says Dr. Brotman. Even chewing gum should come under suspicion. Some people get abdominal cramps and diarrhoea when they chew sugar-free gum that's made with the sweetener sorbitol. Dairy foods and beverages such as ice cream and milk are other common offenders that can make you feel more gassy and bloated, as are many high-sugar or high-fat foods. If you suspect a food is causing the problem, take it out of your diet for a few days. If the stomach-ache disappears, you've found your culprit, says Dr. Brotman.

Welcome a little BRAT into your home. When you are ready to eat a little something, try the BRAT diet—bananas, rice, applesauce, or toast. These foods are all easy for your stomach to digest. "Don't rush back into solid food by eating a steak dinner," says Dr. Brotman.

Stay regular. Constipation can certainly lead to stomach distress, so make sure that you're getting a healthy dose of fibre every day. Shoot for 25 grams of fibre each day, says Dr. Gebhard. Include apples, bran, cabbage, and raw vegetables in your diet—and drink eight eight-ounce glasses of water a day to help keep you regular. "Peel the apple if the skin is hard for you to chew or digest," adds Dr. Gebhard.

Don't overfill with fibre. Believe it or not, stomach problems can also be caused by too much of a good thing—specifically, fibre. For some people, eating more fibre than they are accustomed to can cause wind and abdominal bloating, says Dr. Gebhard. It's best to introduce fibre into your diet slowly and a little at a time. Dr. Gebhard recommends starting with 10 to 15 grams a day, increasing by 5 grams each week to 25.

Eat mindfully. "Mindful eating" is paying attention to the role of food in your daily life, says Amy Saltzman, MD, an internist for the Institute for Health and Healing at the California Pacific Medical Centre. "By bringing attention to when, what, where, and how you eat, you may improve not only your digestion but also the quality of your life," says Dr. Saltzman. "Try eating a mindful meal. Prepare the food with attention to what will be satisfying—and eat when you are hungry." When you sit down to eat, be sure to go slowly, Dr. Saltzman adds. Concentrate on eating, and taste each bite before you swallow.

Ditch dairy. If drinking milk or eating ice cream seems to fuel your intestinal distress, you could be lactose intolerant. That means your body isn't producing enough of the lactase enzyme to break down lactose, the sugar found in milk and other dairy products.

Most adult Blacks, Asians, Native Americans, and some Whites have difficulty digesting milk because they have little or no lactase. To discover whether lactose intolerance is causing your discomfort, eliminate all dairy products from your diet. Wait three days, then add an eight-ounce glass of non-fat milk to your diet. If you can safely drink that glass of milk every day without any adverse reaction, it is all right to slowly reintroduce other dairy products such as non-fat yoghurt and cheese, adding a new food every few days. If discomfort returns, you may have found your problem, says Dr. Lamb.

Relief is available in the form of dietary supplements that make dairy foods more digestible such as Lactaid and Dairy Ease. Lactaid also makes milk that has been pre-treated with the lactase enzyme. It is available in most major grocery stores in the dairy section.

Say goodbye to chocolate. Eating chocolate can cause heartburn, especially when it follows a big meal, says Dr. Lamb. That is because chocolate relaxes the valve connecting the oesophagus to the stomach. When the valve loosens, acid splashes up into the oesophagus, causing heartburn.

Forgo feeding frenzies. Eat slowly, chew your food well, and don't guzzle down drinks. Does that sound like your mother talking? Well, she has a chorus of agreement: It's what stomach experts recommend, too. Food that's chewed well first, and mixed with saliva, is easier to digest, according to John C. Johnson, MD, director of Emergency Medical Services at Porter Memorial Hospital in Valparaiso, Indiana. Need help slowing your chomper speed? Try changing your eating environment. Instead of eating over the kitchen sink, set a place at the table. Add soft music and candlelight and you can't help but slow down.

Graze, don't gorp. Stomachs are very sensitive to over-stuffing. "A distended stomach can cause sharp pain and can be very uncomfortable for some people," says Dr. Johnson. If you're one whose stomach cramps up when you just dig right in, try eating smaller, more frequent meals.

Hold off on eating if you're upset. Anxiety and eating don't mix. "When you're tense, the blood supply to your digestive system is reduced, making it hard to digest food," says Steven Fahrion, Ph.D., a clinical psychologist. While there are many ways to relax, one of the fastest and easiest is with deep, slow, deliberate breathing, Dr. Fahrion says. As you exhale, imagine tension leaving your body.

Stick with noncaffeinated drinks. Coffee and colas make a tense stomach only worse, Dr. Johnson says. Try water, fruit juices or a tummy-taming herbal tea.

Go easy on cold fluids. Leave chugalugging for the fraternity boys. Too much of your favourite icy cold beverage, downed too fast, can send your stomach into temporary but painful spasms.

Give your guts a time-out. Allow a half-hour or more for big meals to move through your stomach before you engage in heavy-duty activities, recommends Dr. Johnson. "Exercise diverts blood from your digestive system to your arms and legs increasing your chances for stomach and intestinal cramps," he explains.

Chicken out cramps. Nobody knows why, but chicken soup soothes stomach and abdominal cramps and cleans out the digestive system, says Wanda Filer, MD, a family practice physician.

Fill up on fluids. It's important to keep up your fluid intake—especially if you have diarrhoea, Dr. Gebhard says. "You want to avoid becoming dehydrated," he explains. "You might try Gatorade or another drink with electrolytes in it." If you're having difficulty drinking because of excess vomiting, see your doctor.

Juice up. In *The Complete Book of Juicing* naturopathic physician Michael Murray, N.D., suggests an apple juice cocktail flavoured with ginger, mint and fennel. All three are potent carminatives, natural substances that help dispel wind and facilitate digestion, according to Dr. Murray. To prepare, juice a 1/4-inch-thick slice of fresh ginger wrapped in half of a handful of mint leaves, followed by half of a small fennel bulb and two sliced apples.

Helpful vitamins and supplements:

Line up vitamins. Foods high in the antioxidant vitamins A, C, and E are very important to maintain the integrity of the intestinal lining, says Priscilla Skerry, a naturopathic and homeopathic doctor. Fruit is vitamin-rich, but since you don't want to irritate your stomach with sugar (or pesticides), focus mainly on organic vegetables, she adds. To load up on vitamin A, eat orange vegetables such as carrots, sweet potatoes, and squash. Cold-pressed salad or cooking oils are one of the top sources of vitamin E (it is important they are labelled "cold-pressed" to assure that the vitamin is preserved). Almonds and sunflower seeds are also vitamin E-rich. Broccoli, cauliflower, potatoes, cabbage, and green and sweet red peppers are high in vitamin C. Try to eat four to six servings of vegetables daily and some fruit in season to keep your stomach running smoothly.

Think zinc. This antioxidant mineral does wonders for the stomach, Dr. Skerry adds. "The most absorbable form is zinc picolinate. If you take it as a supplement, make sure that the tablet has some copper in it. A good ratio is seven to one. Your daily dose of zinc can be up to 15 milligrams, which means that you also need to take approximately 2 milligrams of copper."

Beat it with baking soda. Dissolve a teaspoon of baking soda in warm water, toast to a calmer belly, and drink up, says David Peura, MD, a gastroenterologist. Baking soda has been used to relieve upset stomachs for generations, and with good reason: It works. Just don't use it every day, he says.

Choose charcoal. "I don't believe there is a gastric problem that doesn't respond to activated charcoal," says Agatha Thrash, MD, a medical pathologist. For quick relief of stomach ache, mix two to three tablespoons of activated charcoal powder (available in most health food stores and some pharmacies) with a little water in the bottom of a tall glass. "Stir gently, or the powder flies everywhere," she says. Continue stirring and adding water a little at a time until the glass is full, then drink it with a straw.

Everyday prevention:

Go easy on the pain relievers. Aspirin, ibuprofen, and other nonsteroidal anti-inflammatory drugs (NSAIDS) can irritate the stomach liming and break down its protective mucous layer, causing discomfort, says Dr. Lamb. In the long term, over-use can lead to ulcers or kidney problems. "An aspirin a day to prevent strokes or heart attacks is safe and remains a good idea. A few people, however, will have irritation with just a few doses," he says.

Keep a diary. To help you identify what precipitates your stomach-aches, you may want to try writing down everything you eat as well as all of the stress-producing situations you face, advises Marvin Schuster, MD

Stay vertical. If your stomach-ache is due to overeating, don't follow the meal with time on the couch, says Dr. Peura. "The food wants to go south, but if it can't, it's going to go north. If you lie down or bend over, there's more of a chance that the food contents will come up.

Easing the pain with exercise:

Speed things up with a little walk. If you're feeling full after a sumptuous repast, try "walking it off" before you resort to antacids. Light exercise especially walking, helps speed the movement of digested food through you bowels. "This may reduce stomach cramps by allowing the stomach to empty faster," Dr. Johnson says.

Take a yoga class. Is your stomach in turmoil over something that happened at the office? Yoga offers one solution for preventing stomach-aches and other symptoms of stress "because it puts us in close touch with our bodies and our minds and warns us when stress is looming," says Richard Miller, Ph.D., a clinical psychologist. Because of this early warning, we can intervene with breathing, meditation, massage, and other relaxation strategies. Many yoga classes are offered through adult night-school classes, and at fitness centres.

Herbal help:

Call on camomile. Camomile tea is an age-old and, many believe, effective herbal remedy to ease a sore belly, says Mike Cantwell, MD Try two or three six-ounce cups a day, between meals. Camomile decreases stomach activity, and helps coat the stomach as well, says Dr. Cantwell. You can find the tea in most grocery stores. Follow the directions on tea-bag packages, or if you are using loose dried camomile flowers, steep one teaspoon of camomile in boiling water for 10 to 15 minutes. Very rarely, camomile can cause an allergic reaction when ingested. People who are allergic to closely related plants such as ragweed, asters, and chrysanthemums should drink the tea with caution.

Tea up. Mom was only half fight when she suggested a nice hot cup of tea. "Tea, particularly peppermint tea, can calm down your stomach, but it should be warm—not hot," says Dr. Ruderman. "You're also better off with lukewarm beverages. Something too hot or too cold can induce a spastic response in your stomach, which increases pressure and pain." Other helpful herbal teas to try include valerian, fennel, ginger, rosemary and lemon balm.

Pick up some peppermint. If you have bowel spasms or trapped wind, peppermint oil stops the aching, says Tori Hudson, a naturopathic physician. Peppermint oil is available in capsule form in health food stores. "Take one capsule two or three items a day between meals until your cramping goes away," says Dr. Hudson. The essential oil peppermint's great for easing gastric discomfort, says aromatherapist Michael Scholes. "Peppermint was used for years to flavour after-dinner mints, because it's a very effective digestive," says Scholes. But, he cautions, most of today's peppermint candies do not contain the essential oil and probably wouldn't help your stomach-ache. He suggests sucking on a sugar cube flavoured with a single drop of peppermint oil whenever your stomach feels a bit queasy.

Go ginger. "Cut a piece of ginger and suck on it," advises Allan Magaziner, D.O., a nutritional medicine specialist. He says that ginger helps calm activity in the stomach. A cup of ginger tea can also help, he adds. Ginger tea is available in tea bag form in most health food stores.

Hands-on help:

Press the points. Press both Sp 16 points, situated below the edge of the rib cage, a half-inch in from each nipple line, says Michael Peed Gach, Ph.D., author of *Acupressure's Potent Points*. "These are instinctual spots

What makes stomachs rumble?

A rumbly stomach may get your attention, but should it demand your concern? "You can't do much about stomach gurgling-and there's no need to," says William B. Ruderman, MD "To understand this condition-called borborygmus-think of your stomach as a giant mixmaster. When you eat, your stomach grinds up and mixes the food you've eaten to help digestion. The gurgling you hear is the noise created as the intestines squeeze this solution through."

to press," Dr. Gach explains. "You're pressing these points when you bend over and hold your stomach." He suggests holding the points for one minute while breathing deeply.

Work out stress. Tension and stress can cause plenty of stomach pain. To help relieve stress, put some regular exercise into your weekly routine. Try walking for half an hour three days a week, says Dr. Filer. When you're active, you'll also find that your bowel movements become more regular, which is helpful if constipation is causing your abdominal distress.

Use your imagination. Imagery can be a powerful weapon against stomach-ache, according to Barbara Dossey, R.N., author of *Rituals of Healing: Using Imagery for Health and Wellness.* Picture a bright light that is powerful and penetrating glowing within you. Now picture a beam that has a soft, healing colour spreading from this light. Allow this beam's healing colour to fill your stomach with calm and quiet. Now imagine the colour slowly flowing out of your stomach and into your small intestine like a tiny sailboat riding on smooth waves. Follow it down through your large intestine and into your rectum, gently healing and soothing your digestive tract as it goes. Dossey recommends that you use this imagery for 15 to 20 minutes twice a day.

Stubbed Toe

The pain: A throbbing digit that's just collided with an inanimate object.

The cause: Researchers have determined that a toe is moving at a speed of 40 to 50 miles per hour when it collides with, say, a table leg. Imagine a car colliding with your foot and you get the idea. This explains why stubbing your toe can do so much damage. "You can tear soft tissue or a tendon around a toe joint or the metatarsal joint, which is where the toe attaches to the foot," says Phyllis Ragley, D.P.M., a podiatrist. "You can even break a bone."

See a doctor if:
...you have marked, persistent swelling, with discolouration that extends up toward the ankle.
...you have difficulty bearing weight on the toe.
...you have abnormal positioning of the toe.

Quick relief:
Get it checked. To be on the safe side, experts say, you should have your doctor examine your stubbed toe. That way you can be sure you haven't done any serious damage. "People blow it off," says Rock Positano, D.P.M. "Then four or five years later, the toe is killing them. It turns out there's a fracture line and arthritis."

Just chill. "Apply ice to your toe right away," says Glenn Gastwirth, D.P.M. "The sooner you do so, the sooner you'll reduce the swelling. That's important because swelling puts pressure on the tissues, which in turn puts pressure on the nerves within the tissues. And that contributes a great deal to the pain." Dr. Ragley suggests massaging the toe with an ice cube for 10 to 15 minutes every hour or two. "But don't do this if you have diabetes or a circulatory problem," she cautions. "The ice can limit circulation in your toe."

Put a hold on heat. Don't use any type of heat treatment on a stubbed toe, advises David C. Novicki, D.P.M. "Anything hot will immediately dilate torn blood vessels," he says. "That will lead to the build-up of fluid in the toe."

Attend to a broken nail. The impact between toe and immovable object can cause the nail to tear or break off. "If the nail is still partially attached, cover it with an adhesive bandage to give it a chance to reseat itself," says Dr. Ragley. "If it doesn't reattach or fall off within a few days, clip off the wobbly end."

Ongoing care:

Keep it up. "Stay off your feet as much as you can-especially for the first 24 to 36 hours after the injury," Dr. Ragley says. "And keep your toe elevated, even if you just have your foot resting on a box 6 inches off the floor. What you don't want is for your foot to be hanging down, with blood running into it. That will increase swelling."

Leave your toe unwrapped. Don't bandage a stubbed toe yourself, Dr. Ragley advises. "You may not wrap it correctly—and if it's fractured, you may do more harm than good," she says. Leave this step to the professionals.

Loosen your bedding. Before you hit the sack, untuck your sheets and blankets so that they put less pressure on your toe, Dr. Gastwirth says. "Downward pressure can bend your toe and add to the soreness," he explains.

Open wide. Make sure your shoe provides ample space for your injured toe, Dr. Ragley says. Choose an open-toed slipper or a sandal over a closed shoe. This will help protect your toe from additional pressure, she explains.

Choose stiff shoes. "Wear a shoe that has a less flexible sole," Dr. Gastwirth says. "It will act much like a splint or a cast, preventing your toe from bending. Your toe will heal much faster if it doesn't bend so much."

Tread carefully. Until you have your toe examined, try not to bend it or put pressure on it when you walk, Dr. Gastwirth says. "You could have a hairline fracture, and pressure would enlarge the crack and possibly displace the bone," he explains. "Shift your weight to your heel as much as possible." But don't overdo it, he cautions. Overcompensating could cause problems elsewhere in the foot or in the knee or hip.

Sunburn

The pain: An inflammation of the skin that results from overexposure to the ultraviolet radiation in sunlight, ranging from a mild burn with redness and stinging that dissipates quickly to a second-degree burn, in which your skin will actually blister and ooze.

The cause: Energy from the sun causes biochemical changes within the skin itself, ending with inflammation. The inflammation—a burn—causes damage to the skin. Repeated sunburn can harm your skin, breaking down its elastic tissues, causing wrinkles, and increasing your risk of skin cancer.

See a doctor if:

...you experience chills, nausea, fever, faintness, or fatigue as a result of sunburn.

...you develop a second-degree or severe burn.

...your burn is accompanied by purple blotches or discolouration, excessive blistering, or intense itching.

...the sunburn looks infected. Telltale signs of infection include red streaks or yellow pus.

Medication:

If the label of your prescription medication says, "Avoid the sun," don't overlook it, says Jonathan Weiss, MD, assistant clinical professor of dermatology. This warning label means that you'll sunburn more easily or become more sensitive to light as a side effect of taking the drug, says Dr. Weiss. Ignoring the "shun the sun" warning can give you more than a severe sunburn; it can affect how well the medicine does its job.

Among the drugs that commonly cause "photosensitivity" reactions are:

Tricyclic antidepressants like amitriptyline (Elavil).

Medications often prescribed as antihistamines, like promethazine (Phenergan).

Tetracycline (such as Achromycin), used to treat infections and control acne.

Sulfa antibacterial drugs, such as the combination sulfamethoxazole and trimethoprim (Bactrim).

Oral medicines for diabetes such as glipizide (Glucotrol or Glibenese).
Diuretics like hydrochlorothiazide (Esidrix).

If you're taking pills or liquid medications, your skin will resume its normal sun-sensitivity shortly after you stop taking the drug. But if you're using external salves or ointments on your skin, the photosensitive effects can continue after you stop applying it—so continue to maintain the precautions, says Dr. Weiss.

Remedies:

Preempt pain. When you know you've spent too much time in the sun, take aspirin or another nonsteroidal anti-inflammatory drug (NSAID) before you start feeling the burn, says Dr. Weiss. These over-the-counter medications offer two kinds of sunburn relief: They knock out pain and they reduce inflammation and swelling. If taken soon enough, these drugs can help keep inflammation down and keep a sunburn from getting worse, says Dr. Weiss. He suggests taking the maximum dosage given by the package directions for 48 hours following the sunburn.

Cool it. The best way to soothe sun-sizzled skin is to apply cool water as quickly as possible to prevent the sunburn from getting worse, says D'Anne Kleinsmith, MD, a dermatologist. She recommends cold wet compresses and cool baths to bring down the heat of a sunburn. Do not apply ice, says Dr. Kleinsmith, because it could further injure the skin that's already been irritated by sunburn.

Just add milk. Whole-milk compresses are an excellent remedy for any kind of burn, says John F. Romano, MD, clinical assistant professor of dermatology. Dip gauze or a clean washcloth into milk, lay it on your sunburned skin, and leave the compress in place for 20 minutes or so, suggests Dr. Romano. Repeat every two to four hours, using milk that's room temperature or slightly cooler, but not ice-cold. Since milk leaves a residue that will soon have your skin smelling "sour," rinse yourself off with cool water afterward, he adds.

Say "aloe." Aloe vera gel is probably the most soothing treatment you can apply to a sunburn, says Dr. Weiss. Apply it as needed to alleviate the pain and dryness of sunburned skin. You can buy bottles of the pure gel in health food stores. Or try growing the plants around your house, and then just slice open a leaf and slather on the gel when needed.

Make yourself moisturised. Bland moisturisers (those without fragrances or irritating ingredients) such as Cetaphil cream or Eucerin cream can comfort sun-damaged skin, says Dr. Weiss. Smoothing on cream after a cool bath helps to lock moisture into parched skin, he says. Also, moisturisers with menthol or eucalyptus can add a cooling sensation.

Soothe with hydrocortisone ointment. An over-the-counter hydrocortisone ointment, either 0.5 percent or 1 percent, may help keep down inflammation and swelling, according to Dr. Weiss. Ointments are preferable to hydrocortisone creams since creams can contain preservatives that can sting irritated or blistered skin. Apply as directed on the label.

Flush your system. If your skin swells from a sunburn, that causes you to lose fluids from the rest of your body. To replace that fluid, you need to drink lots of water. Dr. Weiss suggests you drink at least eight eight-ounce glasses of water a day until the sunburn no longer gives off heat.

Practice prevention. Your first line of defence should be a sunscreen. Get in the habit of putting it on every morning. Dr. Weiss recommends the use of products with an SPF (sun protection factor) of at least 15. Also check the label to be sure that the lotion is designed to protect against both UVA (the deep penetrating rays) and UVB (the sunburn-causing rays). Dr. Weiss recommends looking for zinc oxide or titanium dioxide among the ingredients. These are inert, opaque compounds that block almost the entire spectrum of damaging rays, he says, without exposing you to the irritating effects of chemicals like para-aminobenzoic acid (PABA) found in many other sunscreens.

Apply sunscreen liberally—use about the amount that would fill a shot glass—per application for the average-size person. Apply evenly on all exposed skin, including the lips, nose, ears, neck, scalp (if hair is thinning), hands, feet, and eyelids, taking care not to get the product in your eyes, says Dr. Weiss. Be sure to put the sunscreen on 30 minutes before you go out, he adds. It takes about that long before it will protect you fully.

Know when your time is up. If you are careful to reapply sunscreen after getting wet, you can safely stay outside as long as the sunscreen promises. For instance, if you use an SPF 15 sunscreen, you can stay outside 15 times longer without burning than you could by not wearing sunscreen. If you would begin to burn after 8 minutes with no sunscreen, you can stay out for 120 minutes without burning by wearing SPF 15 sunscreen. But you can't "layer" sunscreens. Once your two hours is up, you can't reapply more sunscreen and stay out for another 120 minutes. Also, wearing an SPF 15 and an SPF 30 sunscreen does not make for SPF 45, says Dr. Weiss.

Cover up. Loose-fitting, long-sleeved shirts and pants or long skirts provide the greatest protection from the sun's rays. Tightly woven cloth is best, says Dr. Weiss. A simple rule of thumb is to hold the fabric up against the light: the closer the weave, the better the protection.

Don a hat and shades. Dressing for the sun should also always include a broad-brimmed hat and UV-protective sunglasses, says Dr. Weiss. He suggests a brim of about four inches all around and sunglasses that will block at least 99 percent of both UVA and UVB radiation.

Avoid peak exposure. Your chances of developing a sunburn are greatest between 10:00 a.m. and 3:00 p.m., when the sun's rays are strongest at all latitudes. The risk drops considerably before and after those times, says Dr. Weiss. If you're not wearing a watch, you can judge the sun's intensity by the length of your shadow—when it's shorter than you are, the sun is at its most intense. It's also easier to burn more severely on a hot day because the heat increases the effects of ultraviolet radiation. In addition, you'll burn faster at high altitudes and in the mountains because there is less atmosphere to block ultraviolet rays, he adds.

Beware of clouds. People often discount the risk of getting sunburned on cloudy or overcast days. But you can't let your guard down even when the sun is in hiding, says Dr. Weiss. Up to 80 percent of ultraviolet rays can penetrate the clouds.

Go for oats. There are several effective topical treatments for sun exposure, beginning with the old folk remedy of taking an oatmeal bath, says Kathy Foulser, N.D. Simply pour about 1½ ounces of ground oatmeal, which is sold in drugstores under brand names like Aveeno, into comfortably warm water and soak for 15 minutes. Because sunburn essentially produces skin inflammation, it's helpful to take herbs with strong anti-inflammatory properties, says Dr. Foulser. She recommends either flaxseed oil or evening primrose oil, both of which contain gamma-linoleic acid—more easily remembered by the initials GLA. The body transforms GLA into several hormones, most significantly prostaglandin, which is a potent anti-inflammatory. When you put more GLA into your system, your body has increased power to reduce inflammation.

The essential fatty acids in these two oils provide another benefit: They are good for overall skin health, says Dr. Foulser. She recommends taking one tablespoon a day of flaxseed oil or six capsules daily of evening primrose oil for long-term use. "If you want, you can take more, because these oils are quite safe," she adds. Be sure to check the labels of these supplements for information on recommended dosages.

Up your antioxidants. Whenever your skin burns, cells are damaged. This damage is caused by free radicals, which are free-roaming, unstable molecules that are seeking to stabilise themselves by stealing electrons from healthy cells. As a result of this cell damage, free radicals can cause premature wrinkling, and in the case of repeated sun exposure, even skin cancer. If you take antioxidants, substances that scavenge free radicals in the body, you can speed healing and prevent rapid cell damage. At your chemist or health food store, you will find plenty of antioxidant combination products on the shelf. Alternatively, you can choose to take separate supplements of vitamin C, vitamin E, and beta-carotene, all of which have strong antioxidant properties, says Dr. Foulser.

Mix an aloe-lavender "smoothie." Aloe vera and lavender essential oil combine to cool sunburn, reduce swelling and redness, and prevent infection, says herbalist Mindy Green, co-author of *Aromatherapy: A Complete Guide to the Healing Art*. To make an herbal soother, combine 4 ounces of aloe vera juice, ½ teaspoon lavender oil, 1 teaspoon of apple cider vinegar, and 2 capsules (400 international units each) of vitamin E oil (to use the oil, just prick the capsule with a clean needle or knifepoint, then squeeze out the oil.) Or you can buy a small jar of vitamin E oil, says Eversole. Shake the mixture before applying it. Gently pat your aloe vera smoothie on painful, inflamed sunburn. Reapply as needed to keep skin cool and comfortable, Green says.

Cool down with tea. The tannic acid in tea soothes sunburn pain, says Gayle Eversole, R.N., Ph.D. "Just make regular tea with black or orange pekoe, and when it's cool, pat it on your sunburned skin," she suggests. "The tannic acid actually helps restore the natural acid balance of your skin. Sunburn throws off that balance, contributing to the pain," Eversole notes. While some herbal teas also contain tannins, the high tannin content of regular black tea makes it the top choice when it comes to soothing sunburned skin.

The tannins also prompt proteins in the top layers of your skin to form a protective covering, "kind of like a natural bandage," notes Sharol Tilgner, N.D., a naturopathic physician. You can pat the tea onto your skin with your fingertips or soak a cotton ball in the tea and apply it. Start using this remedy as soon as you notice sunburn pain. If pain returns, reapply as needed, says Eversole.

Pat on St. John's wort or calendula. For a cooling splash or compress, combine 1 part St. John's wort or calendula tincture with 9 parts cool water, Dr. Tilgner suggests. Pat it on sunburned areas or soak a clean cloth in the mixture and lay on scorched skin for at least 15 minutes. St.-John's-wort can relieve pain caused by nerve damage, Dr. Tilgner says, and, in one study, it also helped heal burns. Calendula is a traditional skin mender that has been shown in research studies to also have anti-inflammatory activity. The cool water also helps ease sunburn pain and swelling.

Bathe in apple-cider vinegar. Another plant-based product, apple-cider vinegar, can also soothe sunburn pain, Dr. Tilgner says. For all-over sunburn relief, try adding a cup to a bathtub full of cool water, and soak. Or apply it directly to the skin. "Apple-cider vinegar is astringent. It soothes sunburn pain much the way black tea does," Dr. Tilgner notes.

Wipe with white vinegar. White vinegar applied directly on the skin with a cloth two or three times a day may take away the sting of sunburn, says John Crellin, MD, Ph.D., professor of the history of medicine at Memorial University of Newfoundland Faculty of Medicine in St. John's.

Pop some antihistamines. Over-the-counter drugs like Benadryl and Chlor-Trimeton (Piriton) will reduce swelling and itching. They should be taken once every 6 hours for the first 48 hours after you've burned, Dr. Schreiber says.

Jump into a cool tub. This will help reduce swelling. A bath is better than a shower because it's less traumatic to your skin.

Be soothed by vegetables. Boil some lettuce in water, then strain it and let the liquid cool for a few hours in the refrigerator before applying it to your skin with cotton balls, recommends Lia Schorr, a New York City skin care specialist and author of *Lia Schorr's Seasonal Skin Care*. Other vegetables that produce results? Thinly sliced pieces of raw cucumber, potato or apple can be placed on sunburned areas such as the forearm. The coolness from the vegetables is soothing and might help reduce inflammation.

Double your dosage of pain reliever. "Probably the best thing you can do is to take two times the recommended amount of ibuprofen or another pain reliever for the first two doses and then go to the recommended dose, advises Dr. Romano. Doubling the usual dosage of ibuprofen or aspirin helps block a chemical in your body that causes pain. But check with your doctor, since some people have a reaction to aspirin. And remember not to give aspirin to children because of the risk of Reye's syndrome.

Eat for vitamin E. A regular dose of vitamin E is thought to do a host of good. "It also decreases the inflammation you can get from sunburn," says Karen E. Burke, MD, Ph.D., a dermatologist who has studied the effects Of vitamin E. Good food sources of vitamin E include whole grains such as wheat germ, vegetable oils-especially sunflower and soybean oil-and nuts. If you choose to purchase vitamin E supplements, be sure to read the small print: You should get only the natural form.

Or try baking soda and cornstarch. Another recipe for relief, also from the kitchen cabinet: Mix 1/4 cup of baking soda and 1/4 cup of cornstarch into a tub of tepid water and soak yourself, adds Dr Roth.

Don't be too clean. While you have sunburn, stay away from highly fragrant bubble baths, soaps, colognes and perfumes, according to Thomas Gossel, Ph.D., R.Ph. They may be too drying and irritating to your already parched skin. Stick with mild soaps and don't scrub too hard when you wash.

Give 'em a raise. A burn on your lower leg and ankles can cause a lot of swelling. To prevent that, keep your feet elevated as much as possible— higher than the level of your heart, says Bryan C. Schultz, MD

Read the label. Some ointments intended for sunburn relief contain allergy-causing ingredients, Dr. Schultz says. "Skin that's inflamed is more susceptible to an allergic reaction," he explains. "It affects only a small number of people—but when you have a sunburn, you don't want to experience an allergic reaction besides." If you're allergy-prone, you may want to ask your doctor or pharmacist to recommend a product.

Get homeopathic help. For a mild sunburn, put 20 drops of Calendula tincture in four ounces of water and bathe with it until the pain goes away, says Mitchell Fleisher, MD If the skin is itchy, prickly and stinging, Dr. Fleisher suggests using a mixture of 20 drops of Urtica urens tincture and four ounces of water to bathe the skin. He says you can also take a 6C or 12C dose of Calendula or Utrica urens every two to three hours as needed. If the skin is swollen and bothered by heat and feels better with an application of cold, he says to try taking a 12C or 30C dose of Apis every two to three hours.

Cool with cucumber. The cucumber is often used for soothing burns, notes pharmacognosist Albert Leung, Ph.D. Simply slice open a cucumber and wipe it directly on your skin. Or try applying some mashed eggplant to your skin—it has a folk reputation as a sunburn treatment.

Wipe with witch hazel. In one study, researchers found that witch hazel worked pretty well as a sunburn treatment. You can buy a commercial solution and apply it straight from the bottle in a compress. Or try one teaspoon of witch hazel combined with one teaspoon of honey and a beaten egg white. Or mix one teaspoon each of witch hazel, olive oil and glycerin and give that a try.

Get aid from an amino acid. One study found that l-selenomethionine, a natural amino acid, reduces skin damage caused by sunburn. The study was done by Karen E. Burke, MD. The amino acid is effective applied to the skin and taken orally. Dr. Burke recommends taking 100 micrograms a day during the summer months and 200 micrograms a day for anyone with a family history of any kind of cancer. (Brazil nuts are particularly rich in this nutrient).

Know your SPF!

Sunscreens are a simple way to protect yourself while enjoying the outdoors. They take less than 5 minutes to apply all over your body. Look for the sun protection factor, called SPF, on a sunscreen product. The SPF works like this: If your unprotected skin burns in 10 minutes, an SPF of 6 will allow you to stay out in sun for 60 minutes before you burn. The greater the SPF, the higher the protection and the longer you can stay out in the sun. An important factor affecting how you'll react to sun is your skin type. People of Celtic backgrounds with fair skin burn easily, for example. If you're not sure about your skin type and the recommended SPF for you, use this sunscreen finder:

Skin Characteristics	Recommended SP
Always burns easily, never tans	15 or more
Always burns easily, tans slightly	15 or more
Burns moderately, tans gradually	10 to 15
Burns slightly, always tans well	6 to 10
Rarely burns, tans liberally	4 to 6

Swimmer's Ear

The pain: First the ear feels blocked and itchy, then it becomes red, tender and swollen. Sometimes it swells shut or starts draining a milky liquid. It's also very sensitive to the touch— if you put your finger on the triangular piece of cartilage in front of the ear canal and it really hurts, you probably have swimmer's ear.

The cause: Swimmer's ear is caused by an infection of the outer ear canal by fungus or bacteria. The condition begins when water gets stuck in the ear for a day or two, making the ear canal soggy and vulnerable to infection. Anything that traps moisture in the ear can trigger this condition by creating a warm, moist environment that's hospitable to germ growth.

See a doctor if:

...you have a discharge from the ear, especially a foul-smelling yellowish or milky discharge.
...you have hearing loss.
...you have sudden sharp pain in the ear.

Medication:

Swimmer's ear usually clears up readily with antibiotic eardrops, which your doctor can prescribe. If the ear is too swollen, the doctor can place a wick in the ear canal which will draw the solution into the ear. Antibiotic drops are used for three to five days.

Quick relief:

Blow-dry your ears. Swimmers get lots of ear infections. They spend almost as much time with water-clogged ears as they do with wet hair. "Swimmer's ear may be prevented by keeping the ear canal dry," says Anu Sheth, MD "And blow-dryers make it a breeze." The warm air evaporates trapped moisture. Just be careful not to toast your own or anybody else's ears. Use a warm—never hot—dryer setting on low speed and test the temperature on your wrist after the hair dryer has been running a bit. Hold the dryer as far as you can from your ear and slowly move it back and forth for a few minutes.

Pad the blow. Set a heating pad on low, and place it over the painful ear as long as needed until you feel relief. The dry heat can help ease the pain, says Mark K. Mandell-Brown, MD, an otolaryngologist. Heat promotes blood flow, bringing infection-fighting white blood cells to the area. You can do this as often as you want.

Block the pain. Aspirin or paracetamol can provide relief. (Don't give aspirin to kids because of the risk of Reye's syndrome.)

Try a hydrocortisone cure. "If the ear canal starts to dry out and itch, people may start to scratch and pick at it," says Robert A. Dobie, MD To eliminate the itch, he suggests using an over-the-counter 1 percent hydrocortisone cream. Apply it with your fingers at the recommended dose for about two weeks. If the irritation remains or worsens in that time, check with a doctor about using a more potent treatment.

Try peroxide. Place a few drops of chemist-variety peroxide in the ear, says Laura Orvidas, MD Its antibacterial action can quell minor cases of swimmer's ear.

Everyday prevention:

Pull and tip. After you get out of the pool or shower, remember this infection preventer. Pull your earlobe down and tilt your head. Then wiggle the earlobe to shake the water out of each ear, says Dr. Sheth. This motion helps straighten your ear canal and let trapped water escape.

Play defence with drops. You can also prevent ear infections by using home-made ear drops of equal parts rubbing alcohol and distilled white vinegar, says Dr. Sheth. Put three or four drops in each ear after swimming, she advises. This won't make your ears more moist. As the alcohol evaporates, it absorbs some water that has collected in the ear. And the vinegar helps to discourage the growth of bacteria and fungi in that warm-water medium.

Put a plug in it. "The first thing to do to prevent a recurrence is to keep water out of the ear, so wearing earplugs makes sense," Arnold Schuring, MD If you don't have any or have nothing else available, you can use vaseline-coated cotton balls. Remember to wear these while showering if you are susceptible to water retention in your ears.

Drop in prevention. To dry ears after swimming or getting wet, use an over-the-counter antiseptic eardrop. If used in the "itching" stage, it may also prevent infection. To get the drops into your ear, tilt your head so that the treated ear points upward. Pull the top of your ear upward and backward to coax the liquid into the ear canal. Now wiggle your ear, which helps get the drops down farther. Now return your head to upright to let the drops drain out. Or put four or five drops of isopropyl (rubbing) alcohol in each ear and follow the same procedure.

Don't de-wax. No matter how desperate you are, do not use cotton swabs to remove earwax. This can contribute to swimmer's ear by scratching the ear canal, giving the infection a place to start. In addition, you need to keep the wax inside to protect and lubricate. When you do clean your ears, don't dig for wax, just wipe the outer ear with a clean washcloth.

Keep your head above water. "Bath water is loaded with all the germs from your body in a very small amount of water," says Dr. Dobie. A dunk that puts your ears underwater could create a soggy situation that leads to infection. So even if you've put your body in the tub for a long soak, keep your ears high and dry.

Oil up. Repeated soaking and drying removes protective oil from the ear's tissue-thin skin, which can lead to other problems. To avoid that, put two or three drops of baby oil in your ears before you go into the water, says Jerome C. Goldstein, MD And if dry skin is very severe, a few drops of baby oil or vegetable oil applied with a dropper at bedtime will restore missing oil.

Play with putty. Silicone putty earplugs can help protect infection-prone ears. Make a ball of silicone bigger than the entrance to the ear canal and much it so that it covers the opening but doesn't go deep inside. Don't use hard plugs on tender ears, because they can abrade the skin.

Tennis Elbow

The pain: The first sign is usually soreness or a dull ache on the outside of the elbow joint that gets worse when you grasp something. Eventually, the pain may radiate down the top of your forearm, sometimes all the way to your wrist.

The cause: You don't have to play tennis to get tennis elbow. In fact, about 95 percent of folks with this condition never set foot on a court. Instead, they garden, they type, they turn wrenches, they carry briefcases—activities that require them to repeatedly rotate the elbow or flex the wrist, usually while gripping a heavy object.

See a doctor if:

...your elbow pain is extreme or persists for more than a month, you should consult your doctor.
...if your elbow is red and swollen and you have chills and fever.

Quick relief:

Let your elbow rest. If swelling and soreness have already set in, your elbow needs at least three weeks' rest from playing tennis, says Susan Perry, a physical therapist. And while you're resting it, take some other measures to relieve the pain.

Cool down that elbow. You can soothe that sore elbow by rubbing it with a paper cup filled with ice (fill the cup with water and freeze it) or a resealable plastic bag filled with ice cubes and wrapped in a towel. "Just don't leave the ice on any longer than 10 to 20 minutes," says Perry. Apply the ice no more than four times a day, with at least an hour between icings, she suggests. A bag of frozen peas (or other small vegetables) also works well as a reusable elbow ice pack, says Perry.

Stick with an old standby. A nonsteroidal anti-inflammatory drug (NSAID) such as aspirin or ibuprofen can relieve pain and swelling, says Philip A. Bauman, MD But you should stop taking the medication once you resume a normal level of activity. "You want to be aware of any pain that occurs so you know when you're straining the area," he explains.

Everyday prevention:

Lift right. "A lot of business professionals get tennis elbow because they're lifting their briefcases with their arms extended—and that pulls the forearm tendon," says Perry. If you often tote a bulging briefcase or other heavy object, she suggests holding the case close to your side when you lift it from floor to desk.

Brace yourself. Try an elbow support, Dr. Bauman suggests. "It prevents you from contracting the extensor muscle when you move your hand," he explains. (The extensor muscle pulls on the lateral epicondyle, a bony protuberance on the forearm that is involved in tennis elbow.) "It also reminds you to give the injured area a rest." You can buy one of these devices in a chemist or a medical supply store.

Pick up where you left off. You can ease back into your normal routine when your elbow no longer bothers you. "As a general rule, there should be no pain associated with day-to-day tasks before you move on to something more demanding," Dr. Bauman says. "Give yourself time to see how your elbow reacts. Don't overdo it just because you don't feel pain right away."

Easing the pain with exercise:

Prepare by stretching. Before playing a tennis rematch with your club's top seed, consider using proper forearm stretching and strengthening technique. Here's what Perry suggests: Extend your right arm in front of you until your elbow is straight. With palm down, slowly bend your wrist until your fingers are pointing toward the ground. Using your left hand, gently press the top of your right hand until you feel a tension stretch on the top of your forearm. Without any movement, hold for 15 seconds. Repeat with the other arm.

Now extend your right arm in front of you with the palm up. Using your left hand, gently press as if you wanted to push your right wrist down. But don't move the arm: Hold for 15 seconds, keeping up the pressure. Repeat with the opposite wrist. This exercise stretches the bottom of your forearm, says Perry.

After stretching, try strengthening. After you've stretched your forearms, help strengthen them with these exercises: Place your forearm on a desk with the wrist over the edge, palm up. Grip the handle of a hammer in your extended hand. (You can also use a two-pound can of vegetables or soup.) Slowly curl your hand up, then down, flexing the wrist, repeating 20 times. Change hands and repeat.

Get stronger still with swivels. Swivelling your arm while holding a heavy object is another way to build strength. Holding a hammer in your right hand, sit up straight, with your right elbow against your side. Lift your forearm until it's parallel with the floor. Now, still holding the hammer, twist your wrist 20 times, as if you were turning a doorknob. Repeat with the other hand.

Check your swing. "If you play tennis and have tennis elbow, you probably have a poor backhand technique," says Perry. Instead of leading with your elbow on your backhand, Perry says you should get your racquet in front when you hit a backhand shot. "If you can't find the problem yourself, take a tennis lesson from a professional and have him check out your swing,' Perry adds.

Change your frame. Using a metal racquet? If you've got tennis elbow, you're better off switching to a different kind, says Allan Levy, M. D. While metal frames transmit the shock of ball contact to your poor, beleaguered elbow, other kinds better absorb the blow, he says. "Wooden racquets are better than metal, but you just can't buy them anymore." Next best? "A composition racquet or one made with graphite will certainly help, as long as it's not too large or strung too tightly," says Dr. Levy. Also, be on the lookout for new experimental ceramic racquets, which are supposed to eliminate tennis elbow. But if you're unwilling to part with your metal racquet, slightly loosening the strings should help, says Dr. Levy.

Herbal help:

Put a cap on it. Made from a derivative of hot peppers (capsaicin) and commonly used for shingles, Zostrix is extremely effective at zapping elbow pain, says Craig Hersh, MD, a sports injuries specialist. This topical over-the-counter ointment, available at most chemists, works as a temporary anaesthetic when rubbed on the sore area, he says. "It doesn't work on inflammation—it works at the nerve level, blocking the transmission of pain."

Think ginger. To spice up your heat treatment, try a ginger compress, says Arthur H. Brownstein, MD His instructions: Boil some freshly grated gingerroot, then allow it to cool to a tolerable temperature. You want it to be as hot as you can comfortably stand. Then soak a washcloth in the brew and place it over your elbow. The ginger helps draw out toxins and speeds the healing process, he explains.

Try homeopathy. The homeopathic remedy Ruta graveolens can help soothe a sore elbow, says Cynthia M. Watson, MD She recommends taking a 6X dose every hour while your pain is severe, then three or four times a day as your condition improves. (The notation 6X refers to the remedy's potency, which is indicated on the label.) You will find Ruta graveolens in health food stores and wherever homeopathic remedies are sold.

Hands on help:

Use soothing strokes. Relaxing the surrounding muscles can take some of the pressure off an aching elbow, Dr. Brownstein says. "Gently massage the full length of your forearm muscle from your elbow to above your wrist-not just where you feel pain."

Press the right point. To relieve the pain of tennis elbow, try this acupressure technique: press the outside of your knuckle on the pinkie finger of your opposite hand.

Testicular Pain

The pain: Pain in the testicles or scrotum which may be accompanied by sweating, nausea, dizziness and abdominal pain.

The cause: Testicular problems aren't just generated by errant blows. A long list of conditions from infections to broken internal plumbing can generate pain in the testicles or scrotal area. The damage from a blow usually isn't as bad as it feels. Because the testicles move about inside the scrotum, they usually bounce back, so to speak, without ever sustaining serious injury. When their mobility doesn't protect them and serious injury does occur, the usual result is a rupture or hematocele.

Blows to the testicles are so painful because the testicles are connected to nerves in a different way from, say, your hands. When nerves around muscles get tweaked, the pain is very specific to the location-a necessary function for dealing with the external world. But when internal organs get hit, the pain tends to be deeper and more widespread. in the testicle's case a blow causes pain throughout the abdomen that can be accompanied by sweating, nausea and dizziness. "Remember that the testicles are visceral organs that have migrated outside the body. Pain for them is different," says Durwood E. Neal, Jr., MD

See a doctor if:

...the pain hasn't subsided in an hour or so. See a doctor fast. You might have a rupture or torsion, which means you could be in danger of losing a testicle.
...ice makes the pain worse.

Quick relief:

Ease with ice. Apply an ice bag to your scrotum to ease the pain and swelling, says James Nolan, MD, a urologist. Place the ice in a resealable plastic storage bag and wrap a hand towel around the bag as a buffer to deaden the shock of the cold. Do this for 10 to 20 minutes at a time, for two or three times immediately following the injury. If pain persists or is severe, you should see a doctor. "If you put an ice compress on your testicles and suddenly the pain gets worse, it's a pretty gross indicator that you have torsion," Dr. Neal says. If that happens, see a doctor immediately.

A Painful Twist of Fate

Torsion is probably the most painful of testicular problems. It occurs when one of your two spermatic cords twists in on itself, cutting off the blood supply. These cords normally hold your testicles like a piñata in your scrotum. Unless untwisted, the testicle will die a slow and painful death, swelling to the size of a grapefruit before shrinking to the size of a pea. "Your testicle is like any other body part that needs blood. When the blood is choked off, the testicle will swell, inflame, then atrophy," says Dr. Neal.

Torsion mostly occurs in teens and children, but it can occur in adults. It sometimes happens when your testicles are jostling around during athletics, when you're wearing tight-fitting underwear or even when you're sleeping. But regardless of how torsion begins, it must end with a trip to the doctor. If you think you have torsion, don't delay—you have only four to eight hours before facing permanent damage.

Torsion, condition in which the blood supply to the testicles is cut off, requires immediate attention. "Of course, you don't want to rule out torsion if the pain doesn't worsen with ice."

Get them up. Elevate your scrotum by lying down and putting a rolled-up towel between your thighs, says Dr. Nolan.

Try the hot stuff. If ice isn't doing the trick, then try heat to ease the pain and swelling. Place a heating pad wrapped in a towel or a warm compress on your painful privates. "Heat sometimes helps, like ice, but remember neither is going to cure the problem. You might feel a little better, but you still need help," warns Marc S. Cohen, MD

Go rest, young man. If you get hurt during an athletic event, don't be a hero. Take yourself out of the game and get some rest right away, advises Thomas Douglas, MD By all means, avoid heavy lifting or straining until you are symptom free, and then gradually resume your usual activities, adds Dr. Nolan.

Try a pain-reliever. An over-the-counter pain-reliever can help, says Dr. Nolan. "I usually tell patients to take Tylenol or a nonsteroidal anti-inflammatory such as Motrin if there is only mild to moderate pain as a result of the injury," Dr. Nolan says.

Keep 'em snug. For the next few days after a testicular injury, wear snug-fitting, supportive underwear, if you don't already, says Dr. Douglas. This takes weight off the tender cord of the testicle, he says.

Everyday prevention:

Do a self-exam. Guys should inspect and feel their testicles every one to two months, says Dr. Nolan. Learn their shape and size. Then, if you do get injured or, worse, develop a tumour there, you will be able to recognise any changes that would prompt consultation with a doctor.

Place your jewels in a cup. Baseball catchers normally wear a protective cup to spare them the agony of a foul ball to the testicles, and other athletes should do the same, when possible, says Dr. Douglas. "You don't have to be a catcher. A ball can take a funny hop on the infield," he says. He advises wearing a cup if you play any sport where you might get hit in the groin.

Wear an athletic supporter. Okay, maybe you don't wear a protective cup because you can't run as well with one. You should at least wear a jockstrap, says Dr. Douglas. It may offer some protection. "I think that you see more injuries in guys who are not wearing them," says Dr. Douglas. "it does make a difference. I think testicles are more likely to get injured hanging down in the heat of battle."

Bag it. Since sexually transmitted diseases are common causes of testicular pain, use common sense and wear a condom during sex, especially if you're having sex with multiple partners or are unsure of your partner's sexual history. Putting your manhood under wraps might be the easiest thing you can do to prevent testicular pain-and an unwanted sexual souvenir.

Infectious Fiends

Infections are a common cause of testicular pain in adult men. Lots of things can cause infections, with the biggest culprit being bacteria acquired through a sexually transmitted disease. Here are the common infections that can make your testicles testy.

Epididymitis is inflammation of the epididymis-spaghetti-like tubes inside the scrotum that are coiled up behind each testicle and store and carry sperm. The infection is usually characterised by swelling of the epididymis and feelings of pain—sometimes severe pain. Several things can irritate your epididymis. In younger and sexually active men the cause frequently is a sexually transmitted disease. In older men and men who aren't sexually active, a urinary or prostate infection is usually at fault. And in physically active men, particularly weight lifters, epididymitis can occur when pressure on the back causes fluid from the prostate and epididymis to back up when you strain.

Bacterial infections of the urinary tract, kidney or prostate can cause pain in your testicles and even the whole groin area. Often treated with antibiotics, these infections are sometimes accompanied by painful urination, lower back pain or fever.

Orchitis is inflammation of the testicles themselves. It's usually caused by bacteria and is marked by swelling, heaviness and pain of the testicles.

Sexually transmitted diseases are common causes for testicular pain. The worst offenders are gonorrhea and chlamydia, which can cause orchitis as well as penile discharge and painful urination.

Meet the Cele Family ("Ouch"!)

We'll call these testicular problems celes because their names end with that suffix. The word cele refers to a noncancerous tumour, a swelling or some type of problem with a body cavity, and when it comes to ticking off your testicles, all these definitions can apply.

Except for hematoceles, which occur mostly from physical injuries, many of these conditions develop for no apparent reason. They're just part of the problems that come with a man's plumbing.

Here are the common celes to watch out for.

A varicocele is a varicose vein in your scromatacord, a collection of nerves, arteries, veins and lymphatic channels that run to and from the testicle. "It may or may not be something you notice, though sometimes it feels like a dull pain or a dragging sensation, or even like a bag of worms inside the scrotum," says Marc S. Cohen, MD The feeling often subsides after lying down.

A hydrocele is a collection of fluid, usually in the membrane lining the inside of your scrotum. A hydrocele may go unnoticed, but it may feel like a dull ache or a sensation of heaviness in the scrotum. "Because a hydrocele surrounds the testicle, it may mask an underlying condition," says Dr. Cohen.

A hematocele is a hydrocele, except that the pooled fluid is blood. It's often painful because it's usually caused by physical damage, like a blow to the testicles. You can use a flashlight in a dark room to help spot a hematocele in your scrotum. "Unlike other hydroceles, light won't pass through a hematocele," explains Dr. Cohen.

A spermatocele is a sperm-filled cyst growing on or near your testicular tubes. Most times you won't even know it exists unless you feel it during a testicular self-exam. "Though it's usually not painful, a spermatocele is what causes guys to joke about having a third testicle," Dr. Cohen says. "It feels like a round ball above your testicle. A spermatocele lights up under a flashlight in a darkened room."

Tinnitus

The pain: constant, annoying ringing, buzzing, hissing, or thumping noises. Because it is the real perception of a phantom sound, it can be difficult for the people around someone with tinnitus to understand what the person is going through, says Stephen Nagler, MD "Just because the sound exists only in your head doesn't mean you're crazy. The tinnitus sufferers have lost their silence. It's an incredible loss. It's incredibly real," Dr. Nagler says.

The cause: While this condition can be caused by a build-up of ear wax or allergies, it is often due to damage to the nerve cells in the ears. The damage can come about in a number of ways. With some people, it starts after they've been exposed to loud noises or taken medicine that caused ear damage. Alcohol abuse can also lead to tinnitus, as can an overdose of caffeine. It could also be the result of direct damage to some portion of the ear, such as blockage in the tiny arteries that feed blood to the ears, hardening of the tiny bones in the inner ear, or viral infections that damage the inner ear. Even high blood pressure can be a contributing factor. With so many possible causes, it's important to try to figure out what's causing your tinnitus, with the help of your doctor, says William H. Slattery III, MD

Medication:

More than 70 medicines, prescription and over-the-counter, can cause ringing in the ears as a side effect. The most common are:

Aspirin

Narcotics such as morphine (Duramorph) and codeine

Nonsteroidal anti-inflammatory drugs such as ibuprofen (Motrin)

Antidepressants such as fluoxetine (Prozac) and amitriptyline (Elavil)

Some of the same drugs that can cause tinnitus symptoms are also used to relieve them, notes Michael Seidman, MD, medical director of the Tinnitus Centre at the Henry Ford Hospital in Detroit. Talk to your doctor about trying a different medication if you suspect that one you are taking is causing tinnitus or making it worse.

See a doctor if:

...ringing in your ears (or any other tinnitus-related sound) lasts for more than 24 hours.

...you experience a ringing in one ear accompanied by any bleeding or discharge from the ear.
...you have numbness of the face, balance disturbance, and headaches along with the ringing.

Quick relief:

Mask the noise. Some people with tinnitus can mask the ringing. To determine if masking can help you, try this simple faucet test: Go to the kitchen sink and turn the water on full force. If the sound of that running water makes it impossible or very difficult for you to hear your tinnitus, then wearable tinnitus maskers will probably work for you, says Jack Vernon, Ph.D. You could purchase these maskers from some audiologists.

Let the band play on. Keep soft, gentle music playing in the background. Classical music is a good bet, doctors say. Although it seldom masks the tinnitus, it can be soothing.

Listen to the sounds of nature. You may not be able to have a waterfall, an ocean wave, or a rain shower in your living room, but you can buy tapes of these natural noises. Play these noises softly to help cover up the tinnitus. They are unlikely to distract you. You are trying to avoid sounds that can attract attention, otherwise you will not be able to do something else, says Pawel Jastreboff, Ph.D., Sc.D., director of the University of Maryland Tinnitus and Hyperacusis Centre.

Throw open a window. It's low-tech and simple. If you open your windows, the sounds of the outside world can help distract you from your tinnitus, Dr. Jastreboff says. The rustling of the wind, street noises, and birds chirping provide neutral background sounds that will distract you from your tinnitus but won't distract you from whatever task is at hand.

Play that shower! In the "mask that sound" department: "Some people can't hear their tinnitus when they take showers," says Dr. Vernon. Of course, you can't stay in the shower all day, but you can carry shower sounds around with you. Dr. Vernon suggests making a long-playing tape of a running shower. When the tinnitus gets bad, listen to the tape through headphones, he recommends. (The idea is to find a band of tones that includes your tinnitus tone but is more acceptable to listen to.)

Nutritional remedies:

Mind your menu. Caffeine and several other food items such as alcohol and the simple sugars found in candy bars can aggravate tinnitus, says Michael Seidman, MD Try noncaffeinated beverages including sodas and more complex carbohydrates such as pretzels for snacks.

Dr. Nagler has also found that chocolate, spices, and red wine can temporarily aggravate tinnitus. He advises patients to make a prudent decision about whether to enjoy these foods or not. Though they don't do permanent damage, they can sometimes increase the risk of having a temporary problem.

Helpful vitamins and supplements:

Make it a multi. Take a multivitamin/mineral supplement of vitamins A, B12, C, and E as well as the minerals magnesium, selenium, and zinc. Various studies have shown that all of these nutrients play roles in protecting your ears from damage caused by excessive noise or poor circulation. "I advise all my patients with tinnitus to take a good multivitamin," says Dr. Seidman. Read the label to make sure that the multi you choose fits the bill.

Add a niacin supplement. Niacin also improves circulation and may help tinnitus symptoms. Begin by taking 50 milligrams twice a day. If you have no response after two weeks, you may increase the dosage by 50 milligrams a week up to a maximum of 250 milligrams a day. Dr. Seidman warns that niacin may produce an uncomfortable pins-and-needles or flushing sensation, so you can try a "no-flush" niacin if you have these side effects from taking it. Note: Doses of niacin above 100 milligrams per day should only be taken under your doctor's supervision.

Protect with magnesium. An essential mineral, magnesium, can help protect your ears from noise-induced damage, Dr. Slattery says. "I would recommend that everyone, especially those who already have some hearing loss, make sure they are getting adequate amounts of magnesium." It's not known exactly how the magnesium helps. But when it is in short supply and there's a lot of exposure to noise, the energy stores are depleted in the cells of the inner ear. Those cells can become exhausted, and that in turn can lead to cell damage or destruction. Low magnesium levels can also cause blood vessels to constrict, affecting the tiny arteries leading to your inner ear. When the arteries constrict even farther in reaction to loud noises, the result is tinnitus. If you're often in a noisy environment, make sure you're getting 400 milligrams from food and supplements, Dr. Slattery says. Most people get less than this amount from food, with men averaging about 329 milligrams and women 207 milligrams a day. Make sure that your multivitamin/mineral supplement has enough magnesium to make up the difference, he advises.

Bet on the Bs. Your body needs vitamin B12 to manufacture myelin, the fatty sheath that wraps around nerve fibres, insulating them and allowing them to conduct their electrical impulses normally. That's apparently important for ears as well as the rest of your body.

The same Israeli researchers who found that magnesium helped protect ears also found that 47 percent of a group of 113 army personnel with tinnitus had a B12 deficiency. All the people low in B12 received injections of 1,000 micrograms weekly for about four months. At the end of that time, when their hearing and tinnitus were evaluated, all of them reported some improvement in their tinnitus, including a decrease in loudness.

If your tinnitus is accompanied by memory problems, depression, or difficulty walking, talk to your doctor about having your blood levels of

B12 checked. It's possible that you may not be absorbing the vitamin properly and need injections.

Everyday prevention:

Be smart about your schedule. Because tinnitus can be worse in the evenings when the noises of the day have quieted down, plan to use your noise generators at these times. Extremely high levels of noise, such as that made by chain saws, can trigger a bout of tinnitus or make the condition worse for a few hours, says Dr. Jastreboff. Wear earplugs for protection if you will be exposed to very loud sounds.

Be ready for an MRI. Seniors who may have to undergo magnetic resonance imaging (MRI) for other health reasons should wear earplugs during the scan. Dr. Vernon has had patients whose tinnitus was triggered by the loud noise an MRI machine makes.

Protect your ears from loud noises. Your best bet is to avoid high volume situations whenever possible, advises Maurice H. Miller, Ph.D. But when you can't, at least plan to wear earplugs whenever you are exposed to potentially hazardous noise levels—for example, when using a lawn mower, vacuum cleaner, or hair dryer or when attending a rock concert or wedding reception. And when loud noise comes up unexpectedly, simply hold your ears shut with your fingers until it quiets down.

Skip the smokes and drinks. "Restrict the nicotine, alcohol, tonic water and caffeine you consume," suggests Robert E. Brummett, Ph.D. If you find that it helps to cut out one or all of these, consider a permanent vacation from the noise provoker.

Don't take aspirin. People with tinnitus who take aspirin daily (for arthritis, for example) should try a different anti-inflammatory drug if possible, suggests Dr. Brummett. Aspirin can cause or worsen tinnitus. Some of the other anti-inflammatory drugs can also cause or worsen tinnitus, but not in everyone. By working with your doctor, you can try some of the alternative drugs until you find one that you can tolerate.

Give yourself a dose of distraction. "Getting distracted from tinnitus surely will help," says Dr. Vernon. "Focus on some outside things: Help other people. Join some volunteer groups. Don't retire!" he suggests. "people with tinnitus need to enrich rather than restrict their lives."

Seek pleasing surroundings. Be alert to environmental conditions that lessen the noise, Dr. Vernon says. He tells of one woman who entered a floral shop and felt her tinnitus stop. Looking around she noticed a recirculating water fountain. She put one in her bedroom and has slept well since.

Herbal help:

Try some ginkgo biloba. This herb may help circulation in the inner ear, says Dr. Seidman. He says some of his tinnitus patients swear by it for relief. If you take ginkgo biloba, Dr. Seidman advises that you to purchase tablets with a 50-to-1 or 24 percent strength and take them three times a day. Allow three to six months for the herb to work. Natural remedies take longer to show their effectiveness, he says.

Try homeopathy. In his book *The Family Guide to Homeopathy*, Andrew Lockie, MD, suggests that taking one of the following 6C remedies three times daily for up to two weeks may help control tinnitus. If you have a raring sound in your ears accompanied by giddiness and deafness, try Salicylic acidum, says Dr. Lockie. If you have roaring with a tingling sensation and your ears feel clogged up, he recommends Carbonium sulpuratum. Kali iodatum is a good remedy for long-standing ringing in the ears with no other symptoms, he says. All of these remedies are available in many health food stores.

Beat it with black cohosh. In her interesting feminist herbal book, *The Roots of Healing*, Deb Soule, Maine herbalist, spins the tale of a professional flutist neighbour of hers who had been troubled for years by tinnitus. This neighbour took black cohosh tincture for a few weeks, and his tinnitus almost disappeared. He became a disciple of herbalism. Deb adds that black cohosh and ginkgo are a good combination.

Seek zinc. Noting that zinc deficiency seems to be associated with tinnitus and certain kinds of hearing loss, Melvyn Werbach, MD, author of *Nutritional Influences on Illness*, suggests taking 60 to 120 milligrams of zinc a day.

Avoid these herbs. If tinnitus bothers you, don't take aspirin or aspirin-like herbs—willow bark, meadowsweet and wintergreen. High doses of aspirin may cause ringing in the ears. "I've also seen reports that a few other herbs may aggravate tinnitus, among them cinchona, black haw and uva ursi," says Dr. James Duke.

Temporomandibolar Disorder (TMD)

The pain: Pain in the joints and muscles of your face. Your jaw may lock when you try to open and close your mouth, and you may find that it's painful to chew. The pain and chewing difficulty may also be associated with a clicking sound. It's not unusual for TMD patients' complaints to include earaches and headaches as well as the more common jaw and facial pain.

The cause: Dentists named this painful condition TMD, after the temporomandibular joints, which are little jaw-operating hinges right in front of each of your earlobes. It might be that you've had a defect in the joint since you were born and some lifestyle factor has prompted the pain. Other things can cause it, too, such as being socked in the jaw, for instance, or a head injury, possibly from a fall or accident. And although stress often contributes to TMD, it can also be triggered if you spend long periods with your mouth open (during dental work, for instance), if you have poor posture, or if you grind your teeth. The pain is the facial equivalent of a leg cramp—cramped, blood-starved muscles.

See a doctor if:

...you experience TMD symptoms.
...your ability to function normally is limited—if you cannot open your mouth wide enough to eat, for instance.

Quick relief:

Ice it and heat it. Wrap an ice cube in a paper towel and rotate it over the temporomandibular joint for up to 20 seconds. Remove it as soon as the area feels numb. Next, apply ,moist heat. (You can use a cloth wrung out in very warm water or a moist heat pack wrapped in a small towel for this.) Leave the moist heat on for just a minute. Rub the area gently. If that doesn't give you the relief you want, wait 5 minutes and begin the process again. You may even need a third round for maximum relief. "For some people, this helps for a few hours. For others, it brings all-day relief," says Sylvan Lande, D.D.S. "It depends upon how acute the pain is."

Take a potato break. Relaxing your jaw whenever possible relieves clenching and muscle tension and helps prevent pain. Try relaxing with moist heat. "Boil a potato, wrap it in a towel, and hold it against your cheek for 10 to 15 minutes to relax the muscle," suggests Ira Schneider, D.C., a chiropractor. Just be careful to let it cool a bit first so that you don't burn yourself.

Try aspirin. Over-the-counter analgesics such as aspirin and ibuprofen may help to relieve an occasional acute attack. And they can be particularly helpful when your jaw pain is due to arthritis. But if you find yourself relying on drugs for long-term relief from TMD, you should discuss nondrug forms of therapy with your doctor or dentist.

Try heat for chronic pain. To promote healing, apply moist heat (hot towels or a hot shower) for 20 minutes for mild to moderate pain, says Greg Goddard, D.D.S.

Unlock your jaw. For some unlucky folks temporomandibular disorder has a nasty habit of making the jaw lock in place. "It's usually caused by a muscle going into spasm," explains Ira Klemons, D.D.S., Ph.D. Here's what he suggests you do if this should happen to you: Go to a quiet room, sit down, close your eyes. Relax and count to 60 in your head. "This prevents a panic reaction, which would make the problem worse, and allows your jaw to slip back into its normal position," he says.

Everyday prevention:

Straighten up. If you jut out your chin and hunch your shoulders forward, as many of us do unconsciously, you're making the muscles around your mouth work harder because it's harder to keep your mouth closed. This extra effort puts extra strain on the temporomandibular (tm) joint. Although it may seem unrelated at first glance, correcting your posture is one of the most important ways to relieve jaw pain, says Bernadette Jaeger, D.D.S.,

For correct posture, your ears, shoulders, and hips should all be in a straight line, says Dr. Jaeger. You'll achieve that alignment if you move your shoulders back and allow them to relax. Then lift your chest, straighten your hips, and let your knees relax. In this position, your neck and facial muscles as well as your TM joint do only the amount of work needed to hold your head up. If you're not used to this posture, it may seem uncomfortable at first. And you might want to post some reminders around your home or work area; just a vertical line on a Post-It Note will do the trick. As you work at improving your posture, it will become second nature, says Dr. Jaeger. You may feel an immediate improvement in your jaw, or it might take several weeks.

Open your mouth and say "N." When you work at keeping your jaw closed—actually clenching or grinding your teeth—you'll need to try some tactics to unlock your jaw muscles. Putting your tongue in its proper place can help. Just say the letter "N," says Dr. Jaeger. When you do, you put your tongue on the roof of your mouth behind your top front teeth. In the "N" position, your upper and lower jaws are slightly apart even if your lips are closed, she notes. When you start checking yourself, you might want to set an alarm or a signal on your computer (if you're near a workstation) for every two hours that will remind you to check whether your tongue is in this position. Of course, when you eat or talk, your tongue is no longer in this position, but get used to returning to "N" when you finish.

Slow down. Eating more slowly helps prevent overtiring your jaw. It's the difference between running a mile and walking it. If your jaw hurts after gulping down a meal in record time, take it easy the next time.

Eat smaller meals. For a jaw with TMD, eating a full-course meal can be like running a marathon, so try eating several small meals instead. Noting that many people with TMD continue with a meal even when they have jaw pain, Patricia Rudd, director of physical therapy at the Centre for Orofacial Pain in San Francisco says, "Let pain be your guide, and stop eating when your jaw starts to hurt," she says. You can make your condition worse if you ignore the pain.

Use your jaw wisely. If you are prone to jaw pain, don't crunch on ice or chew gum, pencils, or your fingernails. These habits can cause more pain than you realise, says Thomas R. Feder, D.D.S.

Don't bite off more than you can chew. Taking huge bites of a sandwich can put your joints at risk for TMD. "When you are eating, don't open your jaw wider than is necessary," says Dr. Feder. Cut your food up into small pieces, adds Dr. Schneider. Steer clear of chewy, crunchy foods that may traumatise your jaw joint, he says.

Bite right at night. You may be a jaw-clencher without being aware of it. Lots of people clench their jaws and grind their teeth when they are asleep. A dental appliance called a bite guard or night guard can help. "A bite guard widens the space between the teeth slightly so that the muscle can't clench as tightly," says Dr. Feder. If your dentist agrees that this device may help you, he can prescribe one that will fit your mouth properly.

Stop that yawn. One way to break a yawn is to gently bite down. If you have TMD, the likelihood is that your ligaments are already stretched beyond their comfort zone, Dr. Rogal says. A yawn will just put more stress on them.

Protect yourself from old man winter. "You should always wear a scarf and hat during cold weather," says dentist Barry Kayne, D.D.S. "You want to keep your head and neck as warm as possible in order to maintain good blood flow." With good blood flow, there's less inflammation and less muscle pain.

Drink decaf and stop smoking. Avoid caffeine, whether in coffee, tea or cola. It can make the muscles in the area of your jaw even more tense. Puffing on a cigarette, cigar or pipe forces you to protrude your lower jaw, and that can make TMD pain even worse. Also, smokers are more sensitive to pain than non-smokers, and heal more slowly.

Easing the pain with exercise:

Work out. TMD, like lower back pain, is a chronic condition, says Dr.

TMD No-No's.

The things that most of us do unconsciously with our jaw can spell disaster to someone with temporomandibular joint disorder (TMD). Among some well-practised habits that need to be broken, here are things to avoid. Don't:

Cradle a phone between your neck and shoulder.

Hang heavy bags or pocketbooks on your shoulder when you walk.

Carry children or heavy objects.

Prop your head or chin on your hand for long periods, ala Rodin's Thinker.

Lie on your stomach with your head tilted to one side.

Lie on your back with your head propped forward to read or watch TV.

Grit your teeth or clench when lifting weights or other heavy objects (if you must lift weights, be aware of this!).

Goddard. "When you get chronic pain and you become sedentary, you deplete your own endorphins, your own painkiller in your body," he says. "By exercising and producing your own natural opiates, you reduce the pain that you feel." He recommends low-impact exercises to minimise pressure on the joints, three or four times a week for 20 to 30-minute intervals.

Stretch it out. Here's a simple neck exercise recommended by Dr. Jaeger that will really help ease some of the tension that gets into your jaw. To position yourself for this exercise, find a chair with a hard seat, a straight back, and arms. Put your hands on the arms of the chair and hold that position while you straighten up, making sure that your ears are in line with your shoulders. Now you're ready to begin. Do the stretch once slowly.

Inhale. As you exhale slowly through your nose, gradually lean your head to the left. Try to bring your ear as close to your left shoulder as you can without raising your right shoulder or rotating your head.

When your ear is near your shoulder, hold the position for 30 seconds, breathing normally.

Raise your head slowly and reverse direction, leaning your right ear toward your right shoulder.

Hands-on help:

Do some rubbernecking. Sometimes, massaging the muscles on either side of the neck also helps prevent the tension that can lead to TMD pain, says Dr. Schneider. Using your fingertips, just massage the muscles gently, especially near the jawline, to ease tension in the face and jaw.

Press where it hurts. Use your fingertips to probe for tender spots that may be radiating pain, suggests David Nickel, a doctor of Oriental medicine and a licensed acupuncturist. Press the spot and slowly increase pressure. Or press on and off a few seconds at a time. Like acupuncture, acupressure is thought to ease an ache by stimulating the release of the body's own pain-relieving chemicals. One spot to try is called the Jaw Chariot—it's located above the end of your jaw.

Rub circles around the pain. Massage the muscles of your jaw joint just as you would an aching calf or tense shoulders, suggests Jocelyn Granger, a registered massage therapist. Beginning with light pressure, use your fingertips to make small circles in front of your ears. Massage helps to relax muscles and thus reduces pain. It may also help to improve tissue elasticity and so make your jaw easier to open.

Mind over malady:

Use your imagination. Researchers at the University of Washington's School of Dentistry use mental images to treat TMD pain. Under their guidance, people with TMD do deep abdominal breathing, progressive relaxation, and guided imagery to learn to relax their whole body, and especially their shoulders, neck, and jaw. A mental scene that people find particularly soothing, for example, takes you to a sunlit meadow. There, at the edge of the woods, is a summer cabin, complete with a front porch and—you guessed it—a screen door. That screen door is your jaw, hanging loosely on its hinges, perfectly inert, not giving a hoot if a fly or two find their way into the cabin. "By putting themselves into this sort of scene, teeth apart, lips barely touching, breathing deeply, face smooth and peaceful, drained of all energy, people can experience the feeling of letting the tension melt out of their muscles," says Leanne Wilson, Ph.D., a clinical psychologist who works with TMD patients.

Tongue Pain

The pain: Sores, bites, injuries or other types of tongue pain or discoloration.

The cause: Bites and other minor injuries are probably the most common cause of tongue pain, but they are by no means the only cause. "Your tongue can hurt in the absence of injury," says Kenneth M. Hargreaves, D.D.S., Ph.D. "The lymph nodes under the tongue can become swollen as the result of an infection or even some forms of cancer. The ducts in the salivary glands under the tongue can get blocked." Tongue pain can also be a symptom of allergies or iron deficiency or a side effect of certain medications.

See a doctor if:
...an ulceration in your mouth doesn't heal within 7 to 10 days.
...you have persistent inexplicable sores, especially on the sides of your tongue.
...you have tongue pain and diabetes.
...you have tongue pain and have recently been through menopause.
...you have tongue pain and wear dentures.
...you have tongue pain and take prescription drugs regularly.
...your tongue is redder than normal and looks bald (the entire surface or just the edges look smooth and shiny).
...your tongue is bleeding severely.
...discolouration or coating on the tongue—especially if it's white, curdlike or stringy—does not disappear with regular brushing.

Medication:
Many drugs—such as Darvon (Dolasan) and other analgesics or tetracycline and other antibiotics—change the balance of bacterial flora in the mouth, says J. Frank Collins, D.D.S. That allows certain stronger strains to grow like dandelions in a spring lawn. If you're taking medications and your tongue changes colour or begins to develop a growth, he recommends that you continue to brush your tongue regularly. And ask your doctor if you can discontinue the medication you're on or take something less likely to tint your tongue as a side effect.

Quick relief:

Compress a bleeding tongue. An accident to—or accidental bite of—your tongue can be awfully painful, not to mention frightening. Tightly press a wet handkerchief, face towel or piece of sterile gauze over the injured spot. This will usually bring the bleeding under control without stitches or help from a doctor.

Taste some tea. Pressing a wet tea bag (regular tea, not herbal) against a tongue wound may help the blood clot more quickly, thanks to the tannin in tea leaves. Firmly press a handkerchief or towel over the tea bag.

Bide your time. Your mouth can heal quite quickly on its own because it has such a quick turnover of cells. For this reason Dr. Hargreaves says, "doing nothing will usually work just fine. Hang in there a few days."

Rinse and spit. Gargling with warm salt water each time you brush your teeth can provide temporary relief, experts say. If you have high blood pressure or heart disease, be aware that many commercial mouth rinses contain a lot of sodium. To limit the amount you absorb, says Lawrence Wolinsky, D.MD, Ph.D., don't swallow the rinse-just swish it around in your mouth, then spit it out. You might also want to talk to your dentist about using a prescription rinse containing lidocaine viscous (such as Xylocaine Viscous). "It's a topical agent for the treatment of sore gums, denture sores, and tongue irritation," says Howard S. Glazer, D.D.S., "It can provide short-term pain relief."

Apply an anaesthetic. Look for an over-the-counter medication called Orajel, says Thomas F. Razmus, D.D.S., "Orajel is a topical anaesthetic, so it will reduce the pain," he says. "And it sticks to wet tissue, so it serves as a protective coating for any lesions in the mouth."

Grab your toothbrush. Whenever you notice a discolouration or coat on your tongue, the first recourse is to use a toothbrush on it, says Dr. Collins. "If it doesn't come off with brushing, and it persists for a couple of days, then go see the dentist and ask what the problem is. if it does come off and your tongue returns to normal, just keep on brushing."

Nutritional remedies:

Choose foods wisely. You can easily aggravate a mouth sore by eating the wrong foods. Most experts recommend avoiding anything salty, spicy, or acidic-and that includes orange juice and tomato juice. You can reduce the acidity of these beverages by diluting them with water, says Dr. Wolinsky. That way they won't burn when you swallow them.

Dodge diet drinks. Certain foods may cause discomfort or burning for people with geographic tongue (a benign condition in which smooth red patches on the tongue seem to change location from time to time), Dr. Collins says. "I've seen some people with it who are irritated by diet drinks or spearmint oil in chewing gums," he says. You'll have to experiment with eliminating different drinks or foods from your diet to see if it eases the soreness.

Pain That's Aflame

You might have expected a burning sensation had you sipped from a cup of too-hot coffee or chowed down on super-spicy buffalo wings. But you have done neither, and your tongue still feels as though it's on fire.

You could have a condition known as burning tongue syndrome. "It feels as if you're holding a match to your tongue," says Ira Klemons, D.D.S., Ph.D., "It's a horrible, constant pain."

While burning tongue syndrome has been linked to everything from deficiencies of iron and niacin to menopause, Dr. Klemons has found that it usually accompanies head or facial pain. "At least 70 percent of patients have other symptoms in and about the head and face," he says. And when those symptoms are relieved, the tongue pain tends to go away, too.

Here are a few other culprits that you should be aware of. Note: If you suspect that you have burning tongue syndrome, you should see your dentist for proper diagnosis and treatment.

Medications. Antihistamines, antidepressants, tranquillisers, and drugs for high blood pressure and heart problems can all contribute to burning tongue syndrome. "Tell your dentist what kind of medication You're taking," says Thomas F. Razmus, D.D.S. "You may have to live with burning tongue syndrome because you need the medication, but at least you'll know the source of the problem."

Mouth-care products. A burning tongue can signal an adverse reaction to toothpaste or mouthwash. "A fair number of people have trouble with tartar-control toothpaste," Dr. Razmus notes. "They develop a slimy coating and a burning sensation on their tongues." You might consider changing types or brands of toothpaste or cutting back on mouthwash, using it every other day instead of once a day or more.

Yeast infections. Oral candidiasis—a yeast infection of the mouth—is common in people who have been on long-term antibiotics, says Dr. Razmus. "When you wipe out the 'normal' bacteria in the mouth, the yeast take over, and that can cause a burning tongue," he explains. Talk to your doctor or dentist about weaning yourself from the antibiotic or switching to another kind. Women who have histories of vaginal yeast infections also seem more prone to oral candidiasis, Dr. Razmus says.

Helpful vitamins and supplements:

Get checked for deficiencies. "Tongue pain can be a symptom of a nutrient deficiency, usually in the B-complex vitamins," says Dr. Glazer. "It could also indicate anaemia." He recommends that you ask your doctor or dentist to run tests to rule out these conditions.

Everyday prevention:

Bag the butts. Cigarette smoke is an irritant that can make your tongue pain even worse, says Dr. Glazer. You would be much better off if you quit huffing and puffing.

Maintain your routine. While the thought of wielding a toothbrush near your throbbing tongue may make you bristle, it is more important now than ever. Brushing regularly—the usual recommendation is three to five times a day—will keep your mouth free of food debris.

Fix your choppers. A jagged tooth or a poorly fitting denture can make your tongue sore, says Jay W. Friedman, D.D.S. See your dentist to have the proper repair work done.

Look for suspicious spots. Inspect your tongue in a mirror for any lesion or ulceration. The Academy of General Dentistry recommends that you do this every month or if your tongue is painful. And don't just look at the surface. Check the sides and underneath, too. If you notice something, observe it for a week to 10 days. "If it doesn't go away, have it checked by your dentist—especially if it has no apparent cause," Dr. Friedman says.

A painful sore that can be traced to a specific injury is actually less ominous than a painless one that you don't become aware of until you happen to spot it in the mirror or your dentist notices it during a routine exam. "The more common types of mouth cancer begin without any soreness," Dr. Friedman notes. "That's another reason why it's good to have regular (twice yearly) oral examinations."

Don't blame your teeth. If you develop a sore (painful or not) on the side of your tongue, schedule a visit with the doctor. It could be a mouth ulcer or cold sore. But for some reason, the sides are a favourite site for oral cancer, Dr. Collins advises. "You might think it's caused by scraping against a sharp tooth, but it doesn't have anything to do with a tooth," he says. "Teeth don't usually cause sores on your tongue."

Toothache

The pain: Various types of dental discomfort.

The cause: The most common source of tooth pain is tooth decay. As decay progresses, bacteria invade the pulp—the mass of blood vessels and nerves at the centre of the tooth—and activate pain receptors there. "It hurts when you bite down or drink something cold," says Kenneth M. Hargreaves, D.D.S., Ph.D., "And sometimes it just throbs for no apparent reason."

A cracked tooth also produces pain, but you may feel it only when you bite a certain way. "The pressure of biting opens the crack further," explains Richard Price, D.MD Then there's dental hypersensitivity, which occurs when tubules that make up a tooth's root are exposed-usually by toothbrush abrasion or erosion. When this happens, Dr. Hargreaves says, sugary sweets, ice-cold beverages, and other fare can stimulate the pain receptors inside the tubules. So every meal becomes an oral obstacle course as you try to manoeuvre food and drink past the sensitive tooth without triggering an agonising reaction.

See a doctor if:

...you have a toothache. Seek dental care for a toothache even if the pain diminishes or disappears completely, advises Richard D. Fischer, D.D.S., past president of the International Academy of Oral Medicine and Toxicology. Although it may not be still provoking pain, an abscess or other underlying cause of your toothache could still be damaging your teeth and gums. A prompt visit to a dentist can prevent lengthy, expensive treatments like root canal therapy.

...you feel a sharp or recurring pain in one or more teeth.

...in addition to a toothache, you have bleeding or swollen gums.

...you feel tooth pain when eating or drinking, especially cold or hot foods and beverages.

...you have a toothache in the left lower jaw. "A toothache that is due to an imminent heart attack usually occurs in the left lower jaw and should be brought to the immediate attention of your doctor or dentist," says Dr. Fischer.

Quick relief:

Lay on the ointment. Consider using an over-the-counter tooth pain ointment such as Anbesol or Orajel (Bonjela Gel), Dr. Fischer suggests. Be sure to follow the directions on the label.

Make some waves. Swishing warm salt water around in your mouth can help reduce gum swelling, disinfect abscesses, and relieve tooth pain. Mix a teaspoon of salt into an eight-ounce glass of warm water and use as needed for discomfort, Dr. Fischer says. Swish each mouthful for 10 to 30 seconds, focusing the salt water on the painful area as much as possible. Repeat until the glass is empty. Do this as needed throughout the day, he suggests. If you have high blood pressure and are on a sodium-restricted diet, use Epsom salt instead of table salt, he says. Epsom salts are made with magnesium and, unlike table salt, shouldn't adversely affect your blood pressure.

Keep your mouth shut. Hold a mouthful of very warm water for a couple of minutes or until the pain subsides, then spit it out and repeat if the pain comes back. If heat doesn't work, try the same procedure with cold water. Pop a pain-reliever. Simply taking a 325-milligram aspirin tablet every four to six hours can dampen a lot of tooth pain and gum inflammation, says Robert Henry, D.MD If you can't tolerate aspirin, then try taking 200 milligrams of ibuprofen every four hours, Dr. Henry suggests. Ibuprofen is a potent anti-inflammatory that is gentler on the stomach than aspirin. If you do use aspirin, never put it directly on the tooth or gums, Dr. Henry urges. Remember aspirin is an acid. Keeping it in your mouth for more than a few seconds can cause a painful burn that will only complicate the treatment of your toothache.

Chill out. Wrap an ice pack in a towel and apply it to the outside of your mouth for 15 to 20 minutes every hour until your pain subsides, Dr. Fischer suggests. The ice will reduce swelling and calm agitated nerve endings in your aching tooth.

String it up. Sometimes a toothache is caused by something as simple as trapped food between the teeth. These food particles actually irritate the gums, but the pain can radiate into the surrounding teeth, says Flora Parsa Stay, D.D.S., author of *The Complete Book of Dental Remedies.* So try rinsing your mouth with warm water to loosen any food particles. Then floss or use a water-irrigating device to clean between your teeth. But even if this technique relieves your pain, you should still consult a dentist to make sure other, more complex dental problems aren't contributing to your toothache, she says.

Make a breakthrough. Decrease the pain that accompanies the emergence of a new wisdom tooth by chewing something hard like pretzels. This may help the tooth break through your gums sooner. Unfortunately, this process can occur off and on unpredictably for a week, or a lifetime. Some wisdom teeth never come in completely; if yours doesn't break through in a week or so, see your dentist.

Numb it with benzocaine. "Benzocaine is a local, over-the-counter anaesthetic that works well if there is a large cavity or damage to the tooth surface," says William P. Maher, D.D.S., "It numbs things. The closer you can get it to the pulp, the better it works." Several easy-to-apply, brand-name oral gels and ointments contain this numbing agent. Dab the gel on the entire tooth surface and surrounding gum with your finger or a cotton swab. If you have a visible cavity, get the gel inside the cavity area.

Take charge with charcoal. For quick relief of a toothache, try a charcoal compress, says Agatha Thrash, MD, a medical pathologist. Mix a heaping tablespoonful of activated charcoal powder (which is sold in most health food stores and some pharmacies) with enough water to make a paste, apply it to a strip of gauze and bite down on the gauze "so that the paste squashes around your aching tooth," says Dr. Thrash. "Your tooth should feel better in ten minutes."

Nutritional remedies:

Beware traumatic foods. Most tooth sensitivity is caused by tooth decay and gum disease. But sometimes you can wound a tooth or tear the gum around it by making it chew a particularly hard or crunchy food. If you have touchy teeth, steer clear of hard pretzels, peanut brittle, or any food that requires jaw power, says Charles H. Perle, D.MD

Eat temperately. If your teeth are giving you pain, don't eat hot with cold. "If you do, you are just asking for tooth sensitivity," says Dr. Perle. Avoid temperature extremes, and especially avoid combinations like cold ice cream followed by hot coffee.

Helpful vitamins and supplements:

Load up on minerals. Increasing your intake of calcium and magnesium can help soothe nerves and temporarily ease tooth pain, Dr. Fischer says. He suggests taking 500 milligrams of calcium and 200 to 300 milligrams of magnesium at the first sign of a toothache. Note: People with heart or kidney problems should not take supplemental magnesium. Also, supplemental magnesium may cause diarrhoea in some people.

Vitalise with vitamin C. Vitamin C is one of the essential vitamins that work for the growth and regeneration of normal tissues. "Vitamin C helps fight gum disease," says Joffie Pittman, D.D.S. He recommends that people get 60 milligrams to gain the greatest benefit from it. Good sources of vitamin C include citrus fruits and vegetables such as broccoli and red peppers.

Beware chewable C. Some studies suggest that chewable vitamin C tablets can damage tooth enamel. The evidence isn't decisive. But take a nonchewable supplement to be on the safe side, Dr. Perle recommends.

Everyday prevention:

Choose the right tool. "Use a soft-bristle nylon toothbrush," says Dr. Perle.

A toothache that isn't a toothache

Sometimes you may develop pain in teeth that are perfectly healthy. Doctors call this referred pain, which simply means that the real problem lies in another part of your body. "If you have a dull ache that seems to affect several teeth as opposed to a single tooth, it might be referred from the muscles and joints of the face or head," notes Ira Klemons, D.D.S., Ph.D., director of the Centre for Head and Facial Pain in South Amboy, New Jersey.

One common cause of false toothaches is temporomandibular disorder (TMD). Consider whether you're experiencing any of these common TMD symptoms: pain when you compress your jaw, difficulty opening your mouth more than 1 1/4, inches, or clicking or grating sounds when you open and close your mouth.

A sinus infection can also mimic a toothache, says Howard S. Glazer, D.D.S., "It's called maxillary sinusitis," he says. "It's an impingement on the nerve endings of the tooth caused by pressure build-up in the sinus cavity. There's nothing wrong with the tooth itself."

This condition is especially common during winter, when colds are more prevalent, says Richard Price, D.MD, But it can occur during the summer, too-especially in people who have allergies.

"The patient can't describe exactly where the pain is," Dr. Price says. "If we can't diagnose the problem, we prescribe a three-day regimen of decongestants. That usually clears it up."

A hard toothbrush may actually be too tough on the gums, he explains.

Brush up on your brushwork. Brushing teeth up and down is not the right way to brush. 'This technique can increase periodontal disease because food particles are being brushed into the gums," says Dr. Pittman. Dentists suggest that you start with some up-and-down brushing to be sure that you clean out the crevices at the gum line but that you finish with some side-to-side strokes. "Move the toothbrush in and out along the gum line, tilting it at a 45-degree angle against your gum. You have to be sure to brush the particles of food away from the gum," says Dr. Pittman. Don't forget to brush the lingual side of the teeth, which is the inside area of your teeth that your tongue touches.

Be picky about your paste. If you have had problems with tooth sensitivity in the past, try using a toothpaste specifically formulated for sensitive teeth. "This can help give you temporary relief," says Dr. Perle. Check the chemist for brands that are specifically labelled for sensitive teeth. Or ask your dentist what brand he recommends, he suggests.

Rinse, please. A topical fluoride rinse helps keep teeth in tip-top shape. "It can make teeth less sensitive," says Dr. Perle. Fluoride rinses combine with material inside the tooth to seal up pores, he adds. Dr. Pittman stresses that

fluoride rinses are an adjunct, not a replacement, for brushing and flossing.
Gloss with floss. Flossing prevents decay between teeth and keeps the gums healthy. "If the gums are healthy," says Dr. Perle, "you don't get gum recession and, consequently, tooth sensitivity."
Cease the smoke. Cigarettes have a bad reputation for discolouring teeth, turning them yellowish, but their ingredients may do other damage as well. "Smoking increases the amount of tartar that builds up on your teeth, which causes more plaque to build up," says Dr. Pittman. "When this occurs, you are at greater risk of bone loss and tooth sensitivity."
Desensitise your teeth. Some people's teeth are plain oversensitive. Teeth whose roots are exposed due to gum disease or brushing too hard can become very sensitive. Hypersensitivity can also result from tiny cracks, broker, fillings, or decay. Desensitising toothpaste can help. For 2 minutes, rub a cotton swab dabbed in the toothpaste along the gum line of the sensitive teeth. Repeat the procedure each morning and night for two weeks, then once or twice a week as the sensitivity diminishes. If it doesn't, see your dentist to check for deeper problems.

A dental technique called iontophoresis, involving the application of fluoride, can help, too. The procedure takes about 2 minutes per tooth. Sensitivity is usually alleviated after two or three treatments.
Stop sucking. Hard candies and sugar-coated lozenges are among the most pervasive promoters of tooth decay, says Dr. Pearle. "In my experience, sucking candies are more devastating than a chocolate bar. The solution gets in between the teeth and all over the place."
Stick a straw in it. If you must drink sugary sodas, do so only with a straw and take small sips. Don't swish the soda around your teeth, and you won't cause further decay to the tooth. "Your throat is thirsty, not your teeth," says Dr. Perle.

Easing the pain with exercise:

You may want to exercise...or not. "Most people with a throbbing toothache just want to sit still-and that is probably best," says Thomas Lundeen, D.MD, "On the other hand, physical activity, especially of the aerobic type, may produce enough endorphins (the body's natural pain relievers) that the pain will be greatly reduced." If you can, try a brisk walk or jog. But don't force yourself to keep going if the pain gets worse.

Hands-on help:

Rub it down. Rub an ice cube into the V-shaped area where the bones of your thumb and forefinger meet in the hand on the same side as the toothache. Researchers at McGill University in Canada found that numbing the hand this way for about 7 minutes cuts the intensity of toothaches by about half, apparently by blocking the passage of toothache pain impulses along nerve pathways in your brain. If you don't have ice handy, try holding the spot with your thumb on top of the webbing and your index finger underneath, then squeezing the webbing. Angle the pressure toward the bone that connects the index finger to the hand, says Michael Reed Gach, Ph.D., author of *Acupressure's Potent Points.* He cautions that pressing this point can cause uterine contractions and is not recommended for pregnant women.

Press the point. For temporary relief of toothache, you can massage the sensitive points just above the corner of the jaw on the affected side. Press the spots off and on, for a few seconds at a time, to relieve pain.

Flex your fingers. Manipulating points near the tips of your fingers can also relieve dental pain, says Dean Sluyter, a certified reflexologist. (In reflexology you heal the body by working specific points on the feet and hands.)

According to Sluyter, each finger of each hand equals one or two teeth on your upper or lower jaw—that is, your thumbs correspond to your front teeth, your index fingers to your eye-teeth, and so on. If your toothache is halfway back on the right side of your mouth, you should work the point on the middle finger of your right hand. And if it's a left molar that's hurting, you should work the point on your left pinkie. The points themselves are located just below the cuticles of your fingernails. To find the point you want to work, Sluyter says, rest your hand on something stable, like a tabletop. Using the index or middle finger of your other hand, probe just below the cuticle of the finger that corresponds to your sore tooth. Feet for a point that's a little sensitive or tender. Apply steady, firm pressure to it for 30 to 60 seconds. "You usually feel a sudden shift-your finger or your tooth doesn't hurt as much," Sluyter says.

Herbal help:

Gnaw a knot of cloves. Take a couple of cloves from a spice rack, and place them between your aching tooth and your cheek. They can help soothe the pain, says Dr. Fischer. Let the hard, seedlike cloves soak in your mouth's saliva for several minutes to soften them up. Then gently chew on them—like you would on a toothpick—so the soothing oils within the cloves are released into the area surrounding the aching tooth. Leave the cloves in place for about 30 minutes or until the pain subsides. Continue this treatment as needed until you can see a dentist, he suggests.

Get clove oil. Oil of clove has proven very effective in anaesthetising a toothache. Use a preparation available over-the-counter at chemists, not pure clove oil, which can irreversibly damage nerves. Drop a small amount of the preparation directly onto the sore tooth, or dab some onto a cotton ball and place it over the tooth.

Invite your teeth to tea. Herbal teas made with camomile or echinacea often can quell mild toothache pain, Dr. Stay says. Both of these herbs are available at most health food stores. To prepare a camomile tea, add 2 tablespoons of dried camomile flowers to 2 cups of boiling water, and steep for 10 minutes. As for echinacea, add 4 tablespoons of the dried herb to 8 cups of boiling water, and steep for 10 minutes. After they have been strained, you can drink either of these teas as needed for pain, Dr. Stay says. You can also buy these teas premade in the tea section at your health food store. They may not be as strong as the do-it-yourself version, but they're a little more convenient.

Note: Very rarely, camomile can cause an allergic reaction when ingested. People allergic to closely-related plants such as ragweed, asters, and chrysanthemums should drink the tea with caution. Don't use echinacea if you have autoimmune conditions such as lupus, tuberculosis, or multiple schlerosis. Don't use it if you're allergic to plants in the daisy family such as camomile and marigold.

Picture yourself pain-free. Your imagination is a powerful healer that can help you dampen tooth pain, Dr. Fischer says. To try it, imagine swimming in ice-cold water or playing in the snow. Feel the chill of the water or snow penetrating your hands and feet so that they are almost numb. Now imagine that feeling of numbness enveloping your aching tooth, soothing it as if you were rubbing it with snow until all of the pain is gone, says Deena Margetis, certified clinical hypnotherapist specialising in dental care. Doing this imagery for one to two minutes as needed may relieve much of your pain, she says.

Get homeopathic help. Belladonna, magnesia phosphorica, and other homeopathic remedies may help relieve your toothache, Dr. Fischer says. If you have a throbbing toothache that develops suddenly, try a 30X dose of Belladonna every 30 to 60 minutes until the pain begins to ebb, Dr. Fischer suggests. If cold weather or foods worsen your tooth pain and light pressure on the jaw make it feel better, reach for a 30X dose of Magnesia phosphorica every 30 to 60 minutes as needed. If you develop a toothache after a fall or blow to the mouth, try a 30X dose of Arnica every 30 minutes as needed, he suggests.

Get ginger going. A compress made with this hot spice seems to help alleviate toothache pain, says James A. Duke, author of *The Green Pharmacy.* "I'd add more heat to such a compress myself, in the form of red pepper. Both ginger and red pepper seem to work like the old mustard plasters," says Dr. Duke. They act as counterirritants, meaning that the surface irritation of the ginger or red pepper helps to diminish the deeper toothache pain.

To make a compress for your tooth, mix the powdered spice or spices in enough water to form a gooey paste. Then dip in a small cotton ball and wring it out. Apply the cotton directly to the tooth without letting it touch your gum. If you can't stand the heat, rinse your mouth and try some other remedy.

Mind over malady:

Breathe deeply and listen up. "Soothing music and deep breathing bring about a relaxed state, which can help alleviate some toothache pain," says

Dr. Lundeen. Researchers at the University of Washington in Seattle have discovered that slow rhythmic music effectively reduces your awareness of much acute pain, including dental pain, by distracting your attention and generating pleasant moods and images. So sit back, turn on the stereo, and let the dulcet tones of your favourite crooner chase away your toothache blues.

Shift your attention. Focus on your pain and rate it from zero to ten, with ten being the worst pain you've ever experienced and zero being no pain. Now concentrate on places in your body that feel calm and are pain-free, such as your left foot or your right ear. Keep searching deeper into your body and mind for pain-free points. As you refocus your attention on the calm parts of yourself, the pain in your tooth will fade into the background, says Neil Fiore, Ph.D., author of *The Road Back to Health: Coping with the Emotional Aspects of Cancer.* Use this technique whenever you have pain or worry about pain. If the pain increases, call your doctor.

Ulcers

The pain: Typically ulcer pain is a burning, gnawing or aching pain just below the breastbone that's relieved by eating food but recurs two to three hours after eating a meal. Sometimes that pain is so strong that it awakens you during the night. Ulcer pain is also described as soreness, an empty feeling or hunger, and some older people have no pain at all. Other symptoms include indigestion, heartburn and nausea. For many ulcer sufferers, the first sign that something is wrong is stomach bleeding, evidenced by vomiting or blood in the stool.

The cause: Despite what many have thought for years, anyone at any age can get ulcers. The problem starts when a chronic sore develops either in the protective lining of the stomach or in the part of the intestine just below the stomach, which is called the duodenum. When your stomach's caustic acid seeps over this sore, you will know it by the burning pain you feel, says Martin Brotman, MD, a gastroenterologist.

Science now knows that although stress and diet are not entirely to blame for ulcers. The real cause is a bacteria—Helicobacter pylori, to be precise. It is found in the stomach of nearly all people with duodenal ulcers and in four out of five people with gastric ulcers. (A duodenal ulcer is an irritation in your duodenum, the upper part of the small intestine. A gastric ulcer is on the wall of the stomach itself.) It is pretty tough to avoid infection with H. pylori. In the United States, up to 50 percent of the population harbours the organism. Fortunately, only about 20 percent of this group develops an ulcer. There is evidence that most people get infected as children, and the bacteria just doesn't kick into destructive gear until years later.

See a doctor if:

...you have burning abdominal pain—especially when your stomach is empty—or if you are awakened at night by this pain. Any ulcer should be checked by a doctor.
...If you are coughing up or vomiting material that looks like coffee grounds or if your stools have turned black. An untreated ulcer may bleed, leading to vomiting of blood or blood in your stools.

Medication:

Ironically, agonising ulcers not caused by Helicobacter pylori bacteria often develop from the use of common pain relievers. "The family of drugs known as nonsteroidal anti-inflammatory drugs (NSAIDs) interferes with the body's ability to maintain its protective lining in the stomach and intestine," says W. Steven Pray, Ph.D., R.Ph., a professor of non-prescription drug products. NSAID-related ulcers occur more frequently among people over the age of 60 because they use these drugs more often than younger people do. If you need a pain reliever and you have an ulcer, are recovering from one, or simply want to avoid problems with ulcers, ask your doctor if acetaminophen (paracetamol) would be suitable, says Dr. Pray.

Popularly used over-the-counter and prescription NSAIDs include:

Aspirin, ibuprofen, naproxen sodium (Aleve or Naprosyn), ketoprofen (Orudis KT), diclofenac (Voltaren or Voltacol), etodolac (Lodine), and oxaprozin (Daypro), which are prescribed to relieve mild to moderate pain and inflammation.

Medications like Tagamet and Zantac are "for sure" quick cures for peptic ulcers, says gastroenterologist Chesley Hines, MD These prescription drugs partially block the production of stomach acid, giving the stomach lining a chance to heal. Pain relief is almost instantaneous, he says, "and cure rates are very high. You can expect total healing of the wound in four to six weeks." Side effects are insignificant. Because ulcers can come back, you may need to take a maintenance dose. And because the drugs are so effective in relieving symptoms, you may think you can stop when the pain is gone. Don't: Give the ulcer time to heal.

Your doctor may want to run tests to see if you're infected with H. pylori. If you are, the next step may be to take antibiotics. Studies have shown that the bacteria can be eradicated in 90% of those who undergo "triple therapy" —treatment with two antibiotics plus a third drug.

Quick relief:

Perk up with pink. Over-the-counter stomach remedies like Pepto-Bismol can coat the stomach and provide temporary relief from acid, says Roger Gebhard, MD, professor of medicine. Follow the instructions on the bottle when using any bismuth product such as this, as excessive use can be harmful, he says.

For pain, take acetaminophen. If you have been taking aspirin or other over-the-counter anti-inflammatory medication for pain, switch to acetaminophen (paracetamol). Aspirin and other anti-inflammatories such as ibuprofen can increase your risk of ulcer and irritate the stomach lining, says Dr. Brotman.

Use over-the-counter antacids. These drugs can heal an ulcer, at least temporarily, according to Naurang Agrawal, MD, a gastroenterologist. To help ease ulcer discomfort, try the following schedule: Take two tablespoons of antacid one hour after a meal, three hours after a meal, at bedtime and whenever you have pain. Antacids are safe, although high doses may cause diarrhoea or constipation, according to Dr. Agrawal.

Nutritional remedies:

Eat small. Although you might notice acid pain most when you have an empty stomach, the act of eating also signals the stomach to secrete acid to digest food. To keep that acid at manageable levels, try to eat smaller, more frequent meals, rather than three big meals, says Dr. Gebhard.

Don't hold the onions. As a precautionary measure, add onions to your sandwiches, salads, and other meals. A study in the Netherlands found that the odorous sulphur compounds found in onions help fight the H. pylori bacteria, linked with ulcers and stomach cancer.

Can the citrus. Avoid high-acid citrus foods and juices—they may aggravate ulcer symptoms, says Marie L. Borum, MD, professor of medicine.

Abstain from alcohol. If you like a cocktail or a glass of wine with dinner, scratch it but scratch it from your diet while your ulcer is mending, says Dr. Brotman. Alcohol stimulates acid production. What's more, alcohol can irritate the stomach lining.

Easy on the milk. Dairy products, such as milk and yoghurt, used to be recommended for those with ulcers. It is now known that they stimulate acid secretion, so it is probably not good to use them to soothe ulcer pain, says Dr. Gebhard.

Choose vegetables for your vittles. Fibre and vitamin A from vegetables and fresh fruits may help protect against ulcers. In a study at the Harvard School of Public Health, researchers studied the relationship of dietary factors and ulcer risk in nearly 50,000 men ages 40 to 75 years. Those with a higher consumption of fruits and vegetables were found to be nearly one-third as likely to develop ulcers than men who didn't add those foods to their fare. How fibre is of benefit in the reduction of ulcer risk is not yet understood, but the researchers believe that vitamin A may help protect the lining of the stomach and duodenum by increasing mucous production there.

Multiply and divide your meals. Food neutralizes the stomach acid that causes ulcers, so you may be able to reduce ulcer pain by eating more frequently. Some people have less ulcer upset if they eat six small meals a day instead of three full-size meals, according to Thomas Brasitus, MD, professor of medicine.

Banish the food culprits. Doctors used to supply a hit list of foods to strike from the diet, including a lot of yummy fare. No longer. Now it's up to you to decide.

"The foods that bother people seem to vary with each individual," says David Earnest, MD, professor of medicine.

Those foods might be the classic arsonists such as pepperoni pizza and very hot chilli. "Obviously, spicy foods may bother some people," says Dr. Earnest. But foods that sound soothing, such as milk, ice cream or chicken soup, could be part of the problem. So play watchdog with your diet, and drop the symptom aggravators from your menu.

Go sour on sweets. You may want to cut back on your consumption of sugar, says Melvyn Werbach, MD, a physician who specialises in nutritional medicine and the author of *Healing with Food*. "The more refined sugar in your diet, the greater your risk of developing an ulcer-probably because sugar stimulates the secretion of stomach acid," he explains.

Eat earlier. Ulcer patients often wake up in the middle of the night with gnawing pain in their guts. "Researchers have found that the secretion of stomach acid during the night can be reduced by eating dinner earlier in the evening," reports Dr. Werbach. "Less acid secretion should mean less ulcer pain overnight—and perhaps faster healing."

Snack. Food can either be part of the problem or part of the solution. It's your choice. If you have late-night discomfort, a snack of bread or crackers can serve as a good sponge for stomach acid and bring temporary relief, says Thomas Gossel, Ph.D., registered pharmacist and professor of pharmacology and toxicology.

Heal with honey. Honey has been used in folk medicine for all kinds of stomach troubles. Researchers at King Saudi University College of Medicine in Saudi Arabia found that raw, unprocessed honey strengthens the lining of the stomach. And a laboratory study at the University of Waikato in New Zealand found that a mild solution of honey made from the nectar of the manuka flower, native to New Zealand, was able to completely stop the growth of ulcer-causing bacteria. The reason is that honey contains substances that appear to build up the stomach's protective lining. They also appear to have potent antibacterial abilities, says Patrick Quillin, R.D., Ph.D., vice president of nutrition for the Cancer Treatment Centres of America.

Dr. Quillin recommends using only raw, unpasteurized honey for easing an ulcer, since heat-processed honey doesn't contain any of the beneficial substances. Try taking 1 tablespoon of raw, unprocessed honey at bedtime on an empty stomach. You can do this every day to help the ulcer heal. Continue this sweet treatment indefinitely to help prevent them from coming back, he adds.

Try a healing culture. Yoghurt's healing ability stems from the living stowaways it contains—live, healthful bacteria in every creamy cupful. "These are friendly bacteria that will compete with the bacteria that cause ulcers," says Dr. Quillin. The helpful bacteria in yoghurt, such as Lactobacillus bulgaricus and L. acidophilus, hustle for elbow room inside the stomach. Get enough of these beneficial bacteria in your system, and the ulcer-causing bacteria will find themselves outnumbered and unwelcome.

In addition, a natural sugar in yoghurt called lactose breaks down into lactic acid during digestion. This helps restore a healthful acidic environment in the intestines, says Dr. Quillin. When you have an ulcer, try eating 1 cup of yoghurt three or four times a day for a couple of weeks. When you combine yoghurt therapy with any medical treatment you may be using, you can expect to shorten the course of your ulcer by about a third, says Dr. Quillin. Incidentally, when buying yoghurt, took for brands labelled "live and active cultures," which contain the beneficial live bacteria.

Go ape. Bananas are an old folk remedy for many gastrointestinal problems because they soothe the digestive tract. And studies with experimental animals suggest that bananas do, in fact, have an anti-ulcer effect. One researcher noted that "bananas may be another useful addition to such well-established anti-ulcer foods as raw cabbage, green tea, garlic and legumes."

Follow an Eastern diet. In Ayurveda, the traditional medical discipline of India, the presence of an ulcer indicates an imbalance of pitta, says Brian Rees, MD, medical director of the Maharishi Ayur-Veda Medical Centre in Pacific Palisades, California. Ayurvedic practitioners believe that pitta is one of three basic qualities, or doshas, that determine an individual's constitutional body type. Dr. Rees recommends following a diet that pacifies pitta. That means cutting down on foods with salty, sour, or pungent tastes as well as foods that are fermented or fried.

Helpful vitamins and supplements:

Guzzle glutamine. Drinking one litre a day of fresh, raw cabbage juice throughout the day may help, says Priscilla Skerry, a naturopathic and homeopathic doctor. Cabbage is high in glutamine, a nonessential amino acid. "Glutamine helps the healthy stomach cells regenerate and stimulates the production of mucin, which protects the stomach lining," Dr. Skerry says. To make your own, slice then juice or blend an ordinary green cabbage, says Dr. Skerry. "It's not bad tasting," she says.

Everyday prevention:

Be smoke-free. If you smoke, you have yet another reason to quit. Not only can smoking delay the healing of existing ulcers, it may also help cause them, says Melissa Palmer, MD, a gastroenterologist and liver specialist.

Herbal help:

Feel great with ginger. Ginger is considered an herbal remedy to help protect against ulcers. Take it in capsules, in root form, or as tea, says Mindy Green, director of education services at the Herb Research Foundation in Boulder, Colorado. You will find ginger in these forms at many chemists and natural food stores. Fresh gingerroot is available in most grocery stores. To make tea from fresh ginger, cut a quarter-inch slice of a one-inch-round chunk of gingerroot, place it in a pot containing a cup of water, and simmer it for 10 to 15 minutes in a cup of water. While fresh ginger is safe when used as a spice, some forms of ginger aren't recommended for everyone. Ginger may increase bile secretion, so if you have gallstones, do not use therapeutic amounts of dried root or powder without guidance from a health care practitioner.

Heal with homeopathy. Arsenicum album is one homeopathic remedy available in health food stores that can help burning pain and the anxiety that often accompanies an ulcer. "Take three 30X or 30C pellets when the symptoms are acute," says Dr. Skerry. "You can repeat that in a half-hour if you need to, but if the symptoms don't ease within an hour, then discontinue its use because this isn't the right remedy."

Ask for aloe. Aloe vera gel is an excellent treatment for ulcers, says David Frawley, O.MD, director of the American Institute of Vedic Studies in Santa Fe, New Mexico. He says to take one to two teaspoons three times daily, mixing it with enough honey or a nonacidic fruit juice to disguise the taste if you wish. "Aloe vera gel has a milder taste than the other bitter herbs, although it still doesn't taste very good," Dr. Frawley says. Aloe vera gel is safe to drink, he adds, but make sure you buy a product meant for internal use, not a gel that's for external use only. Ask your Avurvedic practitioner or herbalist to recommend a brand that won't have a laxative side effect.

Ulcers are a symptom of excess pitta dosha, says Vasant Lad, B.A.M.S., M.A.Sc., director of the Ayurvedic Institute in Albuquerque, New Mexico. For angry, hateful feelings accompanied by a burning sensation in the stomach, Dr. Lad recommends drinking a mixture of one cup of hot milk and one teaspoon of arrowroot powder (available in the baby food section of many supermarkets). Or you can make a tea by combining equal portions of cumin, coriander and fennel seeds and steeping roughly a teaspoon of this mixture in a cup of hot water for roughly ten minutes. Dr. Lad says to use this drink when your ulcer flares up or as a preventive measure whenever you're feeling angry.

Lick it with licorice. German physicians have always been more open to herbal medicine than doctors in the United States, and they have researched herbal alternatives extensively. Commission E, the body of scientists that advises the German counterpart of the Food and Drug Administration, approves licorice as an ulcer treatment. This recommendation is based on the medical traditions of Asia, the Middle East and Europe, plus literally dozens of scientific studies.

"Licorice contains several anti-ulcer compounds, including glycyrrhizic acid," says James A. Duke, Ph.D., author of *The Green Pharmacy.* Licorice and its extracts are safe for normal use in moderate amounts, up to about three cups of tea a day. However, long-term use—daily use for longer than six weeks—or ingestion of excessive amounts can produce symptoms such as headache, lethargy, sodium and water retention, excessive loss of potassium and high blood pressure.

These side effects, however, can be largely eliminated by using a slightly processed form of the herb called deglycyrrhizinated licorice (DGL). Commercial licorice preparations containing DGL are readily available in natural food stores that sell herbs. If you have an ulcer, this is the preferred form of licorice to take. "If you'd like to take licorice from time to time as an ulcer preventive, you can do what I do," says Dr. Duke. "When you're brewing some other herbal tea, add a little licorice. Licorice by itself makes a sweet, pleasant-tasting tea, and when added to other teas, it serves as a sweetener."

Yell for yellowroot. If the late Alabama herbalist Tommie Bass's experience with yellowroot can be believed, this herb is worth a try. (Yellowroot is an antibiotic that should work by helping to control H. pylori bacteria. "I personally would try a teaspoon of yellowroot tincture in juice or tea once or twice a day before moving on to the antibiotics my doctor might prescribe for ulcer," says Dr. Duke. If you're already taking anti-biotics, however, do not make this switch without first discussing it with your doctor. Be warned: Untreated H. pylori virus is linked to stomach cancer, so you must take this condition seriously.

Cure with calendula. Calendula, sometimes known as pot marigold, has antibacterial, antiviral and immune-stimulating properties. Calendula has been shown to alleviate symptoms of chronic stomach inflammation, what doctors call hypersecretory gastritis, a condition that has been associated with ulcers. Clinical trials in Europe suggest that this herb may also be useful for treating ulcers. You can make a tea with the dried herb or take a tincture. "I personally enjoy a cup or two of tea made with about five teaspoons of fresh calendula flowers. It's especially good with lemon balm and lemon," says Dr. Duke. If you have hay fever, however, you might want to avoid taking this herb, because people who are allergic to ragweed might react to calendula as well. If you take it and have a reaction—itching or any other discomfort—discontinue use.

Cure with camomile. "Several herbalists I admire recommend camomile tea for ulcers, notably Rudolf Fritz Wiess, MD, the dean of German medical herbalists and author of *Herbal Medicine*," says Dr. Duke. Dr. Wiess writes that for stomach ulcers, "the remedy of choice is camomile. There can be no other remedy more tailor-made, including all synthetic products." Widely used as a digestive aid in Europe, camomile is uniquely suited to treating digestive ailments, including ulcers. This is because it combines anti-inflammatory, antiseptic, antispasmodic and stomach-soothing properties. "If I had an ulcer, I'd take my camomile tea with licorice," says Dr. Duke.

Grab some garlic. Garlic is a potent, broad-spectrum antibiotic. Paul Bergner, editor of *Medical Herbalism,* suggests that those who are wary of pharmaceutical antibiotics for ulcer treatment might want to try a course of garlic therapy. This would involve eating nine raw cloves a day. You can chop the garlic and mix it with any food that makes it palatable, such as carrot juice. Try blending two raw cloves of garlic with one carrot, for instance. "I tried it, and the combination tasted better than I thought it would. It's a painless way to take a couple of cloves of garlic," says Dr. Duke. You can also try whipping up an anti-ulcer gazpacho, heavy on the garlic and red pepper.

Daydream your ulcer away.

The digestive system probably is the most susceptible to mental imagery of all the body's systems, says Martin Rossman, MD, clinical associate at the University of California Medical School in San Francisco, co-director of the Academy for Guided Imagery in Mill Valley, California, and author of *Healing Yourself: A Step-by-Step Program for Better Health through Imagery*. When you have an ulcer, you want to control your stomach's acid production. First, relax. When you've reached a relaxed state, begin to focus on your ulcer. Imagine what it looks like. "Then we play 'Fix the Picture,'" Dr. Rossman says. "What would this look like if it was all better?" So imagine your stomach lining perfectly pink and without holes.

Next, he says, "Imagine a movie of the ulcer progressing to health." You may want to imagine it anatomically: first an ulcerous sore, then more blood flowing to it, bringing immune cells to scour and clean it. Then blood lays down a protective coating over the cleaned wound, and new pink healthy cells begin to grow over it. If you have problems figuring out what an ulcer looks like, look at pictures in an anatomy book or, better yet, medical journals.

Or if you're more abstractly inclined, Dr. Rossman suggests you might "imagine a fire in your stomach, and the healing process would be bringing cooling water down, through fire hoses or waterfalls or rivers, quenching the fire, then seeing regeneration or healing of the tissue." The more spiritually oriented person "might see a healing figure laying on hands, another might see white light coming in from their higher self or the universe."

"The key is to start with your own picture of what the problem is," he says. "Be receptive to the image your mind produces an image of what your stomach lining would look like if it were perfectly healthy, and imagine a healing process to follow through from illness to health."

If you have trouble conjuring up your own image, you might want to try "The Mermaid," an all-purpose visualisation for digestive problems described by Gerald Epstein, MD, in his book *Healing Visualisations: Creating Health through Imagery*.

First close your eyes and breathe in and out three times. Imagine a mermaid with golden hair and a silvery blue body and tail. See her travelling through your digestive tract in a smooth, rhythmical manner. Have her touch the ulcer and see it heal completely. Then have her complete her journey to make sure everything else is in order. When she's finished, breathe out and open your eyes. Do "The Mermaid" three times a day-early morning, twilight, and at bedtime-for up to 3 minutes. Repeat it in three cycles of 21 days on and 7 days off.

Get gentian. This is one of several bitter herbs traditionally used to aid digestion. Commission E reports that the bitter compounds in gentian stimulate the flow of saliva and stomach secretions. Studies with experimental animals suggest that gentian might also be useful in the treatment of ulcers. Herbal pharmacologist Daniel Mowrey, Ph.D., author of *The Scientific Validation of Herbal Medicine and Herbal Tonic Therapies*, recommends using gentian along with ginger, goldenseal and licorice root to treat ulcers.

Pick pineapple. Like cabbage, pineapple is fairly well endowed with glutamine, a compound with experimentally verified anti-ulcer effects. Pineapple also contains bromelain, a general digestive aid.

Risk red pepper. Many Americans believe that hot spices cause ulcers. "The truth is, they don't. In fact, they may even protect the stomach and duodenal lining against them." Says Dr. Duke. Capsaicin, the compound that gives red pepper its heat, has been shown to prevent ulcers in experimental animals that were given high, ulcer-causing doses of aspirin.

Beat it with bilberry and blueberry. Both of these fruits contain compounds known as anthocyanosides. In studies with experimental animals, these compounds have been shown to offer significant protection against ulcers. They help stimulate the production of mucus that protects the stomach lining from digestive acids.

Make it meadowsweet. Like willow bark, meadowsweet is a type of herbal aspirin. Aspirin in high doses causes ulcers, so it might seem strange to recommend it as an ulcer treatment. Many prominent herbalists do, however, among them British herbalist David Hoffmann, author of several good herbals, including *The Herbal Handbook*. The active compounds in meadowsweet are salicylates. Aspirin, on the other hand, is nothing but salicylates. Hoffmann says that while pure salicylates do indeed cause ulcers, whole meadowsweet helps prevent and treat them despite its salicylate content.

Try a rhubarb remedy. In a Chinese study of 312 people with bleeding ulcers, rhubarb helped improve some 90 percent within a few days. "I'd be careful when using this herb, as it's also a powerful laxative. If you experience diarrhoea, cut back the amount you're taking or discontinue use altogether.," says Dr. Duke.

Take turmeric. This culinary herb, used in Indian and Asian curry dishes, might be called the poor person's ulcer treatment. In a good study by physicians in Thailand, turmeric (250-milligram capsules taken three times a day) relieved ulcer pain only about half as well as pharmaceutical antacids after six weeks. However, the antacid was eight times more expensive than the turmeric. If you're low on dough, this herb might be a good way to go, Dr. Duke says.

Try stress relief. "Classic studies have presented strong evidence of a stress component in ulcer development," according to Steven Fahrion, Ph.D., clinical psychologist. Not all researchers agree. But studies suggest that stress increases stomach acid production and decreases blood flow. And if there's anything an ulcer-prone stomach doesn't need, it's more acid.

Many stress relief techniques are recommended by doctors, including deep breathing, moderate physical exercise and mind relaxation techniques such as meditation, yoga, visualisation or listening to relaxation tapes.

For ulcer sufferers, Dr. Fahrion recommends a stomach-warming technique. Spend some time every day in a quiet, relaxed state and try to visualise warmth, increased blood flow and decreased acid secretion in the stomach area. This technique can "relax" blood vessels, allowing greater blood flow to the stomach area.

Urinary Tract Pain

The pain: You need to go to the bathroom. Again. When you go, hardly any urine trickles out. And when it does, it burns. Within half an hour you get the urge again, so you go again—with the same results.

The cause: Bacteria enter the urethra, or urine tube, that enters the bladder, and set up shop. If the infection is limited to the urethra, it's called urethritis. More often than not, the infection travels farther up the tract and into the bladder, which is called cystitis (or, simply, a bladder infection). Unless treated promptly, a bladder infection can move to the kidneys, leading to a more serious condition called pyelonephritis.

Women are especially prone to UTIs. In fact, one in every five women experiences a UTI during her life. The reason is partly structural. Since a woman's urethra is shorter than a man's, bacteria can travel up to her bladder quickly. Even though men are less susceptible in general, their odds of getting UTIs increase as they get older. In men, however, the problems usually stem from some urinary obstruction—such as a kidney stone or an enlarged prostate—or from a medical procedure involving a catheter. In fact, any abnormality of the urinary tract that obstructs the flow of urine sets the stage for an infection. People with diabetes also have a higher risk of a UTI because of changes in their immune systems. Any disorder that suppresses the immune system raises the risk of a urinary infection.

See a doctor if:
...you think you have a urinary tract infection.
...antibiotics don't relieve the symptoms within 72 hours
...your symptoms include blood in the urine, pain in the lower back or flank, fever, nausea or vomiting.

Medication:
While no medications are believed to make you more prone to urinary tract infections (UTIs), you may already be on medication that can help you avoid UTIs. Hormone replacement therapy (HRT) reduces the risk of UTIs, says Dorothy M. Barbo, M.D. The urethra is sensitive to oestrogen, explains Dr. Barbo. Lack of oestrogen can cause the tissues of the urethra to become dry, thinned out, and more prone to injury and infection, which puts

postmenopausal women at increased risk for UTIs. Oestrogen improves circulation in all the tissues of the genital tract and makes them more resilient and less susceptible to infection. This UTI protection is an added benefit of oestrogen replacement, she says.

Quick relief:

Fix yourself a baking soda cocktail. "At the first sign of symptoms, mix half a teaspoon of baking soda in an eight-ounce glass of water and drink it," says Kristene E. Whitmore, M.D., chief of urology and director of the Incontinence Centre at Graduate Hospital in Philadelphia. The baking soda raises the pH (acid-base balance) of irritating, acidic urine.

Drink water, on the hour. Drink one glass of water every hour for eight hours, continues Kimberly A. Workowski, M.D. "Drinking a lot of fluids will increase urine flow," explains Dr. Workowski. "This will wash out the bacteria that are attempting to adhere to the cells lining your urethra. Drinking plenty of water will also help dilute and flush out the substances that are causing the irritation. Drink enough water so that your urine is clear. Aim for at least eight or ten glasses of water a day." "Hydration is the best thing that you can do for a UTI," adds Dr. Whitmore.

Apply soothing heat. To ease the pain sometimes associated with urinary tract problems, place a heating pad on your lower abdominal area, says Dr. Workowski.

Sit, soak and soothe. To relieve the pain and cramping sometimes associated with a UTI, try a warm sitz bath, says Phillip Barksdale, M.D., a urogynecologist. Fill your bathtub with three to four inches of warm water and sit in the water for 10 to 15 minutes.

Nutritional remedies:

Reach for cranberry juice. "According to a study in the Journal of the American Medical Association, cranberry juice can prevent bacteria from sticking to cells that line the urinary tract," says Dr. Workowski. "Plenty of anecdotal evidence says that cranberry juice works," adds Dr. Whitmore. "I know it works for my patients."

Dilute the juice. Doctors caution that in some with urinary tract sensitivity, cranberry juice can act as an irritant. "Some of my patients get worse when they drink a lot of cranberry juice," warns Linda Brubaker, M.D. "That might be because of its high acid content." Dr. Whitmore suggests diluting the juice. If that doesn't help, stop drinking the juice altogether, says Dr. Brubaker.

Nix other offenders. Whether you have a simple irritation or an infected urinary tract, the last thing that you need are known bladder irritants. The most notorious bladder irritants are citrus, tomatoes, aged cheeses, chocolate, spicy foods, caffeine, alcohol and nicotine, says Dr. Whitmore. For certain individuals, anything carbonated—especially beer or soda— may irritate your bladder and make you go more frequently or urgently, says Kallhoff. Vitamin C supplements may also be a problem, says Dr. Brubaker.

Avoid artificial sweeteners. "Artificial sweeteners are among the worst offenders," says Dr. Whitmore. So if you have a UTI, avoid them.

Cut back on alcohol. People who are prone to bladder infections should limit their intake of alcohol to no more than one drink per day, says Larrian Gillespie, M.D., author of *You Don't Have to Live with Cystitis*. (That's one 12-ounce glass of beer, 5 ounces of wine, or 1/2 ounces of hard liquor.) That's because alcohol "temporarily interferes with the brain chemical that causes the bladder muscles to contract efficiently."

Helpful vitamins and supplements:
C up. Take 2,000 milligrams of vitamin C every day for up to three days. Vitamin C inhibits the growth of bacteria, says Richard J. Macchia, M.D., professor of urology. Note: Taking more than 1,200 milligrams of vitamin C a day may cause diarrhoea in some people. If this happens to you, switch to a buffered supplement.

Everyday prevention:
Carry a bike bottle with you. So suggests Jean Kallhoff, advanced registered nurse practitioner at a Urology Clinic. "It's handy, it's easy to carry and it reminds you to drink water throughout the day."

Toss out douches and sprays. Feminine hygiene sprays may irritate the urinary tract, say doctors.

Don't hold it. Even though it might be painful to urinate when you have a UTI, don't resist the urge, says Dr. Barbo. In general, you should try to empty your bladder completely every three to four hours. "It's a wise way to prevent bacterial infection and hasten recovery if you already have one," she says. Urinating frequently helps to eliminate bacteria before they have a chance to multiply.

Have a seat after sex. Women should urinate after they have sexual intercourse, says Dr. Barbo. During sexual intercourse, bacteria may enter the urethra. By urinating, you help wash out the invaders right away.

Wear non-restrictive clothing. Women should avoid clothes that constrict the genital area, says Dr. Barksdale, particularly control-top pantyhose and tight jeans. Clothes with tight crotches put pressure on the inflamed urethral opening, he says, and can force bacteria back up the urine tube. Skirts, loose pants, and knee-highs are far more comfortable and therapeutic when you have a UTI, he says.

Take off that bathing suit. Avoid wearing a wet bathing suit for long periods of time, adds Dr. Barksdale. "Bacteria love to grow in warm, moist areas," he says. "A wet swimsuit provides an ideal environment for bacteria that cause UTI, so you are asking for trouble."

Keep moving. Even though the discomfort of a UTI may make you want to take to your bed, doctors say it is best to stay active since mobility aids bladder function, says Dr. Barksdale. "Exercise is always beneficial for the bladder, and it helps to get your mind off your discomfort."

Clean with care. Keep infections at bay by cleaning the vaginal area with a front to back motion, says Dr. Barbo. Many women were taught to wipe from back to front after a bowel movement, which can spread bacteria from your anus to your urethral opening, she says. Proper wiping can prevent a significant number of UTIs, especially among women who get them recurrently.

Don't shrink. The decongestants that people take for colds and allergies have the power to shrink swollen nasal membranes by constricting tiny blood vessels inside the nose. The problem is that they can also constrict the neck of your bladder. This side effect cuts down the flow of urine and sets you up for a bladder infection. "When there is a high pollen count, doctors will see a wave of cystitis. That's because people are taking decongestants," says Dr. Gillespie.. If you have an allergy, she suggests talking to your doctor about one of the new allergy medicines that do not contain decongestants.

Change your position. Dr. Gillespie says that the standard missionary position for sex can increase the chances of bladder infections if the man is too high up on a woman's pelvis. In that position, he puts pressure on the opening of the urethra, and the up-and-down thrusting motion also drags the urethra up and down. "It quickly becomes sore and swollen," she says. To avoid this problem, she recommends more of a rocking motion. The most bladder-friendly missionary position is "hipbone to hipbone," with the man rocking forward into the woman and then back, according to Dr. Gillespie.

Double-check your diaphragm. About a decade ago, says Dr. Gillespie, many women were being fitted with large diaphragms to more effectively block sperm. Unfortunately, these big diaphragms also obstructed the urethra, impeding the flow of urine, which can lead to a UTI. Don't get a diaphragm larger than 65 millimetres in circumference, Dr. Gillespie advises. And make sure that your diaphragm has a soft rim, which compresses more easily when you urinate and puts you at less risk for a bladder infection than diaphragms that are rigid. If you are using a diaphragm that is too large or too rigid, talk to your gynaecologist about changing, she suggests.

Take out the tampon. Do you get a bladder infection around your period? The problem may be your tampon. "The super-size tampons can compress or obstruct the neck of the bladder, altering the urinary flow rate so that you can't void efficiently," says Dr. Gillespie. The solution, she says, is to remove the tampon before every urination. You may want to quit using tampons and use pads instead.

Pick cotton. Wear cotton underwear. Bacteria grow in warm, moist environments. Cool, absorbent cotton won't allow bacteria to thrive. Cotton underwear is especially helpful if you are experiencing external discomfort such as swelling, rawness, or dryness, says Betsy Foxman, Ph.D.

Skip the panty hose for a month. You may be getting UTIs because you wear nylon panty hose and synthetic underwear, says Dr. Foxman. Switch to stockings and cotton underwear to discourage colonisation of bacteria. If you still end up with an infection, at least you know that your undergarments aren't causing the problem.

Switch condoms. Condoms have been associated with UTI'S, too, says Dr. Foxman. By all means, don't stop using condoms when you have sex. But if you are getting UTIs, try switching to a different type of condom. For example, if you use a spermicidally treated condom, try a lubricated condom instead, says Dr. Foxman. If you have been using a lubricated condom, try a condom with a different type of lubricant.

Easing the pain with exercise:

Watch your back. To maximise your urinary performance and minimise your risk of urinary tract infections, take good care of your back, advises Dr. Gillespie. The nerves that control the operation of your bladder originate in the section of the spine that constitutes your lower back, the lumbar curve. When the lower back becomes weak, she says, the nerve currents to the bladder are also reduced. "Like a weak battery, the current-deprived bladder does not function well. It does not empty efficiently and may leave residual urine, which can lead to infections,' she says. Here are some everyday back strainers to avoid.

Stair-climbing machines. "Stairclimbing machines are not designed properly for the female pelvis," says Dr. Gillespie, "and they cause side-to-side weakening in the spine. I get a lot of women off the stairclimbers, and their bladder infections stop." (These machines don't affect men the same way.)

Vacuuming. Don't push and drag the vacuum with your arm, advises Dr. Gillespie. Instead, walk forward and backward with the machine so that you are not bending over and straightening.

High heels. High heels are fine for some women, says Dr. Gillespie. In fact, some women actually stand straighter when they are wearing high-heeled shoes. But for others, the added height results in an additional curve to the lower back, called lordosis. If you are experiencing back pain, experiment with not wearing high heels, and see if that makes a difference.

Herbal help:

Soak with herbs. Sitting in an herbal sitz bath can help relieve the external burning of a UTI and hasten healing, says Feather Jones, a professional herbalist. She recommends using uva-ursi and marshmallow root powder. To make this soothing soak, boil 1 gallon of water and add a handful of powdered uva-ursi leaves (approximately 1 ounce by weight). Steep for 20 minutes, then strain. Add 1 ounce of marshmallow powder. Transfer the brew to a large pan, be sure the water is comfortably warm, and soak for 20 minutes. Jones suggests doing this once or twice a day for several days or as long as it's needed. "Uva-ursi is an astringent, so it will help reduce swelling, and the marshmallow root soothes irritated tissues," says Jones. You can find powdered uva-ursi and marshmallow root in some health food stores or purchase them through the mail.

Use a tincture trio. When combined, uva-ursi, corn silk, and echinacea tinctures are known as urinary tract antiseptics. Because uva-ursi tincture can be irritating by itself, it's usually mixed with other tinctures (also called extracts). Jones suggests 10 drops of uva-ursi tincture, 10 drops of corn silk tincture, and 10 drops of echinacea tincture. Add this tincture to 1/2 cup of water or a noncitrus juice and drink to help as an antiseptic in the urinary tract, she says. You can buy one-ounce bottles of the tinctures already combined at health food stores.

Smooth on a salve. A salve made from chickweed and calendula can ease the burning of a UTI, says Ellen Kamhi, R.N., Ph.D., an herbalist. To make the salve, put a handful of each herb in a nonaluminium pan and cover them with 2 to 3 cups of extra-virgin olive oil. Warm the mixture over low heat for 30 minutes. Discard the herbs, then mix in 1 tablespoon of melted beeswax per 2 cups of olive oil. Let it cool. Apply the salve to irritated tissue as needed. You can store the salve in the refrigerator for up to a year, says Dr. Kamhi..

Some herbalists say that chickweed soothes irritated tissue, while calendula contains glycosides and carotenoids that reduce swelling. Both of these herbs are sold in bulk in some health food stores and through mail order. Health food stores also carry ready-made salves made with these ingredients.

Pick parsley. Parsley is an excellent diuretic, says Varro E. Tyler, Ph.D., professor emeritus of pharmacognosy and author of *Herbs of Choice.* This herb contains myristicin and apiol, compounds that are thought to help increase the output of urine by increasing the flow of blood to the kidneys. To make a tea, pour a cup of boiling water over a few sprigs of crushed fresh parsley or 1 teaspoon of dried parsley. Let the herb steep for 5 to 10 minutes, then strain and drink. Consume one cup two or three times a day until the infection clears up, says Dr. Kamhi. (Using parsley as a vegetable condiment during pregnancy is fine, but don't use it as a tea in high amounts, she cautions.)

For convenience, consider cranberry capsules. Cranberry also comes in capsule form. And, like cranberries, the capsules are safe for pregnant women, says Eric Yarnell, N.D., a naturopathic doctor, who is on the board of the Botanical Medicine Academy. He suggests taking two or three capsules containing at least 400 milligrams each of cranberry extract every day until the infection clears up.

Make a berry tea. If at all possible, Dr. Kamhi prefers a tea made from whole cranberries. She recommends purchasing fresh, organically grown berries (available in health food stores or in the organic food section of supermarkets) in the fall, when they're harvested. "Stock up, put them in plastic bags, and pop them into the freezer," says Dr. Kamhi. "You'll have them all year long." To make fresh cranberry tea, place a handful of berries in a pot and cover them with water. Gently simmer the berries (don't boil) for 30 to 45 minutes. When the berries are white and the water is bright red, discard the berries, let the tea cool, and drink. If the flavour is too tart, add a drop or two of stevia as a sweetener. Drink three to four cups a day until the infection clears up. If you can't find fresh cranberries, use the dried variety, says Dr. Kamhi. Fill a tea ball with dried cranberries, place the ball in a cup of boiling water, steep for 20 minutes, and drink. Consume three to four cups a day during an infection.

Make tea with a triple punch. Besides using cranberries, you might want to try drinking tea made with equal parts of buchu, corn silk, and couch grass (also known as triticum or dog grass), recommends Douglas Schar, a practising medical herbalist in London, editor of the *British Journal of Phytotherapy,* and author of *Backyard Medicine Chest.* To make the tea, add 1 teaspoon of each herb to 1 cup of boiling water and steep for 10 to 15 minutes. Drink three cups a day until the unpleasant sensations have subsided. "This tea is especially good for a sudden, painful bladder infection," says Schar. "You'll feel better in a matter of days." Buchu contains pulegone, a volatile oil that kills some bacteria in the urine, while the corn silk acts as a diuretic, says Schar. The couch grass contains anti-inflammatory substances that help to soothe burning and inflammation. (Do not take buchu while pregnant.)

Build resistance with echinacea. First used by Native Americans, echinacea has been shown in clinical tests to stimulate the immune system. Researchers aren't sure why echinacea works, but they think it boosts the production of interferon and properdin, two protein substances that resist viruses and bacteria. Some people take echinacea in tea or tincture form, but Schar doesn't recommend the tincture, as he says it tastes "real bad." Some people like the tea, and some people don't. Thus, you may prefer to take capsules. Schar suggests taking two 500-milligram capsules of pure echinacea root three times a day for three to six months to end the cycle of repeated UTIs.

Heal with goldenseal. "Goldenseal 'is an excellent mucous membrane tonic," says Schar. It's also a powerful antimicrobial agent, and herbalists have used it for the last century to treat infections. Schar recommends taking four 500-milligram capsules of goldenseal root a day. It can take up to three months for the herb's healing properties to take full effect, he notes, but during that time, you're likely to get fewer UTIs that pass more quickly. Do not take goldenseal if you are pregnant, however.

Varicose Veins

The pain: Enlarged, twisted, and swollen veins that usually appear just under the skin of the inner calves or on the back of the legs, but can also appear on the thighs. Varicose veins aren't just a cosmetic problem. They can make your legs swell more easily than normal or make them feel heavy and tired. They can also aggravate muscle cramps.

The cause: The heart can pump blood to the toes in one beat, but it needs to pump a full five beats before the blood can make the return trip up your legs. The constant uphill battle against the force of gravity eventually takes its toll on our veins. When you have varicose veins, it means that the blood returning to your heart is extremely sluggish. Within the veins, the valvelike mechanisms that help maintain upward blood flow aren't doing their job any more. It may get to the point where blood is simply pooling in the veins rather than moving along as it should. Such blood vessel damage can set the stage for thrombosis, or clotting.

See a doctor if:

...you think you have varicose veins.
...your legs develop a brownish, purplish discolouration with itching or scaling, particularly around the ankles.
...you notice signs of possible clot in the vein: a hard lump on the vein that doesn't disappear even after you elevate your leg, localised pain and swelling with redness, or a burning feeling in the leg
...you develop new symptoms or aching and fatigue of your legs suddenly get worse.

Medication:

Smaller varicose veins can be removed with an office procedure called sclerotherapy. A solution is injected into the vein, which irritates the lining, causing it to contract and shrivel. Eventually, the vein closes down entirely and the scar tissue it leaves behind is re-absorbed into the body. In severe cases, you may need surgery to partially or totally remove a bulging vein. Treatment with lasers can help erase the smallest offenders. Talk to a dermatologist or vascular surgeon who specialises in treating varicose veins to discuss your options.

Quick relief:

Give them some support. Graduated compression stockings will give your circulation a boost and reduce the circumference of the veins. "Like a stretched-out sock, veins become stretched out from pooling blood, and they lose their ability to contract," says Kevin Welch, MD, a dermatologist. "Put compression stockings on before you get out of bed in the morning and wear them all day." The compression level of graduated stockings, which is measured in millimetres of mercury (mmHg) is greatest at the ankle and decreases gradually up the length of the leg to promote blood flow toward the heart. Wear moderate compression stockings rated in the 15 to 20 mm Hg range, or labelled Grade 1 or 2. They are available at chemists.

Do not substitute ordinary support pantyhose for graduated compression stockings. "Support hose is a misnomer," says Dr. Welch. "Support hose provide uniform compression from foot to thigh. Since the upper part of the leg is so much larger, this creates a binding atmosphere. The compression at the top of the stocking may actually be greater at the thigh or calf than the ankle, which can force blood down the leg instead of toward the heart."

Take two aspirin every day. "One of the easiest ways to get relief is to take half an aspirin every morning and every night," says Luis Navarro, MD, director of the Vein Treatment Centre at Mount Sinai School of Medicine. "Not only does aspirin help relieve any pain you might have from varicose veins, it also increases blood mobility."

Put gravity on your side. Elevate your legs above the level of your heart three or four times a day for 5 to 10 minutes, says Gabriel Goren, MD, a vascular surgeon. Prop your feet up on pillows or sit in a reclining chair with your feet up. Getting gravity on your side, you will help drain excess fluid from the legs and relieve discomfort. "The gravitational drainage will reduce elevated venous pressure and will ease the discomfort," he says.

Nutritional remedies:

Fill up on fibre. Straining to have a bowel movement puts a lot of pressure on the veins of your lower body, and over time, it can promote the development of varicose veins in your legs, says Decker Weiss, N.MD, a naturopathic doctor. "I've had patients who, once they have their constipation problem under control, see their varicose veins improve, especially the haemorrhoid type," he says. To prevent constipation, it's best to eat foods that contain a mixture of fibre, such as beans, fruits and vegetables, and whole grains. If you also need to take a fibre supplement, find one that contains both soluble and insoluble fibres, Dr. Weiss advises. Whatever kind of fibre you're getting, also make sure you drink at least eight glasses of water and other fluids every day.

Enjoy some juice. Fresh fruit juices can be very helpful for those with varicose veins, says Cherie Calbom, M.S., a certified nutritionist and co-author of *Juicing for Life.* Dark-coloured berries such as cherries, blackberries and blueberries contain anthocyanins and proanthocyanidins, pigments that strengthen the walls of the veins, Calbom explains. She adds that pineapples are rich in the enzyme bromelain, which helps prevent blood clots, an uncommon but serious complication of varicose veins.

"Juicing provides these nutrients in much higher concentrations than you can get by just eating the fruits, " says Calbom. She suggests drinking eight ounces of fresh berry or pineapple juice, alone or diluted with another fruit juice, once or twice a day for maximum benefit.

Watch your salt intake. Salt in the diet contributes to swelling, according to Dr. Navarro. "So if you have a propensity toward swelling, you're better off restricting the amount of salt you consume." Avoid salting your meals, and look for low-salt or sodium-free packaged products. And watch out for fast food that's usually high in salt.

Helpful vitamins and supplements:

Break up bumps with bromelain. Bromelain, an enzyme that's extracted from the core of green pineapple, can help prevent the development of the hard and lumpy skin found around varicose veins, says Joseph E. Pizzorno Jr., N.D., president of Bastyr University of Naturopathic Medicine. People with varicose veins have a decreased ability to break down fibrin, one of the compounds involved in formation of blood clots and tissue scarring, Dr. Pizzorno says. In healthy veins, a substance called plasminogen activator helps break down fibrin, but veins that are varicose have decreased levels of plasminogen activator.

Bromelain acts similarly to plasminogen activator to help break down fibrin, so it's particularly helpful for varicose veins, says Dr. Pizzorno. It can also help people who have a tendency to develop phlebitis, or blood clots in leg veins. Try taking 500 to 750 milligrams of bromelain on an empty stomach two or three times per day, Dr. Pizzorno recommends. If you take it with meals, it simply works as a digestive enzyme and is used up in your intestines rather than passed along to your bloodstream.

Bolster with bioflavonoids. Even if you seem destined to get varicose veins, the powerful antioxidant and anti-inflammatory properties of bioflavonoids might help make the walls of your veins stronger, says Stephen T. Sinatra, MD, a cardiologist.

"Bioflavonoids can help protect the structural integrity of the vascular walls and help prevent free radical stress inside the vessel," he says. Two bioflavonoids that seem to promote vascular health are grapeseed and pycnogenol, commonly called oligomeric proanthocyanidins or OPC's. In one study, OPC's demonstrated powerful antioxidant activity by being able to trap the free-roaming, unstable molecule that can do so much cell damage. In fact, the antioxidant ability of OPC's was found to be many times greater than that of vitamin C and vitamin E. If you have varicose veins, you should take about 200 to 300 milligrams of grapeseed extract or pycnogenol a day with meals for at least six months, says Dr. Sinatra. If your discomfort improves, you can continue taking the supplement indefinitely.

C an improvement. Vitamin C is needed to help your body manufacture two important connective tissues, collagen and elastin. "Both of these tissues help to keep vein walls strong and flexible," says Dr. Pizzorno. Vitamin C may be especially important if you bruise easily or have broken capillaries, which may show up on your skin as tiny spider veins, he says. He recommends 500 to 3,000 milligrams of vitamin C daily.

Beat it with B's. Some doctors also recommend a combination of B vitamins, especially to people who have a history of blood clots. It's especially important to make sure that you're getting enough of the B vitamins folic acid, B12, and B6, Dr. Weiss says.

"I recommend B vitamins to all my patients with heart or circulatory problems as part of a high-potency multivitamin," says Dr. Weiss. If people have absorption problems, he will recommend B12 injections. Otherwise, you can take B-vitamin supplements in pill or capsule form.

Ease with E. Sometimes, vitamin E is also recommended for varicose veins because it may help to reduce the chance of blood clots forming in veins, Dr. Pizzorno says. "Vitamin E helps keep platelets, blood components involved in clotting, from sticking together and from adhering to the sides of blood vessel walls," he says. Research shows that reducing platelet stickiness with vitamin E may help people who are at particularly high risk for blood clotting problems, such as those with Type I (insulin-dependent) diabetes. Taking 200 to 600 international units a day should be sufficient, Dr. Pizzorno says. If you've had bleeding problems, however, or are taking prescription anticoagulants to help prevent clotting, get your doctor's okay before you take vitamin E.

Everyday prevention:

Watch your weight. Excess weight, especially in the abdominal area, presses on the veins in the upper thigh and groin, causing them to weaken. Circulation slows, resulting in increased pressure in the veins. If you are more than 15 percent over your ideal body weight, chances are the excess pounds are putting stress on your veins in one way or another, says J. A. Olivencia, MD, a vascular surgeon. "When people are overweight, they become less active. Their clothing may be tight and constrict blood flow." And that constriction will only make varicose veins worse.

Shower at night. Your morning shower may be a lifelong habit, but when you have varicose veins, the wake-up cascade of hot water is an invitation for discomfort early in the day. "At night, during sleep in the horizontal position, even bad veins can regain a more narrow shape," says Dr. Goren. "Heat in the early hours of the morning will immediately distend the veins." This will make them more prominent and more uncomfortable for you.

Stay out of the hot tub. People with varicose veins should avoid soaking in a hot tub or whirlpool bath no matter what time of day it is. The hot water

---

When to coddle your veins

If you already have varicose veins, exercise won't help, and it might make them worse, says Brian McDonagh, MD, founder and medical director of the Vein Clinics of America. When you start walking or cycling, your calf muscles pumping action generates even more turbulent blood flow in your varicose veins, distorting and distending them further. This is why young, athletic males have some of the largest varicose veins.

Although Dr. McDonagh still favours exercise, it's because it benefits your overall health, not because it helps your veins. Comfortably snug support stockings, worn either before or after your workout, may help minimise the negative impact of exercise on varicose veins. If you do strength-training exercises, use smaller weights and do more repetitions to trait without aggravating a vein problem. If you run, run on dirt, grass or cinders rather than asphalt. Remember that once you have varicose veins, your best bet is to go to a clinic that specialises in treating them.

---

just makes your veins swell, says Dr. Goren. Also avoid very hot baths or showers.

Sit when you can. "Don't sit if you can walk, and don't stand if you can sit," advises Deborah Foley, MD, an internist. "If you have a job that requires you to stand for long periods of time, try to work it so that you can sit down once in a while." You should also try to walk around for at least ten minutes every 1 1/2 hours.

Don't be cross. Crossing your legs puts pressure on your veins and ultimately blocks the flow of blood in your legs.

Seek snug footwear. Your shoes can provide an extra measure of support in the foot and ankle area, which is just where you need it, Dr. Foley says. "You want the highest level of compression at the lowest part of your body," she notes. Just be sure your shoes aren't so snug that they actually make your feet hurt.

Stop smoking. Researchers have found that varicose veins are more common in smokers because puffing away interferes with the way the body regulates fibrin, a blood-clotting protein.

Avoid high heels. High heels increase the pressure in the veins and reduce the ability of your calf muscle to pump. "Wearing heels occasionally will not cause problems," says Dee Anna Glaser, MD "If worn regularly, though, high heels alter your ability to contract your calf muscles." That, in turn, makes it harder to pump blood back up to your heart.

Don't toast your tootsies. Ah, the heat from a warm, cozy fire. Doesn't it feel good on a pair of cold feet on a cold winter night? That soothing feeling, however, is short-lived. Heat dilates the blood vessels and encourages additional fluid retention and discomfort in the veins, says Dr. Goren. The same principal applies to any heat source at the floor level. Close heating registers or reposition furniture so that heat is not blowing on your feet while you are sitting down, says Dr. Olivencia.

Pull panty hose on while you're still in bed. Whether you use regular support hose or compression support hose, "keep the stockings by your bed at night and put them on before you get out of bed in the morning, before gravity pulls blood through the valves to pool," says Toby Shaw, MD

Free your thighs. Avoid garments that constrict at the groin. Tight girdles and regular panty hose—which do not have the graduated, structured give of support hose—put pressure on leg veins and encourage them to stretch. Tilt your bed. One simple remedy is to place bricks or blocks of wood under your bed's footboard, so your feet will be raised a few inches, suggests Andrew Lazar, MD, assistant professor of clinical dermatology. But check with your doctor first if you have a history of heart trouble or difficulty breathing during the night.

Hold the hormones. "The hormones of pregnancy are the greatest kick-start to vein disease," says Brian McDonagh, MD, founder and medical director of Vein Clinics of America. "Then after pregnancy, when hormone levels decrease, we see improvement." This is one of the indicators that hormones play a role in bringing out varicose and spider veins. So if you are considering hormone-replacement therapy, be aware that high levels of hormones may increase your chances of getting varicose veins. Birth control pills are another source of high hormone doses.

Shun the sun. Sunburn on your legs breaks down the supporting fibre of the veins and makes them less elastic. Just sunbathing, for that matter, dilates veins and promotes blood pooling.

Go for gotu kola. The herb gotu kola is particularly good for varicose veins and also has a reputation as an anti-ageing herb, says Roberta Bourgon, N.D., a naturopathic doctor. This herb seems to be able to strengthen the sheath of tissue that wraps around veins, reduce formation of clogging scar tissue, and improve blood flow through affected limbs. "It's really more of a preventive measure than a cure," says Dr. Bourgon. "If you know you're prone to varicose veins, this can help you slow down or perhaps prevent the problem." Even if it doesn't help the varicosity itself, gotu kola often improves the symptoms of varicose veins, including pain, numbness, and leg cramps, Dr. Bourgon says. Try taking 60 to 120 milligrams a day in capsules, she says.

Run hot and cold. After eliminating contributing factors such as obesity, constipation and clothing that has tight waistbands, try alternating hot and cold baths to stimulate circulation in the legs, suggests Agatha Thrash, MD, a medical pathologist. Use two buckets or plastic wastebaskets tall enough to submerge the legs up to the knees. Fill one container with enough comfortably hot water to cover the lower legs and the other container with the same amount of cold water. Soak your feet and legs in the hot water for about three minutes, then immerse them in the cold water for about 30 seconds.

Repeat three times, finishing with the cold soak. You'll need to use this treatment once a day for at least one month to see results, according to Dr. Thrash. if you have diabetes, you should use warm (not hot) water, she adds.

Easing the pain with exercise:

Flex those muscles. Don't stand or sit in one place for more than a few minutes at a time. "The blood in your weakened veins will pool. The pressure will increase and fluid will accumulate in the ankles and calves," says Dr. Goren. To prevent blood from pooling in the veins when you are sitting, wiggle your toes and flex your feet and ankles several times every 10 minutes to work the leg muscles that help pump the blood back to the heart. If you are at work or travelling, get up and walk around at least once an hour for 3 to 4 minutes. If you have to stand in one place, get the calf pump moving by moving up and down on your tiptoes.

Take a walk. Walking reduces the pressure in your veins by one-third. "Staying active will set your calf muscle pump in motion. Blood will be pushed uphill toward the heart, and the pressure in your veins should drop," says Dr. Goren. The improved muscle tone that you develop as a result of regular walking will also improve circulation. "A weak muscle doesn't pump as well as a strong one," says Dr. Olivencia. "A walking program is the simplest and most effective way to make the calf muscle pump work more efficiently." Slowly work up to one hour of walking, three times a week.

Build up calf strength. Dr. Navarro also recommends strength training, using weights or exercise bands to provide resistance. Strength training exercises that beef up your calf muscles are most likely to help prevent varicose veins, he says.

Invert your legs with yoga. Yoga poses that position your legs above your head can temporarily reverse the pooling of blood associated with varicose veins, says Carrie Angus, MD, medical director for the Centre for Health and Healing at the Himalayan International Institute of Yoga Science and Philosophy in Honesdale, Pennsylvania.

"Lie on the floor on your back, with your legs and feet raised up against a wall, for about five minutes," suggests Dr. Angus. "With this pose, gravity helps to push the blood back to the heart." To make this pose more comfortable, Dr. Angus suggests putting a pillow under your hips. Repeat once or twice a day. (if you have a history of back trouble, you may want to check with your doctor before trying this pose.)

Herbal help:

Round up some horse chestnut. In a study, people with varicose veins were divided into two groups. One group took 50 milligrams a day of horse chestnut. The other group used compression stockings, which are commonly recommended by doctors as a way to relieve the discomfort of varicose veins. After 12 weeks, researchers found that both groups had an almost identical reduction of swelling in their legs.

Horse chestnut contains compounds called bioflavonoids. When you take this herb, the bioflavonoids seem to move into the bulging varicose veins, says Dr. Weiss. "I'd recommend it as a first-line treatment along with correcting constipation," he says.

Horse chestnut seed extract—the supplement form that's used—has anti-edema properties, which means that it helps prevent the build-up of fluids. It also helps prevent inflammation, and it can decrease fluid leakage from capillaries by reducing the number and size of the small pores in the capillary walls. Horse chestnut also improves the tone of blood vessels so veins become more elastic. With this boost in elasticity, they can contract more strongly and relax better, Dr. Weiss says.

How much you'll need to take depends on what kind of horse chestnut you buy. If you get a standardised extract of horse chestnut seed, use an amount that provides you with a daily dose of 50 milligrams of escin, one of the active ingredient, Dr. Weiss says. Reduce the dose after symptoms improve, he advises. There have been some reports of side effects such as itching, nausea, and stomach discomfort. If you experience these side effects, simply stop taking horse chestnut for a while until the symptoms go away. Horse chestnut may also interfere with the action of other drugs, however, especially blood thinners such as warfarin (Coumadin), so check with your doctor before you try this remedy. Horse chestnut is best used as a minor ingredient in an overall formula that includes other herbs, says herbalist Betzy Bancroft, a professional member of the American Herbalists Guild. Look for such formulas that contain some horse chestnut; they are most often available through mail order. Don't take horse chestnut during pregnancy or while breastfeeding.

Make your own "vein tonic." Although it's almost impossible to reverse varicose veins once they're established, this make-at-home formula can prevent them from getting any worse, Bancroft notes. Using herbal tinctures, combine 2 parts ginkgo, 1 part ginger, and 1 part cinnamon. Take 30 drops of the tincture, mixed with another liquid such as tea, juice, or water, three times a day, recommends Bancroft. Take this remedy for about four weeks, then re-evaluate your condition. Ginkgo is highly effective in the treatment of various blood vessel disorders, Bancroft says. Ginger benefits the cardiovascular system, and as a bonus, it helps lower cholesterol.

Try butcher's broom. The herb butcher's broom is high in rutin, a component of vitamin C that actually helps tone up vein walls, says Claudia Wingo, R.N., a member of the National Herbalists Association of Australia. She adds this herb to a varicose vein formula that may also help improve the function of the circulatory system. Other herbs in the formula include cramp bark, which is high in flavonoids; buckwheat, which is also rich in rutin; ginkgo, which may improve peripheral circulation; hawthorn, believed to strengthen blood vessels and heart muscle; rosemary, a circulatory stimulant, and butcher's broom, which is thought to constrict blood vessels and is used extensively in Europe for varicose veins and haemorrhoids.

Make this varicose vein tonic by combining 1 part each of hawthorn, ginkgo, cramp bark, and buckwheat with one half part butcher's broom. Add 3 to 4 drops of food-grade rosemary essential oil per 8 ounces of tincture. Take two millilitres three times a day for two months, then gradually decrease the dosage. This tincture tastes bitter; try mixing it with 8 ounces of water or orange juice to dissipate the taste.

Make a massage lotion. When varicose veins make your legs feel tired and sore, give yourself a 10-minute rubdown while seated with your legs up on an ottoman. Then keep your legs elevated for at least a half-hour before you resume other activities, advises Wingo. Use equal parts of distilled witch hazel and strong comfrey infusion. Add a few drops of essential oil of cypress, which is available in health food stores. Massage the lotion directly on the area that hurts or apply it to compresses held in place with an elastic bandage for up to an hour. Comfrey is traditionally known as a skin-healing herb, and witch hazel is a soothing astringent. Oil of cypress is an astringent that's considered soothing and relaxing. Use dry comfrey only, and do not apply to broken skin. Never massage directly on varicose veins, warns Elaine Stierman, L.M.T., a massage therapist.

Try an aromatic compress. Applying a cold compress soaked with witch hazel and essential oils to your legs helps soothe varicose veins, says Valerie Cookstey, R.N., holistic nurse and aroma practitioner and author of *Aromatherapy: A Lifetime Guide to Healing with Essential Oils.*

To prepare the solution, put one-half cup to one cup of distilled witch. hazel lotion in a bowl and refrigerate it for at least one hour. Then add six drops of cypress (Cupressus sempervirens) essential oil, one drop of lemon (Citrus timonum) essential oil and one drop of bergamot (Citrus bergamia) essential oil. These oils and the cold witch hazel have an astringent effect—they shrink small blood vessels near the surface of the skin, temporarily reducing minor swelling, explains Cooksley.

To make the compress, soak a cloth in the bowl, then apply it to the affected area on your legs for 15 minutes. Elevate your feet on a few pillows as you apply the compress: That position helps the blood leave the legs and return to the heart. "The compress is very effective. You feel immediate relief as the swelling in the area goes down," she says.

Give homeopathy a try. Pulsatilla, a homeopathic remedy taken from the windflower plant, boosts circulation of stagnant blood, says Andrea Sullivan, Ph.D, a naturopathic and homeopathic physician. Recommended dosages vary from woman to woman. To determine how much you should take of this remedy, consult a homeopath or a naturopath, suggests Dr. Sullivan. Pulsatilla may not work for everyone with varicose veins, she says.

Wipe with witch hazel. Witch hazel comes in two commercial preparations, water extracts (witch hazel water) and alcohol extracts (tincture of witch hazel). Both are soothingly astringent, which makes witch hazel a popular external herbal treatment for various skin conditions from bruises to varicose veins. Studies with laboratory animals have shown that this herb helps strengthen blood vessels. Commission E endorses using witch hazel extracts externally to treat both haemorrhoids and varicose veins. Simply wipe the affected area with a cotton ball that has been dipped in the extract.

Tincture of witch hazel can be taken internally for varicose veins, says the *Lawrence Review of Natural Products*, a respected newsletter. Or to make a tea, steep one to two teaspoons of dried witch hazel leaves in a cup of boiling water for ten minutes. You can drink two to three cups a day.

Let lemon help. Lemon peel helps relieve varicose veins. It contains substances known as flavonoids, including rutin, that reduce the permeability of the blood vessels, especially the capillaries.

Add onions. Onion skin is one of our best sources of the compound quercetin. Like rutin, quercetin reportedly decreases capillary fragility. To get the full benefit of the quercetin, you should cook with whole, unpeeled onions whenever possible and discard the skin before serving.

Bet on bilberry. Bilberry helps circulation by stimulating new capillary formation, strengthening capillary walls and increasing the overall health of the circulatory system. Related berries, which have the same benefits, include blackberries and blueberries.

Get ginkgo. Ginkgo is an all-around circulation booster. It's most widely known for its ability to increase blood flow through the brain, but it also improves circulation elsewhere in the body. German physicians use ginkgo preparations for treating varicose veins. However, large oral doses may be required, and that might prove expensive.

To use this herb, you need to buy a 50:1 extract, which will be specified on the label. No toxic side effects have ever been reported from using these standardised leaf extracts, although amounts higher than 240 milligrams daily may cause diarrhoea, irritability and restlessness.

Seek Spanish peanut. The healing agent here is not the goobers themselves but rather their reddish, papery skins. Peanut skins are one of the better dietary sources of oligomeric procyanidins (OPCs), which are compounds that decrease capillary fragility and permeability, thus helping to prevent and treat varicose veins.

Add assorted essential oils. Aromatherapists suggest massaging the affected area with the essential oils of cypress, juniper, lavender, lemon and marjoram. The oils should be diluted before they come in contact with the skin, so add a few drops of the oils of your choice to a couple of tablespoons of any vegetable oil. This massage treatment can't hurt, and it might help. Just don't ingest essential oils, as even a small amount can be toxic.

Wind

The pain: Abdominal pain, discomfort or bloating that accompanies excessive flatulence.

The cause: The average person passes wind 14 to 20 times a day, which may seem like a lot, but it's actually perfectly normal. One common cause of flatulence is swallowed air, says Harris Clearfield, MD, professor of medicine. Men who chew gum or eat too quickly tend to gulp down a lot of air, which, of course, is made of windes. Most beers and sodas are as well; the wind carbon dioxide is what accounts for their fizziness—and yours, too. Whatever the cause, wind builds up in the digestive tract. Your body has to get rid of it either by belching or by passing it out the rectum.

The foods we eat, however, are often the more likely cause of flatulence—in particular, fibre-rich foods like broccoli, bran, and beans. Because these complex carbohydrates aren't fully digested in the small intestine, undigested bits travel to the colon where they're fermented by bacteria, causing wind. For people who are lactose-intolerant, dairy products cause wind. Lactose intolerance is caused by a deficiency of lactase, an enzyme needed to break down the milk sugar lactose in the small intestine. Lactose is happily broken down by the bacteria that live in your colon, but wind is the unfortunate by-product.

See a doctor if:
...you have persistent bloating, cramping, and pain. Your doctor can rule out serious conditions such as diverticulitis, peptic ulcer disease, or a hiatal hernia.
...you have wind and unexplained weight loss.
...your pain is more severe than you've had before.

Nutritional Remedies:
Ration the wind supply. "Most flatulence originates in the carbohydrates of foods we eat," says Roger Gebhard, MD, professor of medicine. "If there are certain foods you suspect are causing the flatulence, cut those foods out of your diet for three days to see if it reduces the problem. By that time you'll know, and you can quickly use trial and error to discover the worst offenders." Beans, vegetables high in cellulose (like broccoli and cauliflower),

dairy products, and foods or supplements high in fibre are the most common problems, says Dr. Gebhard. Of course, all these contribute to a healthy diet, he points out, so you don't want to eliminate them completely. But cutting back on the one causing the most problems may make a big difference.

Lose the lactose. If cheese or milk products are chief offenders (and they are for some men), don't give up the pizza yet. Try over-the-counter digestive aids like Lactaid or Lactinex. They'll help digest the milk sugar lactose before it reaches the colon (where it ferments and causes wind), says Dr. Gebhard.

Choose "safer" dairy. Hard cheeses contain very small amounts of lactose. Chocolate milk is kind to those with lactose intolerance because the cocoa and sugars slow down the rate of digestion, allowing the small intestine more time to break down the lactase. You may also find that you can tolerate ice cream pretty well—the high levels of fat and sugar slow down digestion. But if you are watching your intake of fat and calories, you will want to keep portions small, cautions Dennis Savaiano, Ph.D.

Get a little culture. The active culture Lactobacillus acidophilus found in some yoghurts—look for it on the label—not only digests the lactose in the yogurt but also may help to digest the lactose in other dairy products. To get the benefit, you need to eat them at the same meal, says Dr. Gebhard.

Train your body to digest dairy

The intestinal bacteria in the colon that produce wind are incredibly adaptable, says Dennis Savaiano, Ph.D., professor of nutrition and dean of the school of consumer and family sciences at Purdue University in West Lafayette, Indiana. "When we gradually feed people increasing amounts of milk, their colon bacteria change so that they more easily handle milk sugar. When people adapt to dairy in this way, they have very little wind when we give them lactose."

To study this adaptation process, Dr. Savaiano first "challenged" people who had trouble digesting lactose with high levels of the milk sugar, then measured their wind production. Not surprisingly, they produced excessive wind. Then he gave them the equivalent of one cup of milk three times a day with each meal. Over a period of 10 days, he gradually increased that amount to the equivalent of two cups of milk at each meal. After 10 days, he again challenged them with high levels of lactose. "They generated no extra wind," he says. "They produced the same amount of wind as they would have had they been living on a lactose-free diet. Essentially, we turned them into digesters."

Dr. Savaiano suggests that you try the same experiment on yourself. Once you have adapted, he says, you can dine freely on low-fat dairy products.

Run 'em under the faucet. Canned beans are a great convenience. Before cooking canned beans, drain off the liquid and rinse the beans in water to remove the wind-causing carbohydrates that leached out of the beans' skin. "This reduces flatulence—no two ways about it," says Dr. Oliveri.

Give them a good soak. Another way to stifle those problematic beans is to soak them in a pot of water overnight, then pour out and refill before cooking, says James Duke, Ph.D., author of *The Green Pharmacy.* This helps to remove the offending carbohydrates. Better yet, add a small whole carrot to the pot of beans after soaking them, he suggests. Carrots can help soothe the digestive tract.

Visit the drugstore. By dashing your food with the enzyme alpha-galactosidase (found in over-the-counter products like Beano), you can break down the offending sugars in beans before they make you break wind. Or try an O-T-C wind reducer with the ingredient simethicone, which helps wind bubbles to coalesce so you can pass the wind more easily.

Step up to the vegetable plate—slowly. "I tell anyone who is thinking of increasing the fibre content of their diet to go very slowly," says Dr. Oliveri. To increase your fibre, he suggests adding one additional serving of a fruit or vegetable to your diet per week, until you have reached your daily minimum of five servings per day.

Go easy with bran. If you are thinking of adding extra fibre to your diet with bran, you will want to do it gradually, says Dr. Clearfield. "People who are going to eat bran cereals should start with small amounts until their bowel adjusts to it." He suggests adding two to three tablespoons of All-Bran or 100% Bran cereals to your regular cereal every day for a week. Then add another tablespoon or two for the next week. "Keep increasing the amount of bran cereal and decreasing the amount of regular cereal until you are eating nothing but bran cereal," he advises.

Scale your supplement intake. Dr. Oliveri recommends a similar strategy if you want to get extra fibre from a fibre supplement like Metamucil or Citrucel (Fybogel or Celevac). "Start off with one tablespoonful a day for the first week, then add one tablespoon a week until you reach the dosage recommended on the label."

Stick with it. Any new addition to your diet like a high-fibre supplement or eight-bean chilli recipe may cause flatulence in the short term. But if you continue to get your fill of fibre, your body may adjust, says Dr. Gebhard. So if a food or supplement is important to your health, don't give it up because of a one-time wind attack. Start small and gradually increase the amount you're taking in, he recommends. You might try adding about five grams of fibre a day more than you're used to for one week, then an additional five the next week, and so on until you are consuming 25 to 35 grams of fibre per day. Over time, your body might produce less wind in response.

Beware of bubbly. Since drinking carbonated beverages can also increase the amount of wind in your stomach, cut back on the amount of soda and beer you drink, says Dr. Clearfield.

Counteract with Kombu. A sea vegetable available in most Asian grocery stores, kombu can help neutralise foods that trigger flatulence, says Allan Magaziner, D.O., a nutritional medicine specialist. If you're boiling broccoli, for instance, put a little strip of kombu in the pot while you're cooking.

Everyday prevention:

Chug some charcoal. To reduce flatulence, try taking two activated charcoal capsules as needed. Purified and steamed, each bit of the porous activated charcoal helps trap intestinal windes in some people, says Dr. Gebhard.

Swallow slowly. Wolfing down your lunch may leave you howling later, so to speak. To avoid swallowing the excess air that could turn you into a wind giant, try to be more conscious of the need to slow down while you eat. You may be able to avoid flatulence in the first place, says Dr. Gebhard. Eating frequent small meals rather than a few large ones may also help.

Stamp out sorbitol. Sorbitol, another sugar our bodies have trouble digesting, is used as an artificial sweetener in sugar-free gums, candies, and many dietetic foods, reports Dr. Gebhard. It's also found naturally in certain fruits such as apples, pears, prunes, and peaches, but only the concentrated form packed into food products causes flatulence problems. If you consume a lot of these products, try cutting back, he suggests.

Go easy on C. Some people develop wind and diarrhoea when they take too-large doses of vitamin C. If this happens to you, reduce your dose until your symptoms subside. You may find that you can take the same amount of vitamin C if you break it up into smaller doses—say, 400 milligrams twice a day instead of 800 milligrams at once.

Herbal help:

Tame it with tea. Brew a tea with one to two teaspoons of anise or fennel seeds per cup of boiling water and steep for 10 minutes, suggests William Keller, Ph.D., chairman of the department of pharmaceutical sciences at the McWhorter School of Pharmacy. Drink as much as you want of this brew between meals, whenever you want relief, says Dr. Keller. Other wind-relieving teas, available premade in many supermarkets, include peppermint, ginger, and chamomile.

Spice things up. Herbs known as carminatives may help the problem by soothing the digestive tract, says Dr. Duke. Among these are anise seed, basil, bergamot, coriander, dill, fennel, lemon balm, marjoram, oregano, peppermint, rosemary, sage, and thyme. Adding a touch of one or more of these herbs to your food or tea can be a flavourful way to solve the problem.

Cure with camomile. Camomile relieves flatulence by mildly sedating and soothing the digestive tract. To make a soothing tea, add 1 full tablespoon of whole dried flowers to 1 cup of hot water and steep for 15 minutes. If you prefer to use fresh camomile, that's okay, too. Just double the amount: If the recipe calls for 1 teaspoon of dried herbs, use 2 teaspoons of fresh. Drink the tea often throughout the day.

Counteract wind-producing foods. Beans and low-fat dairy products are excellent sources of protein, calcium, and other nutrients that are critical for women. You can still eat those foods and avoid wind by having anti-wind spices along with them, says David Frawley, O.MD, a doctor of Oriental medicine, director of the American Institute of Vedic Studies in Santa Fe, New Mexico, and author of *The Yoga of Herbs and Ayurvedic Healing.* The spices will help your body digest the food. Flavour beans with cumin. Have ginger with milk and cayenne with cheese. Vary the amount according to your tastes.

Chew fennel after meals. Aromatic herbs such as fennel, a perennial plant that produces aromatic seeds, can help the body absorb wind in the intestine. "That's why when you go to Indian restaurants, you see a little bowl of fennel seeds on the table," says Daniel Gagnon, executive director of the Botanical Research and Education Institute. "Indians are smart. That country is very crowded." Start by flavouring your food with fennel and other aromatic spices such as cardamom seeds, basil, and mint. If you're not accustomed to eating highly seasoned food, you may need to give yourself some time to tolerate such flavours, so slowly increase the amount of seasoning you use in your cooking, says Dr. Frawley. If you're eating as much spice as you can and still have excessive wind, try two or three capsules (1/2 to 1 gram) of any of those spices after your meal, says Dr. Frawley. Or chew a teaspoon of raw fennel seeds after meals. They are available at health food stores, most supermarkets, and some gourmet shops.

Get ayurvedic aid. A mixture of one teaspoon of grated fresh ginger pulp and one teaspoon of lime juice, taken immediately after eating, can prevent excess winds and lower abdominal pain, says Vasant Lad, B.A.M.S., M.A.Sc., director of the Ayurvedic Institute in Albuquerque, New Mexico.

Get help from homeopathy. A 30C dose of Carbo vegetabilis taken once or twice a day may stop a sudden acute attack of flatulence, says Judyth Reichenberg-Ullman, N.D., a naturopathic physician and co-author of *The Patent's Guide to Homeopathic Medicine.*

Easing the pain with exercise:

Give yourself a morning massage. People who eat big meals or wind-generating foods late at night can expect to have a wind-filled stomach when they wake the next day. Here's an easy exercise to release unwanted wind before your feet hit the floor:

Lie flat on you back in bed.

Place the open palm of your right hand on the lower right side of your belly just above your pelvic bone. This is the seven o'clock position.

Press firmly and begin kneading that spot with you fingers.

Move your right hand clockwise to the 11 o'clock spot, just below your ribs on the right side.

Repeat the firm pressure and finger kneading.

Repeat these actions at the one o'clock and five o'clock spots, moving across and down the left side of your belly.

You can get rid of a lot of wind anytime by massaging your belly in a clockwise circle.

Ease the pressure. Lie down on your back with your knees bent, then raise each knee toward your chest until you feel relief. This exercise relieves the pressure in your lower abdomen.

Windburn

The pain: Dry, parched skin resulting from prolonged exposure to wind.

The cause: "Whenever your skin is exposed to severe wind, it loses moisture quickly and becomes dry and chafed, especially if it's cold," says Patricia Farris Walters, MD, clinical assistant professor of dermatology. "The physical friction of the wind also agitates dry skin." Frequently, windburn comes hand in hand with sunburn, so skin gets a double whammy of dryness and redness. With skiing you're often at high altitudes, where the air is very thin and dry, which adds to skin chapping, says D'Anne Kleinsmith, MD, a staff dermatologist.

See a doctor if:
...you notice any sign of infection such as crusting, scaling, or oozing.
...your skin turns very white or starts to blister and you have a lot of pain. Seek medical attention at once. You may have frostbite.

Quick relief:
Gently rewarm the skin. If you treat damaged skin gently, it is more likely to heal quickly, according to John P. Heggers, MD, at the Shriners Burns Institute in Texas. Avoid exposing your skin to extreme temperature changes, he warns, and when you come indoors, allow the heat of the room to defrost your body. Dot it turn on the heat lamp or stand next to a roaring fire.

Cozy up to a warm compress. "First, gently try to warm the area to take away the sting," suggests Evelyn Placek, MD, a dermatologist and doctor of internal medicine. Get inside to a warm area and put a lukewarm compress (a washcloth soaked in warm water) on your skin. "Don't make water too hot, because that will dry your skin even more and remove oils from the surface," she says.

Wash with TLC. Cleanse tender skin with warm—not hot—water, and a rich, creamy, gentle soap that won't dry it, such as Basis, Dove, Oil of Olay liquid cleanser or Cetaphil liquid, recommends Dr. Kleinsmith. Handle your skin gently without rubbing. And don't overwash, because water strips away the oil that your skin needs to hold in moisture, she advises.

Use a heavy-duty moisturiser. Right after washing, while your skin is still damp, put on a moisturizer to help seal in and add back moisture. "Vaseline, or other pure petroleum jelly, is an even better bet than moisturisers, which can contain irritating ingredients," says Dr. Placek. "A thin coat of petroleum jelly goes a long way," says Dr. Walters. "It's soothing and protective." If you're acne-prone, however, choose a moisture cream that's labelled "noncomedogenic" (non-acne-forming) instead of Vaseline or generic petroleum jelly, which may actually worsen or exacerbate acne, says Dr. Kleinsmith.

Reapply. Whatever you choose to use, reapply it two or three times a day until your windburn is healed, says Dr. Placek.

Boost healing with antibiotic ointment. "Bacitracin (Cicatrin), Polysporin (Polyfax) or some other topical antibiotic ointment in a petrolatum base will help fight infection while it soothes and heals skin," says Dr. Placek.

Go for a vitamin D ointment. Aquaphor Healing Ointment, available by the tube at chemists, can also help heal windburn. "It's a combination of the antibiotic Polysporin and a vitamin D ingredient, Panthenol, which soothes chapped, dry skin," says Dr. Placek. And it comes in a mild, pure, petrolatum and mineral oil ointment, which soothes and hydrates skin. The vitamin D and antibiotic ointments can be combined for extra protection and healing, she notes.

Coat irritated skin with cortisone. An over-the-counter preparation of cortisone ointment will help reduce inflammation and redness. "Use ointment, not cream, which contains preservatives that can sting tender skin," suggests Dr. Walters.

Elevate it. Occasionally there is noticeable swelling in windburned areas. Dr. Heggers recommends elevating windburned hands and feet while they are being rewarmed to minimise the swelling.

Pop a pill for the pain. Aspirin will ease any soreness and discomfort associated with windburn, says Rodney Basler, MD, a dermatologist. And because it's an anti-inflammatory, it will help speed the healing process as well.

Everyday prevention:

Wrap things up. Your nose, lips and ears are particularly susceptible to windburn, notes W. Steven Pray, Ph.D., R.Ph. So wear earmuffs or a woolly hat, with a scarf or face mask to cover your nose and lips.

Block the wind. "The best way to protect yourself from the wind is with a barrier," says Carol Frey, MD She recommends wearing a shell made from Gore-Tex or other synthetics. Zipping it high over the chin and pulling the hood around your face will shield your skin from that parching arctic breeze.

Know the wind chill factor. The wind chill factor is sometimes more of an indication of the weather conditions than the temperature. As the wind chill sends the temperature plummeting, the chance of injury rises, says Dr. Frey. So check the weather report before you head outdoors for those bracing winter activities.

Put your best face forward. If you know you're going to be spending time outside in conditions that produce windburn, then don't wash your face or shave beforehand, advises Dr. Basler. "Doing so removes your skin's natural oils, which offer protection against the environment," he explains.

Don't forget your sunscreen. Just because it's not swimsuit weather doesn't mean that you can't get a sunburn. "The sun is often a factor in complaints of windburn," says dermatologist David Margolis, MD He recommends wearing a moisturiser and a sunscreen on days that you're out in cold, dry, windy weather. Look for a product with a sun protection factor (SPF) of at least 15.

Lay it on your kisser. Your lips are especially vulnerable to windburn. Make sure you give them extra protection. Dr. Basler suggests using a lip balm with sunscreen (such as Blistex, Blistese or Chap Stick).

Don't stick out your neck. "The most vulnerable square inch on your body is the front part of your neck," Dr. Basler says. "The skin there is very thin, and it doesn't get much protection." Dr. Basler suggests wrapping a terry-cloth towel around your neck. It's actually much better than a wool scarf, he notes: "Wool is irritating to the skin, especially if you're sweating. A towel is much less irritating and more absorbent." You can also wear a turtleneck, of course. Just make sure it's made from cotton, not wool or a synthetic fabric, he says.

Wrist Pain

The pain: Pain, burning or aching in the wrist, which may be accompanied by tingling, decreased sensation or numbness.

The cause: "There are basically two types of wrist injury," says Joel Press, MD. "One is acute, such as a sprain or a fracture. The other is overuse, caused by the repetitive motion of activities such as typing." If the tendons of your wrist are abused by repeated forceful movements, they can become irritated and inflamed, and swell up. In time the tendons close in on the median nerve, causing pain and other symptoms of carpal tunnel syndrome. You may be awakened at night by tingling and burning in your hand. Inflamed tendons retain fluid and can cause nocturnal discomfort. During sleep, when your arm is relaxed, the fluid has difficulty circulating properly and builds up pressure in the area. Your wrist is vulnerable to this kind of injury from overuse, but water retention during pregnancy can also cause swollen tissues and carpal tunnel syndrome.

Injuries such as dislocations or broken bones can also cause wrist pain. In fact, it's even possible to break your wrist and not know it at first. The pain and throbbing only later become noticeable, and you may also notice a clicking or grinding sound coming from the joint.

See a doctor if:
...you sustain an acute wrist injury such as a fracture or a sprain.
...wrist pain lasts for more than a few days.
...if you have wrist pain so severe that it keeps you from carrying out daily activities like eating, dressing or working.
...if the pain is so severe that it wakes you from sleep three nights in a row.

Medication:
To tell exactly where the injury has occurred and whether there is any nerve damage, your doctor may recommend a procedure called an electromyelogram (EMG). During this test your physician will measure the condition of your muscles in the injured area by inserting needles with electrodes into the muscles and reading the electrical signals. This helps to locate where the nerve is injured and the extent of the damage. This isn't

necessary for everybody, but it may be called for if the location of your injury isn't readily apparent.

In more painful cases, the doctor may inject cortisone directly into the carpal canal to reduce the pain and swelling.

In more serious carpal tunnel syndrome cases, surgery may be required to relieve the pressure against the nerve and blood vessels. This is outpatient surgery. You're in and out in a day. It usually requires only a local anaesthetic, says David Rempel, MD, an assistant professor of medicine and a biomedical engineer.

Quick relief:

Do no further harm. Protecting your wrist from further damage is often the first step in healing it. So if you're pretty sure why your wrist is starting to hurt—for example, you've been tapping away at the computer keyboard on an all-nighter—ease up. If you can't stop completely—for example, if typing is your job—some physicians recommend that you alternate the typing with your other work duties. Modify your work habits, if you can. Take frequent breaks, and try to keep your hands and wrists in a straight line, not bent up or down. The doctor may prescribe splints as a gentle reminder, though many people only wear them at night.

Chill out. Using an ice pack on the pain may be helpful, says Bogard. Apply mineral oil to the skin where the pack will be placed. Put a damp towel over the oil and place the ice pack on the towel. Cover the pack with added towels for insulation. Leave the pack in place for 10 to 20 minutes, he advises. Check your skin every 5 to 10 minutes. If the skin turns white or blue (which would indicate a potential for frostbite), remove the ice pack immediately.

Turn on the heat. Once any swelling subsides—or if your wrist simply feels stiff and achy—heat can help, says Arthur H. Brownstein, MD, a physician. His instructions: Rub vinegar on your wrist, cover it with plastic, then apply a heating pad (wrapped in a towel) for about 20 minutes. You can repeat this treatment every hour as needed.

Raise your hand. Elevation is not as crucial for an injured wrist as for an injured ankle or knee, says Joel Press, MD Still, it can help keep any swelling down. "Just be sure to prop your wrist so that it's above heart level," he advises.

Opt for over-the-counter relief. A nonsteroidal anti-inflammatory drug (NSAID) such as ibuprofen or naproxen (Aleve or Naprosyn) can ease your discomfort, experts say. Choose the one that works best for you. "Patients have individual responses to these drugs," notes Edward A. Rankin, MD

Think sink. Warm water can soothe aches in your wrists, says Jane Katz, Ed.D., author of *The New W.E.T. Workout.* Submerge your hand over the wrist in a sink full of warm water. Pivoting your wrists, do 10 hand circles to the right, then 10 to the left. This exercise improves the range of motion in your wrist and increases the oxygen-carrying blood flow to your wrists and fingers, says Dr. Katz. "The beauty of exercising in water is that your muscles get resistance from all directions," she adds.

Keep still. For a more severe case of tendonitis, immobilising the joint with an elastic wrist support (also called a wrist splint) may provide some relief, says Dr. Rankin. You'll find these devices at chemists and medical supply stores. He suggests wearing one while you sleep-to prevent your wrist from twisting awkwardly-as well as during your waking hours, when your wrist is in use. "The support should keep your wrist in about a 10-degree dorsiflex position," he advises. In other words, if your palm is facing downward, your wrist should be bent slightly upward. Note: Do not wear a wrist support to treat a severe sprain or fracture, Dr. Press advises. See your doctor instead.

Everyday prevention:

Break it up. If you must use your wrist, John Cianca, MD, assistant professor of physical medicine and rehabilitation recommends taking frequent breaks from repetitive tasks. "Instead of typing for an hour straight, for example, type for 15 minutes and then rest your wrist for a bit," he says.

Don't be a leaner. Leaning on your elbows—when you sit at a desk, for example—can worsen wrist pain, says Ed Laskowski, MD It puts pressure on the ulnar nerve, which runs all the way down your arm into your wrist and hand.

Ease back into it. A wrist that has been immobilised may become stiff from lack of use, Dr. Brownstein notes. Some gentle stretching can help restore flexibility. Dr. Brownstein suggests pressing on a tabletop with the palm of your hand. "Bend your wrist until you reach the angle of pain, then back off just a hair," he says. "By riding the edge of discomfort and stopping just before you feel pain, you're doing beneficial stretching." Hold this position for as long as you find comfortable, working up to 2 minutes. Repeat three to four times daily.

Easing the pain with exercise:

Build some muscle. You can prevent future wrist pain by strengthening the muscles in your forearms, Dr. Cianca says. He recommends holding a 6-ounce can of tomato paste in each hand and flexing your wrists back and forth 15 to 20 times. Or you can simply squeeze a tennis ball in each hand, he says. Squeeze the ball for 5 seconds and release, then repeat 12 to 15 times.

Stretch and strengthen. The key to beating wrist pain is to make sure that your wrists are as limber and as strong as they can be. Experts suggest that you combine stretching exercises (to enhance your range of motion) and strengthening exercises (to build up the tendons, ligaments, and muscles in the wrist area). "Remember to warm up your hands first. Hands must be warm in order to work correctly," says Robert Markison, MD, a hand surgeon. There's nothing like a proper stretch to get the tendons, ligaments, and muscles in the wrist area warmed up, say doctors and physical therapists.

Count to five. Ask a five-year-old his age and he will likely declare "five," raise his hand, and spread all five fingers as proof. The same gesture can be a curing stretch, says Thomas Meade, MD, an orthopedic surgeon. Place your hand out in front of you as if you were stopping traffic. With your arm extended, spread your fingers as far apart as possible. Hold that position for at least 20 seconds. Repeat it five times, then relax and do the same stretch with your other hand. "Your muscles and tendons won't remember this stretch unless you hold it for at least 20 seconds," says Dr. Meade. "You should be able to feel your muscles get more rubbery and stretchy with time."

Halt and stretch. You can use that crossing guard "Stop" pose for this stretch, too. First, extend one arm in front of you at shoulder level and parallel to the ground, with your wrist bent and your palm facing out. Then, use your other hand to gently pull back the fingers of your extended hand. Hold for 20 seconds, then relax. Repeat five times, then switch hands and repeat. The goal is to feel the muscles, ligaments, and tendons stretching in your fingers, hand, wrist, and forearm, says Dan Hamner, MD, a physiatrist and sports medicine specialist.

Grab for the door. All you need for this stretch is an imaginary front door, says Michael Ciccotti, MD, an orthopedic surgeon. Extend your right arm in front of you with your palm facing the ground, then pretend that you are turning a doorknob slowly to the left, then slowly back to the right. Try 10 of these rotations, then switch hands and do 10 more. "This exercise helps make the joints in the wrist more supple," explains Dr. Ciccotti.

Strike up the band. A thick rubber band can actually be a piece of workout equipment. Try this rubber resistance regimen, suggested by Teri Bielefeld, P.T., a physical therapist and certified hand therapist. Extend your right arm in front of you with the palm up. Slip a thick rubber band over the crease on the inside of your palm. Placing your left hand under your right hand, grab the other end of the rubber band. As your left hand slowly pulls the rubber band down, counter by trying to bend your right hand up at the wrist. Feel the resistance. Try 10 times and then repeat, switching hands.

Then turn your right hand palm down and do the same thing. As your left hand slowly tugs downward, try to flex your right hand up, once again using your wrist. Feel the resistance. Try 10 times, then switch hands and repeat. "You're working on resistance with the wrist motion so that neither the wrist nor the rubber band wins," Bielefeld says.

Play shadow games (stretching exercise). Relive those childhood days of making shadow animals on your bedroom wall at night. This exercise mixes fun with flexibility, says Bielefeld. Of course, you can do this anywhere, anytime.

Raise your right hand as if you were being sworn in to testify in court.

Keep your fingers relaxed.

Gently bend your right hand forward at the wrist so that your hand resembles a swan's head.

Use your other hand to push down gently on the top of the swan's head." Hold for five seconds, then gently bring your hand back into the starting position. Hold for five seconds. Repeat four times.

Tug on a towel (strengthening exercise). Roll up a hand towel, then grasp it with both hands. Keep your left hand still as you turn your right hand as though you were wringing out excess water, first in one direction, then the other. Repeat, turning with your left hand, says Mary Ann Towne, P.T., a physical therapist. "When you are wringing a towel, you are both strengthening and stretching the muscles in your wrist," explains Towne.

Go fly fishing. Fly fishing is a good wrist-strengthening exercise as long as you don't overdo it, says Dr. Ciccotti. "It is a wonderful recreational sport as long as you prepare by doing some wrist stretches. The back-and-forth action flexes and extends the muscles. Using muscles rapidly requires strength and force. You are also stretching the joint capsule around your wrist."

Pedal in the air. Try this imaginary hand-pedalling exercise. Extend both arms in front of you and pretend that your fingers are holding onto bicycle pedals. Making a forward circular motion with your arms, move the imaginary pedals forward. Make sure that you flex your wrists as you pedal. You should feel the muscles in your wrists, forearms, and elbows warming up, says Dr. Ciccotti. Gradually work up to three minutes of continuous exercise.

Wave goodbye to pain. This range-of motion exercise is designed to stretch the muscles in the wrist area. Extend your right arm straight in front of you with the palm down. Bend your wrist down, then raise it as if you were doing a slow-motion wave. Do 10 waves with each wrist three times a day, says Bielefeld.

Do the twist. For this flexibility builder, extend your right arm straight in front of you and cup your right elbow with your left hand. Keeping your right elbow still, rotate your right wrist, slowly turning your palm up and then down. Do this for 20 to 30 seconds and then repeat for a total of five repetitions. You should be able to feel the muscles in your arm twisting. Then switch arm positions and repeat with the other wrist. Try this exercise three times a day, suggests Bielefeld.

Herbal help:

Treat it gingerly. A compress made from ginger can draw out toxins and accelerate the healing process, Dr. Brownstein says. To make the compress, simply boil some grated gingerroot, allow it to cool, place it in a moist washcloth, and lay the washcloth over your wrist. The washcloth should be as hot as you can tolerate, he notes. Leave it on for 15 to 20 minutes, and repeat every other hour.

Yeast Infection

The pain: Vaginal itching, discharge, redness and pain. Yeast can cause trouble in other places, too. It can grow in your mouth and throat, a condition called thrush, which shows up as creamy-white patches. Yeast can also become a stubborn tenant in your fingernails or toenails.

The cause: When it comes to chronic or recurring infections, the epicentre of the problem is often the intestines rather than the vaginal area, according to many naturopathic doctors. Candida albicans, the organism that most frequently causes yeast infections, can sometimes become overgrown in your intestines. Bacteria that exit the gastrointestinal tract can migrate into the vagina. In these cases, the vaginal area can become infected repeatedly, says Lorilee Schoenbeck, N.D., a naturopathic doctor.

See a doctor if:
...you haven't been diagnosed with a yeast infection within the past two months.
...you experience a white, "cottage cheese-like" vaginal discharge with a yeasty odour.
...you experience itching and irritation in the vulvar folds, the area outside the vagina, or both.
...you experience pain during urination or sexual intercourse.
...self-treatment doesn't help.

Quick relief:
Use a non-prescription remedy. "For the average yeast infection, over-the-counter antiyeast suppositories and creams such as Gyne-Lotrimin or Monistat 7 (Carestan or Gyno-Daktoin) are very effective," says Kathleen McIntyre-Seltman, MD, professor of medicine in the Department of Obstetrics/Gynaecology at the University of Pittsburgh School of Medicine. "If you've had an infection before and recognise the symptoms, go ahead and use one."

Lean back and apply. To reduce leakage from your vagina, use suppositories and creams at bedtime, suggests Janet Engle. Place the applicator as far into your vagina as possible by inserting it while squatting slightly or, even better, while lying on your back with your knees bent and pulled toward your chest. Wear a sanitary pad or panty liner during treatment to protect your clothing, suggests Dr. McCombs.

Give applicators a hot scrub. If you use an anti-yeast cream, you're probably reusing the applicator. "Wash the reusable applicators in hot soapy water," says Jack Galloway, MD

Ask for the quick treatment. If you dread the thought of using vaginal cream for seven nights, ask your doctor about prescribing a stronger dose of the over-the-counter creams containing clotrimazole or niconazole. These only need to be used for three days. Better yet, one-day treatments of tioconazole (Vagistat-1 or Trosyl) and clotrimazole (Mycelex-G or Canestan) are available, too. And your doctor can prescribe a pill called fluconazole (Diflucan) for yeast infections. Mild nausea can be a side effect, says.

Take every last pill. Be sure to take your full course of whatever antibiotic that your doctor has prescribed, says Dr. Kathleen McIntyre-Seltman. Cutting treatment short just because you feel better invites a recurrence, since you've only wiped out some of the fungus.

Blow it away. After a shower or bath, blow-dry the vaginal area. Yeast needs moisture to survive. Set your blow dryer on cool, and position the dryer six to eight inches from the vaginal area.

Sit in a sitz. Frequent douching should be avoided, since it can be too irritating to those with yeast infections. But there's an easy cleansing solution for your vaginal area. Fill the bathtub to hip height with warm water. Then add 1/2 cup of salt (enough to make the water taste salty) and 1/2 cup of vinegar. Stay in this sitz for about 20 minutes.

Nutritional remedies:

Crunch on carrots. According to doctors in the Department of Obstetrics and Gynaecology at Albert Einstein College of Medicine of Yeshiva University in New York City, eating carrots and other foods rich in beta-carotene—a natural substance that's converted into vitamin A in the body—may offer protection against yeast infections. In one study, vaginal cells in women with yeast infections had significantly lower levels of beta-carotene than the vaginal cells in women who did not have yeast infections. The doctors theorise that benefit may be due to beta-carotene's ability to boost the immune system. Besides carrots, spinach, broccoli, sweet potatoes and apricots all contain plentiful amounts of beta-carotene.

Eat C and E. Foods that are high in vitamins C and E can also play a protective role, says Paul Reilly, a naturopathic doctor. "These vitamins stimulate the immune system to activate specialised cells which are a primary defence against things like yeast," he says. You an get plenty of vitamin C by eating a variety of fruits and vegetables. Vitamin E is found mainly in vegetable oils. To get more vitamin E in your diet without all the fat, Dr. Reilly recommends having several servings a day of nuts and seeds. An even better source of vitamin E is wheat germ.

Is it another yeast infection?

You've consulted a doctor for a previous yeast infection, and now you seem to be getting the same symptoms again. You may be able to save the time and expense of a return visit to the doctor by going to the chemist and buying a strip of pH paper-litmus paper.

Moisten the paper with a small amount of vaginal discharge. (The discharge must be wet to react to the paper.) "If you have a yeast infection, your pH will be between 4 and 4.5 or less," says Ellen Yankauskas, MD "With other types of vaginitis, the pH tends to be higher."

If the litmus test confirms your suspicions, you may simply want to resume treatment with an over-the-counter cream. But if it's not effective after three days, Dr. Yankauskas says, you should definitely see your doctor again.

Watch out for sugar and unrefined starch. If you are prone to yeast infections, William Crook, MD, author of *The Yeast Connection Handbook*, advises to cut way down on simple white sugar, brown sugar, honey, and molasses. If you actually have yeast infection, you should cut out those sugars entirely until the infection is under control. The same holds true for unrefined starches—like pasta and white bread—because they break down into simple sugars in the intestines. "Yeast thrives on sugar and starches," he says.

Eat some allies. Because the vaginal itching, redness, and pain can drive you absolutely nuts, you have to take care of the immediate outbreak first, says Dr. Schoenbeck. Lactobacillus acidophilus is your ally because it's a type of good bacteria that helps keep candida in check. When the level of acidophilus is down, candida starts growing like wild. This is frequently the case if you have recently taken antibiotics for an infection or if you're continuously taking antibiotics for acne. In the process of killing off infectious bacteria, antibiotics inadvertently kill off acidophilus as well, giving candida an extra chance to flourish. One way to get more acidophilus is to eat yoghurt that has live cultures.

Ease up on alcohol. Yeast loves alcohol almost as much as it loves sugar, Dr. Crook says. "Alcohol is easy for yeast to break down and digest."

Avoid foods that contain yeast. This includes yeast-raised breads, sourdough bread, and fermented foods such as beer and vinegar.

Be wary of moulds. This includes aged cheeses, mushrooms, dried fruits, fruit juices (unless they are freshly made), peanuts, and peanut butter. "People with yeast overgrowth tend to be hypersensitive to these sorts of foods and can develop a multitude of symptoms when they eat them," Dr. Crook says. It is safe to eat foods that contain proteins such as eggs, lean meat, chicken, and dairy products without sugar.

Cure with cranberry. Arbutin, a compound found in cranberries (and bearberries and blueberries), helps treat candida infections, according to naturopaths Joseph Pizzorno, N.D. and Michael Murray, N.D., authors of *A Textbook of Natural Medicine.*

Enjoy some juice. Women may be able to speed the healing of yeast infections and to prevent recurrences with daily doses of cranberry or blackberry juice, according to Elaine Gillaspie, N.D., a naturopathic physician. If you can't find fresh or frozen berries, "be sure to use unsweetened cranberry concentrate, not bottled cranberry juice, since most brands are loaded with sugar or corn syrup, which encourages the build-up of yeast," she cautions. And because even fresh berry juices are rich in natural sugars, she suggests diluting four ounces of juice with an equal amount of water to get an eight-ounce serving. She also recommends juicing a clove of fresh garlic and adding it to your vegetable juices. "Nothing prevents yeast overgrowth as well as garlic does," says Dr. Gillaspie.

Helpful vitamins and supplements:

Cure with capsules. Acidophilus also comes in supplement form. Acidophilus capsules can help re-establish normal intestinal health when taken orally, says Dr. Schoenbeck, but she recommends taking the capsules only when you have an active yeast infection or are having a problem with recurring infections. Taking oral doses of acidophilus for just two to four weeks can help decrease candida in both your vagina and your intestines, she says. That makes you less prone to repeat infections. Look for acidophilus capsules that are refrigerated and contain at least one billion organisms per capsule. Dr. Schoenbeck recommends two capsules before breakfast and two before dinner, one hour before each meal, for one month. At the end of the month, see your medical practitioner to be certain that the infection is gone.

Acidophilus capsules can also help with prevention. If your doctor prescribes antibiotics, you can help prevent a yeast outbreak by starting the acidophilus capsules at the same time as your prescription. Continue taking the capsules for just two weeks, says Dr. Schoenbeck.

Everyday prevention:

Try a vinegar douche. Flushing your vagina with a dilute solution of vinegar and water occasionally—no more than once a week—may help prevent yeast infection recurrences. "This makes the vagina a little more acidic, which is bad for yeast." Mix two tablespoons of white vinegar with one quart of water and use a standard douching bulb, available at chemists. Doctors advise against using commercial douches—or douching any more often than once a week. Douching kills off "good" Lactobacilli bacteria in the vagina, leaving Candida to run wild, says Dr. McIntyre-Seltman.

Apply apple cider. An old folk remedy, douching with diluted apple-cider vinegar, really works, says Kathleen Maier, a physician's assistant. It restores the vagina's pH balance, she says. To 2 cups of water, add ¼ cup of organic apple-cider vinegar and douche using a douche bag or a commercial douche bottle whose contents have been discarded. For the first three days, douche twice a day with this solution, says Maier. For the next four days, douche once a day. Many doctors discourage women from douching more than once a month, at most, so if you decide to follow this procedure, check with your health-care practitioner as to how often you should douche, based on your individual health history.

Apply yoghurt. Some people believe that yoghurt, which contains bacteria that are cousins to the "good" bacteria in the vagina, may help the good bacteria repopulate, says Dr. McIntyre-Seltman. If you are going to try this remedy, be sure to use plain, unsweetened yoghurt containing live cultures and apply it to your vaginal opening at bedtime.

Skip the soap. Never wash inside the vagina with soap, or you may have an allergic reaction that leads to a yeast infection. The vagina has a self-cleaning mechanism in no need of soaps or lotions.

Clothe in cotton. "Candida likes moist, warm environments to grow in," says Vesna Skul, MD, medical director of Rush Centre for Women's Medicine. Keep dry and cool by wearing cotton underwear, loose clothing and panty hose with a cotton crotch, she suggests.

Add cornstarch. "Sprinkling a little cornstarch in your groin area helps absorb moisture," says Kimberly A. Workowski, MD.

Double-check your antibiotics. Long-term or repeated use of antibiotics is a common cause of yeast problems. "Antibiotics are overprescribed, especially for respiratory infections and for ear infections in children," says Dr. Crook. Try to avoid them when possible. Ask your doctor if an antibiotic is the only answer to your medical problem.

Try no-frills toiletries. Avoid bubble baths, scented tampons, coloured toilet paper and other products with dyes, perfumes and other chemicals that can irritate vaginal tissue, says John Willems, MD, associate clinical professor of obstetrics/gynaecology. White toilet paper is your best bet.

Go for vaginal ventilation. Vaginal yeast infections are by far the most common variety. One reason is that yeast thrives in warm, moist places. Experts suggest that, when possible, you might want to go without underwear. Sleeping in the buff—or at least without panties under your nightshirt—will help.

Loosen your jeans. Tight pants are not a good idea if you are prone to vaginal yeast infections. Favour loosefitting clothes. Dresses and skirts are the best fashion choice for fighting these kinds of infections.

Snuff the puff. Many dusting powders contain starch. And a fungus like yeast grows well in starch. So you don't want to use any of these powders in the vaginal area.

Keep panty liners to a minimum. A lot of women who wear panty liners every day get chronic yeast infections, says Annamarie Hellebusch, a nurse-practitioner. The plastic on the bottom of the liner traps moisture, so

Take Yeast Infections to the Cleaners

Perhaps the best weapons for treating yeast infections are in your laundry room. But you have to use special tactics to conquer Candida albicam, which can survive regular wash-and-dry cycles. Here are the basics.

Go soak. Soak panties in water for 30 minutes or more before washing them.

Scrub-a-dub-dub. After soaking, scrub the crotch of your panties with unscented detergent before putting them into the washing machine, advises candida specialist Marjorie Crandall, Ph.D., of Yeast Consulting Services in Torrance, California.

Double-rinse. Make sure panties are rinsed thoroughly, since residues from soaps and detergents can intensify vaginitis, according to John Willems, MD, associate clinical professor of obstetrics/gynaecology at the University of California, San Diego, and a researcher at the Scripps Clinic and Research Foundation in La Jolla.

Get 'em hot. Studies have found that the heat-sensitive candida die when panties are touched up with a hot iron.

try not to wear them daily, she says. And don't wear deodorant liners, because the chemicals in the deodorant can cause irritation and promote yeast overgrowth.

Have your partner checked. It's rare, but yeast infections may be sexually transmitted. This can happen particularly if your partner is not circumcised.

Take a scratch test. If your yeast infections persist, you may be allergic to Candida, and allergy shots of Candida extract can help prevent further problems. Ask you doctor to refer you to an allergist for skin testing.

Prime your prescription. If you know you get frequent yeast infections, ask for anti-yeast infection medication whenever your doctor puts you on antibiotics.

Easing the pain with exercise:

Exercise without restraint. Tight exercise clothes invite yeast infections on two counts: You're usually sweating in them, and their tightness interferes with cooling air circulation. A pair of running shorts is better than running tights, because air can circulate in them. And look for sportswear with an open, rather than tight, weave.

Ditch your wet swimsuit. Walking around in a clingy wet swimsuit is an invitation to yeast proliferation, says Kristene E. Whitmore, MD "Buy two identical swimsuits," she suggests. "After a dip, rinse your suit in clear water and put on the dry suit. No one needs to know that you changed suits."

Herbal Help:

Get garlic. Garlic is one of the best things to take for yeast infections," says naturopathic doctor Tori Hudson, N.D., professor at the National College of Naturopathic Medicine, and author of *Women's Encyclopedia of Natural Medicine.* It is both antifungal and immunity-boosting, she says. Two garlic capsules a day are enough to protect against yeast, according to Dr. Hudson. It's best to take enteric-coated capsules because the coating prevents the active ingredients in garlic from breaking down in the stomach. Look for garlic capsules that contain 4,000 milligrams of allicin, which is the antifungal agent found in garlic, she says.

Choose your herb. Herbs such as Oregon grape root extract, teatree oil extract, and lavender extract all help reduce the amount of candida growing in the intestines. "There are supplements on the market that contain all of these extracts, but they are hard to find. I'd ask an alternative practitioner to prescribe one of these," Dr. Schoenbeck says. She recommends taking two tablets three times a day. After a month, visit your medical practitioner to be sure your yeast infection is gone.

Defend with echinacea. Another herb that helps with yeast infections and has been well-studied is echinacea. A German study found that women taking antifungal medicine plus an echinacea extract had only a 10 percent recurrence of yeast infections. In the study, this group was compared to women who only took antifungal medicine. Nearly 60 percent of the non-echinacea group had recurrent infections.

Go for goldenseal. Another great anti-yeast herb is goldenseal, says Dr. Schoenbeck. Like Oregon grape, goldenseal contains berberine, a chemical that has antibiotic properties and works particularly well against yeast. You can buy echinacea and goldenseal separately or in combination capsules. Whichever you choose, take them daily as directed on the product you buy. If the capsules are 450 milligrams of an echinacea and goldenseal combination, for instance, a typical dose would be two or three capsules daily with water.

Squirt on an herbal rinse. "Herbal rinses are the best," says Aviva Romm, a certified professional midwife, herbalist and author of *The Natural Pregnancy Book.* They're cooling, soothing, and antimicrobial, which means that they attack the bad organisms and leave the good ones intact," she adds.

To make Romm's herbal rinse, blend equal parts of dried calendula, yarrow flowers, lavender, and comfrey root. Put 2 ounces of the mixture in a 2-quart pot and cover with 2 quarts of boiling water. Cover and steep for 30 minutes. Allow the infusion to cool to lukewarm and strain. Add 4 ounces of the infusion to a peri bottle (a plastic squeeze bottle designed for washing the outer genital area available at surgical or medical supply stores and some chemists) and squirt the mixture over your vaginal area after you urinate, suggests Romm. Alternately, you can saturate a washcloth with the infusion and apply it as a compress to the vaginal area for several minutes. Repeat several times a day until the solution is used up, advises Romm. You can store the herbal rinse in the refrigerator for up to three days. The calendula eases inflammation and, like lavender, is antimicrobial. Comfrey root is soothing and contains allantoin, which promotes cell growth and helps heal any little fissures or irritations. The yarrow, an astringent, eases inflammation and tones the tissue.

Douche with Aviva's rinse. If your vaginitis is very uncomfortable and there's no possibility that you're pregnant, Romm suggests using the herbal rinse described above as a douche, once a day for a week. If you want to try this remedy, check with your health-care practitioner about how often you should douche. If overused, douching can dry out the vagina and upset its natural balance. "If you try this, use a regular douche bag and fill it with about two cups of the herbal rinse. Keep the tip very low in the vaginal canal and let the rinse flow very slowly," advises Romm. Alternately, you can purchase a premixed commercial douche, empty the contents completely into the sink, and fill the bottle with the herbal rinse. Then use as described, Romm suggests.

Take a powder. You should keep the area around your vulva dry, because a moist environment encourages the growth of yeast, fungi, and bacteria, suggests herbalist Rosemary Gladstar, author of *Herbal Healing for Women*. She recommends using this fine herbal "yoni powder" whenever you feel the need.

   1 cup fine white clay (available in many health food stores)
   1/2 cup cornstarch
   2 tablespoons black walnut hull powder
   2 tablespoons myrrh powder
   1 tablespoon goldenseal powder
   1-2 drops tea tree essential oil

Using a wire whisk, mix the ingredients together. Put some in a clean spice jar with a shaker top for easy application. The remainder can be stored in a glass jar with a tight-fitting lid. Keep the mixture away from moisture and it will last indefinitely.

Add aloe. "Aloe vera gel is very cooling, and it quells inflammation fast," says Romm. "You can use the gel fresh from an aloe plant or buy pure aloe vera gel from a health food store. Apply it to the vaginal area as often as needed."

Blend a healing formula. This formula, a blend of tinctures (also called extracts), provides immune-system support and can be used along with any local or other treatment for bacterial vaginitis and trichomoniasis, says Dr. Hudson. (But don't use it if you are pregnant.)

   Blend 1/4 ounce of licorice tincture, 1/4 ounce of echinacea tincture, 1/4 ounce of usnea tincture, and 1/4 ounce of goldenseal tincture. Using a standard measuring spoon, take 1/2 teaspoon of the tincture mix three times a day for 10 to 14 days, advises Dr. Hudson.

   Licorice is considered a blood purifier and is used to quell internal inflammation. Echinacea stimulates the immune system, helping it increase the body's resistance to bacterial infection. Some herbalists report that usnea eliminates trichomonas, and goldenseal contains berberine, which fights bacterial infections.

Add pau-d'arco. Pau-d'arco contains the anti-yeast compounds lapachol and beta-lapachone. Lapachol is the weaker of the two, but its anti-yeast action is still comparable to that of the prescription anti-yeast medication ketaconazole (Nizoral).

Say ivy. Ivy leaves are active against candida and quite a few bacteria. Commission E endorses using 0.3 gram (that's just a pinch of dried herb) for various chronic inflammatory conditions, and that seems like a reasonable dose for fighting yeast infections as well. You can steep the herb in hot water for about 10 to 15 minutes and drink the tea.

Be smart with sage. Sage contains a mixture of anti-candida compounds. You could take sage tea as a beverage or use it as an astringent douche. If you're using it as a douche, you might add a drop or two of teatree oil, a potent anti-yeast herbal product.

Soothe with spicebush. Studying 54 plant species for antimicrobial effects, American scientists found that an extract of spicebush bark strongly inhibited Candida albicans. "Throughout Appalachia, spicebush tea has long been a favourite, proving once again the wisdom of much folk medicine," says Dr. James Duke, leading herbal expert.

Medical Advisors

Abel, Peter M., MD, director of cardiovascular disease and prevention at the Cardiovascular Institute of South Louisiana.

Abraham, Guy, MD, researcher who has conducted extensive research into PMT and menstrual discomfort, and former professor of obstetrics and gynaecologic endocrinology.

Aesoph, Lauri, N.D., naturopathic physician specialising in integration of natural and conventional therapies.

Agrawal, Naurang, MD, staff gastroenterologist at the Ochsner Clinic in New Orleans.

Aldoori, Walid H., MD, Sc.D., former research fellow in the department of nutrition and epidemiology at the Harvard School of Public Health.

Allen, Karen, a senior physical therapist in the office of environmental health and safety at the University of Virginia in Charlottesville

Alschuler, Lisa, N.D., naturopathic physician and chair of the department of botanical medicine at Bastyr University in Washington.

Altchek, David, MD, assistant professor of orthopaedic surgery at Cornell University Medical College in New York City.

Altura, Burton M., MD, professor of physiology and medicine at the State University of New York, Health Science Centre.

Anderson, Dale L., MD, coordinator of the Minnesota Act Now Project and author of Muscle Pain Relief in 90 Seconds.

Anderson, Eric G., MD, family practise physician in California.

Anderson, Owen, Ph.D., editor of Running Research News.

Andrews, Karen, MD, a consultant in the department of physical medicine and rehabilitation at the Mayo Clinic in Rochester, Minnesota

Andrews-Miller, Sharleen, faculty member at the National College of Naturopathic Medicine in Portland, Oregon, and associate medicinary director at the college's public clinic.

Angus, Carrie, MD, medical director for the Centre for Health and Healing at the Himalayan International Institute of Yoga Science and Philosophy in Honesdale, Pennsylvania.

Anshel, Jeffrey, O.D., optometrist in Carsbad, California, and author of Healthy Eyes-Better Vision.

Appa, Yohini, Ph.D., director of research and development for the Neutrogena Corporation in Los Angeles, California.

Archer, Sanford, MD, associate professor of otolaryngology.

Arena, John, Ph.D., professor of psychology at the Medical College of Georgia School of Medicine and director of the Pain Evaluation and Intervention Program at the Department of Veterans Affairs Medical Center, both in Augusta.

Arnold, Bill, MD, rheumatologist and chairman of the Department of Medicine at Lutheran General Hospital in Park Ridge, Illinois.

Astion, Donna, MD, associate chief of foot and ankle service for the Hospital for Joint Diseases, Orthopaedic Institute in New York City.

Backer, Howard, MD, physician who practises emergency sports and wilderness medicine.

Bailey, Steven, naturopathic doctor at the Northwest Naturopathic Clinic in Portland, Oregon, and member of the American Association of Naturopathic Physicians.

Baldwin, Hilary E., MD, assistant professor of dermatology and director of dermatologic surgery at the State University of New York Health Science Centre at Brooklyn.

Balin, Arthur K., MD, medical director of the Sally Balin Medical Centre for Dermatology and Cosmetic Surgery in Pennsylvania, and co-author of The Life of the Skin.

Bancroft, Betzy, professional herbalist of the American Herbalists Guild (AHG) and manager of Herbalists and Alchemists, an herbal medicine company in Washington, New Jersey.

Barber, Anne, O.D., optometrist and director of program services at the Optometric Extension Program Foundation in Santa Ana, California.

Barbo, Dorothy M., MD, professor of obstetrics and gynecology and director of the Center for Women's Health at the University of New Mexico in Albuquerque.

Bar-David, Tzvi, D.P.M., podiatrist with Columbia Presbyterian Medical Centre in New York City.

Bark, Joseph, MD, past chairman of the Department of Dermatology at St. Joseph's Hospital in Lexington, Kentucky, and author of Your Skin.

Barksdale, Phillip, MD, urogynecologist.

Barnard, Neal, MD, author of Foods That Fight Pain.

Barr, Ronald G., MD, director of Child Development at Montreal Children's Hospital in Quebec.

Barringer, Tom, MD, family physician in Charlotte, North Carolina, who is a fitness runner.

Basler, Rodney, MD, dermatologist in private practise in Lincoln, Nebraska, and assistant professor of internal medicine at the University of Nebraska Medical Centre in Omaha.

Bass, Tommie, herbalist in Alabama experienced with yellowroot.

Bauman, Phillip A., MD, clinical instructor in orthopaedic surgery at the Columbia University College of Physicians and Surgeons and associate attending physician of orthopaedic surgery at St. Luke's /Roosevelt Hospital Centre, both in New York City.

Beck, David E., MD, chairman of the department of colon and rectal surgery at the Ochsner Clinic in New Orleans.**Beckett, Edward, D.P.M.,** podiatrist in Pennsylvania.

Beckstead, Don, MD, family practise physician in Pennsylvania.

Beller, George, MD., professor of medicine and head of the Division of Cardiology at the University of Virginia School of Medicine in Charlottesville.

Bemben, Michael, Ph.D., associate professor of exercise science in the department of health and sport sciences at the University of Oklahoma in Norman

Benedet, Rosalind, R.N., breast health nurse specialist with the California Pacific Medical Centre.

Benjamin, Den E., Ph.D., muscular therapist and president of the Muscular Therapy Institute in Cambridge, Massachusetts.

Bergfeld, Wilma, MD, head of clinical research in the Department of Dermatology at the Cleveland Clinic Foundation.

Bergner, Paul, clinical director of the Rocky Mountain Centre for Botanical Studies in Colorado, and editor of Medical Herbalism.

Berndtson, Keith, MD, integrative medicine specialist at American WholeHealth Centres in Chicago.

Berryhill, James J., Ph.D., naturopathic doctor in Decator, Georgia.

Beutner, Karl R., MD, Ph.D., associate clinical professor and researcher in the department of dermatology at the University of California in San Francisco

Bielefeld, Teri, P.T., physical therapist and certified hand therapist.

Bihova, Diana, MD, dermatologist in New York City, and author of Beauty from the Inside Out.

Binnie, Willia H., D.D.S., professor and chairman of diagnostic sciences at Baylor College of Dentistry in Dallas, Texas.

Blager, Florence B., Ph.D., professor in the department of otolaryngology at the University of Colorado School of Medicine.

Blair, Glenn O. MD., director of the Bair PMS Center Topeka, Kansas.

Blau, J. N., MD, FRCP, FRC Path, medical director of City of London Migraine Clinic.

Blaurock-Busch, Eleanor, Ph.D., director of Trace Minerals International.

Block, Sidney, MD, rheumatologist in Maine.

Borum, Marie L., MD, assistant professor of medicine in the division of gastroenterology and nutrition at George Washington University Medical Centre in Washington, D.C.

Bourgon, Roberta, N.D., naturopathic doctor.

Bove, Mary, N.D., naturopathic physician with the Brattleboro Naturopathic Clinic in Vermont, licensed midwife, and member of Britain's National Institute of Medical Herbalists.

Bowman, Warren, MD, medical director for the National Ski Patrol who lives in Cooke City, Montana, just outside Yellowstone National Park

Bowsher, David, M.A., MD, Ph.D., FRCP (Edinburgh), research director of the Pain Research Institute in Liverpool.

Bracker, Mark, MD, clinical professor of sports medicine in the division of family medicine at the University of California, San Diego, School of Medicine in La Jolla.

Brady, Greg J. D.O., a dermatologist and partner at Advanced Dermatology in Allentown, Pennsylvania

Brasington, Richard, MD, director of clinical services in the division of rheumatology at Washington University School of Medicine.

Brasitus, Thomas, MD, professor of medicine and director of gastroenterology at the University of Chicago Pritzker School of Medicine.

Braver, Richard T., D.P.M., sports podiatrist and director of the Active Foot and Ankle Care Centre in New Jersey.

Brett, Jennifer, N.D., naturopathic doctor at the Wilton Naturopathic Centre in Stratford, Connecticut

Brice, Sylvia, MD, dermatologist at the University of Colorado Health Sciences Centre in Denver.

Bright, Ross, MD, medical director of the Psoriasis Medical Centre in Palo Alto, California.

Brodsky, Michael A., MD, professor of medicine in cardiology at the University California Medical Centre at Irvine.

Brody, Samantha, N.D., naturopathic doctor specialising in women's health in Portland, Oregon.

Brotman, Martin, MD, gastroenterologist at the California Pacific Medical Centre in San Francisco.

Brownstein, Arthur H., MD, physician in Princeville, Hawaii, and clinical instructor of medicine at the University of Hawaii School of Medicine in Manoa.

Brubaker, Linda, MD, director of the Section of Urogynecology and Reconstructive Pelvic Surgery at Rush-Presbyterian- St. Luke's Medical Center in Chicago

Brummett, Robert E., Ph.D., a pharmacologist at the Oregon Hearing Research Center in Portland.

Buchness, Mary Ruth, MD, chief of dermatology at St. Vincent's Hospital and Medical Centre in New York City.

Budoff, Penny Wise, MD, Women's Medical Centre in New York.

Burg, Richard M., MD, colon and rectal surgeon in private practise in New York State.

Burke, Karen E., MD, Ph.D., dermatologist who has studied the effects of vitamin E.

Butler, Sharon, author of Conquering Carpal Tunnel Syndrome and Other Repetitive Strain Injuries.

Cady, Roger, MD, director of the Headache Care Centre in Missouri.

Calbom, Cherie, M.S., certified nutritionist in Washington, and co-author of Juicing for Life.

Caldron, Paul, D.O., clinical rheumatologist and researcher at the Arthritis Centre in Phoenix.

Campanelli, Eve, Ph.D., holistic family practitioner in Beverly Hills, California.

Campbell, Bruce, MD, otolaryngologist at the Medical College of Wisconsin in Milwaukee.

Campbell, Don, Mozart Effect Resource Centre.

Cantwell, Mike, MD, clinician and coordinator for clinical research at The Institute for Health and Healing at the California Pacific Medical Center in San Francisco

Carlson, Karen J., MD, instructor at Harvard Medical School and director of Women's Health Associates at Massachusetts General Hospital.

Carlston, Michael, MD, assistant professor in the department of family and community medicine at the University of California, San Francisco, School of Medicine.

Carpenter, Sue Ellen, MD, obstetrician and gynaecologist with the Emory Clinic in Atlanta.

Carrico, (Back pain chapter, p. 48)

Case, William S., president of Case Physical Therapy in Houston, Texas.

Chaffin , Don, Ph.D., University of Michigan in Ann Arbor.

Chamberlain, David, Ph.D., president of the Association for Pre- and Perinatal Psychology and Health in San Diego.

Charm, Robert, MD, professor of gastroenterology and internal medicine at the University of California.

Chester, Alexander C., MD, clinical professor of medicine at Georgetown University Medical Center in Washington, D.C.

Chou, Loretta, MD, assistant professor of orthopaedic surgery at Stanford University School of Medicine.

Chow, Effie, R.N., Ph.D., certified acupuncturist and Qigong master at the East/West Academy of Healing Arts in San Francisco.

Christensen, Alice, founder and executive director of the American Yoga Association in Sarasota, Florida.

Cianca, John, MD, assistant professor of physical medicine and rehabilitation and director of the sports and human performance medicine program at Baylor College of Medicine in Houston, Texas.

Ciccotti, Michael, MD, orthopaedic surgeon, director of sports medicine at the Rothman Institute at Thomas Jefferson University in Philadelphia, and a team physician for the U.S. Women's National Soccer Team.

Clark, Sheryl, MD, dermatologist.

Clarkson, Priscilla, Ph.D., professor and associate dean in the department of exercise science at the University of Massachusetts School of Public Health and Health Sciences in Amherst

Clary, Andy, head trainer for the University of Miami football team in Florida.

Clearfield, Harris R., MD, professor of medicine and section chief of the division of gastroenterology at the Allegheny University of the Health Sciences in Philadelphia.

Cockerell, Clay J., MD, associate professor of dermatology and pathology.

Cohen, David E., MD, clinical instructor of environmental sciences at the Columbia University School of Public Health.

Cohen, Jay, O.D., associate professor at the State University of New York College of Optometry in New York City.

Cohen, Marc, MD, associate professor of surgery and urology at the University of Florida College of Medicine in Gainesville.

Collins, Frank, D.D.S., a dentist in private practice in Jacksonville, Florida

Collins, John G., N.D., naturopathic physician and associate professor at the National College of Naturopathic Medicine in Oregon.

Collins, Liz, N.D., naturopathic doctor at The Natural Childbirth and Family Clinic in Oregon.

Conn, Doyt, MD, senior vice president of medical affairs for the Arthritis Foundation of the U.S. Nutritional Remedies.

Cookstey, Valerie, R.N., holistic nurse, aroma practitioner, and author of Aromatherapy: A Lifetime Guide to Healing with Essential Oils.

Cowin, Richard, D.P.M., director of Cowin Foot Clinic of Florida.

Cox, James L., O.D., behavioural optometrist with the College of Optometrists in Vision Development in Bellflower, California.

Cracchiolo, Andrea III, MD, orthopaedic surgeon.

Crandall, Marjorie, Ph.D., candida specialist with Yeast Consulting Services in Torrance, California.

Crellin, John, MD, Ph.D., professor of the history of medicine at Memorial University of Newfoundland Faculty of Medicine in St. John's.

Crook, William, MD, author of The Yeast Connection Handbook.

Crowe, Sheila, MD, gastroenterologist and assistant professor of medicine in the Department of Internal Medicine in the Division of Gastroenterology at the University of Texas Medical Branch in Galveston.

Cullen, Margaret, registered occupational therapist, certified hand therapist, and director of hand therapy at the University of California, San Diego, Hand and Upper Extremities Centre in La Jolla.

Culpeper, Nicholas, British herbalist.

Cummings, Ian, MD, director of emergency services at the Day Kimball Hospital in Putnam, Connecticut.

Cykiert, Robert, MD, assistant professor of ophthalmology at New York University Medical Centre in New York City.

Dall, Bruce, MD, orthopaedic spine surgeon.

Dalton, Katharina, MD, author of PMT: The Essential Guide to Treatment Options.

Danberg, Susan C., O.D., optometrist in private practise in Glastonbury, Connecticut.

Daniel, C. Ralph III, MD, clinical professor of dermatology at the University of Mississippi Medical Centre in Jackson.

Danoff, Dudley, M.D., senior attending urologist at Cedars-Sinai Medical Center in Los Angeles and author of Superpotency

Davis, Anne L., MD, associate professor of clinical medicine at New York University.

De la Tour, Shatoiya, herbalist and founder of Dry Creek Herb Farm and Learning Centre in California.

DerMarderosian, Ara, Ph.D., professor of pharmacognosy and medicinal chemistry at Philadelphia College of Pharmacy and Science.

Devor, Eric J., Ph.D., professor of psychiatry at the University of Iowa Hospitals and Clinics in Iowa City.

DeWitt, Donald, MD, clinical professor of family medicine at East Carolina University School of Medicine in Greenville, North Carolina.

Diamond, Robert, D.P.M., podiatrist affiliated with Muhlenberg Hospital Centre in Pennsylvania.

Diamond, Seymour, MD, director of the Diamond Headache Clinic in Chicago.

DiFiori, John P., MD, assistant professor of family medicine, sports medicine specialist in the department of family medicine at the University of California, Los Angeles, and a team physician in the department of intercollegiate athletics.

DiPalma, Jack A., MD, professor of medicine and director of the division of gastroenterology at the University of South Alabama College of Medicine in Mobile.

Dobie, Robert A., MD, chairman of the Department of Otolaryngology at the University of Texas Health Science Center at San Antonio.

Dossey, Barbara, R.N., author of Rituals of Healing: Using Imagery for Health and Wellness.

Doughty, Susan, R.N., nurse practitioner at Women to Women, a clinic in Maine.

Douglas, Thomas, MD, staff urologist at DeWitt Army Community Hospital in Fort Beivoir, Virginia.

Drugge, Rhett, MD, dermatologist in Stamford, Connecticut, who is president and founder of the Internet Dermatology Society, and chief editor of the Electronic Textbook of Dermatology.

Drusine, Helen, massage therapist who works with professional ballet and Broadway dancers in New York City.

Duke, James A., Ph.D., world's foremost authority on healing herbs, botanical consultant, retired ethnobotanist and toxicology specialist with the U.S. Department of Agriculture who specialises in medicinal plants, and author of The Green Pharmacy.

Dunas, Felice, Ph.D., licensed acupuncturist and author of Passion Play.

Dunne-Boggs, Nancy, doctor of naturopathy at Bitterroot Natural Medicine in Montana.

Dweck, Monica, MD, ophthalmologist in Pennsylvania who specialises in eyelid problems.

Earnest, David, MD, professor of medicine at the University of Arizona College of Medicine Health Sciences Centre in Tucson and chairman of the Clinical Practise Section for the American Gastroenterological Association.

Edelberg, David, MD, assistant professor of medicine at Rush Medical College in Chicago.

Edwards, Robert A., Somerset School of Massage Therapy.

Elftman, Nancy, certified orthotist/pedorthist (professional shoe fitter) in La Verne, California.

Eliot, Robert S., MD, director of the Institute of Stress Medicine in Wyoming.

Elson, Melvin, MD, medical director of the Dermatology Centre in Nashville.

Elta, Grace, MD, gastroenterologist in the gastroenterology division of the University of Michigan.

Engle, Janet, Pharm. D., clinical associate professor of pharmacy practice at the University of Illinois at Chicago

Epstein, Gerald, MD, psychiatrist in New York City and author of Healing Visualizations: Creating Health through Imagery.

Epstein, Michael, MD, founder of Digestive Disorders Associates in Maryland.

Epstein, William, MD, professor of dermatology at the University of California, San Francisco, School of Medicine.

Erick, Miriam, R.D., senior perinatal nutritionist at Brigham and Women's Hospital in Boston, Massachusetts, and author of Take Two Crackers and Call Me in the Morning.

Erickson, James C., MD, professor of anaesthesiology.

Evans, Priscilla, N.D., a naturopathic doctor at the Community Wholistic Health Center in Chapel Hill, North Carolina (sciatica)

William J. Evans, Ph.D., director of the Nutrition, Metabolism, and Exercise Laboratory at the University of Arkansas for Medical Sciences in Little Rock (muscle soreness)

Eversole, Gayle, R.N., Ph.D., a nurse-practitioner, medical herbalist and professional member of the American Herbalists Guild (AHG) in Everett, Washington

Fagan, Kim, MD, sports medicine physician at the Alabama Sports Medicine and Orthopaedic Centre in Birmingham.

Fahrion, Steven, Ph.D., clinical psychologist and director of the Centre for Applied Psychophysiology at the Menninger Clinic in Topeka, Kansas.

Fallon, Patrick, P.T., physical therapist with the Texas Back Institute.

Fanizzi, William J., MD, senior physician and director of paediatrics for the Broward County Public Health Unit in Florida.

Fay, Hope, N.D., naturopathic doctor in Seattle, Washington.

Feder, Robert J., MD, Los Angeles otolaryngologist who teaches singing at the University of Southern California School of Music.

Feder, Thomas R., D.D.S., a dentist in private practice in Santa Monica,California.

Feingold, David, MD, chairman of the Department of Dermatology at Tufts University School of Medicine.

Feldman, William, MD, (Stomach pain, p. 492)

Ferentz, Kevin, MD, associate professor of family medicine at the University of Maryland School of Medicine in Baltimore.

Ferrante, Michael, MD, University of Pennsylvania Medical Centre in Philadelphia.

Fields, Karl B., MD, professor of family medicine at the University of North Carolina.

Filer, Wanda, MD, family practise physician in York, Pennsylvania.

Fiore, Michelle, MD, dermatologist.

Fiore, Neil, Ph.D., author of The Road Back to Health: Coping with the Emotional Aspects of Cancer.

Fischer, Richard D., D.D.S., dentist in Virginia, and a past president of the International Academy of Oral Medicine and Toxicology.

Fisher, Thomas, M.D., a dermatologist in private practice in Chicago.

Fishman, Harold, MD, California dermatologist.

Flatley, John A., MD, clinical instructor of surgery at the University of Missouri School of Medicine.

Fleisher, Mitchell, MD, family practise physician and homeopath in Colleen, Virginia.

Fliegelman, Emanuel, D.O., professor emeritus of obstetrics and gynaecology and director of the human sexuality program at the Philadelphia College of Osteopathic Medicine.

Flint, Margi, professional member of the American Herbalists Guild (AHG) who practises in Massachusetts.

Foley, Deborah, MD, internist at Northwest Community Health Care in Arlington Heights, Illinois.

Foster, Steven, noted Arkansas herbalist and photographer, and co-author of Encyclopaedia of Common Natural Ingredients.

Foulser, Kathy, N.D., a naturopathic doctor at the Ridgefield Center for Integrative Medicine in Connecticut.

Fox, James M., MD, orthopaedic surgeon and knee specialist, and author of Save Your Knees.

Foxman, Betsy, Ph.D., associate professor of epidemiology at the University of Michigan School of Public Health in Ann Arbor

Francis, Gary, M.D., director of the coronary intensive care unit at the Cleveland Clinic Foundation

Frank, Barbara, MD, gastroenterologist and clinical professor of medicine at Allegheny University of the Health Sciences.

Frawley, David, O.M.D., doctor of Oriental medicine, professional member of the American Herbalists Guild (AHG), director of the American Institute of Vedic Studies in Santa Fe, New Mexico, and author of The Yoga of Herbs and Ayurvedic Healing.

Freedman, Robert, Ph.D., director of the Behavioural Medicine Laboratory at Wayne State University.

Freeman, Ellen, Ph.D., director of the University of Pennsylvania Medical Centre PMT Program.

Freilich, Abraham R., MD, dermatologist and assistant clinical professor of dermatology at Downstate Medical Centre New York.

Freitag, Frederick G., D.O., spokesperson for the U.S. National Headache Foundation.

Frey, Carol, MD, chief of the Foot and Ankle Service and associate clinical professor of orthopaedic surgery at the University of Southern California School of Medicine.

Fried, Carl, P.T., physical therapist at K Valley Orthopaedics in Kalamazoo, Michigan.

Fried, Walter I., MD, Ph.D., clinical assistant professor of ophthalmology at University of Health Sciences/Chicago Medical School.

Friedlaender, Mitchell H., MD, director of corneal services in the Division of Ophthalmology at the Scripps Clinic and Research Foundation in La Jolla, California, and co-author of 2/20: A Total Guide to Improving Your Vision and Preventing Eye Disease.

Friedman, Jay W., D.D.S., a dental consultant in Los Angeles and author of Complete Guide to Dental Health

Friend, John, a Iyengar yoga instructor in Spring, Texas

Fries, James F., MD, associate professor of medicine at Stanford University School of Medicine.

Fuhrmann, Joe, MD, director of the Amwell Health Centre in Belle Mead, New Jersey, and author of Fasting and Eating for Health.

Gach, Michael Reed, Ph.D., director of the Acupressure Institute in Berkeley, California, and author of The Bum Back Book and Acupressure's Potent Points.

Gadd, Michele A., MD, participating surgeon at the Comprehensive Breast Health Centre Division of Surgical Oncology at Massachusetts General Hospital.

Gagnon, Daniel, executive director of the Botanical Research and Education Institute, and owner of Herbs, Etc., in Santa Fe, New Mexico.

Galloway, Jack, MD, clinical professor of obstetrics and gynaecology at the University of Southern California School of Medicine in Los Angeles.

Garay, Kenneth F., MD, director of the Centre for Sinus and Nasal Disease in New York City.

Gardner, Leslie, herbalist in Sebastopol, California, professional member of the American Herbalists Guild (AHG), and staff member at the California School of Herbal Studies in Forestville.

Garfinkel, Marian, Ph.D., health educator and certified senior yoga teacher in Philadelphia.

Gastwirth, Glenn, D.P.M., deputy executive director of the American Podiatric Medical Association.

Gattefosse, Rene-Maurice, French chemist who discovered the burn-healing power of lavender by accident.

Gazsi, Michael, N.D., naturopathic doctor in Connecticut.

Gebhard, Roger, MD, professor of medicine in the division of gastroenterology at the University of Minnesota in Minneapolis.

Gerson, Scott, MD, expert in Ayurvedic medicine.

Gersten, Dennis, MD, San Diego psychiatrist and publisher of Atlantis, a bimonthly imagery newsletter.

Gibson, Gary R., MD, assistant professor of medicine at Northeastern Ohio University College of Medicine in Warren.

Gibson, Gretchen, D.D.S., director of the geriatric dentistry program at the Veterans Administration Medical Centre in Dallas, Texas.

Gillaspie, Elaine, N.D., naturopathic physician in Portland, Oregon.

Gillespie, Larrian, MD, author of You don't Have to Live with Cystitis.

Gillerman, Hope, board-certified teacher of the Alexander Technique.

Ginsburg, Robert, MD, director of the Cardiovascular Intervention Unit at the University of Colorado Health Science Centre

Ginsburg, Robert, MD, director of the Centre for Advanced Cardiovascular Therapy in California.

Giordano, Joseph M., MD, professor and chief of surgery at George Washington University Hospital in Washington, D.C.

Gladstar, Rosemary, author of Herbal Healing for Women and several other herb books.

Glaser, Dee Anna, MD, assistant professor of dermatology and internal medicine at the St. Louis University School of Medicine.

Glazer, Howard S., D.D.S., a dentist in Fort Lee, New Jersey, and past president of the Academy of General Dentistry

Goddard, Greg, D.D.S., assistant clinical professor of restorative dentistry at the University of California, San Francisco, Center for Orofacial Pain.

Goldberg, Norman J., MD, professor of medicine at the University of California.

Goldberg, Stephen R., D.D.S., dentist in New York City.

Goldstein, Jerome C., MD, executive vice president of the American Academy of Otolaryngology/ Head and Neck Surgery in Alexandria, Virginia.

Goren, Gabriel, M.D., vascular surgeon and director of the Vein Disorders Center in Encino, California.(Varicose veins, p. 555)

Gossel, Thomas, Ph.D., R.Ph., registered pharmacist, professor of pharmacology and toxicology, and dean of the College of Pharmacy at Ohio Northern University in Ada.

Gottlieb, Sidney, MD, cardiologist at Johns Hopkins Medical Institution.

Granger, Jocelyn, registered massage therapist.

Grayson, Leonard, MD, clinical associate allergist and dermatologist at Southern Illinois University School of Medicine.

Green, Mindy, herbalist, director of education services at the Herb Research Foundation in Boulder, Colorado, and co-author of Aromatherapy: A Complete Guide to the Healing Art.

Greenberger, Paul, MD, professor of medicine in the Division of Allergy and Immunology at Northwestern University Medical School.

Greene, Hinda, D.O., internal medicine and emergency medicine physician at Cleveland Clinic

Hospital in Fort Lauderdale, Florida.

Greenwood, Sadja, MD, assistant clinical professor of gynaecology at the University of California, San Francisco, Medical Centre.

Gregory, Patricia, R.D., dietician at Shands Hospital at the University of Florida.

Grieve, Maude, author of Modern Herbal.

Grillone, Gregory, MD, assistant professor of otolaryngology, head and neck surgery, at Boston University School of Medicine and director of the Voice Centre at Boston Medical Centre.

Gross, Charles, MD, professor of otolaryngology.

Grossbart, Ted, Ph.D., instructor in the department of psychiatry at Harvard Medical School, senior associate and clinical supervisor for the department of psychiatry at Beth Israel Hospital, clinical psychologist in Boston, and author of Skin Deep: A Mind/Body Program for Health Skin.

Grossier, Daniel, MD, dermatologist at Clara Mass Medical Centre in New Jersey.

Grubb, Debra, MD, director of the Natural Choice Birth Centre in California.

Gutgesell, Margaret, MD, Ph.D., associate professor of pediatrics at the University of Virginia Health Science Center in Charlottesville.

Gwaltney, Jack, MD, professor of medicine and head of the division of epidemiology and virology in the department of internal medicine at the University of Virginia in Charlottesville.

Haas, Elson, MD, director of the Preventive Medical Centre of Marin in San Rafael, California, and author of Staying Healthy with Nutrition.

Haberman, Frederic, MD, sports dermatologist and clinical instructor of medicine at Albert Einstein College of Medicine in New York City.

Halderman, Scott, MD, D.C., Ph.D., associate clinical professor of neurology at the University of California

Hale, Douglas, D.P.M., podiatrist at the Foot and Ankle Centre of Washington in Seattle.

Halpern, Dr. Steven, Inner Peace Music.

Hambrick, Ernestine, MD, colon and rectal surgeon at Michael Reese Hospital in Chicago.

Hamlet, Murray, D.V.M., U.S. Army Research Institute of Environmental Medicine.

Hammons, John L., Ph.D., staff chemist at Procter & Gamble Company in Cincinnati, Ohio.

Hamner, Dan, MD, physiatrist and sports specialist in New York City.

Harden, Norman, MD, director of the pain clinic at the Rehabilitation Institute in Chicago.

Hargreaves, Kenneth M., D.D.S., Ph.D., associate professor in the divisions of endodontics and pharmacology at the University of Minnesota Medical School in Minneapolis

Harig, James, M.D., associate professor of medicine in the Department of Digestive and Liver Diseases at the University of Illinois College of Medicine in Chicago

Harris, David, MD, clinical professor of dermatology at Stanford University School of Medicine.

Hartigan, Carol, MD, physiatrist who specialises in spine rehabilitation.**Harvey, Birt, MD,** professor of paediatrics at Stanford University School of Medicine in California.

Hass, Frederick, MD, general practitioner in California, and author of The Foot Book.

Hausauer, Heidi, D.D.S., assistant clinical professor at the University of the Pacific School of Dentistry.

Hauser, Ross, MD, director of Caring Medical and Rehabilitation Services at Beulahland Natural Medicine Clinic in Thebes Park, Illinois

Healy, Helen, N.D., naturopathic doctor and director of the Wellspring Naturopathic Clinic in Minnesota.

Hecht, Leon, N.D., naturopathic physician at North Coast Family Health Centre in Portsmouth, New Hampshire.

Heggers, John P., Ph.D., professor in the department of surgery, microbiology, and immunology at the University of Texas Medical Branch and director of clinical microbiology at the Shriners Burns Institute, both in Galveston.

Heinerman, John, Ph.D., medical anthropologist and author of Heinerman's Encyclopedia of Fruits, Vegetables and Herbs and many other books related to healing with herbs and foods.

Helm, Thomas, MD, assistant clinical professor of dermatology and pathology at the State University of New York.

Hening, Wayne, MD, Ph.D., research neurologist.

Henry, Robert, D.M.D., dentist in Lexington, Kentucky, and past president of the American Society for Geriatric Dentistry.

Herrera, Jorge, MD, spokesperson for the American Gastroenterological Society.

Hersh, Craig, MD, sports injuries specialist.

Hetherington, Susan E., Dr.Ph., certified nurse-midwife, sex therapist, and professor in the School of Nursing at the University of Maryland.

Hiatt, William, MD, professor of vascular medicine at the University of Colorado Health Sciences Centre.

Hines, Chesley, MD, gastroenterologist.

Hoffman, David, British herbalist and author of The Herbal Handbook.

Hoffman, Ronald L., MD, director of the Hoffman Centre for Holistic Medicine in New York City.

Hoffman, Wendy, certified childbirth educator and labour assistant in Pennsylvania.

Hollander, Joseph, MD, professor emeritus of medicine at the University of Pennsylvania Hospital.**Hollingsworth, Helen, MD,** associate professor of medicine at Boston University School of Medicine.

Homansky, Flip, MD, ringside physician in Las Vegas who has worked more than 250 championship boxing matches.

Hopman, Ellen Evert, master herbalist in Amherst, Massachusetts; professional member of the American Herbalists Guild (AHG); and author of Tree Medicine, Tree Magic.

Howell, Patricia, professional herbalist.

Hudson, Tori, N.D., naturopathic physician and professor at the National College of Naturopathic Medicine in Oregon.

Huemer, Richard P. MD., holistic practitioner in Lancaster, California

Huppin, Lawrence Z., D.P.M., podiatrist at the Foot and Ankle Centre of Washington in Seattle.

Hurley, Ben F., Ph.D., director of the exercise science Laboratory at the University of Maryland College of Health and Human Performance in College Park.

Iglarsh, Annette Z., Ph.D., vice president of Theraphysics, a rehabilitation managed-care corporation, and president of the Orthopedic Section of the American Physical Therapy Association.

Irwin, John, MD, author of Arthritis Begone!

Isernhagen, Susan, P.T., physical therapist and director of Isernhagen WorkSystems in Duluth, Minnesota.

Jacknowitz, Arthur, Pharm.D., chairman of clinical pharmacy at West Virginia University School of Pharmacy.

Jackson, Judith, aromatherapist in Greenwich, Connecticut, and author of Scentual Touch: A Personal Guide to Aromatherapy.

Jacobs, Danny, MD, surgeon at Brigham and Women's Hospital and assistant professor of surgery at Harvard Medical School.

Jacobs, Stephen, MD, professor of urology at the University of Maryland School of Medicine.

Jacques, Jacqueline, N.D., naturopathic physician and specialist in pain management in Portland, Oregon.

Jaeger, Bernadette, D.D.S., associate professor of diagnostic sciences and orofacial pain at the University of California, Los Angeles, School of Dentistry.

Jaffe, Philip, MD, assistant professor of gastroenterology at the University of Arizona College of Medicine.

Janowitz, Ira, P.T., certified professional ergonomist for the ergonomics program at the University of California ergonomic San Francisco/Berkeley.

Jastreboff, Pawl, Ph.D., Sc.D., director of the University of Maryland Tinnitus and Hyperacusis Centre.

Jimenez, Ramon, MD, chief of staff at O'Connor Hospital in California, and president of the California Orthopaedic Association.

Johansen, Olaf, MD, colorectal surgeon.

Johnson, John C., MD, director of Emergency Medical Services at Porter Memorial Hospital in Valparaiso, Indiana, and a past president of the American College of Emergency Physicians.

Johnson, Jonas T., MD, professor of otolaryngology at the University of Pittsburgh School of Medicine.

Johnson, Judy, R.N., nurse in dermatology office in Alaska.

Jones, Carl, R.N., board-certified enterostomal therapy nurse, certified childbirth educator in Jefferson, New Hampshire, and author of Mind over Labour and Childbirth Choices Today.

Jones, Charles, D.P.M., dean and vice president of academic affairs at the Dr. William School College of Podiatric Medicine.

Jones, David, MD, medical director of the Spine and Sport Medical Centre in Orange, Texas.

Jones, Feather, professional member of the American Herbalists Guild (AHG) and director of the Rocky Mountain Centre for Botanical Studies in Colorado.

Jones, Jeffrey, MD., director of the department of emergency medicine at Butterworth Hospital in Grand Rapids, Michigan.

Jones, Keith, head trainer for the Houston Rockets basketball team.

Kakita, Lenore S., MD, clinical assistant professor of dermatology at the University of California, Los Angeles, and an adviser to the American Academy of Dermatology.

Kalin, David, N.D., a family practitioner in Largo, Florida

Kalina, Robert E., MD, chairman of ophthamology at the University of Washington.

Kallhoff, Jean, advanced registered nurse practitioner at the Urology Clinic at the University of Washington Medical Centre in Seattle.

Kamhi, Ellen, R.N., Ph.D., herbalist in Oyster Bay, New York, professional member of the American Herbalists Guild (AHG), and host of the syndicated radio show ìNatural Alternatives.î

Kaminski, Mitchell, Jr., MD, clinical professor of surgery at the Finch University of Health Sciences/The Chicago Medical School.

Kaplan, Robert-Michael, O.D., behavioural optometrist and consultant in vision care in British Columbia.

Karlstadt, Robyn, MD, gastroenterologist at Graduate Hospital in Philadelphia.

Karp, Carol L., MD, assistant professor ophthalmology at the Bascom Palmer Eye Institute/University of Miami School of Medicine.

Kassiner, Marilyn MD, neurologist.

Katz, Jane, Ed.D., professor of health and physical education at the City University of New York, world

Masters champion swimmer, member of the 1964 U.S. Olympic performance synchronized swimming team, and author of The New W.E.T. Workout.

Katz, Philip, MD, director of the Comprehensive Chest Pain and Swallowing Centre at Allegheny University.

Kauvar, Kenneth, MD, assistant clinical professor of ophthalmology at the University of Colorado School of Medicine in Denver. and author of Eyes Only.

Kayne, Barry, D.D.S., clinical assistant professor at the University School of Dental Medicine

Kechijian, Paul, MD, clinical associate professor of dermatology and chief of the nail section at the New York University Medical Centre.

Keenan, Mary Ann, MD, chairman of the Department of Orthopaedic Surgery at the Albert Einstein Medical Centre in Philadelphia.

Keller, William, Ph.D., chairman of the department of pharmaceutical sciences at the McWhorter School of Pharmacy at Stamford University in Birmingham, Alabama.

Kempczinski, Richard F., MD, chief of vascular surgery at the University of Cincinnati College of Medicine.

Kessler, Jo, licensed nurse-practitioner and certified sex therapist in San Diego.

Keville, Kathi, California herbalist.

Kimmelman, Charles P., MD, professor of otolaryngology at Manhattan Eye, Ear and Throat Hospital.

Kintz, Mary, P.T., orthopaedic physical therapist at Raleigh Community Sports Medicine and Physical Therapy in North Carolina.

Klaper, Michael A., MD, nutritional medicine specialist in Florida.

Klass, Perri Elizabeth, MD, author of Baby Doctor.

Kleinsmith, D'Anne, MD, cosmetic dermatologist at William Beaumont Hospital in Royal Oak, Michigan.

Klemons, Ira, D.D.S., Ph.D., director of the Centre for Head and Facial Pain in South Amboy, New Jersey.

Klima, Carrie, R.N., certified nurse-midwife and assistant professor at the Yale University School of Nursing.

Kluka, Evelyn, MD, director of paediatrics otolaryngology at Children's Hospital in New Orleans.

Koch, Kenneth L., MD, professor of medicine.

Koff, Irwin, MD, general practitioner in Kahuku, Hawaii who is certified in acupuncture.

Kowalsky, Susan, N.D., naturopathic doctor in Norwich, Vermont.

Krall, Elizabeth, Ph.D., epidemiologist and associate professor at Boston University School of Dental Medicine.

Kramer, Karl, MD, clinical professor of dermatology at the University of Miami School of Medicine.

Kramer, Neal, D.P.M., podiatrist practising in Pennsylvania.

Krasner, Diane, R.N., specialist in chronic wound care.

Krassner, Devra, doctor of naturopathic medicine and homeopathy in Maine.

Krevsky, Benjamin, MD, gastroenterologist and professor of medicine at Temple University School of Medicine in Philadelphia.

Kroser, Joyann, MD, gastroenterologist at Presbyterian Medical Centre and assistant professor of medicine at the University of Pennsylvania, both in Philadelphia.

Krueger, Gerald, MD, professor dermatology.

Kruzel, Thomas, N.D., naturopathic doctor in Portland, Oregon, and member of the American Association of Naturopathic Physicians.

Kunkel, Robert, M.D, migraine specialist at the Cleveland Clinic Foundation in Ohio

Lad, Vasant, B.A.M.S., M.A.Sc., director of the Ayurvedic Institute in Albuquerque, New Mexico.

Lahr, Christopher, MD, director of Complete Colon Care in South Carolina, and author of Shining Light on Constipation.

Lakowski, Ed, MD, co-director of the Sportsmedicine Centre at the Mayo Clinic in Minnesota.

Lamb, Geoffrey C., MD, associate professor of internal medicine at the Medical College of Wisconsin in Milwaukee

Lamping, Kathleen, MD, associate clinical professor of ophthalmology at Case Western Reserve University in Cleveland, Ohio.

Lande, Sylvan, D.D.S., professor of dentistry at the University of Southern California School of Dentistry

Lane, Alfred T., MD, associate professor of dermatology and paediatrics at Stanford University School of Medicine in California.

Lanyi, Valery, MD, clinical associate professor of rehabilitation medicine at New York University Medical Centre.

Lapides, Jack, MD, urologist in Michigan.

Lark, Susan, MD, author of Fibroid Tumours and Endometriosis.

Laskowski, Ed, MD, co-director of the Sportsmedicine Center at the Mayo Clinic in Rochester, Minnesota

Laux, Marcus, N.D., naturopathic doctor in California, and co-author of Natural Women, Natural Menopause.

Lawrence, Steven, MD, orthopaedic surgeon.

Lazar, Andrew P., MD, associate professor of clinical dermatology.

Lebowitz, Bruce, D.P.M., director of the podiatric clinic of the Johns Hopkins Bayview Medical Centre in Baltimore, Maryland.

Lee, Alison, MD, pain-management specialist and

acupuncturist with Barefoot Doctors, an acupuncture and natural-medicine resource centre in Ann Arbor, Michigan.

Lee, Bob, O.D., assistant professor of optometry and co-ordinator of computer vision services at Southern California College of Optometry in Fullerton.

Lee, Linda, MD, assistant professor of medicine in the Division of Gastroenterology at Johns Hopkins University School of Medicine in Baltimore, Maryland.

Leff, Edmund, MD, proctologist in Arizona.

Leung, Albert, Ph.D., pharmacognosist (natural product pharmacist), author of Chinese Herbal Remedies, and co-author of Encyclopaedia of Common Natural Ingredients.

Levi, Ernest, D.P.M., podiatrist in private practise in New York City.

Levine, Jon, MD, rheumatologist at the University of California at San Francisco.

Levine, Laurence, D.D.S., MD, associate clinical professor of otolaryngology at Washington University School of Medicine in St. Louis.

Levine, Suzanne, D.P.M., adjunct clinical instructor at New York College of Podiatric Medicine and clinical assistant podiatrist at Wycoff Heights Medical Centre, both in New York City.

Levy, Allan, MD, director of the Department of Sports Medicine at Pascack Valley Hospital in Westwood, New Jersey, and team physician for the New York Giants professional football team and the New Jersey Nets professional basketball team.

Levy, Leonard A., D.P.M., professor of podiatric medicine and past president of the California College of Podiatric Medicine in San Francisco.

Lezak, Myron B., MD, gastroenterologist in Florida.

Liberman, Jacob, O.D., Ph.D., Colorado optometrist.

Light, Kenneth, MD, medical director of San Francisco Spine Centre.

Lillis, Kathy, MD, a pediatric emergency medicine physician at Childrens Hospital of Buffalo in Buffalo, New York

Lipelt, Michael, N.D., D.D.S., naturopathic physician, biological dentist, and licensed acupuncturist at Stillpoint Family Health Services in California.

Lisse, Jeffrey R., MD, professor of medicine and director of the division of rheumatology at the University of Texas Medical School at Galveston.

Litt, Jerome Z., MD, assistant clinical professor of dermatology at Case Western Reserve University School of Medicine in Cleveland, Ohio, and author of Your Skin: From Acne to Zits.

Little, Hunter, MD, clinical professor of ophthalmology at Stanford University School of Medicine in Palo Alto, California.

Lockie, Andrew, MD, author of The Family Guide to Homeopathy.

Loening-Baucke, Vera, MD, paediatrician at the University of Iowa Hospitals and Clinics.

Lombard, Jay, MD, co-author of The Brain Wellness Plan.

Loney, Deborah, MD, otolaryngologist.

Lotke, Paul, MD, professor of orthopaedic surgery at the University of Pennsylvania Medical Centre.

Low, Samuel, D.D.S., associate professor and director of graduate periodontology at the University of Florida College of Dentistry.

Low Dog, Tieraona, MD, physician at the University of New Mexico Hospital and member of the Alternative Medicine Research Group.

Lowe, Nicholas J., MD, clinical professor of dermatology at the University of California.

Lundeen, Thomas, D.M.D., co-director of the Clinical Pain Program at the University of North Carolina in Chapel Hill

Lupo, Mary, MD, associate clinical professor of dermatology at Tulane University School of Medicine in New Orleans.

Luttkus, Becky, head instructor at the National Academy of Nannies of Denver.

Lynch, James M., MD, team physician.

Lynn, Martin, D.P.M., podiatrist at the Seattle Foot and Ankle Centre.

McAlindon, Tim, MD, assistant professor of medicine at the Boston University School of Medicine.

McAndrews, Jerome F., D.C., spokesperson for the American Chiropractic Association.

McClave, Stephen, MD, gastroenterologist and associate professor of medicine at the University of Louisville School of Medicine in Kentucky.

McClenon, Anne, N.D., naturopathic doctor at the Compass Family Health Centre in Massachusetts.

McCombs, Janet, Pharm.D., clinical assistant professor at the Univeristy of Georgia College of Pharmacy in Athens.

McDonagh, Brian, MD, founder and medical director of the Vein Clinics of America.

McIntyre-Seltman, Kathleen, MD, professor of medicine in the Department of Obstetrics/Gynaecology at the University of Pittsburgh School of Medicine.

McMullan, Dickie, MD, opthalmologist in private practise in Atlanta, Georgia.

McNally, Peter, D.O., chief of gastroenterology at Evans Army Hospital in Colorado Springs, Colorado, and spokesperson for the American College of Gastroenterology.

McNeal, Glennis, public information director at the Psoriasis Foundation.

McQuade Crawford, Amanda, professional member of the American Herbalists Guild (AHG), and member of Britain's National Institute of Medical Herbalists.

McShefferty, John, Ph.D., president of the Gillette

Research Institute.

Mabry, Richard, MD, professor in the department of otorhinolaryngology at the University of Texas Southwestern Medical Center at Dallas.

Macchia, Richard J., MD, professor and chairman of the department of urology at the State University of New York Health Science Centre.

Magaziner, Allan, D.O., nutritional medicine specialist and head of the Magaziner Medical Centre in Cherry Hill, New Jersey.

Magnuson, Thomas H., MD, expert in gallstone disease and assistant professor of surgery in the department of surgery at the John Hopkins University School of Medicine in Baltimore, Maryland.

Maharam, Lewis, MD, president of the Greater New York Regional Chapter of the American College of Sports Medicine and medical director of the Metropolitan Athletics Congress in New York City

Maher, William P., D.D.S., assistant Professor of endodontics at the University of Detroit Mercy School of Dentistry

Maier, Kathleen, physician's assistant and herbalist in Virginia, professional member of the American Herbalists Guild (AHG), and director of the Dreamtime Centre for Herbal Studies in Virginia.

Mandel, Steven, MD, clinical professor of neurology at Jefferson Medical College and attending physician at Thomas Jefferson University Hospital, both in Philadelphia.

Mandell-Brown, Mark K., MD, otolaryngologist.

March, Robert, MD, associate professor of cardiovascular surgery at Rush Presbyterian St. Luke's Medical Centre in Chicago.

Margolis, David, MD, dermatologist.

Markison, Robert, MD, hand surgeon and associate clinical professor of surgery at the University of California, San Francisco.

Marmar, Earl, MD, orthopaedic surgeon at Einstein Medical Centre in Philadelphia.

Marshutz, Nancy, R.N., nurse-midwife at the Natural Childbirth Institute and Women's Health Centre in Los Angles.

Martin, Dan, MD, clinical associate professor of obstetrics/gynaecology at the University of Tennessee, and a reproductive surgeon at Baptist Memorial Hospital, both in Memphis.

Marty, David, MD, otolaryngologist in Jefferson, Missouri, and author of The Ear Book.

Mason, Joel, MD, nutritionist and gastroenterologist with the U.S. Department of Agriculture Human Nutrition Research Centre on Aging at Tufts University in Boston.

Massey, Patrick, MD, Ph.D., internist at Alexian Brothers Medical Centre in Illinois.

Mauskop, Alexander, MD, director of the Downstate Headache Centre in New York.

Meade, Thomas, MD, orthopaedic surgeon and medical director of the Sports Medicine and Human Performance Centre in Pennsylvania.

Meletis, Chris, N.D., naturopathic physician and medicinary director at the National College of Naturopathic Medicine in Portland, Oregon.

Melzack, Ronald, Ph.D., McGill University and past president of the International Association for the Study of Pain.

Menacker, Marjorie, D.P.M., podiatrist in Virginia.

Mendoza, Guillermo, MD, chief of allergy for Kaiser-Permanente in California.

Meserole, Lisa, R.D., N.D., naturopathic doctor and past chairman of the department of botanical medicine at Bastyr University in Seattle.

Messer, Stephen, N.D., naturopathic physician in Oregon, and dean of the summer school of the National Centre for Homeopathy in Virginia.

Metcalfe, Melissa, N.D., naturopathic doctor in Los Angeles, California.

Metzger, Deborah A., MD, Ph.D., director of the Reproductive Medicine Institute of Connecticut in Hartford.

Meyer, Thomas, MD, associate professor of medicine at the University of Colorado in Denver

Micheli, Lyle, MD, director of the Sports Medicine Division at Boston Children's Hospital and associate clinical professor of orthopaedic surgery at Harvard Medical School.

Michelson, James, MD, associate professor of orthopaedic surgery at Johns Hopkins School of Medicine in Baltimore, Maryland.

Middaugh, Susan, Ph.D., research psychologist in the department of physical medicine and rehabilitation at the Medical University of South Carolina College of Medicine in Charleston.

Mikesky, Alan, Ph.D., director of the Human Performance and Biomechanics Laboratory at Indiana University-Purdue University in Indianapolis

Milburn, Alison, Ph.D., health psychologist who specialises in chronic pain and former co-director of the Chronic Pelvic Pain clinic at the University of Iowa Hospitals and Clinics in Iowa City.

Miller, Emmett, MD, mind-body specialist and author in Nevada City, California.

Miller, Margot, P.T., physical therapist.

Miller, Maurice H., Ph.D., professor of audiology and speech language pathology in the School of Education at New York University in New York City

Miller, Richard, Ph.D., clinical psychologist and co-founder of the International Association of Yoga Therapists in California.

Miller, Richard A., D.O., avid runner and dermatologist in private practise in Florida.

Miller, Susan, Ph.D., assistant professor of otolaryngology and director of the Centre for the Voice at Georgetown University Medical Centre in Washington.

Mindell, Earl, Ph.D., professor of nutrition at Pacific Western University and author of Earl Mindell's Supplement Bible.

Molnar, Marika, P.T., director of West Side Dance Physical Therapy in New York City.

Molony, David, Ph.D., licensed acupuncturist and executive director of the American Association of Oriental Medicine Pennsylvania.

Molony, Ming Ming, O.M.D., licensed acupuncturist and doctor of Oriental medicine in private practise in Catasauqua, Pennsylvania.

Monica, Monica L., MD, Ph.D., opthalmologist in New Orleans and spokesperson for the American Academy of Ophthalmology.

Montgomery, Owen, MD, obstetrics/gynaecology specialist at Thomas Jefferson University Hospital.

Moore, Michael, one of America's leading herbalists, and author of Medicinal Plants of the Desert and Canyon West.

Moore, Willow, N.D., chiropractor and naturopathic doctor in Owings Mills, Maryland.

Morency, Patrice, sports injury management specialist in Oregon.

Morgan, Brian L., Ph.D., research scientist with the Institute of Human Nutrition at Columbia University College of Physicians and Surgeons in New York City.

Morrow, Geraldine, D.M.D., past president of the American Dental Association, and a dentist in Anchorage, Alaska.

Mostow, Steven R., MD, professor of medicine at the University of Colorado, chairman of the American Thoracic Society's committee on the prevention of pneumonia and influenza, and chairman of medicine at the Rose Medical Centre in Denver.

Motto, Stephen G., DM, Dip Sports Med, D M S Med, DipMedAc, musculo-skeletal physician with a specialty in sports medicine at London Bridge Hospital.

Mountfield, Janet A., MD, general practitioner in Toronto.

Mowrey, Daniel, Ph.D., director of the American Phytotherapy Research Laboratory and author of The Scientific Validation of Herbal Medicine and Herbal Tonic Therapies.

Mulcahy, John J., MD, Ph.D., professor of urology at the Indiana University Medical Centre.

Murray, Alexander H., MD, head of the division of dermatology at Dalhousie University Faculty of Medicine in Halifax, Nova Scotia.

Murray, Michael, N.D., naturopathic physician, author of The Complete Book of Juicing and co-author of A Textbook of Natural Medicine as well as several other scholarly books on nutritional and naturopathic healing.

Murray-Doran, Lisa, N.D., naturopathic doctor and instructor at the Canadian College of Naturopathic Medicine in Toronto.

Murrell, George A., D.D.S., prosthodontist in Manhattan Beach, California.

Nagler, Stephen, MD, director of the Southeastern Comprehensive Tinnitus Clinic in Atlanta

Navarro, Luis, MD, director of the Vein Treatment Centre at Mount Sinai School of Medicine.

Neal, Durwood E. Jr., MD, associate professor of surgery, microbiology and internal medicine at the University of Texas Medical Branch in Galveston.

Neezon OR Nezezon, Stephen A., MD, yoga teacher and staff physician at the Himalayan International Institute of Yoga Science and Philosophy in Honesdale, Pennsylvania.

Nelson, Dan, MD, associate professor of ophthalmology at the University of Minnesota in Minneapolis and chairman of the department of ophthalmology at the Health Partners-Regions Hospital in Saint Paul.

Nelson, William D., N.D., naturopathic physician in private practise in Colorado.

Neville, Helen, R.N., paediatric nurse at Kaiser-Permanente Hospital in California

Nevitt, Michael C., Ph.D., assistant adjunct professor of epidemiology and biostatistics.

Newsome, Paual, O.D., optometrist and spokesperson for the Better Vision Institute in Charlotte, North Carolina.

Nezhat, Camran, MD, director of the Fertility and Endoscopy Centre for Special Pelvic Surgery in Atlanta.

Ni, Maoshing, Ph.D., doctor of Oriental medicine, licensed acupuncturist, and director of Tao of Wellness, a professional acupuncture corporation in California.

Nicholas, Stephen, MD, associate director of the Nicholas Institute of Sports Medicine in New York City and team physician for the New York Jets and Islanders

Nickel, David, O.M.D., certified acupuncturist and doctor of Oriental medicine in Santa Monica, California, and author of Acupressure for Athletes.

Niebyl, Jennifer, MD, professor and head of obstetrics and gynaecology at the Hospitals and Clinics at the University of Iowa in Iowa City.

Nirschl, Robert, MD, assistant professor of orthopaedic surgery at Georgetown University School of Medicine.

Nogueras, Juan, MD, colon and rectal surgeon at the Cleveland Clinic in Florida.

Nohr, Don, captain of the Cypre Prince, a fishing boat that plies the choppy waters off British Columbia.

Nolan, James, MD, urologist.

Nolan, Michael F., Ph.D., physical therapist and associate professor of anatomy and neurology at the University of South Florida College of Medicine in Tampa.

Norelli, Charles, MD, sports medicine specialist.

Norris, Mark, MD, professor of anaesthesiology, obstetrics, and gynaecology and chief of the section of obstetric anesthesiology at Washington University School of Medicine in St. Louis.

Northrup, Christiane, MD, assistant clinical professor of obstetrics and gynaecology at the University of Vermont College of Medicine.

Novicki, David C., D.P.M., president of the American College of Foot and Ankle Surgeons.

O'Dell, Jim, MD, professor and chief of rheumatology at the University of Nebraska Medical Centre.

Odom, Richard, MD, dermatology department at the University of California, San Francisco.

O'Donnell, Judith, MD, assistant professor of medicine in the division of Infectious Diseases at Allegheny University of the Health Sciences in Philadelphia, Pennsylvania, and a medical specialist for the Sexually Transmitted Disease Control Program at the Philadelphia Department of Public Health.

Ohashi, Wataru, founder of the Ohashi Institute in New York City.

Oleson, Terry, Ph.D., chair of the Department of Behavioral medicine at the California Institute in Los Angeles

Olivencia, J. A., MD, vascular surgeon.

Oliveri, Eugene, D.O., gastroenterologist and professor of medicine at Michigan State University College of Osteopathic Medicine in East Lansing, Michigan.

Oppenheim, Michael, MD, author of The Complete Book of Better Digestion.

Orengo, Ida, MD, associate professor of dermatology at Baylor College of Medicine in Texas.

Orkin, Bruce, MD, assistant professor of colon and rectal surgery at the George Washington University School of Medicine and Health Services.

Ornish, Dean, MD, director of the Preventive Medicine Research Institute in California, and author of Dr. Dean Ornish's Program for Reversing Heart Disease.

Orvidas, Laura, MD, senior associate consultant and instructor in the Department of Otorhinolaryngology at the Mayo Clinic in Rochester, Minnesota.

Palmer, Melissa, MD, gastroenterologist and liver specialist in private practise in New York City.

Panos, Maesimund, MD, homeopathic physician and co-author of Homeopathic Medicine at Home.

Panush, Richard S., MD, chairman of the department of medicine at Saint Barnabas Medical Centre in Livingston, New Jersey.

Parker, Richard, D.O., staff physician with the San Diego Sports Medicine Centre.

Pascarelli, Emil, MD, professor of clinical medicine and a repetitive strain injury specialist at Columbia Presbyterian Medical Centre in New York City.

Pascualy, Ralph, MD, medical director of the Sleep Disorders Centre at Providence Medical Centre.

Payne, Larry, Ph.D., director of the Samata Yoga Centre in Los Angeles, California, and chairman of the International Association of Yoga Therapists.

Perle, Charles H., D.M.D., a dentist in Jersey City, New Jersey; a spokesperson for the Academy of General Dentistry; and a member of the Council on Communications of the American Dental Association (ADA).

Perlmutter, David, MD, neurologist and author of Lifeguide.

Perricone, Nicholas V., MD, associate clinical professor of dermatology at Yale University School of Medicine.

Perry, Susan, P.T., physical therapist specialising in sports medicine.

Pesanelli, William, P.T., physical therapist and director of Boston University's Rehabilitation Services in Boston.

Petersen, Paula, MD, Ph.D., attending physician at Cedars-Sinai Medical Centre in Los Angeles, California.

Peterson, John, MD, Ayurvedic practitioner in Muncie, Indiana.

Peura, David, MD, gastroenterologist and professor of medicine in the division of gastroenterology and hepatology at the University of Virginia Health Sciences Centre in Charlottesville

Pfeiffer, Ronald F., M.D., associate professor of neurology and pharmacology at the University of Nebraska Medical Center in Omaha.

Phelps, Dennis, athletic trainer with the Athletic Rehab Care Clinic in California.

Pittman, Joffie, D.D.S., general director and medical administrator of the Henry J. Austin Health Center in Trenton, New Jersey

Pizzorno, Joseph E. Jr., N.D., naturopathic doctor, founding president of Bastyr University in Seattle, author of Total Wellness, and co-author of A Textbook of Natural Medicine.

Placek, Evelyn, MD, dermatologist and doctor of internal medicine in private practise in Scarsdale, New York.

Plancey, Robert, M.D., assistant clinical professor of medicine at the University of Southern California.

Planer, Paul, O.D., behavioural optometrist in Atlanta and past president of the International Academy of Sports Vision in Pennsylvania.

Positano, Rock, D.P.M., co-director of the Foot and Ankle Orthopedic Institute at the Hospital for Special Surgery in New York City

Post, Judith, D.M.D., dentist in private practise in Montclair, New Jersey.

Postman, Marshall, MD, allergist in private practise in Nevada.

Potthoff, Ellen, D.C., N.D., chiropractor and naturopathic physician in California.

Pray, W. Steven, Ph.D., R.Ph., professor of pharmaceutics at Southwestern Oklahoma State University in Weatherford

Press, Joel, MD, associate professor of clinical physical medicine and rehabilitation at Northwestern University Medical School in Chicago.

Pribitkin, Edmund, MD, otolaryngologist.

Price, Richard, D.M.D., clinical instructor at the Henry Goldman School of Dentistry at Boston University

Primavera, Joseph P. III, Ph.D., psychologist at the Jefferson Headache Centre in Philadelphia, Pennsylvania.

Primos, William A. Jr., MD, practitioner of primary-care sports medicine in North Carolina.

Printz, Don W., MD, president of the American Society of Dermatology and a dermatologist in Atlanta.

Putnam, Marian H., MD, paediatrician.

Quatrochi, Kathlyn, N.D., naturopathic physician and herbalist in California, and author of The Skin Care Book: Simple Herbal Recipes.

Raether, Paul, MD, marathoner and physical medicine specialist at the Kaiser-Permanente Medical Centre in Portland, Oregon.

Ragley, Phyllis, D.P.M., podiatrist and vice president of the American Academy of Podiatric Sports Medicine.

Raichur, Pratima, doctor of naturopathy, Ayurvedic practitioner, and author of Absolute Beauty.

Rakowski, Robert, D.C., chiropractic physician, acupuncturist, and clinic director of the Natural Medicine Centre in Houston.

Rankin, Edward A., MD, chief of orthopedic surgery at Providence Hospital in Washington, D.C.

Rapoport, Alan, MD, director of The New England Centre for Headache.

Rask, Michael, MD, chairman of the American Academy of Neurological and Orthopaedic Surgeons and the American Board of Ringside Medicine and Surgery.

Ravick, Arnold, D.P.M., podiatrist at Capital Podiatry Associates in Washington, D.C.

Razmus, Thomas F., D.D.S., associate professor in the department of diagnostic services at the West Virginia University School of Dentistry in Morgantown

Redwine, David, MD, director of the Endometriosis Institute in Bend, Oregon.

Rees, Brian, MD, medical director of the Maharishi Ayur-Veda Medical Centre in Pacific Palisades, California.

Rees, Terry D., D.D.S., chairman of the department of periodontics and director of the Stomatology Centre at Baylor College of Dentistry in Dallas, Texas.

Reese, Vail, MD, dermatologist with the Dermatology Medical Group of San Francisco.

Reichenberg-Ullman, Judyth, N.D., naturopathic physician in Edmonds, Washington, and co-author of The Patient's Guide to Homeopathic Medicine.

Reid, Sheila, therapy co-ordinator at the Spine Institute of New England.

Reilly, Kevin, D.C., a certified chiropractic sports physician and owner of Reilly Chiropractic Health and Fitness in Columbus, Ohio

Rempel, David, MD, assistant professor of medicine at the University of California, San Francisco, and a bio-medical engineer.

Rennard, Stephen, MD, chief of pulmonary and critical care medicine at the University of Nebraska Medical Centre in Omaha.

Resnick, Edward J., MD, professor of orthopaedic surgery at Temple University Hospital in Philadelphia.

Rich, Brent S. E., MD, staff physician at Arizona Orthopaedic and Sports Medicine Specialists and team physician at Arizona State University.

Richards, David, MD, orthopaedic surgeon at the Lexington Clinic Sports Medicine Centre in Lexington, Kentucky.

Richie, Douglas, Jr., D.P.M., clinical instructor of podiatry at University of Southern California Medical Centre.

Robb, Leon, MD, director of the Robb Pain Management Group in Los Angeles, California.

Robbins, Lawrence, MD, founder of the Robbins Headache Clinic in Northbrook, Illinois, and co-author of Headache Help.

Roberts, Richard, MD, associate chair and professor of family medicine at the University of Wisconsin Medical School.

Rodu, Brad, D.D.S., professor and chairman of the department of pathology at the University of Alabama School of Medicine in Birmingham.

Roe, Jedd, MD, assistant professor of emergency medicine at the University of Colorado School of Medicine.

Rogal, Owen J., D.D.S., executive director of the American Academy of Head, Facial, and Neck pain and TMJ Orthopedics and author of Mandibular Whiplash.

Romano, John F. MD, dermatologist and clinical assistant professor of medicine at The New York Hospital-Cornell Medical Centre in New York City.

Romm, Aviva, certified professional midwife, herbalist, and professional member of the American Herbalist Guild (AHG) who practises in Bloomfield Hills, Michigan, and is the author of The Natural

Pregnancy Book.

Rooney, David, MD, family physician in Pennsylvania.

Rose, David, MD, Ph.D., chief of the division of health and endocrinology at the Naylor Dana Institute in New York

Rose, Jeanne, practising herbalist and aromatherapist in San Francisco, California, chairman of the National Association for Holistic Aromatherapy, and author of Aromatherapy.

Rosen, Lester, MD, professor of clinical surgery at Penn State University Hospital.

Rosoff, Mark, emergency medical technician and director of the Front Range Institute for Safety in Colorado.

Ross, David, D.C., practitioner at Rockridge Family Chiropractic in Oakland, California.

Rossman, Martin L., MD, clinical associate at the University of California Medical School in San Francisco, co-director of the Academy for Guided Imagery in Mill Valley, California, and author of Healing Yourself: A Step-by-Step Program for Better Health through Imagery.

Rosson, Constance L., MD, general medicine practitioner.

Roth, Harry, M.D., professor of clinical dematology at the University of California, San Francisco. (Sunburn, p. 501)

Rothenberg, Amy, doctor of naturopathy in Amherst, Massachusetts, and editor of the New England Journal of Homeopathy.

Rothfeld, Glenn S., MD, clinical assistant professor at Tufts University School of Medicine and author of Natural Medicine for Arthritis.

Roubenoff, Ronenn, MD, associate professor of nutrition and medicine at Tufts University.

Rucker, Karen, MD, Virginia Commonwealth University

Rudd, Patricia, director of physical therapy at the Centre for Orofacial Pain in San Francisco.

Ruderman, William B., MD, practising physician in gastroenterology.

Ruml, Lisa, MD, assistant professor of medicine at the University of Texas Southwestern Medical Centre.

Russell, Nancy, MD, internist in Missouri, and member of the American Holistic Medical Association.

Russman, Marina, MD, anesthesiologist and pain-management specialist.

Russo, Nick, D.D.S., vice-president of the Academy of General Dentistry in Chicago.

Rutherford, William H., D.P.M., clinical instructor in the podiatry section at Howard University School of Medicine in Washington, D.C.

Sachs, Gregory, MD, assistant professor of medicine at Columbia University College of Physicians and Surgeons in New York City.

Saltzman, Amy, MD, internist for the Institute for Health and Healing at the California Pacific Medical Centre.

Sanders, Barbara, Ph.D., chairman of the physical therapy department at Southwest Texas State University.

Sarnoff, Deborah S., MD, assistant clinical professor of dermatology at New York University in New York City.

Saviano, Dennis, Ph.D., professor of nutrition and dean of the school of consumer and family sciences at Purdue University in West Lafayette, Indiana.

Saxby, Charlotte, MD, ophthalmologist with the Group Health Cooperative of Puget Sound in Seattle.

Scala, James, Ph.D., nutritional biochemist and lecturer at Georgetown University School of Medicine in Washington, D.C.

Schar, Douglas, practising medical herbalist in London, editor of the British Journal of Phytotherapy, and author of Backyard Medicine Chest.

Schatz, Mary Pullig, MD, doctor, yoga instructor, and author of Back to Health: A Doctor's Program for Back Care Using Yoga.

Scheiber, Dr., (Sunburn, p. 500)

Scher, Richard K., MD, nail specialist and professor of dermatology at the Columbia-Presbyterian Medical Centre in New York City.

Schncider, Ira, D.C., chiropractor.

Schneider, Meir, Ph.D., licensed massage therapist, founder of the Centre and School for Self-Healing in San Francisco, and creator of the Meir Schneider Self-Healing Method.

Schneider, Myles J., D.P.M., podiatrist in Virginia, and co-author of The Athlete's Health Care Book.

Schoenbeck, Lorilee, N.D., naturopathic doctor.

Scholes, Michael, aromatherapist of Aromatherapy Seminars in Los Angeles.

Schor, Jacob, N.D., president of the Colorado Association of Naturopathic Doctors.

Schorr, Lia, New York City skin care specialist and author of Lia Schorr's Seasonal Skin Care.

Schosser, Robert, MD, chief of the division of dermatology at the University of Kentucky A. B. Chandler Medical Centre in Lexington.

Schreiber, Michael, M.D., dermatologist and senior clinical lecturer at theUniversity of Arizona School of Medicine in Tucson.

Schultz, Bryan C., MD, clinical associate professor at Loyola University of Chicago Stritch School of Medicine. (Sunburn, p. 501)

Schuring, Arnold, MD, otologist in Warren, Ohio.

Schuster, Marvin M., MD, chief of the Department of Digestive Diseases at Francis Scott Key Medical Centre in Baltimore.

Schwingl, Pamela, Ph.D., senior epidemiologist at Family Health International in North Carolina.

Seidman, Michael, MD, medical director of the Tinnitus Centre at the Henry Ford Hospital in Detroit.

Selner, Allen, D.P.M., podiatrist at the Medstar Foot and Ankle Centre in California.

Seltzer, Samuel, D.D.S., professor emeritus of endodontology at the Temple University School of Medicine and Dentistry in Philadelphia.

Serage, Houshang, MD, assistant professor of orthopaedic surgery at the University of Okalahoma Science Centre and director of the Orthopaedic and Reconstructive Centre, both in Oklahoma City.

Severson, Jessica, MD, clinical researcher in dermatology.

Shah, Meena, D.D.S., a dentist in Lake Grove, New York.

Shapira, Eric Z., D.D.S., dentist in Half Moon Bay, California, and spokesperson for the Academy of General Dentistry.

Shaw, Toby, MD, associate professor of dermatology at Allegheny University of the Health Sciences MCP-Hahnemann School of Medicine in Philadelphia.

Shay, Kenneth, D.D.S., chief of dental services at the Veterans Affairs Medical Centre in Michigan.

Sheftell, Fred, MD, psychiatrist, headache specialist, and co-founder of the New England Centre for Headache in Connecticut.

Shelton, Clough, MD, associate clinical professor of otolaryngology at the University of California, Los Angeles, and member of the House Ear Institute at the University of Southern California.

Shepard, Richard, D.D.S., dentist in Colorado.

Sheth, Anu, MD, lead physician at the Egleston Children's Health Care Center in Dunwoody, Georgia

Ship, Jonathan, D.M.D., associate professor and vice chairman in the department of oral medicine, pathology, and surgery at the University of Michigan School of Dentistry and director of hospital dentistry at the University of Michigan Medical Centre, both in Ann Arbor.

Siegel, Sheryl, MD, neurologist.

Sierpina, Dr. Victor S., University of Texas Medical Branch.

Silbert, Barbara, D.C., N.D., chiropractor and naturopathic doctor in Newburyport, Massachusetts, and president of the Massachusetts Society of Naturopathic Physicians.

Silverman, Sol, D.D.S., professor of oral medicine at the University of California, San Francisco.

Simon, Richard, MD, orthopaedic surgeon.

Simons, Anne, MD, assistant clinical professor of family and community medicine at the University of California.

Sinatra, Stephen T., MD, director of the New England Heart Centre in Connecticut, and author of Optimum Health and Heartbreak and Heart Disease.

Singleton, Kenneth, MD, physician in private practise in Bethesda, Maryland.

Sinks, Thomas, Ph.D., epidemiologist with the Centres for Disease Control and Prevention in Atlanta, Georgia.

Skerry, Priscilla, naturopathic and homeopathic doctor in private practise in Portland, Maine.

Skul, Vesna, MD, medical director of Rush Centre for Women's Medicine in Chicago.

Slakter, Jason, MD, attending surgeon in the Department of Ophthalmology at the Manhattan Eye, Ear and Throat Hospital.

Slattery, William H. III, MD, director of clinical studies at the House Ear Institute in Los Angeles.

Sluyter, Dean, certified reflexologist.

Smith, Ed, herbalist.

Smith, Howard R., MD, chief of rheumatology at Meridia Huron Hospital and adjunct professor of medicine at Case Western Reserve University School of Medicine, both in Cleveland.

Snarr, Carol, R.N., psychophysiological therapist (one who teaches biofeedback and other mind/body skills) at the Life Sciences Institute in Kansas.

Soloman, glen, MD, headache expert and consultant to the Cleveland Foundation.

Sonis, Stephen, D.M.D., professor of oral medicine at the Harvard School of Dental Medicine.

Soppe, Glenn G., MD, San Diego physician who lectures on aquatic bites and stings.

Soule, Deb, Maine herbalist and author of The Roots of Healing.

Spieler, Eric, D.M.D., lecturer in dental medicine at the University of Pennsylvania School of Dental Medicine.

Spierings, Egilius, MD, Ph.D., neurologist and headache specialist in Massachusetts.

Spilken, Terry, D.P.M., podiatrist at the New York College of Podiatric Medicine.

Spraker, Lana, master instructor who has taught tai chi for more than 25 years and certified Alexander Technique instructor.

Stanish, William D., MD, associate professor of surgery at Dalhousie University in Halifax and director of the Orthopaedic and Sports Medicine Clinic in Nova Scotia.

Stansbury, Jill, N.D., assistant professor of botanical medicine, chair of the botanical medicine department at the National College of Naturopathic Medicine in Portland, Oregon, and a naturopathic doctor in Battle Ground, Washington.

Stark, James, MD, physiatrist at the Centre for Sports Medicine in San Francisco.

Starlanyl, Devin, MD, physician in New Hampshire, and author who has fibromyalgia.

Stay, Flora Parsa, D.D.S., dentist in California, and author of The Complete Book of Dental Remedies.

Steele, John, aromatic consultant in Los Angeles, California.

Steinhagen, Randolph M., MD, associate professor of surgery at Mountain Sinai Medical Centre.

Steirman, Elaine, L.M.T., massage therapist.

Stengler, Mark, N.D., naturopathic physician in Carlsbad, California, and author of The Natural Physician: Your Health Guide for Common Ailments.

Stephens, Robert, Ph.D., chairman of the Department of Anatomy and director of sports medicine at the University of Health Sciences College.

Stiles, Kristin, N.D., naturopathic doctor at the Complementary Medicine and Healing Arts Centre in New York.

Stillerman, Elaine, L.M.T., licensed massage therapist on the staff of the Swedish Institute of Massage in New York City, and author of Mother-Massage.

Stoltz, Sarah, MD, neurologist.

Stone, Jenny, certified athletic trainer and manager of clinical programs in the division of sports medicine for the U.S. Olympic Committee in Colorado Springs.

Stone, Kathleen, D.P.M., podiatrist in private practise in Glendale, Arizona.

Strauss, Richard H., MD, sports medicine doctor at Ohio State University College of Medicine in Columbus.

Strauss, Stephen, MD, chief of the Laboratory of Clinical Diseases.

Subotnick, Steven, D.P.M., N.D., Ph.D., clinical professor of biomechanics and surgery at the California College of Podiatric Medicine in Hayward, a specialist in sports medicine, and author of Sports and Exercise Injuries.

Sugar, Sam, MD, doctor in Illinois.

Sullivan, Andrea D., Ph.D., naturopathic and homeopathic physician and author of A Path to Healing.

Sullivan-Durand, Jane, MD, behavioural medicine physician in Contoocook, New Hampshire.

Surrell, James, MD, colorectal surgeon at the Ferguson Clinic in Grand Rapids, Michigan.

Sutcliffe, Jenny, Ph.D., DPP, MBBS, MCSP, former Senior Lecturer in Paediatric Neurology, Great Ormond Street Hospital, London, chartered physiotherapist, and author of The Reader's Digest Body Maintenance Manual.

Swanstrom, Lee, MD, associate clinical professor in the department of surgery at Oregon Health Sciences University in Portland.

Swezey, Robert, MD, medical director of the Arthritis and Back Pain Centre in California.

Syrop, Steven, D.D.S., director of the TMD-facial pain program at Columbia University School of Dental and Oral Surgery in New York City.

Taintor, Jerry F., D.D.S., endodontist in Memphis, Tennessee.

Talley, Nicholas, MD, Ph.D., associate professor of medicine at the Mayo Clinic in Rochester, Minnesota.

Taub, Larry R., MD, assistant professor of ophthalmology and director of comprehensive ophthalmology at Emory University School of Medicine.

Taylor, Pamela, doctor of naturopathy in private practise in Moline, Illinois.

Thomas, Charles, Ph.D., physical therapist at Desert Springs Therapy Centre in California, and co-author of Hydrotherapy: Simple Treatments for Common Ailments.

Thomassy, John E., D.C., chiropractor in private practise in Virginia Beach, Virginia.

Thornton, Yvonne S., MD, visiting associate physician at the Rockefeller University Hospital in New York City and director of the perinatal diagnostic testing center at Morristown Memorial Hospital in New Jersey

Thrash, Agatha, MD, medical pathologist and co-founder and co-director of Uchee Pines Institute, a natural healing centre in Seale, Alabama.

Tilgner, Sharol, N.D., naturopathic physician, professional member of the American Herbalists Guild (AHG), and president of Wise Woman Herbals in Creswell, Oregon.

Tourles, Stephanie, licensed aesthetician in Massachusetts, and author of The Herbal Body Book.

Towne, Mary Ann, P.T., physical therapist.

Traub, Michael, N.D., naturopathic doctor and director of the integrated residency program at North Hawaii Community Hospital in Kamuela OR naturopathic physician in private practise in Kailua Kona, Hawaii.

Turk, Dennis C., Ph.D., John and Emma Bonica professor of anesthesiology and pain research at the University of Washington School of Medicine in Seattle.

Tyler, Varro E., Ph.D., professor of pharmacognosy at the School of Pharmacy and Pharmacal Sciences at Purdue University in West Lafayette, Indiana, and author of The Honest Herbal and Herbs of Choice.

Ullis, Karlis, MD, assistant clinical professor at the University of California, Los Angeles, UCLA School of Medicine.

Upton, Roy, herbalist.

Van Ost, Lynn, P.T., clinical specialist.

Van Pelt, William, D.P.M., podiatrist in Houston, Texas, and former president of the American Academy of Podiatric Sports Medicine.

Veenstra, Mark, MD, orthopaedic surgeon.

Vernon, Jack, Ph.D., professor emeritus of otolaryngology at Oregon Health Sciences University in Portland and a board member of the American Tinnitus Association

Walters, Patricia Farris, MD, clinical assistant professor of dermatology at Tulane University School of Medicine in New Orleans and a spokesperson for the American Academy of Dermatology.

Warnock, William, N.D., neuropathic doctor in Shelburne, Vermont.

Wartenberg, Alan, MD, assistant professor of medicine at Tufts University School of Medicine and director of the addiction-recovery program at Faulkner Hospital, both in Boston, Massachusetts.

Waslaski, James, sports massage therapist at the Centre for Pain Management and Clinical Sports Massage in Florida, and author of International Advancements in Event and Clinical Sports Massage.

Watson, Cynthia Mervis, MD, family practise physician specialising in homeopathic and herbal therapies in Santa Monica, California, and author of Love Potions.

Webster, Guy F., MD, Ph.D., professor of dermatology at the Jefferson Medical College of Thomas Jefferson University in Philadelphia.

Weed, Susan, herbalist and herbal educator from New York, and author of the Wise Woman series of health books.

Weil, Andrew T., MD, director of the integrative medicine program at the University of Arizona College of Medicine in Tucson, and author of several books, including Eight Weeks to Optimum Health, Spontaneous Healing and Natural Health, Natural Medicine.

Weil, Carl, emergency medical technician and director of Wilderness Medicine Outfitters in Colorado.

Weiner, Cheryl, D.P.M., podiatrist in Columbus, Ohio, and president of the American Association for Women Podiatrists.

Weiss, Decker, N.D., naturopathic doctor.

Weiss, Eric A., MD, assistant professor of emergency medicine at Stanford University Medical Centre and author of Wilderness 911.

Weiss, Eric G., MD, staff colorectal surgeon at Cleveland Clinic.

Weiss, Jonathan, MD, dermatologist and assistant clinical professor of dermatology at Emory University School of Medicine in Atlanta.

Weiss, Rudolph Fritz, MD, Germany's leading herbal physician and author of Herbal Medicine, used in German medical schools.

Welch, Kevin, MD, dermatologist.

Werbach, Melvyn, MD, physician in Los Angeles who specialises in nutritional medicine and author of Healing with Food.

Wescott, Wayne, Ph.D., strength training consultant.

Wheeler, Anthony, M.D., a neurologist in private practice in Charlotte, North Carolina

Whitaker, Julian, MD, founder and president of the Whitaker Wellness Centre in Newport Beach, California.

White, Augustus A. III, MD, professor of Orthopaedics Surgery at Harvard Medical School.

Whitehead, E. Douglas, MD, urologist and co-director of the Association for Male Sexual Dysfunction.

Whitmore, Kristene E., MD, chief of urology and director of the Incontinence Centre at Graduate Hospital in Philadelphia.

Wiebelt, Frank, D.D.S., chairman of the Department of removable Prosthodontics at the College of Dentistry at the University of Oklahoma Health Sciences Centre.

Wilkinson, Marcia, MA, DM, FRCP, Honorary Medical Director, City of London Migraine Clinic (now retired) and author of a number of popular books on migraine/headaches.

Willard, Terry, Canadian herbalist, president of the Canadian Association of Herbal Practitioners, and author of Textbook of Modem OR Modern Herbology.

Willems, John, MD, associate clinical professor of obstetrics/gynaecology at the University of California.

Williams, James E., O.M.D., doctor of Oriental medicine.

Williams, Maureen, N.D., naturopathic physician at the New England Centre for Integrative Health in Hanover, New Hampshire.

Williams, Melvin, Ph.D., exercise physiologist at Old Dominion University in Norfolk, Virginia

Williams, Saralyn R., MD, toxicologist and emergency physician at the San Diego Regional Poison Centre.

Wilson, A. P., MD, gastroenterologist and professor of medicine at Duke University Medical Centre in Durham, North Carolina.

Wilson, Leanne, Ph.D., clinical psychologist who works with TMD patients.

Wilson, Virginia N., co-founder of the Restless Legs Syndrome Foundation and author of Sleep Thief, Restless Legs Syndrome, a guide to coping with RLS.

Wingo, Claudine, R.N., member of the National Herbalists Association of Australia.

Winston, David, founding and professional member of the American Herbalists Guild (AHG) and a clinical herbalist in New Jersey.

Witkowski, Joseph A., MD, clinical professor of dermatology.

Wolf, Jacqueline, MD, gastroenterologist and assistant professor of medicine at Harvard Medical School and co-director of the Inflammatory Bowel Disease Centre at Brigham and Women's Hospital.

Wolfe, M. Michael, MD, chief of gastroenterology at Boston University School of Medicine.

Wolinsky, Lawrence, D.M.D., Ph.D., professor of oral biology at the University of California, Los Angeles, School of Dentistry

Wong, Randolph, MD, plastic and reconstructive

surgeon and director of the burn unit at Straub Clinic and Hospital in Honolulu.

Woods, Wendy, P.T., physical therapist at K Valley Orthopaedics in Michigan.

Workowski, Kimberly A., MD, assistant professor of medicine in the Division of Infectious Diseases at Emory University in Atlanta, Georgia.

Worwood, Valerie Ann, British aromatherapist and author of The Fragrant Mind.

Wotton, Elizabeth, N.D., naturopathic doctor at Compass Family Health Centre in Plymouth, Massachusetts.

Wright, Eileen Marie, MD, staff physician at the Great Smokies Medical Centre in North Carolina.

Wurtman, Judith, Ph.D., researcher at the Massachusetts Institute of Technology.

Wynne, Michael, Ph.D., associate professor in the department of otolaryngology, head and neck surgery, at the Indiana University School of Medicine in Indianapolis.

Yanick, Paul, Ph.D., research scientist in Pennsylvania.

Yankauskas, Ellen MD, director of the Women's Centre for Family Health in Atascadero, California.

Yarnell, Eric, N.D., naturopathic doctor who is on the board of the Botanical Medicine Academy.

Yeh, Yu-Yan, Ph.D., researcher on the healing properties of garlic.

Young, Jess R., MD, chairman of the Department of Vascular Medicine at the Cleveland Clinic Foundation.

Zampieron, Eugene, doctor of naturopathy in Connecticut, professional member of the American Herbalists Guild (AHG), and co-author of The Definitive Guide to Arthritis.

Zarling, Edwin J., MD, associate professor of medicine at Loyola University Medical Centre in Illinois.

Zirul, Evany, D.O., professor of clinical medicine at the University of Health Sciences in Kansas City, Missouri, and assistant professor of clinical medicine at the University of Kansas

Zunka, Craig, D.D.S., past president of the Holistic Dental Association in Front Royal, Virigina.

Index